SALEM HEALTH

ADDICTIONS & SUBSTANCE ABUSE

SALEM HEALTH

ADDICTIONS & SUBSTANCE ABUSE

Volume 1

Editor
Robin Kamienny Montvilo, RN, PhD

SALEM PRESS
A DIVISION OF EBSCO PUBLISHING
Ipswich, Massachusetts   Hackensack, New Jersey

Note to Readers

The material presented in *Salem Health: Addictions and Substance Abuse* is intended for broad informational and educational purposes. Readers who suspect that they or someone they know has any disorder, disease, or condition described in this set should contact a physician without delay. This set should not be used as a substitute for professional medical diagnosis. Readers who are undergoing or about to undergo any treatment or procedure described in this set should refer to their physicians and other health care providers for guidance concerning preparation and possible effects. This set is not to be considered definitive on the covered topics, and readers should remember that the field of health care is characterized by a diversity of medical opinions and constant expansion in knowledge and understanding.

Library of Congress Cataloging-in-Publication Data

Addictions and substance abuse / editor, Robin Kamienny Montvilo.
   p. cm. – (Salem health)
  Includes bibliographical references and index.
  ISBN 978-1-58765-959-1 (set) – ISBN 978-1-58765-960-7 (volume 1) – ISBN 978-1-58765-961-4 (volume 2) – ISBN 978-1-58765-963-8 (ebook set) 1. Substance abuse–Treatment–United States. 2. Drug abuse–Treatment–United States. 3. Alcoholism–Treatment–United States. 4. Cognitive therapy. I. Montvilo, Robin Kamienny.
  RC563.A356 2012
  362.29–dc23
              2012020279

PRINTED IN THE UNITED STATES OF AMERICA

Contents

Publisher's Note

Salem Health: Addictions and Substance Abuse presents essays on a variety of topics concerning substance abuse and behavioral addictions and their related issues. In 2011, the U.S. Centers for Disease Control and Prevention (CDC) reported that more Americans died from the effects of drug abuse than from traffic accidents; similarly, the CDC attributes the death of nearly 80,000 Americans annually to the excessive consumption of alcohol. These startling statistics, coupled with the staggering rise in deaths from prescription drug misuse in the twenty-first century, have thrown the spotlight on how the allied health community and society at large approach, track, and treat alcohol and drug dependency and other addictive behaviors.

As addictions and their related disorders continue to escalate, so has society's understanding and treatment of them, from increased and more thorough comprehension of maladaptive behavior to a clearer picture of the physiological effects of substance abuse, both in the short and long term. Also of pertinence is the growing awareness of the role that substance abuse and addiction plays in society, whether through glorification or stigmatization in the media lens or experienced firsthand in a dysfunctional home or social setting by a parent or child, and the agencies and preventative strategies in place to curb abuse and its effects. *Salem Health: Addictions and Substance Abuse* surveys the decades of progress in understanding and treating addictive behaviors and substance abuse, analyzing trends and treatment, offering historical and technical background, and providing both a socioeconomic and psychological and physiological understanding of the influence and impact of addiction and substance abuse.

Salem Health: Addictions and Substance Abuse is a valuable addition to the Salem Health series, which includes both print and electronic versions of *Salem Health: Cancer* (2009), *Salem Health: Psychology and Mental Health* (2009), *Salem Health: Genetics and Inherited Conditions* (2010), *Salem Health: Infectious Diseases and Conditions* (2011), *Salem Health: Complementary and Alternative Medicine* (2012), and the core set *Magill's Medical Guide*, Sixth Edition (2011).

SCOPE AND COVERAGE

This A-Z encyclopedia arranges over 325 essays covering all aspects of addictions and substance abuse, including diseases or conditions, substances of abuse, treatment and addiction overviews, organizations and foundations dedicated to treatment and prevention, physiological and psychological issues and behaviors, trends and statistics, and social contexts and concerns related to substance abuse and treatment such as advertising and media influence, aging, ethnicity, and children and substance abuse. The essays, written for nonspecialists by medical professionals, professors in science and medicine, and medical writers, will appeal to science and premedical students, students of psychology and addictive behaviors, students of drug abuse epidemiology and public health issues, public library patrons, and librarians building collections in science, health, and medicine, or related fields.

Salem Health: Addictions and Substance Abuse examines the various concepts and models of both the addiction and its associated behaviors and impulses and the therapeutic and treatment practices that enable an individual to regain the traction of an addiction and abuse-free life. Comprehensive essays on drug and alcohol abuse constitute the core coverage, while a significant number of essays survey behavioral addictions and disorders, as well as the sociocultural and economic impact of addiction. Essays, where applicable, provide overviews of prevention, diagnosis, and treatment, and outline causes, risk factors, and symptoms. The encyclopedia's scope also embraces ethical questions raised by the convergence of alternative therapy and addiction and the legalized use of substances of abuse in the allied health field. Also prominent in the set is the discussion of the preventative and educational work of the government and other agencies in addressing addictions and substance abuse.

ORGANIZATION AND FORMAT

Essays are alphabetized and vary in length from one to five pages and include ready-reference top matter that contains the topic category and definition.

- CATEGORY lists the focus of the essay.
- Diagnosis and Prevention
- Health Issues and Physiology

- Psychological Issues and Behaviors
- Social Issues
- Substance Abuse
- Substances
- Treatment
- ALSO KNOWN AS provides alternative names used, where applicable.
- DEFINITION introduces, defines, and describes the essay topic.

Substance abuse essays include the following sections: Causes, Risk Factors, Symptoms, Screening and Diagnosis, Treatment and Therapy, and Prevention. Substances of abuse essays include the following sections: Status and Classification, Source, Transmission Route, History of Use, and Effects and Potential Risks. Essays covering associated organizations, programs, and treatment centers offer the following sections: Background, Dates established or founded, and Mission and Goals. Essays covering diagnosis, physiology, prevention, psychological issues, socials issues, treatment, and other topics related to behavioral addictions and substance abuse will include subsections chosen by the author as they suit the particular topic. These topical subheads divide the main text and guide readers through the essay.

All entries end with a byline, including the author's credentials, a list of sources for further reading, often with annotations, and several web sites for further study. Additionally, the SEE ALSO section lists cross-references to other essays of interest within the set. The reference set also features over 70 sidebars and graphs and more than 120 photographs chosen to enhance the information offered.

SPECIAL FEATURES
The articles in the *Salem Health: Addictions and Substance Abuse* are arranged alphabetically by title. Both volumes offer a Complete List of Contents for easy identification of desired topics. The value of this encyclopedic guide is enhanced by the wealth of appendices and other resources and tools, ranging from a geographical listing of treatment centers and programs to a cross-referenced list of substances of abuse. Other appendices that supplement the set include a glossary that provides hundreds of definitions of commonly used scientific and medical terms and concepts related to behavioral addiction and substance abuse; pharmaceutical treatments, categorized by brand name; a bibliography which offers citations for both classic and recently published sources for additional research; and a time line which details major developments in addictions and substance abuse. Lastly, a category index appears at the end of each volume and a comprehensive subject index can be found at the conclusion of volume 2 and includes entries that direct readers to related topics throughout the set.

ACKNOWLEDGMENTS
The editors wish to thank the many medical practitioners and other scholars who contributed to this new edition; their names and academic affiliations and other credentials appear in the list of contributors that follows.

ABOUT THE AUTHOR
Robin Kamienny Montvilo, RN, PhD, is a Professor of Psychology and Chair of the Chemical Dependency/Addiction Studies Program at Rhode Island College. She is a member of the Steering Committee of the Institute for Addiction Recovery at Rhode Island College and serves on the Board of Directors of the National Neimann-Pick Disease Foundation. She has also served as a consultant for the International Certification and Reciprocity Consortium, acting as a Subject Matter Expert for the creation of the Co-Occurring Disorders Certification Exam. A member of the American Psychological Society, the Eastern Psychological Association, the Gerontological Society of America, the International Coalition for Addiction Studies Education, and the National Association of Neonatal Nurses, Professor Montvilo has more than one hundred presentations and publications within the fields of psychology, chemical dependency and addiction studies, and nursing. Previously, she served as a staff nurse in a Neonatal Intensive Care Unit for thirty years. She serves as a manuscript reviewer for several psychology and nursing journals and is a frequent contributor to Salem Press publications,

Editor's Introduction

Addictions and substance abuse have existed for many thousands of years. There is evidence that alcohol use was prevalent in Egypt as early as 8000 BCE. Cannabis (marijuana) seeds were eaten in China nearly 8,000 years ago. Ancient Sumerians used opium nearly 6,000 years ago. One of the first known uses of the term "addiction" was by the Archbishop of Canterbury in Shakespeare's *Henry V*, written just prior to 1600, and the term became widely used in the medical field in the 1800s. There is evidence that behavioral addictions, related to gambling and sexual activity, for example, also existed in ancient times.

While addictions and substance abuse clearly hold a place in history, they occur much more commonly today. The number of substances that are now abused and the number of behavioral addictions are skyrocketing, as evidenced by the number of entries in these volumes. As substance abuse and addictions became more common, the United States government became involved in trying to regulate drug use, prevent substance abuse, and establish treatment protocols. This began in 1929 with the establishment of the Narcotics Division of the US Public Health Service. In the subsequent decades, more government agencies were established to deal with substance abuse, including the Drug Enforcement Agency (DEA), the Alcohol, Drug Abuse, and Mental Health Administration

(ADAMHA), and the Substance Abuse and Mental Health Services Administration (SAMHSA). In the twenty years since SAMHSA was formed, the fields of mental health and substance abuse have typically been combined into the broader field of behavioral health.

Today, we continue to see some individuals with addiction problems, others with mental health problems, and many more who suffer from co-occurring disorders (having a mental health problem along with some form of addiction). Commonly seen addictions include substance abuse (to alcohol or various forms of drugs) as well as behavioral addictions (to sex, or shopping, or exercise, or various forms of technology). There has also been movement away from viewing addiction as something that is voluntary and needs to be punished, to treating it as a disease like other chronic disorders such as diabetes and heart disease, with the recognition that relapse is a part of recovery.

It is hoped that the entries in these volumes will clarify the topic of substance abuse and addictions from ancient times to the present. A deeper understanding of the problem may help to foster its prevention, facilitate treatment, and lead to a better understanding of recovery.

Robin Kamienny Montvilo, RN, PhD
Rhode Island College

Contributors

Christopher M. Aanstoos, PhD
University of West Georgia

Richard Adler, PhD
University of
    Michigan—Dearborn

Wendell Anderson, BA
American Medical Writers
    Association

Tammi Arford, MA
Northeastern University

Bryan C. Auday, PhD
Gordon College

Allison C. Bennett, PharmD
Duke University Hospital

R. L. Bernstein, PhD
New Mexico State University

Lillian J. Breckenridge
Oral Roberts University

Michael A. Buratovich PhD
Spring Arbor University

Byron D. Cannon, PhD
University of Utah

Christine M. Carroll, RN, BSN,
    MBA
American Medical Writers
    Association

Jack Carter, PhD
University of New Orleans

Paul J. Chara, PhD
Northwestern College

Ruth M. Colwill, PhD
Brown University

Ronna F. Dillon, PhD
Southern Illinois University

Sally Driscoll, MLS
State College, Pennsylvania

Karen Nagel Edwards, PhD
Midwestern University

Anthony J. Fonseca, PhD
Nicholls State University

Rebecca J. Frey, PhD
Yale University

Jennifer L. Gibson, PharmD
Excalibur Scientific, LLC

Lenela Glass-Godwin, MS
Texas A&M University/Auburn
    University

P. Graham Hatcher, PhD
University of Alabama

Julie Henry, RN, MPA
Myrtle Beach, South Carolina

Christine G. Holzmueller, BLA
Glen Rock, Pennsylvania

Glenn Hutchinson, PhD
Decatur, Georgia

April D. Ingram, BS
Kelowna, British Columbia

Pamela Jones, MA
Emerson College/Tufts Univer-
    sity School of Medicine

Stefanie M. Keen, PhD
University of South Carolina,
    Upstate

Patricia Griffin Kellicker, BSN
Upton, Massachusetts

Camillia King
Huntsville, Alabama

Diana Kohnle
Platte Valley Medical Center

Tracy Ksiazak, PhD
Converse College

Laurie LaRusso, MS, ELS
University School of Nutrition
    Science and Policy

Amanda Lefkowitz, MA
Rockville Centre, New York

Lisa M. Lines, MPH
University of Massachusetts
    Medical School

Marianne M. Madsen, MS
University of Utah

Katia Marazova, MD, PhD
Paris, France

Monica L. McCoy, PhD
Converse College

Eugenia F. Moglia, BA
Glen Cove, New York

Robin Kamienny Montvilo, RN,
    PhD
Rhode Island College

Debra L. Murphy, PhD, MPH
Huston-Tillotson College

Elizabeth Marie McGhee Nelson,
    PhD
Independent Scholar

David A. Olle, MS
Eastshire Communications

Michelle Petrie, PhD
University of South Carolina, Aiken

Nancy A. Piotrowski, PhD
Capella University

John Pritchard
Richmond, Vermont

Claudia Daileader Ruland, MA
Johns Hopkins University

Amy Scholten, MPH
Inner Medicine Publishing

Jason J. Schwartz, PhD
Los Angeles, California

Martha A. Sherwood, PhD
Kent Anderson Law Office

Laura B. Smith
Swampscott, Massachusetts

Mark Stanton, PhD
Azusa Pacific University

Annie Stuart
Pacifica, California

Linda R. Tennison, PhD
College of Saint Benedict/Saint John's University

Eugenia M. Valentine, PhD
Xavier University of Louisiana

Patrice La Vigne
American Medical Writers Association

C. J. Walsh, PhD
Mote Marine Laboratory

Mary C. Ware, PhD
SUNY, College at Cortland

Robert J. Wellman, PhD
Fitchburg State University

Barbara Woldin, BS
American Medical Writers Association

Robin L. Wulffson, MD
FACOG (Faculty, American College of Obstetrics and Gynecology)

Complete List of Contents

Volume 1

Volume 2

Complete List of Contents

A

Abstinence-based treatment

CATEGORY: Treatment

ALSO KNOWN AS: Minnesota model of addiction treatment

DEFINITION: Abstinence-based treatment of drug and alcohol addiction is based on addiction as a disease. According to this treatment model, no cure exists for the disease of addiction. Through counseling and continued support, the addicted person can recover as long as he or she maintains lifelong abstinence from drugs and alcohol.

HISTORY

Abstinence-based treatment was first developed at Willmar State Hospital and Hazelden Treatment Center in Minnesota in 1949. The treatment was targeted at "hopeless" alcoholics and was based on the principles of Alcoholics Anonymous (AA). Borrowing from the twelve-step meetings of AA, developed in the 1930s, these alcoholic treatment centers added residential treatment that included lectures, open discussions, small group therapy, and peer interaction.

First known as the Willmar or Hazelden model, and then the Minnesota model in the 1970s, abstinence-based treatment centers became the predominant model for treating both alcohol and drug abuse in the 1980s. Private treatment in twenty-eight-day residential treatment centers dominated the treatment landscape but was affected by cost-cutting managed-care by the 1990s.

Most abstinence-based treatment now occurs in outpatient settings. Treatment focuses on individualized treatment plans, family involvement, and frequent use of group meetings such as AA, Narcotics Anonymous, and Al Anon. Studies show that more than 90 percent of drug and alcohol treatment programs in the United States are abstinence-based, and most use the twelve-step program of AA as a core principle.

BASIC PRINCIPLES

The first treatment principle is that all addiction, no matter the substance, is caused by lifelong physiological, social, and psychological disease processes. No cure exists for the disease of addiction, but recovery is possible through peer support and positive change. This principle removes the guilt that is associated with addiction and focuses on the disease instead of the addicted person. The addicted person begins by admitting that the disease makes him or her powerless over drugs and alcohol.

Recovery involves taking responsibility for the disease and making necessary changes in thinking and behavior. This type of cognitive behavioral therapy may include individual and group therapy. Personal change may include recognizing denial and other self-defeating behaviors and replacing these negative thoughts with gratitude, honesty, forgiveness, and humility. For many addicts and alcoholics, key components of successful abstinence include a spiritual awakening, faith in a higher power, and faith in the power of being part of a recovery community. A final principle is that without continued abstinence, addiction is a progressive and ultimately fatal disease.

BASIC COMPONENTS

Diagnosis should begin with a comprehensive evaluation that recognizes that addiction is a social, biological, and psychological disease. The initial phase of treatment may require medically supervised detoxification. Comorbid diseases related to alcohol or drug abuse and dual diagnosis such as bipolar disorder, attention deficit/hyperactivity disorder, or depression should also be recognized and treated.

Treatment for primary addiction may include the use of control-craving drugs, individual cognitive behavioral therapy, group therapy, family therapy, and relapse prevention therapy. Abstinence-based treatment may be adapted to a long period of residential treatment or may occur through outpatient care. Because this treatment considers addiction a lifelong disease, addicts are encouraged to attend after-care programs and twelve-step meetings, where they can benefit from the reinforcement of core principles and the support of other recovering people.

SUCCESS AND CRITICISM

Abstinence-based treatment is often criticized for having a low success rate, but because relapse is accepted as part of the natural course of the disease of addiction, it is difficult to give much credence to studies that look at one-year or even five-year success rates. Many addicted people fail initial treatment, have several relapses, and then continue with many years of sustained abstinence. According to the National Institute on Drug Abuse, relapse rates for addictions are similar to those for other chronic diseases, such as diabetes, hypertension, and asthma.

The abstinence-based treatment model also is criticized for being one-size-fits-all; for not allowing other treatment options, such as the harm-reduction model; for not being adaptable to persons who cannot accept the spiritual concept of a higher power; and for encouraging unattainable goals. These criticisms and alternatives are under discussion and study.

Still, most experts agree that abstinence should be the first and primary goal of addiction treatment. In the United States, therefore, abstinence-based treatment remains the treatment of choice for drug and alcohol addiction.

Christopher Iliades, MD

FURTHER READING

Ries, Richard, and Shannon C. Miller. *Principles of Addiction Medicine.* Philadelphia: Lippincott, 2009. A respected text for physicians and mental health professionals on all aspects of drug and alcohol addiction from the American Society of Addiction Medicine.

Scott, Christy K., et al. "Surviving Drug Addiction: The Effect of Treatment and Abstinence on Mortality." *American Journal of Public Health* 101.4 (2010): 737–44. Print. This study examines the effect of abstinence on mortality in a population of substance abusers. Concludes that a chronic disease paradigm is the best approach to addiction treatment.

Spicer, Jerry. *The Minnesota Model: The Evolution of the Multidisciplinary Approach to Recovery.* Center City, MN: Hazelden, 1993. Describes how the blend of behavioral science and the philosophy of Alcoholics Anonymous became the treatment model for all abstinence addiction treatment.

WEBSITES OF INTEREST

American Society of Addiction Medicine
http://www.asam.org

"The Definition of Addiction." AddictionsandRecovery.org
http://www.addictionsandrecovery.org/definition-of-addiction

Resources for Medical and Health Professionals. National Institute on Drug Abuse
http://www.drugabuse.gov/nidamed

"Treating Addiction, Transforming Lives." Hazelden
http://www.hazelden.org

See also: Alcoholics Anonymous; Hazelden Foundation; Minnesota Model; Outpatient treatment; Relapse.

Addiction

CATEGORY: Health issues and physiology
DEFINITION: The term *addiction* does not appear in the diagnostic criteria of substance abuse problems outlined by the American Psychiatric Association, in part because of the concern that words like *addiction* and *addict* are pejorative and could result in unnecessary stigmatizing of persons with drug and alcohol problems. Instead, problems associated with substance use are categorized not as addictions but as substance abuse or substance dependence.

THE COSTS OF ADDICTION

According to the National Institute on Drug Abuse, the societal cost of drug and alcohol addiction, in terms of lost productivity, crime, and health-care associated costs, is more than $600 billion per year. Perhaps an even greater cost, but one that is far more difficult to calculate, is the harm of addiction to those addicted and the "collateral damage" that often occurs to the loved ones of the addicted individual.

Most people can think of someone in their lives—a friend, partner, parent, or child—who is affected by addiction. Addiction is far too common, and its effects can be devastating. Researchers are making considerable progress in understanding the illness, and with greater understanding should come better treatment and more reason for hope.

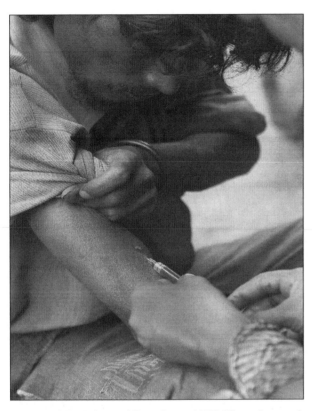

A drug addict injects a fellow abuser. (AFP/Getty Images)

DIAGNOSTIC CATEGORIES RELATED TO ADDICTION

Substance abuse involves a set of maladaptive behaviors associated with the taking of drugs, behaviors that include the failure to fulfill one's responsibilities, run-ins with the law, social or interpersonal problems, and engaging in risky, potentially dangerous behavior. Substance dependence is associated with changes in the way a person responds to drugs over time. Common changes indicating substance dependence are tolerance (the need for increasing doses to maintain drug effects) and withdrawal (unpleasant symptoms associated with drug removal). Additional criteria for substance dependence include the tendency to escalate drug use; taking the drug more frequently, in greater doses, or for longer periods of time; loss of control over drug use; and an inability to limit one's use.

To the extent that the symptoms associated with dependence and abuse are relatively clear and precise, they are valuable as diagnostic categories.

Symptoms do not, however, capture all meanings associated with the term *addiction*. The terms *substance abuse* and *substance dependence* have been limited to behaviors associated with addictive substances, even though in modern use the term *addiction* has been expanded to include excessive, compulsive, or destructive habits that have nothing to do with drugs. For example, persons are *workaholics* or *shopaholics*, two terms reflecting society's belief that a person can be addicted to working or to shopping, respectively. The concept of addiction also is commonly applied to compulsive eating, gambling, sexual behavior, and even web surfing.

GENERAL FEATURES OF ADDICTION

Because the term *addiction* includes many kinds of behaviors, one might wonder if it remains possible to extract common features of addiction that are associated with these behaviors in a relatively objective way. A number of common elements are indeed associated with addictions.

Addictions occur with behavioral rewards. Behavioral rewards include experiences that a person wants, experiences for which a person is willing to behave in a particular way. In short, the objects of addictions always feel good, at least in the beginning. While certain potentially addicting drugs and behaviors may, indeed, be harmful in all circumstances, this is not true across the board. There is nothing inherently unhealthy in things that feel good, or in the tendency to engage in certain behaviors to obtain those things. These behaviors have evolved, and they are tendencies that have served well for human survival.

The problem with addiction is that the effect of the behavioral reward changes in particular ways. With time and repeated exposure, a person's reaction to the behavioral reward changes in three observable ways. First, the person may develop a tolerance and then experience withdrawal. More and more of the behavioral reward will be needed to get the same amount of pleasure (tolerance), and the behavior may need to continue to keep feeling pleasure (withdrawal).

The presence of tolerance and withdrawal has been used as the primary indicator of addiction in years past. However, a person can vary in the extent to which he or she experiences tolerance and, especially, withdrawal, in his or her addiction, even with drugs such as alcohol, which produce symptoms of physical dependence.

In addition, other changes in a person's reaction to behavioral rewards also typically accompany the development of addictions. For example, the value of the addictive behavior, relative to other possible behaviors, changes. The person's behavioral repertoire shifts from one in which variable behaviors and responses occur to a far narrower focus, in which behaviors associated with the addiction come to predominate. Finally, the person seems to lose control of the addiction. Once he or she gets started with the behavior in question, they "overdo it" in ways that they did not intend and that they frequently regret. Efforts to permanently curtail or eliminate the addiction are extraordinarily difficult. Relapse, or returning to the behavior after successfully staying away from it for a time, is a common problem.

MODELS OF ADDICTION

Many different models, from widely diverse theoretical orientations within the field of psychology and medicine, have been proposed to account for addiction. Some consider addictions to be learned behaviors. These behavioral models focus on the role of conditioning processes in the development of addiction. Other models (social models) emphasize the role of other people (peers, family, society) in addictive behavior.

Other experts have sought to explain addiction in terms of personality variables, emphasizing the role of inner conflict or inadequate psychological coping mechanisms. Finally, numerous biological models search for the root of addictive behaviors in genetics and neurochemistry. It seems likely that a complete understanding of addiction may ultimately require a synthesis of several, if not all, of these approaches.

Linda R. Tennison, PhD

FURTHER READING

DiClemente, Carlo C. *Addiction and Change: How Addictions Develop and Addicted People Recover.* New York: Guilford, 2003. Describes the common features of addictive behavior, broadly defined, and discusses the development of and recovery from addictions as a stage theory.

Hart, Carl L., and Charles Ksir. *Drugs, Society, and Human Behavior.* 14th ed. New York: McGraw-Hill, 2010. An easy to read, entry-level textbook on substances of abuse.

Julien, Robert M., Claire D. Advokat, and Joseph E. Comaty. *A Primer of Drug Action.* 12th ed. New York: Worth, 2011. An excellent, thorough text covering uses and effects of both psychiatric substances and drugs of abuse.

WEBSITES OF INTEREST

American Psychological Association. Psychopharmacology and Substance Abuse Division
http://www.apa.org/divisions/div28

American Psychological Association. Society of Addiction Psychology Division
http://www.apa.org/divisions/div50

American Society of Addiction Medicine
http://www.asam.org

See also: Models of addiction; Psychological dependence; Risk factors for addiction; Science of addiction; Substance abuse

---

Addiction medications

CATEGORY: Treatment

DEFINITION: Addiction medications are drugs used to treat substance use disorders. The drugs are best used when combined with psychosocial treatment.

INTRODUCTION

Addiction is a brain disease. Once a person becomes addicted, changes typically occur in the body and the brain that make these systems function differently than before the development of the addiction. The functional (and perhaps structural) changes to the brain that occur with addiction can sometimes be treated with medications that allow the brain to function normally in the absence of the drug.

Medications are available for the treatment of opiate, alcohol, and cocaine use disorders and for nicotine use. Each of these medications will be considered individually here. No medication exists for the treatment of methamphetamine addiction, but about one-half dozen are being studied.

A pellet of naltrexone is shown. Naltrexone blocks the effects of heroin and other opium-derived drugs by binding to the same receptors in the brain that illegal drugs would. (AP Photo)

Many of the medications used in the treatment of addiction are used "off-label." In other words, the medications are used for addiction even though they have been approved by the US Food and Drug Administration (FDA) to treat other disorders, such as depression, muscle spasms, insomnia, and nausea. Only those medications currently legal to use in the United States (including those used off-label) are presented here. When available, both the clinical name and the more commonly used name will be included. The common name will appear in parentheses.

Many of the medications discussed fall under one of three categories: antagonist, full agonist, or partial agonist. An antagonist is a substance that binds to receptor cells so tightly that it will block any other substance from binding to that cell. Antagonists also bind to the cell without stimulating the cell or otherwise causing a response. Examples of antagonists include naltrexone and ondansetron.

A full agonist is similar to an antagonist in that it completely binds to a receptor cell. Unlike antagonists, however, full agonists will activate that receptor site. Examples of full agonists include morphine and topiramate (a gamma-aminobutyric acid, or GABA, agonist).

Partial agonists, like agonists, bind to receptor cells and activate them, but they cannot bind fully, so the receptor is only partially activated. Examples of partial agonists include varenicline and buprenorphine.

Medications are wonderful tools in the treatment of both physical and mental illnesses and disorders. It should be noted, however, that patients receiving medication also should receive psychosocial treatment.

MEDICATIONS FOR ALCOHOL ADDICTION

Alcohol is a central nervous system depressant. It works by interfering with communication between nerve cells and by interacting with the receptors on some cells. Alcohol suppresses excitatory nerve pathway activity (for example, glutamine) and increases inhibitory nerve pathway activity (for example, GABA). Thus, alcohol lowers inhibitions, which is why it is often found to be a significant factor in violent and sexually motivated crimes. Medications used (or under study) to treat alcohol use disorders include baclofen, campral (Acamprosate), disulfiram (Antabuse), naltrexone (ReVia or Vivitrol), ondansetron (Zofran), and topiramate (Topamax).

Baclofen. Baclofen treats muscle tightness and cramping or spasms that are often associated with spinal cord injury, spinal cord disease, or multiple sclerosis. The drug is a derivative of GABA and works with alcohol dependence by decreasing withdrawal symptoms and cravings. These effects are achieved by inhibiting the activation of the receptors in the brain that become stimulated during withdrawal.

Campral. The FDA approved campral for the treatment of alcohol use disorder in 2004. Before this time, campral was used widely across Europe in the treatment of alcohol use disorders. Campral works by stimulating GABA receptors and thereby reducing the negative symptoms a person may experience when attempting to abstain from alcohol.

Disulfiram. Disulfiram has been used to treat alcohol use disorders since the 1950s. Originally thought to work well as a treatment for parasites, experts began to notice that persons who took the medication and who also drank alcohol became ill. The medication disrupts the metabolism of alcohol, resulting in a hangover type of physical illness. The physical effects caused by disulfiram in persons also ingesting alcohol include headache, flushing nausea, dizziness, and vomiting.

Naltrexone. Naltrexone is an antagonist; it binds to the mu (μ) opioid receptors in the brain, but it does not stimulate them. This is important because naltrexone is used to treat addictions but does so without causing euphoria, like some addiction medications. Naltrexone is available in two different administrations: oral and injection.

The oral version of naltrexone, ReVia, was approved for the treatment of alcohol use disorders in 1995. However, because it must be taken daily, its effectiveness varies for those who are not medication compliant or not committed to treatment. In addition, side effects may be substantial because the medication levels vary throughout the day. The injection form of naltrexone, Vivitrol, was approved in 2006. Vivitrol is a long acting, once-a-month, injection that works the same way as ReVia, but it has fewer side effects and better medication compliance.

Ondansetron. Ondansetron is an antiemetic that reduces the nausea and vomiting that often accompany chemotherapy treatment. Ondansetron is a serotonin receptor antagonist and works by reducing the activity of the vagus nerve, thereby blocking the sensation of the need to vomit. This medication also has been studied as a treatment for other disorders, including alcohol use disorder, and although it is not approved for this, it can be prescribed off-label.

Topiramate. Topiramate treats epilepsy; however, research also indicates that it may be useful as a treatment for alcohol, cocaine, and nicotine dependence. Topiramate is a glutamate antagonist and a GABA agonist. It works by blocking the glutamate receptors and by increasing the effects of GABA, which help to calm over-excited nerve cells. Topiramate has been shown useful in the treatment of alcohol dependence. Topiramate has a number of side effects, including weight loss, impaired memory and concentration, numbness and tingling of extremities (although this side effect is transient), and the development of kidney stones.

MEDICATIONS FOR COCAINE ADDICTION
Cocaine is a stimulant of the central nervous system derived from the coca plant (not to be confused with the cocoa plant, which is used for chocolate). Cocaine is a serotonin-norepinephrine-dopamine reuptake inhibitor, which means that cocaine can increase alertness, euphoria, energy, motor activity, and feelings of competence. However, it also can result in anxiety, paranoia, restlessness, delusions, hallucinations, and tachycardia. Medications used (or under study) to treat cocaine use disorders include baclofen, disulfiram, gabapentin (Gabitrol), and modafinil (Provigil), and the dietary supplement N-acetylcysteine (NAC).

Baclofen. Baclofen, which is used to treat muscle spasticity (found in persons with multiple sclerosis), also has been studied as a potential treatment for cocaine addiction. Baclofen is said to work by decreasing the effects of dopamine in the brain and, thereby, reducing cocaine-induced euphoria.

Disulfiram. Disulfiram, which is used to treat alcohol use disorders, also has been studied as a treatment for cocaine disorders. In one study conducted at Yale University, disulfiram was found to work well in decreasing cocaine use. Similar to its effect with alcohol users, the study showed that is caused cocaine users to become physically ill. This research has since been replicated.

Gabapentin. Gabapentin is an anticonvulsant medication used to treat seizure disorders, depression, and pain. The medication also has been studied as a treatment for cocaine use disorders. The medication works by making cravings less intense and by lessening the severity of any relapse to cocaine use. Because of these positive effects, however, some doctors are hesitant to prescribe gabapentin for cocaine use disorders; it is believed that the medication will reinforce cocaine use rather than discourage it.

Modafinil. Modafinil is FDA approved for the treatment of narcolepsy and other sleep disorders. It also has been studied in the treatment of cocaine use disorders. However, findings have proven inconclusive.

N-acetylcysteine. N-acetylcysteine is an over-the-counter herbal supplement with purported antioxidant effects. It has been used to treat everything from carbon monoxide poisoning to acetaminophen overdose. Its effectiveness in treating cocaine use disorders has not been determined.

MEDICATIONS FOR METHAMPHETAMINE ADDICTION
Methamphetamine is a synthetic drug. Although chemically similar to amphetamine, its effects are

much longer lasting. Methamphetamine is a central nervous system stimulant with euphoric effects similar to those found with cocaine. Methamphetamine works by increasing the release of dopamine in the brain. No approved medications are on the market to treat methamphetamine addiction, and no medication is used off-label to treat methamphetamine addiction. However, a few drugs are under study, including paroxetine (Paxil), ondansetron, and gabapentin.

Paroxetine. Paroxetine is indicated for the treatment of mood disorders (depression and anxiety) and obsessive-compulsive disorder and panic disorder. It also is under study for the treatment of methamphetamine abuse.

Ondansetron. Ondansetron, used to treat alcohol use disorders, is FDA approved as an antinausea drug that may work to block specific binding sites for the neurotransmitter serotonin. Some preliminary studies have indicated that ondansetron may block the effects of methamphetamine.

Gabapentin. Gabapentin, in addition to being a potential medication for the treatment of cocaine use disorders, also may be a viable option for the treatment of methamphetamine use disorders.

MEDICATIONS FOR NICOTINE ADDICTION

Nicotine is a stimulant found in tobacco and tobacco products. The American Heart Association reports that nicotine dependence is one of the most difficult addictions to break. Some medications, including bupropion (Wellbutrin) and varenicline (Chantix), and other products, such as nicotine replacements, are available to assist persons addicted to nicotine. The use of bupropion and varenicline in nicotine addiction treatment, however, has been linked to serious side effects, including depression and suicidal ideation. Nicotine replacement products (such as patches and gum) provide the user with nicotine, but they do not have the harmful carcinogens that accompany many of the delivery systems (such as smoking or tobacco chewing).

Bupropion. Bupropion is a well-known antidepressant that has been used in the treatment of nicotine dependence. The drug works by reducing the urge to smoke.

Varenicline. Varenicline is a nicotine receptor partial agonist. It works by decreasing the cravings for nicotine and by decreasing the pleasurable effects of nicotine consumption.

MEDICATIONS FOR OPIATE ADDICTION

Opiates are narcotic analgesics (painkillers) that are derived from the poppy plant and from several artificial means. Opiates work by binding to specific receptors in the brain. Because the human body creates its own form of opiate, the brain has specific receptors created just for this substance. The receptors where opiates bind typically control movement, digestion, mood, the experience of pain, and, most problematic, body temperature and respiration.

Opiate use disorders vary and can include addiction to heroin and painkillers (such as vicodin and oxycodone). Medications used to treat opiate use disorders include buprenorphine, methadone, and naltrexone.

The FDA approved buprenorphine in 2002 as a treatment for opiate use disorders. The drug works by binding to the same receptors as opiates, but because it is a partial agonist it does not completely fill the receptor; therefore, little euphoria is achieved when taken as prescribed. A doctor prescribes buprenorphine, and induction (introduction of buprenorphine into the system) can be done in a doctor's office rather than at a substance abuse treatment facility. The effects of buprenorphine can last up to three days, so unlike the common drug methadone, daily doses are not required.

There are two different formulations of buprenorphine: Subutex and Suboxone. Subutex contains only buprenorphine and is the formulation used during the first few days of induction. Suboxone includes both buprenorphine and naloxone. Naloxone is a powerful substance that blocks the effects of opiates and is often used to treat opiate overdose. When combined with buprenorphine, it greatly reduces the abuse potential of this medication.

Methadone. Methadone, perhaps the best-known medication to treat opiate use disorders, is a synthetic opiate and a narcotic pain reliever similar to morphine. It has been used in the treatment of opiate addiction since the 1960s. Methadone is a full mu (μ) opioid agonist and works by binding to this receptor and by preventing other opiates from binding to that same receptor. However, methadone, if given in the incorrect dosage or through certain routes, can result in euphoria similar to that of illicit opiates.

Withdrawal from methadone can take several weeks to several months and has been described as more difficult to withdraw from than other opiates. Methadone is taken orally and is typically taken daily.

Naltrexone. Naltrexone, in addition to treating alcohol use disorders, also has been shown to be effective in the treatment of opiate use disorders. When used for opiate use disorders, naltrexone works as it does for alcohol: It binds tightly to the mu (μ) opioid receptors and prevents any other drug from binding to those same receptors. The binding action reduces cravings for the substance and also prevents the high that is normally experienced from opiate use. Because naltrexone is an antagonist, it is powerful enough to push the opiates out of the receptors to bind to them. This is important because naltrexone will place a patient into precipitated withdrawal from opiates if the patient has not abstained from opiates before receiving naltrexone.

There are two ways to administer naltrexone: orally (ReVia) and through an intramuscular injection (Vivitrol). Both forms are FDA approved for the treatment of opiate use disorders.

Desirée A. Crèvecoeur-MacPhail, PhD

FURTHER READING

Anglin, M., et al. "Longitudinal Effects of LAAM and Methadone Maintenance on Heroin Addict Behavior." *Journal of Behavioral Health Services and Research* 36.2 (2009): 267–82. Print. Discusses a study where the effects of LAAM were compared with methadone, whereby LAAM outperformed methadone in treatment retention and treatment suppression of heroin use.

Diehl, A., et al. "Why Is Disulfiram Superior to Acamprosate in the Routine Clinical Setting? A Retrospective Long-Term Study in 353 Alcohol-Dependent Patients." *Alcohol and Alcoholism* 45.3 (2010): 271–77. Print. This study compared disulfiram with acamprosate and found that in the short term, disulfiram produced results that were inferior to those of acamprosate. At follow-up, the acamprosate group had better treatment attendance and greater cumulative abstinence.

Dranitsaris, G., P. Selby, and J. C. Negrete. "Meta-Analyses of Placebo-Controlled Trials of Acampro-

sate for the Treatment of Alcohol Dependence: Impact of the Combined Pharmacotherapies and Behavior Interventions Study." *Journal of Addiction Medicine* 3.2 (2009): 74–82. Print. Details a meta-analysis that examined the effects of acamprosate and naltrexone and found that both drugs are effective in treating alcohol use disorders.

Johnson, B. A., et al. "Improvement of Physical Health and Quality of Life of Alcohol-Dependent Individuals with Topiramate Treatment." *Archives of Internal Medicine* 168.11 (2008): 1188–99. Print. Reports the outcomes of a study that examined the effect of topiramate on the physical and psychosocial well-being of the participants. Examined body mass index, blood pressure, and liver enzymes.

Kahan, M., et al. "Buprenorphine: New Treatment of Opioid Addiction in Primary Care." *Canadian Family Physician* 53.3 (2011): 281–89. Print. Discusses the use of buprenorphine for the treatment of opioid dependent persons in primary care.

Mattick, R. P., et al. "Methadone Maintenance Therapy versus No Opioid Replacement Therapy for Opioid Dependence." *Cochrane Database of Systematic Reviews* 3 (2009): CD002209. Web. Discusses the results of a study comparing methadone with opiate treatments that do not use opioid replacement therapy.

WEBSITES OF INTEREST

The Addiction Recovery Guide
http://www.addictionrecoveryguide.org/medication

Office of Alcoholism and Substance Abuse Services. New York State
http://www.oasas.ny.gov/AdMed/meds/meds.cfm

US National Library of Medicine
http://www.ncbi.nlm.nih.gov/pubmedhealth/s/
drugs_and_supplements/a

See also: Addiction medicine; Baclofen; Bupropion; Methadone; Naltrexone

Addiction medicine

CATEGORY: Treatment

ALSO KNOWN AS: Addiction treatment; medical treatment for addictions

DEFINITION: Addiction medicine is a medical specialty certified through the American Board of Addiction Medicine. Addiction medicine is founded on the premise that successful treatment for substance and behavioral addictions is best handled through a combination of medical intervention and psychotherapy or twelve-step programs.

OVERVIEW AND HISTORY

The concept of addiction medicine refers to newer treatment methods for substance and behavioral addictions that are based on the disease model rather than on the more prevalent behavioral model adopted by psychologists. Just as diabetes and other chronic diseases are treated with both pharmaceuticals and lifestyle changes, so too is addiction best treated as a brain disease; a growing number of medical experts are accepting this view.

The American Society of Addiction Medicine (ASAM) has officially represented the medical viewpoint for alcohol and drug addiction treatment in the United States since 1988, when ASAM was recognized as a national medical-specialty society by the American Medical Association. In 2007, ASAM founded the American Board of Addiction Medicine to certify specialists; in 2011 the first residencies offering clinical and research opportunities were established. ASAM now views most addictions as chronic diseases, including nicotine and prescription drug dependence, and behavioral addictions such as pathological gambling, sex addiction, and exercise addiction.

PHARMACOLOGIC INTERVENTIONS

The basis for pharmacologic intervention is founded in research that has shown that addiction alters the chemistry of the brain. The ability of the addictive substance or behavior to stimulate dopamine secretions in the mesolimbic reward pathway is the source for the pleasure sensation that drives addiction.

In time, an addiction can severely damage the neurons and brain circuits, resulting in impaired cognitive ability and other serious health issues. The right medication can block or counteract the euphoria

Dr. Drew Pinsky, a radio host and cable television personality, was tabbed as the "national face of addiction medicine." (FilmMagic)

caused by dopamine release or can help to repair an injured brain. While the use of medicine to treat addictions has gained favor, such an approach remains controversial, as medications have their own side effects and can sometimes become addicting too.

A medical treatment plan for a substance addiction usually begins with a medication that will help curb the cravings and alleviate the pain and suffering of the detoxification (detox) stage. The most commonly used medicines for alcohol detox are the benzodiazepines (tranquilizers such as Serax, Valium, and Ativan). For withdrawal from heroin, patients are usually given the synthetic opioid methadone. Other medications used for withdrawal from opiates (oxycodone, codeine, morphine, and others) include buprenorphine (Subutex), an opioid partial agonist; and Suboxone, a combination of buprenorphine and the opioid antagonist naloxone (Narcan, Narcanti).

In addition, patients might be given a benzodiazepine; an anti-inflammatory drug such as ibuprofen

(Motrin); a drug for diarrhea, such as loperamide (Imodium, Maalox, and others); and other medications. Varenicline (Chantix) or bupropion (Zyban) is prescribed for nicotine withdrawal when over-the-counter nicotine replacement therapy is ineffective. Clonidine (Catapres), an opioid agonist, is also sometimes used for nicotine and opiate withdrawal.

To prevent patient relapse, physicians usually prescribe a maintenance drug that blocks the receptor sites responsible for the sense of euphoria and cravings. For alcohol avoidance, the US Food and Drug Administration (FDA) permits naltrexone (Vivitrol, ReVia, Depade), acamprosate calcium (Campral), and disulfiram (Antabuse). For opiate avoidance, methadone, naltrexone, and buprenorphine are prescribed most often. The FDA has been reviewing topiramate (Topamax), a drug used to prevent epileptic seizures, for use in alcohol addiction treatment, and the proprietary Prometa treatment program, also used for opiate addiction treatment.

Medications for stimulant (cocaine, methamphetamine) and cannabis (marijuana) addictions are being developed. Other medications also might be prescribed when depression, anxiety, or other mental disorders are present.

BEHAVIORAL AND THERAPEUTIC INTERVENTIONS

As with the American Psychological Association's promotion of psychotherapy, twelve-step programs, family and couples therapy, and counseling for treating addictions, ASAM also believes that a multifaceted approach is usually best in treating addictions.

A central tenet of addiction medicine is that pharmacological intervention can set the stage for more successful therapeutic intervention. Once an addict is no longer physically addicted and once related mental disorders are under control, the brain becomes more receptive to treatment involving the modification of behavior and thoughts.

Addiction medicine recognizes the value of therapy to uncover the underlying thoughts that are often at the root of an addiction and to help patients recognize the triggers for their behavior. Therapeutic intervention also can improve self-esteem or help with the recovery from depression or anxiety. Health and wellness counseling, contingency management, and educational programs also are typical components of an addiction medicine plan.

Sally Driscoll, MLS

FURTHER READING

Freed, Christopher R. "Addiction Medicine and Addiction Psychiatry in America: Commonalities in the Medical Treatment of Addiction." *Contemporary Drug Problems* 37.1 (2007): 139–63. Print. Compares and contrasts treatment philosophies between the medical and psychiatric communities.

Quenqua, Douglas. "Medicine Adds Slots for Study of Addictions." *New York Times*, July 11, 2011, A11. Print. Examines the implications of the first accredited residencies in addiction medicine.

Ries, Richard K., et al. *Principles of Addiction Medicine.* 4th ed. Philadelphia: Lippincott, 2009. A standard reference for the medical profession that covers diagnosis, assessment, pharmacology, ethical and legal issues, and other topics.

Smith, David E. "Editor's Note: The Process Addictions and the New ASAM Definition of Addiction." *Journal of Psychoactive Drugs* 44.1 (2012): 1–4. Print. This excellent introduction to addiction medicine presents recent research that supports medical intervention for behavioral addictions.

---. "The Evolution of Addiction Medicine and Its San Francisco Roots." *Journal of Psychoactive Drugs* 42.2 (2010): 199–201. Print. This article traces the history of the concept of addiction medicine not just to San Francisco, but to the 1700s.

Urschel, Harold C. III. *Healing the Addicted Brain.* Naperville, IL: Sourcebooks, 2009. A popular book that explores the science behind addiction medicine. Usable as a self-help guide or for resources for further study.

WEBSITES OF INTEREST

American Board of Addiction Medicine
http://abam.net

American Society of Addiction Medicine
http://www.asam.org

National Institute on Drug Abuse
http://www.drugabuse.gov/related-topics/treatment-research

See also: Abstinence-based treatment; Detoxification; Halfway houses; Harm reduction; Rehabilitation programs

Addictive personality

CATEGORY: Psychological issues and behaviors

DEFINITION: Although a composite personality type predisposed to addiction has long been a popular concept, numerous studies to date have failed to uncover that type. Prevalent in earlier literature is the notion of a character flaw that leads inevitably to addiction. Modern research into addiction and personality, however, owes considerably more to neurobiology and neuroimaging than to psychodynamics. Research now focuses on broad-based personality traits—primarily impulsivity and disinhibition—that are linked to addictive behavior and are anatomically seated in the brain.

PERSONALITY COMPONENTS OF ADDICTION

Unplanned, spontaneous reaction to a stimulus without regard for adverse consequences is the hallmark of impulsivity. Insensitivity to consequences is a critical prerequisite for addiction. Impulsivity impels the choice of immediate rewards over the promise of delayed, albeit greater, rewards. Early in addiction, impulsivity is a strong impetus for experimenting with drugs.

Disinhibition is a close relation to impulsivity; it is a tendency to engage in risk-taking, sensation-seeking behaviors without constraints. Like impulsivity, disinhibition involves a loosening of self-regulatory controls and a disregard for the potentially disastrous consequences of maladaptive behavior. Both traits closely dovetail with the salient elements of addiction: behavior that confers a pleasure, benefit, or relief from an internal stress; behavior that has escaped the person's control; and behavior that is continued despite negative consequences.

Addiction cannot be understood without the concept of executive function. An umbrella term rather than an individual trait, *executive function* is a kind of supervisory cognitive process that integrates complex processes and mechanisms that govern behavior. The purview of executive function, which is anchored within the prefrontal cerebral cortex, includes reasoning skills, purposeful decision making, and the capacity to fend off distraction. Conscious control of thoughts and actions is implicit in executive function. When the interaction of emotional processing with behavioral restraints becomes impaired, addictive behavior and compulsions can take hold. Deficits in these mechanisms predispose and contribute to addiction.

IMPULSE-CONTROL DISORDERS AND ADDICTION

In accord with current research findings, the term *addiction* is likely to encompass behaviors and substances. Impulse-control disorders (ICDs) are a group of related behavioral disorders listed in the fourth edition of the *Diagnostic and Statistical Manual of Mental Disorders* (DSM-IV). The traditional ICDs include pathologic gambling, kleptomania, and trichotillomania (compulsive hair pulling). Other considered candidates for the ICD designation are compulsive Internet use, compulsive shopping, and compulsive sexual behavior.

The person with an ICD cannot resist the impulse to engage in potentially harmful behavior despite negative consequences—even possible criminal charges. Some internal tension precedes the behavior, which the behavior alleviates. A person with an ICD is typically a high scorer on measures of impulsivity and sensation-seeking. Descriptions of disinhibition, impulsivity, substance addiction, and behavioral addiction have obvious parallels; loosened controls and lessened restraints are integral to all. Distinctions between ICDs and substance addictions have blurred, in particular because similarly impaired neurophysiologic mechanisms underlie both.

Pathologic gambling has been termed a behavioral, or nondrug, addiction. It has been extensively studied as a model of the addiction process, in part because it does not cause the confounding effects of drugs on the brain. Defective processing of rewards and punishment, implicated in substance addiction, is a characteristic of compulsive gamblers. Sensitivity to monetary gains and losses alike is decreased. Pathologic gamblers will choose immediate monetary gains over the promise of higher, but delayed, gains. Known as delay discounting, this pattern reflects maladaptive decision making and impaired executive functioning. The trait predicts relapse in pathologic gambling.

CHANGES IN THE BRAIN

Whether it involves a substance or a behavior, addiction has a neurobiologic basis. The compulsions and lack of control that characterize addiction have counterparts in the brain's neurophysiology. Neuroimaging techniques have made it possible to trace addiction-related personality traits to metabolic activity in specific parts of the brain.

Regions of the prefrontal cerebral cortex exercise control over most facets of personality that participate in addiction: notably, decision making and regulation of emotion-laden behavior. In addition to inhibitory control functions, frontal cortical regions govern the reward-related behavior that is impaired in addicted persons. Chronic substance abusers have shown, in studies that measure neuropsychologic traits, deficits in decision making and in executive and inhibitory abilities. These impairments parallel abnormalities in areas of the prefrontal cortex observed in neuroimaging studies.

Abnormal metabolic activity in persons with substance dependence has been observed in the orbitofrontal cortex, a specific area in the prefrontal cortex (directly behind the forehead). This region is thought to be a major participant in critical executive functions—emotional processing, impulse control, working memory. Dysfunction in the orbitofrontal cortex impairs the ability to assess future consequences. It is the orbitofrontal cortex that will direct a decision to set aside immediate gratification in favor of greater delayed rewards.

Involvement of the neurotransmitter dopamine is further evidence of neural participation in addictive processes. Dopamine is believed to act on mechanisms of expectation and reward. Cocaine and amphetamines both increase dopamine levels and dopaminergic transmission. Appetizing food and addictive drugs have a comparable effect in raising levels of extracellular dopamine.

Personality traits that pervade neurophysiologic and neuropsychologic studies of addiction also emerge in genetic studies. Genes apparently make an early contribution to addictive behaviors, determining expression of the vulnerabilities that promote addiction. The finding of high heritability for behavioral disinhibition is based on samples of adolescent monozygotic and dizygotic twin pairs. Genetically determined predisposition to behavioral disinhibition, which is related to early-onset substance addiction, is expressed in parts of the brain affecting impulsivity and reward systems. Genetic studies have linked several genes to impulsivity and addiction. Alcohol, nicotine, and cocaine addictions have particularly strong genetic roots.

Judith Weinblatt, MS, MA

FURTHER READING

Erickson, Carlton K. *The Science of Addiction: From Neurobiology to Treatment.* New York: Norton, 2007. Neuroscience findings are written in understandable terms. Includes a glossary.

Holloran, Patricia. *Impaired: A Nurse's Story of Addiction and Recovery.* New York: Kaplan, 2009. In telling her own story, the author disputes the idea that addiction is a character flaw.

Van Wormer, Katherine, and Diane Rae Davis. *Addiction Treatment: A Strengths Perspective.* 2nd ed. Stamford, CT: Cengage, 2007. A college-level textbook with real-life examples and a pragmatic approach to addiction treatment.

WEBSITES OF INTEREST

"Addiction." American Psychological Association
http://www.apa.org/topics/addiction

Drug Abuse." MedlinePlus
http://nlm.nih.gov/medlineplus/drugabuse.html

See also: Addiction; Behavioral addictions: Overview; Impulse control disorders; Risk factors for addiction; Science of addiction

---

Adult children of alcoholics

Category: Psychological issues

Definition: According to estimates by the nonprofit Children of Alcoholics Foundation (CAF), there are more than 26.8 million adult children of alcoholics (ACOA) in the United States in the early twenty-first century. Children brought up in alcoholic or otherwise dysfunctional homes often are exposed to emotional, psychological, or physical abuse, and the scars left by an alcoholic parent can last long into adulthood.

A CHALLENGING JOURNEY

Adult children of alcoholics (ACOA) suffer from a wide range of negative effects because of their disrupted family backgrounds, including a fourfold increase in the likelihood of becoming alcoholics themselves, higher rates of mental disorders, higher rates of marrying into alcoholic families, and higher rates of becoming separated or divorced from their spouses. Typical ACOA tendencies can affect critical elements of life, including romantic relationships, parenting style, career goals, and finances.

Trust and security, two necessities for successful long-term relationships, do not come easily for many ACOAs, who grew up in insecure homes and may choose to isolate themselves from others. In addition, because many alcoholic parents were often more pre-occupied with drinking than with caring for their children, ACOAs often have a strong need for affection, which can manifest itself as possessiveness, jealousy, and oversensitivity. The strong desire to be loved can lead ACOAs to inspire dependency in their own children. ACOAs' need for approval can also lead them to overspend or pay beyond their means to please others. Also, many ACOAs had to mature early and assume the responsibilities that the alcoholic parent could not fulfill, which can create an overdeveloped sense of responsibility in ACOAs and contribute to feelings of inadequacy and loss of control.

FINDING HELP

The depth to which alcoholism affects ACOAs' daily lives depends on a wide range of variables, from their own personalities and coping skills to the extent to which their parent's alcoholism affected their early developmental years. All ACOAs can benefit from learning strategies that will help them overcome negative behaviors and chart courses for healthy futures, but no single method works best for everyone. Options include:

Reading. Find the latest books and research, both in print and online, about alcohol abuse and the way it can affect family life.

Talking. Confide in a close friend or family member who can understand your feelings and respect your privacy without judgment.

Counseling. Meet with a psychologist or certified social worker who can help you focus on your future, not the pains of the past. Sometimes talking with a stranger can be more therapeutic than talking with a friend.

Joining. Become a part of a free support group that meets in person or in a private online chat forum to find out how other ACOAs have overcome barriers to happiness. Twelve-step programs, such as Al-Anon and Adult Children of Alcoholics (ACA), can be particularly empowering.

Elissa Sonnenberg, MSEd

FURTHER READING

Ketcham, Katherine, William F. Asbury, Mel Schulstad, and Arthur P. Ciaramicoli. *Beyond the Influence: Understanding and Defeating Alcoholism.* New York: Bantam, 2000. Emphasizes that alcoholism is a disease, not a weakness of character. Explains the neurological nature of alcoholism and lists in detail various treatment options.

Ludwig, Arnold. *Understanding the Alcoholic's Mind: The Nature of Craving and How to Control It.* New York: Oxford University Press, 1989. An examination of the methods that can be used for a successful recovery from alcoholism.

Miller, William R., and Kathleen M. Carroll, eds. *Rethinking Substance Abuse: What the Science Shows, and What We Should Do about It.* New York: The Guilford Press, 2010. Covers treatment and prevention of substance abuse based on the best science available. Incorporates various perspectives, including social-environmental, genetic, behavioral, developmental, and neurobiological.

WEBSITES OF INTEREST

Adult Children of Alcoholics World Service Organization, Inc.
http://www.adultchildren.org

Al-Anon/Alateen
http://www.al-anon.alateen.org/

Children of Alcoholics Foundation
http://www.coaf.org

See also: Families and substance abuse; Marriage/partnership and alcoholism; Parenting and alcoholism

Advertising for alcohol

CATEGORY: Social issues

DEFINITION: Advertising for alcohol involves the use of various media in stores, shops, newspapers, and magazines, and on billboards, television, radio, websites, film, and clothing to entice and persuade persons to buy and consume products containing alcohol. Certain venues, particularly sporting events and concerts, also promote alcohol products because these venues are commonly sponsored by distributors of alcohol. Alcohol advertising especially influences youth.

ALCOHOL AS IMAGE

Since the ancient Greeks celebrated Dionysus, the god of wine, theater, and ecstasy, a connection has endured among alcohol, media, and sensuality. In addition to sharing a profound appeal to the senses, alcohol, theater, and ecstasy offer an escape from the mundane and a sense of liberation. The view of intoxication as a celebration and a rite of passage continues to this day, anchored by the many messages modern society reflects in its depictions of alcohol through advertising.

Echoes of Dionysus reverberate throughout much modern advertising for alcohol, which often touts youth, sexual prowess, beauty, and athleticism. Initiation into manhood, quite often involving male bonding through modern-day sporting events, is

This advertisement for Curtis Gin dates back to the mid-twentieth century. (SSPL via Getty Images)

rarely viewed as complete without alcohol. Alcohol advertisers carefully create their own myths about alcohol normalcy, portraying a world where the successful people drink and all drinkers are rewarded.

Through advertising, young people in particular learn to associate alcohol with social acceptance. Those who abstain are promptly left behind and dismissed. Young people are especially susceptible to the lure of alcohol advertising. The images depicting alcohol's social benefits are wildly exaggerated and distorted by alcohol advertising, and many young people tend to accept the misconception that drinking will somehow improve their lives.

Instead of finding the advertised camaraderie and companionship, many will find themselves, years later, abusing alcohol alone. Alcohol advertising frequently sells one reality but delivers another.

ALCOHOL ADVERTISING AND YOUTH

The legal age to buy alcohol in all fifty US states is twenty-one years. Many people argue that some alcohol advertising campaigns are designed specifically to appeal to the youth market, despite the legal barriers to consumption. One such compelling argument was frequently made about the advertising mascot Spuds McKenzie, a highly appealing 1980s ad image of a bull terrier dog, the original "party animal."

Wearing sunglasses, a bandana, a Hawaiian shirt, and headphones, and holding a Bud Light beer, Spuds was depicted in tropical locales and surrounded by beautiful, scantily clad young women. First appearing to acclaim in a 1987 Bud Light commercial during the broadcast of the Super Bowl, Spuds, throughout the late 1980s, rode skateboards, raced horses, drove convertibles, maneuvered surfboards, played Frisbee, and combed beaches.

Sales of Bud Light beer soared during the Spuds ad campaign, which not only marketed the alcoholic beverage but also sold millions of dollars of Spuds paraphernalia: everything from T-shirts to caps to plush toys. Antidrinking groups responded by arguing that the campaign targeted children and teenagers. In 1989, Mothers Against Drunk Driving claimed that Anheuser-Busch, the maker of Bud Light, was deceptively marketing alcohol to children and demanded that Spuds ads cease promoting the beer. An investigation of the ad campaign by the Federal Trade Commission (FTC) ensued, and although the FTC found no wrongdoing by Anheuser-Busch, the company nevertheless terminated the campaign in 1989.

Anheuser-Busch again ignited controversy in the 1990s with its Budweiser Frogs ad campaign. First appearing as a Super Bowl television commercial in 1995, the Budweiser Frogs depicted three frogs, Bud, Weis, and Er, who lived on a log in a swamp behind a bar and croaked "Budweiser" rhythmically. In 1996, a study revealed that considerable numbers of nine- to eleven-year-old children could easily identify the Budweiser Frogs and associate them with beer, but were unable to recognize or identify various children's cartoon figures. Antidrinking groups again accused the alcohol industry of targeting children.

Shortly thereafter, another study revealed that when asked to name US presidents, most eight- to twelve-year-old children could name few but had no difficulty naming a variety of brands of beer. In spite of these negative reports, the Budweiser Frogs campaign continued for many years; it is recognized in the adverting industry as one of most successful marketing campaigns in history.

ALCOHOL AND SPORTING EVENTS

The alcohol industry is a frequent sponsor and promoter of sporting events, many of which appeal to a large percentage of fans who are minors. From the Super Bowl to the World Series to auto racing to college basketball, the alcohol industry spends billions of sponsorship and advertising dollars each year, specifically targeting an audience of sports fans, many of them younger than twenty-one years.

The alcohol industry provides a lucrative source of funding for collegiate sports, especially the National Collegiate Athletic Association's (NCAA) annual basketball championships (known as March Madness), but some critics argue that the price for this funding is too high, owing to the toll it levies in the form of underage drinking. The NCAA's playoff and championship games, for instance, welcome millions of children and minors as viewers each year, who are subjected to the same degree of intense alcohol advertising as adults. Although the alcohol industry maintains that it is advertising its products so rigorously during such sporting events only to establish brand loyalty among adults who already drink, March Madness nonetheless draws millions of underage viewers.

According to the National Institute on Alcohol Abuse and Alcoholism (NIAAA), studies reveal a greater propensity among young people to initiate drinking at a younger age if they are heavily exposed to alcohol advertising. Moreover, the NIAAA cites evidence demonstrating that the younger a person begins to drink, the greater the likelihood that he or she will become an alcoholic. For example, statistically, the NIAAA reports that a person who begins drinking by age fifteen years is four times as likely to become a heavy drinker and dependent on alcohol than a person who begins drinking at age twenty-one years.

Children, drawn to watch their favorite sports teams and athletes, are ill equipped to decipher the deceptive messages of alcohol advertising. Youths often come away from watching such sporting competitions with a false sense of normalcy, believing that alcohol consumption as portrayed by advertising is ubiquitous, harmless, fun, and inconsequential, regardless of age or circumstance. Fans attending both collegiate and professional sporting events sponsored by alcohol companies have recently become increasingly dismayed and alarmed at the escalation of public drunkenness and violence occurring among fans, an environment that is growing increasingly unsafe for children.

Mary E. Markland, MA

FURTHER READING

Bryant, Jennings, and Mary Beth Oliver. *Media Effects: Advances in Theory and Research.* 3rd ed. New York: Routledge, 2009. Provides convincing evidence of recent studies that supports a direct correlation between increased exposure to alcohol advertising and an earlier initiation into drinking by youths.

Lankford, Ronnie. *At Issue: Alcohol Abuse.* Farmington Hills, MI: Greenhaven, 2007. Examines the ways in which alcohol advertising contributes to underage drinking, specifically by targeting youths in ad campaigns.

Sheehan, Kim. *Controversies in Contemporary Advertising.* Thousand Oaks, CA: Sage, 2004. Analyzes beer, wine, and hard-liquor advertising, comparing and contrasting its appeal statistically to different genders, age groups, ethnic groups, and socioeconomic groups.

Tardiff, Joseph. *Teen Alcoholism.* Farmington Hills, MI: Greenhaven, 2008. Argues that college sporting events, and the National Collegiate Athletic Association in particular, should ban funding and sponsorship by alcoholic beverage companies.

Wechsler, Henry, and Bernice Wuethrich. *Dying to Drink: Confronting Binge Drinking on College Campuses.* Emmaus, PA: Rodale, 2002. Discusses scientific studies that demonstrate that the greater the volume of discount and point of sale advertising of alcoholic beverages within the proximity of college campuses, in the form of happy hours and such, the greater the amount of alcohol that is consumed by college students.

WEBSITES OF INTEREST
Alcoholics Anonymous
http://www.aa.org

Center on Alcohol Marketing and Youth
http://www.camy.org

Mothers Against Drunk Driving
http://www.madd.org

National Institute on Alcohol Abuse and Alcoholism
http://www.niaaa.nih.gov

See also: Advertising for tobacco products; Media and substance abuse

Advertising for tobacco products

CATEGORY: Social issues
DEFINITION: Tobacco companies advertise their products, namely cigarettes, cigars, and smokeless tobacco, in newspapers and magazines, on billboards, in retail stores, and at sporting events. Advertising in the United States for tobacco products is banned, however, from television, radio, and the web by the Federal Trade Commission, but motion pictures still promote tobacco products through what is called product placement.

THE "JOE CAMEL" CAMPAIGN
Of all the advertising campaigns launched by the tobacco industry, R. J. Reynolds Tobacco Company's marketing for Camel brand cigarettes was by far the most notorious and controversial. In 1988, in an attempt to create "replacement smokers" for those long-term smokers who were sick and dying, R. J.

Reynolds introduced the enormously popular and youth "friendly" animated character Joe Camel. An engaging, wisecracking, and easygoing character, "Old Joe" was an instant success among young people. Few people realize that R. J. Reynolds's Joe Camel was a nod to the Durham bull, a similarly popular anthropomorphic character at the turn of the twentieth century. The Durham bull advertised roll-your-own cigarettes by rebelliously kicking up its heels and making humorous remarks.

Through R. J. Reynolds's marketing campaign, Joe Camel was popularized on billboards and in magazines and newspapers, which became saturated with the Joe Camel image. The character was selling not only Camel cigarettes but also a huge amount of Joe Camel paraphernalia—everything from T-shirts, to baseball caps, to underwear.

In 1991, the American Medical Association sparked debate when it published a study revealing that 90 percent of six-year-old children who were surveyed could recognize and identify Joe Camel, roughly the same percentage who could recognize and identify Mickey Mouse. By contrast, only 67 percent of adults surveyed could identify Joe Camel and directly associate the character with cigarettes.

After filing a lawsuit against R. J. Reynolds for deceptive advertising practices and liability, a San Francisco law firm later revealed an astronomical spike of several hundred percent in revenue from youth market shares between 1988 and 1992 that was specifically attributable to the Joe Camel advertising campaign. In 1997, following public outcry and after the US Congress threatened stricter legislation, R. J. Reynolds settled the lawsuit, agreeing to terminate Joe Camel-related advertisements and agreeing to pay the State of California $10 million to fund antismoking education for youth.

Shortly thereafter, R. J. Reynolds changed its ad campaign by replacing Joe Camel the cartoon character with an image of a true camel, an image that was designed to appeal to adults and an image that still represents Camel cigarettes.

In the end, though, it was the phenomenal success of the Joe Camel advertising campaign that did more than anything else to incense and inflame the public. The ad campaign encouraged public, school, and legislative support for subsequent antismoking campaigns around the United States.

LEGISLATING DECEPTIVE TOBACCO ADVERTISING

In 1900, only one in 100 Americans smoked, but that percentage soon rose. During World War I, smoking became immensely popular in both the United States and in Europe, in part because the US military distributed free branded cigarettes to its troops. By the 1930s, the Federal Trade Commission began regulating the false advertising claims made by tobacco companies. Throughout the nineteenth and early twentieth centuries, it had been commonplace for tobacco products to be advertised by doctors and surgeons, who claimed that smoking had all-around health benefits.

Beginning in 1920, tobacco brands, especially Lucky Strike, began advertising campaigns that targeted women, appealing to American women's new-found status as "liberated" voters after the passage of the Nineteenth Amendment to the US Constitution (1920). The ads promised women that smoking would make them more slender, trim, and attractive, a claim repeated fifty years later with the branding of Virginia Slims cigarettes.

The 1930s witnessed en masse the first detrimental fallout of smoking's ever-growing popularity, as doctors began treating huge numbers of patients for lung cancer, a disease otherwise rarely seen. Increasing numbers of medical reports and studies worldwide began to draw direct correlations between the upsurge in smokers and the spike in certain kinds of cancer.

Smoking was further popularized during World War II, when free cigarettes were provided to the troops, as they were during World War I. Also, tobacco companies continued to deny medical reports, and their ads continued to portray smoking as healthy. Hollywood similarly intensified the glamorous appeal of smoking in its films. Consequently, by 1950, approximately 50 percent of American adults smoked cigarettes.

After more than a decade of continued research that further linked smoking and cancer, the US Office of the Surgeon General (in 1964) proclaimed smoking to be hazardous to one's health and to be a direct cause of lung cancer. In 1965, Congress passed

A Marlboro billboard uses cowboys to advertise cigarettes. (Getty Images)

the Cigarette Labeling and Advertising Act, which required cigarette manufacturers to place a warning label on each pack of cigarettes. The first label warned consumers that cigarette smoking "might" be hazardous to their health; in 1969, Congress passed additional legislation, the Public Health Cigarette Smoking Act, which required the warning label on cigarettes packs to be more definitive: "Warning: The Surgeon General Has Determined That Cigarette Smoking Is Dangerous to Your Health." The act also banned all advertising for cigarettes on television and radio.

BIG TOBACCO MASTER SETTLEMENT AGREEMENT

Throughout the 1970s and 1980s, scientific studies continued to confirm the harm of tobacco products, yet the tobacco industry continued to deny this fact in its advertising. By the 1990s, with escalating numbers of lawsuits against the tobacco industry for fraudulent misrepresentation, wrongful death, criminal negligence, and criminal liability, an increasing number of cases were decided in favor of injured and, oftentimes, deceased smokers. Moreover, as enormous amounts of taxpayer dollars were being used to treat sick and dying smokers, state attorneys general began to sue tobacco companies to recoup lost revenue from state budgets. As juries awarded plaintiffs ever larger settlements, the tobacco industry began to search for a way to stop the increasing litigation.

Finally, in 1998, R. J. Reynolds, Brown and Williamson, and Philip Morris (three major entities of what came to be called Big Tobacco) were bound to the Master Settlement Agreement (MSA), the largest financial settlement in US history. In addition to severely restricting tobacco advertising, the MSA mandated annual Big Tobacco payments of millions of dollars to state governments for ongoing governmental efforts to control tobacco use, especially among youths. The MSA also led to widespread antismoking advertising campaigns, such as the Truth campaign, which encouraged youth to stop or avoid smoking.

The MSA also made illegal all advertising and selling of tobacco products to any person younger than age eighteen and made it illegal to use any cartoon or animation to advertise tobacco products. This provision would ensure against the recurrence of any marketing campaign reminiscent of the Joe Camel campaign that had targeted children in earlier

decades. The MSA additionally placed Big Tobacco advertising under the regulation and control of the US Food and Drug Administration, a provision later reinforced with congressional legislation.

Mary E. Markland, MA

FURTHER READING

Califano, Joseph, Jr. *High Society: How Substance Abuse Ravages America and What to Do About It.* New York: Public Affairs, 2007. Discusses the ways in which tobacco companies target women, children, and ethnic and racial minorities in their advertising campaigns. Covers the Virginia Slims, X, Dorado and Rio, and Joe Camel campaigns.

Hudson, David, Jr. *Smoking Bans.* Philadelphia: Chelsea House, 2004. Traces a chronological history of governmental legislation and restriction of tobacco following landmark tobacco litigation in the United States, beginning with the first US Supreme Court's tobacco-related decision in 1900.

Hyde, Margaret. *Know About Smoking.* New York: Walker, 1995. Concrete information about the abusive cycle of smoking, how tobacco advertisers exploit that cycle through advertising, and how to combat and break tobacco's circle of entrapment.

White, Larry. *Merchants of Death: The American Tobacco Industry.* New York: Random House, 1991. Beginning its discussion in the early 1950s, this book details the enormous political power of tobacco lobbyists and their ability to manipulate Congress and public perception while continuing to knowingly market harmful tobacco products.

Williams, Rodger. *At Issue: Teen Smoking.* Farmington Hills, MI: Greenhaven, 2009. Examines the specific nature of tobacco advertising as it relates to teenagers, and addresses the ways in which marketing literacy campaigns can increase teenagers' awareness of tobacco advertising tactics.

WEBSITES OF INTEREST

American Cancer Society
http://www.cancer.org

Campaign for Tobacco-Free Kids
http://www.tobaccofreekids.org

Stanford Research into the Impact of Tobacco Advertising. Stanford School of Medicine
http://tobacco.stanford.edu

"Tobacco Control Advocacy." American Lung Association
http://www.lungusa.org/stop-smoking/tobacco-
control-advocacy

US Office of the Surgeon General
http://www.surgeongeneral.gov

See also: Advertising for alcohol; Media and smoking

Aerosols

CATEGORY: Substances
ALSO KNOWN AS: Dusters; whippets
DEFINITION: Aerosols are inhalants that use propellants to release a substance from a pressurized container into the air. Examples of aerosols include computer and electronic duster sprays, air fresheners, spray paint, whipped-cream dispensers, whipped-cream dispenser chargers (whippets), and cooking, hair, and deodorant sprays. The propellants and solvents in these devices can be abused like other volatile substances, such as nitrites, and solvents, such as paint thinners and correction fluid.
STATUS: Legal in the United States and worldwide
CLASSIFICATION: Noncontrolled substance
SOURCE: Aerosols are sold in cans that contain propellants such as nitrous oxide or solvents such as toluene.
TRANSMISSION ROUTE: Inhalation

HISTORY OF USE

Aerosols make up a unique category of abused substances, as they are not drugs and were not formulated to produce intoxicating effects. Aerosols are, however, easily obtained and, as such, are more commonly abused by children and adolescents. Most users are adolescents (ages twelve to seventeen years), and in the United States, users are more likely to be poor and to live in impoverished communities, where aerosols are inexpensive and easy to obtain.

Aerosol abuse remains a significant problem, a fact contradicting the results of three surveys in the United States that tracked aerosol and inhalant abuse. The surveys had reported a declining trend in aerosol abuse since the late 1990s, but they also had relied on self-reporting and focused on specific age ranges, so they may provide an incomplete picture of abuse trends.

Reported abuse rates are higher among Hispanics, Native Americans, and Caucasians in the United States, and while national survey data does not show significant gender differences in overall use of inhalants, males are more likely to abuse inhalants over a sustained period of time. Information from the National Poison Data System indicates that nearly 75 percent of cases reported to poison control centers involve boys. Whereas boys and girls report use equally, boys are more likely to have severe incidents requiring immediate medical intervention. Other studies have shown an association between eating disorders and inhalant abuse, and have shown an increased likelihood of abuse among persons living in rural areas or small towns.

Historically, inhalant abuse became a widespread problem in the United States during Prohibition, when ether was inhaled as a substitute for drinking alcohol. Abuse shifted mainly to the inhalation of glue, gasoline, and paint fumes during the 1950s. Aerosol spray abuse did not become common until the 1980s, as propellants in products produced before the 1980s generally contained chlorinated fluorocarbons (CFCs), which, based on their properties as refrigerator coolants, froze the lungs of a person who inhaled the fumes. Manufacturers' replacement of CFCs with more environmentally friendly propane and butane led to an increase in the number of people abusing the products. Later data indicated that computer dusters and spray paint are two aerosol products with the highest abuse rates.

EFFECTS AND POTENTIAL RISKS

Inhalation of aerosol propellants leads to effects similar to those of alcohol intoxication. Symptoms include loss of coordination, slurred speech, euphoria, dizziness, and lightheadedness. Some people also experience hallucinations or delusions. The effects do not last as long as alcohol intoxication, however, and they generally subside after a few minutes. This leads users to repeatedly inhale the substance to attempt to extend the effects. Repeated inhalation can lead to headaches, nausea and vomiting, and loss of inhibitions. Addiction can occur, but is not common.

One study found that toluene, a solvent contained in spray paint, can activate the dopamine system in the brain, however. As this system plays a role in the rewarding effects of most drugs of abuse, this particular type of aerosol abuse may be more likely to lead to addiction.

A major concern with aerosol abuse is that the products displace air in the lungs and can lead to oxygen deprivation or hypoxia. Brain cells are particularly sensitive to hypoxia, and repeated abuse of such substances can lead to memory loss, learning difficulties, and conversational problems. Long-term abuse can destroy myelin, the protective fatty tissue surrounding nerve fibers. Myelin destruction eventually leads to muscle spasms, tremors, and difficulty with walking and other motor activities.

In addition, inhaling highly concentrated amounts of solvent or propellant from aerosol sprays can lead to heart failure and to a condition referred to as sudden sniffing death, which can occur within minutes of inhalation. Death also can occur from severe hypoxia, which leads to suffocation; the chances of this occurring are increased when the substance is inhaled in a closed area or from a paper or plastic bag.

Certain substances also can lead to unique irreversible effects. Hearing loss, central nervous system damage, and brain damage can result from sniffing the toluene component of spray paint. Peripheral neuropathies and limb spasms can result from sniffing the nitrous oxide contained in whipped-cream dispensers. Toluene also can lead to kidney and liver damage.

Although aerosol and other inhalant abuse remains a problem, no clear treatment guidelines exist. This may due to the fact that aerosol dependence and abuse are not generally recognized by clinicians and because treatment is focused on other substances of abuse. Also, most abusers are adolescents who may not wish to seek treatment; also, age limits keep adolescents from enrolling in clinical trials, which could lead to intervention.

Karen Nagel Edwards, PhD

FURTHER READING

Konghom, Suwapat, et al. "Treatment for Inhalant Dependence and Abuse." *Cochrane Database of Systemic Reviews* 12 (2010). Web. 30 Jan. 2012. A review of the treatment methods available for inhalant dependence and abuse. No studies met the authors' inclusion criteria; this was believed to be because inhalant abusers do not wish to seek treatment and tend to abuse many substances. Any substance abuse treatment they receive tends to focus on other substances of abuse.

Marsolek, Melinda R., Nicole C. White, and Toby L. Litovitz. "Inhalant Abuse: Monitoring Trends by Using Poison Control Data, 1993–2008." *Pediatrics* 125 (2010): 906–13. Print. A comprehensive overview of poison control data as it relates to inhalant abuse; focuses on demographic and geographic trends, particularly among teenagers.

Perron, Brian E., and Matthew O. Howard. "Adolescent Inhalant Use, Abuse, and Dependence." *Addiction* 104 (2009): 1185–92. Print. A research report comparing adolescents with documented psychiatric inhalant-use disorders to inhalant users without a diagnosis and to nonusers.

WEBSITES OF INTEREST

Alliance for Consumer Education. Inhalant Abuse Prevention Program
http://www.inhalant.org

"Inhalants." *National Institute on Drug Abuse*
http://www.drugabuse.gov/drugs-abuse/inhalants

Office of National Drug Control Policy
http://www.whitehouse.gov/ondcp

See also: Gateway drugs; Inhalants abuse

Age and addiction

CATEGORY: Social issues

DEFINITION: There is no age limit for addictions. Babies are born addicted to the illicit drugs and prescription medicines that their mothers abused while pregnant, and addiction to a wide range of substances and behaviors is endemic among teenagers and young adults. Although not as widely recognized, older adults also suffer addictions.

A HIDDEN PROBLEM

A nationwide survey in the United States revealed that between 2000 and 2008, admissions for addiction treatments for people age fifty years and older in-creased by 70 percent, while overall this age group grew by only 21 percent. About 60 percent of these addiction-treatment admissions included persons seeking treatment for alcohol abuse, about 16 per-cent were for heroin addiction, and about 11 percent were for cocaine addiction.

A study released by the Substance Abuse and Mental Health Services Administration (US Depart-ment of Health and Human Services) in 2010 showed that the aging of the baby-boom generation (made up of persons born from 1946 through 1964) has led to a sharp increase in the abuse of illicit drugs by adults older than age fifty years. Researchers concluded that the need for addiction-treatment services for Ameri-cans age fifty years and older would double by 2020.

The scope of the problem of addiction among older adults is unknown, largely because many cases go unreported. In addition, the elderly and their families often deny the problem. For example, family members might excuse an older rela-tive's gambling addiction as a harm-less hobby, or they might argue that heavy alcohol use is an entitlement for a relative after a long, hard life. Also, many older people rarely admit they have a problem. They rationalize that they are experienced and wise and able to handle any situation. This way of rationalizing is especially true for people addicted to prescription med-ications. The symptoms of addiction are often less evident in older people than they are in younger people. For example, many older adults addicted to alcohol or drugs indulge at home, so they are less likely to drive a ve-hicle and to risk arrest while intoxi-cated. Also, many elderly persons live alone, making it difficult for others to notice problems with drinking or with drug abuse. Furthermore, many elderly persons are retired, so common determiners of addiction, such as work absenteeism or poor job performance, are poor determiners of addiction in the elderly.

Addiction in older adults often goes unrecognized, even by health professionals. Symptoms of addictions are mistaken for diseases common to old age, such as high blood pressure, dementia, stroke, Parkinson's disease, and sleep disorders. Moreover, most of the medical and psychological screening tests for addiction are de-signed for younger people, making the tests inade-quate for older adults.

SUBSTANCES AND BEHAVIORS

Using a working definition of *addiction* as "a physio-logical or psychological dependence on a substance or behavior to the extent that its withdrawal causes extreme distress to the user," addictions in older adults are the same as those in younger people. How-ever, two substances, alcohol and prescription medi-cations, and two behaviors, gambling and watching television, appear to be particularly troublesome for older adults.

Alcohol is the drug most often abused by older adults. In a survey of adults between ages sixty years

A 53-year-old drug addict lights up a pipe filled with heroin in a room at an elderly home for drug addicts in Rotterdam, Netherlands. (Jerry Lampen/ Reuters/Landov)

and ninety-four years, some 62 percent reported drinking alcohol regularly and 13 percent admitted to heavy use of alcohol. In many cases, alcohol addiction leads to other problems for the elderly. Older adults addicted to alcohol are three times more likely to already have or to develop another mental disorder.

Prescription medications rank as the second most commonly abused substance among older adults and include sedatives, antidepressants, sleeping pills, and pain relievers, especially the narcotic analgesics. The National Institute on Drug Abuse (NIDA) reported that people age sixty-five years and older received about 33 percent of all medications prescribed by doctors in the United States, yet this group makes up only 13 percent of the US population. According to NIDA, some 18 percent of adults age sixty years and older abuse prescription drugs. Older adults take prescription medications three times more frequently than the general population and are more likely to disregard dosing directions, often choosing to self-medicate instead. To compound the problem, NIDA reported that, in general (for some drugs), older adults receive prescriptions with higher doses and with longer dosage times than younger adults receive.

Gambling has become a popular pastime of older adults. In one survey, 73 percent of study participants said they had engaged in some form of gambling in the previous year. Studies have revealed that throughout North America, about 4 percent of all adult gamblers are addicted to gambling, about the same percentage as older gamblers. However, considering that the older adult segment is the fastest growing segment of gamblers, the actual number of addicted gamblers (known as pathological gamblers) is greater than ever. Researchers in New Jersey found that 4 percent of gamblers age fifty-five years and older are problem gamblers and that 2 percent are pathological gamblers. Nearly 11 percent of persons age sixty-five and older in primary care facilities in Pennsylvania are at-risk gamblers. In Missouri, 4 percent of participants in that state's compulsive gamblers program are older than age sixty-five years.

Television watching, too, can become an addiction, according to many mental health professionals. About 97 percent of older adults watch television regularly, more so than any other age group. For many older adults, especially those living alone or with limited mobility, television is a companion and watching television is an activity that helps them cope with their problems. Watching television is considered an addiction when a viewer cannot stop watching at a chosen time, when he or she wants to but cannot watch less, when he or she complains that watching replaces other activities and takes up too much time, and when he or she is uneasy and experiences withdrawal symptoms when not watching for a time.

AGE-RELATED FACTORS

Some adults carry an addiction into their later years. Most baby boomers with an addiction to illicit drugs, for example, continue a pattern of abuse that began for them in the 1960s and 1970s. However, not many drug addicts, or alcoholics, live to old age because of the devastating physical effects of lifelong addiction.

Other adults switch addictions when they get older. Studies of the chemistry of addiction are helping to explain why some people and not others become addicted. A seminal study prepared for the National Academy of Sciences in 1983 identified certain personality traits that can contribute to the onset of addiction. A person with an addictive personality, for example, might have been addicted to heroin when young but may have switched to prescription drugs later in life.

Other adults become addicted only in their later years. Many elderly persons turn to substances and behaviors that become addictions as a way to cope with growing older. The factors that contribute to addiction, at any age, are complex, but certain circumstances and elements are unique to older people.

In general, as people reach their sixties they are more vulnerable to compulsive behaviors such as gambling. Older people experience many more types of loss than do younger people—loss of physical and mental capabilities; loss of older family members, of spouses, and of friends in the same age group; loss of earning power; and loss of status in society, especially following retirement and particularity in a society that reveres youth. Older adults deal with more serious medical conditions, such as heart disease, Parkinson's disease, hearing loss, and dementia. Following retirement, many people are unsure how to spend their time and are unaware of social opportunities and community resources. Boredom and loneliness plague many older people.

The consequences of addiction are, in many cases, more serious for older people than for younger people. The aging body processes substances differently than the young body. The level of alcohol or drug use, for example, considered light or moderate in the younger body, is often dangerous to the organs and systems of the older body. Recovery from substance abuse takes longer in the older body. Older people, on average, are more likely to be taking more medications than younger people and, thus, risk serious problems when combining medications with alcohol or illicit drugs. Finally, financial losses are more difficult to recoup for persons, such as the elderly, who often live on fixed incomes.

Addiction affects a person's self-esteem, coping skills, and relationships, which, when combined with the other losses common in later life, can lead to other serious mental illnesses. Clinical depression, although not specifically a disease of age, afflicts many older people. The link between clinical depression and addiction is well established.

Treatment for addictions in older people is similar to treatment for younger people, with the exception that most older addicts receive treatment for co-occurring disorders (two or more diseases present at the same time). On the positive side, health professionals report that once older adults enter treatment, they achieve greater success than any other age group.

Wendell Anderson, BA

FURTHER READING

Colleran, Carol, and Debra Jay. *Aging and Addiction: Helping Older Adults Overcome Alcohol or Medication Dependence.* Center City, MN: Hazelden, 2002. A guide for family members and friends of addicts.

Gurnack, Anne, Roland Atkinson, and Nancy Osgood. *Treating Alcohol and Drug Abuse in the Elderly.* New York: Springer, 2002. A handbook for health and social services professionals.

Nakken, Craig. *The Addictive Personality: Understanding the Addictive Process and Compulsive Behavior.* Center City, MN: Hazelden, 1996. Explains how addiction starts and discusses the mind-set of the addict.

WEBSITES OF INTEREST

"Aging, Alcohol, and Addictions." *University of South Florida, Gerontological Society of America*
http://gsa-alcohol.fmhi.usf.edu/GSA-Alcohol.htm

"Increasing Substance Abuse Levels Among Older Adults Likely to Create Sharp Rise in Need for Treatment Services in Next Decade." *US Substance Abuse and Mental Health Services Administration*

http://www.samhsa.gov/newsroom/advisories/1001073150.aspx

See also: Addiction; Elderly and addictions; Gender and addiction; Risk factors for addiction; Socioeconomic status and addiction

---

Alcohol abuse and alcoholism: In depth

Category: Substance abuse
Definition: Alcohol abuse is a disorder characterized by a desire for alcohol and the continuation of drinking despite alcohol-related occupational, legal, health, and family problems. Alcohol abuse can progress to alcohol dependence or alcoholism. Alcoholism is a condition in which a person becomes physically dependent on alcohol and drinks to avoid withdrawal symptoms.

CAUSES

It is estimated that nearly 17.6 million people in the United States abuse alcohol or are considered alcoholics. Alcohol problems are highest among young adults, age eighteen to twenty-nine, and lowest among adults age sixty-five and older. Several factors contribute to alcohol abuse and alcoholism, including genetics, brain chemistry, social pressure, emotional stress, chronic pain, depression or other mental health problems, and problem drinking behaviors learned from family and friends.

RISK FACTORS

A risk factor is anything that increases one's likelihood of getting a disease or condition. It is possible to develop alcoholism without any of the risk factors listed below. However, the more risk factors an individual has, the greater the likelihood of developing alcoholism. The following factors can increase the risk of alcoholism:

Gender. Alcohol abuse is five times more likely in men than in women. Men are more likely to be binge drinkers and alcoholics than women. However, the incidence of alcoholism in women has been on the rise in the past thirty years. Women tend to become alcoholics later in life than men, but the condition has a faster progression in women.

Family history. Alcoholism tends to run in families. The rate of alcoholism in men with no alcoholic parents is approximately 11 percent. For men with one alcoholic parent, the rate of alcoholism is approximately 30 percent. A family history of alcoholism is also seen in women, although the link is somewhat weaker. Children of alcoholics may learn problematic drinking habits from observing their parents' behavior, or they may inherit a genetic vulnerability to developing alcoholism.

Genetic factors. Some studies suggest that genetic factors affect the way a person's body processes and responds to alcohol. This may also influence an individual's risk of becoming an alcoholic.

Cultural factors. Alcoholism is more of a problem in some cultures than in others. For example, rates of alcoholism are high in Europe and the United States where alcohol consumption is common and socially acceptable. In American culture, alcohol is often used as a social lubricant and a means of reducing tension. Among religious groups that abstain from drinking alcohol, such as Mormons or Muslims, the incidence of alcoholism is minimal. Higher rates of alcohol abuse and alcoholism are also related to peer pressure and easy access to alcohol.

Psychological vulnerability. Researchers have found that certain psychological factors increase an individual's risk for alcohol abuse and alcoholism. These factors include having high self-expectations, having a low frustration tolerance, feeling inadequate and unsure of one's roles, needing an inordinate amount of praise and reassurance, and having a tendency to be impulsive and aggressive.

Psychiatric disorders. Researchers have found high rates of alcohol abuse disorders among people with anxiety disorders, depression, antisocial and other personality disorders, schizophrenia, and other substance abuse disorders, such as smoking and illicit

---

An Interview with a Former Alcoholic

Rick began drinking when he was twelve years old; he did not realize drinking was a problem until his early twenties. As a son of an alcoholic mother and being an alcoholic himself, he felt angry, isolated, and constantly full of fear. Now, after twenty-three years of sobriety, he speaks openly and honestly about his alcoholism and recovery. He is married and has three daughters, ages eighteen, sixteen, and ten years.

Q: What was your first sign that something was wrong? What symptoms did you experience?

A: It's difficult to say exactly what was the first sign that something was wrong, because, if I'm honest—and in retrospect—I can say that there were signs right from the very start of my drinking: drinking for the effect, to get attention, to fill an emotional void, blacking out. Probably the first time I really remember knowing that there was a problem with my drinking was in my early twenties. I never drank in moderation. One drink and I was off to the races. Often the first drink appeared to be totally innocent—just a beer between friends, or a shot of Russian vodka to "take the edge off," or a civilized glass of wine at an art opening—and before I even knew what was happening, I was drunk and doing crazy things.

In terms of physical symptoms, I experienced blackouts almost from the very beginning of my drinking, at around age twelve. Later, in my early twenties, I experienced the shakes, vomiting, dehydration, slurred speech, paranoid and irrational fears, and a lack of impulse control.

Q: What was the diagnosis experience like?

A: I am one who never was "officially" diagnosed—I never went to a treatment center or medical facility directly for my alcoholism. For the last few years of my drinking, I referred to myself as an alcoholic, though I didn't really comprehend what that meant. For me, it was a convenient way of justifying my drinking, like, "Why do you think I got drunk at the picnic. I'm an alcoholic, that's why." I used the term to deflect criticism, in the sense of denigrating myself before anyone else got the chance to do so.

Q: What advice would you give to anyone living with alcoholism?

A: There are two aspects of alcoholism: living with it in yourself and living with it in someone else. Both aspects need examination. I grew up in an alcoholic household, but never thought that had any impact on myself or my siblings. Well, I was wrong. Subsequently, when I developed alcoholism myself, I thought I was only hurting myself, that I didn't have an impact on anybody else. Again, I was wrong.

Alcoholism causes pain—emotional, physical, and spiritual pain. It is pain that is largely avoidable. It is pain that is largely self-induced.

drug use. People with attention deficit hyperactivity disorder also have a higher rate of alcoholism (and other substance use disorders), as do those with post-traumatic stress disorder. People suffering from psychological disorders may begin using alcohol to manage their symptoms; repeated use can then develop into dependence.

SYMPTOMS

Alcoholism is characterized by an extremely strong craving for alcohol, a loss of control over drinking, and a physical dependence on alcohol. In contrast, alcohol abuse is defined as a pattern of drinking that results in one or more of the following situations within a twelve-month period: repeated problems at work, school, or home due to drinking; risking physical safety by drinking in situations that are dangerous, such as driving or operating machinery; recurring trouble with the law, such as being arrested for driving under the influence of alcohol or for physically hurting someone while drunk; and continuing to drink despite alcohol-related difficulties. Denial that an alcohol problem exists is common.

Alcohol abuse often progresses to alcohol dependence or alcoholism. Alcoholism involves a powerful "craving," or uncontrollable need for alcohol. This craving overrides the ability to stop drinking. Symptoms of alcohol dependence include craving a drink of alcohol, the inability to stop or limit drinking of alcohol, and the need for greater amounts of alcohol to feel the same effect. Withdrawal symptoms if alcohol is stopped include nausea, sweating, shaking, anxiety, and increased blood pressure. Seizures are an extreme symptom of withdrawal.

Alcoholism may also lead to physical symptoms caused by the destructive effects of alcohol on the body. Symptoms include high blood pressure, yellowing of the whites of the eyes and/or skin (jaundice), flushed face, spidery veins showing through the skin around the umbilicus and on the face, enlarged liver, dyspepsia and ulcers, and easy bruising or bleeding. Other physical symptoms that may result include general shakiness, weakness of the wrists and ankles, numbness and tingling, impaired memory, fast heart rate, shrunken testicles and erectile dysfunction, and increased susceptibility to infections and cancer.

There are a myriad of risks associated with alcoholism. Alcoholism can increase the risk of accidents and injury, including motor vehicle accidents and falls; domestic violence, murder, and suicide; family dysfunction and failed relationships; lost jobs and earnings; problems with the law, including drunk driving; and depression.

Drug interactions are also of concern when dealing with alcoholism, especially if the individual is diagnosed with certain cancers. These include cancer of the liver, esophagus, throat, larynx, and pancreas. Other concerns are pancreatitis, diabetes, or hepatitis. Gastrointestinal problems, such as bleeding, diarrhea, hemorrhoids, ulcers, and inflammation of the esophagus, are also affected and caused by alcoholism.

The excessive use of alcohol and alcoholism also increases the risk of nerve damage; sexual disorders, including impotence and reproductive problems; postoperative complications (infections, bleeding, and delayed healing); neurological problems and brain damage (in long-term use); liver damage, including cirrhosis; heart and circulatory problems; pneumonia and acute respiratory distress syndrome; osteoporosis; peripheral neuropathy; hormonal problems in both sexes; fetal alcohol syndrome (in the babies of women who drank during their pregnancy); malnutrition; disorders of the immune system; and increased risk of infection.

SCREENING AND DIAGNOSIS

It may not be easy for an individual to accept the fact that he or she needs help for an alcohol problem. Nevertheless, the sooner help is provided, the better the chances for a successful recovery. In our society, some people may perceive alcohol problems as a sign of moral weakness. As a result, one may feel that to seek help is to admit some type of shameful defect in oneself. However, taking steps to identify a possible drinking problem has an enormous payoff: a chance for a healthier, more rewarding life.

The purpose of screening is early diagnosis and treatment. Screening tests are usually administered to people without current symptoms, but who may be at high risk for certain diseases or conditions. Screening tests for alcohol abuse and alcoholism usually involve simple questionnaires, either verbally administered by a doctor or given in written form. Several of the most commonly used tests include the CAGE, the Michigan Alcoholism Screening Test (MAST), Self-Administered Alcoholism Screening Test (SAAST), the Alcohol Dependence Scale (ADS), the Alcohol Use Disorders Identification Test (AUDIT), and the T-ACE Test.

Some healthcare providers use a single question for screening: "When was the last time you had more than five drinks (for men) or four drinks (for women) in one day?" About 50 percent of all individuals who have a problem with drinking alcohol will answer "within three months" to this question.

A diagnosis of alcohol abuse or alcoholism is often based on an initial assessment, physical examination, and psychological evaluation. Typically, a doctor will ask a number of questions about alcohol use to determine whether the patient is experiencing problems related to drinking. A physical examination may include blood tests to determine the size of red blood cells; to check for a substance called carbohydrate-deficient transferrin (CDT), a measure of alcohol consumption; and to check for alcohol-related liver disease and other health problems, such as gamma-glutamyltransferase (GGT).

A patient may also be evaluated for psychiatric disorders that often co-occur with alcoholism, such as anxiety disorders and depression. He or she may be evaluated by a doctor or be referred to a mental health professional.

TREATMENT AND THERAPY

The type of treatment one receives depends on the severity of alcoholism and the resources that are available in the community. Treatment may be on an inpatient or outpatient basis and may include detoxification (the process of safely getting alcohol out of one's system), medications to help prevent a relapse once drinking has stopped, individual or group counseling, and referral to community resources, including support groups.

In order to manage the disease, a patient will have to make some permanent lifestyle changes. The following strategies can help an individual stay away from alcohol and reduce the risk of relapse: socializing without alcohol, including avoidance of bars; refraining from keeping alcohol in the home; avoiding situations and people that encourage drinking; befriending nondrinking individuals and engaging in activities that do not involve alcohol consumption; attending support groups, such as Alcoholics Anonymous; identifying potential relapse triggers; and developing coping strategies for difficult situations.

Eating a healthful diet and learning stress reduction techniques, such as deep breathing, meditation, and yoga, are also helpful, along with basic rest and relaxation.

Certain medications can help alleviate symptoms of alcohol withdrawal and help to prevent relapse. Medications are usually prescribed alongside counseling or other psychosocial treatment. Also, alcoholism and alcohol abuse are usually treated with a combination of medications, rather than just one medication. Treatment will vary on a case-by-case basis.

Naltrexone is used to help an individual stay away from alcohol, but it is not a cure for addiction. It may work by blocking the cravings for alcohol. It will not, however, prevent one from experiencing the effects of alcohol. Naltrexone is available as a pill (ReVia) and an injection in the muscle (Vivitrol).

Disulfiram (Antabuse) helps overcome a drinking problem by making the individual very sick if they drink alcohol. However, it does not "cure" alcoholism. While this medicine is being taken, and for fourteen days before an individual begins taking it, he or she should not drink even the smallest amount of alcohol. They should also not use any foods, products, or medicines that contain alcohol, nor should they come into contact with any chemicals that contain alcohol while using this medicine. Symptoms of this medication may include nausea and vomiting, chest pain, dizziness or fainting, sweating and flushing, difficulty breathing, confusion and weakness, rapid heartbeat, and drowsiness.

Acamprosate (Campral) reduces the craving for alcohol by inhibiting a chemical in the brain called gamma aminobutyric acid (GABA). Several studies have indicated that it may help a patient remain abstinent. Possible side effects include diarrhea and headache.

Benzodiazepines are anti-anxiety drugs that may be used to relieve withdrawal symptoms of alcoholism and reduce the risk of seizures. These drugs produce a sedative effect and are fast-acting. Benzodiazepines are usually not used for long periods of time because they can lead to dependence and may cause withdrawal symptoms when discontinued.

Selective serotonin reuptake inhibitors (SSRIs) affect the concentration of the neurotransmitter serotonin, which plays a role in anxiety and depression. SSRIs may be used to reduce cravings for alcohol. They are also helpful if the individual has a coexisting psychiatric problem, such as an anxiety disorder or depression. Improvement is usually seen in four to six weeks after beginning treatment.

The anti-anxiety drug Buspirone (BuSpar) may be used in the treatment of alcoholism and withdrawal symptoms, as well as a coexisting anxiety disorder. It takes from two to four weeks for improvement to be evident. For this reason, this drug is not useful for treating acute anxiety and insomnia. The primary advantages of Buspirone are that it is less sedating than benzodiazepines, and it does not result in physical dependence or tolerance. Buspirone should be taken with food to increase absorption.

In addition to medications, alcoholism treatment programs use counseling and group therapy to help a person stop drinking. Most alcoholics need help to recover from their disease. With support and treatment, many people are able to stop drinking and rebuild their lives.

Self-help groups are the most commonly sought source of help for alcohol-related problems. Alcoholics Anonymous (AA) is one of the most well-known self-help groups. AA emphasizes person-to-person relationships, group support, and commitment to recovery. Meetings consist mainly of discussions about the participants' problems with alcohol and testimonials from those who have recovered. AA outlines twelve consecutive activities, or steps, that an individual should achieve during the recovery process.

Psychotherapy is also an option, as a number of cognitive and behavioral therapies may be beneficial in the treatment of alcohol abuse and alcoholism. These approaches target thoughts and behaviors that may contribute to the abuse of alcohol. Cognitive-behavioral interventions have been shown to improve mood and reduce substance abuse. In addition, aversive conditioning is a behavioral approach in which the consumption of alcohol is associated with a wide range of noxious stimuli. Another approach, self-control training, can help to reduce the intake of alcohol without totally abstaining. A variety of coping skills and stress management techniques may also be used.

Motivational enhancement therapy (MET) is based on the assumption that one has the responsibility and capacity for change. A therapist begins by providing individualized feedback about the effects of drinking. Working closely together, the patient and the therapist will explore the benefits of abstinence, review treatment options, and design a plan to implement treatment goals. Often, it is helpful to involve a non-alcoholic spouse or significant other in a treatment program. This can increase the likelihood that the patient will complete therapy and continue to abstain after treatment ends.

Behavioral-marital therapy (BMT) combines a focus on drinking with efforts to strengthen marital relationships. BMT involves shared activities and the teaching of communication and conflict evaluation skills. Couples therapy may also be combined with learning and rehearsing a relapse prevention plan. Among alcoholics with severe marital and drinking problems, the combination approach produces improved marital relations and higher rates of abstinence.

Brief interventions involve counseling from primary care doctors or nursing staff during five or fewer standard office visits. In brief interventions, the patient will receive information on the negative consequences of alcohol abuse. They will also learn about strategies and community resources to help achieve moderation or abstinence. Most brief interventions are designed to help individuals if they are abusing alcohol and are at risk for developing alcoholism. They are designed to help reduce alcohol consumption. If they are already alcohol-dependent, however, they are encouraged to enter specialized treatment with the goal of complete abstinence. There are no surgical treatments indicated for the treatment of alcoholism.

Amy Scholten, MPH

FURTHER READING

Bellenir, Karen, and Amy Sutton. *Alcoholism Sourcebook*. Detroit: Omnigraphics, 2007. Basic consumer information about alcohol use, abuse, and dependence, with statistics on physical and social pathology.

Brown, Stephanie, and Virginia Lewis. *The Alcoholic Family in Recovery: A Developmental Model*. New York: Guilford Press, 1999. Provides a developmental model of recovery with specific stages. The focus is the recovery process for the family system, rather than just recovery for the alcoholic.

Encyclopedia of Drugs, Alcohol & Addictive Behavior. Detroit: Macmillan Reference, 2009. A source of historical information about alcoholism and its effects.

Ethen, Mary K., et al. "Alcohol Consumption by Women Before and During Pregnancy." *Maternal and Child Health Journal* 13 (2009): 274–285. A study of the prevalence, patterns, and predictors of alcohol use before and during pregnancy in the United States.

Seixas, Judith. *Children of Alcoholism: A Survivor's Manual.* New York: Harper & Row, 1986. Focuses on children of alcoholics and the problems they face.

WEBSITES OF INTEREST

Al-Anon and Alateen
http://www.al-anon.alateen.org/

Alcoholics Anonymous
http://www.aa.org/

National Institute on Alcohol Abuse and Alcoholism
http://www.niaaa.nih.gov/

See also: Alcohol: Short- and long-term effects on the body; Birth defects and alcohol; Drunk driving; Parenting and alcoholism; Stress and alcohol; Substance abuse; Support groups

---

Alcohol abuse and alcoholism: Overview

CATEGORY: Substance abuse

DEFINITION: Alcohol abuse is characterized by excessive or problematic alcohol consumption. It can progress to alcoholism. Alcoholism is a condition characterized by a physical dependence on alcohol and an inability to stop or limit drinking.

RISK FACTORS AND SYMPTOMS

Several factors can contribute to alcohol abuse and alcoholism, including genetics, brain chemistry, social pressure, emotional stress, chronic pain, depression or other mental health problems, and problem drinking behaviors learned from family or friends. Other factors that increase the chance of developing alcoholism include a family history of alcohol abuse (especially for men whose fathers or brothers are alcoholics), alcohol use at an early age (beginning when younger than fourteen years), illicit drug use, peer pressure to drink, easy access to alcoholic beverages, the presence of psychiatric disorders, and cigarette smoking.

It is common for a person to deny an alcohol problem, and alcohol abuse can occur without physical dependence. Symptoms of alcohol abuse include repeated work, school, or home problems due to drinking; risking physical safety to drink; recurring trouble with the law, often involving drunk driving or violent behavior; and continuing to drink despite alcohol-related difficulties. Symptoms of alcoholism include craving alcohol; an inability to stop or limit drinking; needing greater amounts of alcohol to feel the same effect; giving up activities in order to drink or recover from alcohol; drinking that continues even when it causes or worsens health problems; and wanting to stop or reduce drinking, but being unable.

It is also important to understand and recognize withdrawal symptoms. Drug withdrawal is an unpleasant physical reaction that occurs when a

Health officials are working to spread the word that alcoholism is a health danger and not just a social taboo. (AP Photo)

substance-dependent person suddenly stops using drugs or alcohol. Withdrawal symptoms may include nausea, sweating, shaking, anxiety, increased blood pressure, and hallucinations and seizures (known as delirium tremens). The brain, nervous system, heart, liver, stomach, gastrointestinal tract, and pancreas are all damaged by alcoholism.

DIAGNOSIS

To help with diagnosis, doctors ask a series of questions to assess possible alcohol-related problems:

- Have you tried to reduce your drinking?
- Have you felt bad about drinking?
- Have you been annoyed by another person's criticism of your drinking?
- Do you drink in the morning to steady your nerves or cure a hangover?
- Do you have problems with a job, your family, or the law?
- Do you drive under the influence of alcohol?
- Blood tests may be done to look at the size of red blood cells and to check for alcohol-related liver disease and other health problems.

TREATMENT

Treatment for alcohol abuse or dependence is aimed at teaching patients how to manage the disease. Most professionals believe that this requires giving up alcohol completely and permanently. The first and most important step is recognizing a problem exists; successful treatment depends on the desire to change. A doctor can help an individual withdraw from alcohol safely. Recovery may require supervised care in a detoxification center. Certain medications can help to relieve some of the symptoms of withdrawal and to prevent relapse. A doctor may prescribe medication to reduce cravings for alcohol. Medications used to treat alcoholism and to prevent drinking include naltrexone (ReVia, Vivitrol), which helps to block the cravings for alcohol; disulfiram (Antabuse), which will make individuals sick if they drink alcohol; and acamprosate (Campral), which reduces cravings for alcohol. Additionally, a study showed that an anti-convulsant drug, topiramate (Topamax), may reduce alcohol dependence.

Therapy helps individuals to recognize alcohol's dangers. Education raises awareness of underlying issues and lifestyles that promote drinking. In therapy, recovering alcoholics work to improve

Alcohol

Alcohol is a colorless liquid made up of a hydroxyl derivative of hydrocarbons. Common alcohols include ethanol (used in alcoholic beverages), methanol, and propanol (used as a solvent and an antiseptic). Consumption of ethanol can lead to changes in behavior and addiction. Alcohol is obtained by fermentation of plant matter containing sugar or starch; however, beverages containing higher alcoholic content are obtained by distillation.

The euphoric affects of ethanol are triggered by the inhibition of glutamate receptors and by the activation of dopamine and serotonin reward systems in the brain. Alcohol has both short- and long-term effects. Short-term effects include dehydration and intoxication. Consumption of large amounts of alcohol in a short time usually leads to coma, life-threatening respiratory depression, or death. Intake of ethanol by pregnant women can harm the fetus. Long-term heavy drinking can cause liver cirrhosis, neuropathology, immune system problems, and increased susceptibility to cancer. Alcohol addiction is also a leading cause of homicide and suicides.

There exist some benefits from small to moderate consumption of alcohol in longer periods of time. These benefits include lower risk of heart attack and ischemic strokes, and increased levels of HDL (good) cholesterol.

coping skills and learn other, more adaptive ways of dealing with stress or pain. Additionally, recovery groups, such as Alcoholics Anonymous (AA), help many people to stop drinking and stay sober. AA members meet regularly and provide support for each other throughout the recovery process. Family members may also benefit from attending meetings of Al-Anon, as living with an alcoholic can be a painful, stressful situation. The general statistics on treatment outcomes for alcoholism indicate that one year after attempting to stop drinking, one-third of patients achieved total abstinence, one-third resumed drinking but at a lower level, and one-third had relapsed completely. Most professionals who treat alcohol abuse and dependence believe that complete abstinence is the only effective way to recover.

Debra Wood, RN

FURTHER READING

Bellenir, Karen, and Amy Sutton. *Alcoholism Sourcebook.* Detroit: Omnigraphics, 2007. Basic consumer information about alcohol use, abuse, and dependence, with statistics on physical and social pathology.

Blane, Howard T., and Kenneth E. Leonard, eds. *Psychological Theories of Drinking and Alcoholism.* New York: Guilford Press, 1999. Provides an overview of the psychology of alcoholism from leaders in the field, including thoughts on emotions, genetics, and neurobiology related to drinking.

Ketcham, Katherine, William F. Asbury, Mel Schulstad, and Arthur P. Ciaramicoli. *Beyond the Influence: Understanding and Defeating Alcoholism.* New York: Bantam, 2000. Emphasizes that alcoholism is a disease, not a weakness of character. Explains the neurological nature of alcoholism and lists treatment options in detail.

WEBSITES OF INTEREST

Alcoholics Anonymous
http://www.alcoholics-anonymous.org/

National Council on Alcoholism and Drug Dependence
http://www.ncadd.org

Substance Abuse and Mental Health Services Administration
http://www.oas.samhsa.gov

See also: Alcohol: Short- and long-term effects on the body; Caffeinated alcoholic drinks; Intoxication; Physiological dependence; Psychological dependence; Substance abuse; Trends and statistics: Alcohol abuse

---

Alcohol abuse and alcoholism: Treatment

CATEGORY: Treatment

ALSO KNOWN AS: Alcohol addiction; alcohol dependency

DEFINITION: Alcoholism is a chronic condition in which a person depends on regular ingestion of alcoholic beverages. Alcoholics are unable to control their drinking and continue to drink even if doing so interferes with their health, interpersonal relationships, or job. Alcohol abuse refers to excessive drinking—enough to cause problems in daily life—without complete dependence upon the substance.

CRITERIA MARKING ALCOHOL DEPENDENCY

A wide range of treatment programs are available to persons who are alcoholics or who otherwise abuse alcohol; however, many problem drinkers deny that they have a problem or simply refuse to obtain help. A person who meets any three of the following criteria is considered to be alcohol dependent: drinks more or longer than one intends; unable to stop or cut down on alcohol consumption; needs more alcohol to get the same effect; has withdrawal symptoms when no alcohol is consumed; spends an increasing amount of time drinking or recovering from drinking; neglects other activities because of drinking; and continues to drink despite negative consequences. According to the National Institute on Alcohol Abuse and Alcoholism, approximately 5 percent of Americans

---

Michigan Alcoholism Screening Test (MAST)

Created in 1971 by Melvin Selzer, MAST is a twenty-five-item structured interview to detect for the presence of alcohol dependence. It does not directly assess the frequency and quantity of alcohol consumption.

Interview questions require a yes or no response and include items such as whether drinking has ever created problems between the respondent and his or her family, whether the respondent has ever lost a job because of his or her drinking, and whether the respondent has ever been in a hospital because of drinking. Individual items receive a weighted score of zero, one, two, or five points when answered in a manner that indicates the interviewee may be an alcoholic.

MAST may be used either for research or for clinical purposes. However, because it is a screening instrument only, the confirmation of MAST scores with more thorough diagnostic procedures is often necessary for clinical purposes.

currently meet these criteria, and more than 10 percent meet these criteria at some time in their lives.

PROBLEM RECOGNITION

Many people with alcoholism deny that they have a problem; thus, treatment is initiated by a triggering event or by the urging of another person. A triggering event may be a conviction for driving under the influence, a serious health condition (such as pancreatitis or cirrhosis of the liver), or a threat of divorce, job loss, or loss of child custody. A spouse, relative, coworker, or boss may be influential in initiating treatment. However, some alcohol abusers ignore a triggering event or advice from others and sink deeper into alcohol abuse or alcoholism. For example, some alcoholic women stop drinking if they become pregnant, but some do not, even knowing that their drinking will harm their developing fetus.

In addition to confronting one's own drinking problem, an alcoholic must be willing to admit that he or she is an alcoholic or a recovering alcoholic. The term *recovered alcoholic* should be avoided because it implies that the person is fully recovered and will never return to drinking. As alcoholics can attest, some alcoholics return to drinking, even after treatment and short- or long-term sobriety.

TREATMENT OPTIONS

A number of treatment options are available to problem drinkers; these options vary by individual circumstances. In some cases, a brief intervention by a health care professional may be sufficient. Other cases require enrollment in an outpatient program, which includes counseling. More severe cases require an inpatient program. For some alcohol abusers who are not dependent upon alcohol, cutting back on alcohol consumption may be possible and may allow the person to return to a normal lifestyle. Persons with alcohol dependence, as most health care professionals and support groups recommend, should completely abstain from alcohol. However, some experts advocate continued moderate alcohol intake. Despite this alternative therapy, the preponderance of evidence supports complete abstinence.

Alcoholics also should be cautioned that alcohol is present in a number of medications (both prescription and over the counter). Alcohol is a common component of, for example, cough medication and mouthwash.

Often, alcoholics abuse other substances, such as cocaine, marijuana, and prescription drugs, so treatment programs also should include therapy for addiction to these substances. Tobacco contains nicotine, which is highly addictive. Some treatment programs include smoking (or chewing) cessation in their programs, while others focus on the abuse of alcohol and other substances, excluding tobacco.

The following steps are involved in treating alcohol abuse and alcoholism:

Detoxification. For alcoholics and for some persons with alcohol dependency, detoxification (or detox) is necessary. Sedatives are often necessary to reduce withdrawal symptoms, which include shaking, confusion, or hallucinations. Collectively, these symptoms are termed *delirium tremens* (DTs). Withdrawal may require up to one week and usually requires inpatient care at a hospital or a treatment center.

Reprogramming. A recovering alcoholic, with the help of health care professionals skilled in alcohol abuse treatment, can learn new life and coping skills and can formulate a treatment plan. The plan should include behavior modification techniques, counseling, goal-setting, and the use of self-help manuals and web resources.

Psychological counseling. Counseling on an individual or group basis is an essential treatment component. Group therapy is particularly valuable because it allows interaction with other alcohol abusers, and it increases the awareness that one's problems are not unique. Therapy may include the presence of a spouse or other family members. Family support is a significant component of the recovery process.

Medication. Following medication for detox, long-term pharmaceutical treatment may be used. Oral medications available for treatment include disulferam, acamprosate, and naltrexone. Disulferam (Antabuse), which is taken by mouth, produces unpleasant physical reactions when taken in combination with alcohol, such as flushing, headaches, nausea, and vomiting. Disulferam does not reduce the craving for alcohol; however, acamprosate (Campral) may reduce alcohol craving. Naltrexone (ReVia) also may reduce the urge to drink; furthermore, it blocks the pleasant sensations associated with the consumption of alcohol. One problem with oral medications is this: If a person wants to return to drinking, he or she can simply stop taking the medication.

Follow-up support. Aftercare programs and support groups are essential if the recovering alcoholic is to avoid (or manage) relapses and deal with the necessary life changes to maintain sobriety. Regular attendance at a support group such as Alcoholics Anonymous (AA) is often a component of follow-up care. Follow-up often includes psychological and medical care. Alcoholism commonly is a component of other mental health disorders. For these cases, psychological counseling or psychotherapy may be recommended. Treatment for depression or anxiety also may be a part of follow-up.

Alcoholics commonly have medical conditions that require treatment. These conditions include hypertension (high blood pressure), diabetes, heart disease, and liver disease (cirrhosis of the liver). If an alcoholic remains sober, some medical conditions may decrease in severity or resolve.

Beyond counseling and medication, other modalities may be helpful. For example, in September 2010, researchers released the results of a clinical trial on a unique new therapy that applies electrical stimulation to a major nerve emanating from the brain. The technique, trigeminal nerve stimulation, achieved an average of a 70 percent reduction in symptom severity in an eight-week study period.

INPATIENT TREATMENT

For persons with a serious alcohol abuse problem, inpatient care is often necessary. These programs include detox followed by counseling, group therapy, and medical treatment. A benefit of an inpatient program is that it greatly reduces the risk of a patient gaining access to alcohol or other harmful substances. For anyone who receives inpatient care, regular outpatient follow-up is essential.

Many medical centers include treatment for substance abuse, including alcoholism. Stand-alone facilities also can be found throughout the United States and other developed nations. Some provide care in a basic, clinical setting while others function in a resort-like setting. One well-known facility is the Betty Ford Center (in Rancho Mirage, California), which was founded by former US first lady Betty Ford. The one-hundred-bed nonprofit residential facility offers inpatient, outpatient, and day treatment for alcoholism and other substance abuse problems. It also provides prevention and education programs for family members (including children) of substance abusers.

SUPPORT GROUPS

Many support groups are available to an alcoholic who admits he or she has a problem and who wants a life without dependence upon alcohol. Treatment centers may have their own support groups or may refer patients to outside programs. A recovering alcoholic may have to try many different resources before finding the best fit.

Alcoholics Anonymous. The primary goal of the well-known international support group AA is to help alcoholics stay sober. AA was founded in 1935 by Bill Wilson, a New York stock broker, and Bob Smith, an Ohio surgeon, in Akron, Ohio. Both had been "hopeless drunks." The organization claims more than 2 million members. New members are encouraged to avoid drinking but to do so "one day at a time" instead of "swearing off [alcohol] forever."

AA is established in more than 180 nations; members in each group usually meet once or twice a week. Two main types of meeting are held: open and closed. In open meetings, speakers describe how they drank, how they discovered AA, and how AA has helped them. Relatives, friends of members, and anyone interested in the organization may attend. Closed meetings, which are for alcoholics only, consist of group discussions involving questions, shared thoughts, and discussions of personal problems.

AA has no formal government; the membership elects a chairperson, a secretary, and other group officers. The sole function of these persons is to ensure that the meetings run smoothly. No membership dues are assessed. The organization pays for expenses from donations.

Al-Anon and Alateen. Al-Anon (which includes Alateen for younger members) is a support group for friends and families of problem drinkers. The organization estimates that each alcoholic usually impacts the lives of a minimum of four other persons; thus, alcoholism is a family disease. Al-Anon and Alateen are open to affected persons whether or not the alcoholic in their lives is still drinking. Al-Anon and Alateen report more than 24,500 groups meeting in 135 countries. The meetings are anonymous and confidential; no dues or fees are required for membership.

RELIGIOUS SUPPORT

Churches and synagogues often sponsor support for alcoholics. Members can avail themselves of services, which are often integrated with other organizations and social services in the community. Sometimes, an alcoholic who has no religious faith can get help by first accepting a religious faith. Although nonsectarian and nondenominational, AA, for example, is a faith-based organization as exemplified by its twelve-step program, which, in part, acknowledges the existence of a supreme being.

GENETIC FACTORS

Significant evidence exists that genetic factors play a part in whether or not a person becomes an alcoholic. The interaction of genes and environmental factors that influence alcohol dependence is a complex scientific topic. For most people with alcohol dependence, many factors are involved.

Since 1989, the US-government-funded Collaborative Studies on the Genetics of Alcoholism (COGA) has been tracking alcoholism in families. COGA researchers have interviewed more than 14,000 people and have sampled the DNA (deoxyribonucleic acid) of 262 families. Researchers have found evidence for the existence of several alcohol-related genes. COGA researchers are increasingly convinced that different types of alcoholics are representative of a number of genetic variations. Researchers are using the accumulated data to identify drugs that can help treat an alcoholic based on his or her specific DNA profile. Most drugs on the market for the treatment of alcoholism merely reduce alcohol craving. Compliance is a problem too, and these drugs are not effective for everyone.

Recognized genetic factors in developing alcoholism include the following: Children of alcoholics have a high risk of alcohol abuse, a risk that is present even if the children are raised in homes without alcohol abuse; the sons of alcoholic fathers have nine times the normal risk of becoming alcoholics themselves; people with a certain gene become inebriated with just one or two drinks (thus, they are often discouraged from abusing alcohol); if one identical twin is an alcoholic, the other twin has a 76 percent risk of alcoholism; many Asians have genes that cause them to quickly metabolize alcohol (this causes a rapid heartbeat and nausea; thus, reducing their risk of becoming alcoholics); a rare gene present mainly in Finnish people makes them susceptible to severe impulsivity and alcoholism; a dopamine-receptor gene enhances pleasure from alcohol; friends often choose friends with the same

genetic variation; and genes regulating neuropeptide Y are linked to stress and withdrawal symptoms from alcohol.

Robin L. Wulffson, MD

FURTHER READING

Fisher, Gary, and Thomas Harrison. *Substance Abuse: Information for School Counselors, Social Workers, Therapists, and Counselors.* 5th ed. Upper Saddle River, NJ: Merrill, 2012. Incorporating clinical examples with solid research, this text provides counselors and social workers with a detailed overview of alcohol and other drug addictions.

Ketcham, Katherine, and William F. Astbury. *Beyond the Influence: Understanding and Defeating Alcoholism.* New York: Bantam, 2000. Defines *alcoholism* as "a genetically transmitted neurological disease" and not the result of a character defect or moral weakness. Explains in exhaustive detail the effects of "the drug alcohol" on the human body and brain in both alcoholics and nonalcoholics.

Ludwig, Arnold. *Understanding the Alcoholic's Mind: The Nature of Craving and How to Control It.* New York: Oxford UP, 1989. Informative text for those who treat alcoholics, who live with alcoholics, or who are alcoholics.

Miller, William R., and Kathleen M. Carroll, eds. *Rethinking Substance Abuse: What the Science Shows, and What We Should Do about It.* New York: Guilford, 2010. Reviews what is known about substance abuse and offers overviews of biological, psychological, and social factors involved in the treatment of substance abuse. Also anticipates developments and evaluates them for their impact on prevention and treatment.

Seixas, Judith, and Geraldine Youcha. *Children of Alcoholism: A Survivor's Manual.* New York: Harper, & Row 1986. Focuses on children of alcoholics and the problems they face.

WEBSITES OF INTEREST

Al-Anon and Alateen
http://www.al-anon.alateen.org

Alcoholics Anonymous
http://www.aa.org

National Institute on Alcohol Abuse and Alcoholism
http://www.niaaa.nih.gov

See also: Alcoholics Anonymous; Betty Ford Center; Group therapy for substance abuse; Halfway houses; Intervention; Outpatient treatment; Relapse; Sober living environments; Sponsors; Support groups

Alcoholics Anonymous

CATEGORY: Treatment

DEFINITION: Alcoholics Anonymous is a worldwide voluntary association that promotes a program of total abstinence, adherence to a step program for personal reformation, attendance at meetings, volunteer service to recover from alcoholism, and volunteer service to help others achieve recovery.

DATE: Established June 1935

BACKGROUND

Alcoholism, the compulsion to consume alcohol in quantities that seriously undermines physical health and normal functioning in society, is an enormous social problem without a quick or clear solution. For the alcoholic in the United States in 1935, few options were available. Prohibition, which attempted to combat alcohol abuse by making alcohol illegal, had been repealed after proving to be a dismal failure.

Physicians and psychiatrists, using the best knowledge available, had scant success keeping alcoholics sober, and they increasingly refused to treat them. The only faith-based programs that had much success were those, such as the Church of Jesus Christ of Latter-Day Saints, that demanded unswerving allegiance and major lifestyle changes.

In 1934, an alcoholic stockbroker in New York named Bill Wilson, who had a history of failed treatment for alcohol abuse, became involved with the Oxford Group, a movement of personal transformation that was nonsectarian but explicitly Christian. The Oxford Group followed a series of six steps for reforming one's life. Wilson achieved sobriety and had a profound spiritual experience during his last bout of detoxifying from alcohol. He wanted to share his experience with other alcoholics.

In Akron, Ohio, one year later, discouraged and once again tempted to drink, Wilson tried the only thing he knew that would keep him sober: reaching out to another alcoholic. Alcoholics Anonymous (AA) dates its foundation from Wilson's meeting with surgeon Bob Smith, another alcoholic, in the spring of 1935.

AA as such did not actually take shape until 1939, when the newly established Alcoholic Foundation published the first edition of the book *Alcoholics Anonymous*, consisting of Wilson's personal story, a description of the problem of alcoholism, an outline of the program's twelve-steps process, advice to employers and families, advice on how to spread the program's message, and thirty-nine personal stories of recovery from alcoholism gleaned from a membership of roughly one hundred persons. Wilson approached businessman John D. Rockefeller Jr., hoping for major philanthropic support, which was not forthcoming. Rockefeller did, however, offer advice on making the organization self-supporting. He also underwrote some expenses during the early years and provided valuable publicity. AA soon established an office in New York to field inquiries and to provide support to people wanting to form new AA groups.

After an article in the *Saturday Evening Post* provided nationwide exposure to AA, membership in AA rose from about two thousand persons in 1940 to about six thousand persons in 1941. Membership continued to rise, reaching about one hundred thousand in 1950, the year of the first international convention of AA in Cleveland, Ohio. Membership passed the one million mark around 1970 and was slightly more than two million in 2001. (These figures are based on self-reporting by registered groups and are not precise.) Since 1990, membership growth in the United States and in Canada has leveled off, while growth continues in other parts of the world.

The organizational structure of today's AA dates from 1951, when Wilson turned over directorship to a general service conference consisting of delegates elected by representatives of AA groups. This body determines AA policy. Between annual conferences, a board of trustees determines the day-to-day running of the central organization. Individual groups have a high degree of autonomy, and the higher levels have no coercive power over them.

MISSION AND GOALS

The mission and goals of AA are neatly summarized in a statement that appears in most literature distributed by AA's general service office. The statement is read at the beginning of many meetings:

Alcoholics Anonymous is a fellowship of men and women who share their experience, strength and hope with each other that they may solve their common problem and help others to recover from alcoholism. The only requirement for membership is a desire to stop drinking. There are no dues or fees for AA membership; we are self-supporting through our own contributions. AA is not allied with any sect, denomination, politics, organization or institution; does not wish to engage in any controversy, neither endorses nor opposes any causes. Our primary purpose is to stay sober and help other alcoholics to achieve sobriety.

Throughout its years of operations, AA has adhered closely to its primary purpose: avoiding involvement in politics and leaving to treatment programs any recovery concerns for other addictions and compulsions. AA remains entirely self-supporting, and it receives no funding from government agencies or private foundations and refuses large contributions from individual members. Operating expenses are low because volunteers perform most functions.

AA MEETINGS
Critical to the success of AA is that it remains open to anyone wishing to make use of its services. The fundamental unit of AA is the meeting, offered one or more times each week, free of charge, and open to anyone seeking support. Meetings are available in all but the most remote communities, and urban areas offer many types of groups, including those in foreign-languages and those that are same-gender only. Meeting participants elect representatives who act as a sort of legislature. In urban areas meetings form an intergroup to maintain an office and answering service, handle public information, and carry the AA message to prisons and other institutions.

With the rise of the treatment-center industry, AA is no longer the first entry into recovery for the majority of alcoholics, although about one-third still follow this route exclusively. AA cooperates with treatment programs, providing literature and holding meetings in facilities when requested to do so.

A valuable feature of AA that is not provided by any treatment program is ongoing sobriety support, which can last a lifetime. The average length of sobriety of

The Twelve Steps of Alcoholics Anonymous

Alcoholics Anonymous adopted its program of twelve steps in 1939. These steps, outlined here, have remained a crucial part of the organization.

1. We admitted we were powerless over alcohol—that our lives had become unmanageable.
2. Came to believe that a Power greater than ourselves could restore us to sanity.
3. Made a decision to turn our will and our lives over to the care of God as we understood Him.
4. Made a searching and fearless moral inventory of ourselves.
5. Admitted to God, to ourselves, and to another human being the exact nature of our wrongs.
6. Were entirely ready to have God remove all these defects of character.
7. Humbly asked Him to remove our shortcomings.
8. Made a list of all persons we had harmed, and became willing to make amends to them all.
9. Made direct amends to such people wherever possible, except when to do so would injure them or others.
10. Continued to take personal inventory and when we were wrong promptly admitted it.
11. Sought through prayer and meditation to improve our conscious contact with God as we understood Him, praying only for knowledge of His will for us and the power to carry that out.
12. Having had a spiritual awakening as the result of these steps, we tried to carry this message to alcoholics, and to practice these principles in all our affairs.

Source: Alcoholics Anonymous Big Book. *4th ed. New York: Alcoholics Anonymous World Services, 2001.*

people in AA exceeds eight years, with many members remaining abstinent for twenty or more years. Those who remain sober but who continue to go to meetings are at these meetings not necessarily because they are tempted to drink; often, they find the ongoing social support of a group of like-minded people to be helpful in meeting life's challenges.

There is a saying that AA is for people who want AA, not for those who need AA. The organization does not conduct interventions or engage in high-pressure advertising, and it deals directly with the alcoholic rather than with family members, employers, or the courts. Meetings and attendees differ a good deal on the degree to which they will work with outside agencies on a particular case. The principle of anonymity dictates that meetings and sponsors not keep records of attendees' progress. This anonymity and the spiritual aspect of the program have led many court diversion programs, for example, to avoid AA and to embrace professional counseling.

The core of a person's recovery program in AA is working the twelve steps, usually with a sponsor who is an experienced AA member. These steps involve admission of powerlessness (step 1), reliance on a higher power (steps 2, 3, 6, 7, and 11), examination of conscience (steps 4, 5, and 10), identifying people one has harmed and then making amends (steps 8 and 9), and working with others (step 12).

Critics accuse the program of being a cult that "brainwashes" participants. The spiritual aspect, based on a higher power of the member's understanding, is flexible enough to accommodate a wide range of religious beliefs but proves a stumbling block both to atheists and to religious fundamentalists.

AA membership in the United States and Canada is 85.1 percent white and 67 percent male; the average age of participants is forty-seven years. These figures mirror the demographics of people likely to have problems with alcohol, though not the population as a whole. Younger members are often addicted to street drugs as well and are encouraged to attend Narcotics Anonymous. The proportion of women at meetings has risen, as drinking has become more socially acceptable for them and as women are more visible in the workplace, making problems of alcohol-related job performance in women more prominent. Also more common to AA is the participation of those also addicted to prescription medications and those who are being treated for major psychiatric disorders.

Though not a panacea or cure for alcohol addiction on a societal level, AA has helped several million people at the individual level achieve sobriety. AA's success has spawned more than one hundred anonymous-type twelve-step programs of varying utility.

Martha A. Sherwood, PhD

FURTHER READING

Alcoholics Anonymous. 4th ed. New York: Alcoholics Anonymous World Services, 2001. Includes the unrevised text of the 1939 edition, introductions to all four editions, and forty-two personal stories of recovery spanning sixty years of AA operation. Considered the AA bible.

Alcoholics Anonymous Comes of Age: A Brief History of AA. New York: Alcoholics Anonymous World Services, 1985. Texts of talks given by Bill Wilson and other key figures at the AA General Service Conference in 1955. Includes a detailed time line.

Dick B. *The Oxford Group and Alcoholics Anonymous.* Seattle: Glen Abbey, 1992. A history of AA written by a long-time AA member. This work is not part of official AA literature.

Hartigan, Francis. *Bill W.: A Biography of Alcoholics Anonymous Cofounder Bill Wilson.* New York: St. Martin's Press, 2000. A well-researched, balanced account, presenting a favorable picture of Wilson and the organization free from mythology.

Wilson, William. *Twelve Steps and Twelve Traditions.* New York: Alcoholics Anonymous World Services, 1952. A manual for working the twelve steps of AA, by the cofounder of the organization.

WEBSITES OF INTEREST

The Addiction Recovery Guide
http://www.addictionrecoveryguide.org/resources/recovery

Alcoholics Anonymous
http://www.aa.org

Hazelden
http://www.hazelden.org/

See also: Abstinence-based treatment; Alcohol abuse and alcoholism: Treatment; Group therapy for substance abuse; Outpatient treatment; Sponsors; Support groups; Twelve-step programs for addicts

Alcohol poisoning

CATEGORY: Health issues and physiology
ALSO KNOWN AS: Binge drinking; ethanol poisoning; isopropyl alcohol poisoning; methanol poisoning
DEFINITION: Alcohol poisoning is an illness caused by consuming a large amount of alcohol in a short time. It usually occurs after binge drinking, in which

a person rapidly ingests five or more drinks in sequence. Alcohol poisoning also can result in coma and death. The amount of alcohol in the body is usually measured as blood alcohol content (BAC) and is expressed as the percentage of alcohol per liter of blood. Alcohol consumption is also measured by the number of drinks a person consumes.

CAUSES

Most alcohol poisoning cases are caused by ethanol (C_2H_5OH), which is a component of alcoholic beverages, namely beer, wine, and hard liquor. Ethanol has been produced by the fermentation of sugar since antiquity. Other alcohol poisoning cases are caused by methanol (CH_3OH) or isopropyl alcohol (C_3H_8O). Methanol is primarily used in the production of other chemicals; it is sometimes used as an automotive fuel. Isopropyl alcohol is a component of rubbing alcohol and is widely used as a solvent and a cleaning fluid.

All forms of alcohol are flammable and colorless, and all are readily available in the marketplace. Although the purchase of alcoholic beverages in the United States is generally restricted to adults age twenty-one years and older, minors often obtain the product through a third party, sometimes even their parents, without difficulty.

RISK FACTORS

A number of factors increase the risk of becoming ill through alcohol poisoning. They include the following:

- *Rate of drinking*. The more rapidly a person consumes a given amount of alcohol, the more likely the risk of alcohol poisoning. One to two hours are required to metabolize one drink.
- *Gender*. Young men age eighteen through twenty-five years are the most likely to experience alcohol poisoning; however, women are more susceptible to alcohol poisoning than men because they produce less of an enzyme that slows the release of alcohol from the stomach.
- *Age*. Teenagers and college-age youth are more likely to engage in binge drinking; however, the majority of these drinking-related deaths occur in persons age thirty-five to fifty-four years. This older age group often does not metabolize alcohol as readily as younger persons and is more likely to have an underlying health problem that increases the risk.

Hangover

A hangover is the body's way of indicating that overindulging in alcoholic beverages is unhealthy. An effective treatment for hangovers would undermine the body's own defense system against drinking too heavily. It is important to understand how alcohol consumption and hangovers are related.

After a person stops drinking, his or her blood alcohol concentration (BAC) begins to drop. Hangover symptoms peak around the time the BAC is 0.0. Alcohol acts as a diuretic (increases urine output), leading to dehydration and the loss of electrolytes. Although alcohol initially acts as a sedative, drinking actually disrupts the sleep cycle, causing a person to wake up fatigued. Finally, acetaldehyde, a toxic byproduct of the body's breaking down of alcohol, causes many hangover symptoms.

There is no scientific evidence to support any method to rid the body of hangover symptoms. However, hangover remedies remain well known and often used, despite the evidence. Strong black coffee, for example, is a favorite among persons with a hangover, who reason that a jolt of caffeine will restore energy to their body. However, caffeinated beverages, like alcohol, are diuretics and only worsen dehydration.

Additionally, the modest benefits of acetaminophen (Tylenol) may not be worth the increased risk of liver toxicity that can occur in the presence of alcohol. Ibuprofen and aspirin are safer for the liver, but they may worsen any stomach irritation caused by drinking excesses. One should not expect to recover by drinking more alcohol. The additional alcohol will be metabolized, and the unavoidable hangover will return as the person's BAC drops.

- *Body mass*. A heavier person can drink more alcohol than a lighter person and still register the same BAC. For example, a 240-pound man who drinks two cocktails will have the same BAC as a 120-pound woman who consumes one cocktail.
- *Overall health*. Persons with kidney disease, liver disease, heart disease, or other health problems may metabolize alcohol more slowly. A person with diabetes, for example, who binge drinks might experience a dangerous drop in blood sugar level.

- *Food consumption.* A full stomach slows the absorption of alcohol, so drinking on an empty stomach increases the risk.
- *Drug use.* Prescription and over-the-counter drugs might increase the risk of alcohol poisoning. Ingestion of illegal substances, such as cocaine, methamphetamine, heroin, and marijuana, also increases the risk.

SYMPTOMS

Alcohol poisoning symptoms include confusion, stupor, or unconsciousness; respiratory depression (slow breathing rate); irregular breathing (a gap of more than ten seconds between breaths); slow heart rate; low blood pressure; low body temperature (hypothermia); vomiting; seizures; and pale or blue skin.

SCREENING AND DIAGNOSIS

The BAC is a definitive test for alcohol poisoning. Persons with alcohol poisoning often have a BAC of 0.35 to 0.5 percent. By way of comparison, a person is considered to be driving under the influence in all US states if his or her BAC is 0.08 percent or higher. Other blood tests include those that check a person's complete blood count (CBC) and those that check levels of glucose, urea, arterial pH (acid), and electrolytes.

TREATMENT AND THERAPY

Treatment consists of supportive measures until the body metabolizes the alcohol. This includes insertion of an airway (endotracheal tube) to prevent vomiting and aspiration of stomach contents into the lungs; close monitoring of vital signs (temperature, heart rate, and blood pressure); provisions of oxygen; medication to increase blood pressure and heart rate, if necessary; respiratory support, if necessary; maintenance of body temperature (blankets or warming devices); and administration of intravenous fluids to prevent dehydration. In such cases, glucose should be added if the person is hypoglycemic, that is, if the person has low blood sugar (also, thiamine is often added to reduce the risk of a seizure). Another form of treatment is hemodialysis (blood cleansing), which might be needed for a dangerously high BAC (of more than 0.4 percent). Hemodialysis also is necessary if methanol or isopropyl alcohol has been ingested.

PREVENTION

The best prevention against binge drinking is education, especially of persons who participate in at-risk activities. Young men make up the group with the highest risk of alcohol poisoning. Often, young men have a sense of invincibility and they may disregard helpful advice from any source. Peer pressure is probably the best deterrent; however, it also is a factor that can encourage binge drinking. Furthermore, children with a good parental relationship are less likely to drink to excess.

Robin L. Wulffson, MD

FURTHER READING

Fisher, Gary, and Thomas Harrison. *Substance Abuse: Information for School Counselors, Social Workers, Therapists, and Counselors.* 5th ed. Upper Saddle River, NJ: Merrill, 2012. Incorporating clinical examples with solid research, this text provides counselors and social workers with a detailed overview of alcohol and other drug addictions.

Ketcham, Katherine, and William F. Asbury. *Beyond the Influence: Understanding and Defeating Alcoholism.* New York: Bantam, 2000. The authors define *alcoholism* as "a genetically transmitted neurological disease," and not something that results from a character defect or from moral weakness. Explains in detail the effects of "the drug alcohol" on the human body and brain in both alcoholics and non-alcoholics.

Miller, William R., and Kathleen M. Carroll, eds. *Rethinking Substance Abuse: What the Science Shows, and What We Should Do about It.* New York: Guilford, 2010. Reviews what is known about substance abuse and offers overviews of biological, psychological, and social factors involved in the treatment of substance abuse. It also anticipates developments and evaluates them for their potential impacts on prevention and treatment.

Olson, Kent R., et al., eds. *Poisoning and Drug Overdose.* 6th ed. New York: McGraw-Hill, 2012. A resource for poison control centers, toxicologists, and health care practitioners for the diagnosis, treatment, and management of poisonings caused by exposure to industrial, therapeutic, illicit, and environmental chemicals.

See also: Alcohol: Short- and long-term effects on the body; Blood alcohol content (BAC); Intoxication

---

Alcohol: Short- and long-term effects on the body

CATEGORY: Health issues and physiology
DEFINITION: Ethanol, the type of alcohol found in alcoholic beverages, is a colorless, flammable substance with psychoactive (mind-altering) properties. The amount of alcohol in the body is usually measured as the blood alcohol content (BAC), expressed as the percentage of alcohol per liter of blood. Moderate intake of alcohol can have some health benefits; however, excessive or prolonged use has many detrimental effects on the body.

SHORT-TERM EFFECTS

Alcohol is absorbed into the bloodstream through the lining of the stomach, so measurable amounts can be present within five minutes of ingestion. If alcohol is consumed after eating a heavy meal, its absorption is slowed. Alcohol is metabolized (broken down) in the liver. One to two hours are required to metabolize one drink.

Alcohol is a central nervous system (CNS) depressant; small amounts can produce euphoria and relaxation while large amounts can result in coma or death. Furthermore, moderate alcohol intake (a maximum of one or two drinks per day) may have some health benefits; excessive and regular consumption can be severely detrimental to one's health.

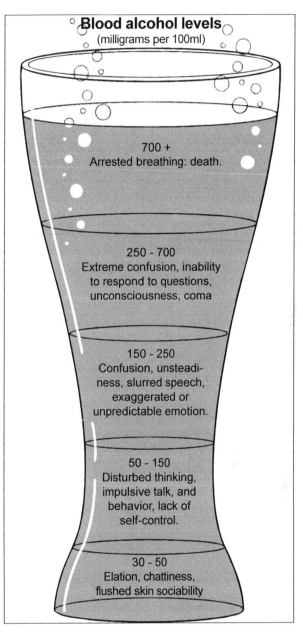

Blood alcohol levels
(milligrams per 100ml)

700 +
Arrested breathing: death.

250 - 700
Extreme confusion, inability to respond to questions, unconsciousness, coma

150 - 250
Confusion, unsteadiness, slurred speech, exaggerated or unpredictable emotion.

50 - 150
Disturbed thinking, impulsive talk, and behavior, lack of self-control.

30 - 50
Elation, chattiness, flushed skin sociability

The presence of 30-50 milligrams of alcohol per every 100 milliliters of blood represents one average drink (a glass of beer or wine or an ounce of hard liquor). People who abuse alcohol may not stop drinking unitl much higher levels result in confusion, unconsciousness, coma, or even death. (Hans & Cassidy, Inc.)

Different degrees of BAC produce different effects, including euphoria, lethargy, mental confusion, stupor, vomiting, and coma. These effects are outlined here.

Euphoria (BAC of 0.03 to 0.12 percent). Symptoms include improved mood, increased sociability, increased self-confidence, increased appetite, inhibited judgment, impaired fine-muscle coordination, and flushed appearance. At this level, the person may laugh more readily, be friendlier, become more socially aggressive, or do things he or she would not normally do. Of note, a BAC of 0.08 percent, the threshold for driving under the influence, is set for every US state.

Lethargy (BAC of 0.09 to 0.25 percent). Symptoms include impaired comprehension and memory, sedation, slowed reflexes, blurred vision, and ataxia (lack of coordination), which is manifested by difficulties in balancing and walking. At this level, the person may forget phone numbers, addresses, or where he or she has parked a car. Driving or operating machinery could result in serious injuries or fatalities. If walking, the person could trip or fall.

Mental confusion (BAC of 0.18 to 0.30 percent). Symptoms include pronounced confusion, labile emotions (abrupt mood changes, laughing or crying readily), increased ataxia, decreased pain sensation, slurred speech, staggering, sensory impairment (sight, hearing, and touch), vomiting, and dizziness, which is often associated with nausea. This level is sometimes referred to as falling-down-drunkenness, and the person at this level of intoxication is severely impaired.

Stupor (BAC of 0.25 to 0.40 percent). Symptoms include severe ataxia, vomiting, unconsciousness (may be intermittent), slowed heart rate, slowed respirations, and urinary incontinence. At this level, death can occur from respiratory depression or from vomiting (if while unconscious, the person aspirates vomit into his or her lungs).

Coma (BAC of 0.35 to 0.50 percent). Symptoms include unconsciousness, markedly depressed reflexes (for example, pupils do not respond to light), severe respiratory depression, and severely slowed heart rate. At this level the drinker has alcohol poisoning, and death at this point is not uncommon.

Aftereffects from an acute drinking episode persist for up to twenty-four hours. Consumption of alcohol within several hours before going to sleep results in the drinker falling asleep more promptly. Consumption of one alcoholic beverage may increase total hours of sleep and may decrease awakening during the night. Higher consumption, however, results in the disruption of sleep patterns and prevents a restful night's sleep. The person falls asleep promptly; however, once most of the alcohol has been metabolized, the person experiences (because of a rebound effect) episodes of wakefulness and light, unproductive sleep. The following morning, the person who consumed two or more alcoholic beverages awakens fatigued and may experience a hangover, which can include headache, nausea, thirst, sensitivity to light and noise, diarrhea, and dysphoria (depression, anxiety, and irritability). Some of these symptoms are caused by dehydration, which can occur even with moderate alcohol consumption.

A single episode of drinking at the euphoric level (BAC of 0.03 to 0.12 percent) can have long-term consequences. Inappropriate comments or behavior while under the influence can result in the breakup of a relationship or the loss of a job. Driving under the influence—even if below the legal limit of 0.08 percent—can result in a traffic accident, which might cause serious injuries.

LONG-TERM EFFECTS

In general, regular abusers of alcohol fall into two categories of use: alcoholism and alcohol abuse. Alcoholism is a chronic condition in which a person depends on regular ingestion of alcoholic beverages. Alcoholics are unable to control their drinking and continue to drink even when doing so interferes with their health, interpersonal relationships, and work.

Alcohol abuse is excessive drinking—enough to cause problems in daily life—without the person having complete dependence on alcohol. The long-term effects of regularly consuming more than one or two alcoholic beverages are profound and include medical, neuropsychiatric, and social problems. Both alcoholics and alcohol abusers are more susceptible to the long-term effects of alcohol abuse. These are caused by the direct effects of alcohol on the body and by resultant poor nutrition. Heavy drinkers may have a poor diet because much of their caloric intake often comes from alcoholic beverages.

Long-term alcohol abuse has medical, neuropsychiatric, and social consequences. Medical effects include diabetes, an impaired immune system, kidney infections and kidney failure, pneumonia, gastritis (inflammation of the stomach) and esophagitis (inflammation of the esophagus), and the following, all of which are common in alcoholics:

Cancer. Includes many forms of cancer, such as throat, esophagus, stomach, colon, rectum, liver, and kidney cancers. The combination of tobacco and alcohol markedly increases the risk of cancer, particularly cancers of the mouth and throat.

Cardiovascular disease. Hypertension (high blood pressure), heart failure, cardiomyopathy (damage to the heart muscle), and stroke.

Pancreatitis (inflammation of the pancreas). Acute pancreatitis is the sudden onset of inflammation, which may result in death. Chronic pancreatitis can continue for many years and can ultimately lead to death.

Ulcers of the stomach or duodenum (upper portion of the stomach). A perforated ulcer is a life-threatening situation.

Cirrhosis of the liver. This condition can lead to liver failure and death. Cirrhosis can produce portal hypertension (increased blood pressure in the venous system within the liver). Portal hypertension can produce esophageal varices (dilated blood vessels in the esophagus). Esophageal varices are prone to rupture and can result in a fatal hemorrhage.

Vitamin deficiencies. Vitamin deficiencies, which are usually caused by a poor diet, can result in a number of severe health problems.

Obesity. The appetite-stimulating effect of alcohol coupled with the calories in alcohol can result in obesity in some alcohol abusers.

Long-term neuropsychiatric effects of alcohol abuse include confusion; impaired memory; dementia; antegrade amnesia (also known as blackouts, the loss of memory following an episode of heavy drinking); tremors; peripheral neuropathy (numbness of the feet and hands); hallucinations (auditory and visual); fear, anxiety, and a sense of impending doom; an obsession with drinking; sexual dysfunction, including decreased libido and erectile dysfunction (inability for a male to get an erection); and delirium tremens, or DTs (tremors or convulsions). DTs occur during an episode of withdrawal from alcohol.

Long-term social effects of alcohol abuse include traffic fatalities or injuries to self or others, dysfunctional home life, spousal battery, child abuse, disruption of interpersonal relationships outside the home, injury or accidents at work, loss of a job or promotion, and codependency (a condition in which an alcoholic manipulates or controls others, such as his or her spouse, children, friends, and coworkers).

FETAL ALCOHOL SPECTRUM DISORDER

Fetal alcohol spectrum disorder (FASD) is a general category for the long-term effect of alcohol consumption on the fetus of a pregnant woman who also is an alcoholic. FASD involves varying degrees of physical and mental abnormalities. The best known and most thoroughly researched form of FASD is fetal alcohol syndrome (FAS).

Children with FAS are often born with a low birth weight and have varying degrees of facial abnormalities, mental retardation, CNS disorders,

Mixing Different Types of Alcohol

Is there any truth to the saying, "beer before liquor, never been sicker; liquor before beer, you're in the clear"? Beliefs about the sequence of drinking may stem from the rate at which the body processes alcohol. The liver can efficiently process one standard-sized alcoholic drink per hour only, although men can process more alcohol per hour than can women. What constitutes one drink? Twelve ounces of beer, five ounces of wine, and one shot (1.5 ounces) of hard liquor are generally equivalent in their alcohol content.

The amount of alcohol in the blood rises more quickly after drinking liquor than after drinking beer. If a person drinks liquor before beer, he or she is likely to feel the effects of the alcohol sooner. This may encourage one not to consume as much, decreasing the chances of getting sick from overdoing it. Drinking beer before liquor, on the other hand, may make one feel ill because, having had little or no immediate effect from the beer, a person may be motivated to consume higher concentrations of alcohol by drinking shots or drinking stronger mixed drinks.

A more scientific explanation for the common belief is that different types of alcohol contain different amounts of compounds called congeners. Drinks that contain high quantities of congeners may increase hangover symptoms. Clear beverages like vodka, gin, and white wine contain less congeners than darker drinks like brandy, whisky, rum, and red wine. Mixing the congeners may increase stomach irritation.

skeletal abnormalities, and heart defects. The facial abnormalities include microcephaly (small head and brain), small eyes, thin upper lip, and a small, upturned nose. The CNS disorders include vision and hearing problems, poor coordination, learning disabilities, and sleep problems. The skeletal abnormalities include deformities of the limbs, joints, and fingers. The heart defects include atrial septal defects (defects in the wall separating the upper heart chambers) and ventricular septal defects (defects in the wall separating the lower heart chambers).

Two other forms of FASD are alcohol-related neurodevelopmental disorder (ARND) and alcohol-related birth defect (ARBD). Persons with ARND may have intellectual, behavioral, and learning disabilities. During childhood, they tend to perform poorly in school and have difficulties with mathematics, attention, judgment, memory, and impulse control. Persons with ARBD have abnormalities that include hearing problems and problems of the heart, skeletal system, and kidneys.

Affected children cannot be cured; however, the following factors can improve a child's quality of life: early recognition of the disorder (before the age of six years); enrollment in special education programs; and a nurturing, stable, home environment. FASD is preventable if a woman stops drinking when she learns that she is pregnant.

A February 2011 study found that counseling about alcohol use during pregnancy is often inadequate. A study of 12,611 women who delivered infants from 2001 through 2008 found that, despite the substantial number of women who continue to consume alcohol during pregnancy, health care providers do not routinely assess alcohol consumption or counsel all women about alcohol's harmful effects. As with other alcohol-related disorders, nutrition and other factors (such as abuse of prescription drugs or illegal substances) play a role in the development of FASD.

A safe level of alcohol consumption, which will prevent FASD, is not known; however, no cases of FASD have been reported in which the pregnant woman consumed an occasional alcoholic beverage or even consumed a larger amount on a few occasions. A large study (11,513 children) published by researchers at University College London in October 2010 found that children at age five years who were born to women who drank one or two alcoholic beverages per week during pregnancy were not at increased risk for any behavioral or cognitive problems.

ALCOHOL COMBINED WITH OTHER SUBSTANCES

Many abusers of alcohol also abuse other substances. Sometimes, the combination has a synergistic effect—the combined effect is significantly more harmful than either substance alone. These harmful effects can occur with both short- and long-term use of alcohol plus another substance or substances. These substances include tobacco, marijuana, CNS depressants, CNS stimulants, prescription drugs, and over-the-counter (OTC) medications.

Tobacco. The combination of alcohol and tobacco greatly increases the risk of many types of cancers. The risk of oral (mouth and tongue) cancer is extremely high in smokers (or tobacco chewers) who also drink alcohol in excess. Smoking is a particularly difficult habit to quit. For example, studies have found that heroin addicts who had given up the drug for more than one year found it more difficult to quit smoking than breaking a heroin habit. Other studies have found that it is more difficult to quit smoking than to quit using cocaine.

Marijuana. Marijuana is a commonly used recreational drug and is frequently used with alcohol. The combination of the two can be particularly lethal. When a marijuana smoker also has overindulged in alcohol, vomiting is not uncommon. This reaction removes some of the alcohol from the stomach, but this reflex is suppressed with marijuana. As a result, more alcohol remains in one's system, increasing the result of alcohol poisoning. Even small amounts of alcohol and marijuana increase the risk of a traffic accident. Alcohol slows reaction time and alertness, and marijuana further impairs the driver. For example, marijuana reduces the frequency of a driver's visual searches (that is, of looking right and left before entering an intersection or before changing lanes).

CNS depressants. Alcohol is a CNS depressant. Co-ingestion (mixing) of alcohol and other CNS depressants, such as heroin, barbiturates, tranquilizers, analgesics (pain relievers), and sedatives, is particularly harmful. Reports have shown that more than 70 percent of fatal heroin overdoses are caused by the co-ingestion of heroin and another depressant, such as alcohol. The drug interaction can lead to depressed breathing and slowed heart rate, resulting in unconsciousness. The unconscious state can progress to coma and death.

While unconscious, the person may vomit and aspirate the vomitus into his or her lungs, which frequently causes death. A 2010 study found that alcohol is more detrimental to one's health than is heroin.

CNS stimulants. CNS stimulants, such as cocaine, methamphetamine, and caffeine, interact with alcohol. Researchers have found that cocaine and alcohol combine in the liver to produce cocaethylene, which intensifies the euphoric effect of cocaine. Cocaine by itself has been associated with sudden death; however, cocaethylene is associated with a greater risk of sudden death than cocaine alone.

Methamphetamine is a potent stimulant. Studies have suggested that when combined with alcohol, it increases the risk of alcohol poisoning. Caffeine is a mild stimulant, compared with cocaine and methamphetamine. However, the combination of alcohol and caffeine has added risks. Not uncommonly, a person who has overindulged is offered a cup of coffee to "sober up." However, the caffeine in the coffee does not improve sobriety—it merely produces a state of wide-awake drunkenness. The increased alertness coupled with the augmented self-confidence from alcohol increases the risk of unsafe activity, such as driving an automobile.

Prescription or nonprescription medication. Many prescription drugs, such as antipsychotics and antidepressants, interact with alcohol. In addition, some OTC products, such as sleep aids and cold remedies, also may have an interaction. It is prudent for one taking any medication to read the label of the medication before consuming alcohol.

MODERATE ALCOHOL INTAKE

Moderate drinking (up to three drinks per occasion or seven drinks per week) may have some health benefits. This level of drinking might reduce the risk of heart disease, of dying from a heart attack, and of developing gallstones, and it might possibly reduce the risk of stroke and diabetes. Drinking red wine might be particularly beneficial. The so-called French paradox observes that the French have a relatively low incidence of coronary artery disease, despite high rates of smoking, low rates of exercise, and high rates of diets that are relatively high in saturated fat. The answer to this paradox might lie in the consumption of red wine by the French.

Red wine contains resveratrol, which is an antioxidant. Experimental evidence shows that resveratrol may have anti-inflammatory, anticancer, and blood-sugar-lowering properties, all of which promote cardiovascular health. Despite the positive evidence, the health benefits of resveratrol are subject to controversy. The appetite-stimulating properties of alcohol have been found to benefit the elderly, whose health can suffer from a lack of appetite. A variety of tonics containing alcohol are on the market, and they often improve appetite. They also often improve sleep patterns.

Robin L. Wulffson, MD

FURTHER READING

Fisher, Gary, and Thomas Harrison. *Substance Abuse: Information for School Counselors, Social Workers, Therapists, and Counselors.* 4th ed. Boston: Allyn & Bacon, 2008. Incorporating actual clinical examples with solid research, this text provides counselors and social workers with a detailed overview of alcohol and other drug addictions.

Ketcham, Katherine, and William F. Asbury. *Beyond the Influence: Understanding and Defeating Alcoholism.* New York: Bantam, 2000. The authors define *alcoholism* as "a genetically transmitted neurological disease," and not the result of a character defect or moral weakness. They explain in exhaustive detail the effects of "the drug alcohol" on the human body and brain in both alcoholics and nonalcoholics.

Ludwig, Arnold. *Understanding the Alcoholic's Mind: The Nature of Craving and How to Control It.* New York: Oxford UP, 1989. Informative text for those who treat alcoholics, live with alcoholics, or who are alcoholics.

Miller, William R. *Rethinking Substance Abuse: What the Science Shows, and What We Should Do about It.* New York: Guilford, 2010. Reviews what is known about substance abuse and offers overviews of biological, psychological, and social factors in the treatment of substance abuse. Anticipates future developments and evaluates them for their possible impact on prevention and treatment.

WEBSITES OF INTEREST

Al-Anon and Alateen
http://www.al-anon.alateen.org

Alcoholics Anonymous
http://www.aa.org

National Institute on Alcohol Abuse and Alcoholism
http://www.niaaa.nih.gov

See also: Alcohol poisoning; Birth defects and alcohol; Blood alcohol content (BAC); Fetal alcohol syndrome; Liver disease and alcohol use; Pregnancy and alcohol; Withdrawal

Alternative therapies for addiction

CATEGORY: Treatment
DEFINITION: Alternative therapies are therapies other than prescription medication, behavioral therapy, or other types of conventional therapy to treat addiction.

INTRODUCTION

Many types of alternative therapies have historically helped persons who suffer with substance addiction. Generally, these therapies are not scientifically proven, but anecdotal evidence and some scientifically based studies show they can ease cravings and the side effects of withdrawal. Alternative therapies work in different ways with different types of people and with different kinds of addictions. Alternative therapies usually can be safely used as part of a comprehensive addiction relief program.

ACUPUNCTURE

Acupuncture is part of the whole-body treatment program of ancient Chinese medicine. It treats addiction and addictive tendencies as an imbalance of qi, the body's life energy. By correcting the imbalance of qi, the body can use its natural energy to ease withdrawal symptoms, such as headaches, depression, nausea, sweating, and insomnia. With qi restored, the body may even be able to achieve the balance it needs to overcome an addiction.

Some studies using acupuncture for different types of addiction have shown success rates as high as 50 percent. It is thought that acupuncture increases the amount of endorphins in the body, thus easing the cravings that accompany addiction and even removing the need for the addictive substance.

Passionflower

The herb passionflower is thought to have mild sedative properties and has been suggested as an aid to drug withdrawal. A fourteen-day, double-blind trial enrolled sixty-five men addicted to opiate drugs and compared the effectiveness of passionflower combined with the drug clonidine and with clonidine alone.

Clonidine is used widely to assist in narcotic withdrawal. It effectively reduces physical symptoms, such as increased blood pressure. However, it does not help emotional symptoms, such as drug-craving, anxiety, irritability, agitation, and depression. These symptoms can be severe, and they often cause addicts in drug treatment programs to end participation.

In this fourteen-day study, the use of passionflower with clonidine significantly eased the emotional aspects of withdrawal compared with the use of clonidine alone. However, more research is necessary to prove this treatment's effectiveness.

Auriculotherapy, which is a form of acupuncture that uses points on the ears to treat the entire body, is usually the type of therapy used for addiction treatment. Five points on the ear are stimulated, and if a person does not need treatment daily, small pellets may be taped over the acupressure points. The patient is given instructions on how to press on the points to stimulate them frequently to help deal with addictive desires.

Acupuncture is a long-term treatment, often spanning several months, and it is usually used with other therapies, such as counseling. One study showed that in people with severe alcohol addiction, those who received a placebo acupuncture treatment had twice the number of relapses than those who received true acupuncture treatment. Studies with acupuncture therapy also have shown success with nicotine and cocaine addiction. In one hospital where acupuncture was used with methadone treatment for heroin addicts, acupuncture treatment alone was so well received that the methadone portion of the treatment was discontinued. Acupuncture also can be helpful with other addictions, such as overeating.

HOMEOPATHY

Homeopathic remedies have been used historically to combat cravings and desires, to minimize general addictive tendencies, and to counteract the negative side effects of substance abuse. Homeopathy is a whole-body type of treatment. Before recommending a remedy, practitioners consider the substance to which a patient is addicted, whether the patient has addictive tendencies, the patient's symptoms, and the patient's personality traits.

For example, a person who has an addiction to opium, morphine, or alcohol and who also has insomnia may be helped by a remedy involving *Avena sativa* (oat), while someone with an alcohol addiction who is anxious and irritable may fare better with carboneum sulphuratum. Another time-honored homeopathic remedy for addiction is white bryony, which is used for eating addiction accompanied by insecurity.

Homeopathy is considered by some to be a pseudoscience, but some studies show that it is at least as successful as a placebo, and with some types of addiction it is more successful than a placebo. Homeopathy is assumed to be generally harmless and, thus, may be recommended as an alternative therapy.

MEDITATION

Meditation practices, including yoga and qi gong, attempt to help alleviate withdrawal symptoms. These practices can reduce anxiety, improve concentration, ease depression, and promote a sense of calmness and peace that may help an addict regain a sense of control. These practices encourage a deep interior and exterior self-awareness that may help a person face difficulties and challenges, both in dealing with addiction and withdrawal and in dealing with life challenges. A religious or spiritual component may be involved with meditation, so this type of therapy may appeal to certain persons and not to others. Meditation is often used with traditional or other alternative therapies to boost success in overcoming addictions.

A common type of meditation used in addiction treatment is Vipassana meditation, which attempts to help a person avoid the blame that may accompany thoughts about an addictive substance and to rather accept the reality of the thought or thoughts. One is taught that when an addictive thought or craving arises, one should observe and accept the thought but not act upon it and then refocus energy and attention more positively.

Meditation helps with self-esteem and provides positive affirmations to improve confidence, both of which can help a person overcome addictive tendencies.

OTHER ALTERNATIVE THERAPIES

Nutritional therapy. Persons with addictions are often malnourished and suffer damage to major body organs, such as the liver. Nutritional therapy—adding dietary supplements such as vitamins and minerals to the body—attempts to overcome or correct some of these deficiencies and to aid in detoxifying the body. Supplements that have shown nutritional promise are zinc, vitamin C, beta-carotene, vitamin E, selenium, calcium, magnesium, and the B vitamins, particularly thiamine. Some persons believe that nutritional therapy can restore balance to the brain, and that this balance eliminates the need for an addictive substance.

Herbal medicine. Herbs are another type of therapy that may help ease withdrawal symptoms and reduce cravings. Some helpful herbs for addiction are catnip, chamomile, peppermint, skullcap, and St. John's wort. These herbs are thought to work with the nervous system to provide relief. They may also calm the brain and help with any depressive tendencies. Herbs must be used carefully, as many can have serious side effects.

Hypnotherapy. Hypnotherapy is a controversial alternative therapy for addiction, with many people claiming good results while others dismissing this type of therapy as a sham. It seems that the best results are obtained with less serious addictions, such as nicotine and behavioral addictions. It also seems that results depend heavily on the type of person with the addiction. Persons who are receptive to hypnotic suggestion and who believe that the therapy works generally have the most success.

Hypnotherapists attempt to find the root of the addiction in "buried" thoughts and actions. By confronting the thoughts and behaviors that cause the addiction, one can, theoretically, recover from it. Hypnotherapists use post-hypnotic suggestion to help persons with addiction avoid addictive substances, overcome the need for the substance, and ease cravings.

Other types of alternative therapies thought to help with addiction-related cravings and to possibly address some of the underlying issues that led to the addiction include relaxation (breathing exercises, progressive muscle relaxation, guided imagery, and creative visualization), biofeedback training, massage, and chiropractic treatment.

Marianne M. Madsen, MS

FURTHER READING

Hoffman, Jeffrey A. *Living in Balance: 90 Meditations for Recovery from Addiction.* Center City, MN: Hazelden, 2011. Describes the basics of meditation practice and suggests meditations specific to overcoming addiction for the first ninety days, a critical period in changing behaviors.

Marohn, Stephanie. *The Natural Medicine Guide to Addiction.* Charlottesville, VA: Hampton Roads, 2004. Discusses a variety of alternative approaches to addiction treatment, including meditation, acupuncture, and nutritional therapy.

O'Connell, David F., and Charles N. Alexander. *Self-Recovery: Treating Addictions Using Transcendental Meditation and Maharishi Ayur-Veda.* New York: Routledge, 1995. Describes the basics of transcendental meditation practice with specific theory, research, and clinical studies on how it applies to addiction recovery.

Tian, X., and S. Krishnan. "Efficacy of Auricular Acupressure as an Adjuvant Therapy in Substance Abuse Treatment: A Pilot Study." *Alternative Therapies in Health and Medicine* 12.1 (2006): 66–69. Print. Explains this type of therapy and its theory and practice. Describes results from a pilot study.

Wager, Kim, and Sue Cox. *Auricular Acupuncture and Addiction: Mechanisms, Methodology, and Practice.* New York: Churchill, 2009. Discusses acupuncture theory. Chapters on treatment protocol and analysis of updated research in modern biomedical concepts and ancient Chinese medical practices.

WEBSITES OF INTEREST

Addiction Recovery Guide.org
http://www.addictionrecoveryguide.org/holistic

AltMD.com
http://www.altmd.com/Articles/Meditation-for-Addiction

Auroh.com
http://auroh.com/addiction/homeopathic-treatment-for-addiction.php

ProjectMeditation.org
http://www.project-meditation.org/a_bom1/drug_addiction_meditation.html

See also: Addiction medicine; Behavioral therapies for addiction; Treatment methods and research

---

Amphetamine abuse

CATEGORY: Substance abuse

DEFINITION: Amphetamine abuse is the repeated, high-dose, nonmedical use of amphetamines, which are potent, highly addictive central nervous system stimulants. Abuse continues despite the user's inability to function normally at home, school, and work.

CAUSES

Amphetamines are rapidly absorbed once ingested. When they reach the brain, they cause a buildup of the neurotransmitter dopamine. This leads to a heightened sense of energy, alertness, and well-being that abusers find to be pleasurable and productive for repetitive tasks. Tolerance develops rapidly, leading to the need for higher doses.

Amphetamines are easy to obtain, often through diversion from legal use, and they are relatively inexpensive. Using them does not carry the social stigma or legal consequences associated with the use of other stimulants, such as methamphetamine and cocaine.

RISK FACTORS

Amphetamine abuse is widespread and has been present almost since their introduction for medical use in the 1930s. Amphetamines were widely abused by soldiers during World War II to maintain alertness during long hours on duty. They are still used by some military personnel in combat settings.

After the war, amphetamines became popular among civilians, especially students who used them to keep awake for studying and as appetite suppressants and recreational drugs. By the 1960s, about one-half of all legally manufactured amphetamines were diverted for illegal use. With greater control over distribution of commercially manufactured amphetamines, manufacture by clandestine laboratories increased dramatically. In addition, the Internet has become a popular source for nonprescription amphetamines.

Abuse now occurs primarily among young adults (age eighteen to thirty years). A common venue for their abuse is the rave, an all-night music and dance concert or party. Use among males and females is evenly divided, except for intravenous use; in this case, males are three to four times more likely to use the drug intravenously. Abusers can rapidly become both physically and psychologically dependent on amphetamines, with a compulsive need for the drug.

SYMPTOMS

Physical symptoms of amphetamine abuse include euphoria, increased blood pressure, decreased or irregular heart rate, narrowing of blood vessels, dilation of bronchioles (the breathing tubes of the lungs), heavy sweating or chills, nausea and vomiting, and increases in blood sugar. High doses can cause fever, seizures, and cardiac arrest.

Frequent, high-dose abuse can lead to aggressive or violent behavior, ending in a psychotic state indistinguishable from paranoid schizophrenia. Features of this state include hallucinations, delusions, hyperactivity, hypersexuality, confusion, and incoherence. One such delusion is formication, the sensation of insects, such as ants, crawling on the skin. Long-term use can result in permanent memory loss.

SCREENING AND DIAGNOSIS

Routine blood and urine testing do not detect amphetamines in the body. Abusers who use pills or who snort amphetamine leave no outward signs of the abuse. Smokers may use paraphernalia to use the drug. Abusers who inject the drug will have needle marks on their skin.

A change in behavior is the primary clue to amphetamine abuse. The abuser develops mood swings and withdraws from usual activities and family and friends. Basic responsibilities and commitments are ignored or carried out erratically. The abuser becomes hostile and argumentative. Any change in a person's appearance, such as sudden weight loss, or in behavior, such as agitation or change in sleep patterns, should be addressed. Such changes may indicate amphetamine abuse. Experts recommend that parents focus their concern with the youth's well-being, and not on the act of abuse.

TREATMENT AND THERAPY

Symptoms of amphetamine withdrawal can develop within a few hours after stopping use. Withdrawal symptoms include nightmares, insomnia or hypersomnia (too much sleep), severe fatigue or agitation, depression, anxiety, and increased appetite. Severe depression can produce suicidal thoughts. Withdrawal symptoms usually peak within two to four days and resolve within one week.

No specific medications are available for directly treating amphetamine abuse. However, antidepressants can be helpful in the immediate and post-withdrawal phases. Some research suggests that serotonergic uptake inhibitors, such as fluoxetine, might be helpful in treating amphetamine abuse.

The National Institute on Drug Abuse recommends psychotherapeutic intervention utilizing a cognitive behavioral approach. Such an approach helps the abuser learn to identify counterproductive thought patterns and beliefs and to change them so that his or her emotions and actions become more manageable. The abuser is also taught how to improve coping skills to address life's challenges and stresses. Narcotics Anonymous and amphetamine-specific recovery groups are also helpful.

PREVENTION

As there are medical indications for amphetamines, experts recommend that prescription formulations be kept from potential abusers. Pill counts should be taken regularly. Young people should be taught the differences between medical use and illegal abuse. Parents should ensure that their children are not attracted to social settings or activities where amphetamine abuse is or might be encouraged or tolerated.

Ernest Kohlmetz, MA

FURTHER READING

Abadinsky, Howard. *Drug Use and Abuse: A Comprehensive Introduction.* 7th ed. Belmont, CA: Wadsworth, 2011. Focuses on what drugs are abused, how they are abused, and how abuse is treated or prevented. Amphetamine abuse is covered in chapter 12.

Julien, Robert M. *A Primer of Drug Actions.* 11th ed. New York: Worth, 2008, A concise, nontechnical guide to the mechanisms of action, side effects, uses, and abuses of psychoactive drugs. A section in chapter 7 discusses amphetamines.

Kuhn, Cynthia, Scott Swartwelder, and Wilkie Wilson. *Buzzed: The Straight Facts about the Most Used and Abused Drugs from Alcohol to Ecstasy.* 3rd ed. New York: Norton, 2008. Contains an informative, easy-to-read section on hallucinogens and their effects.

Lowinson, Joyce W., et al., eds. *Substance Abuse: A Comprehensive Textbook.* 4th ed. Philadelphia: Lippincott, 2005. A comprehensive textbook. Chapter 16 covers amphetamines.

WEBSITES OF INTEREST

"Amphetamines and Related Disorders." Encyclopedia of Mental Disorders
http://www.minddisorders.com/A-Br/Amphetamines-and-related-disorders

Narcotics Anonymous
http://www.na.org

National Institute on Drug Abuse
http://www.nida.nih.gov

See also: Controlled substances and precursor chemicals; Recreational drugs; Stimulant abuse; Stimulants: Short- and long-term effects on the body

Anabolic steroids

CATEGORY: Substances

ALSO KNOWN AS: Anabolic-androgenic steroids; gym candy; pumpers; roids; stackers

DEFINITION: Anabolic steroids are synthetic formulations structurally related to testosterone, the male sex hormone. The steroids are used illicitly to increase muscle size and strength.

STATUS: Legal in the United States for specific medical applications. Nonmedical use is illegal.

CLASSIFICATION: Schedule III controlled substance in the United States (possession, buying, and selling are illegal); schedule IV controlled substance in Canada (buying and selling are illegal); legal in Mexico

SOURCE: Diversion from medical and veterinary practices and suppliers, produced in clandestine laboratories, and smuggled. Sold at gyms, in schools, and the web.

TRANSMISSION ROUTES: Intramuscular injection, pills, creams, and gels

HISTORY OF USE

Although commonly called anabolic steroids, these drugs are more correctly identified as anabolic-androgenic steroids. They have both anabolic properties, which promote the growth of skeletal muscle, and androgenic properties, which promote the development of male sexual characteristics.

Synthetic testosterones were first developed in the 1930s in Europe. After World War II they were used by sports officials in the Soviet bloc, especially East Germany, to enhance athletic strength and performance in both males and females. In 1956, John Ziegler, a US Olympic Team physician, developed methandrostenolone, which in 1958 became the first anabolic steroid licensed in the United States for medical use. Eventually, the danger and long-term risk of the use of anabolic steroids as muscle enhancers became

Former Major League Baseball player Barry Bonds was convicted on one count of obstruction of justice in relation to his use of performance enhancing drugs. (Getty Images)

apparent. The steroids were banned from use in Olympic competitions in 1976.

The US Anabolic Steroids Control Act was passed in 1990, making anabolic steroids a schedule III controlled substance in the United States. Anabolic steroids now are used in medicine primarily to treat men with hypogonadism (low production of testosterone by the testes) and to treat boys with delayed puberty. The steroids also are used to facilitate tissue regrowth in persons with severe burns and to treat severe weight loss in persons with acquired immune deficiency syndrome.

The illegal use of anabolic steroids, including among professional athletes, remains a major problem. Newer formulations based on molecules not screened by existing tests are always being developed. These newer steroids are popular among teenage boys, especially those participating in competitive sports, most notably wrestling, football, and weightlifting. Abusers take doses of anabolic steroids in quantities ten to one-hundred times greater than those doses used in medicine.

Anabolic steroids, including formulations of bolderone and nandrolone, are usually injected. Methandrostenolone, oxymetholone, and stanozole are taken as pills. Steroid gels, creams, and transdermal patches are less effective when used alone, but many abusers employ a "stacking" regimen, in which topical, oral, and injectable formulations are combined to increase the total effect and to avoid detection of high levels of any one steroid in testing. New formulations of anabolic steroids that are not specifically restricted or that are not detectable using current screening methods are being developed and distributed. Fifty-nine anabolic steroids have been identified as controlled substances in the United States.

EFFECTS AND POTENTIAL RISKS

Unlike most other abused drugs, anabolic steroids do not cause immediate euphoria or other pleasurable feelings. They are used to promote rapid muscle growth and weight gain (also called bulking up) and to increase strength and sports prowess over time. A common adverse effect of high, prolonged dosing is "roid rage," in which one experiences mood swings, anxiety, irritability, and aggressiveness.

Abusers do not become physically addicted to anabolic steroids, but they can develop a compulsive reliance on them. Depression, headache, fatigue, loss of appetite, and insomnia may result if the drugs are discontinued. Depression may be long-lasting and can lead to suicidal thoughts and actions. In males, long-term abuse suppresses the sex drive, lowers or halts sperm production, and causes shrinking of the testicles. Severe acne may develop. These adverse effects are reversible. Feminine characteristics, including breast development, may occur because some of the excess testosterone produced is converted into the female hormone estradiol. Such changes cannot be reversed.

In females, abuse leads to the emergence of masculine characteristics, including extra muscle deposits, deeper voice, thicker and coarser body hair, male-pattern baldness, disruption of the menstrual cycle, and enlargement of the clitoris. Some of these changes are irreversible. Among younger abusers, high testosterone levels in the body can prematurely signal bones to stop growing and, thus, can stunt growth. In both males and females, steroid abuse contributes to the risk of heart attack and stroke. High levels of testosterone negatively impact cholesterol levels. Levels of bad cholesterol (low-density lipoprotein, or LDL) are increased, while those of good cholesterol (high-density lipoprotein, or HDL) are decreased. This causes a buildup of plaque in the arteries (atherosclerosis), which decreases or eventually blocks blood flow to the heart, leading to a heart attack, or blood flow to the brain, leading to a stroke. Liver disease too is a rare but potential risk of steroid abuse. Blood-filled cysts that develop in the liver may rupture and cause life-threatening internal bleeding. Kidney failure also can occur. Abusers who share or use contaminated needles are at risk of infection with HIV (human immunodeficiency virus) or with the hepatitis B or C viruses.

Ernest Kohlmetz, MA

FURTHER READING

Gold, Mark S., ed. *Performance-Enhancing Medications and Drugs of Abuse.* Binghamton, NY: Haworth, 2007. A series of articles on steroid abuse that first appeared in the *Journal of Addictive Disease* (2007).

Kuhn, Cynthia, Scott Swartwelder, and Wilkie Wilson. *Buzzed: The Straight Facts about the Most Used and Abused Drugs from Alcohol to Ecstasy.* 3rd ed. New York: Norton, 2008. Chapter 11 discusses the risks involved in steroid abuse.

Minelli, Mark J. *Drug Abuse in Sports: A Student Course Manual.* 7th ed. Champaign, IL: Stipes, 2008. Detailed information presented in an easy-to-read outline format. Contains a separate section on anabolic steroids.

Rosen, Daniel M. *Dope: A History of Performance Enhancement in Sports from the Nineteenth Century to Today.* Westport, CT: Praeger, 2008. A thorough presentation of the history of the use of anabolic steroids and other performance-enhancement drugs.

Yasalis, Charles E., ed. *Anabolic Steroids in Sport and Exercise.* Champaign, IL: Human Kinetics, 2000. Each chapter is written by an expert in the field. Chapters 1 and 2 are on the history of use, chapters 6 through 8 are on effects.

WEBSITES OF INTEREST

"Anabolic Steroids." NIDA for Teens. National Institute on Drug Abuse
http://teens.drugabuse.gov/facts/facts_ster1.php

"Steroids: Anabolic-Androgenic." National Institute on Drug Abuse
http://www.drugabuse.gov/publications/infofacts/steroids-anabolic-androgenic

See also: Controlled substances and precursor chemicals; Steroid abuse; Substance abuse

Anesthesia abuse

CATEGORY: Substance abuse

DEFINITION: Anesthesia abuse is the intentional use of anesthetic agents for recreational and nonmedical purposes. Anesthetic agents are potent medications with mind-altering effects and include inhaled gases such as nitrous oxide, intravenous medications such as propofol, and local anesthetics such as cocaine.

CAUSES

As with any addiction, biological and environmental factors contribute to anesthesia abuse. Addicts have a genetic predisposition and a chronic, compulsive need for the substance of choice. For the anesthesia abuser, these substances include a variety of potentially addictive agents. Generally, insatiable cravings compel chronic use (abuse) of a particular drug, which results in damage to internal organs. However, because many anesthesia drugs have the potential to cause apnea or paralysis within seconds, abuse of anesthetic agents can lead to death.

RISK FACTORS

Although laypersons abuse anesthesia drugs, the most frequently cited anesthesia abusers are anesthesia providers such as certified registered nurse anesthetists, medical residents, and anesthesiologists. Easy access to anesthetic medications enables anesthesia providers to experiment with controlled substances such as fentanyl and other opioids, which are highly addictive.

Anesthesia providers often work long and irregular hours under stressful conditions with access to anesthetic agents. Propofol abuse is increasingly popular because the substance has a short half-life and is quickly eliminated from the body. Nitrous oxide, commonly known as laughing gas, is an inhaled anesthetic that also is abused. The primary risk of inhaled nitrous oxide is hypoxia, which results from inadequate oxygen supply to the body's tissues and particularly the brain.

SYMPTOMS

A variety of symptoms occur from using common anesthetic medications. These symptoms (and their symptom-producing medications) include amnesia and anxiolysis (midazolam), pain relief (opioids), and sedation and apnea (opioids and propofol). Abusers experience impaired functioning because of these drugs. The dose associated with abuse is often less than that required for general anesthesia. However, the effects of anesthetic medications are dose dependent and may also lead to dysphoria and mood changes. Therefore, abusers may exhibit behavioral changes; may appear fatigued, irritable, euphoric, dysphoric, drowsy, or depressed; or may simply appear out of character. Recognition of these signs is imperative to protect the abuser and to aid health care providers who have a legal responsibility to report colleagues known or suspected of chemical dependency. This not only protects the abusers but also the patients under their care.

SCREENING AND DIAGNOSIS

The screening test commonly used to confirm drug use is typically a urine drug screen. However, many anesthetic medications (such as fentanyl, propofol, naltrexone, and ketamine) are not included in standard drug screens and must be specifically requested. Because of the short half-lives of these anesthesia drugs, many are quickly eliminated from the body and, therefore, are difficult to detect. In some cases, the metabolites of these drugs can be detected in urine samples, while hair samples fulfill other testing needs. Although more expensive than urine testing, hair-sample testing can detect chronic exposure to certain drugs; urine drug screens are limited to detecting drug use only within hours or days of use.

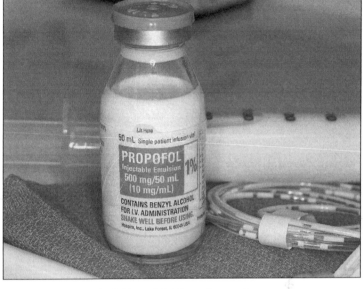

A bottle of the anesthetic Propofol. (Getty Images)

TREATMENT AND THERAPY

The American Association of Nurse Anesthetists and the American Society of Anesthesiologists are two national organizations that govern the practice of anesthesia providers. These organizations and many others not affiliated with medical and nursing personnel recommend inpatient treatment for persons with chemical dependency.

Short- and long-term therapy combined with support-group attendance and abstinence monitoring offer the highest success rates. Various peer assistance groups are available to monitor and assist those undergoing treatment. Narcotics Anonymous offers a twelve-step program that protects anonymity and offers the addict a structured plan for recovery that includes admitting loss of control over the compulsion (the repeated use of anesthetics) and the aid of a sponsor to evaluate mistakes made by the addict. In return, the addict offers help to others who have the same type of addiction.

PREVENTION

The US Drug Enforcement Administration (DEA) establishes standards and substance schedules and enforces these standards to prevent and control drug abuse. The DEA has plans to treat propofol as a controlled substance, and doing so would institute more accountability and address the overwhelming availability of the drug to anesthesia providers. Random drug screening in accordance with the US Substance Abuse Mental Health Services Administration's guidelines and employing the proper chain of custody are two methods that various organizations use to deter and detect drug abusers, including anesthesia abusers.

Virginia C. Muckler, CRNA, MSN, DNP

FURTHER READING

Bryson, Ethan O., and Jeffrey H. Silverstein. "Addiction and Substance Abuse in Anesthesiology." *Anesthesiology* 109.5 (2008): 905–17. Print. An excellent overview that covers manifestations, legal issues, diagnosis and treatment, prognosis, prevention, and testing methodologies.

Sinha, Ashish C. "The Drug-Impaired Anesthesia Provider." *Audio-Digest Anesthesiology* 50.7 (2007). Print. Through use of several studies, discusses incidence, influencing factors, reasons for suspicion, intervention, treatment, and therapy.

WEBSITES OF INTEREST

"Diprivan Abuse Rare but Deadly." Farley Center
http://www.farleycenter.com/resources/articles/2009-10-09/diprivan-abuse-rare-deadly

Narcotics Anonymous Recovery Literature
http://www.na.org/?ID=ips-eng-index

Peer Assistance. American Association of Nurse Anesthetists
http://www.aana.com/resources2/health-wellness

See also: Barbiturates; Fentanyl; Ketamine; Nitrous oxide; Opioid abuse

Anhedonia

CATEGORY: Health issues and psychology
DEFINITION: Anhedonia is the failure or inability to feel pleasure from activities that are pleasurable for most people. Some of these activities are eating, sports, listening to music, sexual activity, and interacting with other people.

CAUSES

Anhedonia is associated with substance abuse, depression, schizophrenia, and some neuroses. It is thought that anhedonia reflects a problem in the dopamine pathways of the brain. Research has used functional magnetic resonance imaging to examine the brains of persons with depression and anhedonia. This research showed less activity in the ventromedial prefrontal cortex, ventral striatum, and amygdala of the brain. These areas of the brain are involved in reactions to pleasant and unpleasant occurrences.

Clinical depression is often associated with anhedonia. However, not all persons with depression have anhedonia, although it is common. Persons with anhedonia often have a flat affect; have a loss of interest in eating, sexual activity, and other normal daily activities; avoid eye contact; and withdraw or isolate themselves. With schizophrenia, it is thought that the chemical imbalance that causes this condition also causes anhedonia.

Anhedonia is fairly common in drug addicts after withdrawal, particularly from cocaine and amphetamines. Withdrawal appears to deplete dopamine, serotonin, and other neurotransmitters involved with feeling pleasure. Also, chronic substance abuse causes changes in the functioning of the brain. These changes affect emotions and are more likely to occur in persons whose substance withdrawal, called protracted withdrawal, has taken longer than usual. A person with long-term addictions appears to have permanent damage to the pleasure pathways in his or her brain, damage that is characterized by apathy.

Serious losses that cause depression also can trigger anhedonia. These losses include the loss of a loved one; physical trauma; serious illness; extreme stress, such as living through a disaster; and other life-altering happenings. In these instances, the anhedonia will pass eventually, as will the depression.

TREATMENT

The most common treatments of anhedonia are antidepressant medications, cognitive-behavioral psychotherapy, and group milieu therapy. Other treatments for anhedonia include regularly scheduled exercise, setting goals, spending time with other people, yoga, art and music therapy, and sunlight and fresh air. The antidepressants most commonly used are the selective serotonin reuptake inhibitors and the selective serotonin and norepinephrine reuptake inhibitors.

The therapist working with a withdrawing substance abuser should inform the patient that he or she may continue to have withdrawal symptoms after the acute withdrawal period or detoxification. If necessary, the patient's doctor should prescribe medications to counter these symptoms.

Ideally, the therapist should encourage his or her patient to be active both physically and mentally, and should suggest that the patient join an appropriate support group. Many recovering addicts need to relearn good sleep habits. The therapist should assist them with this as well.

Christine M. Carroll, RN, BSN, MBA

FURTHER READING

Brynie, Faith. "Depression and Anhedonia." *Psychology Today*, 21 Dec. 2009.
Hatzigiakoumis, D. S., et al. "Anhedonia and Substance Dependence: Clinical Correlates and Treatment Options." *Frontiers in Psychiatry* 2 (2011). Web. http://www.frontiersin.org/addictive_disorders/10.3389/fpsyt.2011.00010/full
Substance Abuse and Mental Health Services Administration, Center for Substance Abuse Treatment. "Substance Abuse Treatment Advisory: Protracted Withdrawal." Web. http://hap.samhsa.gov/products/manuals/advisory/pdfs/SATA_Protracted_Withdrawal.pdf.

WEBSITE OF INTEREST
Substance Abuse and Mental Health Services Administration
http://www.samhsa.gov

See also: Depression; Schizophrenia and addiction; Stress and drug abuse; Substance abuse; Withdrawal

Anorexia nervosa

CATEGORY: Psychological issues and behaviors
DEFINITION: Anorexia nervosa is an eating disorder characterized by a persistent fear of gaining weight. The disorder leads to excessive weight loss, severe distortions in body image, a body mass index that is significantly below normal, a refusal to maintain a normal weight, and a cessation of menstruation in women. Anorexia affects both females and males, and it can have serious physiological consequences, ranging from loss of bone mass to death.

CAUSES
Anorexia nervosa (or anorexia) is caused by a complex constellation, including sociocultural messages about eating and body image, by a lack of effective coping strategies, and by stressful events or life transitions. Also, the disorder may be caused by biological predispositions or cognitive vulnerabilities. There is no single trajectory for the development of anorexia, however. Comprehensive multimodal eating disorder assessments reveal that each person with anorexia may have a unique causal

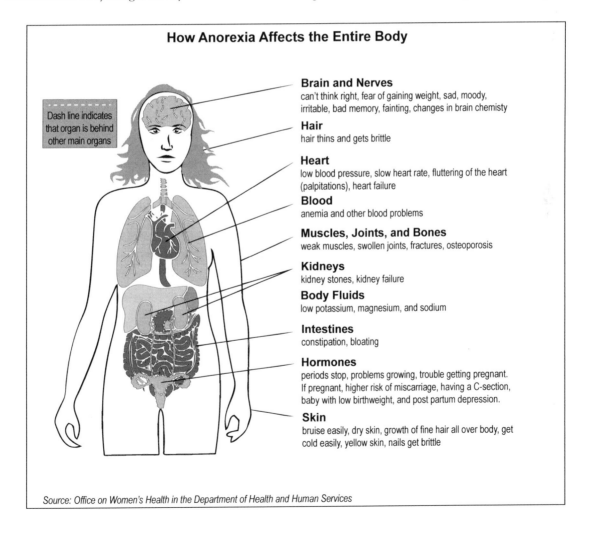

How Anorexia Affects the Entire Body

Dash line indicates that organ is behind other main organs

Brain and Nerves
can't think right, fear of gaining weight, sad, moody, irritable, bad memory, fainting, changes in brain chemisty

Hair
hair thins and gets brittle

Heart
low blood pressure, slow heart rate, fluttering of the heart (palpitations), heart failure

Blood
anemia and other blood problems

Muscles, Joints, and Bones
weak muscles, swollen joints, fractures, osteoporosis

Kidneys
kidney stones, kidney failure

Body Fluids
low potassium, magnesium, and sodium

Intestines
constipation, bloating

Hormones
periods stop, problems growing, trouble getting pregnant. If pregnant, higher risk of miscarriage, having a C-section, baby with low birthweight, and post partum depression.

Skin
bruise easily, dry skin, growth of fine hair all over body, get cold easily, yellow skin, nails get brittle

Source: Office on Women's Health in the Department of Health and Human Services

history for this disorder, although both genetic and environmental factors play a role.

RISK FACTORS

The greatest risk factors for developing anorexia are being a female between the ages of fourteen and eighteen years and living in a society that links cultural perceptions of attractiveness with thinness. Other risk factors include stressful life events, family dysfunction, perfectionism, and obsessive-compulsive behaviors or thought patterns. Additionally, persons who have a biological parent or sibling diagnosed with anorexia have an increased likelihood of developing the disorder.

SYMPTOMS

Anorexia has both physical and psychological symptoms. Physical symptoms include loss of menstrual periods, significant weight loss that leads to a weight that is more than 15 percent below normal for the person's height, and maintenance of a weight that is less than 85 percent of the normal weight for a person's height. Additional physical effects and medical complications can include growth of soft and downy hair called lanugo, low blood pressure, osteoporosis, muscle loss and weakness, fatigue, dehydration, and heart failure.

Psychological symptoms of anorexia include a preoccupation with weight and an intense fear of gaining weight, a distorted perception that one is "fat" even when severely underweight, resistance or refusal to maintain a normal body weight, significant and progressive restriction of food intake, excessive anxiety about one's body or appearance, self-evaluation with an unusually strong emphasis on physical appearance, food rituals, and social withdrawal. Some people with anorexia may engage in purging (vomiting) or in compensatory behaviors such as excessive exercise or laxative use.

SCREENING AND DIAGNOSIS

A comprehensive screening and assessment for anorexia involves collaboration between a physician and a therapist. The therapist will ask the patient about symptoms, background information, weight and body image issues, abnormal eating behaviors, weight control measures, general functioning, family and social experiences, mental health history, and medical history. The doctor will perform a physical examination and will typically run a variety of tests, including tests of organ functioning, electrolytes, heart irregularities, and bone density. The doctor also will ask specific questions about the patient's eating behaviors, physical symptoms, and medical history. The doctor and therapist will then share the results of their comprehensive assessments with the patient and will then discuss treatment options.

TREATMENT AND THERAPY

A variety of comprehensive treatment options for anorexia are available, and the choice of treatment is determined by the severity of the disorder. Patients whose illnesses have not reached a dangerous level may attend weekly or biweekly counseling sessions with a therapist, participate in group therapy, meet with a registered dietitian for assistance in meal planning, and have regular appointments with a physician for monitoring of physical functioning. Family therapy may also be integrated to address any family concerns or stressful life events that are affecting the patient, and to address family members' concerns about their loved one with anorexia.

Partial hospitalization or inpatient treatments may be necessary for patients with increasingly severe medical instability or other co-occurring mental health concerns. In such programs, patients receive intensive medical monitoring and intervention, frequent and intensive individual and group therapy services, and supplemental treatments such as art therapy. The length of treatment for anorexia varies by client and is determined by the client's willingness to engage in treatment, the client's other coping resources, and the severity of symptoms.

PREVENTION

The best way to prevent anorexia is to challenge sociocultural messages about thinness and attractiveness. Emphasizing a positive body image and valuing a person for her or his unique qualities and behaviors, rather than for physical appearance, will decrease the risk of eating disorders.

Tracy Ksiazak, PhD

FURTHER READING

American Psychiatric Association. *Diagnostic and Statistical Manual of Mental Disorders.* 4th ed. Arlington, VA, 2000. Outlines the symptoms, causes, and prevalence rates for anorexia nervosa and related disorders. Diagnostic categories provide a common language for all mental health professionals in the United States.

Brumberg, Joan Jacobs. *Fasting Girls: The History of Anorexia Nervosa*. New York: Vintage, 2000. Reviews the historical rise of prevalence of anorexia from the medieval era to the present. Explores contextual influences on eating disorders, such as the role of women in society, religious influences, and education.

Costin, Carolyn. *The Eating Disorders Sourcebook: A Comprehensive Guide to the Causes, Treatments, and Prevention of Eating Disorders*. 3rd ed. New York: McGraw-Hill, 2006. Provides accessible information about trends and controversies in the treatment of eating disorders. Explores a variety of underlying causes for anorexia.

Grilo, Carlos M., and James E. Mitchell, eds. *The Treatment of Eating Disorders: A Clinical Handbook*. New York: Guilford, 2010. Comprehensively reviews research and theory on the treatment of anorexia from medical, cognitive-behavioral, nutritional, and family therapy perspectives. Addresses treatment of eating disorders in diverse patients of varying levels of severity.

WEBSITES OF INTEREST

National Alliance on Mental Illness
http://www.nami.org

National Eating Disorders Association
http://www.edap.org

See also: Behavioral addictions: Overview; Bulimia; Children and behavioral addictions; Depression; Women and behavioral addictions

Antabuse

CATEGORY: Treatment

ALSO KNOWN AS: Disulfiram

DEFINITION: Antabuse (disulfiram) is classified as an aldehyde dehydrogenase (ALDH) inhibitor and is considered an alcohol-aversive drug. Persons taking disulfiram while also ingesting alcohol will experience a disulfiram-ethanol reaction. This reaction involves a multitude of symptoms, including flushing, sweating, and nausea. Even small amounts of alcohol can produce this pharmacologic response. It is important to remind persons taking disulfiram that alcohol can be absorbed by the body even from common substances such as mouthwash or topical toners. This absorption can lead to a disulfiram-ethanol reaction, also known as acetaldehyde syndrome.

HISTORY OF USE

Disulfiram was discovered in the United States in 1937 by E. E. Williams when employees for the chemical plant Williams worked at were exposed to disulfiram and later experienced physical discomfort upon ingesting alcohol. One of the first medications specifically indicated for alcohol abuse, disulfiram was approved by the US Food and Drug Administration in 1951. Disulfiram was first used in high doses, up to 3,000 milligrams (mg), and was regularly used in the treatment of persons with alcohol dependence or abuse. These high dosages often led to undesired, adverse effects and, on rare occasions, deaths.

Dosing recommendations now are much more conservative. Patients should start with 500 mg as a single daily dose. After one to two weeks, depending on response, the dose may be decreased to a range of 125 to 250 mg daily. Therapy should continue until the patient and the patient's caregiver decide that a full recovery has been achieved; this may take up to a few years in some patients. These dosing requirements represent the minimum drug concentration necessary to achieve the amount of physical discomfort targeted, should the patient ingest alcohol.

Initially used in persons with alcohol dependence, disulfiram also has shown potential benefit in persons addicted to cocaine. Multiple clinical trials on the use of disulfiram for the treatment of cocaine dependence and methamphetamine dependence are in various stages of completion. Disulfiram is estimated to be used by about two hundred thousand alcoholics in the United States. The number of persons treated with disulfiram is far fewer than the estimated seventeen million or more persons with alcohol dependence or abuse in the United States.

EFFECTS AND POTENTIAL RISKS

Disulfiram inhibits aldehyde dehydrogenase (ALDH), the enzyme that converts acetaldehyde to acetate in the liver during the metabolism of alcohol. In the absence of disulfiram, acetaldehyde is quickly converted to acetate. Acetaldehyde levels are increased because of the inhibition of ALDH, which leads to the constellation of adverse effects. The adverse effects occur immediately and can include, at a mild level, headache, facial flushing, and sweating. Effects experienced in a moderate reaction can include nausea, tachycardia, hyperventilation, hypotension, and respiratory difficulties. In the most severe reactions, persons can experience serious cardiovascular decomposition, which could lead to death. The severity of the reaction depends on both the dose of disulfiram and the amount of alcohol ingested.

This medication should not be given to anyone without their knowledge and should not be given less than twelve hours after alcohol ingestion because of the risk of an unintended disulfiram-ethanol reaction. Even upon discontinuation of disulfiram treatment, the drug can remain in circulation for up to fourteen days, and alcohol must be avoided during this whole period.

Adherence is another hurdle to success with disulfiram. Studies have shown that supervised medication ingestion or other incentives to take the medication may result in higher rates of adherence. Side effects that occur even without ingestion of alcohol, although generally mild, include drowsiness, headache, and taste disturbances and can lead patients to stop taking the medication.

Disulfiram is available in tablet form and may be crushed and mixed with liquids. Disulfiram use can increase liver function tests into abnormal values and should be monitored before therapy initiation and again a few weeks after beginning therapy. Often, patients with alcohol dependence have underlying liver dysfunction.

Allison C. Bennett, PharmD

FURTHER READING
Pani, P. P., et al. "Disulfiram for the Treatment of Cocaine Dependence." *Cochrane Database of Systematic Reviews* 20.1 (2010): CD007024. Web. 8 Feb. 2012. Systematic review that includes the results of seven randomized clinical trials comparing disulfiram with placebo or an alternate pharmacological intervention for the treatment of cocaine dependence. Authors concluded there was no sufficient evidence to warrant disulfiram use for the treatment of cocaine dependence.
Soghoian, Samara, Sage W. Wiener, and Jose Eric Diaz-Alcala. "Toxicity, Disulfiram." *WebMD.* Aug. 2008. Web. 9

Mar. 2011. Detailed information on the metabolism of disulfiram and on signs of toxicity. Includes a section on other agents that may cause a similar reaction to that seen with disulfiram and alcohol.
Suh, Jesse J., et al. "The Status of Disulfiram: A Half of a Century Later." *Journal of Clinical Psychopharmacology* 26 (2006): 290–302. Print. A review of disulfiram, including information on other alcohol-aversive drugs, such as calcium carbamide and metronidazole. Includes brief sections on studies and the use of disulfiram implants.
Wright, Curtis, and Richard D. Moore. "Disulfiram Treatment of Alcoholism." *American Journal of Medicine* 88 (1990): 647–55. Print. Review of disulfiram usage. Includes tables with brief reviews of trials investigating disulfiram in persons with alcohol dependence.

WEBSITES OF INTEREST
"Alcoholism." MedlinePlus
http://www.nlm.nih.gov/medlineplus/alcoholism.html

Clinical Trials.gov
http://www.clinicaltrials.gov

See also: Addiction medications; Alcohol abuse and alcoholism: Treatment; Baclofen; Naltrexone

Anticholinergics

CATEGORY: Substances
ALSO KNOWN AS: Angel's trumpet; crazy tea; devil's seed; devil's snare; devil's trumpet; ditch weed; Jamestown weed; Jimson weed; locoweed; madhatter; stinkweed; thornapple
DEFINITION: Anticholinergics, such as Jimson weed, are plants that contain euphoria- and delirium-inducing properties.
STATUS: Legal in the United States
CLASSIFICATION: Noncontrolled substance
SOURCE: Jimson weed is the common name for the plant *Datura stramonium,* a member of the family Solanacea. It is native to most of the United States.
TRANSMISSION ROUTE: All parts of Jimson weed contain anticholinergic compounds. The plant is

abused by smoking the dried leaves, ingesting the seeds, or drinking teas made from its leaves.

HISTORY OF USE

Anticholinergic medications, directly derived from plants such as *Datura* species, are used for treating asthma, gastrointestinal disorders, diarrhea, bed-wetting, and motion sickness. Such anticholinergic plants contain the alkaloids atropine, hyoscyamine, and scopolamine, all potent inhibitors of the neurotransmitter acetylcholine.

The anticholinergic plant Jimson weed has been used for hundreds of years by Native Americans as a medicine and in religious and social rituals. The ingestion of *Datura* species of plants in Jamestown, Virginia, reportedly caused British soldiers during the Revolutionary War to behave bizarrely.

In modern times, Jimson weed is abused mostly by teenagers and adolescents, and it is usually used one time because of its unpleasant adverse effects. Other anticholinergic plants and medications have the potential for abuse, but most people who routinely use these agents have a significant history of drug abuse, personality disorders, or schizophrenia. In many cases, the overuse and inappropriate use of anticholinergic medications are attempts to treat adverse effects of certain antipsychotic agents. Sometimes, anticholinergic medications are combined with other illegal street drugs, such as heroin, to enhance the effect of the illicit drug.

EFFECTS AND POTENTIAL RISKS

Symptoms of anticholinergic toxicity, which may appear within minutes of ingestion of plant extracts, include increased heart rate, dry mouth, agitation, nausea, vomiting, incoherence, disorientation, auditory and visual hallucinations, dilated pupils, slurred speech, urinary retention, and high blood pressure. High doses may cause seizures, paralysis, coma, or death. Anticholinergic toxicity also may cause damage to liver and muscle tissues, and it can cause cardiac arrhythmias. The anticholinergic effects may last for several days.

Jennifer L. Gibson, PharmD

FURTHER READING

Centers for Disease Control and Prevention. "Jimsonweed Poisoning Associated with a Homemade Stew: Maryland, 2008." *Morbidity and Mortality Weekly Report* 59.4 (2010): 102–4. Print.
Graeme, Kimberlie A. "Anticholinergic Plants (Tropane Alkaloids)." *Wilderness Medicine*. Ed. Paul S. Auerbach. 5th ed. Philadelphia: Mosby, 2007.
Wiebe, Tannis H., Eric S. Sigurdson, and Laurence Y. Katz. "Angel's Trumpet (*Datura stramonium*) Poisoning and Delirium in Adolescents in Winnipeg, Manitoba: Summer 2006." *Paediatric and Child Health* 13.3 (2008): 193–96. Print.

WEBSITES OF INTEREST

"Drugs and Chemicals of Concern: Jimson Weed (Datura stramonium)." US Drug Enforcement Administration
http://www.deadiversion.usdoj.gov/drugs_concern/jimson_w.htm

"Jimson Weed Poisoning." Medline Plus
http://www.nlm.nih.gov/medlineplus/ency/article/002881.htm

See also: Hallucinogen abuse; Hallucinogens: Short- and long-term effects on the body; Psychosis and substance abuse

Anxiety

CATEGORY: Psychological issues and behaviors
DEFINITION: Many people feel anxious when faced with a challenge, and for some, that anxiety can help them to better perform a given task. Anxiety also can be useful when it alerts people to potential threats or dangers. In these situations, anxiety can help a person to be aware of his or her surroundings, and to act accordingly. However, for some people, anxiety can become overwhelming and interfere with their everyday lives, manifesting as anxiety disorder. Common anxiety disorders include generalized anxiety disorder, panic disorder, obsessive-compulsive disorder, post-traumatic stress disorder, and social anxiety disorder.

ANXIETY DISORDER SYMPTOMS

To understand how anxiety can lead to addiction or how addiction can lead to anxiety, it is important to know the symptoms of anxiety disorder. Symptoms can vary depending on the type of anxiety disorder.

Generalized anxiety disorder (GAD). GAD is characterized by persistent, excessive, unrealistic worry about things that may or may not be consequential. A diagnosis of GAD is made when this excessive worrying about everyday stressors lasts for a minimum of six months. In addition to excessive worrying, symptoms of GAD may include muscle tension, fatigue, restlessness, difficulty sleeping, irritability, stomach pain, and diarrhea.

According to the Anxiety Disorders Association of America (ADAA), GAD affects 6.8 million adults (3.1 percent of the US population). Women are two times more likely to be affected than are men.

Panic disorder. Panic disorder is characterized by feelings of impending doom or death. These feelings occur frequently and without warning, sometimes even while the person is sleeping. People with panic disorder also may live in fear of a recurring panic attack. In addition to feelings of impending doom, symptoms of panic disorder may include sweating, chest pain or pressure, irregular heartbeat, a feeling of choking or being smothered, dizziness, a fear of "going crazy," a sense of unreality, a tingling sensation, chills or flushing, and feeling the need to escape.

ADAA statistics show that approximately six million American adults experience panic disorder each year. Women are two times more likely to be affected than are men.

Obsessive-compulsive disorder (OCD). OCD is characterized by persistent thoughts or impulses that may lead to ritualistic behaviors and routines. People with OCD may spend hours focusing on obsessive thoughts and performing compulsive rituals, such as hand washing, counting, or checking things to try to rid themselves of their obsessive thoughts and feelings. Symptoms of OCD may include obsessive, irrational worry about dirt or germs, excessive concern with order and symmetry, fear that negative thoughts or impulses will cause actual harm to self or others, preoccupation with losing objects that have little or no value, excessive cleaning, repeatedly checking and rechecking things, and repeating the same phrase or the same action multiple times throughout the day.

The International OCD Foundation estimates that between two and three million adults and around one-half million children and teenagers in the United States have OCD. The disorder affects men, women, and children equally.

Post-traumatic stress disorder (PTSD). PTSD is characterized by frightening thoughts and memories of a traumatic event, such as a sexual assault, war, a natural disaster, a serious accident, or the sudden death of a loved one. People with PTSD often feel as though they are reliving the traumatic event. Other symptoms of PTSD include flashbacks, nightmares, emotional numbness, avoidance of places or situations that may trigger memories of the trauma, difficulty sleeping, and agitation.

According to the ADAA, approximately 7.7 million Americans age eighteen years and older have PTSD. Women are twice as likely as men to be affected.

Social anxiety disorder. Social anxiety disorder is characterized by an unreasonable fear of social situations. People with social anxiety disorders live in fear that they will say or do something that will embarrass or humiliate themselves in front of other people. Other symptoms of social anxiety disorder may include avoidance of social situations, rapid heartbeat, sweating, shaking, muscle tension, nausea, vomiting, and diarrhea.

ADAA statistics show that approximately fifteen million American adults suffer from social anxiety disorder. The disorder usually begins around the age of thirteen years.

HOW ANXIETY CAN LEAD TO ADDICTION

For people with anxiety disorders, the symptoms can become uncomfortable, and sometimes even overwhelming. To cope, many of these persons turn to drugs and alcohol to relieve their symptoms. Turning to drugs and alcohol is known as self-medicating. Central nervous system depressants, such as alcohol, marijuana, and opiates, are commonly used to self-medicate or to help relieve anxiety symptoms. Long-term use of any of these substances can lead to addiction.

In time, people who use drugs or alcohol to self-medicate will build a tolerance to the drug or the alcohol, so that they will eventually need to increase the amount that they are using to get the same effect. For example, someone who may at first have one or two drinks to relax at the end of the day may suddenly find that three, four, or more drinks are needed to relax. A person who began taking one pain pill a day to relieve anxiety symptoms may suddenly need two or three pills a day to get the same relief. This is how self-medicating can lead to substance abuse.

In addition to substance abuse, other problems are associated with self-medicating. These problems include the following: The relief from self-medicating is temporary, the side effects of long-term drug or alcohol use can be severe, and the underlying cause of the anxiety remains untreated.

HOW ADDICTION CAN LEAD TO ANXIETY

Not only can anxiety be a cause of substance abuse; anxiety also can be an effect of substance abuse. Certain substances, such as caffeine, cocaine, and methamphetamines, can cause panic attacks, GAD, and other physical symptoms of anxiety. Anxiety symptoms caused by substance abuse include irregular heart rate, flushing, dizziness, sweating, nausea, and difficulty sleeping. These symptoms can last long after the effects of the drug wear off and can make the person want to use again.

Additionally, withdrawal from alcohol or opiates can cause symptoms of anxiety. Anxiety symptoms caused by alcohol or opiate withdrawal include sweating, rapid heartbeat, difficulty sleeping, flushing, agitation, shakiness, nausea, and diarrhea. Therefore, a person who is self-medicating to avoid anxiety may actually be increasing his or her anxiety levels through substance abuse and subsequent withdrawal.

THE CYCLE OF ANXIETY AND ADDICTION

Anxiety and substance abuse often coexist in a vicious cycle. Central nervous system depressants are often used to relieve anxiety, but as withdrawal symptoms set in, anxiety is increased. This leads the person with the anxiety disorder to repeat the self-medicating behavior. When anxiety is caused by addiction, the anxiety that is caused by the substance abuse is often "self-treated" with more substance abuse.

Julie Henry

FURTHER READING

Barclay, Laurie. "Self-medication of Anxiety Linked to Substance Use Disorders." *Archives of General Psychiatry* 68 (2011): 800–07. Print. Presents the results of a national survey showing that self-medication in anxiety disorders is associated with a high risk for substance use disorders.

Mayo Foundation for Medical Education and Research. "Anxiety." 13 Feb. 2012. Web. http://www.mayoclinic.com/health/anxiety/DS01187. An overview of anxiety, including a definition, symptoms, types of anxiety disorders, causes, risk factors, diagnosis, and treatment options.

Rodriguez, Diana: "Double Trouble: Anxiety and Substance Abuse." http://www.everydayhealth.com/anxiety/anxiety-and-substance-abuse-double-trouble.aspx. 13 Feb. 2012. An article about the connection between substance abuse and anxiety.

WebMD.com. "Anxiety Disorders." 13 Feb. 2012. Web. http://www.webmd.com/anxiety-panic/guide/mental-health-anxiety-disorders. A detailed description of common types of anxiety disorders, symptoms, causes, diagnosis, and treatment options.

WEBSITES OF INTEREST

Anxiety Disorders Association of America
http://www.adaa.org

National Institute of Mental Health
http://www.nimh.nih.gov

National Institute on Drug Abuse
http://www.drugabuse.gov

Substance Abuse and Mental Health Services Administration
http://www.samhsa.gov

See also: Addiction; Anxiety medication abuse; Obsessive-compulsive disorder (OCD); Panic disorders and addiction; Post-traumatic stress disorder and addiction; Self-medication; Valium

Anxiety medication abuse

CATEGORY: Substance abuse

ALSO KNOWN AS: Anxiolytic medication abuse

DEFINITION: Anxiolytic medications are typically prescribed to reduce the symptoms of anxiety and panic attacks. Anxiety medication abuse occurs when these drugs are used for reasons other than what is instructed by a health care provider. The drugs may have been prescribed for a medical reason or may have been obtained illegally. They are taken more frequently, at a greater dose, or for a longer period of time than directed to produce changes in one's mental or physical state.

CAUSES

The most commonly abused class of anxiety medications is the benzodiazepines, and the most frequently abused benzodiazepine is alprazolam (Xanax) because of the increasing frequency with which physicians are prescribing this medication. Other common types of benzodiazepines are clonazepam (Klonopin), diazepam (Valium), and lorazepam (Ativan). Additional classes of anxiety medications, such as selective serotonin reuptake inhibitors (SSRIs), are not as popular with abusers, although there are case reports in the medical literature of recreational use of SSRIs and other anxiety drugs. Tolerance and physical dependence may occur after a short time of abuse, causing people to use larger quantities of medication to produce the same effects and to avoid withdrawal symptoms, respectively.

RISK FACTORS

Persons who abuse anxiety medications are more often non-Hispanic, Caucasian, adolescent or young adult males, although all ethnicities, ages, and genders have been reported to misuse anxiolytic drugs. Adolescents are at particularly high risk because of the ability to safely obtain the substance from a friend or from a family member who is prescribed the medication.

Alcohol users and persons with a psychiatric diagnosis are also at high risk for anxiety medication abuse. Those who are contemplating suicide are more likely to add benzodiazepine medications to alcohol. Abusers of illegal drugs, such as opiates (heroin and methadone), marijuana, and cocaine, often also abuse anxiolytic drugs. However, it is more likely for an illicit substance abuser to secondarily abuse a

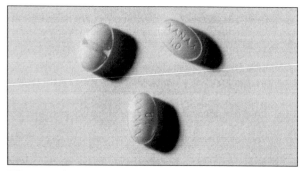

The most frequently abused benzodiazepine is alprazolam (Xanax) *because of the increasing frequency with which physicians are prescribing this medication.* (Tom Pennington/MCT/Landov)

benzodiazepine than it is for a benzodiazepine abuser to secondarily begin abusing other illegal substances.

SYMPTOMS

While these drugs are typically considered safe and effective when taken in prescribed doses, they may lead to significant and life-threatening symptoms when abused. Benzodiazepines are intended to produce a calming and drowsy sensation to reduce anxiety or panic attacks by depressing the central nervous system. Persons who abuse the drug seek the euphoria or extreme sleepiness that occurs when taken in excess quantity. When combined with other illegal substances, especially opiates, the benzodiazepines often enhance or extend the other drug's high. Additionally, anxiety medication may counteract the unwanted effects of abusing other illegal substances.

Adverse effects of abuse include confusion, lack of coordination, impaired memory, tachycardia, hallucinations, and coma. Although rare, case reports of death have been documented. Some but not all publications in the medical literature found that when compared with other benzodiazepines, the greatest risk for death is with Xanax abuse. Withdrawal symptoms, such as nausea, tremors, abdominal cramps, sweating, and seizures, may result from sudden discontinuation of the drugs.

SCREENING AND DIAGNOSIS

A urine drug-screen will detect the presence of benzodiazepines, although a health care provider would need to determine if the test was positive because of a legal prescription or if the substance was being abused. Because anxiety medication abuse often occurs in conjunction with other illegal substance or alcohol abuse, physicians should screen patients for concurrent disorders before prescribing anxiety medications. Inquiring about other psychological diagnoses also may help identify persons at risk for abusing the prescription.

TREATMENT AND THERAPY

As with many substances of abuse, a gradual tapering off of the anxiety medication may help with the detoxification process and with minimizing withdrawal symptoms. Persons who abuse anxiety medications seek treatment less frequently than those who abuse illegal substances or alcohol; those who have an addiction may be referred to Narcotics Anonymous or Pills Anonymous to complete a twelve-step program. Individual or group inpatient or outpatient therapy has proven effective for treating underlying anxiety, coexisting mental health disorders, or substance abuse problems.

PREVENTION

Physicians should take care when prescribing medications to ensure that their patients have not recently been evaluated by other physicians. Many people who abuse anxiety medications are known to "doctor shop," that is, they simultaneously seek the care of multiple physicians for the same prescription. Pharmacists should verify that a patient is not filling excessive prescriptions for the medication and that the prescription is not fraudulent. Also, parents and child caretakers who are prescribed benzodiazepines should be sure that children do not have access to the prescribed medications.

Janet Ober Berman, MS, CGC

FURTHER READING

Forrester, Mathias. "Alprazolam Abuse in Texas, 1998–2004." *Journal of Toxicology and Environmental Health,* part A, 69 (2006): 237–43. Print. Study details the growing trend of Xanax abuse, especially among adolescents.

Hernandez, S., and L. Nelson. "Prescription Drug Abuse: Insight into the Epidemic." *Clinical Pharmacology and Therapeutics* 88.3 (2010): 307–17. Print. A summary of networks and studies that collect data on prescription drug abuse and of commonly misused substances, including anxiolytics.

WEBSITES OF INTEREST

National Institute on Drug Abuse
http://drugabuse.gov

Substance Abuse and Mental Health Services Administration
http://samhsa.gov

See also: Anxiety; Benzodiazepine abuse; Panic disorders and addiction; Valium

---

Autoerotic asphyxiation

CATEGORY: Behavioral addictions
ALSO KNOWN AS: Hypoxphilia
DEFINITION: Autoerotic asphyxiation, also known as hypoxphilia, is an act of reducing the flow of oxygen to the brain to heighten sexual arousal and orgasm. The blood flow to the brain is reduced by self-hanging, intentional strangling, or suffocation. Autoerotic asphyxiation is most commonly practiced by males and is usually a solitary act. Autoerotic asphyxiators use cords, belts, ropes, neckties, scarves, or plastic bags to strangle or suffocate themselves while masturbating. Autoerotic asphyxiation is also practiced with a partner as a form of sexual masochism.

CAUSES

There is no known cause for autoerotic asphyxiation. Some experts believe the practice may be related to childhood trauma, such as sexual abuse. Others believe it may stem from an anxiety about death. The anxiety is relieved, and sexual gratification is obtained, by repeatedly "cheating death."

RISK FACTORS

There are no known factors that predispose a person to engage in autoerotic asphyxiation. People who practice autoerotic asphyxiation are often involved in otherwise healthy relationships. However, there are some comorbidities that can be associated with the practice of autoerotic asphyxiation, including mood disorders, anxiety disorders, and other forms of masochism, sadism, and fetishism.

People who play the choking game as adolescents or teenagers also may be predisposed to practicing autoerotic asphyxiation. The choking game is "played" by depriving the brain of oxygen through strangulation or by hugging a person from behind until he or she passes out. The choking game produces a feeling of euphoria and, therefore, is used as a means of getting high.

SYMPTOMS

Autoerotic asphyxiation is a dangerous practice that can end in death. Because it is normally a solitary act that is practiced behind locked doors, it may be difficult to determine if a person is at risk. However, there are some signs and symptoms, including the following: unexplained bruises on the neck; bloodshot eyes; bed sheets, belts, ties, or ropes tied in strange knots and found in unusual places; frequent, severe headaches; disorientation after being alone; wearing high-neck shirts or scarves in warm weather; locked bedroom or bathroom doors; and wear marks on bed posts or closet rods. Aside from death, there are some potential complications that are associated with autoerotic asphyxiation, including heart attack and permanent brain damage.

SCREENING AND DIAGNOSIS

Each year, as many as one thousand people in the United States are found dead—naked or partially naked—hanging by their necks in their bedroom closets (or in similar positions). Sexual paraphernalia is often found nearby.

People who practice autoerotic asphyxiation do not intend to kill themselves. They often devise some sort of safety mechanism that is intended to prevent accidental death in case they lose consciousness. Safety mechanisms may include slip knots or hanging from something that is shorter than they are. These safety mechanisms often fail because the person becomes disoriented and is unable to take the necessary steps to restore the flow of oxygen. Many people also mistakenly believe that autoerotic asphyxiation with a partner is safe because they assume that the partner can remove the object that is cutting off the flow of oxygen after the person who is being asphyxiated loses consciousness.

It is difficult to diagnose autoerotic asphyxiation because it often goes undetected until it results in death. People who practice autoerotic asphyxiation tend to go to great lengths to keep it a secret; most do not discuss it with peers, parents, or clinicians.

Screening for autoerotic asphyxiation requires that clinicians be knowledgeable about autoerotic asphyxiation, its signs and symptoms, and other related risky behaviors, such as the choking game. It may be helpful for clinicians to begin a discussion about autoerotic asphyxiation with people who are assumed to be engaging in the practice by approaching the subject in a nonsexual way. Instead of focusing on the sexual aspects or autoerotic asphyxiation, the clinician could focus on the dangers of getting high by self-hanging, strangulation, or suffocation.

TREATMENT AND THERAPY

Treatment for autoerotic asphyxiation may include a combination of cognitive behavior therapy and medication. Common medications for the treatment of autoerotic asphyxiation include selective serotonin reuptake inhibitors and anti-androgens.

PREVENTION

Education is key to the prevention of autoerotic asphyxiation. Education about the dangers of the choking game and about autoerotic asphyxiation may take place both at home and as part of sex education classes at school.

Once the behavior has started, many children begin looking for a way to perform autoerotic asphyxiation safely, so they need to be told that there is no safe way to do it. Clinicians should also be educated about autoerotic asphyxiation. Education could be incorporated into medical, nursing, and psychology curricula, and into primary care, psychiatry, and emergency medicine residency programs.

Julie Henry

FURTHER READING

Cowell, Daniel. "Autoerotic Asphyxiation: Secret Pleasure, Lethal Outcome." *Pediatrics* 124.5 (2009): 1319–24. Print. A research study designed to increase pediatricians' knowledge of autoerotic asphyxiation and increase awareness of its typical onset among youth.

Hucker, Stephen. "Hypoxphylia/Auto-Erotic Asphyxia." Web. 13 Feb. 2012. http://www.forensic-psychiatry.ca/paraphila/aea.htm. An article about autoerotic asphyxiation that includes a description, characteristics, information about potential comorbidities, and treatment options.

MedicineNet.com. "Paraphilias." Web. 13 Feb. 2012. http://www.medicinenet.com/paraphilia/article. htm#. An overview of paraphilias, including behaviors that are considered paraphilias, as well as causes and treatment options.

Sheleg, Sergey, and Edwin Ehrlich. *Autoerotic Asphyxiation: Forensic, Medical, and Social Aspects.* Tucson, AZ: Wheatmark, 2006. A comprehensive examination of autoerotic asphyxiation from the perspective of forensics, medicine, and sociology.

Warner, Jennifer. "Some Docs in the Dark about Choking Game." Web. 13 Feb. 2012. http://www. webmd.com/parenting/news/20091214/some-docs-in-the-dark-about-choking-game. A description of the choking game that outlines symptoms and preventive measures.

WEBSITE OF INTEREST

American Academy of Pediatrics
http://www.aap.org

See also: Anxiety; Behavioral addictions: Overview; Choking game; Marriage/partnership and behavioral addictions

B

Baclofen

CATEGORY: Treatment

ALSO KNOWN AS: Lioresal

DEFINITION: Baclofen is a skeletal-muscle relaxant, primarily administered for the treatment of reversible muscle spasticity and mobility impairments associated with spinal cord injury, multiple sclerosis, cerebral palsy, or various neuralgias. It has been investigated as a treatment for addiction and dependence disorders.

HISTORY OF USE

Baclofen was developed to control seizures in persons with epilepsy; however, its effectiveness for this treatment has been inadequate. Instead, baclofen has evolved into a treatment of choice for spasticity related conditions.

Baclofen was introduced as a possible addiction treatment when physician Olivier Ameisen self-treated his alcohol addiction with high-dose baclofen. His results were published in a self-case study report in the journal *Alcohol and Alcoholism* in 2005, prompting the public and the medical community to evaluate the use of baclofen to treat addiction.

EFFECTIVENESS

According to research, baclofen suppresses symptoms and cravings associated with alcohol dependence and reduces symptoms of alcohol withdrawal. Baclofen works by activating the gamma amino-butyric acid (B) receptors in the central nervous system. Baclofen is safe and effective, even in persons with alcohol-related liver damage. Baclofen possesses no abuse potential, has limited drug interactions, and causes fewer side effects than traditional medications used to treat alcohol dependence.

Baclofen is also being investigated as a treatment for cocaine- and opioid-dependence and abuse disorders. Large-scale clinical trials are needed to prove the long-term safety and effectiveness of baclofen in the treatment of substance abuse disorders.

PRECAUTIONS

High doses of baclofen can cause excessive drowsiness, dizziness, psychiatric disturbances, and decreased muscle tone that may impair daily function. Overdoses of baclofen may precipitate seizures, slowed breathing, altered pupil size, and coma. Abrupt discontinuation of baclofen can result in withdrawal symptoms, including hallucinations, disorientation, anxiety, dizziness, memory impairments, and mood disturbances.

Owing to increased publicity regarding baclofen as a potential treatment for addictions, some people have turned to illegally buying baclofen over the Internet in an attempt to control their addictions. As with any medication, baclofen should be used only under the guidance and supervision of a trained medical professional.

Jennifer L. Gibson, PharmD

FURTHER READING

Ameisen, Olivier. "Complete and Prolonged Suppression of Symptoms and Consequences of Alcohol-Dependence Using High-Dose Baclofen: A Self-Case Report of a Physician." *Alcohol and Alcoholism* 40.2 (2005): 147–50. Print.

---. *The End of My Addiction.* New York: Farrar, 2008.

Leggio, Lorenzo, J. C. Garbutt, and G. Addlorato. "Effectiveness and Safety of Baclofen in the Treatment of Alcohol Dependent Patients." *CNS and Neurological Disorders Drug Targets* 9.1 (2010): 33–44. Print.

Swift, Robert, and Lorenzo Leggio. "Adjunctive Pharmacotherapy in the Treatment of Alcohol Dependence." *Evidence-Based Addiction Treatment.* Ed. Peter M. Miller. New York: Academic, 2009.

WEBSITES OF INTEREST

The Alcoholism Guide. New Alcoholism Treatment: Uncovering Baclofen Alcohol Treatment
http://www.the-alcoholism-guide.org/new-alcoholism-treatment.html

Medline Plus: Baclofen Oral
http://www.nlm.nih.gov/medlineplus/druginfo/
   meds/a682530.html

*New York State Office of Alcoholism and Substance Abuse
   Services, Addiction Medications: Baclofen (Lioresal)*
http://www.oasas.ny.gov/AdMed/FYI/fyibaclofen.
   cfm

See also: Addiction medications; Alcohol abuse and
alcoholism: Treatment; Self-medication; Treatment
methods and research; Withdrawal

Barbiturates

CATEGORY: Substances
ALSO KNOWN AS: Barbies; barbs; block busters; blue
   devils; dolls; downers; goofballs; nembies; phen-
   nies; pinks; rainbows; red birds; red devils; reds;
   sleepers; stoppers; yellow jackets; yellows
DEFINITION: Barbiturates are a family of central
   nervous system depressant drugs with considerable abuse potential. Historically, they have
   played important roles in the treatment of sleep
   disorders, anxiety, seizures, and muscle spasms.
   Largely replaced by benzodiazepines, they retain
   clinical usefulness mainly as anticonvulsants and
   anesthetics.
STATUS: Prescription drugs
CLASSIFICATION: Schedule II, III, or IV controlled
   substances
SOURCE: Barbiturates are synthetic compounds with
   no natural sources.
TRANSMISSION ROUTE: Routes of administration include oral (common) and intravenous and rectal
   (infrequent). As with other depressants, persons
   who abuse barbiturates obtain them by getting
   multiple prescriptions, often by forging them, and
   by buying products from the illicit drug market.

HISTORY OF USE

In 1864, German scientist Adolf Von Baeyer synthesized barbituric acid by condensing urea and malonic
acid. The name reportedly came from a friend of the
discoverer, or from the day of Saint Barbara. The acid
itself did not induce any effect on the central nervous

Medicines Classified as Barbiturates

- Amytal sodium
- Butisol sodium
- Luminal
- Nembutal sodium
- Phenobarbital
- Seconal sodium

---

system. Subsequently, more than twenty-five hundred
barbiturate compounds with pharmacological properties have been obtained.

In 1903, Emil Fischer and Joseph von Mering discovered an effective sedative, diethylbarbituric acid
or barbital, which entered medicine under the trade
name Veronal. Another barbiturate, phenobarbital
(Luminal), was introduced in 1912.

By the mid-twentieth century, barbiturates became
the most widely used sedative-hypnotic medication
and the most popular substances of abuse. Their lipid
solubility rendered them quick to act and increased
their hypnotic properties, but it decreased the duration of action. Collectively referred to as downers,
barbiturates were taken alone or with ethanol to
produce a feeling of relaxation and euphoria. In the
United States, barbiturate abuse and addiction markedly increased in the 1950s and 1960s. The drugs became especially popular with actors and entertainers,
as a way to cope with stress and uncertainty. (Elvis
Presley chronically overused barbiturates, and an
empty bottle of pentobarbital [Nembutal] was found
on Marilyn Monroe's nightstand after her death.) As
safer drugs for people with sleep disorders became
available, the use of barbiturates for this purpose
declined.

The beginning of the twenty-first century, however,
saw a modest increase in the popularity of barbiturates as substances of abuse. According to a national
survey on drug use and health by the US Substance
Abuse and Mental Health Services Administration,
in the first years of this century an estimated 3.1 million people age twelve years and older had misused
barbiturates. Deaths caused by overdose and suicide
attempts using barbiturates still occur.

Barbiturates today are used clinically for anesthesia, pediatric sedation, status epilepticus treatment, and seizure prevention, and, in certain instances, for cases of traumatic brain injury. Some barbiturates are used to treat insomnia. Lesser known uses for barbiturates include treatment of essential hand tremor, cyclic vomiting, and hyperbilirubinemia in neonates. Among advocates of euthanasia and among those who commit suicide, barbiturates remain one of the most commonly employed drugs. Pentobarbital is the drug of choice for veterinary anesthesia and euthanasia.

EFFECTS AND POTENTIAL RISKS

Barbiturates are classified according to their duration of action. The effects of ultra-short-acting drugs, such as Pentothal (used in surgical settings), last less than one hour. Short-acting barbiturates (such as Nembutal and Seconal) act for three to four hours and are more likely to be abused. The effects of intermediate-acting barbiturates (such as Amytal) last for six to eight hours, and those of long-acting barbiturates (such as Veronal and Luminal) last approximately twelve hours.

Like other sedative-hypnotic drugs, barbiturates produce relaxation or sleep. The mechanism underlying their effect is thought to be an enhancement of the neural inhibition induced by the neurotransmitter gamma-aminobutyric acid.

At regular doses, the effects of barbiturates vary depending on the user's previous experience with the drug, the setting of use, and the mode of administration. A particular dose taken in the evening, for example, may induce sleep, whereas it may produce relaxed contentment, euphoria, and diminished motor skills during the day. Some users report sedation, fatigue, unpleasant drowsiness, nausea, vomiting, and diarrhea. A paradoxical state of excitement or rage also can occur. Users may experience a "hangover" phenomenon the day after drug administration. Hypersensitivity reactions, sensitivity to sunlight (photosensitivity), decreased sexual function, and impaired memory also have been reported. Tolerance to sedative and hypnotic effects develops after regular use.

Above-regular dosage of barbiturates induces a state of intoxication similar to that caused by ethanol. This resemblance, and tolerance development, may prompt some users to increase their drug intake. Mild intoxication is characterized by drunk-like behavior with slurred speech, unsteady gait, lack of coordination, abnormal eye movements, and an absence of alcohol odor.

The therapeutic dosage of any barbiturate is close to the lethal dose. Because of this narrow therapeutic window, severe intoxication or drug-induced death can easily occur. Intentional or accidental overdose results in extreme drowsiness, respiratory depression (with slow breathing), hypotension, hypothermia, renal failure, decreased reflexes, and, ultimately, coma and death. A person with suspected barbiturate overdose should be seen by a physician without delay.

Barbiturate use can cause both psychological and physical dependency and severe, even life-threatening, withdrawal symptoms (such as anxiety, insomnia, tremors, increased heart rate, delirium, and seizures). Persons who want to stop taking this medication should do so under medical supervision only. Concomitant use of other sedative hypnotics, such as alcohol and benzodiazepines, leads to potentially dangerous synergistic effects.

Mihaela Avramut, MD, PhD

FURTHER READING

Doweiko, Harold E. *Concepts of Chemical Dependency.* 7th ed. Belmont, CA: Brooks, 2009. An accessible textbook that includes a discussion of barbiturate effects and abuse.

Goldberg, Raymond. *Drugs across the Spectrum.* 6th ed. Belmont, CA: Wadsworth, 2010. A popular drug textbook with a subchapter discussing the effects of barbiturates and the health implications of their use.

Lynton, Richard. "Barbiturates." *Haddad and Winchester's Clinical Management of Poisoning and Drug Overdose.* Eds. Michael W. Shannon, Stephen W. Borron, and Michael Burns. 4th ed. New York: Saunders, 2007. A well-written, authoritative chapter on barbiturates and their pharmacology, uses, and overdose potential.

Shannon, Joyce Brennfleck, ed. *Drug Abuse Sourcebook.* 3rd ed. Detroit: Omnigraphics, 2010. A comprehensive resource for information on the abuse of depressants, including barbiturates.

WEBSITES OF INTEREST

"CNS Depressants." *National Institute on Drug Abuse*
http://www.drugabuse.gov/publications/research-reports/prescription-drugs/cns-depressants

US Drug Enforcement Administration. Drug Information:
   Barbiturates
http://www.justice.gov/dea/concern/b.html

See also: Anesthesia abuse; Controlled substances
and precursor chemicals; Depressants abuse; Prescription drug addiction: Overview; Stress and drug
abuse

Behavioral addictions: Overview

CATEGORY: Psychological issues and behaviors
DEFINITION: Behavioral addictions are patterns of
   behavior that follow a cycle similar to that of substance dependence. Behavioral addictions begin
   when a person experiences pleasure in association with a behavior, initially as a way of enhancing his or her experience of life and, later, as a
   way of coping with stress. The process of seeking
   out and engaging in the behavior becomes more
   frequent and ritualized, until it becomes a significant part of the person's daily life. The person
   experiences urges or cravings to engage in the
   behavior that intensifies until he or she carries
   out the behavior again; these urges or cravings
   usually lead to relief and elation. A person who
   cannot control or stop an activity, even after experiencing adverse consequences, has become a
   behavioral addict.

TYPES OF BEHAVIORAL ADDICTIONS

Compulsive Gambling Addiction
A person is said to have a gambling addiction when
they feel compelled to gamble and do so regardless
of monetary loss. The person takes game-playing, in
which a person has a chance to win, to an extreme
level. Compulsive gamblers feel a rush or a high from
gambling that further motivates them.
   Causes. People who have a family history of addiction may be more likely to become gambling addicts
themselves. Some research points to a biological component. Gambling addicts may have a deficiency of
the neurotransmitter serotonin in the brain. Other
causes of gambling addiction include emotional
immaturity, having friends and associates who are

involved in gambling, having low self-esteem, and experiencing stress without an outlet.
   Symptoms. Persons with a gambling addiction may
exhibit several behavioral symptoms, including becoming defensive if someone expresses concern
about their gambling habits, borrowing money or
selling belongings so they can continue to gamble,
feeling anxious or depressed when they are unable to
gamble, lying about how much they are betting and
how much they have lost, and taking time from work
or family life to gamble.
   Consequences. Gambling addicts will likely have
financial, relational, and, in some cases, legal problems. They may be unable to pay their bills. Relational
problems may develop because a loved one or a family
member may have a problem with the addict's excessive gambling and spending. Gamblers desperate for
money may resort to illegal activities to support their
addiction.
   Treatment and therapy. The first step in getting help
is acknowledging the symptoms and admitting that
there is a problem. A program such as Gamblers
Anonymous can be effective. Staying in recovery involves avoiding places that offer gambling and finding
friends who do not gamble. The addict is encouraged
to find new strategies for dealing with stress, because
stress can act as a trigger and cause a relapse.

Sex Addiction
Sex addiction is a compulsive need or desire to have
sex, to masturbate, to participate in one-time sexual
affairs, to regularly use prostitutes, to engage in voyeurism, or to obsessively think about sex. A sex addict
uses sex to get a rush, to deal with stress, or to escape
from negative feelings. For sex addicts, sexual activities interfere with their everyday lives.
   Causes. Family history may influence whether a
person becomes a sex addict. Having a parent who
acted out sexually increases the likelihood that a
child will grow up thinking the behavior is appropriate. Growing up in a home with distant or abusive
parents also may lead to sexual addiction. Another
cause may lie in brain chemistry. Antidepressant
medications help to control symptoms, indicating
that the problem has to do with insufficient levels
of certain neurotransmitters in the brain. The act of
having sex and an orgasm releases a powerful feeling
of euphoria, prompting the addict to continue the
behavior.

Symptoms. Sex addicts may have much sex, but not necessarily enjoyable sex. They use sex as a coping mechanism instead of a way to interact with a partner. Some of their behaviors may involve looking at pornography, excessive masturbation, exhibitionism, extramarital affairs, multiple sexual partners, voyeurism, phone sex, and inordinate viewing of Internet pornography.

Consequences. The negative consequences of sex addiction include arrest and criminal charges; debts from buying pornography, paying for prostitutes, or phone sex; sexually transmitted diseases; and relationship problems, including separation and divorce.

Treatment and therapy. The first step in treatment is to stop the behavior. A period of abstinence gives the person time to focus on finding the cause of the addiction. Treatments can include individual or group therapy sessions at a rehabilitation center. The addict must learn new coping skills and learn how to have healthy sexual relationships. Lifelong abstinence is not the goal. Support groups such as Sex Addicts Anonymous may be helpful, and prescribed medications such as Prozac or Anafranil can help to deal with the obsessive-compulsive aspect of the addiction.

Pornography Addiction

A person is considered to be addicted to pornography (porn) if that person's interest in looking at pornographic images goes from something that is a casual part of life to the focus of a good portion of their time and energy. A person addicted to porn uses this medium as a way to deal with stress, worries, or emotional upset and to get a high from seeing images that feed into their sexual fantasies. Porn addicts accumulate large collections of porn or spend a great deal of time viewing Internet porn.

Causes. For some porn addicts, the cause of their addiction can be traced to childhood. The addict may have been exposed to inappropriate images as a child and may have then fixated on and fantasized about what they had seen. Others may have begun using porn as a way to cope with physical, emotional, or sexual abuse experienced in childhood.

Symptoms. A person who is addicted to porn may devote a large amount of time to thinking about pornographic images and to planning porn viewing. They spend much time watching porn in secret or they visit strip clubs or adult bookstores excessively, while lying about their activities. These persons may even forgo

sexual relations in favor of looking at porn. Persons addicted to porn may be unable to have successful sexual relationships because their views of sex have become skewed by this addiction.

Consequences. Being addicted to porn can have several negative consequences, both for the addict and for the spouse or partner. Relationships are often strained if one person is addicted to porn and the other is repulsed by it. A porn addict also may have sexual performance problems, preferring porn over physical sex. This can result in significant problems for those with a partner.

Treatment and therapy. A porn addict can get help from a therapist who works with clients individually with cognitive-behavior therapy, or they can investigate rehabilitation centers that provide treatment programs. A person who has "quit" porn needs follow-up care and support from other former porn addicts to avoid returning to former patterns of addiction.

Compulsive Eating Disorder: Food Addiction

For a food addict, the obsession with food goes well beyond enjoying a good meal. A food addict's obsession with food is out of control, even when he or she understands the dangers associated with eating too much food. When not actually eating, food addicts are thinking about their next snack or meal. Food is their "drug" of choice, and many food addicts eat much more food then they need as a form of self-medication.

Causes. Food addicts often eat to improve their mood and to deal with negative feelings. They may suffer from low self-esteem and depression. Some eat because they associate certain foods with comfort. A person who is feeling depressed or stressed may turn to foods containing high amounts of sugar or fat because of the effect these ingredients have on the brain. These foods act in the same way as endorphins, the body's "feel good" hormones, and the food addict gets a kind of high after eating them. However, after the effect has worn off, the person feels guilty and more depressed. Brain scans reveal that the mere sight or smell of favorite foods triggers a spike in dopamine, a brain chemical linked to reward and motivation.

Symptoms. Food addicts may display a number of signs that point to a problem with their relationship with food. These signs can include cravings for certain kinds of foods, eating in secret or hiding food, eating when not hungry, eating past the point of feeling full or even to the point of feeling sick, feeling guilty about what and how much they eat, spending much time thinking about what they ate or what they plan to eat next, and turning to food to relieve stress or to deal with unpleasant emotions.

Consequences. The effects of food addictions are serious. Food addicts may develop eating disorders such as bulimia, which involves binging and purging. They might also gain unhealthy amounts of weight, putting them at risk for a host of health problems and diseases, including high blood pressure, heart disease, and diabetes. The most prominent complications of food addiction are weight gain, obesity, and chronic illness, all of which can lead to death.

Treatment and therapy. A therapist can help a food addict avoid eating food for comfort. The addiction may be a symptom of an underlying condition, such as abuse, which needs to be addressed to help the client learn to have a more healthy relationship with food and discover how to stop compulsive overeating. A support group such as Overeaters Anonymous or Food Addicts in Recovery Anonymous also can be part of the treatment process. As most food addicts tend to have low self-esteem and depression, a group such as Emotions Anonymous also might help the person learn how to have a better relationship with food.

Exercise Addiction

Exercise can be a great way to stay in shape, release stress, and fight disease. However, exercising, or working out, excessively, especially when not overweight, can quickly become a problem. Exercise addiction and extreme fixation on physical fitness are compulsive behaviors that may be quite difficult to stop without appropriate treatment.

Causes. People may develop an exercise addiction if they have a poor body image. To a person addicted to exercise, what matters is not weight but how he or she perceives his or her own body. Many exercise addicts are fit and may not be considered by others to be overweight. One of the positive effects of engaging in exercise is the release of endorphins. These hormones give a feeling of euphoria after exercising. The exercise addict may fall into a pattern of continuing to exercise to excess to try to experience these sensations. It also is possible that the exercise addict turns to physical activity to cope with the stresses of everyday life.

Symptoms. Exercise addicts may have various motivations for their behavior, including a desire to control their body weight or shape, a feeling of inexplicable dread if exercise is not performed, or feeling the need to achieve an exercise-induced high. Exercise addicts may have rigid fitness schedules to which they always adhere. They may compulsively exercise alone to avoid attracting the attention of trainers and gym staff. Addicts will exercise even when they are sick or injured. They may miss social obligations in order to exercise and may choose exercise over spending time with friends and family. They may feel guilty when unable to exercise, may experience withdrawal symptoms when unable to exercise, may repeatedly exercise for more than two hours daily, may fixate on weight loss or calories burned, or may suffer frequent injury from over-exercising.

Consequences. A person can exercise so much that they lose too much weight, become undernourished, and develop nutrition-related health problems. Women may lose so much weight that they stop menstruating. Psychological and social effects also occur. Exercise addicts may always be tired or irritable because of the demands of their fitness routines, and they might isolate themselves socially because they are preoccupied with exercising.

Treatment and therapy. Recovering exercise addicts need to learn how to limit their level of physical activity to moderate levels. Therapy and medications for obsessive-compulsive disorder may help addicts to deal with the urge to exercise to excess. Counseling with a psychologist or psychiatrist can help uncover and address deeper problems. The goal of treatment is to help the addict learn how to exercise enough to stay healthy, without becoming obsessed again.

Compulsive Shopping Addiction

Shopping addiction, also known as oniomania, is considered to be an impulse control disorder. Shopping addiction involves the uncontrolled urge to spend. Shopping addicts may feel compelled to buy items they do not need or want, and they get a rush from the experience itself. They use shopping as a way to cope with anxiety or stress, and they may not feel fulfilled or happy unless they have made a purchase. Despite efforts to stop reckless spending, the shopping addict is unable to change his or her behavior.

Causes. A shopping addiction may be caused by low self-esteem. A person may seek to compensate by spending money. Social pressure to keep up with the spending of others also might be a factor. For some, shopping becomes a way to self-medicate; the person might go shopping to improve his or her mood or to soothe hurt feelings. Other reasons why a person may turn to shopping as a coping mechanism include attempting to deal with symptoms of depression, difficulty handling intense emotions such as anger, lacking impulse control, and needing acceptance.

Symptoms. Some people get a rush from spending money. They will hide their purchases from loved ones and attempt to cover their actions to hide their addiction. Addicts will likely have money problems. They may be unable to pay their bills and may have to borrow and go into debt to finance their addiction.

Consequences. Compulsive spending continues for a certain time only before the addict has to deal with the consequences. Shopping addicts often will find themselves in financial trouble.. Foreclosure and even bankruptcy can be consequences of a severe shopping addiction, a situation that can result in marriage and relationship problems.

Treatment and therapy. If the shopping addict is depressed or has obsessive-compulsive disorder, medications may be prescribed as part of a treatment plan. Seeing a therapist is another part of treatment. The goal is to get to the root of the addictive behavior. Cognitive-behavioral counseling can help the addict avoid shopping as a way to deal with other issues. Shopping addiction treatment also needs to deal with the financial fallout of excessive spending.

Gerald W. Keister, MS

FURTHER READING

Ebert, M. H., P. T. Loosen, and B. Nurcombe. *Current Diagnoses and Treatment in Psychiatry.* New York: McGraw-Hill, 2000. A comprehensive reference for answering day-to-day questions on psychiatric diseases and disorders. Clearly describes behavioral addictions.

Frances, A., H. A. Pincus, and M. B. First, eds. *Diagnostic and Statistical Manual of Mental Disorders (DSM-IV-TR).* Arlington, VA: American Psychiatric Association, 2000. This clinical reference, the gold standard for psychiatry, presents descriptions of addictive behaviors that are easily understood by general readers.

Sadock, B. J., and V. A. Sadock, eds. *Kaplan and Sadock's Comprehensive Textbook of Psychiatry.* Philadelphia: Lippincott, 2000. Contains detailed descriptions of various behavioral addictions, written for clinicians but comprehensible to the general reader.

WEBSITES OF INTEREST

Emotions Anonymous
http://www.emotionsanonymous.org

Gamblers Anonymous
http://www.gamblersanonymous.org

Overeaters Anonymous
http://www.oa.org

Sex Addicts Anonymous
http://saa-recovery.org

See also: Body modification addiction; Bulimia; Children and behavioral addictions; Cleanliness addiction; Compulsions; Exercise addiction; Food addiction; Gaming addiction; Internet addiction; Marriage/partnership and behavioral addictions; Media and behavioral addictions; Men and behavioral addictions; Parenting and behavioral addictions; Pornography addiction; Sex addiction; Shopping/spending addiction; Television addiction; Trends and statistics: Behavioral addictions; Women and behavioral addictions; Work issues and behavioral addictions

Behavioral addictions: Treatment

CATEGORY: Treatment

ALSO KNOWN AS: Compulsive behavior: process addictions; psychological addictions

DEFINITION: A behavior or activity becomes an addiction when it interferes with daily functioning and causes emotional, social, or physical harm. The most common behavioral addictions are compulsive shopping, workaholism, pathological gambling, overeating, and exercise (most often bodybuilding and running). Other common behavioral addictions are sex, Internet, tanning, and computer gaming. Sometimes a person will present more than one addiction, as is often the case with gambling and alcohol abuse. Behavioral addictions are also commonly tied to another mental disorder, as obsessive compulsive disorder and eating disorders.

OVERVIEW AND ASSESSMENT

As behavioral addictions share similarities with drug and alcohol addictions, obsessive-compulsive disorders (OCDs), and impulse control disorders (ICDs) such as kleptomania and pyromania, their treatment plans can be similar. Unlike a treatment goal for substance abuse addictions, however, behavioral addictions do not usually require total abstinence, as clients must still eat, work, shop, exercise, and so forth.

The one exception to the nonabstinence rule is pathological gambling, as it is usually treated as a substance addiction, with recovery tied closely with abstinence. In other cases, a period of temporary abstinence might be required until the client can resume the activity normally. In all cases, the primary goal of most behavioral addiction treatment plans is the formation of healthy behaviors and habits.

Mental health experts do not know the causes of most behavioral addictions, although most agree that they stem from some combination of physiologic, social, genetic, and psychological etiologies, and thus their treatment plans vary greatly. The selection of an effective treatment plan for an addictive behavior begins with an initial assessment of the client.

Examples of commonly used diagnostic and screening tools include the workaholism battery, Minnesota impulsive disorder interview, compulsive buying scale, sexual addiction screening test, Massachusetts gambling screen, exercise dependence questionnaire, bodybuilding dependency scale, Internet addiction test, and online cognition scale. As research is still being conducted on behavioral addictions, tests and surveys are devised regularly, such as the Yale food addiction scale and the Dutch work addiction scale.

The American Psychiatric Association's *Diagnostic and Statistical Manual of Mental Disorders* (DSM) is the standard starting point for the diagnosis of pathological gambling, currently classified as an OCD not elsewhere classified; however, experts have proposed that gambling be moved in the revised DSM to a new category—addiction and related disorders—along with substance addictions. Other psychological addictions are either not included in the DSM or fall under a miscellaneous category, as with sexual disorders not otherwise specified.

As a high comorbidity exists between behavioral addictions and substance dependence and other mental disorders, clients are often tested also for depression, anxiety, post-traumatic stress disorder, and other disorders. Treatment plans are personalized and may involve individual, couples, group, and family therapy; a twelve-step program; or pharmacological intervention. Most clients are treated as outpatients, but some may require treatment at an inpatient facility or a hospital. In either case, successful treatment depends on the willingness of the client to be treated.

THERAPY

Cognitive-behavioral therapy (CBT) now represents the most common approach to treating process addictions, as neither cognitive therapy nor behavioral therapy proved to be completely effective by itself. There are as many different approaches to CBT as there are addictions, although these schools and approaches tend to share more similarities than differences, including the ultimate goal of empowering the client to take charge of his or her life in a healthy manner.

Most CBT treatment plans are administered in steps or phases over a period of usually no less than two months, although intensive residential programs might be shorter and include both individual and group sessions, with couples or family therapy when relevant. Flexibility and personalization are key to the most successful therapy programs.

CBT focuses on the client's thoughts because cognitions, rather than external influences or stimuli, are believed to be the primary sources for the addiction. This focus is also the foundation for the highly popular rational-emotive behavior therapy school, a precursor of CBT.

In CBT, while listening to the client discuss his or her behavior, the therapist can help the client to identify the thoughts that tend to trigger the behavior or trigger the emotions that cause the behavior. The therapist also helps the client to overcome any negative personality issues, such as low self-esteem or antisocial attitudes; irrational or distorted thoughts, such as overconfidence (which is common among pathological gamblers); or the belief that a person's worth is based on ownership of consumer goods, which is common among compulsive shoppers. The therapist then suggests alternative activities, deterrents to the behavior, and strategies to avoid the places, people, or objects associated with the behavior. The therapist also teaches relevant skills, including problem solving, critical thinking, stress management, or social skills, and introduces such techniques as deep breathing and mindfulness to help ground the client.

Drawing upon behavioral therapy, CBT also might include covert sensitization techniques, in which a patient learns to associate the undesirable behavior with an aversive image that usually elicits a strong, negative reaction. For example, an exercise addict who thinks about working out should, instead of visualizing a physically fit body, try to visualize a black widow spider spinning a web across a treadmill.

Behavioral interventions also make up a typical part of treatment. For example, a compulsive shopper might be asked to destroy all credit cards, perhaps keeping a bank card for emergencies, and entrust that card to another family member. A sex addict might be required to move his or her computer into the kitchen or another busy room of the house, where a lack of privacy might inhibit the person from viewing pornography.

CBT is especially goal-oriented and structured, and it relies heavily on homework, with reading assignments, self-monitoring exercises, and practice scenarios. Clients might be asked to keep a log or journal that details the time and place when they entered into the addictive behavior, along with their moods and other contributing factors.

Insight-oriented therapy, a type of psychotherapy that might be combined with cognitive therapy or CBT, attempts to uncover the unconscious conflicts that might be causing the behavioral addiction. Such conflicts could be responsible not only for the addiction but also for problems with relationships, work, and other aspects of life. Once uncovered, the client gains control over his or her life and is able to assume full responsibility for his or her behavior.

Hypnosis may be used to draw out unconscious thoughts or events that could be contributing factors to the addiction. By using special induction techniques, the therapist can encourage the client to fall into a trance, or a heightened state of relaxation. Once in this state, the therapist can make positive suggestions intended to replace negative thoughts or memories.

Couples therapy involves the spouse or partner of the addicted client and may resemble marriage counseling in that communication and sexuality are often primary topics, or it might focus on developing specific skills, such as effective budgeting, particularly relevant to shopping addicts, or house cleaning and organizational skills, especially relevant to hoarders. Family counseling, which can involve the client's children, siblings, parents, grandparents, or other relatives, is an especially important component of a treatment plan when relationships have become dysfunctional.

Group therapy can be similar to couples or individual therapy but offers the added benefit of peer support and the opportunity to learn from others. The most common type of group therapy is the twelve-step program devised by Alcoholics Anonymous (AA). AA's model has been adopted for use by Sex Addicts Anonymous, Gamblers Anonymous, Debtors Anonymous, Shopaholics Anonymous, and other organizations. Twelve-step therapies also are considered types of CBTs, as they engage the client in the active process of identifying and changing his or her behavior.

The first steps in this model involve getting the client to admit that he or she is unable to control his or her behavior and then recognizing a higher power can give one the strength to change. The client then asks for help and forgiveness, and through a spiritual awakening learns new behaviors while also receiving the benefits of a support group and the positive feelings that come with helping others overcome their addictions.

Secular programs, such as Rational Recovery's Addictive Voice Recognition Technique program, require a person to assume responsibility rather than placing oneself in the hands of a higher being. Related to the twelve-step programs is SMART Recovery's Four-Point Program, which is used to treat pathological gambling.

Successful therapy also involves relapse-prevention planning. The therapist will ensure that the client is well equipped to monitor and assess his or her behavior and to deal with moments of weakness and the general hurdles of life that sometimes cause setbacks. Planning might simply involve compiling a list of affirmations, alternative activities, or people that the client can call upon if needed, or a more elaborate course of action.

PHARMACOLOGICAL INTERVENTION

Drugs are administered as part of a treatment plan for behavioral addictions when therapy alone is insufficient and when other mental disorders are present. While research on the effectiveness of pharmacological interventions in treating behavioral addictions is limited, most of the medications prescribed are associated with treating substance addictions or OCD, and they have been documented as useful in treating some behavioral addictions.

The most commonly prescribed medications for treating addictions are the opioid receptor antagonists, such as naltrexone (Revia, Depade, Vivitrol), which is known to reduce cravings in recovering alcoholics and to block the "pleasure-feeling" effects of opioids (heroin, cocaine, oxycodone). For this reason, naltrexone has proven useful also in treating pathological gambling and sex and shopping addictions (as well as other behavioral addictions).

Antidepressants, particularly the selective serotonin reuptake inhibitors (SSRIs) such as fluoxetine (Prozac, Sarafem), paroxetine (Paxil, Pexeva), sertraline (Zoloft), and citalopram (Celexa), are often prescribed to treat depression, which tends to have a high comorbidity with compulsive buying, eating disorders, and some other addictions. Mood stabilizers such as lithium (Lithobid), commonly prescribed for treating bipolar disorder, a mental illness often present in substance abusers, may be prescribed for some process addictions too.

Antiandrogen drugs, prescribed for clients with a paraphilia disorder (pedophilia, zoophilia, necromania, and others), can lower the levels of or inhibit production of testosterone and androgens (male sex hormones) and have some demonstrative success in treating nonparaphilic sex addictions as well. Antiandrogens tend to be prescribed only after SSRIs have proven ineffective. Other medications also might be prescribed when a client is experiencing suicidal thoughts, anxiety, or another mental or medical condition.

ALTERNATIVE TREATMENTS AND SELF-HELP

Alternative, or holistic, therapies and techniques can complement a traditional treatment plan or be undertaken instead of medicine or psychotherapy. Alternative treatments are often an important part of residential treatment-center programs, where clients undergo a full daily schedule of therapy sessions.

The expressive therapies—dance, music, art, creative writing, and drama—are especially useful in treating children, young adults, seniors, and persons with limited verbal communication skills. These creative therapies allow addicts to explore deep emotions and thoughts; they also teach new skills that can build self-esteem and support personal growth.

Alternative medicine therapies include laser, acupuncture, biofeedback, homeopathy, and herbal medicine. As with yoga, tai chi, qigong, massage, meditation, drumming, and laughter and humor therapy, these types of activities help people relax and decrease stress, while they simultaneously teach new skills and provide healthy diversions from the negative behavioral addiction.

Any healthy activity or diversion that offers positive rewards can help with recovery from an addiction. These activities include nature walks, taking care of a pet, and taking a vacation away from the source of the addiction. Most addicts also will benefit from exercise and nutritional programs.

Self-help is another form of alternative therapy, although only the most motivated addicts will find success with this type of treatment. The best books are written by mental health experts with extensive experience treating a particular addiction, and they are structured to follow the CBT model used to treat their own clients. Personal experience with a particular addiction also can prove insightful. In general, the best books emphasize goal setting, include exercises for self-reflection, and teach a variety of skills.

Sally Driscoll, MLS

FURTHER READING

Benson, April Lane, ed. *I Shop, Therefore I Am: Compulsive Buying and the Search for Self.* Northvale, NJ: Aronson, 2000. This collection of essays includes a variety of treatment plans for shopping and spending addictions.

Collins, George, and Andrew Adleman. *Breaking the Cycle: Free Yourself from Sex Addiction, Porn Obsession, and Shame.* Oakland, CA: New Harbinger, 2010. This self-help book for men offers insights into the nature and recovery of sex addictions from a former addict turned mental health expert.

Dobson, Keith S., ed. *Handbook of Cognitive-Behavioral Therapies.* 3rd ed. New York: Guilford, 2009. This standard reference text includes chapters on treating couples, children, and teenagers, and has been updated to include newer types of CBT.

Duarte, Garcia Frederico, and Florence Thibaut. "Sexual Addictions." *American Journal of Drug and Alcohol Abuse* 36.5 (2010): 254–60. Print. Discusses the classification of excessive nonparaphilic sexual behavior and pharmacological treatment.

Grant, Jon E. *Impulse Control Disorders: A Clinician's Guide to Understanding and Treating Behavioral Addictions.* New York: Norton, 2008. Examines the etiology, assessment, and treatment of impulse control disorders and how they are related to substance addictions.

Grüsser, Sabine M., Ulrike Albrecht, and Nina Ellen Kirschner. "Diagnostic Instruments for Behavioural Addiction: An Overview." *GMS Psycho-Social-Medicine* 4 (2007). Web. 18 Apr. 2012. http://www.ncbi.nlm.nih.gov/pmc/articles/PMC2736529. This article discusses various tools for assessing sex, exercise, shopping, work, and Internet addictions.

Hartston, Heidi. "The Case for Compulsive Shopping as an Addiction." *Journal of Psychoactive Drugs* 44.1 (2012): 64–67. Print. Discusses the similarities between compulsive shopping and substance addictions on dopamine levels in the brain and argues for similar treatment plans.

Ladouceur, Robert, and Stella Lachance. *Overcoming Pathological Gambling: Therapist Guide.* Treatments that Work Series. New York: Oxford UP, 2007. Although this book is intended for mental health experts, students and general readers will appreciate the examples of diagnostic tools and other information.

Yapko, Michael D. *Trancework: An Introduction to the Practice of Clinical Hypnosis.* 4th ed. East Sussex, England: Brunner, 2012. This standard, updated work can be used as an entry point for students or referred to by professionals.

Young, Kimberly S., and Christiano Nabuco de Abreu. *Internet Addiction: A Handbook and Guide to Evaluation and Treatment.* Hoboken, NJ: Wiley, 2010. Two internationally known mental health experts offer the latest research on online gambling, cybersex, and gaming addictions.

WEBSITES OF INTEREST

Addiction Treatment
http://www.addictiontreatmentmagazine.com

American Society of Clinical Hypnosis
http://asch.net

Association for Behavioral and Cognitive Therapies
http://www.abct.org

Medline Plus: "Compulsive Gambling"
http://www.nlm.nih.gov/medlineplus/compulsivegambling.html

See also: Addiction medications; Gamblers Anonymous; Group therapy for behavioral addictions; Overeaters Anonymous; Screening for behavioral addictions; Support groups; Treatment methods and research

---

Behavioral therapies for addictions

CATEGORY: Treatment
ALSO KNOWN AS: Behavior therapy; cognitive-behavioral therapy
DEFINITION: Behavioral therapies, which have their roots in learning principles, focus on observable antecedents to behavior and on the consequences of the actions on the self and others. Cognitive-behavioral therapies add a person's thoughts as factors in maintaining and causing behavior.

THE BEHAVIORAL PERSPECTIVE

From the behavioral perspective, an addiction is a maladaptive way to cope with difficulties and to satisfy unmet needs in life. Behaviorally, the person who is addicted to drugs or alcohol is experiencing a learned sequence of behaviors acquired over time in response to problems or circumstances in life.

An addiction is a learned behavior that may have resulted from observing other persons coping with stressors through the use of substances. An addiction also can develop after a person has a rewarding experience with the physiological effects of alcohol or drugs. Once a person finds that the depressive or stimulating properties of drugs or alcohol have desirable effects, that person will use the substances to cope with stressors and other negative states. Substance abuse can become a preferred coping behavior, as substances work fairly rapidly. Also, ingesting these substances usually takes little effort. Repeatedly using a substance to cope with personal or situational problems leads to an addictive pattern of abuse.

Addiction from the behavioral perspective can be summarized as follows: a stressor triggers the need for coping, a substance is obtained and used, its effects are experienced, the negative feelings from the stressor are blunted, and, consequently, the substance is used in greater quantities to mitigate personal or situational problems. This learned pattern then becomes an addiction from which the person is unwilling or unable to break.

LEARNING THEORY FOUNDATIONS

The behavioral therapies for addictions are based upon the early research conducted by Ivan Pavlov and B. F. Skinner. Pavlov studied the concept of classical conditioning, in which a neutral stimulus that previously did not evoke any positive or negative response could be conditioned to produce a positive or negative response. This classical conditioning paradigm involved the pairing of the neutral stimulus with a reward or punishment. When associated with a rewarding stimulus, a positive response to the neutral stimulus emerged. A negative or punishing stimulus when paired with the neutral stimulus would produce a negative or avoidance response.

Skinner is known for his work with operant conditioning, which showed the power of positive reinforcement or reward in producing and maintaining responses. Skinner showed that a person will learn behavior that has been positively reinforced and will keep responding to earn the reward.

The foundations of classical and operant conditioning demonstrate that the pattern of addiction can be explained through the application of learning principles. Neutral settings may become classically conditioned to promote substance use and abuse through the power of rewards. Operant conditioning strengthens the behaviors associated with addictions, as the substance may initially manage stressors in a person's life and then reward the person for engaging in the addictive actions. The behavioral therapies focus on reversing the previous patterns of classical and operant conditioning that produced the addiction patterns.

TREATMENT FROM THE BEHAVIORAL PERSPECTIVE

The behavioral therapies for addictions focus on the emotional or situational factors that promote episodes of substance use and on the underlying factors that maintain the behaviors. These therapies seek to break the learned pattern that promotes addiction and to replace the maladaptive pattern with new adaptive behaviors. The triggers for the learned pattern are identified as the antecedents for the maladaptive addiction. This helps a therapist determine the occasions or reasons for the substance use.

A number of antecedents to the pattern of maladaptive substance use exists, so therapists seek to identify what has produced the pattern of addiction. Some common triggers or antecedents are social pressures, interpersonal conflicts, depressive moods, anger or frustration in life, chronic pain, poor role models, or settings where substances are routinely abused. Once a pattern has been learned, a number of factors can contribute to its maintenance.

The addictive pattern can continue because of the physiological effects of a substance, because of a reduction in anxiety, or because of social reinforcement from others with similar addictions. For each person affected, treatment involves identifying the most common and powerful triggers or antecedents and developing behavioral strategies to learn effective ways to manage the triggering factors that had created the learned pattern of addiction.

Treatment can be difficult because each person may have significant behavioral deficits to overcome. Some persons may never have learned the coping skills or behaviors that would help them to handle personal or situational distress. Behavioral therapies not only try to break the pattern of addiction but also try to overcome skill deficits that keep a person from facing problems in an adaptive fashion.

COPING SKILLS

To overcome the detrimental long-term consequences of addictive behavior, treatment includes coping-skills training, a behavioral therapy designed to achieve abstinence and to learn adaptive behaviors. This training involves an initial functional analysis to determine the role of the addiction in the person's life. Functional analysis shows what skills are lacking in the person's behavioral repertoire, especially those skills needed to cope with situational or personal stressors, and shows how addictive behaviors have been used as ways to cope.

The clinical interview is used for the functional analysis in conjunction with a variety of assessment instruments. These instruments provide objective measures to identify the extent of the addiction behaviors. It has often been found in the functional analysis that a person's emotional state is closely tied to the addiction. Feelings of depression, anxiety, loneliness, inadequacy, estrangement, and weakness are often inadequately managed because the person lacks effective coping skills. Substance use and abuse or some other behavioral addiction become conditioned responses to unpleasant emotional states.

With the completion of the functional analysis, behavioral therapy then enters a treatment planning phase that focuses on skills to overcome addictive behavior. Two major categories of skills make up the treatment planning phase: intrapersonal and interpersonal.

Intrapersonal skills involve the person's decision-making patterns and problem-solving capabilities. Intrapersonal-skills training helps to improve a person's ability to think through stressor situations (and anticipate problems) and then to select adaptive ways of coping with the situation or feeling. New ways of acting and thinking about problems or feeling states can be reinforced, resulting in a new pattern of behavior learned through the assistance of a behavioral therapist.

Interpersonal-skills training seeks to overcome problems with familial and social interactions. Behavioral therapies attempt to refresh or teach the skills needed for effective interpersonal relationships. The person with a substance abuse problem needs to learn how to refuse invitations from others to take substances and to avoid the social contexts that may reinforce addictive behaviors.

Having inadequate social skills also can contribute to feelings of loneliness and inadequacy. Interpersonal-skills training can bolster self-esteem and enhance a person's resistance to addiction.

TRAINING IN ACTION

Coping-skills training begins with the establishment of specific behavioral goals that focus on the elimination and management of the triggers for substance abuse or behavioral addictions. Behavioral goals, which are regularly reviewed at the beginning of each therapy session, can be covered in an individual, group, or family format. Contingency management, the major technique used in behavioral therapy, attempts to

modify a behavioral response by controlling the consequences of that response. Patients are rewarded when their adaptive behavior adheres with their behavioral goals. Failure to adhere to the behavioral goals in a treatment plan leads to a loss of reinforcement or reward. Contingency management is based upon the basic principles of operant conditioning, which predict that if a good or desirable behavior is rewarded, it is more likely to be repeated.

A component of contingency management is stimulus control. This is a procedure that is used to help a patient avoid or leave a situation that leads to substance abuse or behavioral addictions. Stimulus control is basically learning to pay attention to characteristics in the environment that can promote or trigger the pattern of addiction. Behavioral therapy is expanded for individual patients to whatever areas can promote adaptive function; it can include skill development in the areas of communication, parenting, time management, and occupational training.

Frank J. Prerost, PhD

FURTHER READING

Azrin, Donahue, et al. "Family Behavior Therapy for Substance Abuse and Other Associated Problems: A Review of Its Intervention Components and Applicability." *Behavior Modification* 33 (2009): 495–519. Print. A comprehensive review of the behavioral treatment options for substance abuse that includes specific protocols used in treatment.

Hougue, Aaron, et al. "Family Based Treatment for Adolescent Substance Abuse: Controlled Trials and New Horizons in Services Research." *Journal of Family Therapy* 31 (2009): 126–54. Print. Family therapy is a commonly used modality of therapy for drug addictions. This article provides a good review of the effectiveness of this treatment approach.

Potenza, March, et al. "Neuroscience of Behavioral and Pharmacological Treatments for Addictions." *Neuron* 69 (2011): 695–712. Print. A good overview of the neurobiologic foundations of many addictions. Explains how behavioral therapies can be effective in the treatment of addictions.

Witkiewitz, Katie, et al. "Behavioral Therapy across the Spectrum." *Alcohol Research* 33 (2010): 313–19. Print. A good article that provides a general review of the various behavioral techniques used to treat alcohol abuse.

WEBSITES OF INTEREST

Association for Behavioral and Cognitive Therapies
http://www.abct.org

National Institute on Drug Abuse
http://www.drugabuse.gov

Non-AA Alcohol Treatment Programs. AlcoholismGuide. com
http://www.the-alcoholism-guide.org/alcohol-treatment-programs.html

See also: Alternative therapies for addiction; Cognitive behavioral therapy; Treatment methods and research

Benzodiazepine abuse

CATEGORY: Substance abuse
DEFINITION: Benzodiazepine abuse involves the misuse of benzodiazepine, an anti-anxiety sedative and a controlled substance, often leading to dependence.

CAUSES

Benzodiazepine is used as an anti-anxiety sedative because of its rapid inhibitory effect on nerve activity via gamma-aminobutyric acid (GABA) receptors in the central nervous system (CNS). Benzodiazepines provide relaxation and hypnotic effects therapeutically and can be misused to get high or to come down from the effects of stimulants. Benzodiazepine abuse may be acute (for example, illegal use or accidental overdose from prescription) or may be chronic (for example, repeatedly and deliberately combining with cocaine or alcohol to get high or to self-medicate during alcohol withdrawal). Also, chronic misuse of prescribed benzodiazepines by increasing the dose, duration, or number of prescriptions can result in drug dependency.

Although newer CNS agents for anxiety treatment, such as selective serotonin reuptake inhibitors, are available, benzodiazepines can be taken as needed for sporadic anxiety-inducing circumstances; they also act quickly to relieve acute anxiety. However, these two benefits can cause benzodiazepine abuse. The widespread availability of the drug eases accessibility for nonprescription users; for example, benzodiazepines have been used as date rape drugs, which impair function and, thus, resistance to sexual assault, especially because the drug is difficult to taste when dissolved in a drink.

RISK FACTORS

Although benzodiazepines have lower abuse potential than do older psychotropic drugs, opioids, and stimulants, benzodiazepines remain popular for abuse in combination. Benzodiazepines with rapid onset, such as diazepam, are the most likely to be abused, although short- or intermediate-acting agents, such as alprazolam or lorazepam, may be abused too. Longer-acting agents, such as clonazepam, are associated with fewer cases of rebound anxiety or abuse.

Longer duration of prescription use (more than four weeks) and higher prescribed dosages (greater content or multiple daily doses) both increase the risk of physical dependence and withdrawal symptoms upon drug discontinuation. As tolerance develops to the prescribed dosages, abusive self-medicating behaviors, such as increasing the number of pills or increasing the times a pill is taken without consulting a physician can occur.

Additional risk factors for abuse of a benzodiazepine prescription are combining controlled substance prescriptions, particularly prescribed drugs that have similar CNS activity, and having a history of legal or illegal drug abuse. For example, methadone users often combine diazepam with methadone to increase the effect of the latter drug.

SYMPTOMS

Acute symptoms of benzodiazepine abuse or misuse are less likely to be fatal than benzodiazepine abuse in combination with alcohol. Prominent acute symptoms of abuse are mood changes, increased sleep with trouble awakening, unusual behaviors, and poor focus. With high doses, possible symptoms include confusion, blurred vision, dizziness, weakness, slurred speech, poor coordination, shallow breathing, and even coma.

Chronic symptoms of abuse are more difficult to identify; signs of addiction to a prescribed product include requests for increased doses to provide the same anxiety-relieving effects (drug tolerance) and the use of multiple prescriptions and doctors for the same drugs (drug-seeking behavior). Persons who abuse benzodiazepines chronically may have a changed appearance, changed behaviors, or changed mood, and they may regularly display poor performance at work or home. At times, these symptoms may mimic anxiety disorders themselves.

Long-term benzodiazepine use may lower cognition permanently, with only partial recovery of cognitive abilities upon discontinuation of the benzodiazepine. Seizure risk exists during withdrawal, especially with drugs (such as alprazolam) in the class that have short half-lives.

SCREENING AND DIAGNOSIS

With the exception of acute overdose presenting in an emergency room, screening for benzodiazepine

abuse requires subtle observation by family and health care providers. Chronic abuse may lead users to stop performing their normal duties at home and work; abusers will increasingly neglect themselves and others. Abusers may take benzodiazepines even in unsafe circumstances, such as before driving a vehicle, and may experience legal or family problems. Repeated requests for prescriptions, early pharmacy refills, and hiding medications in different locations are signs of addiction and drug-seeking behavior.

Dependence may be identified as an aid to diagnosing benzodiazepine abuse. When benzodiazepines are used regularly for more than two to three weeks, even at low doses, they begin to lose their inhibitory GABA effects, and higher doses are required to relieve anxiety or to obtain a high. Once this tolerance develops, withdrawal symptoms upon drug discontinuation are also likely and may occur within days of stopping the benzodiazepine.

Withdrawal symptoms also may contribute to a diagnosis of abuse because they differ from rebound anxiety symptoms and appear more similar to the symptoms of alcohol withdrawal. Tremor, insomnia, sweating, and nausea and vomiting are possible. Sensitivity to light and sound are common and directly distinguish withdrawal from symptoms of an underlying anxiety disorder. More severe withdrawal symptoms include agitation, confusion, myoclonic jerks, and seizures.

TREATMENT AND THERAPY

Acute overdose treatment in an emergency room depends upon the amount of time passed since the benzodiazepine was ingested. Within one to two hours of a lethal dose, gastric lavage may be used to flush the stomach. Alternatively, one dose of activated charcoal can be given within four hours of ingestion to bind the drug in the stomach; severe cramps and nausea are possible, and vomiting is a risk. Flumazenil provides an antidote to the sedative effects of benzodiazepines in cases of severe overdose and coma risk; however, its use may cause seizures when given to people who abuse benzodiazepines chronically and who may have become dependent.

Chronic abuse treatment is multifactorial and gradual. A slow tapering of dosage is key to avoiding rebound anxiety or withdrawal symptoms, which may take three to four days after drug discontinuation to begin. At the physician's discretion, a short-acting benzodiazepine such as triazolam may be replaced

---

Common Benzodiazepines

The following common benzodiazepines are used to treat acute mania, alcohol dependence, seizures, anxiety, insomnia, and muscular disorders:

Trade Name	Generic Name
Ativan	lorazepam
Dalmane	flurazepam
Dormicum	midazolam
Halcion	triazolam
Klonopin	clonazepam
Lexotanil	bromazepam
Librium	chlordiazepoxide
Loramet	lormetazepam
Mogadon	nitrazepam
ProSom	estazolam
Restoril	temazepam
Rohypnol	flunitrazepam
Sedoxil	mexazolam
Serax	oxazepam
Valium	diazepam
Xanax	alprazolam

with longer-acting agents in the class, such as chlordiazepoxide (Librium), or with a prescription agent from another class with a similar mechanism, such as gabapentin (an antiseizure drug). Either replacement may be more safely tapered and stopped.

In some persons with chronic anxiety disorder, benzodiazepines cannot be fully discontinued. These persons may remain on very low dosages of the abused drug or another benzodiazepine, under strict observation, to avoid withdrawal and rebound risks and to minimize tolerance or abuse, which is likely with higher dosages, without sacrificing anti-anxiety therapy.

PREVENTION

The key to prevention of acute or chronic benzodiazepine abuse is to lower its availability in prescribed and nonprescribed forms. The drug should be replaced as a prescription with safer and newer anti-anxiety agents. Physical dependence and acute misuse are less likely to occur if longer-acting or alternatively acting agents are prescribed for short time periods with careful physician supervision.

Nicole M. Van Hoey, PharmD

FURTHER READING

"Drug Abuse and Addiction: Benzodiazepines." *Cleveland Clinic: Current Clinical Medicine.* 2nd ed. Cleveland, OH: Elsevier, 2010. A chapter in a medical textbook discussing benzodiazepine's risk for abuse and dependence and examining withdrawal methods and concerns.

Goldman, Lee, and Dennis Ausiello. "Drugs of Abuse: Benzodiazepines and Other Sedatives." *Cecil Medicine.* Eds. Lee Goldman and Dennis Ausiello. 23rd ed. Philadelphia: Elsevier, 2007. Substance abuse section of a medical textbook that explains the therapeutic and misuse effects of prescription drugs, including psychotropics like benzodiazepine.

O'Brien, Charles P. "Benzodiazepine Use, Abuse, and Dependence." *Journal of Clinical Psychiatry* 66 (2006): 28–33. Web. Review article covering topics of benzodiazepine misuse in detail, including comparison of addiction and withdrawal symptoms, causes, and treatment options.

WEBSITES OF INTEREST

"Benzodiazepines: How They Work and How to Withdraw" *Benzo.org*
http://www.benzo.org.uk/manual/bzcha01.htm

CureResearch.com
http://cureresearch.com/b/benzodiazepine_abuse/intro.htm

eMedicine Health
http://www.emedicinehealth.com/benzodiazepine_abuse/article_em.htm

"Mental Health Book: Benzodiazepine Abuse."
Family Practice Notebook
http://www.fpnotebook.com/psych/cd/BnzdzpnAbs.htm

See also: Anxiety; Anxiety medication abuse; Date rape drugs; Panic disorders and addiction; Prescription drug addiction: Overview; Temazepam; Valium

Betty Ford Center

CATEGORY: Treatment
DEFINITION: The Betty Ford Center is a nonprofit alcohol- and drug-addiction treatment hospital located in Rancho Mirage, California.
DATE: Established in October 1982

BACKGROUND

Since its opening, the Betty Ford Center has focused on a singular mission: to provide effective treatment services for alcoholism and other drug dependencies. The center, founded in 1982 by former US First Lady Betty Ford and by Leonard Firestone, a businessman and former US ambassador to Belgium, provides residential treatment services for persons recovering from drug and alcohol addiction. Ford's decision to undertake such a project followed her own treatment for alcohol dependence and opioid analgesic addiction. Following her release from the Long Beach Naval Hospital's Alcohol and Drug Rehabilitation Service in 1978, she pursued the goal of creating a treatment center that emphasized the needs of women.

The center, which sits adjacent to the Eisenhower Medical Center, has one hundred inpatient beds available on its campus and additional lodging for eighty-four clients in its residential day-treatment program. The center's mission from the start has been to provide low-cost treatment usually unobtainable in acute-care hospitals. Also, the center's founders hoped to utilize for care the natural resources available in the area of Rancho Mirage. In a 2011 interview, Ford said, "Leonard Firestone and I realized we wanted a recovery hospital that would be less institutionalized and more of a relaxed setting in these mountains with their serenity and the beauty of them where people would be able to reach a spiritual feeling about their recovery."

Inpatient treatment, residential day-treatment, and intensive outpatient treatment form the core of the nonprofit center's therapy. The licensed, one-hundred-bed recovery hospital facilitates a structured program including daily lectures, group therapy, and counseling sessions. Physicians, nurses, psychologists, spiritual care counselors, activity therapists, registered dietitians, and other staff work together to create individualized treatment plans for each patient and to evaluate their progress.

Specialized support groups are available on an individual basis. From its earliest days, the center has treated women and men suffering from chemical dependency. The center has always reserved one-half of its space for women and one-half for men. Treatment, however, is gender-specific, as women and men reside in separate halls. Following discharge, patients receive a continuing care plan and participate in the focused continuing care program, staying in close contact with the staff for a full year after leaving the center.

More than ninety thousand persons have participated in a program at the center since its doors opened in 1982. The center provides staff and a network of alumni and friends around the world who continue to support one another, long after program participation.

MISSION AND GOALS

The center, an alcohol treatment center and drug rehabilitation clinic for individuals suffering from narcotic and chemical dependency, also provides support for family members and the community at large. Treatment is based on the spiritual principles embodied in the twelve-step recovery program and is integrated with the latest medical and therapeutic treatments.

The Betty Ford Center. (Getty Images)

The center is funded through the Betty Ford Center Foundation, whose mission is to serve as the funding vehicle for the center and for the Betty Ford Institute. The foundation is a vital part of the center and raises money to support the mission of the center through gifts, pledges, and planned-giving programs. The foundation's efforts are entirely nonclinical and are solely charitable. The foundation is the bridge between committed benefactors and those served by the programs and projects of the center and the institute.

The institute was created in 2006 with a mission to conduct and support collaborative programs of research, prevention, education, and policy development that lead to a reduction of the effects of substance use disorders on individuals, families, and communities. In 2008, the institute established the Children's Program Training Academy with the goal of training and certifying service providers in cities around the United States to offer children's programs locally. In 2009 the Professionals in Residence Program and the celebrated Summer Institute for Medical Students were realigned within the institute. Both programs offer an incomparable learning opportunity.

In September 2010, the center introduced a pain management track that allows patients to gain insight into the ways in which pain has changed their ability to think and approach life. The pain management track treats various types of chronic pain, including arthritis, chronic tension-type headaches and migraines, general headaches, fibromyalgia, neuropathies, orofacial pain, and post-laminectomy syndrome.

Camillia King

FURTHER READING

Fessier, Bruce. "History of the Betty Ford Center." *Desert Sun*, 8 Jul. 2011. Web. 6 Mar. 2012. http://www.mydesert.com/article/20110708/NEWS01/110708022/History-Betty-Ford-Center.

Ford, Betty. *Healing and Hope: Six Women from the Betty Ford Center Share Their Powerful Journeys of Addiction and Recovery*. New York: Putnam, 2003.

West, James W. *The Betty Ford Center Book of Answers*. New York: Pocket, 1997.

WEBSITES OF INTEREST

Betty Ford Center
http://www.bettyfordcenter.org

Betty Ford Foundation
http://bettyfordcenterfoundation.org

Betty Ford Institute
http://www.bettyfordinstitute.org

See also: Alcohol abuse and alcoholism: Treatment; Outpatient treatment; Residential treatment; Treatment methods and research; Twelve-step programs for addicts; Twelve-step programs for family and friends

Binge drinking

CATEGORY: Substance abuse
ALSO KNOWN AS: Alcohol poisoning; ethanol poisoning
DEFINITION: Binge drinking is the rapid consumption of five or more alcoholic beverages in succession. Binge drinking often occurs in group settings and can lead to coma and death. The amount of alcohol in the body is usually measured as the blood alcohol content, which is expressed as the percentage of alcohol per liter of blood. Alcohol consumption is also measured by the number of drinks ingested.

CAUSES

Ethanol (C_2H_5OH) is the psychoactive (mind-altering) component of alcoholic beverages, namely beer, wine, and hard liquor. Since antiquity, ethanol has been produced by the fermentation of sugar.

Alcohol is a flammable and colorless liquid and is readily available on the marketplace. Although the sale of alcoholic beverages in the United States and many other developed nations is generally restricted to adults over the age of twenty-one years, minors can often obtain the product through a third party, sometimes even their parents, without difficulty.

Peer pressure is a major factor in binge drinking. Teenagers and young adults who have never consumed alcohol, or who have consumed only an occasional alcoholic beverage, may succumb to peer pressure in a party environment and engage in binge drinking through drinking games. Party attendees are sometimes encouraged to partake in drinking with a beer "bong," which facilitates binge drinking. (A beer bong is a funnel attached to a hose. The drinker lies on his or her back, and one or more bottles of beer are funneled into his or her mouth.)

Significant evidence exists that genetic factors are involved in the development of alcoholism. The interaction of genes and environment is complex and, for most people with alcohol dependence, many factors are involved. Since 1989, the US government-funded Collaborative Study on the Genetics of Alcoholism (COGA) has been tracking alcoholism in families. COGA researchers have interviewed more than fourteen thousand people and sampled the DNA (deoxyribonucleic acid) of hundreds of families. Researchers have found evidence for the existence of several alcohol-related genes. COGA researchers are increasingly convinced that certain types of alcoholics are representative of a number of genetic variations.

RISK FACTORS

The following factors increase one's risk of binge drinking:

Rate of drinking. Rapid consumption of a given amount of alcohol increases the risk of alcohol poisoning. One to two hours are required to metabolize one drink.

Gender. Young men from age eighteen through twenty-five years are the most likely group to engage in binge drinking; thus, they are at the highest risk for alcohol poisoning. However, young women also engage in binge drinking and are more susceptible to alcohol poisoning because women produce less of an enzyme that slows the release of alcohol from the stomach than men.

Age. Teenagers and college-age youth are more likely to engage in binge drinking; however, the majority of deaths from binge drinking occur in persons age thirty-five to fifty-four years. The persons in this age group often do not metabolize alcohol as readily as younger persons and are more likely to have underlying health problems that increase the risk.

Body mass. A heavier person can drink more alcohol than a lighter person and still register the same blood alcohol content (BAC). For example, a 240-pound man who drinks two cocktails will have the same BAC as a 120-pound woman who consumes one cocktail.

Overall health. Persons with kidney, liver, or heart disease, or with other health problems, may metabolize alcohol more slowly. Persons with diabetes who binge drink might experience a dangerous drop in blood sugar level.

Food consumption. A full stomach slows the absorption of alcohol; thus, drinking on an empty stomach increases the risk.

Drug use. Prescription and over-the-counter drugs might increase the risk of alcohol poisoning. Ingestion of illegal substances, such as cocaine, methamphetamine, heroin, and marijuana, also increase the risk.

SYMPTOMS

Symptoms of alcohol poisoning include respiratory depression (slow breathing rate); confusion, stupor, or unconsciousness; slow heart rate; low blood pressure; low body temperature (hypothermia); vomiting; seizures; irregular breathing (a gap of more than ten seconds between breaths); and blue-tinged skin or pale skin.

SCREENING AND DIAGNOSIS

The BAC test is a definitive measure of alcohol in the blood and, hence, of blood poisoning. Persons with alcohol poisoning often have a BAC of 0.35 to 0.5 percent. By comparison, the BAC level that marks driving under the influence is 0.08 percent in all US states. Other screening tests include complete blood count and other tests that check levels of glucose, urea, arterial pH, and electrolytes in the blood.

TREATMENT AND THERAPY

Acute treatment consists of supportive measures until the body metabolizes the alcohol; acute treatment includes insertion of an airway (endotracheal tube) to prevent vomiting and aspiration of stomach contents into the lungs; close monitoring of vital signs (temperature, heart rate, and blood pressure); oxygen administration; medication to increase blood pressure and heart rate, if needed; respiratory support, if needed; and maintenance of body temperature (blankets or warming devices). Acute treatment also includes the administration of intravenous fluids to prevent dehydration (glucose should be added if the person is hypoglycemic, and thiamine is often added to reduce the risk of a seizure). Further treatment includes hemodialysis (blood cleansing), which might be needed for dangerously high BAC levels (more than 0.4 percent).

Hemodialysis also is necessary if methanol or iso-propyl alcohol has been ingested.

Follow-up treatment for binge drinking requires the aid of a health care professional skilled in alcohol abuse treatment. A treatment plan includes behavior-modification techniques, counseling, goal setting, and use of self-help manuals or online resources. Counseling on an individual or group basis is an essential treatment component. Group therapy, which is particularly valuable because it allows interaction with others who abuse alcohol, helps a person become aware that his or her problems are not unique. Family support is a significant component of the recovery process, so therapy may include a spouse or other family member.

Binge drinking may be a component of other mental health disorders. Counseling or psycho-therapy may be recommended. Treatment for depression or anxiety also may be a part of follow-up care. Beyond counseling and medication, other modalities may be helpful. For example, in September 2010, researchers at the University of California, Los Angeles released the results of a clinical trial on a unique therapy that applies electrical stimulation to a major nerve that emanates from the brain. The technique, trigeminal nerve stimulation, reduced participants' depression an average of 70 percent in an eight-week period.

College Binge Drinking

Binge drinking, or heavy episodic drinking, is one of the most serious problems on college campuses. According to the Centers for Disease Control and Prevention, binge drinking is defined as consuming five or more drinks in about two hours for males and consuming four or more drinks in about two hours for females.

Binge drinking not only leads to alcohol overdose (poisoning) but also leads to drunk driving, accidents, poor school performance, risky sexual activity, property damage, illicit drug use, and death. Furthermore, studies suggest that heavy drinking in adolescence is strongly associated with heavy drinking in young adult life. Rather than "growing out" of binge drinking behavior, many young persons "grow into" a pattern of alcohol dependence or abuse.

Care also may include long-term pharmaceutical treatment, including the oral medications disulfiram, acamprosate, and naltrexone. Disulfiram (Antabuse), which is taken orally, produces unpleasant physical reactions to alcohol ingestion; these reactions include flushing, headaches, nausea, and vomiting. Disulfiram, however, does not reduce the craving for alcohol. One drug that can reduce craving is acamprosate (Campral). Another drug, naltrexone (ReVia), may reduce the urge to drink, and it blocks the pleasant sensations associated with alcohol consumption. Oral medications are not foolproof, however; if a person wants to return to drinking, he or she can simply stop taking the medication.

To avoid (or manage) relapses and to help deal with the necessary lifestyle changes to maintain sobriety, aftercare programs and support groups are essential for the recovering alcoholic. Regular attendance at a support group, such as Alcoholics Anonymous, is often a component of follow-up care.

Although death can occur from binge drinking, most alcohol-related fatalities occur in automobile accidents caused by driving under the influence. Also, women who binge drink are vulnerable to sexual assault while in an alcohol-induced stupor. Repeated episodes of binge drinking can result in permanent physical injury and in reduced quality of health. Brain and liver damage is common in repetitive binge drinkers. A young adult who binge drinks often progresses to alcoholism in adulthood.

PREVENTION

The best way to prevent binge drinking is to educate persons who partake in at-risk behaviors. The highest risk for binge drinking occurs among young men, who often have a sense of invincibility and who often disregard advice from any source. Peer pressure is probably the best deterrent; it also is a factor that can encourage binge drinking. Finally, children with a good parental relationship are less likely to drink to excess.

Robin L. Wulffson, MD

FURTHER READING

Fisher, Gary L., and Thomas C. Harrison. *Substance Abuse: Information for School Counselors, Social Workers, Therapists, and Counselors.* 5th ed. Upper

Saddle River, NJ: Merrill, 2012. Incorporating clinical examples with solid research, this text provides counselors and social workers with a detailed overview of alcohol and other drug addictions.

Ketcham, Katherine, and William F. Asbury. *Beyond the Influence: Understanding and Defeating Alcoholism.* New York: Bantam, 2000. The authors define *alcoholism* as "a genetically transmitted neurological disease" and not the result of a character defect or moral weakness. They explain the effects of "the drug alcohol" on the human body and brain in both alcoholics and nonalcoholics.

Miller, William R., and Kathleen M. Carroll, eds. *Rethinking Substance Abuse: What the Science Shows, and What We Should Do about It.* New York: Guilford, 2010. Reviews what is known about substance abuse and offers overviews of biological, psychological, and social factors involved in the treatment of substance abuse. Also anticipates prevention and treatment developments and evaluates them for their overall possible effects.

Olson, Kent R., et al., eds. *Poisoning and Drug Overdose.* 6th ed. New York: McGraw-Hill, 2012. A resource for poison control centers, toxicologists, and health care practitioners for the diagnosis, treatment, and management of poisonings from exposure to industrial, therapeutic, illicit, and environmental chemicals.

WEBSITES OF INTEREST

Al-Anon and Alateen
http://www.al-anon.alateen.org

Alcoholics Anonymous
http://www.aa.org

National Institute on Alcohol Abuse and Alcoholism
http://www.niaaa.nih.gov

National Institute on Drug Abuse
http://www.drugabuse.gov

See also: Alcohol poisoning; Peer pressure; Teens/young adults and alcohol abuse

Bipolar disorder and addiction

CATEGORY: Psychological issues and behaviors

DEFINITION: Bipolar disorder is a mental illness characterized by cycles of depression and mania. This disease, earlier known as manic-depressive disorder, affects nearly six million American adults, or about 2.5 percent of the adult population in the United States. Persons with bipolar disorder are at high risk of substance abuse and suicide. This disease has a high rate of recurrence and, if untreated, has a 15 percent risk of death by suicide.

BACKGROUND

The coexistence of bipolar disorder and addiction is the rule rather than the exception. As many as 60 percent of people with bipolar disorder also will abuse an

Former NFL star Barret Robbins, who struggles with bipolar disorder and substance abuse, famously disappeared on the eve of the 2003 Super Bowl, and two years later was shot by Miami Beach police during a violent struggle. (Tim Chapman/MCT/Landov)

addictive substance during their lifetime, according to the National Alliance on Mental Illness.

The person in the manic phase of bipolar disorder may turn to alcohol or drugs to try to stabilize their condition. An addiction to alcohol or drugs might come about because the person is trying to slow down his or her thought processes long enough to get some rest. Addiction may be the result of, and not the reason for, the manic phase of the illness.

In the depressive stage of the illness, a person is vulnerable to addiction because he or she is looking for something that will help with feelings of hopelessness, isolation, and worthlessness. Alcohol or drugs may be considered a type of anesthetic to help the person escape from these kinds of feelings.

Causes

Persons with bipolar disorder are subject to overwhelming forces that are largely beyond their conscious control, which explains why so many persons with the disorder turn to drugs and alcohol for support and relief. Often, persons with bipolar disorder will use alcohol or drugs to numb their painful and difficult symptoms and to help them cope with their intense feelings. This can lead to a pattern of abuse that can quickly spiral into dependency and addiction.

People suffering with bipolar disorder are three to seven times more likely than others to abuse alcohol or drugs, such as sleeping pills and stimulants (including cocaine and methamphetamines). Drugs and alcohol are abused to increase the natural high of the mania and to self-medicate during depressive episodes.

Symptoms

Bipolar disorder is characterized by drastic mood swings—extreme highs and devastating lows. Some of the symptoms exhibited during manic episodes include an extremely elated, happy mood or an extremely irritable, angry, unpleasant mood; increased physical and mental activity and energy; racing and uncontrolled thoughts; increased talking (speech more rapid than normal); ambitious, often grandiose plans; inflated self-esteem; risk taking; and impulsive activity such as spending sprees; sexual indiscretion; and decreased sleep without experiencing fatigue.

Symptoms of depressive episodes include loss of energy; prolonged sadness; decreased energy and activity; restlessness and irritability; inability to concentrate or make decisions; increased worry and anxiety; less interest or participation in, and less enjoyment of, activities normally enjoyed; feelings of guilt and hopelessness; change in appetite; change in sleep patterns; and thoughts of suicide.

People with bipolar disorder often have difficulty in the workplace. Many of their symptoms can interfere with their ability to show up for work, to do their job, and to interact productively with others.

The consequences of addiction for persons with bipolar disorder are many and include taking drugs or consuming alcohol to regulate, stabilize, or improve their mood. Drugs and alcohol can provide temporary symptom relief, but in time, they worsen the symptoms, resulting in ever-increasing drug or alcohol use. Alcohol and drugs can reduce the effectiveness of bipolar medications and can reduce compliance for bipolar treatment. Stimulant drugs, such as cocaine or methamphetamines, can induce mania and then deep depression, exacerbating symptoms. Withdrawal symptoms can worsen depression.

Screening and Diagnosis

A diagnosis for substance abuse that occurs in persons with bipolar disorder is known as a dual diagnosis. In such cases, the substance abuse can occur during both the manic and the depressive phases.

No diagnostic laboratory tests exist for bipolar disorder. Thus diagnosis occurs through standardized diagnostic criteria to rate and evaluate the person's behavior.

Treatment and Therapy

Treatment for addiction includes psychiatric care and medication. Because bipolar disorder and alcohol and drug addiction often appear together, the symptoms of each disorder overlap, making it difficult to recognize the coexistence of both. The two conditions must be treated in tandem, making dual diagnosis critical to the recovery process.

Effective in treating co-occurring disorders is a residential substance abuse treatment program. This treatment typically includes individual and group counseling, cognitive-behavior therapy, dialectical behavior therapy, twelve-step programs, and other mental health services. Research has shown that the most effective treatment combines supportive psychotherapy and the use of a mood-stabilizer (either lithium, carbamazepine, or divalproex/valproic acid), often with an antipsychotic medication. No research exists to show that any form of psychotherapy is an effective substitute for medication.

PREVENTION

The best recoveries are achieved when individuals with bipolar disorder get effective treatment and faithfully follow that treatment for a lifetime. The patient should regularly see a supportive physician who is knowledgeable about the psychiatric management of this disorder, should learn what symptoms predict the return of this illness and what additional "rescue" medication can be taken, and should learn to trust the warnings given by family and friends when they see early signs of relapse.

Gerald W. Keister

FURTHER READING

Basco, M. R., and A. J. Rush. *Cognitive-Behavior Therapy for Bipolar Disorder.* 2nd ed. New York: Guilford, 2007. Presents a comprehensive overview of therapy for bipolar disorder and examines the coexistence of addiction.

Goodwin, F. K., and K. R. Jamison. *Manic-Depressive Illness: Bipolar Disorders and Recurrent Depression.* 2nd ed. New York: Oxford UP, 2007. A comprehensive presentation of clinical descriptions, diagnoses, and treatments of bipolar disorder. Includes an entire chapter on comorbidities.

Johnson, C., et al. "Convergent Genome-Wide Association Results for Bipolar Disorder and Substance Dependence." *American Journal of Medical Genetics B: Neuropsychiatric Genetics* 150.2 (2009): 182–90. Print. A study on how genetics play a part in the development of bipolar disorder and substance abuse and dependence.

WEBSITES OF INTEREST

"Bipolar Disorder." *National Institute of Mental Health*
http://www.nimh.nih.gov/health/publications/bipolar-disorder/complete-index.shtml

"Drug Abuse and Mental Illness." *National Drug Intelligence Center*
http://www.justice.gov/ndic/pubs7/7343

National Institute on Drug Abuse
http://drugabuse.gov

See also: Addiction; Depression; Mental illness; Suicide and addiction

---

Birth defects and alcohol

CATEGORY: Health issues and physiology

DEFINITION: Fetal alcohol exposure is one of the leading causes of birth defects and developmental disorders. Estimates place the number of children in the United States affected by fetal alcohol exposure at approximately two cases for every one thousand live births.

THE DANGERS OF DRINKING FOR TWO

When a pregnant woman drinks alcoholic beverages, the alcohol in her blood crosses the placenta easily and enters the embryo or fetus through the umbilical cord. Children affected by prenatal exposure to alcohol may suffer lifelong consequences, including intellectual impairment, learning disabilities, and serious behavioral problems.

All drinks containing alcohol can hurt an unborn baby. A standard twelve-ounce can of beer has the same amount of alcohol as a four-ounce glass of wine or a one-ounce shot of straight liquor. In addition, some alcoholic drinks, such as malt beverages, wine coolers, and mixed drinks, often contain more alcohol than a twelve-ounce can of beer. Studies have not been done to establish a known safe amount of alcohol that a woman can drink while pregnant.

Any time a pregnant woman participates in regular drinking increases her chance of having a miscarriage and puts her unborn child at risk for growth deficiencies, learning disabilities, and behavioral problems. Birth defects associated with prenatal exposure to alcohol can occur in the first eight weeks of pregnancy, before a woman even knows that she is pregnant.

Findings from the Centers for Disease Control and Prevention (CDC) show that about one in eight pregnant women reported alcohol use during pregnancy.

FETAL ALCOHOL SYNDROME

Fetal alcohol syndrome (FAS) is caused by alcohol consumption during pregnancy and is one of the leading known causes of mental disability and birth defects. It is characterized by abnormal facial features, including small head size, narrow eye slits, and abnormalities of the nose and lip areas; growth deficiencies; and problems with the central nervous system (CNS).

Children with FAS may have problems with learning, memory, attention span, problem solving, speech, and hearing. These problems often lead to difficulties in school and in getting along with others. FAS is an irreversible condition that affects every aspect of a child's life and the lives of his or her family. FAS is preventable if a woman abstains from alcohol while she is pregnant.

FETAL ALCOHOL EFFECTS
In the past, the term fetal alcohol effects (FAE) was generally used to describe children who did not have all of the clinical signs of FAS, but who had various

Justin Scott, right, gets help walking from his adoptive mother. Scott, 20, who struggles with Fetal Alcohol Syndrome, was born three months early with a .237 blood alcohol level, which took his two-pound body four days to dry out. His mother lived on the street and was inebriated throughout most of her pregnancy. (Bill Roth/MCT/Landov)

problems, including growth deficiency, behavioral problems, or problems with motor and speech skills. FAE has also been used to describe children who have all of the diagnostic features of FAS, but at mild levels. Because experts in the field were unable to agree on a single definition for FAE, the Institute of Medicine (IOM) proposed the terms alcohol-related neuro-development disorder (ARND) and alcohol-related birth defects (ARBD). ARND describes the functional or mental impairments linked to prenatal alcohol exposure, such as behavioral or cognitive abnormalities. These include learning difficulties, poor school performance, poor impulse control, and problems with mathematical skills, memory, attention, and judgment. ARBD describes malformations of the skeletal system and major organ systems. Such malformations may include defects of the heart, kidneys, bones, and auditory system.

TREATMENT AND PREVENTION
There is no cure for either fetal alcohol syndrome or fetal alcohol effects. They are irreversible, lifelong conditions that affect every aspect of a child's development. With early identification and diagnosis, a child with FAS can receive services that can help to maximize his or her potential.

The easiest way to prevent FAS is to abstain from alcohol use during pregnancy. Any amount of alcohol consumed during pregnancy is potentially dangerous to an unborn baby. If a pregnant woman is drinking during pregnancy, it is never too late for her to stop. The sooner a woman quits drinking, the better it will be for both her and her baby. If a woman is not able to quit drinking, she should contact her local social service agency or health plan for alcohol abuse treatment, if needed. If a woman is not yet pregnant, she should use an effective form of birth control until her drinking is under control.

Mothers are not the only ones who can help prevent FAS, however. Significant others, family members, schools, social organizations, and communities alike can help to prevent FAS through education and intervention. Also, emerging research suggests that long-term alcohol abuse among men may alter sperm cells in ways that introduce defects to the fetus at conception. Continued research will help to clarify this link and improve prevention efforts.

Celeste M. Krauss, MD

Levels of Intellectual Disability

Mild

- IQ 50–70
- Slower than normal in all areas
- No unusual physical signs
- Can acquire practical skills
- Reading and math skills up to grades 3–6
- Can conform socially
- Can acquire daily-task skills
- Integrated in society

Moderate

- IQ 35–49
- Noticeable delays, particularly with speech
- May have unusual physical signs
- Can learn simple communication
- Can learn elementary health and safety skills
- Can participate in simple activities and self-care
- Can perform supervised tasks
- Can travel alone to familiar places

Severe

- IQ 20–34
- Significant delays in some areas; may begin walking later than normal
- Little or no communication skills, but some understanding of speech with some response
- Can be taught daily routines and repetitive activities
- May be trained in simple self-care
- Need direction and supervision socially

Profound

- IQ <20
- Significant delays in all areas
- Congenital abnormalities present
- Need close supervision
- Require attendant care
- May respond to regular physical and social activity
- Not capable of self-care

FURTHER READING

Chaudhuri, J. D. "Alcohol and the Developing Fetus— A Review." *Medical Science Monitor* 6.5 (2000): 1031– 41. Describes in detail the various clinical features of fetal alcohol syndrome, based on experimental findings in animals.

"Drinking Alcohol During Pregnancy." *March of Dimes*. March of Dimes Foundation. Nov. 2008. Web. 29 Mar. 2012. Covers the risks of drinking while pregnant, fetal alcohol syndrome (FAS) and fetal alcohol spectrum disorder (FASD), and how to prevent alcohol-related birth defects.

"Drinking and Your Pregnancy." *NIAAA*. National Institute on Alcohol Abuse and Alcoholism. May 2010. Web. 29 Mar. 2012. Lists the risks of drinking while pregnant and resources for getting help if the mother has trouble stopping.

Nayak, Raghavendra B., and Pratima Murthy. "Fetal Alcohol Spectrum Disorder." *Indian Pediatrics* 45.12 (2008): 977–83. Covers the prevalence of FASD, its clinical features, its pathogenesis, and its differential diagnosis.

"Prenatal Exposure to Alcohol." *Alcohol Research & Health* 24.1 (2000):32–41. Reviews how prenatal exposure to alcohol can affect the developing brain of a child in terms of intellect, mental health, and social interactions.

Thackray, Helen M., and Cynthia Tifft. "Fetal Alcohol Syndrome." *Pediatrics in Review* 22 (2001):47–55. Reviews the diagnosis, epidemiology, management, prognosis, and prevention of FAS. Stresses the preventability of maternal alcohol abuse.

"Treating Individuals Affected with FASD." *NOFAS*. National Organization on Fetal Alcohol Syndrome. 2004. Web. 29 Mar. 2012. Information for treating FAS and FASD, from the prenatal period through adulthood.

WEBSITES OF INTEREST

Alcoholics Anonymous
http://www.alcoholics-anonymous.org/

National Institute on Alcohol Abuse and Alcoholism
http://www.niaaa.nih.gov/

National Organization on Fetal Alcohol Syndrome (NOFAS)
http://www.nofas.org/

See also: Alcohol: Short- and long-term effects on the body; Birth defects and drug use; Birth defects and smoking; Fetal alcohol syndrome; Newborn addicts; Pregnancy and alcohol

Birth defects and drug use

CATEGORY: Health issues and physiology

ALSO KNOWN AS: Congenital anomalies and substance abuse; developmental defects and substance abuse

DEFINITION: Birth defects or developmental defects refer to problems that develop in the fetus during the course of prenatal development. Birth defects are physical abnormalities that are present at birth regardless of the cause. One of the common causes of birth defects is drug use during pregnancy.

DRUGS AS TERATOGENS

Teratogens (teratogenic substances) are environmental substances that cause birth (or developmental) defects. Thousands of teratogenic substances exist, and a large number of them are drugs, including over-the-counter (OTC) drugs, prescription drugs, and illegal drugs of abuse.

Nearly all teratogens are most detrimental during the embryonic period (the second to eighth week of pregnancy). It is during this period in which organs form. Exposure to teratogenic substances may interfere with this normal organ formation. While drugs that are taken beyond the eighth week of pregnancy are not likely to cause actual birth defects, they may interfere with normal functioning of organs or may interfere with normal growth, causing intrauterine growth retardation. Drugs, like most other teratogens, affect the fetus when they cross the placenta along with oxygen and nutrients. Aspirin is one of the OTC drugs that is teratogenic, potentially causing bleeding in the pregnant woman and the fetus.

The use of prescription drugs may be necessitated because of a medical condition in the pregnant woman. If this is the case, it is essential for the medical professional to prescribe a drug that is not teratogenic or one that is unlikely to harm the fetus. One formerly common prescription drug, the broad-spectrum antibiotic tetracycline, caused discoloration of primary and secondary teeth in utero. Today, another broad-spectrum antibiotic is used to treat infection, decreasing the likelihood of a resultant birth defect.

Generally, when speaking of birth defects and drug use, one more commonly attributes defects to tobacco (smoking), alcohol, marijuana, stimulants, sedatives, addictive substances (like heroin or cocaine), and hallucinogens, most of which are teratogenic. Smoking tends to cause heart defects and intrauterine growth retardation. Alcohol exposure most typically causes fetal alcohol syndrome. This condition generally involves growth retardation and other physical and cognitive problems. No definite evidence exists about the teratogenic effects of marijuana, although the drug has been implicated in cases of small head circumference, neurological problems, and learning deficiencies. Investigations are ongoing into the effects of marijuana on prenatal development, especially because marijuana is the single most common illicit drug used by pregnant women.

Stimulants (including amphetamines) and sedatives (including phenobarbital) seem to cause developmental defects within the nervous system. Cocaine has been found to cause placental abruptions, causing death of pregnant woman and baby, or premature delivery. Opioids like heroin often cause intrauterine growth retardation and cause infants to be born addicted. Also, newborns addicted to heroin or other opioids are likely to have learning disabilities later in life.

Hallucinogens (like LSD or belladonna) differ from the other categories of drugs in that they can cause birth defects even if they are taken years before pregnancy. Hallucinogens have been found to cause chromosomal damage at the time of use. Because chromosomes in egg cells (ova) and in spermatogenic cells may be damaged, a wide variety of birth defects can occur. Similarly, if hallucinogens are used during early pregnancy, chromosomal damage may occur, leading to various types of birth defects. Many pregnant drug-users use more than one type of drug. This complicates the situation in that drugs may interact to have a significantly different and greater effect on the fetus.

DRUG TREATMENT FOR PREGNANT WOMEN

Pregnant women who use heroin or other opioids are often treated with methadone. While this is an effective immediate treatment, it does not prevent a fetus from being born addicted. Suboxone (also known as buprenorphine) is a newer drug used to treat opioid addiction (first used in the United States for this purpose in 2002). Suboxone is too new to have a clearly known effect on the fetus. The preferred mode of treatment for opioid addicted women remains methadone, simply because of the unknown effects of suboxone on the fetus. Infants born to mothers on heroin, methadone, or suboxone are evaluated using the neonatal abstinence (Finnegan) scale. The use of this scale determines the course of treatment in stopping the use of these substances.

Robin Kamienny Montvilo, PhD

FURTHER READING

Boyd, Susan C., and Leonora Marcellus. *With Child: Substance Use During Pregnancy—A Woman-Centered Approach.* Halifax, NS: Fernwood, 2007. Focuses on the treatment of drug-addicted pregnant women, making the argument that they should be treated as any other pregnant woman with additional emphasis on their substance abuse problem. Attempts to identify best practices in the treatment of the drug-using pregnant woman, encouraging best outcomes.

Huestis, Marilyn A., and Robin E. Choo. "Drug Abuse's Smallest Victims: In Utero Drug Exposure." *Forensic Science International* 128 (2002): 20–30. Print. This study, funded by the National Institute on Drug Abuse, investigated the effects of drug use on prenatal development. It attempted to develop an effective way to monitor drug use in pregnancy, identify tests that could accurately uncover when prenatal drug exposure has occurred, and look at the myriad effects that drug use has on the developing fetus. Emphasizes the importance of adequate treatment for pregnant drug users.

Huizink, Anja C., and Eva J. Mulder. "Maternal Smoking, Drinking, or Cannabis Use During Pregnancy and Neurobehavioral and Cognitive Functioning in Human Offspring." *Neuroscience Biobehavioral Review* 30 (2006): 24–41. Print. Examines the use of tobacco, alcohol, and marijuana during prenatal development and on the effects on future intellectual functioning in the child. While many studies have looked at the physical effects of these substances during pregnancy, this study specifically investigated effects on cognitive functioning. One such commonly found effect is the develop-ment of attention deficit hyperactivity disorder in childhood.

Rayburn, William, F. "Maternal and Fetal Effects from Substance Use." *Clinical Perinatology* 34 (2007): 559–71. Print. This article, written for medical professionals, discusses the effects of drug use on pregnant women and their developing fetuses. Touches on biological and psychological needs of the patients and deals with the ethical and legal issues that result from drug use.

WEBSITES OF INTEREST

March of Dimes
http://www.marchofdimes.com/baby/birthdefects.html

National Center on Birth Defects and Developmental Disabilities
http://www.cdc.gov/ncbddd

See also: Birth defects and alcohol; Birth defects and smoking; Hallucinogens: Short- and long-term effects on the body; Narcotics: Short- and long-term effects on the body; Pregnancy and drug use; Stimulants: Short- and long-term effects on the body

---

Birth defects and smoking

CATEGORY: Health issues and physiology

DEFINITION: It is estimated that between 10 and 25 percent of women smoke during their pregnancies. Incidence rates are especially high among women who are young, single, or poor. Prenatal exposure to nicotine results in many negative effects on the developing fetus, including physical and cognitive problems evident at birth and throughout the lifespan.

MECHANISM OF ACTION

The pharmacologically active ingredient in cigarettes is nicotine. When a woman smokes during pregnancy, the nicotine passes into the bloodstream of her fetus. After nicotine crosses the placenta, the level of nicotine in the fetus exceeds that of the level in the pregnant woman. Nicotine also can constrict blood vessels in the umbilical cord, which decreases the amount of oxygen available to the fetus. The effect of nicotine on fetal development appears to be dose-dependent: The more cigarettes a woman smokes during her pregnancy, the greater the risk to her fetus.

PRENATAL EXPOSURE TO NICOTINE: PHYSICAL EFFECTS

Fetuses exposed to nicotine are less likely to survive pregnancy than are fetuses not exposed. Smoking increases the likelihood of ectopic pregnancy, spontaneous abortion, and placental abruption (in which the placenta detaches from the uterine wall), which can lead to perinatal mortality (death during the end of pregnancy or within the first month after birth).

Fetuses exposed to nicotine prenatally are at a greater risk of being born prematurely, of having a low birth weight (an average weight reduction of 200 grams), of showing heightened tremors and startles, and of having respiratory problems. Prenatal exposure to nicotine also increases the risk of stillbirth and infant mortality. The rate of sudden infant death syndrome is three to four times higher among exposed infants than it is among infants who were not exposed to nicotine before birth.

Research on the relationship between maternal smoking and the risk of congenital birth defects has produced mixed results. While some researchers suggest a link between maternal smoking and, for example, cleft palate, this result is not found in all studies. There is evidence to support an increased risk of cardiovascular anomalies and neural tube defects in infants who were exposed to nicotine before birth. Data from the National Birth Defects Prevention Study also reveals an increase in craniosynostosis (in which the bones in the skull of a fetus close too early) in fetuses carried by women who smoked more than fifteen cigarettes per day while pregnant.

The problems associated with prenatal exposure to nicotine continue beyond infancy. Children who had been prenatally exposed to nicotine continue to be at risk for poor respiratory function during childhood and are more likely to be diagnosed with asthma and wheezing than are children who were not exposed. Children born to women who smoked during their pregnancies are also at an increased risk for developing all types of childhood cancer.

While most of the research in this field has focused on pregnant women who smoke, some new work looking at secondhand smoke suggests that exposure to secondhand smoke may increase fetal risk at a rate that is similar to that seen in women who smoke less than one-half a pack per day while pregnant.

PRENATAL EXPOSURE TO NICOTINE: COGNITIVE EFFECTS

When women smoke during pregnancy, their children have (when tested at three and four years of age), on average, poorer language skills and lower cognitive functioning than children not exposed. Many studies report that children prenatally exposed to nicotine are at an increased risk for intellectual impairment. Furthermore, controlled studies have documented a 50 percent increase in idiopathic mental retardation (in which a low intelligence quotient is not associated with a chromosomal defect).

Children whose mothers smoked during pregnancy also are more likely to be diagnosed with attention deficit hyperactivity disorder than are their peers who were not exposed. In addition to having academic difficulties, children whose mothers smoked during their pregnancies are also more likely to have disruptive behavior disorders. Finally, children exposed to nicotine before birth are at an increased risk of being diagnosed with a psychiatric disorder during childhood, especially if their mothers were heavy smokers.

PATERNAL SMOKING

Although most studies focus on maternal smoking, some researchers have explored the effect of paternal smoking on fetuses and found evidence that men who smoked for years before conceiving a child had children who were at increased risk for developing brain tumors and cancer before the age of five years. Other researchers have reported an increased risk of anencephalus (the absence of a large part of the brain and skull) and of spina bifida (in which some vertebrae are not fully formed, preventing their closure around the spinal cord) in the offspring of fathers who smoked.

Monica L. McCoy, PhD

FURTHER READING

Cnattingius, Sven. "The Epidemiology of Smoking During Pregnancy: Smoking Prevalence, Maternal Characteristics, and Pregnancy Outcomes." *Nicotine and Tobacco Research* 6.2 (2004): 125–40. Print. Reviews the prevalence of smoking by pregnant women in different countries, explores the effectiveness of programs to help women quit smoking, and reviews nicotine's effect on the fetus.

Huizink, Anja, and Eduard Mulder. "Maternal Smoking, Drinking, or Cannabis Use During Pregnancy and Neurobehavioral and Cognitive Functioning in Human Offspring." *Neuroscience and Biobehavioral Reviews* 30.1 (2006): 24–41. Print. While many articles explore behavioral outcomes in newborns, this article is one of the few studies to examine behavioral and cognitive functioning after infancy.

Shea, Alison, and Meir Steiner. "Cigarette Smoking During Pregnancy." *Nicotine and Tobacco Research* 10.2 (2008): 267–78. Print. In addition to reviewing the negative effects of prenatal exposure to nicotine, this article explores the physiological mechanisms that underlie these problems.

Woods, Scott E., and Uma Raju. "Maternal Smoking and the Risk of Congenital Birth Defects: A Cohort Study." *Journal of the American Board of Family Practice* 14.5 (2001): 330–34. Print. This article reviews earlier research on the link between maternal smoking and the risk of congenital birth defects. Presents data based on a study of 18,076 births.

WEBSITES OF INTEREST

Centers for Disease Control and Prevention
http://www.cdc.gov/tobacco/basic_information/
  health_effects/pregnancy

March of Dimes
http://www.marchofdimes.com/pregnancy/
  alcohol_smoking.html

See also: Birth defects and alcohol; Birth defects and drug use; Pregnancy and smoking; Smoking: Short- and long-term effects on the body

Blood alcohol content (BAC)

CATEGORY: Diagnosis and prevention
ALSO KNOWN AS: Blood alcohol concentration
DEFINITION: Blood alcohol content is a measurement of the amount of alcohol in a person's circulatory system at a given time. This measurement is commonly obtained by law enforcement offi-

cers in the field, who check drivers for operating a vehicle under the influence of alcohol. Blood alcohol content is less often used as a measure in medical treatment.

BACKGROUND

Blood alcohol content (BAC) is a measure of the amount of ethanol (or ethyl alcohol) in a person's bloodstream. In the United States, BAC is measured in grams of alcohol per 100 milliliters (ml) of blood. If a person has 0.10 grams of alcohol in his or her bloodstream for every 100 ml of blood, the BAC for that person would be 0.10. Another way to think of BAC is that it is the percentage of a person's blood that is composed of alcohol.

BAC is most often measured to determine if a person is impaired by alcohol while driving. Because drawing blood is an invasive procedure, law enforcement officers usually use a breath analyzer (or breathalyzer) in the field to estimate a person's BAC. Breathalyzer results accurately reflect blood-alcohol levels. In the United States (all states), the legal blood-alcohol limit for drivers who are old enough to legally drink alcohol is 0.08. Some states have stiffer penalties for drivers whose BAC is 0.17 or higher. The legal blood-alcohol limit for persons younger than age twenty-one years is 0.02 in most states, rather than 0.0 because some legal drugs contain small amounts of ethyl alcohol, which, if ingested, could register as alcohol in one's BAC.

RELATIVITY OF BAC LEVELS

Although blood alcohol levels are directly proportional to the amount of alcohol consumed, BAC levels vary significantly from person to person and from situation to situation for the same amount of alcohol. Factors that affect BAC are a person's weight and gender, the length of time in which the alcohol was consumed, the presence or absence of food in the stomach at the time of alcohol consumption, and a person's genetic makeup.

Women's bodies generally contain less water than do men's bodies, so alcohol has a greater relative impact on women. Also, the greater a person's weight, the more that person can consume alcohol before feeling its effects. For instance, a 200-pound man who drank two 12-ounce beers in one hour would likely have a BAC of 0.04, whereas a 120-pound woman drinking the same two beers in the same amount time would likely have a BAC of 0.08.

Food in the stomach at the time of alcohol consumption can keep a person's BAC lower because the alcohol makes its way into the bloodstream at a slower rate. One factor that does not affect BAC is caffeine, which can mask the depressant effects of alcohol but does not improve impaired judgment or increase a person's reaction time while, for example, driving. Finally, a physician may be interested in a patient's BAC if the physician suspects acute alcohol poisoning or when making a diagnosis of alcoholism.

Cathy Frisinger, MPH

FURTHER READING

Dasgupta, Amitava. *The Science of Drinking: How Alcohol Affects Your Body and Mind.* Lanham, MD: Rowman, 2011.

Hingson, R., T. Heeren, and M. Winter. "Lower Legal Alcohol Limits for Young Drivers." *Public Health Reports* 109.6 (1994): 738–44. Print.

Shults, R. A., et al. "Association Between State-Level Drinking and Driving Countermeasures and Self-Reported Alcohol-Impaired Driving." *Injury Prevention* 8 (2002): 106–10. Print.

WEBSITES OF INTEREST

Blood Alcohol Content (BAC) Calculator. University of Oklahoma Police Department
http://www.ou.edu/oupd/bac.htm

DUI/DWI Laws. Insurance Institute for Highway Safety
http://www.iihs.org/laws/dui/aspx

National Institute on Alcohol Abuse and Alcoholism
http://www.niaaa.nih.gov

See also: Alcohol: Short- and long-term effects on the body; Diagnosis methods; Drunk driving

---

Body modification addiction

CATEGORY: Psychological issues and behaviors

DEFINITION: Body modification is the intentional physical altering of one's body, often for aesthetic reasons, by means of piercing and tattooing, for example. Personal modification is mediated by numerous psychological and social constructs (such as religion, culture, self-esteem, and identity development). Literature on body modification addiction is predominantly focused on how to understand, balance, and differentiate issues of self-mutilation versus issues of self-empowerment and identity formation, in the context of a person's unique cultural background.

BACKGROUND

Body modification's long history is rooted in the practice of more clearly marking or imposing meaning upon a particular person by physically changing their appearance. The practice of body piercing and tattooing, for example, has enabled cultures to more closely monitor religious affiliation, social groups, and social status for thousands of years.

Modern understandings of body modification have evolved in nuanced ways. While some cultures continue to use modification rituals in the ways of predecessors, other cultures have seen body modification practices take a more provocative turn, away from tenets of group affiliation or rite-of-passage and toward self-expression and identity formation.

The latter part of the twentieth century and the beginning of the twenty-first century have seen a steep increase in body modification (in both the volume of people choosing to modify their body and in the larger cross-section of society engaging in the practice). Body modification has become so popular that it has become difficult to assign a person to a particular subgroup (or subculture) based solely on the chosen modification. Historically, this was the principal reason why people chose to modify their body.

The most common motivators behind the practice of body modification include art and fashion, individuality (control), group affiliation, and personal transformation. As such, the tenor of body modification research has shifted slightly over the years, away from issues of self-mutilation and toward a greater appreciation for and understanding of how such practices align with one's self-structures and ongoing personal narrative.

Finally, a powerful undercurrent to these motivators is that of addiction. A question that remains is this: What exactly is a person becoming addicted to when his or her body modification rituals intersect with obvious patterns of addictive behavior?

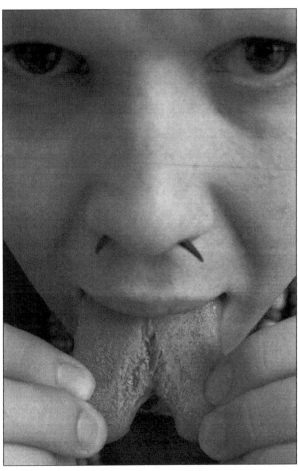

A 25-year-old tattoo artist, who had his tongue split as a form of body art in New York, shows how it has healed. (Chip East/Reuters/Landov)

TRANSITIONAL RESEARCH

Sociological research on issues related to body modification has been largely replaced with research aimed at identifying existing personality structures that make body modification more likely. This transition has been made, in part, because issues of body modification have become so prevalent in society. Body modification is now a mainstream practice, so drawing lines between specific social groups and exploring their derivations has become something of an antiquated notion.

Psychological research has instead taken up the issue of underlying motivational factors and existing personality structures that make it more likely for someone to pursue specific body modification (body piercing, tattooing, and plastic surgery, in particular).

Additionally, while there is a dearth of research focused exclusively on body modification addiction, valuable research is available to help one better understand the mechanisms that lead to addictive behavior. Of particular importance is research that values pluralism and examines body modification addiction through several, competing theoretical modalities.

Modern research is far more collaborative and inclusive when it comes to understanding body modification and treating body modification addiction. Research now considers traditional, well-accepted medical underpinnings of addiction, longstanding sociological precedents inherent to all body modification, and the complex self-processes and personality structures that may predispose people to body modification, all of which has helped advance research in this area. As such, what may have once fallen into the realm of psychopathology is now considered more broadly and more carefully.

MOTIVATORS AND ADDICTIVE BEHAVIOR

An *addiction*, by definition, is a behavior that persists despite negative consequences. In the case of body modification addiction, the negative consequences can include infections (sometimes severe), the perpetuation of unhealthy coping mechanisms, and potential pathological stigma (among others). Underlying these consequences are complex representations and expressions of the self, including prevalent cultural dynamics and experiences in one's early history that led to a specific self-identity.

Considerable research has looked at the most prevalent motivators and personality traits common to people who engage in body modification. This research has helped advance the discussion about how to best identify and treat body modification addiction. It considers, for example, external and internal triggers, conflicts that arise, and factors that interfere with goal-setting and necessary support systems.

Perhaps most important to any treatment of addiction is identifying the motivation in place to help reduce (and ultimately stop) the negative behavior. A preliminary, vital step would be considering why it is that someone is engaged in the behavior in the first place (before even considering why it is that they want to change). Taken together, evaluating motivational factors and personality constructs that contribute to a specific behavior is a crucial first step for any treatment.

With respect to body modification, considerable overlap exists between motivators and personality traits common to those who engage in this behavior. Typically, the average body modifier is one who seeks sensation and control and one who is (often) driven by art and fashion, individuality, group affiliation, and personal transformation. Those addicted to body modification typically strive to hold on to specific memories, experiences, and values (positive and negative).

CURRENT UNDERSTANDINGS

How might one answer a person who asks why he or she cannot stop a child from piercing his or her body? Before answering this question, one may want to consider how body modification addiction differs from other substance-based addictions.

Whereas tracing the derivation of one's substance-based addiction is more "paint-by-numbers" (linear), tracing the derivation of one's body modification addiction is more comparable to a fresco painting, with layers upon layers of factors contributing to the overall portrait. It can be difficult to navigate to a particular place in time, or event, that led to a specific body modification addiction. Instead, it is better to consider the range of factors that can make body modification addiction so complex. This is precisely what modern research is aiming to do.

Discriminative overtones have been largely replaced with questioning and curious inquiry about how (and why) people choose to modify their body, about what is driving their proclivity to do so, and about possible patterns or character traits common to those who modify often. The body has been an artistic canvas for thousands of years. It also has become more than an object. The body has become the vehicle through which people assert control in their lives, transform and heal in the face of trauma, and tell the world how they would like to be identified.

Much has been written about the ways in which people use their body to reclaim some aspect of their life, empower themselves, and express themselves in a therapeutic way. As such, a twenty-first-century understanding of body modification has been elevated by research examining theories of the self and embracing pluralism. What is known about body modification addiction has been greatly enhanced by research into motivational factors and personality constructs common to those who engage in this behavior. Future research should continue this trend, examining the powerful representations of the self and cultural factors that shape human identity.

Joseph C. Viola, PhD

FURTHER READING

Nathanson, Craig, Delroy L. Paulhus, and Kevin M. Williams. "Personality and Misconduct Correlates of Body Modification and Other Cultural Deviance Markers." *Journal of Research in Personality* 40 (2006): 779–802. Print. Examines cultural factors and unique personality constructs inherent to body modification practices. Methods used are predominantly self-report. The use of the word *deviance* separates this research from others that look specifically at issues of personality.

Pitts, V. *In The Flesh: The Cultural Politics of Body Modification*. New York: Palgrave, 2003. Examines the societal and psychological evolution of understandings of body modification.

Suchet, Melanie. "The 21st Century Body: Introduction." *Studies in Gender and Sexuality* 10.3 (2009): 113–18. Print. Outlines competing theoretical formulations common in body modification research, looking specifically at self-structures and incorporating psychoanalytic tenets into body modification research.

Winchel, Ronald M., and Michael Stanley. "Self-Injurious Behavior: A Review of the Behavior and Biology of Self-Mutilation." *American Journal of Psychiatry* 148 (1991): 306–17. Print. Outdated but fascinating analysis of body modification practices and research evolutions. While this article is quite good, it is compelling to consider how the scope of current research has changed since its publication.

Wohlrab, Silke, et al. "Differences in Personality Characteristics Between Body-Modified and Non-Modified Individuals: Associations with Individual Personality Traits and Their Possible Evolutionary Implications." *European Journal of Personality* 21.7 (2007): 931–51. Print. A seminal work comparing personality traits between persons with and without body modifications. Work on gender-related issues is particularly revealing.

Wohlrab, Silke, Jutta Stahl, and Peter M. Kappeler. "Modifying the Body: Motivations for Getting Tattooed and Pierced." *Body Image* 4.1 (2007): 87–95. Print. Discusses the volume of research that looks at the various motivators for body modification and describes in detail the history of research in this area.

See also: Behavioral addictions: Overview; DSM-IV criteria for behavioral addictions; Self-destructive behavior and addiction

---

Brain changes with addiction

CATEGORY: Health issues and physiology

DEFINITION: Neuroscientists agree that the chronic use of drugs and alcohol profoundly affects the brain. As a person develops a dependency on a substance, his or her brain undergoes lasting changes. Because of these changes, a recovering addict is vulnerable to relapse.

PERSONALITY DISORDERS OF THE ADDICTED

With advances in brain-imaging technology, medical experts can now conclude that addiction is not merely a defect in behavior or will, but a disease of the brain. Behavioral experts conclude that personality disorders can lead to substance abuse and can also result from substance abuse.

Until recently, clinicians treating substance abuse did not connect substance abuse disorders to personality disorders. Now, substance abuse treatment usually involves the detection, management, and treatment of a person's underlying personality pathology. A personality disorder is presented as persistent, unusual behavior relative to the cultural expectations for normal behavior, and it is usually observed during childhood or adolescence.

According to specialists Shelley McMain and Michael Ellery in a 2008 article in the *International Journal of Mental Health and Addiction*, persons with a personality disorder are impaired in two or more of the following behavioral functions: impulsivity, interpersonal functioning, affectivity, and cognition. McMain and Ellery, who found that the most common disorders among addicts are antisocial personality, borderline personality, and histrionic personality disorders, recommend "a thorough diagnostic assessment involving screening for personality pathology" for persons seeking treatment for addiction.

According to psychiatrist Raymond Anton, between 40 and 60 percent of persons dependent on alcohol have inherited the tendency to abuse alcohol. Most of these persons are male. Gene studies suggest that certain people are more susceptible to becoming alcoholics. Anton concluded,

> Whether it is heredity (the genes we are born with) or an interaction between these genes and environmental events and/or between genes and substances themselves, there is no doubt that the genetic brain differences are likely to be at the root cause of addiction.

BRAIN RESPONSES IN BEHAVIOR

Scientists agree that alcohol and drugs affect the brain's biochemical processes, altering the way neuroreceptors receive, process, and send information by overtaking the brain's neurotransmitters or by overstimulating the brain's pleasure center. Just as the brain connects the consumption of food and water as necessary for survival, the brain links alcohol or drugs to sustainment. The overuse of substances disrupts the brain's normal biochemical balance and the brain's mechanisms for controlling pain, anxiety, euphoria, and impulsiveness.

Because alcohol and drugs affect biochemical processes in the brain, they also impede the brain's ability to control decision-making and judgment. The desire for the substance of choice becomes an all-consuming desire for the addict, and substance abuse becomes an intrusion into the brain from which the brain will never fully recover.

A person's risk for addiction is linked to the reward and pleasure system in the brain. For many, intense euphoria is experienced when first trying a given substance, according to specialist Timothy W. Parker. The user's brain cultivates a deeper attraction to the reward of the substance. In contrast, once the effects of the substance wear off, the person's mood sinks to a severe low. The brain responds by again craving the substance, and the cycle continues, evolving into addiction. "Although they are motivated to take more of the drug to duplicate the original high," Parker explained, "drug abusers will never again attain that intensity of pleasure. Clearly some reaction in the brain has reduced the effect of the drug. It is interesting that this occurs so rapidly; the brain is a quick study."

This reduction of the effect of the substance characterizes the next stage of addiction. The user ingests higher doses of the substance, increasing tolerance. At this stage, withdrawal symptoms, which are the opposite of the high, persist if the user does not ingest the substance regularly. If a substance's effect is relaxation and numbness, as with heroin, withdrawal symptoms manifest as restlessness, tremors, and pain. Withdrawal from a stimulant like cocaine includes fatigue and depression.

The final stage of substance abuse is recovery: the period after an addict undergoes treatment and is abstaining from the substance. Even when withdrawal symptoms have dissipated, the recovering addict remains extremely vulnerable to a reactivation of a craving for the substance, triggered by social cues and visual stimuli. Even in recovery the addict will continue to be plagued with a condition in the brain that blocks the "just-say-no" solution to substance abuse.

According to Anton in a 2011 article in the *Journal of Law, Medicine, and Ethics*, magnetic resonance imaging scans of the brains of alcoholics and nonalcoholics show chemical differences in the dopamine-activation part (pleasure center) of the brain. Alcoholic brains show much more activity than those of nonalcoholics when processing images of alcoholic substances. Anton further found that even during periods of abstinence, addicts experience a dopamine-receptor deficiency when challenged by alcohol stimuli, leading to pleasure cravings and, consequently, poor judgment.

PHYSICAL BRAIN EFFECTS

Drugs and alcohol influence synaptic transmission in the brain and activate the release of an increased amount of dopamine into the brain's neural circuit. Depending on the substance, two structures in the brain are affected: the ventral tegmental area (VTA) and the nucleus accumbens (NA). VTA neurons influence the NA, which is where dopamine is released. Most drugs either activate VTA or directly affect NA dopamine levels. The ethanol found in alcohol directly increases dopamine release in the NA.

As a person becomes addicted, the tolerance to the substance of abuse increases. Physically, the brain changes to place controls (neuroadaptations) on how the substance affects dopamine release and changes to shut down NA receptors. The amount of dopamine released during ingestion of the substance subsides, causing the person to consume more of the substance to gain the desired level of pleasure. The brain also

releases controls to regulate the addict's emotions, activating moods of anxiety or depression as a sort of "antireward" system. The addict's pursuit of pleasure facilitates higher doses of the substance, leading that person to potentially overdose.

Substance abuse leads to long-term brain changes. The neuroadaptations that the brain produces to control the release of dopamine and to regulate emotions remain with the addict even after treatment and abstinence. Addiction alters the prefrontal cortex of the user, causing the reduction in neuron activity in this part of the brain. Other parts of the brain release a neurotransmitter known as glutamate, which impairs the addict's decision-making ability. Glutamate facilitates impulsiveness and a focus on immediate reward. Consequently, addicts often engage in reckless behavior, and rehabilitated addicts are prone to relapse when faced with substance-related stimuli. The amygdala, or memory part of the brain, is affected as well, enhancing emotional memories associated with being high, thereby making stimuli triggering these memories difficult for the addict to resist.

TREATMENT

In a 2011 editorial, the editors of *Drug Week* asserted that

> Effective prevention and treatment of addiction requires a clear understanding of the complex brain mechanisms that underlie addictive behaviors, and research has provided a fascinating view of how substance abuse hijacks neuronal circuits involved in reward and motivation and causes profound and persistent changes in behavior.

Critical to effective treatment is understanding how substance abuse changes the brain over time. According to Parker, an estimated 90 percent of treated addicts relapse. Many addicts benefit from initial treatment, but clinicians need to better understand how these addicts can remain in recovery that lasts a lifetime.

Central to the Alcoholics Anonymous (AA) approach to treatment, for example, is the notion that the alcoholic has no power over his or her addiction. Assuming that addiction is a chronic life-long condition and that the addict's brain cannot be cured medically, AA treatment involves intervention, group therapy and support, counseling, and accountability.

Pharmaceutical companies are seeking to develop pharmacological cures for addiction. With advances in neuroscience come new pharmaceutical treatments. Some treatments have been designed to make a person physically ill if they ingest a particular substance. Other treatments act as weaning mechanisms. Generally, drug treatment taps the brain's natural dopamine regulators, the brain's inhibiting mechanism (gamma-aminobutyric acid), and the brain's excitatory mechanism (glutamate).

As pharmacologists seek to leverage pharmaceutical breakthroughs to develop remedies for substance abuse, skeptics insist that treating substance abuse with substances will not offer lasting cures. Suggesting that there is more to beating addiction than physically treating the brain, many people warn that the spiritual element of recovery should not be dismissed.

Melissa Walsh

FURTHER READING

Anton, Raymond. "Substance Abuse Is a Disease of the Human Brain: Focus on Alcohol." *Journal of Law, Medicine, and Ethics* 38.4 (2010): 735–44. Print. Contextualizes modern understanding of alcohol and substance abuse and dependency.

McMain, Shelley, and Michael Ellery. "Screening and Assessment of Personality Disorders in Addiction Treatment Settings." *International Journal of Mental Health and Addiction* 6.1 (2008): 20–31. Print. Reviews the psychometrics of several instruments for the screening and diagnosis of personality disorders, which may be useful in addiction treatment settings.

Simon, David, and Deepak Chopra. *Freedom from Addiction.* Deerfield Beach, FL: Health Communications, 2007. Addiction specialists discuss ways to recognize addiction and examine methods for recovery.

Westreich, Laurence M. *Helping the Addict You Love.* New York: Simon & Schuster, 2007. A guide for family members and friends of addicts in leading the addicted into and through treatment and recovery.

WEBSITES OF INTEREST

Narcotics Anonymous
http://www.na.org

Substance Abuse and Mental Health Services Administration
http://samhsa.gov

See also: Alcohol: Short- and long-term effects on the body; Dopamine and addiction; Genetics and substance abuse; Narcotics: Short- and long-term effects on the body; Science of addiction

---

Bulimia

CATEGORY: Psychological issues and behaviors
ALSO KNOWN AS: Bulimia nervosa
DEFINITION: Bulimia is an eating disorder characterized by recurrent binge eating combined with harmful compensatory behavior such as excessive exercise, vomiting, or laxative use. Persons with bulimia feel a loss of control when binge eating and have significant preoccupations with body image, especially thinness. Bulimia can have serious physiological consequences, ranging from tooth decay to electrolyte imbalances that may lead to death.

CAUSES

Bulimia is caused by a complex constellation of factors, including sociocultural messages about eating and body image, stressful events or life transitions, family stress, and a lack of effective coping strategies. There are also biological predispositions or cognitive style vulnerabilities to this disorder. There is no single trajectory for the development of bulimia, although persons with this diagnosis report experiencing the effect of both genetic and environmental factors. Comprehensive eating-disorder assessments reveal that each person with bulimia may have a unique causal history for this disorder.

RISK FACTORS

There are a number of significant risk factors for bulimia, including being a white, adolescent, or young adult female and living in a society in which attractiveness is linked to thinness. Other risk factors include family dysfunction, having pre-existing depressive symptoms or anxiety disorders, and experiencing stressful life events or life transitions. Additionally, individuals who have a biological parent or sibling who has been diagnosed with bulimia have an increased likelihood of developing the disorder.

SYMPTOMS

Bulimia has behavioral and psychological symptoms and a variety of physical effects. Behavioral symptoms include episodes of binge eating, in which the person feels a loss of control and eats a quantity of food that is significantly larger than most people would consume in a similar period of time. Persons with bulimia have an intense concern with weight and appearance, which leads them to engage in unhealthy compensatory behaviors to negate the effects of their binge eating. These compensatory behaviors include purging by vomiting or by using laxatives, excessive exercising, and severely restricting food consumption when not binge eating. This cycle of binge eating and compensatory behaviors will continue regularly, that is, two or more times per week.

As bulimia progresses, symptoms will include depression and anxiety, such as frequent worry, disturbed sleep patterns, and feelings of sadness and ineffectiveness. The person may withdraw from social activities and relationships and may feel great shame about their binge eating and their compensating behaviors.

Physical effects and medical complications of bulimia include tooth decay and esophageal inflammation from vomiting, electrolyte imbalances, menstrual irregularities, dehydration, and possible heart failure. Death too can occur from complications of bulimia.

SCREENING AND DIAGNOSIS

A comprehensive screening and assessment for bulimia involves collaboration between a physician and a therapist. The therapist will ask the patient about symptoms, background information, weight and body image issues, abnormal eating behaviors, weight control measures, general functioning, family and social experiences, mental health history, and medical history. The

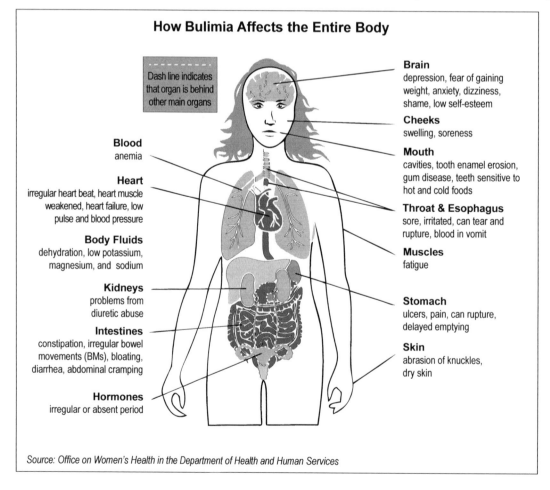

How Bulimia Affects the Entire Body

Dash line indicates that organ is behind other main organs

Brain
depression, fear of gaining weight, anxiety, dizziness, shame, low self-esteem

Cheeks
swelling, soreness

Mouth
cavities, tooth enamel erosion, gum disease, teeth sensitive to hot and cold foods

Throat & Esophagus
sore, irritated, can tear and rupture, blood in vomit

Muscles
fatigue

Stomach
ulcers, pain, can rupture, delayed emptying

Skin
abrasion of knuckles, dry skin

Blood
anemia

Heart
irregular heart beat, heart muscle weakened, heart failure, low pulse and blood pressure

Body Fluids
dehydration, low potassium, magnesium, and sodium

Kidneys
problems from diuretic abuse

Intestines
constipation, irregular bowel movements (BMs), bloating, diarrhea, abdominal cramping

Hormones
irregular or absent period

Source: Office on Women's Health in the Department of Health and Human Services

doctor will perform a physical exam and will typically run a battery of tests, including tests of organ functioning, electrolytes, heart irregularities, and bone density. The doctor also will ask specific questions about the patient's eating behaviors, physical symptoms, and medical history. The doctor and therapist will then share the results of their comprehensive assessments with the patient and will review treatment options.

TREATMENT AND THERAPY

Many comprehensive treatment options for bulimia are available, and the choice of treatment is determined by the severity of the disorder. Patients whose illnesses have not reached a dangerous level may attend weekly or biweekly counseling sessions with a therapist, participate in group therapy, meet with a registered dietitian for assistance in meal planning, and have regular appointments with a physician for monitoring of physical functioning. Family therapy also may be integrated to address any family concerns or stressful life events that are affecting the patient, and to address family members' concerns about their loved one with bulimia. For individuals who have engaged in excessive exercising as a compensatory behavior, treatment may include working with an exercise physiologist to learn appropriate exercise habits.

Partial hospitalization or inpatient treatments may be necessary for patients with increasingly severe medical instability or other co-occurring mental health concerns. In such programs, patients receive intensive medical monitoring and intervention, frequent and intensive individual and group therapy services, and supplemental treatments such as art therapy. The length of treatment for bulimia varies by person and is affected by the patient's willingness to engage in treatment, by other coping resources, and by the severity of symptoms.

PREVENTION

The general way to prevent bulimia is to challenge social and cultural messages that overemphasize the importance of thinness and attractiveness. Promoting messages that emphasize a positive body image and personal value based on qualities and behaviors, rather than on physical appearance, will decrease the risk of eating disorders.

Tracy Ksiazak, PhD

FURTHER READING

American Psychiatric Association. *Diagnostic and Statistical Manual of Mental Disorders.* 4th ed. Arlington, VA, 2000. Outlines the symptoms, causes, and prevalence rates for bulimia and related disorders. Diagnostic categories provide a common language for all mental health professionals in the United States.

Costin, Carolyn. *The Eating Disorders Sourcebook: A Comprehensive Guide to the Causes, Treatments, and Prevention of Eating Disorders.* 3rd ed. New York: McGraw-Hill, 2006. Provides accessible information about current trends and controversies in the treatment of eating disorders. Explores underlying causes for bulimia and explains the contributions of each component of the treatment process.

Grilo, Carlos M., and James E. Mitchell, eds. *The Treatment of Eating Disorders: A Clinical Handbook.* New York: Guilford, 2010. Comprehensively reviews research and theory on treatment of bulimia from medical, cognitive-behavioral, nutritional, and family therapy perspectives. Provides descriptions of how effective therapy for bulimia can be conducted from many theoretical approaches.

Hall, Lindsey, and Leigh Cohn. *Bulimia: A Guide to Recovery.* Carlsbad, CA: Gurze, 2011. Self-help book discusses health strategies for coping, types of treatment for bulimia, and underlying emotional factors.

WEBSITES OF INTEREST

National Alliance on Mental Illness
http://www.nami.org/template.cfm?section=By_Illness

National Eating Disorders Association
http://www.edap.org

See also: Anorexia nervosa; Children and behavioral addictions; Depression; Women and behavioral addictions

Bupropion

CATEGORY: Treatment

ALSO KNOWN AS: Wellbutrin; Zyban

DEFINITION: Bupropion is an antidepressant, but it is also prescribed to help people quit smoking. It can be used in combination with a nicotine replacement product. Bupropion appears to affect two brain chemicals that may be related to nicotine addiction: dopamine and norepinephrine. Bupropion reduces the cravings for cigarettes that smokers experience when they try to quit. The drug also seems to reduce many of the nicotine withdrawal symptoms, including irritability, frustration, and anger.

HISTORY OF USE

Bupropion is a widely prescribed antidepressant, at one time the fourth-most prescribed antidepressant in the United States. It was invented in 1969 by GlaxoSmithKline (then Burroughs Wellcome) and was designed and synthesized by Nariman Mehta. It was approved as an antidepressant in 1985 by the US Food and Drug Administration, withdrawn in 1986 because of concerns over seizures, and reintroduced to the market in 1989, after the maximum dosage was adjusted. Bupropion was approved in 1997 as an aid for smoking cessation (under the name Zyban). Under the name Wellbutrin XL, it has also been approved to treat seasonal affective disorder, a mood disorder prevalent in either the winter or the summer months.

TREATMENT

Patients are instructed to start taking bupropion one week before they plan to stop smoking. It takes about one week for this medication to reach adequate levels in a person's system, and patients are instructed to target a specific quit date during the second week that they are taking bupropion. If a dose is missed, patients are instructed to skip it and to stay with their regular dosing schedule. Taking too much bupropion at one time can cause seizures.

EFFECTS AND POTENTIAL RISKS

Most people do not have side effects from taking bupropion for smoking cessation. If side effects do occur, they can usually be minimized. In addition,

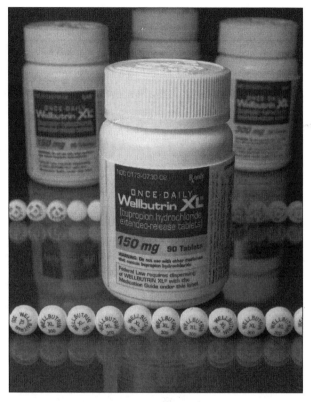

Wellbutrin XL. (JB Reed/Landov)

side effects are most often temporary, lasting only as long as one is taking the medication.

There are rare but serious side effects that patients should be aware of. In some people, medications like bupropion may cause severe mood and behavior changes, including suicidal thoughts. Young adults may be more at risk for these side effects.

Other side effects include anxiety; buzzing or ringing in the ears; headache (severe); and skin rash, hives, or itching. Side effects that may occur frequently or become bothersome include abdominal pain, constipation, decrease in appetite, dizziness, dry mouth, increased sweating, nausea or vomiting, trembling or shaking, insomnia, and weight loss.

Symptoms of an overdose may be more severe than side effects seen at regular doses, or two or more side effects may occur together. They include fast heartbeat, hallucinations, loss of consciousness, nausea or vomiting (or both), and seizures.

Bupropion should not be combined with other medications that lower the threshold for seizures.

These medications include theophylline, antipsychotic medications, antidepressants, Tramadol (Ultram), Tamoxifen, steroids, diabetes drugs, and Ritonavir.

Karen Schroeder Kassel, MS, RD, Med

FURTHER READING

Fiore, M. C., et al. "Treating Tobacco Use and Dependence: 2008 Update." Tobacco Use and Dependence Guideline Panel. Rockville, MD: Department of Health and Human Services, 2008.

Hughes, J. R., L. F. Stead, and T. Lancaster. "Antidepressants for Smoking Cessation." *Cochrane Database of Systematic Reviews* 1 (2007): CD000031. Web.

Wu, P., et al. "Effectiveness of Smoking Cessation Therapies: A Systematic Review and Meta-Analysis." *BMC Public Health* 6 (2006). Web.

WEBSITES OF INTEREST

"Guide to Quitting Smoking." *American Cancer Society*
http://www.cancer.org/Healthy/StayAwayfrom
    Tobacco/GuidetoQuittingSmoking

"Smoking and Tobacco Use." *Centers for Disease Control and Prevention*
http://www.cdc.gov/tobacco

See also: Addiction medications; Smoking cessation; Treatment methods and research

Bureau of Alcohol, Tobacco, Firearms and Explosives (ATF)

CATEGORY: Social issues

DEFINITION: The US Bureau of Alcohol, Tobacco, Firearms and Explosives is a federal law enforcement agency within the US Department of Justice. Among other tasks, the bureau regulates interstate trade and illegal trafficking of alcohol and tobacco products, helping to prevent substance abuse, particularly among minors and young adults.

DATE: Established in its present form in 2003

BACKGROUND

The roots of the US Bureau of Alcohol, Tobacco, Firearms and Explosives (ATF) go back to the earliest days of the United States. In 1789, the first Congress under the US Constitution imposed a tax on imported spirits (alcoholic beverages). This tax was followed in 1791 by a tax on domestic production of alcoholic beverages. Collection of these taxes became the responsibility of the Department of the Treasury. In 1862, Congress created the Office of Internal Revenue within the Treasury. Among its duties were the collection of taxes on distilled alcohol and on tobacco. The following year, three federal agents (called revenuers) were appointed to aid in the prevention, detection, and punishment of tax evaders. During Prohibition (1919–1933), revenuers had a prominent role in combating the illicit importation, production, and sale of alcoholic beverages.

In 1942, responsibility for enforcing federal firearms regulations was transferred to the Alcohol Tax Unit (ATU) of the Bureau (or Office) of Internal Revenue (BIR). In 1952, when the BIR was renamed the Internal Revenue Service (IRS), the ATU expanded to become the Alcohol and Tobacco Tax Division of the BIR. With the passage of the Gun Control Act of 1968, the ATF became responsible for explosives. In 1972, the ATF gained federal jurisdiction over alcohol, tobacco, firearms, and explosives, effectively severing ties to the IRS. In 1982, the ATF was assigned responsibility for investigating commercial arsons.

In 2003, under the Homeland Security Act, the ATF was reorganized into two separate divisions. The tax and trade functions of the agency remain within the Treasury Department as the Alcohol and Tobacco Tax and Trade Bureau (TTB). The law-enforcement functions of the agency were transferred to the Department of Justice as the Bureau of Alcohol, Tobacco, Firearms and Explosives (ATF) in its current form.

MISSION AND GOALS

The mission of the ATF is to enforce laws against violent crimes, criminal organizations, the illegal use and trafficking of firearms, the illegal use and storage of explosives, acts of arson and bombings, acts of terrorism, and the illegal diversion of alcohol and tobacco products. The ATF's motto is At the Frontline Against Violent Crime.

The alcohol and tobacco diversion mission of the ATF is to disrupt and eliminate criminal and terrorist organizations by identifying and arresting offenders who traffic in contraband cigarettes and illegal liquor; to conduct financial investigations in conjunction with alcohol and tobacco diversion investigations to seize and deny further access to assets and funds utilized by criminal enterprises and terrorist organizations; to prevent criminal encroachment on the legitimate alcohol and tobacco industries by organizations trafficking in counterfeit and contraband cigarettes and illegal liquor; and to assist local, state, and other federal law enforcement and tax agencies investigating interstate trafficking of contraband cigarettes and liquor.

SUBSTANCE ABUSE CONCERNS

Although the ATF is not directly involved in combating substance abuse, by regulating interstate trade of alcohol and tobacco and prosecuting those who divert them, the agency contributes to preventing abuse, particularly among minors and young adults. The ATF regulates the content and distribution of all alcoholic beverages in the United States.

One major concern regarding potential abuse, especially among minors and young adults, is the availability of flavored alcoholic beverages (FABs) and alcohol and caffeine energy-drinks. Both have become popular "entry-level" alcoholic drinks for minors and young adults. FABs, or "alcopops," combine fruit juices or other flavorings with beer, wine, or other alcoholic beverages, such as vodka and rum. These drinks appeal to young people because they do not taste or smell like alcohol and users think they do not carry the risk of abuse or serious adverse effects associated with alcohol consumption. Alcohol-caffeine energy drinks also are popular because users believe the caffeine will counter sedation and other adverse effects of alcohol while providing a different and safer high. The US Food and Drug Administration (FDA) has taken action against several brands of such energy drinks that effectively removes them from store shelves.

Another concern of the ATF is online sales of cigarettes. Vendors of these products disregard their responsibility to collect taxes from their customers. They also do not fulfill their obligation to avoid selling to minors. Prosecuting vendors for not fulfilling their tax obligations ends their role as suppliers of tobacco products to minors. In 2005, the major credit card companies were persuaded to no longer accept payments for tobacco products bought online, effectively putting many online cigarette merchants out of business.

A new concern that the ATF may have to address is electronic cigarettes (e-cigarettes), which are battery-operated devices that deliver vaporized, flavored nicotine to the smoker. E-cigarettes are not under ATF jurisdiction, as they are a nicotine by-product rather than a tobacco product. As of September 2010, the FDA had banned e-cigarette machines sold by five companies because of the excessive amount of nicotine and carcinogens that e-cigarettes released in their vapors.

Ernest Kohlmetz, MA

FURTHER READING

Howland, Jonathan, et al. "The Acute Effects of Caffeinated versus Noncaffeinated Alcoholic Beverage on Driving Performance and Attention Reaction Time." *Addiction* 106 (2010): 335–41. Print. A scientific study that shows that consuming a caffeinated beverage after drinking an alcoholic beverage does not counter the adverse effects of alcohol.

Kurian, George T., ed. *Historical Guide to the US Government.* New York: Oxford UP, 1998. Presents detailed information of the early history of the ATF and its predecessors.

Tedeschi, Bob. "E-Commerce Report: Trouble for Online Vendors of Cigarettes." *New York Times* 4 Apr. 2005. Web. http://www.nytimes.com/2005/04/04/technology. Explains how pressuring major credit card companies to not accept payments for tobacco products purchased on the web affected sales of those products.

WEBSITES OF INTEREST

US Bureau of Alcohol, Tobacco, Firearms and Explosives
http://www.atf.gov

US Food and Drug Administration
http://www.fda.gov

See also: Caffeinated alcoholic drinks; Cigarettes and cigars; Crime and substance abuse

C

Caffeinated alcoholic drinks

CATEGORY: Substances

DEFINITION: A caffeinated alcoholic beverage, or CAB, contains alcohol with caffeine as an additive. It is sold in this combined form. Alcoholic beverages that contain caffeine as a natural constituent, such as a coffee flavoring, are not part of the CAB category.

STATUS: Illegal in some US states and in Canada

CLASSIFICATION: Noncontrolled substance

SOURCE: Premixed beverage, usually with a malt or distilled-spirits base

TRANSMISSION ROUTE: Ingested orally

HISTORY OF USE

In 2008, a group of state attorneys general successfully pressed two manufacturers of caffeinated alcoholic beverages (CABs) to stop production of the drinks because of concern for public safety. The attorneys general asked the US Food and Drug Administration (FDA) to review the safety of the drinks, because the FDA had not approved the use of caffeine in any alcoholic beverages. Several states have since banned or restricted the drinks.

The FDA and the Federal Trade Commission warned manufacturers that the marketing and sale of CABs could be considered deceptive and unfair. Additional manufacturers have withdrawn their products from the market.

Hypercaffeinated energy drinks entered the United States market in 1997, with the market value of energy drinks growing to $5.4 billion in 2006. Looking to expand their profits and customer base, manufacturers began experimenting with caffeine-alcohol energy drink formulas. After many CAB-related hospitalizations of college students and underage drinkers in the fall of 2010, the FDA issued warning letters to manufacturers, leading several states to ban the products. Legislation has been initiated in some states to remove CABs from convenience stores and to require that they be sold in liquor stores.

EFFECTS AND POTENTIAL RISKS

The caffeine in a CAB masks the consumer's sense of inebriation, leading to a state of intoxication known as wide-awake drunkenness. In this physical state, a person may drink to the point of alcohol poisoning,

Cans of Four Loko, a fruit flavored malt beverage, are seen in the liquor department of a convenience store. The FDA launched an investigation into the safety of the drinks in 2010. (Getty Images)

putting him or her in danger of blackouts, seizures, acute mania, stroke, impaired driving, sexual assault, or even death.

Caffeine intoxication can lead to high blood pressure, restlessness, insomnia, tremors, rapid heartbeat, psychomotor agitation, major depression, and panic disorder. Users can develop a tolerance for and dependence on alcohol and caffeine. Addiction specialists view this combination as a gateway for other forms of drug dependence. Research shows at least one-quarter of college students mix alcohol and caffeinated energy drinks on their own.

Merrill Evans, MA

FURTHER READING

Benac, Nancy. "United States Food and Drug Administration Signals Crackdown on Caffeinated Alcohol Drinks." *Canadian Medical Association Journal* 183 (2011): E47–48. Print.

O'Brien, Mary Claire, et al. "Caffeinated Cocktails." *Academic Emergency Medicine* 15 (2008): 453–60. Print.

Reissig, Chad J., Eric C. Strain, and Roland R. Griffiths. "Caffeinated Energy Drinks: A Growing Problem." *Drug and Alcohol Dependence* 99 (2009): 1–10. Print.

WEBSITES OF INTEREST

Centers for Disease Control and Prevention
http://www.cdc.gov/alcohol/fact-sheets/cab.htm

US Food and Drug Administration
http://www.fda.gov/Food/FoodIngredientsPackaging/ucm190366.htm

See also: Bureau of Alcohol, Tobacco, Firearms and Explosives (ATF); College and substance abuse; Teens/young adults and alcohol abuse

Caffeine addiction

CATEGORY: Substance abuse

DEFINITION: Caffeine addiction, a dependence on caffeine, is marked by the development of withdrawal symptoms if caffeine is not ingested. Experts are not sure if this dependence should be categorized as an actual addiction because clini-cal studies demonstrate mixed results concerning symptom occurrence and frequency. Also, the *Diagnostic and Statistical Manual of Mental Disorders* of the American Psychiatric Association does not classify caffeine as addictive because data are insufficient to prove that the symptoms of caffeine addiction cause any clinically significant mental or physical impairment.

CAUSES

Caffeine acts as a central and peripheral nervous system stimulant and is considered a mood-altering substance. Caffeine also leads to the release of dopamine in the prefrontal cortex of the brain, an area that reinforces the positive excitatory properties of caffeine. Addiction occurs when a person consumes excessive amounts of drinks or foods that contain caffeine to maximize the positive effects from caffeine and to avoid withdrawal symptoms. Several studies also have demonstrated a genetic predisposition for caffeine tolerance and dependence.

Coffee and cocoa beans, tea leaves, and fruit all contain caffeine and are harvested to manufacture food and drink products. Regular coffee contains more caffeine per serving than either tea or caffeinated cola soft drinks. Energy drinks and over-the-counter caffeine supplements (in tablet form) have become popular among people wanting to consume large amounts of the substance. Medications such as over-the-counter pain relievers and cold and cough medicines also often contain caffeine. Chocolate, cocoa products, and decaffeinated coffee have lower levels of the substance.

RISK FACTORS

Persons who consume a high level of caffeinated products (750 milligrams to 1 gram per day) have the greatest possibility of developing a caffeine addiction; this consumed amount equates to a minimum of five to seven cups of coffee per day. Males, who consume more caffeine on average than females, are at a higher risk for caffeine addiction. Also, smokers and substance abusers are more likely to develop a caffeine addiction. Although scientific literature once showed that young adults ages eighteen to thirty-five years made up the largest group of consumers of caffeine, newer research suggests that young children and adolescents are a rising at-risk population because of media advertisements and the development and marketing of new products that target this demographic.

Caffeine consumption and dependence typically decrease after age sixty-five years because of the adverse effects of caffeine on common age-related health problems.

Symptoms

The effects of caffeine can be observed within thirty to sixty minutes of consuming caffeinated foods or drinks. When ingested in recommended doses, caffeine produces the desired effects of increased alertness and decreased lethargy. Many people do not experience symptoms of excess caffeine intake because they develop a tolerance to the substance. However, overconsumption still may lead to insomnia, nausea, restlessness, mental confusion, and tremors. At high doses caffeine increases the heart rate and causes ringing of the ears and visualized flashes of light. It also may induce cardiac arrhythmias, seizures, respiratory failure, gastrointestinal irregularities, and even, but rarely, death.

Whether or not caffeine withdrawal occurs remains debatable, as some studies have found no evidence of withdrawal and others have reported a 100 percent incidence. Withdrawal symptoms typically begin twelve to twenty-four hours after an abrupt discontinuation of caffeine use, although some persons report withdrawal effects for days or weeks. A variety of withdrawal symptoms has been reported in the literature, such as irritability, headaches, sleepiness, insomnia, tremors, slowness in performing physical tasks (such as working), anxiety, runny nose, and nausea and vomiting.

Screening and Diagnosis

A caffeine addiction diagnosis is controversial, as most reports of this addiction are subjective and cannot be reliably confirmed by randomized clinical trials. The majority of the relevant literature contains case reports from individual examples of caffeine addiction.

No reliable blood or laboratory tests exist to help establish the diagnosis. Therefore, persons who feel they are having a problem with dependence or withdrawal should seek the care of a physician to confirm the diagnosis and to rule out other medical problems.

Treatment and Therapy

As with any substance of addiction, a gradual tapering off of the caffeinated substance may help to minimize withdrawal symptoms. To decrease caffeine intake, one should switch from drinking regular to drinking decaffeinated coffee, tea, or soda. Some people may benefit from outpatient therapy to treat any underlying behavioral addiction. Also, people who have additional substance abuse problems should be treated for the co-occurring addiction issues.

Prevention

The primary means of preventing a caffeine addiction is to abstain from consuming products that contain the substance. To prevent addiction among children and adolescents, parents and caretakers should be educated about caffeine's effects and should be aware of products that contain large amounts of caffeine.

Janet Ober Berman, MS, CGC

Caffeine

A plant alkaloid from numerous sources, caffeine is a central nervous system stimulant used recreationally more than therapeutically. It is found in different concentrations from myriad sources worldwide. Perhaps the best-known sources of caffeine are cacao from Brazil and West Africa, *Camellia sinensis* (green tea) and other tea leaves from Asia and India, and *Coffea arabica* or other coffee bean varieties from the African and South American continents. Caffeine also is found in some shrub-like plants.

Caffeine improves mood and alertness, but anxiety and insomnia occur with high intake. Caffeine antagonizes adenosine receptors and increases dopamine, epinephrine, and adrenaline. It constricts cerebral vasculature to treat vasodilating headaches such as migraines. Caffeine inconsistently increases heart rate and muscle contractions, but it relaxes renal vasculature to increase urination and stomach smooth-muscle and gastric secretions to cause heartburn and to suppress appetite.

Caffeine is an addictive and reinforcing drug that encourages habitual use. More than 80 percent of adults in the United States ingest caffeine by consuming an average of one to two cups of coffee drinks per day. This daily number of caffeine users totals more than that for alcohol or nicotine. Withdrawal starts within twenty-four hours of consumption of as little as two cups of coffee each day, causing headache, poor performance, and depression.

FURTHER READING

Chou, Tony. "Wake up and Smell the Coffee: Caffeine, Coffee, and the Medical Consequences." *Western Journal of Medicine* 157 (1992): 544–53. Print. Provides an overview of the history of coffee as the primary source of caffeine intake.

Dews, P., C. O'Brien, and J. Bergman. "Caffeine: Behavioral Effects of Withdrawal and Related Issues." *Food and Chemical Toxicology* 40 (2002): 1257–61. Print. Details the concepts and controversies of tolerance of, withdrawal from, and dependence on caffeine.

Satel, Sally. "Is Caffeine Addictive? A Review of the Literature." *American Journal of Drug and Alcohol Abuse* 32 (2006): 493–502. Print. Argues that caffeine should not be classified as a substance of addiction and reviews the literature supporting this argument.

Temple, Jennifer. "Caffeine Use in Children: What We Know, What We Have Left to Learn, and Why We Should Worry." *Neuroscience Behavioral Research* 33.6 (2009): 793–806. Print. Summary article that discusses the growing popularity and addiction concerns of caffeine intake in children and adolescents.

WEBSITES OF INTEREST

Behavioral Biology Research Center, Johns Hopkins University
http://www.caffeinedependence.org/caffeine_dependence.html

MedicineNet.com
http://www.medicinenet.com/caffeine/article.htm

See also: Caffeine: Short- and long-term effects on the body; Coffee; Physiological dependence; Stimulant abuse; Stimulants: Short- and long-term effects on the body

Caffeine: Short- and long-term effects on the body

CATEGORY: Health issues and physiology
ALSO KNOWN AS: Caffeinism
DEFINITION: Caffeine, a derivative of methylxanthine found in plants worldwide, is a central nervous system stimulant that causes short- and long-term effects on the body, even with use in coffee, tea, or colas. Although generally regarded as safe as a food additive by the US Food and Drug Administration, caffeine also is a drug with the capacity to harm and to worsen medical problems.

SHORT-TERM EFFECTS

Caffeine is used socially in drinks such as coffee, tea, and colas by a majority of the adult population in the United States; it also is popular worldwide. Although most use in this manner is moderate (such as one to two cups of coffee per day) and likely within safe health boundaries, higher intake and continual moderate use have distinct adverse effects on the health of numerous body systems, including cardiac, gastrointestinal, and renal organs.

Central nervous system (CNS) stimulation by caffeine increases levels of dopamine, epinephrine, and adrenaline in the body to increase alertness, concentration, and mood; insomnia or anxiety can occur at higher doses. With acute use, caffeine constricts blood vessels to ease symptoms of vasodilating headaches, such as migraines, and increases gastric secretions and smooth muscle relaxation in the stomach to cause heartburn pain. Caffeine relaxes the renal vasculature to cause increased urination. Intake during evening hours may result in low energy levels and excessive fatigue the next day.

Caffeine also is an ingredient in many over-the-counter and prescription headache medications because of its own symptom relief and its amplification of other pain-relieving drugs. Dry mouth, poor appetite, and dizziness are possible directly after large caffeine intake, and caffeine acutely worsens existing ulcers and anxiety disorders. Within one hour of ingesting caffeine, some people may feel edgy and have increased heart rate and blood pressure because of caffeine's effects on heart muscle and rhythm. A nursing infant may become jittery or may experience sleep disturbances from caffeine present in the mother's breast milk.

Side effects, particularly mild effects like stomach upset and insomnia, can begin with moderate caffeine doses as low as 50 milligrams (mg). Caffeine circulates in the body within five to thirty minutes and may cause acute effects for up to twelve hours. Its half-life in adults ranges from three to six hours but is shorter in smokers because of enhanced liver metabolism. The half-life increases to five to ten hours in women taking oral contraceptives, nine to eleven hours in pregnant women, and thirty hours in newborns.

Caffeine is metabolized by CYP 450 demethylation twice, and both metabolites are active in the body as well. Several cups of coffee may provide a serum level of 5 to 10 micrograms per milliliter (microg/mL).

LONG-TERM EFFECTS FROM CHRONIC USE

Some chronic effects of caffeine are simply extensions of short-term effects of use. The *Diagnostic and Statistical Manual of Mental Disorders* recognizes four caffeine-related disorders: caffeine intoxication, caffeine-induced anxiety disorder, caffeine-induced sleep disorder, and caffeine-related disorder not otherwise specified.

Caffeinism, a diagnosis similar in part to panic disorder or generalized anxiety disorder, acknowledges the dangers of caffeine in high amounts, particularly with repeated use. High levels of caffeine intake leading to this diagnosis cause anxiety, rapid heart rate and breathing, diarrhea and excess urination, tremors, and increased blood pressure. Irritability and agitation from caffeinism may be indistinguishable from anxiety disorders in the physician's office, so the disorder is best identified by discussing caffeine use during symptom review. Prescribed antianxiety medications are unlikely to improve symptoms of caffeinism if caffeine use continues.

Any amount of chronic caffeine use can lead to abdominal pain, insomnia, irritability, and anxiety. Supposedly beneficial effects of caffeine, such as improved alertness and performance, also become less pronounced with chronic use. Heavy caffeine use has been linked to the development of osteoporosis from bone density loss and to peptic ulcer or gastroesophageal reflux diseases from smooth muscle relaxation and heartburn. Emotional lability (instability), prolonged hypertension, and cardiac disease are possible, and dehydration can occur with continual use.

Caffeine that remains in the body leads to adrenal exhaustion and, hence, tolerance. With tolerance, the body requires even more caffeine to obtain the same mood- and performance-heightening effects. Thus, caffeine is reinforcing, and users will ingest increasing amounts to experience alertness and concentration.

Abrupt caffeine discontinuation causes physiologic withdrawal even with only moderate chronic use (for example, two cups per day). Headache is the primary withdrawal symptom and may be throbbing at first; poor performance and depression over time may occur as a result of the sudden changes in dopamine and adrenaline levels. Renewing caffeine intake relieves withdrawal symptoms temporarily but continues the habitual cycle of caffeine-induced symptoms, tolerance, and withdrawal symptoms. Although caffeine is rarely taken to get high, its narrow therapeutic index of 8 to 20 microg/mL and its variable effects can lead to chronic misuse.

ACUTE INTOXICATION

Overdose, or acute intoxication, is rare from social use. At doses of 5 to 50 grams or serum levels of 100 to 200 mg per kilogram of body weight, caffeine is potentially lethal, although highly sensitive persons may experience severe overstimulation with individual doses as low as 250 mg. Caffeine intake greater than 300 mg per day may cause miscarriage or poor neonatal growth during pregnancy, and intake greater

Soda Drinks

A soda drink is a sweetened, nonalcoholic, carbonated beverage that is made up of various flavoring additives, among other ingredients. There are many different classifications of soda drinks, including regular (with sugar and caffeine), regular decaffeinated, diet (sugar-free), diet decaffeinated, and highly caffeinated. The arousing effects of caffeine paired with the high amounts of sugar make many sodas stimulatory beverages.

Short-term effects of drinking sodas include tooth decay and heartburn from soda's acidic properties. Other short-term effects include developing caffeine dependence, which can lead to caffeine addiction; irregular heartbeat; and high blood pressure. Withdrawal during caffeine addiction can be uncomfortable and dangerous, depending on the severity of the addiction.

Obesity is another danger of drinking soda. Sodas that are not sugar-free have high calorie counts, and drinking these types of soda can lead to the consumption of too many calories and, thus, obesity. Drinking sodas at a young age increases the risk of childhood obesity. Obesity can lead to type 2 diabetes, which in itself can cause kidney damage.

Furthermore, the common sweetener in diet sodas, aspartame, is thought to induce neurological disorders and cancer. However, studies have not linked the compound to these diseases.

than 600 mg per day by pregnant women may induce premature or aborted birth.

Moderate toxicity from overdose (for example, the use of large quantities of energy drinks) causes vomiting, muscle stiffening, and heart muscle irritation. When caffeine levels in the blood are extremely high, intoxication causes metabolic changes in the body, including low potassium levels, high sugar levels, and ketosis. The CNS, cardiac, and musculoskeletal effects can include repeated seizures, muscle posturing and hypertonicity, and ventricular fibrillation or tachycardia.

More severe acute overdose effects involve breathing problems. Pulmonary edema occurs when blood vessels around the lungs dilate, leading to life-threatening blocked airways and hypoxia. Rhabdomyolysis, or muscle cell breakdown, and metabolic acidosis contribute to acute renal failure.

Nicole M. Van Hoey, PharmD

FURTHER READING

"Anxiety: Nutrition–Caffeine." *Integrative Medicine.* Ed. David Rakel. 2nd ed. Philadelphia: Elsevier, 2007. General medicine textbook, with discussion of disease-causing substances from nutrition. Describes the acute and chronic effects of caffeine.

Brecher, Edward M. "Consumers Union Report on Licit and Illicit Drugs: Caffeine." 1972. Schaffer Library of Drug Policy. Web. http://www.druglibrary.org/schaffer/library/studies/cu/cu21.html. An overview of caffeine use and overuse.

Foxx, R. M., and A. Rubinoff. "Behavioral Treatment of Caffeinism: Reducing Excessive Coffee Drinking." *Journal of Applied Behavior Analysis* 12.3 (1979): 335–44. Print. Reports on an early study of caffeinism in three persons and documents the effects of caffeine reduction.

Greden, John F. "Anxiety of Caffeinism: A Diagnostic Dilemma." *American Journal of Psychiatry* 131 (1974): 1089–92. Print. An early journal article examining caffeinism and its symptoms, and differentiating the disorder from anxiety diagnoses.

Griffiths, Roland R., and Geoffrey K. Mumford. "Caffeine: A Drug of Abuse?" *Neuropsychopharmacology: The Fourth Generation of Progress.* Ed. David J. Kupfer. Philadelphia: Lippincott, 1995. Definitive textbook about neurologic effects and psychiatric disorders from pharmacologically active substances, often substances of abuse. Debates caf-

feine benefits and adverse effects and discusses its addictive potential.

James, Jack E. "Acute and Chronic Effects of Caffeine on Performance, Mood, Headache, and Sleep." *Neuropsychobiology* 38 (1998): 32–41. Print. Describes results of a crossover study comparing caffeine with placebo on symptoms of caffeine use and withdrawal.

Lande, R. Gregory. "Caffeine-Related Psychiatric Disorders." *Emedicine Health*, 1 Aug. 2011. Web. 13 Apr. 2012. http://emedicine.medscape.com/article/290113-overview. Comprehensive discussion of caffeine use and overuse and associated psychiatric disorders.

Shannon, Michael W. "Theophylline and Caffeine." *Haddad and Winchester's Clinical Management of Poisoning and Drug Overdose.* Eds. Michael W. Shannon, Stephen W. Borron, and Michael J. Burns. 4th ed. Philadelphia: Elsevier, 2007. Standard toxicology textbook, with discussion of drug intoxication symptoms and treatment that relate to chemical structure and mechanisms of action in the body.

WEBSITES OF INTEREST

Caffeine Awareness Association
http://www.caffeineawareness.org

Herbs2000.com
http://www.herbs2000.com/h_menu/caffeine.htm

NaturalNews.com
http://www.naturalnews.com/012352_caffeine_coffee.html

See also: Caffeine addiction; Coffee; Physiological dependence; Stimulant abuse; Stimulants: Short- and long-term effects on the body

Canada's Drug Strategy (CDS)

CATEGORY: Diagnosis and prevention
ALSO KNOWN AS: National Anti-Drug Strategy
DEFINITION: Canada's Drug Strategy (CDS) was an initiative developed and funded by the federal government of Canada to address the harmful effects of substance abuse and the supply and demand of

illicit drugs. The principles of this strategy were based on four pillars: education and prevention, treatment and rehabilitation, harm reduction, and enforcement and control. CDS is now called the National Anti-Drug Strategy.

DATE: Established 1992

BACKGROUND

The National Drug Strategy in Canada was launched by the Canadian government in 1987 as a five-year program with a $210-million budget (Canadian dollars). After five years, in 1992, this program was merged with the National Strategy to Reduce Impaired Driving, thus creating the initiative Canada's Drug Strategy (CDS). An additional $270-million was allocated to reduce the harmful effects of substance abuse on individuals, families, and communities and to reduce the supply and demand of addictive substances. The strategy focused on balancing drug supply reduction and drug demand reduction.

CDS was developed as a collaborative effort between federal, provincial, and territorial governments, and law enforcement, community groups, addiction agencies, and the private sector. Consultation between government and nongovernment organizations determined seven important components that would need to be applied to create an effective framework for the strategy. The seven components were research and knowledge development; knowledge dissemination; prevention programming; treatment and rehabilitation; legislation, enforcement, and control; national coordination; and international cooperation.

Health Canada provided national coordination and leadership for CDS and was required to report to Parliament and the Canadian public every two years about the direction, advancement, and developments of the program. The CDS provided policy makers and researchers with valuable information, raising the level of understanding about the prevalence and effects of substance abuse in Canada.

In 2001, reports began to emerge that were highly critical of the CDS and its policies, use of funding, and effectiveness. It appeared that there were no measurable outcomes to report and that the total impact of the program was uncertain. This unflattering feedback prompted Canada's prime minister, Stephen Harper, to announce the new National Anti-Drug Strategy (NADS) in October 2007. CDS was transitioned to NADS in 2008.

MISSION AND GOALS

In addition to the four pillars, which included education and prevention, treatment and rehabilitation, harm reduction, and enforcement and control efforts, the strategy acknowledged that for interventions to be effective for individuals, several factors had to be recognized. These factors were gender, age and culture; involvement and buy-in of target groups; attention to the needs of drug users; and the underlying causes associated with substance abuse.

Between 1992 and 1998 the focus of CDS was on school-based drug-prevention programs, although reports from the Canadian Centre on Substance Abuse indicated that illicit drug use among youth increased during this time. When the CDS was renewed in 1998, its primary objective was to reduce the harm associated with alcohol and other drug abuse to families and communities.

The NADS continues to operate on three principle goals: preventing illicit drug use, treating persons with illicit drug dependencies, and combating the production and distribution of illicit drugs.

April D. Ingram, BSc

FURTHER READING

DeBeck, K., et al. "Canada's 2003 Renewed Drug Strategy." *HIV AIDS Policy Law Review* 11.2–3 (2006): 1, 5–12. Print. Reports on a study that examined activities related to the CDS as renewed in 2003. Reviews the effectiveness of the CDS and its national impact in light of current scientific evidence pertaining to the reduction of drug-related harm.

---. "Canada's New Federal 'National Anti-Drug Strategy': An Informal Audit of Reported Funding Allocation." *International Journal of Drug Policy* 20.2 (2009): 188–91. Print. A review of Canada's anti-drug strategy. Reports on the budget intended for drug prevention and treatment initiatives. Concludes that the direction of funds into policy determined from more evidence-based research would improve the program.

Jensen, Eric L., and Jurg Gerber. "State Efforts to Construct a Social Problem: The 1986 War on Drugs in Canada." *Canadian Journal of Sociology* 18.4 (1993): 453–62. Print. Discusses Canada's response to the US War on Drugs with the implementation of its own such program.

Moore, Dawn. *Criminal Artefacts: Governing Drugs and Users.* Vancouver: U British Columbia Press, 2007. Provides case studies from drug treatment courts and addiction treatment programs. Further examines the relationships among law and psychology, treatment and punishment, and conflicting theories of addiction.

Zilkowsky, Diane. "Canada's National Drug Strategy." *Forum on Corrections Research Focusing on Alcohol and Drugs* 13.3 (2001). Reviews the history of Canada's Drug Strategy and reports on results since its implementation and revision. Concludes that the strategy promotes a balance between restricting the supply and reducing demand for drugs, and positions substance abuse as a health rather than enforcement issue.

WEBSITES OF INTEREST

Government of Canada, National Anti-Drug Strategy
http://www.nationalantidrugstrategy.gc.ca

Health Canada, Drug Strategy and Controlled Substances Program
http://www.hc-sc.gc.ca/ahc-asc/branch-dirgen/
    hecs-dgsesc/dscsp-psasc/index-eng.php

See also: Education about substance abuse; Harm reduction; Law enforcement and drugs; Prevention methods and research

Cancer and substance abuse

CATEGORY: Health issues and physiology

DEFINITION: Certain substances, such as tobacco, have an associated cancer risk. Illegal substances can contain carcinogenic additives. Some persons with cancer become addicted to illegal substances and prescription medications during the course of their disease. An estimated 526,000 people in the United States die each year from cancer, most commonly from cancers of the breast, colon, and lung.

CANCER RISKS

Certain substances of abuse, including tobacco, marijuana, alcohol, methamphetamine, cocaine, and heroin, present special risks for the development of cancer.

Tobacco

Tobacco is a well-known carcinogen, and its use is the leading cause of preventable illness and death in the United States. In addition to causing lung, throat, and mouth cancer, it has been associated with cancers of the nasal cavity, esophagus, stomach, pancreas, breast, kidney, bladder, and cervix. Nicotine, which is contained in tobacco leaves, is highly addictive; however, it is not known to be carcinogenic. Nicotine is a vasoconstrictor (blood vessel constrictor), so it increases the risk of cardiovascular disease.

The National Cancer Institute has revealed the following statistics related to cancer and tobacco use in the United States:

- Cigarette smoking causes an estimated 443,000 deaths each year, including approximately 49,400 deaths from exposure to secondhand smoke.
- Lung cancer is the leading cause of cancer-related death among both men and women; 90 percent of lung cancer deaths among men and approximately 80 percent of lung cancer deaths among women are caused by smoking.
- Persons who smoke are up to six times more likely to have a heart attack than are nonsmokers, and the risk increases with the number of cigarettes smoked. Smoking also causes most cases of chronic lung disease.
- In 2009, about 21 percent of adults were cigarette smokers.
- Nearly 20 percent of high school students smoke cigarettes.

Smoking (or chewing) tobacco markedly increase the risk of cancers of the oral cavity (mouth, lips, and tongue). One of the effects of tobacco is that it weakens the immune system, which not only increases the risk of cancer but also increases the risk of infection. Aside from its relationship to cancers of the oral cavity, chewing tobacco also increases the risk of many other cancers and health problems.

Marijuana

Smoked marijuana and smoked tobacco are chemically similar; thus, like cigarettes, the greatest health hazard of marijuana is from smoking the substance. The psychoactive component of marijuana leaves, delta-9-tetrahydrocannabinol (THC), is a relatively safe drug.

Smoked marijuana, however, is a health risk. Thorough scientific analyses have identified at least six thousand of the same chemicals in marijuana smoke present in tobacco. The chief difference between the two plants is that marijuana contains THC and tobacco contains nicotine. Moreover, one of the most potent carcinogens in tobacco smoke, benzo[a]-pyrene, is present in larger quantities in marijuana smoke.

Another factor increasing the carcinogenic risk of marijuana is in the way it is inhaled; marijuana smokers frequently inhale and hold the smoke in their lungs, which increases the amount of tar deposited in the respiratory tract by a factor of about four. Approximately 20 percent of regular marijuana smokers (those who smoke three to four joints a day) have problems with chronic bronchitis, coughing, and excess mucus.

An alternative to smoking marijuana is ingesting it in pastries, drinks, and lollipops. Marijuana leaves also can be baked into brownies and other desserts. Ingested marijuana has no known carcinogenic effect; however, it still has a psychoactive effect, which can result in myriad problems, including social problems, traffic accidents, and dependence.

A problem with ingesting rather than smoking marijuana is that the digestive process markedly slows the onset of psychoactive effects. This makes ingesting less attractive to users of the substance; furthermore, because the onset of marijuana's effect is slowed through ingestion, a large amount of the substance must be consumed, ultimately resulting in an unusually high level of THC in the body.

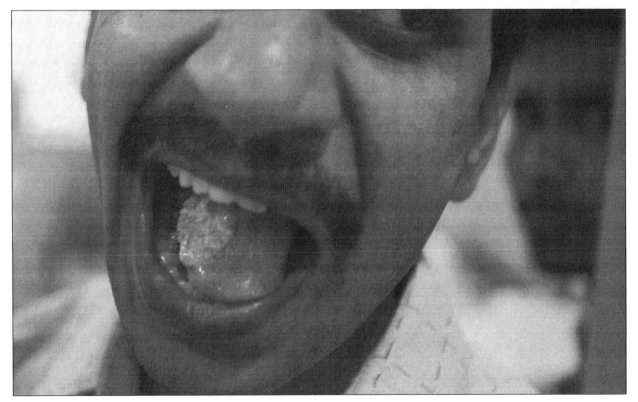

A cancer patient shows his tongue in the outpatient department of Tata Memorial Hospital in Mumbai, India. More than 1 in 10 Indians, or an estimated 140 million people, use 'pan,' a preparation of tobacco wrapped in a leaf, and other forms of smokeless tobacco, according to Healis, a Mumbai-based public health research institute. Its widespread use has given India the highest rate of oral cancer. (Bloomberg via Getty Images)

Alcohol

The combination of alcohol abuse and tobacco use markedly increases the risk of cancers of the oral cavity. Approximately 50 percent of cancers of the mouth, pharynx (throat), and larynx (voice box) are associated with heavy drinking. Even in nonsmokers, a strong association exists between alcohol abuse and cancers of the upper digestive tract, including the esophagus, the mouth, the pharynx, and the larynx.

Alcohol abuse, either alcoholism or binge drinking, also has been linked to pancreatic cancer, particularly in men. The risk has been reported to be up to six times greater than in men who do not abuse alcohol. A possible association may exist between alcohol abuse and other cancers, such as liver, breast, and colorectal cancers. It has been estimated that 2 to 4 percent of all cancer cases are caused either directly or indirectly by alcohol abuse. Alcohol abuse, like cigarette smoking, suppresses the immune system, which in turn increases the risk of developing cancer. These persons often do not seek treatment until the cancer is well advanced.

Methamphetamine

A number of different chemical processes can be used to make methamphetamine; most of the processes include the use of volatile organic compounds, which are emitted gases, some of which have carcinogenic effects. Also, other toxic substances can be produced through the production of methamphetamine. Some of these substances are carcinogenic. Specifically, pancreatic cancer has been associated with methamphetamine use.

Cocaine and Heroin

Cocaine itself is not associated with a cancer risk; however, substances added to cocaine are carcinogenic. One example is phenacetin, which not only can cause cancer but also can induce kidney damage. Heroin and other opiates have no known carcinogenic properties. However, like cocaine, heroin may contain additives that are carcinogenic.

SUBSTANCES USED AND ABUSED BY PERSONS WITH CANCER

Cancer, particularly in advanced stages, can cause extreme pain; thus, persons with cancer are often prescribed opiates to lessen their pain. Marijuana too is used by persons with cancer for pain relief and to reduce the side effects of chemotherapy.

Opiates

An opiate is a drug derived from opium, which is the sap of the opium poppy (*Papaver somniferum*). Opium has been used by humans since ancient times. Many opiates are on the market, including morphine, meperidine hydrochloride (Demerol), hydromorphone hydrochloride (Dilaudid), hydrocodone (Vicodin), and oxycodone (Oxycontin). Heroin is an excellent analgesic, but it is not prescribed for pain relief because of its highly addictive properties compared with other opiates. Another property of opiates is tolerance, which results in the need for increasingly higher doses to achieve the same effect.

Tolerance and addiction are not a major concern for a terminally ill person with cancer but they are a concern for persons with cancer that is in remission or cured. Some of these persons have "exchanged" their cancer for a drug addiction. After completing a drug rehabilitation program, these persons are at high risk to resume the use of opiates. Researchers believe that drug relapse is caused by the stress associated with cancer, combined with the ready availability of psychoactive drugs, both prescription and illegal.

Marijuana

Cancer and its treatment with chemotherapy is associated with side effects such as nausea, vomiting, anorexia (loss of appetite), and cachexia (muscle wasting). Marijuana is effective in reducing these symptoms; therefore, it has been recommended for persons with cancer.

The opinion of scientists at the National Cancer Institute, however, is that pharmaceuticals are available that are superior to marijuana in their effects. These pharmaceuticals include serotonin antagonists such as ondansetron (Zofran) and granisetron (Kytril), used alone or combined with dexamethasone (a steroid hormone); metoclopramide (Reglan) combined with diphenhydramine and dexamethasone; methylprednisolone (a steroid hormone) combined with droperidol (Inapsine); and prochlorperazine (Compazine).

Medical marijuana legislation is a controversial topic in the United States. Despite the controversy, medical marijuana outlets (dispensaries) are increasing in number throughout the country. Their incidence depends on state and federal regulations. Many states have adopted marijuana statutes that are much more liberal than federal statutes.

Although there are legitimate medical uses for marijuana for persons with cancer and other conditions (such as glaucoma), many of the medical marijuana outlets supply the product to almost anyone for any reason. Persons using medical marijuana for either a legitimate or a frivolous reason can develop a dependency on the substance.

Robin L. Wulffson, MD

FURTHER READING

Earleywine, Mitch. *Understanding Marijuana: A New Look at the Scientific Evidence.* New York: Oxford UP, 2005. An overview of this controversial and illegal controlled substance and the scientific evidence of its biological, psychological, and societal impacts.

Fisher, Gary, and Thomas Harrison. *Substance Abuse Information for School Counselors, Social Workers, Therapists, and Counselors.* 4th ed. Boston: Allyn & Bacon, 2008. Incorporating actual clinical examples with solid research, this text provides counselors and social workers with a detailed overview of alcohol and other drug addictions.

Miller, William. *Rethinking Substance Abuse: What the Science Shows, and What We Should Do about It.* New York: Guilford, 2010. Reviews what is known about substance abuse and offers overviews of biological, psychological, and social factors involved in substance abuse treatment. Also anticipates future developments and evaluates them for their possible impact on prevention and treatment.

WEBSITES OF INTEREST

Al-Anon and Alateen
http://www.al-anon.alateen.org

Alcoholics Anonymous
http://www.aa.org

American Cancer Society
http://cancer.org

National Cancer Institute
http://www.cancer.gov

National Institute on Alcohol Abuse and Alcoholism
http://www.niaaa.nih.gov

National Institute on Drug Abuse
http://www.drugabuse.gov

See also: Alcohol: Short- and long-term effects on the body; Esophageal cancer; Laryngeal cancer; Lung cancer; Opioid abuse; Respiratory diseases and smoking; Smoking; Smoking: Short- and long-term effects on the body

Celebrities and substance abuse

CATEGORY: Social issues

DEFINITION: The news media has documented a number of cases of substance abuse among celebrities, with negative impacts ranging from career loss to relationship problems to death.

SUBSTANCE ABUSE PREVALENCE

Although there have been no scientific studies of how often addictions occur among celebrities, popular news sources frequently report celebrity arrests for drunk driving, drug possession, public intoxication, and other criminal offenses related to substance abuse. Many celebrities and public figures, including Betty Ford, Elizabeth Taylor, Melanie Griffith, Drew Barrymore, Keith Urban, Eminem, and Ben Affleck, to name just a few, have openly shared their personal stories of struggle with addictions in interviews and autobiographies.

Substance abuse also has been linked to the deaths of many celebrities. Among celebrities whose cause of death was determined by a coroner to have involved drug or alcohol overdoses or otherwise harmful combinations of legal and illegal substances include Whitney Houston, Michael Jackson, Amy Winehouse, Elvis Presley, Dorothy Dandridge, Marilyn Monroe, John Belushi, Anna Nicole Smith, Janice Joplin, and Heath Ledger.

Other celebrities, such as Lindsay Lohan, Mel Gibson, Robert Downey Jr., and Charlie Sheen, have been in the public eye because of their addictions and substance-abuse-related behaviors. One television reality show, *Celebrity Rehab with Dr. Drew*, documents the lives of celebrities who are seeking inpatient hospital treatment for a variety of addictions.

POSSIBLE CAUSES

By the nature of their work, celebrities are subject to public attention and scrutiny. Often, this attention and scrutiny extends beyond celebrities' work into their personal lives. In 1972 psychologists Thomas

Duval and Robert Wicklund proposed self-awareness theory, a framework that may explain why some celebrities abuse substances to cope with excessive attention.

According to self-awareness theory, when persons engage in activities that draw attention to themselves, they often evaluate themselves negatively because their actual lives do not live up to some high internal standard. When this happens, these persons are likely to experience a drop in self-esteem. Researchers who tested self-awareness theory found that people who are more self-focused, as are many celebrities, are at increased risk for depression, anxiety, and substance abuse. Persons with higher degrees of self-focus also are more likely to have long-lasting negative moods. People may cope with this discomfort by trying to behave in ways that match their internal standards, or they may look for ways to avoid or escape a focus on the self. Some of these escapes include substance use, gambling, sex, shopping, and other addictive behaviors.

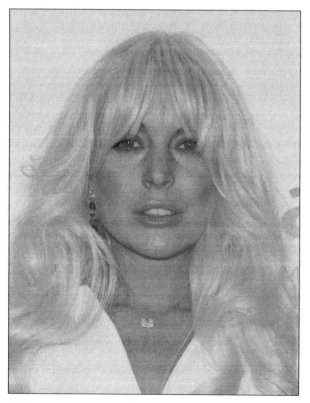

Celebrity Lindsay Lohan, whose fight with substance abuse has kept her in the spotlight, was ordered by a court to attend substance abuse treatment classes. (FilmMagic)

Psychologists Jay Hull and Richard Young documented this phenomenon in a 1983 study in which they asked one hundred twenty men age twenty-one years and older to complete a fake IQ test and a real measure of self-consciousness. The researchers then gave the men fake feedback about their IQ test results, telling them that they had scored poorly on the test.

Afterward, the men were asked to participate in a wine-tasting experiment in which they could moderate the amount of wine they consumed. The researchers found that men who were highly self-conscious and received negative feedback on the fake IQ test drank larger quantities of wine than did men who were less self-conscious. These findings support the theory that highly self-conscious people's alcohol consumption increases in response to a reduction in their self-esteem. It follows that celebrities, whose life experiences force them to be highly self-conscious, also may engage in heavy substance use after receiving negative feedback, such as poor reviews or seeing oneself featured in a tabloid.

Additionally, researchers Lynne Cooper, Michael Frone, and Marcia Russell conducted an online survey and found that both adolescents and adults reported using alcohol both to cope with negative emotions and to increase positive emotions. Additionally, psychological research studies have found that people report increased or inflated self-esteem after consuming alcohol. This research suggests that celebrities may abuse substances as a means to artificially increase their self-perception.

Celebrities also may be likely to abuse substances because of norms of substance use and abuse in celebrity culture. Anthropological research indicates that throughout the world, persons more often than not tend to conform to the accepted social practices and behaviors of their cultures. Like any other human beings, celebrities are motivated to conform to group norms. Young or emerging celebrities may be socialized into a culture in which substance abuse is common, and these celebrities may then later take part in that cultural norm and encourage other celebrities to do the same.

NEGATIVE SOCIAL EFFECTS

Several research studies have documented that people imitate behaviors they observe in others. In a famous study of observational learning, psychologist Albert Bandura and his colleagues Dorothea Ross and Sheila Ross showed children a film of an adult punching, kicking, beating, and insulting a doll. Children who had observed this aggressive behavior were significantly more likely to engage in aggressive play with the doll, imitating the behaviors of the adult and engaging in new aggressive behaviors.

Many other psychological studies have replicated these results, showing that people learn behaviors, both desirable and undesirable, through watching others. Observing celebrities engage in substance abuse increases the likelihood that members of the general public will imitate this behavior.

Other research in psychology suggests that celebrities are particularly influential role models because they have many of the factors that increase the likelihood of others selecting them as models for observational learning. These factors include attention, high social status, attractiveness, and in some cases, similarity in age, gender, or other characteristics. Additionally, celebrities who abuse substances often face less serious legal and financial consequences for their behavior than do noncelebrities. Therefore, those who are observing celebrity behaviors may be more likely to abuse substances themselves, as they do not see their role models experiencing significant negative consequences for their behavior.

Tracy Ksiazak, PhD

FURTHER READING

Bandura, Albert, Dorothea Ross, and Sheila A. Ross. "Transmission of Aggression through Imitation of Aggressive Models." *Journal of Abnormal and Social Psychology* 63.3 (1961): 575–82. Print. This landmark study of children's behavior after viewing adults who punched, kicked, and beat a doll supported Bandura's theory of observational learning. Children who watched adults engaged in aggressive behavior toward the doll were substantially more likely to engage in the same, and similar but new, aggressive behaviors.

Cooper, M. Lynne, et al. "Drinking to Regulate Positive and Negative Emotions: A Motivational Model of Alcohol Use." *Journal of Personality and Social Psychology* 67.5 (1995): 990–1005. Print. In this study, researchers found that both adults and adolescents age thirteen to nineteen years reported that they drank alcohol both to increase positive emotional states and to cope with negative emotional states.

Duval, Thomas S., and Robert A. Wicklund. *A Theory of Objective Self-Awareness.* New York: Academic, 1972. In this book, the authors first proposed self-awareness theory, which states that particular situations increase a person's tendency to examine and critique him- or herself, and that such situations often result in decreased self-esteem.

Hull, Jay G., and Richard D. Young. "Self-Consciousness, Self-Esteem, and Success-Failure as Determinants of Alcohol Consumption in Male Social Drinkers." *Journal of Personality and Social Psychology* 44.6 (1983): 1097–109. Print. Researchers found that after receiving poor results on a fake IQ test, men who were more self-conscious drank larger quantities of alcohol than men who were less self-conscious.

Ingram, Rick E. "Self-Focused Attention in Clinical Disorders: Review and a Conceptual Model." *Psychological Bulletin* 107.2 (1990): 156–76. Print. In a review of numerous research studies on the relationship of self-focused attention to a variety of mental health conditions, the author found that high levels of self-focused attention are found in people with all diagnosed mental health problems.

Mor, Nilly, and Jennifer Winquist. "Self-Focused Attention and Negative Affect: A Meta-Analysis." *Psychological Bulletin* 128.4 (2002): 638–62. Print. In this study, researchers combined statistical data from 226 earlier studies and found that high self-focused attention is strongly linked to depression, anxiety, social anxiety, and negative moods.

Spradley, James, and David W. McCurdy, eds. *Conformity and Conflict: Readings in Cultural Anthropology.* 13th ed. Boston: Allyn & Bacon, 2008. Addresses topics such as cultural norms, differences between cultures, and conformity. Highlights research on norms in a variety of cultures and factors that may affect conformity with those norms.

WEBSITES OF INTEREST

National Institute on Alcohol Abuse and Alcoholism
http://www.niaaa.nih.gov

National Institute on Drug Abuse
http://www.drugabuse.gov

Promises Treatment Centers
http://www.promises.com

See also: Media and substance abuse; Promises Treatment Centers; Substance abuse

Center for Substance Abuse Prevention (CSAP)

CATEGORY: Diagnosis and prevention

DEFINITION: The Center for Substance Abuse Prevention, whose mission is to establish substance abuse prevention programs in communities across the United States, is a branch of the US Substance Abuse and Mental Health Services Administration.

DATE: Established 1988

BACKGROUND

The Center for Substance Abuse Prevention (CSAP) was originally established as the Office for Substance Abuse Prevention (OSAP) in 1988. The Anti-Drug Abuse Act of 1988 established this federal office, which is tasked with coordinating drug prevention initiatives nationwide. Before becoming part of OSAP, CSAP was a center within the Alcohol, Drug Abuse, and Mental Health Administration (ADAMHA), which is itself under the US Department of Health and Human Services. ADAMHA was renamed the Substance Abuse and Mental Health Services Administration (SAMHSA) in 1992.

MISSION AND GOALS

The early mission of CSAP was to bring effective substance abuse prevention to every community in the United States. Now, CSAP's identity has been integrated more closely with that of SAMHSA, so the focus of CSAP is now wider: to reduce the impact of substance abuse and mental illness on communities in the United States.

For CSAP and SAMHSA, the prevention of substance abuse and mental illness involves supporting community efforts that promote emotional health and that work to reduce the rates of mental illness, suicide, and drug use. Additionally, CSAP provides national leadership in the prevention of problems related to alcohol, tobacco, and other drug abuse. CSAP's mission is "to help Americans lead healthier and longer lives." Furthermore, according to the CSAP website:

CSAP promotes a structured, community-based approach to substance abuse prevention through the Strategic Prevention Framework (SPF). The framework aims to promote youth development, reduce risk-taking behaviors, build assets and resilience, and prevent problem behaviors across the individual's life span. The approach provides information and tools that can be used by states and communities to build an effective and sustainable prevention infrastructure.

SAMHSA has eight Strategic Initiatives (SSIs) that provide a roadmap for how CSAP will navigate its goals and focus its work. In addition to prevention of substance abuse and mental illness, CSAP's initiatives address issues related to trauma and justice; military families; recovery support; health reform; health information technology; data, outcomes, and quality for behavioral health care; and public awareness and support. Substance abuse prevention is integrated in all eight SSIs.

In 2009, National Academies Press published *Preventing Mental, Emotional, and Behavioral Disorders among Young People: Progress and Possibilities.* This publication has influenced the field of substance abuse prevention, including the work of CSAP. Instead of focusing on the work of drug abuse prevention alone, this report focused on the interconnecting web that composes youth disorders, including mental health initiatives and suicide prevention efforts.

In summary, CSAP's reorganization reflects an emerging trend in the field of substance abuse prevention, treatment, and recovery that attempts to address the wide array of issues involved in the development of substance abuse and other mental disorders. This consolidation of government health services will help policy makers to address the issue of substance abuse prevention in an integrated, organized, and holistic manner.

Julie A. Hogan, PhD

FURTHER READING

Fisher, Gary, and Nancy Roget. *Encyclopedia of Substance Abuse Prevention, Treatment, and Recovery.* Thousand Oaks, CA: Sage, 2009. An encyclopedia of key concepts and approaches used in the field of substance abuse prevention, treatment, and recovery.

Hogan, Julie, et al. *Substance Abuse Prevention: The Intersection of Science and Practice*. Boston: Allyn & Bacon, 2003. A textbook that orients students and prevention specialists through the science of substance abuse prevention.

O'Connell, Mary Ellen, Thomas Boat, and Kenneth Warner, eds. *Preventing Mental, Emotional, and Behavioral Disorders among Young People: Progress and Possibilities*. Washington: National Research Council, 2009. A report that calls for the advancement of the prevention of mental, emotional, and behavioral disorders and the promotion of mental health of young people a high priority.

WEBSITES OF INTEREST

Center for Substance Abuse Prevention (CSAP)
http://www.samhsa.gov/about/csap.aspx

Substance Abuse and Mental Health Services Administration
http://www.samhsa.gov

See also: Center for Substance Abuse Treatment (CSAT); Prevention methods and research; Substance Abuse and Mental Health Services Administration (SAMHSA)

Center for Substance Abuse Treatment (CSAT)

CATEGORY: Treatment
DATE: Established 1992
DEFINITION: The Center for Substance Abuse Treatment is a US government organization that supports the research work of the US Substance Abuse and Mental Health Services Administration as the provider of substance abuse treatment services, especially for children and adolescents.

BACKGROUND

For eighteen years after its beginning, the work of the Center for Substance Abuse Treatment (CSAT) was a program of the National Institute on Drug Abuse (NIDA), which was responsible both for overseeing research related to substance abuse and for delivery of services to patients. When NIDA became part of the National Institutes of Health in 1992, its focus shifted entirely to research. The provision of services shifted to CSAT and the Center for Substance Abuse Prevention.

MISSION AND GOALS

According to Richard Miller of CSAT, the center's initiatives and programs since 1992 have been based on research findings and the general consensus of experts in the field of addiction. For most people, treatment and recovery work best in a community-based, coordinated system of comprehensive services. Because no single treatment approach is effective for all persons, CSAT supports efforts to provide multiple treatment modalities, evaluate treatment effectiveness, and use evaluation results to enhance treatment and recovery approaches.

Advisors

CSAT's national advisory council was established under Section 502 of the Public Health Service Act (1944) and was originally chartered on December 9, 1992, in keeping with public law. The council advises, consults with, and offers recommendations to the US health secretary, the SAMHSA (Substance Abuse and Mental Health Services Administration) administrator, and the CSAT director concerning issues relating to the activities done by and through the center and to the policies related to such events.

The advisory council can, on the basis of evidence provided, make recommendations to the director of the center concerning actions conducted at the center. The council also reviews applications submitted for grants and cooperative agreements for activities requiring council permission; it also recommends for approval applications for projects that show promise of making valuable contributions to the center's mission. Furthermore, the council can consider any grant proposal made by the organization itself.

The advisory council collects material about studies and services that are ongoing in the United States or other countries and that relate to the issues of substance abuse and mental illness. The council also examines material on issues linked to diseases, disorders, or other aspects of human health that relate to the mission of SAMHSA and its programs.

The director of CSAT permits the council to make such information available through publications for the benefit of public and private health entities, health professions personnel, and the general public. The council may appoint subcommittees and convene workshops and conferences. Management and support services for the council are provided by the center.

Programs

CSAT programs include a treatment helpline (1-800-662-HELP) and the National Recovery Month, which promotes the societal benefits of treatment for substance use and mental disorders, celebrates people in recovery, lauds the contributions of treatment providers, and promotes the message that recovery is possible. National Recovery Month spreads the message that behavioral health is essential to overall health, that prevention works, that treatment is effective, and that people can and do recover.

Another CSAT service is the Substance Abuse Treatment Facility Locator, an online resource for locating drug and alcohol abuse treatment programs. The locator lists private and public facilities that are licensed, certified, or otherwise approved for inclusion by their respective state's substance abuse agency. It also lists treatment facilities administered by the US Department of Veterans Affairs, the US Indian Health Service, and the US Department of Defense.

Margaret Ring Gillock, MS

FURTHER READING

Courtwright, David T. "The NIDA Brain Disease Paradigm: History, Resistance, and Spinoffs." *BioSocieties* 5.1 (2010): 137–47. Print.

DuPont, Robert L. "National Institute on Drug Abuse at Its First Thirty-Five Years." *Drug and Alcohol Dependence* 107.1 (2010): 80–81. Print.

WEBSITES OF INTEREST

Center for Substance Abuse Treatment
http://www.samhsa.gov/about/csat.aspx

National Institute on Drug Abuse
http://www.drugabuse.gov

See also: Center for Substance Abuse Treatment (CSAT); Prevention methods and research; Substance Abuse and Mental Health Services Administration (SAMHSA)

Centre for Addiction and Mental Health (CAMH)

CATEGORY: Diagnosis and prevention
ALSO KNOWN AS: Centre de toxicomanie et de santé mentale
DEFINITION: The Centre for Addiction and Mental Health (CAMH) is the largest mental health and addiction teaching hospital in Canada. It also is an internationally renowned research center in the field of addiction and mental health. CAMH is affiliated with the University of Toronto and is a collaborating center of the Pan American Health Organization and the World Health Organization.
DATE: Established 1998

BACKGROUND

CAMH was formed in 1998 following the merger of the Clarke Institute of Psychiatry, the Addiction Research Foundation, the Donwood Institute, and Queen Street Mental Health Centre. CAMH combines clinical care, research, education, policy, and health promotion to transform the lives of people affected by mental health and addiction issues.

The organization is focused on the assessment and treatment of schizophrenia and mood, anxiety, and personality disorders and of addictions to alcohol, drugs, and pathological gambling. CAMH also includes the Law and Mental Health Programme, which provides forensic psychiatry and forensic psychology services. This program serves as a major research center for these disciplines.

The central facilities of CAMH are located in Toronto in addition to twenty-six satellite facilities within the province of Ontario. The center is affiliated with the University of Toronto and operates as a collaborating center for mental health and addiction issues for the World Health Organization and the Pan American Health Organization.

CAMH offers practical, research-based publications and online resources for professionals and the general public. Journals, newsletters, documents, and websites provide updated information in the areas of substance use and addiction, mental health, concurrent disorders, trauma, policy research, clinical tools, and health promotion.

Research at CAMH is an integral part of the organization and features four areas of scientific focus: clinical research, neuroscience, positron emission tomography (PET), and social and epidemiological research. The research laboratories include a wet lab, an animal facility, two PET scanners, and a cyclotron. A number of scientists associated with CAMH hold prestigious positions as Canadian research chairs, endowed university chairs, or professorships. Research is conducted in collaboration with national and international neural and social scientists to address global issues related to addiction and mental health.

MISSION AND GOALS

The goal of CAMH is to provide a national leadership network for better awareness, prevention, and care of substance abuse and mental health issues. The research generated and the publications produced promote the discovery, sharing, and application of new knowledge that helps to improve the lives of those affected by addiction and mental health problems.

The major mission of the center is to conduct research and develop adequate services. The center's research findings and developments are widely disseminated in Canada and internationally. CAMH also ensures that people in Ontario and the rest of Canada are able to access effective and appropriate services as required in a client-centered practice. In addition to the operation of numerous facilities, the center provides reliable, easily accessible online resources for the general public regarding addiction and mental health.

CAMH promotes continuous learning and evaluation, diversity, collaboration, and accountability. The mission of client-based care incorporates a holistic view of health and recognizes the unique social, physical, psychological, and spiritual needs of each patient and works to incorporate these preferences, needs, aspirations, and cultural beliefs into more effective prevention and treatment programs.

April D. Ingram, BSc

FURTHER READING

Giesbrecht, Norman, Andrée Demers, and Evert Lindquist. *Sober Reflections: Commerce, Public Health, and the Evolution of Alcohol Policies in Canada, 1980–2000.* Toronto: McGill-Queen's UP, 2006.

Mick, Hayley. "Extreme Makeover to Transform City's Premier Mental Health Centre and Queen West." *Globe and Mail,* 3 Oct. 2006. Print.

Moran, James, and David Wright. *Mental Health and Canadian Society: Historical Perspectives.* Toronto: McGill-Queen's UP, 2006.

Shilliday, Greg. "The Donwood Institute: Resort of Last Resort." *Canadian Medical Association Journal* 128.10 (1983): 1220–21. Print.

Steep, Barbara. *Talking About Mental Illness: A Guide for Developing an Awareness Program for Youth.* Toronto: CAMH, 2001.

WEBSITES OF INTEREST

Centre for Addiction and Mental Health
http://www.camh.net

United Nations Office on Drugs and Crime
http://www.unodc.org/treatment/en/Canada_resource_centre_4.html

See also: Canada's Drug Strategy (CDS); Education about substance abuse; Mental illness

Children and behavioral addictions

CATEGORY: Social issues
ALSO KNOWN AS: Soft addictions
DEFINITION: A behavioral addiction is defined as compulsive, repetitive participation in any activity not related to the use of illicit substances to the point that such behavior dominates a person's life, disrupting normal behavior patterns and potentially causing physical, mental, or social harm. Common behavioral addictions among all age groups include those related to gambling, sex, technology, shopping, eating, and exercise. Common behavioral addictions among children include addictions to video

gaming, the Internet and computers, exercise, food, sex, and exercise.

BEHAVIORAL ADDICTIONS

Though the cause or causes of behavioral addictions have not been established, some studies have suggested that behavioral addictions, like physical addictions, may be rooted in brain chemistry. Many researchers believe that the act of engaging in certain activities results in an increase in the production of beta-endorphins in the brain, an increase that leads to a feeling of euphoria. In the case of behavioral addictions, it is thought that repetitive engagement in an activity for the purpose of achieving this euphoric feeling may, in turn, cause a person to become trapped in a cycle of addiction.

Experts also have suggested that the development of behavioral and physical addictions may be related to hereditary factors or environmental influences. For example, in the case of behavioral addictions in children, a child with a parent or parents who engage in some form of addictive behavior may be more likely than other children to engage in the same or similar behaviors at some point in their lives.

Regardless of the cause of their condition, people who suffer from behavioral addictions often exhibit certain characteristics that suggest they have become addicted to a particular activity. Many behavioral addicts become obsessed with the activity and find themselves unable to stop thinking about it. They often continue the activity without regard to how it may be affecting their own lives or the lives of others.

In many cases, the addict's engagement in the activity becomes compulsive, meaning that the addict is driven to continue the activity. Some addicts also experience a loss of control over when or to what degree they will engage in an addictive activity. Other characteristics of behavioral addictions include a tendency to deny that the behavior is causing personal problems. Some addicts also attempt to conceal their behavior from family members or friends.

Some behavioral addicts also encounter physical and mental symptoms related to their condition. Many claim to black out during the activity and are thus unable to remember their actions. In some cases, withdrawal symptoms, such as irritability or restlessness, result when the behavioral addict cannot engage in the addictive behavior. Many behavioral addicts also have depression and low self-esteem.

CHILDREN AND ADOLESCENTS

Children and adolescents are equally prone to developing behavioral addictions as adults. Many children also suffer from the same types of behavioral addictions as adults. Most commonly, children and adolescents struggle with behavioral addictions related to eating, exercise, sex, gambling, and technology, including Internet use.

Behavioral addictions related to eating and diet among children and adolescents often manifest as eating disorders, including binge eating, bulimia, and anorexia nervosa. If left untreated, these eating disorders can lead to serious health consequences and even death.

Exercise-related behavioral addictions are often triggered by the importance placed on sports in the lives of many young people. Some adolescents who are involved in a team or individual sport can easily become obsessed with their performance and may engage in excessive physical training to improve their skills. This, in turn, can lead to the development of anorexia athletica, an exercise addiction wherein the addict feels the need to exercise continually in order to feel normal.

As older children and young teens enter puberty, they become increasingly aware of their sexuality and begin to engage in sexual behaviors. During this period, some teens may come to rely on sex to relieve stress or to cope with other emotional issues. This reliance can, in some cases, lead to sex addiction. Persons who develop such addictions may be unable to control their sexual behavior.

Gambling may seem like a problem faced only by adults, but adolescents are susceptible to gambling addictions too. Much like adults, adolescents become addicted by playing games of chance. Some resort to selling off their personal possessions or securing money from their parents to fund their addiction.

Increasingly, however, the most commonly occurring behavioral addiction among children and adolescents is addiction to video games and the Internet, especially social media. For children and young adults in particular, the Internet has become a vital part of their everyday lives, providing nearly constant access to social networks and a wealth of information and entertainment. This widespread use of computer technology also presents a serious risk of addiction.

Children and adolescents with computer and Internet addictions often spend excessive amounts of time online or engage in other computer activities. Many experts agree that spending more than twenty hours per week on the Internet may indicate an addiction. Other factors that suggest addiction include obsessive preoccupation with the Internet, decreased interest in non-Internet-related social activities, and the onset of withdrawal symptoms when Internet access is not available.

Internet addictions also frequently lead to obsessive behaviors. Many young Internet addicts spend an inordinate amount of time building and maintaining online relationships while disregarding real-life relationships. Others may simply find themselves compulsively surfing the web.

In some cases, technological addictions also can intersect with other common addictions, such as sex addiction. Many adolescents turn to adult chat rooms or online pornography, which is often a highly addictive form of sexual behavior. While more common among adults, the frequent use of online gambling websites also can lead to the development of a gambling addiction.

For many young people, playing video games can become as addictive as Internet use. According to a 2009 Harris Poll, 8.5 percent of video-game players between the age of eight and eighteen years showed signs of addiction. Addiction to video games, online games, and the Internet in general is often driven, among other factors, by the opportunity these technologies provide for escape from reality and retreat into a virtual world where they feel more self-confident.

The consequences of addiction to computers, the Internet, or video games can vary in scope and severity. Excessive use of technology can lead to weight issues caused by skipping meals or eating poorly, by a lack of sleep, and by a decrease in physical activities away from the computer or game console. Technological addictions often also result in a reduction in the amount of time students spend studying, which, in turn, leads to poor academic performance. In some cases, such as viewing content that users must pay to access, technological addictions can result in financial problems. Finally, the continual use of a computer or other technology also can lead to physical health problems, such as carpal tunnel syndrome, eye strain, or back and neck pain.

SOLUTIONS

All forms of addiction have negative consequences for children and adolescents. Parents should be watchful for signs of any behavioral addiction. A variety of treatment options are available for children and adolescents with behavioral addictions. Medical treatments or other forms of therapy can help break the cycle of addiction and encourage the resumption of a normal, healthy lifestyle.

FURTHER READING

Bruner, Olivia, and Kurt D. Bruner. *Playstation Nation: Protect Your Child from Video Game Addiction.* New York: Hachette, 2006. Provides information on how to recognize and prevent video game addiction.

Peele, Stanton. *Addiction Proof Your Child: A Realistic Approach to Preventing Drug, Alcohol, and Other Dependencies.* New York: Crown, 2007. A guide to recognizing and preventing a variety of addictions in children and adolescents.

Young, Kimberly S., and Cristiano Nabuco De Abreu. *Internet Addiction: A Handbook and Guide to Evaluation and Treatment.* Hoboken, NJ: Wiley, 2011. A comprehensive guide to Internet addiction with a strong emphasis on adolescents.

WEBSITES OF INTEREST

Center for Internet Addiction
http://www.netaddiction.com

Childnet International
http://www.childnet-int.org/downloads/factsheet_addiction.pdf

WebMD
http://children.webmd.com/news/20090421/is-your-child-addicted-to-video-games

See also: Behavioral addictions: Overview; Families and behavioral addictions; Parenting and behavioral addictions

China white

CATEGORY: Substances

DEFINITION: China white is a common name for a number of illegally manufactured fentanyl derivatives. These substances, considered designer drugs, are highly potent narcotic analgesics with opiate-like properties.

STATUS: Illegal in the United States and worldwide

CLASSIFICATION: Schedule I controlled substance

SOURCE: China white consists of various synthetic fentanyl derivatives. Most China white is smuggled into the United States from Mexico or is manufactured in illegal clandestine laboratories.

TRANSMISSION ROUTE: China white exists in powder form and resembles street heroin. It can be inhaled, smoked, snorted, or injected.

HISTORY OF USE

Fentanyl was first synthesized in the 1950s by Janssen Pharmaceuticals of Belgium as a fast-acting narcotic analgesic. The modification of the fentanyl molecule by clandestine chemists produced analogs known as designer drugs that are similar to, but more potent than, heroin. In the 1970s, the first fentanyl designer drug created and labeled as China white was alpha-methylfentanyl, a simple derivative with twice the potency of fentanyl. China white gained popularity as a recreational drug among heroin users because it was a cheaper and more potent synthetic alternative.

China white is one of the most addictive, unpredictable, and lethal illegal drugs available. It is more dangerous than legal opioids because of its high potency and unknown purity. It is frequently combined with low quality heroin to increase potency. By the 1980s, China white was responsible for numerous overdose deaths in the United States. As a result, the fentanyl forms of China white are now classified as schedule I controlled substances under the US Controlled Substances Act (1970). Schedule I controlled substances are drugs with high abuse potential and no legitimate medical use. Despite numerous efforts to curb the illegal manufacture of China white, its abuse continues to be a concern.

EFFECTS AND POTENTIAL RISKS

Similar to other opiates, China white acts through opioid receptors to alter the brain's response to pain. It lessens pain sensations and elevates levels of dopamine, the neurotransmitter linked to pleasurable experiences.

China white pharmacologically mimics the effects of heroin but has a quicker onset and a shorter duration. Its short-term effects include a rush of euphoria followed by feelings of peacefulness and physical relaxation. Negative short-term effects include drowsiness, nausea, dizziness, fatigue, and headache.

Many people who use China white do so to achieve greater heroin-like highs. The most immediate and intense "rush" typically occurs through intravenous injection; the high is fast and intense, but brief. However, there is little distinction between a dose that leads to euphoria and one that leads to death.

China white is highly addictive, and physical and psychological tolerance and dependence develop quickly. Long-term use can lead to anxiety and paranoia and can cause many physical problems, including painful constipation, muscle rigidity, tremors, paralysis, and respiratory depression. Accidental overdose and death also are prevalent.

Rose Ciulla-Bohling, PhD

FURTHER READING

Clayton, Lawrence. *Designer Drugs*. New York: Rosen, 1998.

Gahlinger, Paul M. *Illegal Drugs: A Complete Guide to Their History, Chemistry, Use, and Abuse*. New York: Plume, 2004.

Goldberg, Raymond. *Drugs across the Spectrum*. Belmont, CA: Wadsworth, 2010.

Olive, M. Foster. *Designer Drugs*. Philadelphia: Chelsea House, 2003.

WEBSITES OF INTEREST

European Monitoring Centre for Drugs and Drug Addiction
http://www.emcdda.europa.eu/publications/drug-profiles/fentanyl

National Institute on Drug Abuse
http://www.drugabuse.gov/drugpages/fentanyl

US Drug Enforcement Administration
http://www.deadiversion.usdoj.gov/drugs_concern/fentanyl.htm

See also: Controlled substances and precursor chemicals; Designer drugs; Fentanyl; Narcotics abuse

Choking game

Category: Psychological issues and behaviors

Also known as: Airplaning; American dream; black out game; breath play; California high; choke out; cloud nine; fainting; fainting game; flatline; flatliner; gasp; ghost; hanging; Hawaiian high; knock out; natural high; pass out game; purple dragon; rising sun; space cowboy; space monkey; suffocation roulette

Definition: The choking game is an activity in which, most frequently, children, teenagers, and young adults use strangulation to reduce the flow of oxygen to the brain. This reduction in oxygen flow leads to a temporary state of euphoria, or a "high." There are two ways to play the choking game. The first is to apply pressure to the neck using the hands or a ligature, such as a belt, necktie, scarf, or other device, until the person faints or nearly passes out. The second is for one person to take a deep breath and hold it while another grips him or her in a "bear hug" from behind until the first person passes out. The choking game is most commonly "played" by two people, but it can also be played alone.

Causes

There is no known reason why some people participate in the choking game while others do not. Many adolescents mistakenly believe that the game is a safe way to get high because it does not involve drugs or alcohol.

The Internet may also give children a false sense of security about the game. One can find numerous instructional videos on the web that teach how to participate in the choking game, but these videos most often do not include information about the activity's dangers.

Many people also mistakenly believe that if they play the choking game with another person, doing so will be safe. The other player is trusted to remove the object cutting off the oxygen after the person being asphyxiated loses consciousness.

Risk Factors

There are no known factors that predispose a person to begin playing the choking game. Many children who play the game do not otherwise engage in risky activities, such as drug and alcohol use. However, some factors are common to those who play the game, including age and peer pressure. The choking game is most often played by children and young adults age nine to twenty years, and most children learn about the game from other children.

Symptoms

Because many parents have never heard of the choking game, they are not likely to know the signs that their child may be participating. Symptoms that one is playing the game include the following: having unexplained bruises on the neck; having bloodshot eyes; leaving bed sheets, belts, ties, or ropes tied in strange knots and in unusual places; having frequent, severe headaches; being disoriented after being alone; wearing high-neck shirts or scarves, even in warm weather; locking one's bedroom or bathroom doors; leaving marks of wear on bed posts or closet rods; and showing curiosity about the choking game or asphyxiation in general. The choking game is a dangerous practice that can lead to seizures, fractures, retinal hemorrhages, brain damage, stroke, and death.

Screening and Diagnosis

The choking game often goes undetected until the person who has been playing the game dies. It is unknown how many people die each year from playing the game, because many cases are likely classified as suicides. However, most people who play the game do not intend to kill themselves. Those persons who play it alone often devise some sort of safety mechanism that is intended to prevent accidental death in case they lose consciousness. Safety mechanisms may include the use of slip knots or arranging to hang from something that is shorter than themselves. These safety mechanisms often fail because the person becomes disoriented and is unable to take the necessary steps to restore the flow of oxygen.

At minimum, physicians and other clinicians trying to determine whether or not their patients have been playing the choking game need to be knowledgeable about the game and its warning signs. Screening for evidence of the choking game can take place during routine physical examinations or when a patient presents with symptoms. Diagnosis is based on the patient's symptoms and medical history.

TREATMENT AND THERAPY

Treatment for choking game participants may include a combination of cognitive-behavioral therapy and education about the dangers of asphyxiation.

PREVENTION

Education is key to preventing children from playing the choking game. Once the behavior has started, many children begin looking for a way to play the game safely, so they need to be told that there is no safe way to do it.

Parents also should be educated about the choking game, including learning the warning signs. Parents who believe their child may be participating in the game should discuss the dangers with their child and then seek treatment for the child. The child's physician may be able to provide a referral. Even if parents do not believe their child is playing the game, they still should discuss the dangers of the game with their children.

Many clinicians remain unaware of the choking game. Education about the game could be included in continuing education programs. It also could be incorporated into medical, nursing, and psychology curricula and into primary care, psychiatry, and emergency medicine residency programs.

Julie Henry

FURTHER READING

Hitti, Miranda. "CDC Warns of Choking-Game Deaths." *WebMD.com.* 14 Feb. 2008. Web. http://children.webmd.com/news/20080214/cdc-warns-of-choking-game-deaths. An article about the choking game that includes discussion of symptoms and risk factors and outlines the numbers of related deaths.

McClave, Julie L., et al. "The Choking Game: Physician Perspectives." *Pediatrics* 125.1 (2010): 82–87. Print. A survey assessing awareness of the choking game among physicians who care for adolescents.

WEBSITES OF INTEREST

"Doctors Warn of Deadly Choking Game." *American Academy of Pediatrics*
http://www.aap.org

"Facts of the Choking Game." *Dangerous Behaviors Foundation*
http://chokinggame.net/chokinggame

See also: Autoerotic asphyxiation; Behavioral addictions: Overview; Children and behavioral addictions

Chronic bronchitis

CATEGORY: Health issues

DEFINITION: Chronic bronchitis is a condition in which the airways in the lungs become inflamed. The condition persists for a long time or continues to recur following periods of remission. Chronic bronchitis, along with emphysema, is a form of chronic obstructive pulmonary disease (COPD).

CAUSES

With chronic bronchitis, the airways in the lungs become inflamed. When these airways become irritated, thick mucus forms inside the airways, making it difficult to breathe.

The most common causes of chronic bronchitis include cigarette smoking and exposure to secondhand cigarette smoke. Air pollution, infections, and allergens worsen the symptoms of bronchitis.

RISK FACTORS

Cigarette smoking is the single greatest risk factor for developing chronic bronchitis. The more a person smokes and the longer he or she smokes, the greater the risk is of developing chronic bronchitis. Frequent and long-term smoking also increases the risk that the chronic bronchitis will be severe.

Other factors that may increase the chance of developing chronic bronchitis include long-term exposure to chemicals, dust, and other substances that have been inhaled; long-term cigar or marijuana smoking; uncontrolled asthma; and long-term exposure to air pollution.

SYMPTOMS

Symptoms of chronic bronchitis include coughing up mucus, coughing up mucus streaked with blood, and shortness of breath (difficulty breathing). Difficulty breathing may especially occur after mild activity or exercise. Other symptoms include recurring respiratory infections that cause symptoms to worsen; wheezing when breathing; fatigue; swelling of the ankles, feet, and legs; and headaches.

SCREENING AND DIAGNOSIS

To diagnose chronic bronchitis, symptoms of productive cough must have been present for three or more months in at least two consecutive years, and not have been caused by another condition. A doctor will ask about symptoms and medical history and perform a physical examination.

Tests may include breathing tests to check lung function, arterial blood gas tests, chest X-ray (a test that uses radiation to take a picture of structures inside the chest), blood tests to determine complete blood count and oxygen saturation of the blood, exercise stress testing to test lung function, and a CT scan of the chest (a type of X-ray that captures 3-D images of the internal organs).

TREATMENT AND THERAPY

There is no cure for chronic bronchitis, but there are treatments that can reduce symptoms and improve lung function. The best way to reduce symptoms is to stop smoking. Short-acting bronchodilator medications may be prescribed to help open the airways in the lungs and improve breathing. Long-acting bronchodilator medication may be prescribed as well, and steroids may be prescribed to help improve breathing. Antibiotics are rarely prescribed to treat bronchitis. However, they may be needed to treat a lung infection that often accompanies the illness. A small percentage of patients may need chronic antibiotic therapy.

Oxygen therapy can restore oxygen to parts of the body depleted because of chronic bronchitis. Exercise can also help. Breathing exercises can help to improve lung function, and are usually done under the supervision of a respiratory therapist. A regular exercise program can reduce symptoms and improve lung function.

PREVENTION

The best way to prevent chronic bronchitis is to stop smoking, or avoiding smoking altogether for nonsmokers. Early diagnosis and treatment of the condition will preserve lung function and reduce symptoms.

Diana Kohnle

FURTHER READING

Halbert, R. J., et al. "Global Burden of COPD: Systematic Review and Meta-Analysis." *European Respiratory Journal* 28.3 (2006): 523–532. Quantifies the prevalence of chronic obstructive pulmonary disease (COPD) through a systematic review and random effects meta-analysis.

Lopez, A.D., et al. "Chronic Obstructive Pulmonary Disease: Current Burden and Future Projections." *European Respiratory Journal* 27.2 (2006): 397–412. Uses the results from a global burden of disease study to provide estimated and projected statistics about the prevalence of COPD. Also estimates and projects mortality rates resulting from the disease.

Mayo Clinic Staff. "Bronchitis." *Mayo Clinic.* Mayo Foundation for Medical Education and Research. 2012. Web. 29. Mar. 2012. Information about bronchitis, including its definition, symptoms, causes, risk factors, complications, diagnosis, treatment, lifestyle, home remedies, and prevention.

WEBSITES OF INTEREST

American Lung Association
http://www.lungusa.org

Smokefree.gov
http://www.smokefree.gov/

See also: Chronic obstructive pulmonary disease (COPD); Nicotine addiction; Respiratory diseases and smoking; Smoking; Smoking: Short- and long-term effects on the body; Tobacco use disorder

Chronic obstructive pulmonary disease (COPD)

CATEGORY: Health issues

DEFINITION: Chronic obstructive pulmonary disease (COPD) is a progressive illness that makes it increasingly difficult to breathe. In COPD, the airways and air sacs of the lungs become inelastic and inflamed, making it more difficult for oxygen to reach the bloodstream. COPD includes emphysema, which is caused by damage to the air sacs, and chronic bronchitis, a lung disorder of the large airways. Changes to lung tissue differ between the two diseases. However, their causes and treatment are similar.

CAUSES

COPD develops due to inhaling toxins or other irritants. In fact, smoking cigarettes is the leading cause of COPD. A genetic predisposition may make a person's lungs more susceptible to damage from smoke or pollutants (including alpha-1-antitrypsin deficiency), increasing the chances of developing COPD.

RISK FACTORS

Factors that increase the chance of developing COPD include smoking cigarettes, long-term exposure to secondhand smoke, and exposure to pollutants. Other factors include having family members with COPD and having a history of frequent childhood lung infections. Because COPD develops over a long period of time, the risk increases for people fifty years or older.

SYMPTOMS

Early symptoms of COPD include coughing in the morning, coughing up clear sputum (mucus from deep in the lungs), wheezing, and shortness of breath with physical activity. As the disease progresses, symptoms may include increased shortness of breath, a choking sensation when lying flat, fatigue, trouble concentrating, and heart problems. Other progressive symptoms may include weight loss, breathing through pursed lips, desire to lean forward to improve breathing, and more frequent flare-ups (periods of more severe symptoms).

SCREENING AND DIAGNOSIS

A diagnosis from a doctor will include questions about a patient's symptoms and medical history. A physical exam will also be conducted. Tests may include a chest X-ray (X-rays of the chest may detect signs of lung infection), CT scan (a type of X-ray that uses a computer to generate pictures of the structures inside the chest), blood tests to assess the amount of oxygen and carbon dioxide in the blood, and a lung function test.

TREATMENT AND THERAPY

There is no treatment to cure COPD. Instead, treatment aims to ease symptoms and improve the patient's

Nutrition in the Treatment of COPD

There are several ways to treat COPD with nutrition and proper eating:

- Maintain a normal weight; excess weight causes the lungs and heart to work harder.

- Eat a healthy diet that is low in saturated fat and rich in fruits, vegetables, and whole grain foods.

- Eat several small meals during the day; doing so makes breathing easier.

- Avoid gas-producing foods; large meals and excess gas swell the stomach, which pushes up on the diaphragm.

- Drink fluids to keep mucus thin.

quality of life. Such treatments include smoking cessation, environmental management (limiting the number of irritants in the air), and medication. Drugs used to ease COPD may work by opening airways, relaxing the breathing passages, decreasing inflammation, and thinning secretions to bring up mucus from the lungs. Chronic and mild to moderate COPD may require antibiotics. One study found that shorter antibiotic treatment (five days or less) is as effective as longer treatment (more than five days). Additionally, the flu vaccine may help to reduce COPD flare-ups.

A few people can benefit from receiving oxygen. Oxygen is given to improve the air breathed in and to increase the amount of available oxygen. This can improve energy levels and heart and brain function. Special exercises can strengthen chest muscles and make breathing easier. Physical activity builds endurance and improves quality of life. Yoga is an example of an exercise routine that may offer benefits for people with COPD.

A small number of patients may benefit from surgery, such as lung transplants.

PREVENTION

Steps taken to reduce the risk of developing COPD include quitting smoking, avoiding exposure to secondhand smoke, avoiding exposure to air pollution or irritants, and wearing protective gear when exposed to irritants and toxins at the workplace.

Debra Wood, RN

FURTHER READING

COPD Foundation. The COPD Foundation. 2012. Web. 29 Mar. 2012. The COPD Foundation develops and supports programs for research, education, diagnosis, and therapy for those affected by COPD. Their website has educational resources that outline the preventability and treatability of COPD.

COPD Learn More Breathe Better. National Heart, Lung, and Blood Institute. 2012. Web. 29 Mar. 2012. The "COPD Learn More Breathe Better" campaign has resources to increase the awareness of COPD and how to treat it. The campaign encourages those at risk to talk to their health care providers about COPD.

Eisner, Mark D., et al. "Lifetime Environmental Tobacco Smoke Exposure and the Risk of Chronic Obstructive Pulmonary Disease." *Environmental Health: A Global Access Science Source.* Biomed Central Ltd. 12 May 2005. Web. 29 Mar. 2012. Examines the association between lifetime exposure to environmental tobacco smoke (ETS) and the risk of developing COPD.

WEBSITES OF INTEREST

American Association for Respiratory Care
http://www.aarc.org/

American Lung Association
http://www.lungusa.org/

COPD Foundation
http://www.copdfoundation.org

COPD Learn More Breathe Better
http://www.nhlbi.nih.gov/health/public/lung/
    copd/lmbb-campaign/

See also: Chronic bronchitis; Nicotine addiction; Respiratory diseases and smoking; Smoking; Smoking: Short- and long-term effects on the body; Tobacco use disorder

Cigarettes and cigars

CATEGORY: Substance of abuse

DEFINITION: A cigarette is a cylinder of cured and finely cut tobacco wrapped in paper. The paper is ignited and the smoke is inhaled through the mouth into the lungs. A cigar is a larger cylinder of dried and fermented tobacco wrapped in whole-leaf tobacco that is also ignited. Cigar smoke is drawn into the mouth, and nicotine is absorbed through the oral membranes; cigar smoke is not inhaled because its alkalinity is highly irritating to inner mucous membranes.

STATUS: Legal in the United States and most countries for adults. In some Canadian provinces, the legal age is nineteen years. In Japan, the legal age is twenty years. In Kuwait, the legal age is twenty-one years. In Austria, Belgium, France, and the Netherlands, the legal age is sixteen years.

CLASSIFICATION: Regulated by the US Food and Drug Administration as a nicotine delivery system.

SOURCE: The United States grows about 10 percent of the world's tobacco crop; the major tobacco-growing countries are China, India, Brazil, and Turkey. Two-thirds of the American tobacco crop is grown in the states of Kentucky and North Carolina.

TRANSMISSION ROUTE: The nicotine in cigarette smoke is absorbed in the lungs and rapidly acts on the brain to activate pleasure centers and stimulate an adrenaline rush. Small amounts of nicotine in the smoke may be absorbed through the mucous membranes of the nose and mouth. The nicotine in cigar smoke is absorbed slowly through the mucous membranes of the mouth because the smoke is too harsh to be inhaled.

HISTORY OF USE

Smoking tobacco was introduced in Europe in the sixteenth century and in the United States in the seventeenth century. Matches and cigarettes were first commercially produced in the nineteenth century, facilitating the habit of smoking. By 1901, 80 percent of American men smoked at least one cigar a day; that same year, 6 million cigars and 3.5 million cigarettes were sold in the United States.

In 1913, the R. J. Reynolds Tobacco Company introduced Camel cigarettes, and ten years later, Camels were smoked by 45 percent of American smokers. By 1940, the number of cigarette smokers had doubled from that of 1930. Tobacco company advertising and marketing in the twentieth century especially targeted military personnel and women.

In 1950, the first evidence linking lung cancer and tobacco smoking was published in a British medical journal. In 1965, a US federal law mandated that a warning from the US surgeon general be placed on all packages of cigarettes and all cigarette advertising, stating the risks of smoking tobacco. In 1971, cigarette advertising was banned from television. In 1972, Marlboro became the best-selling brand of cigarettes in the world, and it remains the best-selling brand. In 1988, the US surgeon general determined that nicotine was an addictive substance. Nine years later, a US federal judge ruled that the US Food and Drug Administration can regulate tobacco as a drug.

Worldwide, nearly 5.4 million people die annually from tobacco-related illnesses, including heart disease, stroke, and cancer. For every person who dies of a smoking-related disease, twenty people are living with a serious smoking-related disease. Men who do not smoke live 13.2 years longer than men who do smoke, and women who do not smoke live 14.5 years longer than women who do smoke.

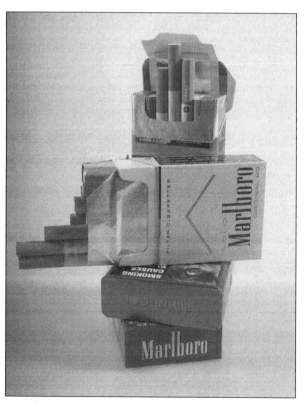

Australia is the first country to ban logos on cigarette packaging, and will require all cigarettes sold there to be in plain packaging from December 1, 2012. (Bloomberg via Getty Images

EFFECTS AND POTENTIAL RISKS

The smoking of tobacco leads to nicotine addiction. Repeated introduction of nicotine into the body causes increased production of dopamine in the pleasure centers of the brain. As the dopamine level drops, the smoker feels depressed and lights the next cigarette or cigar to regain the heightened sense of pleasure and well-being.

Nicotine also stains the teeth and fingers yellow, sours the breath, diminishes the senses of smell and taste, and reduces one's appetite. People who smoke experience hair loss and wrinkle formation at a younger age. Women who smoke have an increased risk of miscarriage, premature labor, and giving birth to an underweight baby.

Along with nicotine, tobacco smoke contains carbon monoxide, which reduces the blood's ability to carry oxygen to cells. To ensure that adequate oxygen reaches vital organs, the body reduces the blood flow to the extremities. Smoking stresses the heart and thereby increases the risks of heart disease and stroke.

The toxicity of tobacco smoke damages the lips, tongue, gums, throat, larynx, esophagus, and lungs. This progressive damage leads to chronic bronchitis and emphysema and an increased likelihood of death from cancer of the mouth, lungs, kidneys, bladder, pancreas, and stomach.

Nonsmokers who breathe environmental, or secondhand, cigarette and cigar smoke are also exposed to the toxins and carcinogens contained in that smoke. Nonsmokers are thus exposed to the same health risks as smokers.

Bethany Thivierge, MPH

FURTHER READING

Bellenir, Karen. *Tobacco Information for Teens: Health Tips about the Hazards of Using Cigarettes, Smokeless Tobacco, and Other Nicotine Products.* Aston, PA: Omnigraphics, 2010. A comprehensive and easy-to-read reference book for middle school and high school students.

Carr, Allen. *The Easy Way to Stop Smoking: Join the Millions Who Have Become Non-Smokers Using Allen Carr's Easy Way Method.* New York: Sterling, 2010. This book helps smokers discover the underlying reasons for smoking and discusses how to handle nicotine withdrawal and how to avoid the temptation to relapse.

Rose, Jed Eugene, et al. "Personalized Smoking Cessation: Interactions between Nicotine Dose, Dependence, and Quit-Success Genotype Score."

Molecular Medicine 16 (2010): 247–53. Print. Discussion of a study that found that the reduction of carbon monoxide levels with nicotine replacement therapy increases the likelihood of successful smoking abstinence.

WEBSITES OF INTEREST

"Harms of Smoking and Health Benefits of Quitting." *National Cancer Institute*
http://www.cancer.gov/cancertopics/factsheet/tobacco/cessation

"Smoking and Tobacco Use." *Centers for Disease Control and Prevention*
http://www.cdc.gov/tobacco/basic_information

"Stop Smoking." *American Lung Association*
http://www.lungusa.org/stop-smoking

See also: Nicotine addiction; Smoking; Smoking: Short- and long-term effects on the body; Tobacco use disorder

---

Cirque Lodge

CATEGORY: Treatment
DEFINITION: Cirque Lodge is a private drug and alcohol rehabilitation facility located in the mountains of Utah. Based on the twelve-step treatment model of Alcoholics Anonymous (AA), Cirque Lodge offers drug and alcohol treatment through a thirty-day residential program.
DATE: Established in 1999

HISTORY

Cirque Lodge was founded in 1999 by entrepreneur Richard Losee, a native of Provo, Utah, and the center's chief executive officer. Losee became interested in drug and alcohol treatment because of his own experience with a family member.

Cirque Lodge is located in Sundance, Utah, in the Wasatch Range of the Rocky Mountains. The name of the treatment center derives from the nearby glacier-carved Cascade Cirque.

Cirque Lodge expanded to include Cirque Studio in 2002. Located in Orem, Utah, this 110,000-square foot facility was built in the 1970s as a television studio for the Osmond family and their television variety show. The studio and lodge are accredited by the Joint Commission on Accreditation of Health Care Organizations.

Because treatment costs at Cirque Lodge may exceed $1,000 per day per person, it has gained the reputation as an exclusive and private treatment center for the rich and famous. Although some celebrities have been associated with Cirque Lodge, most of the center's clients are not celebrities. The center offers some scholarships for clients who cannot afford treatment.

The model of drug and alcohol treatment used by Cirque Lodge can be traced back to 1949. Abstinence-based treatment was first developed at Willmar State Hospital and the Hazelden Treatment Center in Minnesota. Borrowing from the twelve-step meetings of AA, which were developed in the 1930s, these alcoholic treatment centers added residential treatment that included lectures, open discussions, small group therapy, and peer interaction.

Abstinence-based treatment centers became the predominant model for treating both alcohol and drug abuse in the 1980s. Private treatment in twenty-eight-day residential centers dominated the treatment landscape, but was affected by cost-cutting managed health care in the 1990s.

Most abstinence-based treatment now is provided in outpatient settings. Treatment focuses on individualized treatment plans, family involvement, and frequent use of group meetings such as AA, Narcotics Anonymous, and Al Anon. Studies show that more than 90 percent of drug and alcohol treatment programs in the United States are abstinence-based programs that use the twelve steps of AA as a core principle.

MISSION AND GOALS

Cirque Lodge believes that addiction to drugs or alcohol is caused by an uncontrollable impulse in the brain caused by an imbalance of brain chemicals. Center staff acknowledge that heredity and life experiences also contribute to addiction. As the brain becomes accustomed to addictive substances, physical changes in the brain lead to the mental and social symptoms of addiction.

The treatment philosophy at Cirque Lodge is to use the most effective therapies available. This includes learning coping skills from the twelve steps of AA, cognitive behavioral therapy, independent counseling, lectures, group therapy, and peer support. Family involvement is also seen as important, and families are invited to spend four days at the facility to attend a special program. Family members are integrated into group classes and group therapy during this program.

Before beginning the actual residential treatment program, all clients must go through detoxification, if needed. This treatment is offered through a separate licensed detoxification facility. Upon arrival at Cirque Lodge, staff assess the clients and then develop individualized treatment programs. Cirque Lodge also treats co-occurring eating disorders and mood disorders.

In addition to therapy sessions and twelve-step meetings, clients are offered programs in exercise, meditation, journaling, working with horses, hiking, climbing, and organic gardening, and clients can take part in a ropes course and can use a fully equipped art room. The former soundstage at the Cirque Studio houses the indoor ropes challenge course, and it also has an archery range and a lecture hall.

Cirque Lodge staff believe that addiction is a chronic condition and that relapse is a common reality. To address this they provide an active aftercare program, an alumni program, and a guesting program. Clients who have completed treatment at the facility may return without charge for a few days of additional care if needed.

Christopher Iliades, MD

FURTHER READING

Hoffman, John, et al. *Addiction: Why Can't They Just Stop?* New York: Rodale, 2007. A companion book to the HBO television documentary of the same name. Provides a human face to the hidden problem of addiction in the United States and breaks through the myths and misunderstandings that surround addiction and its treatment.

Ries, Richard K., et al., eds. *Principles of Addiction Medicine.* 4th ed. Philadelphia: Wolters, 2009. A respected text for physicians and mental health professionals covering all aspects of drug and alcohol addiction. A text from the American Society of Addiction Medicine.

Spicer, Jerry. *The Minnesota Model: The Evolution of the Multidisciplinary Approach to Recovery.* Center City, MN: Hazelden, 1993. Describes how the blend of behavioral science and the philosophy of Alcoholics Anonymous became the treatment model for all abstinence addiction treatment.

WEBSITES OF INTEREST

American Society of Addiction Medicine
http://www.asam.org

Cirque Lodge
http://www.cirquelodge.com

National Institute on Drug Abuse
http://www.drugabuse.gov/nidamed

"Top Residential 30-60-90 Day Addiction Treatment Centers." *New Life Recovery*
http://www.newliferecovery.net/InPatientAddictionTreatmentRehab

See also: Abstinence-based treatment; Hazelden Foundation; Minnesota Model; Rehabilitation programs; Twelve-step programs for addicts

Cleanliness addiction

CATEGORY: Psychological issues and behaviors
ALSO KNOWN AS: Contamination OCD; germaphobia
DEFINITION: Cleanliness addiction is a type of obsessive compulsive disorder, which consists of unwanted thoughts (obsessions) accompanied by repetitive behaviors (compulsions) intended to reduce the anxiety caused by the unwanted thoughts. Typical obsessions involve contamination, aggression, religious concerns, sexual concerns, and the need for exactness or symmetry. More than one-half of all persons with obsessive compulsive disorder experience contamination fears. For some persons, cleaning obsessively is the main symptom of obsessive compulsive disorder. A person may develop an obsession with contamination, bodily functions, and illness; this obsession manifests as cleanliness addiction.

CAUSES

Researchers do not understand the genetic mechanisms of obsessive compulsive disorder (OCD), though they suspect multiple genes are involved. Genetic links are being investigated. OCD often runs in families, and identical twins have a 70 percent chance of sharing the disorder (fraternal twins have a 50 percent chance of sharing the disorder). Later studies have shown that a streptococcal infection may trigger OCD in children; the infection is known as PANDAS (pediatric autoimmune neuropsychiatric disorders associated with streptococcal infections).

RISK FACTORS

The onset of OCD is usually gradual. It most often begins in adolescence or early adulthood and is surprisingly common. Most people at some time in their lives exhibit some obsessive and compulsive symptoms.

A recent study suggests that fluctuating hormones may trigger OCD symptoms during pregnancy. The same study reports OCD in 30 percent of women observed. A woman may also sometimes develop OCD or see a mild condition worsen in the postpartum stage. Illness may intensify fears about health and cleanliness and increase the compulsive activities associated with those fears. Major life changes and problems at work or school may trigger worries, fears, and obsessions.

SYMPTOMS

Those with contamination OCD have compulsions, intrusive thoughts, or rituals related to cleaning. Cleaning must be done in a certain order or frequency. Worry overwhelms the person, who might think, for example, that a critical spot may have been missed during cleaning. A person with contamination OCD may wash their hands repeatedly until their hands are chapped and even bleeding. This may expose the person to infection.

Washing behaviors are rarely confined to the hands and may include excessive bathing and showering. Rituals might also involve washing clothing and utensils, and house cleaning. Cleanliness addicts may also insist that others adopt the same extreme cleaning behaviors.

OCD can interfere with one's ability to concentrate, and it is not uncommon for a person with OCD to avoid certain situations. For example, someone with cleanliness addiction may be unable to use public restrooms. That person also may have panic attacks when faced with certain situations; they may avoid shaking another person's hand or may avoid public transportation.

People with OCD often miss work or appointments because of compulsions and may even become housebound. Sometimes their pattern of behaviors is confusing to others because it may seem inconsistent. For example, they may have a contamination concern about one specific thing, such as not touching bruised fruit, but be unconcerned about other things (such as gardening manure) that may seem more of a contamination concern to many others.

Unlike adults, children with OCD do not realize that their obsessions and compulsions are excessive. Some experts believe that OCD that begins in childhood may be different from OCD that does not manifest until adulthood.

SCREENING AND DIAGNOSIS

A psychiatrist, psychologist, primary care physician, or nurse with mental health training will usually make a diagnosis of OCD. Many health care professionals use a tool called a structured clinical interview, which contains standardized questions about the nature, severity, and duration of various symptoms. For OCD to be diagnosed, the obsessions and compulsions must demand from the person a minimum of one hour every day and must interfere with normal routines, occupational functioning, social activities, or relationships.

People with contamination obsessions and washing compulsions are sometimes mistaken for hypochondriacs. However, a hypochondriac fears that he or she is already ill and a person with cleanliness addiction fears that he or she may become contaminated (and later, ill). Furthermore, OCD should not be confused with obsessive-compulsive personality disorder (OCPD), which involves, in the case of a cleanliness addict, obsessive concern with cleanliness but a concern that does not cause distress; thus, OCPD is not considered an anxiety disorder.

Dermatologists are often alerted to a cleanliness addiction because of chapped skin or other skin problems that excessive washing can cause. In many cases, family members and friends will urge a cleanliness addict to get help when they see the obsession interfering with the addict's life and the lives of those around him or her.

TREATMENT

Recovery is a process, not a discrete event. There is no cure for this addiction, but cleanliness addiction can be managed. Cognitive-behavioral therapy and antidepressant medications are used to treat the disorder, usually in combination. Cognitive-behavioral therapy involves exposure with response prevention and cognitive therapy.

Exposure involves imagined or actual exposure to things (for example, touching a pet or taking off shoes) that triggers the obsessions and anxiety. Eventually, such exposure will cause little anxiety, if any. This process is called habituation. Response refers to the ritual behaviors that people with cleanliness addiction perform to reduce anxiety. Patients learn to resist the compulsive behaviors. Cognitive therapy focuses on how the person interprets the obsessions. A destructive belief will be objectively challenged and reinterpreted.

Some medication, such as selective serotonin reuptake inhibitors, can increase the levels of serotonin available to transmit messages in the brain, and they have been shown to alleviate the symptoms of 70 percent of persons with OCD. In cases extremely resistant to treatment, brain surgery may be considered.

PREVENTION

There is no known prevention for OCD. However, by adhering to therapy, it can be managed and relapse can be avoided.

Stephanie Eckenrode, BA, LLB

FURTHER READING

American Psychiatric Association. *Diagnostic and Statistical Manual of Mental Disorders.* 4ᵗʰ ed. Arlington, VA, 1994.

Grayson, Jonathan. *Freedom from Obsessive Compulsive Disorder: A Personalized Recovery Program.* New York: Penguin, 2004.

March, John S., and Karen Mulle. *OCD in Children and Adolescents: A Cognitive-Behavioral Treatment Manual.* New York: Guilford, 1998.

WEBSITES OF INTEREST

International OCD Foundation
http://www.ocfoundation.org

National Institute of Mental Health
http://www.nimh.nih.gov

OCDCenter.org
http://www.ocdcenter.org

See also: Addiction; Behavioral addictions: Overview; Obsessive-compulsive disorder (OCD)

Closing the Addiction Treatment Gap (CATG)

CATEGORY: Treatment

DEFINITION: Closing the Addiction Treatment Gap, or CATG, is a private, nonprofit initiative to expand access to quality substance abuse treatment and to increase knowledge about addiction as a disease state. Under CATG sponsorship, millions of dollars have been invested across the United States in the development of state-based and local substance abuse treatment as a stimulus for expansion of quality addiction care. CATG strives to increase awareness of the wide disparity between the number of people who abuse substances and the number who ultimately receive treatment for their addictions.

DATE: Established 2008

BACKGROUND

Alcohol and drug abuse problems lead to about 100,000 deaths each year and affect one in every ten persons in the United States. In 2010, an estimated 23 million people were addicted to an illicit substance. Although this number approaches that of people with diabetes, far fewer people who have an addiction receive treatment for their substance abuse disorders. Of the 23 million addicts reported in 2010, only about 3 million (or 10 percent) received treatment, a gap that remains steady each year.

Addiction is an undertreated condition in part because of the stigma associated with substance abuse and the common belief that addiction is a behavioral choice rather than a chronic, treatable disease. Substance abuse and addiction can develop in any person, regardless of age, gender, or ethnicity, and the impact of addictive behavior affects the addict and his or her family and friends, and also entire communities.

The addiction treatment gap affects low income populations most noticeably. Obstacles to care abound. Addicts are more likely to be on public, not private, health programs; to believe that addiction treatment is inaccessible or unaffordable; and to have little knowledge of the treatment systems or provider referral options available.

The benefits of addressing treatment for this population are numerous. The most emphatic benefit is financial: The costs required to provide substance abuse treatment are substantially lower than the costs of addiction care in emergency rooms, prisons, and chronic-disease management programs. Addiction care is not a burden on the health care system but rather a tactic of cost-effective preventive medicine.

MISSION AND GOALS

The CATG program was established in 2008 by the Open Society Institute, a private organization for global health and social initiatives. CATG is a one-time, three-year grant program that also offers literature and public outreach.

Efforts by CATG to close the treatment gap comprise three tenets: increasing insurance coverage for treatment, increasing public funding for treatment programs, and increasing access to programming by improving its quality and positive outreach. Addiction programs are expanding and their stigma is decreasing because of better health-care provider communication and better quality of professional education. However, community program efforts are still lacking; in 2007, two-thirds of addicts received care within the criminal justice system, and only 7 percent of all care involved physician-provided treatment.

The CATG program seeks to stimulate community- and medical-based efforts on multiple fronts by advocating support for local treatment programs in hospitals and public health settings. As a national advocacy group, CATG intends to begin reducing the treatment gap. However, it intends to do so without providing all the resources necessary to maintain expanded, quality care. Programs funded by or inspired by CATG are part of a long-term solution to provide a flow of public and private contributions into the effort. Closing the gap requires trusted partnerships to increase referrals to community treatment programs and to sustain addiction treatment quality to end the treatment disparity.

CATG acts as a grantor to business, community, public health, and health care centers at the state and local level. Eight sites within the United States have received grants to implement and model bridging strategies; each grant provided about $600,000 in three years to foster successful practices to minimize the treatment gap. Grants were awarded to programs in state government, teaching hospitals, university research centers, and advocacy groups.

Interim grantee achievements reached by 2010 embodied the positive effects of addiction treatment. Successful efforts have provided treatment for addiction as a covered item in basic insurance plans in the state of Wisconsin, added Medicaid programs in multiple states to cover addiction treatment for pregnant women and their children, increased the numbers of medication-assisted treatment programs, provided referrals to community treatment programs, and certified treatment centers to obtain Medicaid or insurance reimbursements. Documented benefits of these CATG programs include dramatically lower overall health care costs and reduced numbers of hospital visits.

CATG also has strengthened other actions that aim to close the addiction treatment gap. The newly founded American Society of Addiction Medicine encourages acceptance of chronic substance abuse as a treatable, lifelong disease and offers guidelines to health professionals about increasing availability and quality of addiction treatment. Nationally, the 2010 Patient Care and Affordability Act mandated health care coverage for every person, despite addiction treatment history. The act includes a provision to expand addiction services as a basic benefit for the care of chronic mental-health conditions.

Future directions to close the addiction treatment gap remain broad, as states develop programs founded on the initiative principles. Opportunities continue to involve new federal and state regulations, better definitions of treatment benefits, integrations of addiction care services into existing health care infrastructures, monitoring of community-based programs to maintain quality and certification, expanded coverage of community-based programs by public and private health insurance, and the reintegration of recovering addicts into all levels of society.

Nicole M. Van Hoey, PharmD

FURTHER READING

Lamb, Sara, Merwyn R. Greenlick, and Denis McCarty, eds. *Bridging the Gap Between Practice and Research: Forging Partnerships with Community-Based Drug and Alcohol Treatment.* Washington, DC: National Academies, 1998. Thorough guide on how to improve the availability of treatment options for substance abuse and to provide treatments that follow updated guidelines for those already receiving care.

Medina-Mora, M. E. "Can Science Help Close the Treatment Gap?" *Addiction* 105.1 (2010): 15–16. Print. Review of the difficulties faced by providers of addiction treatment to reach patients most in need.

O'Brien, A., R. Fahmy, and S. P. Singh. "Disengagement from Mental Health Services: A Literature Review." *Social Psychiatry and Psychiatric Epidemiology* 44.7 (2009): 558–68. Print. Accessible review that helps to determine why more people with substance abuse disorders do not obtain necessary and available services.

WEBSITES OF INTEREST

National Institute on Drug Abuse
http://www.drugabuse.gov/publications/topics-in-brief/nidas-blending-initiative-accelerating-research-based-treatments-practice

Open Society Institute
http://www.soros.org/initiatives/treatmentgap

Spotlight on Poverty and Opportunity
http://www.spotlightonpoverty.org

See also: Alcohol abuse and alcoholism: Treatment; Education about substance abuse; Insurance for addiction treatment; Rehabilitation programs

Club drugs

Category: Substance abuse
Also known as: Designer drugs, psychedelics
Definition: Club drug is a slang term for a wide variety of substances of abuse that generally are used in social situations, such as at clubs or dance parties. Common club drugs include ecstasy, GHB, ketamine, and methamphetamine. Club drugs often have hallucinogenic properties, and may have either excitatory or sedative effects.

CAUSES AND SYMPTOMS

Club drugs are often less expensive and more accessible than other controlled substances, making them particularly attractive to young people who want to experiment with drugs at a rave, dance party, or bar with friends. This desire, combined with a false belief that club drugs are safer than other drugs, can lead people to try drugs and sometimes begin using them regularly. Club drugs are often first used at dance clubs or with friends. The belief that such drugs are natural analogs of prescription drugs or are not illegal fuels a misconception of their safety. Because the drugs are psychedelic, reactions of individual users will vary significantly depending on the user's emotional state, concurrent use of other substances, underlying psychiatric conditions, personality, and past experience with the drugs. Additionally, because these substances are street drugs, their contents are usually subject to some variability, such as being mixed with less expensive drugs, and their quality may vary substantially.

Club drugs go by many different names. They include substances such as gamma-hydroxybutyrate (GHB, Georgia home boy, liquid X), ketamine hydrochloride (ketamine, special K), lysergic acid diethylamid (LSD, acid, blotter), methylenedioxymethamphetamine (MDMA, Adam, ecstasy, X), and Rohypnol (roofies, roach, roche). They also include herbal ecstasy (herbal X, cloud nine, herbal bliss), which is a drug made from ephedrine or pseudoephedrine and caffeine. The effects of club drugs vary, but as a group they cause a number of positive reactions, including euphoria, feelings of well-being, emotional clarity, a decreased sense of personal boundaries, and feelings of empathy and closeness to others. However, they can also cause significant negative reactions, including panic, impaired judgment, amnesia, impaired motor control, insomnia, paranoia, irrational behavior, flashbacks, hallucinations, rapid heartbeat, high blood pressure, chills, sweating, tremors, respiratory distress, convulsions, and violence. It is not uncommon for individuals to mix these drugs with alcohol, prescription drugs, or other illegal drugs. When drugs are taken in combination, the drugs can interact and cause dangerous and unexpected reactions.

TREATMENT AND THERAPY

The effects of club drugs vary by substance and the treatment for drug abuse varies by substance as well. In general, club drugs tend to be seen more in emergency care settings than in primary health care settings. This is because some of the problems that they cause are often critical and require emergency care. For instance, overdose, strokes, allergic shock reactions, blackouts, loss of consciousness, and accidents related to these conditions may require emergency care. Similarly, dehydration and heat exhaustion can result from prolonged periods of dancing or other physical exertion, as can occur in rave situations. Date rapes have been known to occur with these drugs, particularly Rohypnol, and injuries due to sexual assault may also require emergency care.

A person holding ecstasy tablets. (Paul Faith/PA Photos/Landov)

The long-term impact of problems, such as those described above, may require psychotherapy. In addition, problems related to the abuse of or dependence upon club drugs will be addressed in much the same manner as for other substances of abuse. General addiction treatment is advised.

PERSPECTIVE AND PROSPECTS

The dangers of club drugs underscore the continuing need for social awareness of these substances that may otherwise seem harmless. Just because a substance is not listed as an illegal drug does not mean that it cannot be dangerous. Any drug, whether sold over the counter, by prescription, or in any other way, can be misused and be dangerous or even fatal to the user.

While the experimental use of psychedelic substances for psychotherapeutic work may prove beneficial to certain groups of patients, such work is balanced by investigations into neurology, physiology, psychopharmacology, and psychology, which emphasize that the proposed benefits do not outweigh the risks. Continued exploration of the neuronal, developmental, social, and other health effects of using club drugs is necessary as they pose a significant danger to public health, particularly to younger populations.

Nancy A. Piotrowski, PhD

FURTHER READING

Holland, Julie, ed. *Ecstasy: The Complete Guide—A Comprehensive Look at the Risks and Benefits of MDMA.* Rochester, VT: Inner Traditions International, 2001. Discusses the therapeutic potential of ecstasy, its social implications, and its dangers if used unsupervised.

Jansen, Karl. *Ketamine: Dreams and Realities.* Ben Lomond, CA: Multidisciplinary Association for Psychedelic Studies, 2004. A comprehensive overview of ketamine, including its recreational use, use in psychotherapy, the psychedelic experiences it induces, and its benefits and dangers. Includes a treatment plan for ketamine addicts.

Kuhn, Cynthia, Scott Swartzwelder, and Wilkie Wilson. *Buzzed: The Straight Facts About the Most Used and Abused Drugs from Alcohol to Ecstasy.* 3rd ed. New York: W. W. Norton, 2008. Objective summaries and analyses of the most commonly used and abused drugs. Includes the short- and long-term effects of these drugs, how they affect the brain, the "highs" they produce, and when they could be deadly.

O'Neill, John, and Pat O'Neill. *Concerned Intervention: When Your Loved One Won't Quit Alcohol or Drugs.* Oakland, CA: New Harbinger, 1992. A guide to group intervention, based on the authors' experience with families seeking counseling and treatment.

Stafford, Peter. *Psychedelics.* Berkeley, CA: Ronin, 2003. Provides a framework for understanding the information available on psychoactive substances. Covers the origins, varieties, mental and physical effects, and benefits and dangers of psychedelics, particularly LSD.

WEBSITES OF INTEREST

American Council for Drug Education
http://www.acde.org/

National Institute on Drug Abuse
http://www.nida.nih.gov/

See also: Designer drugs; Ketamine; LSD; MDMA; Rohypnol; Teens/young adults and drug abuse

Cocaine Anonymous

CATEGORY: Treatment

DEFINITION: Cocaine Anonymous (CA) is a nonprofit recovery program that was developed for men and women addicted to crack cocaine or any other mind-altering substance, including alcohol. CA aims to provide a community for discussion and bonding in support of the goals of abstinence and longstanding addiction recovery.

DATE: Established 1982

BACKGROUND

Cocaine Anonymous (CA) was established in Los Angeles in November of 1982 by a member of Alcoholics Anonymous (AA). From the charter region, or service area, CA has since spread across the United States into Canada and throughout many European countries. By 1996, two thousand service groups with thirty thousand members existed worldwide.

CA World Services, or CAWS, has become the over-arching global board that provides services and oversees individual service areas, both physical and virtual. CA has a defined online presence that began with the first CA website in 1995. CA Online (CAO) meetings were established in 1997 and were expanded in 1999, receiving full service-area status by CAWS in 2000. In 2010, audio Internet discussion meetings were initiated too, making six online meeting groups available for members worldwide.

CA was formed on the basis of principles from AA (which was established in 1935) for coping with the abuse of cocaine and other illicit substances. The inclusion of all types of substances is validated in part because people addicted to cocaine and other abusive drugs of choice face similar addiction and recovery challenges; in addition, addicts often interchange substances or replace cocaine with new drugs during their struggles for abstinence. CA relies on the group lessons of shared recovery experiences and mutual understanding among longtime and new participants within the community.

The CA program, like AA, models a twelve-step recovery. During the recovery process, group participants progress through steps of acknowledgement, forgiveness, and resolve. The addict begins abstinence by letting go of his or her sense of fault for the addition, continues by asking and accepting forgiveness for past actions, and ultimately identifies a greater spiritual authority.

CA tenets also include twelve traditions, which provide a moral code of themes based on faith, forgiveness, and autonomy to supplement the twelve-step process. The traditions are directives for the individual members and for the larger group, including the CAWS board.

Although initial recovery relies on the CA steps and traditions, CA participation does not end when the twelfth step is completed. Instead, the social network of a person's local recovery group continues to provide positive reinforcement to sustain recovery after the twelve-step process and after any other treatment programs have ended. Leadership roles or simple comfort zones exist in the physical and virtual settings without a time line or defined conclusion; recovery from substance abuse addiction is lifelong, and so too is CA support.

CA meetings are separated by regional service areas, and each regularly scheduled group is identified as a service unit. Each unit is independently supported by contributions from its members and is not affiliated with business or political organizations. Although the meetings follow a traditional format outlined by AA and by CAWS, each unit is autonomous in its decision making and particular needs. Service units are available in rural, suburban, and urban areas; numerous district sites also are often available within a major city. Home groups are the unit meetings at which the addict should feel most comfortable, uninhibited, and open to participation.

To be fully participatory, a member should attend one meeting each day for the first month as an immersive recovery experience. In addition, participants are encouraged to identify a member who has already completed the twelve-step recovery process; sponsorship by a member with a minimum of a one-year history of sobriety in the service unit can guide the new member on his or her own recovery path and promote abstinence on an individual level. In addition, a sponsor can build a close relationship with the new member and can provide deeper guidance and more thorough discussions than the group meetings permit.

MISSION AND GOALS

The primary goal of CA is to provide a local, accessible, and comfortable community for substance abuse addicts to start and maintain their addiction-free lives. One mission of the CA unit for each member through the recovery period is to encourage self-supporting discipline, community involvement, and re-entry into active society after suffering from the disease of substance abuse. CA supports a goal of freedom from addiction as one of its traditions; related tenets focus on God, spirituality, and personal inventory to further support the CA mission of addiction-free living.

To bolster each unit's goal of unity through community outreach, CAWS publishes "Newsgram" each quarter; it is available in print and digital versions. A newsletter subscription can be purchased by members or any website visitors; single copies also can be obtained at service units. Similarly, CAWS released a two-volume series that presents the CA principles through literature and fellowship stories. The first volume, *Hope, Faith, and Courage*, was followed by a second volume of the same title about recovery experiences.

The Hope, Faith, Courage motto is now part of the organization's logo and summarizes the qualities that each member learns to depend on to sustain an addiction-free goal.

Nicole M. Van Hoey, PharmD

FURTHER READING

Cocaine Anonymous World Services. *Hope, Faith, and Courage.* 2 vols. Los Angeles: CAWS, 1993, 2007. Relates the shared experiences of CA members during their recovery to encourage and inspire current recovering members or other readers, such as family and friends.

Kampman, K. M. "What's New to Treat Cocaine Addiction?" *Current Psychiatric Report* 12.5 (2010): 441–47. Print. Discusses medical and behavioral treatment options, which can be administered before or during a twelve-step program, for people addicted to cocaine.

National Institute on Drug Abuse. *Principles of Drug Addiction Treatment: A Research-Based Guide.* 2nd ed. National Institutes of Health Publication No. 09-4180. Bethesda, MD: NIDA, 2009. An evidence-based guide to treating addiction and recovery.

---. *Seeking Drug Abuse Treatment: Know What to Ask.* National Institutes of Health Publication No. 12–7764. Bethesda, MD: NIDA, 2011. Provides the top five questions a person seeking substance abuse treatment for self or another should consider when evaluating treatment options. Considers twelve-step programs as crucial to treatment and recovery success.

WEBSITES OF INTEREST

Cocaine Anonymous
http://www.ca.org

Cocaine Anonymous Online
http://www.ca-online.org

National Institute on Drug Abuse
http://www.drugabuse.gov/publications/infofacts/cocaine

See also: Abstinence-based treatment; Cocaine use disorder; Group therapy for substance abuse; Outpatient treatment; Sponsors; Support groups; Twelve-step programs for addicts

Cocaine use disorder

CATEGORY: Substance abuse

ALSO KNOWN AS: Cocaine abuse; cocaine addiction; cocaine dependency

DEFINITION: The diagnosis of cocaine use disorder is applied when the repeated use of cocaine harms a person's health or social functioning, or when a person becomes physically dependent on cocaine. The powdered form of cocaine can be snorted or dissolved in water and injected, while crack, which is cocaine in a rock crystal form, can be heated and its vapors smoked. Cocaine use disorder is treatable, but recovery is often difficult and may require professional care.

CAUSES

Cocaine is a powerful central nervous system stimulant that causes the brain to release large amounts of the hormone dopamine. Dopamine, a neurotransmitter associated with feelings of pleasure, floods the brain's reward pathways and results in the euphoria commonly reported by cocaine users. As a person continues to use cocaine, a tolerance is developed. This means that more frequent use and higher doses are required to achieve the same feeling of euphoria. Repeated use of cocaine can result in long-term disruptions to the brain's dopamine levels and reward circuitry.

When a cocaine user stops using abruptly, he or she experiences a crash or withdrawal. This results in an extremely strong craving for more cocaine. It also results in fatigue, loss of pleasure in life, depression, anxiety, irritability, and paranoia. These withdrawal symptoms often prompt the user to seek more cocaine.

RISK FACTORS

Being male and between the ages of eighteen and twenty-five years are considered factors that increase one's chances of developing cocaine use disorder.

SYMPTOMS

The short-term effects associated with cocaine use include euphoria, increased energy, mental alertness, decreased need for food and sleep, dilated pupils, increased temperature, increased heart rate, increased blood pressure, erratic or violent behavior, vertigo,

---

Cocaine

Cocaine is a central nervous system stimulant that acts by blocking the reuptake of neurotransmitters such as norepinephrine and dopamine in the brain. Symptoms of cocaine use include agitation; euphoria; sweating; chills; nausea; vomiting; talkativeness; increased sensitivity to sight, sound, and touch; and increased heart rate. High doses or prolonged use of cocaine can cause paranoia. Cocaine also is a cardiac stimulant, and cocaine-related deaths are usually the result of cardiac arrest or seizures that are followed by respiratory arrest.

Cocaine's easy availability and strong addictive potential make it a popular drug of abuse. Additionally, cocaine is rapidly absorbed by and eliminated from the body, leading to a short duration of effects; this prompts cocaine abusers to rapidly repeat doses of cocaine until their supply is exhausted. Cocaine abuse is prevalent across all gender, demographic, and socioeconomic lines.

---

muscle twitches, paranoia, restlessness, irritability, and anxiety. A cocaine overdose can result in a dangerous elevation of blood pressure, leading to stroke, heart failure, or even sudden death

The long-term effects include uncontrollable or unpredictable cravings; increased tolerance; increased dosing; increasing irritability, restlessness, and paranoia; paranoid psychosis; and auditory hallucinations.

Medical complications that may result from cocaine use disorder include heart rhythm abnormalities, heart attack, chest pain, respiratory failure, stroke, seizure, headache, abdominal pain, and nausea.

SCREENING AND DIAGNOSIS

A doctor who suspects cocaine use disorder will ask the patient about symptoms and medical history. He or she will also perform a physical examination. The doctor will ask specific questions about the cocaine use, such as how long the patient has been using the drug and how often.

TREATMENT AND THERAPY

A medical professional should be consulted to develop the best treatment plan for an individual suffering from cocaine use disorder. Treatment programs may be inpatient or outpatient. Treatment programs may require that the patient has already stopped using cocaine prior to treatment or they may involve a supervised detoxification program.

Medications can be used to help manage the symptoms of withdrawal, but there are currently no medications that specifically treat cocaine use disorder. Medications that have shown some promise include modafinil (Provigil), N-acetylcysteine, topiramate (Topamax), disulfiram, agonist replacement therapy, and baclofen. Antidepressants may also be helpful for people in the early stages of cocaine abstinence.

Behavioral therapies to help people quit using cocaine are often the only effective treatment for cocaine use disorder. These therapies use contingency management. With this program, people receive positive rewards for staying in treatment and remaining cocaine-free. Additionally, cognitive-behavioral therapy helps people to learn the skills needed to manage stress and prevent relapse.

Recovery programs such as Cocaine Anonymous provide community support for people seeking to recover from cocaine addiction. In rehabilitation programs, people with cocaine use disorder stay in a controlled environment for six to twelve months. During this time, they may receive vocational rehabilitation and other support to prepare them to return to society.

PREVENTION

The best way to prevent cocaine use disorder is to never use cocaine because the drug is highly addictive. Also, education programs on the dangers of cocaine use have helped to lower rates of cocaine use in the United States since the 1990s.

Krisha McCoy, MS
Theodor B. Rais, MD

FURTHER READING

DuPont, Robert L. *The Selfish Brain: Learning from Addiction.* Center City, MN.: Hazelton, 2000. Discusses the commonalities across different types of addiction in an easy-to-understand manner.

Julien, Robert M., Claire D. Advokat, and Joseph Comaty. *A Primer of Drug Action: A Comprehensive Guide to the Actions, Uses, and Side Effects of Psychoactive Drugs.* 12th ed. New York: Worth, 2010. A nontechnical guide to drugs, written by a medical professional. Describes the different classes of drugs, their actions in the body, their uses,

and their side effects. Basic pharmacologic principles, classifications, and terms are defined and discussed.

Sussman, Steven, and Susan L. Ames. *Drug Abuse: Concepts, Prevention, and Cessation.* New York: Cambridge UP, 2008. A comprehensive overview of issues and concerns related to preventing problems related to drug use; focuses especially on teenagers.

Weil, Andrew, and Winifred Rosen. *From Chocolate to Morphine: Everything You Need to Know About Mind-Altering Drugs.* Rev. ed. Boston: Houghton Mifflin, 2004. Provides basic information about psychoactive substances to the general reader. Psychoactive substances are identified and defined. Also outlines the relationships between different types of drugs, the motivations to use drugs, and associated problems.

WEBSITES OF INTEREST

Cocaine Anonymous
http://www.ca.org

Cocaine Anonymous (Canada)
http://www.ca-on.org

National Institute on Drug Abuse
http://www.nida.nih.gov

Native Alcohol and Drug Abuse Counseling Association of Nova Scotia
http://nadaca.ca

See also: Cocaine Anonymous; Crack; Dopamine and addiction; Withdrawal

Codeine

CATEGORY: Substances
ALSO KNOWN AS: Methylmorphine; morphine methylester; 3-methylmorphine
DEFINITION: Codeine is a drug used primarily as an analgesic, but it also is used in antidiarrheal and antitussive medications.
STATUS: Legal by prescription in the United States; legal outside the United States without a prescrip-

tion if combined with other drugs in relatively small dosages

CLASSIFICATION: Controlled substance: schedule I (derivatives of codeine), II (codeine alone), III (with other analgesics), or V (in cough preparations with other drugs)

SOURCE: Milky fluid of immature seed capsules of the opium poppy plant (*Papaver somniferum*); also synthesized from morphine

TRANSMISSION ROUTE: Oral, intramuscular, subcutaneous, and intravenous

HISTORY OF USE

Codeine was isolated from opium by French chemist Pierre-Jean Robiquet in 1832 and was used in the nineteenth century for pain relief and diabetes control. Near the end of the nineteenth century, codeine was used to replace morphine, another substance found in the opium poppy, because of the highly addictive properties of morphine. Codeine has effects similar to, albeit weaker than, morphine and was not thought to be addictive. Codeine was subsequently used in treatment for morphine withdrawal.

The first detailed report of codeine addiction is thought to be from 1905, and reports by others followed. In the 1930s, concern over the widespread abuse of codeine in Canada was noted. Codeine abuse in the United States was evaluated more fully in the 1960s, leading to inclusion of codeine as a schedule II controlled substance. Schedule II drugs have a high potential for abuse.

Subsequently, among substance abusers, prescription cough syrups containing codeine began to be mixed with soft drinks and candy (in a combination known as lean syrup, sizzurp, or purple drank). The combination remains a substance of concern.

EFFECTS AND POTENTIAL RISKS

Codeine primarily exerts its medicinal effects by being metabolized by liver enzymes to substances that bind to specific receptors in the central and peripheral nervous systems. One of the most potent of these substances is morphine. The codeine metabolites can effectively block the transmission of pain signals to the brain and can inhibit the cough reflex. The metabolites also contribute to the usefulness of codeine in treating diarrhea by affecting, among other things, the contraction of gastrointestinal tract muscles.

Short-term use of codeine provides pain relief and euphoric effects. Some of the more common side effects of codeine ingestion include itching, constipation, dizziness, sedation, flushing, sweating, nausea, vomiting, and hives.

Long-term use of codeine can lead to drug tolerance, necessitating higher doses to achieve the same euphoric effect. Endorphin (natural painkiller) production may be slowed or stopped, causing increased sensitivity to pain if codeine is not used. More serious side effects include respiratory depression, central nervous system depression, seizures, and cardiac arrest.

Jason J. Schwartz, PhD

FURTHER READING

Manchikanti, Laxmaiah, et al. "Therapeutic Use, Abuse, and Nonmedical Use of Opioids: A Ten-Year Perspective." *Pain Physician* 13 (2010): 401–35. Print.

Parker, James N., and Philip M. Parkers, eds. *Codeine: A Medical Dictionary, Bibliography, and Annotated Research Guide to Internet References.* San Diego: Icon, 2003.

Parker, Philip M., ed. *Codeine: Webster's Timeline History, 1888-2007.* San Diego: Icon, 2010.

WEBSITES OF INTEREST

National Institute on Drug Abuse
http://drugabuse.gov/drugpages

Office of National Drug Control Policy
http://www.whitehouse.gov/ondcp/
   prescription-drug-abuse

See also: Controlled substances and precursor chemicals; Painkiller abuse; Prescription drug addiction: Overview

Codependency

CATEGORY: Psychological issues and behaviors
ALSO KNOWN AS: Relationship addiction
DEFINITION: No single definition exists for codependency, but available definitions describe a pattern of unhealthy learned behaviors that generally re-

sult from a psychologically unhealthy family situation. Codependents are often focused on others, rather than themselves, and are unable to communicate or take action in a healthy, productive way about their situation, the relationship, or themselves.

CAUSES

Common causes of codependency include being a child of a drug or alcohol abuser or coming from a home that is dysfunctional in other ways.

RISK FACTORS

Persons who were exposed to a dysfunctional family situation as a child are at risk for developing codependency. This risk is attributed to the difficult realities and premature responsibilities that made it challenging for the child to cope. This risk also is attributed to the lack of role models to demonstrate the appropriate management of emotions and behavior.

SYMPTOMS

There is no universally accepted list of symptoms of codependency; symptoms can vary from person to person and are described differently by different sources. A key characteristic of many codependent persons is caretaking, or feeling responsible for other people and feeling excessively compelled to help other people solve their problems. This can result in overcommitment and a feeling of being constantly under pressure.

Even though codependent persons will take on excessive responsibilities, they also often blame others for their own negative feelings and for their situation. Conversely, some participants in codependent relationships may become extremely irresponsible.

Codependent persons often have feelings of low self-worth, will generally blame themselves for many situations, and will have trouble receiving compliments or praise. Low self-worth is often associated with feelings of guilt as well.

Codependent persons can engage in denial, or "pretending" that uncomfortable situations or feelings are not happening. They also can seem to be rigid and controlled; this can be a result of not wanting to deal with uncomfortable emotions, such as fear and guilt.

It is not uncommon for codependent persons to obsess about specific people or problems and to perceive themselves as unable to get things done or have

---

Enabling

Enabling describes any behaviors by family members, partners, therapists, coworkers, or friends of addicts that allow the addicted person to continue engaging in substance abuse or other self-destructive behavior without facing negative consequences. Enabling is one of the hallmarks of codependency.

A person often begins engaging in enabling behavior because he or she cares about the addict and wants to be helpful and kind. However, enabling actually allows the addict to increase the severity of his or her substance abuse or other self-destructive behavior. Without negative consequences, the addict can continue engaging in denial that he or she has a problem.

Additionally, the addict's tolerance for the drug of choice increases, requiring more of the drug of choice to achieve the same physical and psychological effects. As the addict uses increasingly more of the drug of choice, members of his or her family system engage in more frequent, more severe, and more consequential forms of enabling. Thus, the family system or social system that includes the addict engages in a negative cycle of enabling and addictive behavior.

---

a "normal" life because of these people or problems. They also tend to feel unable to be comfortable or happy with themselves and, as a result, seek happiness from external sources. They often worry that they will be left alone or abandoned and may tolerate abuse in relationships because of this fear. A term often used in association with codependence is *poor boundaries*, meaning that people who are codependent may allow others to treat them inappropriately or to hurt them.

Codependent persons often feel unable to trust themselves or others. They have not learned effective ways to communicate and may use such manipulative strategies as blaming and begging to get what they want from others. They often are uncomfortable with angry emotions.

Codependent persons often are described as engaging in "enabling" behavior, meaning that they enable the person with whom they are in an unhealthy relationship to continue behaviors that are harmful for both of them. For example, an enabler might continue to "cover" for an alcoholic who frequently engages in binge drinking. In such as case, the codependent person might contact the person's place of employment to call in sick for that person or to otherwise lie to help him or her avoid the consequences of the behavior.

People who struggle with codependency for a long period of time may feel withdrawn and depressed and may even consider suicide. They also may become addicted to alcohol, drugs, or other harmful behaviors, such as compulsive or binge eating.

Authors on codependency have identified several ways to broadly categorize patterns that are typical of the condition. For example, the three dimensions of the personality of an addict, as identified by C. Robert Cloniger, are described as novelty seeking, harm-avoidance, and reward-dependence. Codependent persons may gravitate toward either extreme of these dimensions.

In the case of novelty seeking, codependent persons can be high novelty-seeking, exhibiting impulsive behaviors, or low novelty-seeking, with a rigid style of coping. In the reward-dependence dimension, codependent persons can be either eager to help others or appear socially detached and self-willed. In the harm-avoidance dimension, codependent persons can be either excessively pessimistic or anxious, or they can be overconfident and eager to take risks.

Codependent behaviors also have been explained, originally by Sharon Wegscheider-Cruse, in terms of "survival roles" in the family or relationship that arise from a dysfunctional environment. Survival roles include the "family hero," who takes on tremendous responsibilities; the "family scapegoat," who accepts blame; the "lost child," who remains removed from most people; and the "mascot," who attracts attention by acting inappropriately.

SCREENING AND DIAGNOSIS

The diagnosis of codependency is not listed in the *Diagnostic and Statistical Manual of Mental Disorders,* which is used by psychiatrists and other mental health professionals as a diagnostic guide.. However, several personality disorders in the manual contain elements recognized by authors on codependency as being part of the condition.

Many who write about codependency encourage the codependent person to examine his or her own behaviors to determine if he or she is codependent. Self-help groups, including Co-Dependents Anonymous (CoDA) and Nar-Anon, provide checklist-style guidelines for identifying patterns of thought and behavior that indicate codependency. For example, the CoDA patterns of codependency list includes thoughts and behaviors indicative of patterns of denial, low self-esteem, compliance, and control. Nar-Anon lists twelve common characteristics of codependency. Many mental health care professionals, particularly those who work in the area of substance abuse and addiction, are familiar with the characteristics of codependency and can help persons identify dysfunctional patterns and behaviors.

TREATMENT AND THERAPY

Mental health professionals can work with codependent persons in individual or group therapy sessions with the goal of modifying dysfunctional patterns and adopting healthy coping skills. Although much of the focus of treatment for codependency tends to be on the caretaker, it is important to note that the addict or substance abuser in the relationship is also considered to be codependent.

Experts thus suggest that the problems of abuse and addiction cannot be fully resolved if the codependency is ignored. Programs designed to address addiction often involve education for the patient and family on codependency.

Self-help programs including CoDA and Nar Anon provide support and instruction to aid the person in monitoring and modifying his or her own behaviors based on the same twelve-step model that is often employed by substance abusers and addicts in programs such as Alcoholics Anonymous and Narcotic Anonymous.

The twelve steps identified by CoDA begin with "We admitted that we are powerless over others—that our lives had become unmanageable" and progress to a final step of carrying the messages learned through the twelve steps to other codependent persons. CoDA also provides examples of patterns of recovery that can, over time, replace patterns of codependency that most likely developed over many years.

PREVENTION

Literature regarding the prevention of codependency is limited. However, it has been suggested that codependency might be prevented or mitigated by the early employment of healthy coping strategies to deal with dysfunctional behaviors such as drug or alcohol abuse.

Katherine Hauswirth, RN, MSN

FURTHER READING

Beattie, Melody. *Codependent No More*. San Francisco: HarperCollins, 1987. This internationally best-selling book describes codependency in easy-to-understand language with the aid of many examples from real life.

Co-Dependents Anonymous. "Patterns and Characteristics of Codependence." 2010. Web. 16 Apr. 2012. http://www.coda.org/tools4recovery/patterns-new.htm. Lists common characteristics of codependency in a checklist-style format.

---. "The Twelve Steps of Co-Dependents Anonymous." 2010. Web. 16 Apr. 2012. http://www.coda.org/tools4recovery/twelve-steps.htm. Lists the twelve steps subscribed to by CoDA members.

Cruse, Joseph R. *Painful Affairs: Looking for Love through Addiction and Co-dependency*. Deerfield Beach, FL: Health Communications, 1989. A physician describes the similarities between chemical dependency and codependency and provides insights into dysfunctional patterns of behavior.

WEBSITES OF INTEREST

Co-Dependents Anonymous
http://www.coda.org

Mental Health America
http://www.mentalhealthamerica.net/go/codependency

See also: Families and substance abuse; Psychological dependence

Coffee

CATEGORY: Substances
DEFINITION: Coffee is a commonly consumed beverage and one of the most common sources of the stimulant caffeine.
STATUS: Legal in the United States and worldwide
CLASSIFICATION: Stimulant
SOURCE: Coffee bean
TRANSMISSION ROUTE: Coffee is consumed through oral ingestion.

HISTORY OF USE

Coffee has been consumed for centuries and has played a critical role in many societies. The coffee bean originally came from a berry of an Ethiopian shrub. Coffee drinking was believed to have started in Sufi monasteries in Yemen in southern Arabia during the fifteenth century. Coffee's ability to deter sleep made it popular among Sufi monks, who used it to keep themselves alert during nighttime devotions. Coffee was initially banned for secular consumption and also for its stimulating effects, but bans were eventually overturned because of coffee's popularity.

Coffee drinking first spread through the Middle East, then to Europe, Indonesia, and the Americas. Coffeehouses, or their equivalents, became popular first in the Middle East, then in Europe and later in the United States. In the 1950s, the idea of a coffee break was popularized. Specialty coffeehouses arose during the 1970s.

Coffee is the most commonly consumed mood-altering substance worldwide and is the leading source of caffeine in the United States. More than 80 percent of the adults in the United States consume behaviorally active doses on a daily basis. Until recently, coffee was rarely considered an addictive stimulant.

EFFECTS AND POTENTIAL RISKS

Although once thought harmless, coffee consumption, according to numerous studies, can have adverse effects. Physiological effects begin within ten to twenty minutes of consumption, with maximum effects coming within thirty to sixty minutes. Effects substantially diminish after about three hours. Coffee, through the effects of caffeine, has been shown to alter mood, stamina, and heart rate, and it can lead to gastric disturbances, such as heartburn. Caffeine increases heartbeat, respiration, metabolic rate, and stomach acid and can result in tension, irritability, and insomnia.

Risks associated with coffee overconsumption include liver, heart, and pancreatic problems. Coffee drinking also is associated with infertility, birth defects and disorders, sudden infant death syndrome, and the development of fibrocystic breasts.

The typical caffeine in a cup of coffee, approximately 155 milligrams, is enough to produce measurable metabolic effects. Caffeine affects the body

A boy picks ripe coffee beans at a coffee plantation in Nicaragua. Coffee is one of the most common sources of caffeine. (Oswaldo Rivas/Reuters/Landov)

similarly regardless of a person's body size or age, but effects are much more pronounced in children than in adults.

C. J. Walsh, PhD

FURTHER READING

Cherniske, Stephen. *Coffee Blues: Wake up to the Hidden Dangers of America's #1 Drug.* New York: Warner, 1998.

Hanson, Dirk. *The Chemical Carousel: What Science Tells Us about Beating Addiction.* Charleston, SC: Book-Surge, 2008.

Pendergrast, Mark. *Uncommon Grounds: The History of Coffee and How It Transformed Our World.* New York: Basic, 2010.

WEBSITES OF INTEREST

Caffeine Awareness Association
http://www.caffeineawareness.org

National Institute on Drug Abuse
http://www.nida.nih.gov

See also: Caffeine addiction; Caffeine: Short- and long-term effects on the body; Physiological dependence; Stimulants: Short- and long-term effects on the body

Cognitive-behavioral therapy

CATEGORY: Treatment

ALSO KNOWN AS: Relapse-prevention coping skills

DEFINITION: Cognitive-behavioral therapy is a form of psychotherapy in which a person works with a therapist to identify and challenge misperceptions or negative thoughts and their associated undesirable behaviors. The term *cognitive-behavioral therapy* applies not to one specific type of therapy but rather to a group of therapy types that share a similar approach. These therapy types include rational-emotive behavior therapy, rational behavior therapy, rational living therapy, cognitive therapy, and dialectical behavior therapy.

HISTORY AND DEVELOPMENT

Early work by researchers including Ivan Pavlov, John B. Watson, and B. F. Skinner was based on classical behavioral theory, which states that learning is based on interactions with the environment and that behaviors form from exposure to stimuli in the environment. In the 1960s theorist Aaron T. Beck emphasized the impact of each person's thoughts and emotions on behavior, referring to therapy that addressed both thoughts and behaviors as cognitive-behavioral therapy (CBT).

GENERAL USES

CBT has been used widely in the field of psychiatry for disorders including those of mood, thought, personality, and addiction. CBT can occur in either a one-to-one therapist-patient setting or in a group therapy setting.

In the area of addictions and substance abuse, research by G. Alan Marlatt and J. R. Gordon published in the 1980s incorporated CBT concepts into a specific strategy for preventing relapse of negative addictive behaviors. Experts note that CBT may be one of the most studied treatments for addiction, and research has confirmed that this approach has a generally modest but positive effect in persons who have abuse or addiction diagnoses.

The use of CBT with either medication or other psychosocial approaches may provide an added benefit in some cases as compared with CBT alone. While CBT differs in many ways from popular twelve-step programs, such as Alcoholics Anonymous and Narcotics Anonymous, that are often used by people struggling with addictive behaviors, both CBT and twelve-step approaches encourage participants to pursue activities that are incompatible with the addictive behavior and to find ways to combat negative thinking.

Persons who participate in CBT to cope with an addiction or abuse problem work with the therapist to understand patterns in which they repeatedly engage and which promotes ongoing substance abuse and addiction. Persons in therapy learn to identify factors that can trigger relapse of abusive or addictive behaviors and learn how to successfully refuse the substance or behavior of abuse.

CBT participants explore the consequences of continued substance abuse behaviors. Scrutiny of even seemingly small decisions that may affect thoughts, emotions, or behavior, as in the case of an alcoholic who may pass a favorite bar on the way to or from work, is strongly encouraged. CBT emphasizes the successful use of coping skills and the adoption of new activities that are completely unrelated to the abusive behavior.

An important aspect of CBT is identifying thoughts that support continued substance abuse or other addictive behaviors (often referred to as cognitive distortions) and learning to replace these thoughts with more beneficial ones. This process is called reframing. Patients engage in role play or rehearsal that is intended to help them cope with cravings for the addictive substance or behavior, or with high-risk situations, such as being invited to an occasion at which the substance of abuse will be available. Patients are often assigned homework, during which they can practice new thought patterns or skills learned during therapy sessions. Treatment goals are usually well-defined in CBT, and sessions are structured and brief in duration, often limited to twelve to twenty-four weeks.

LIMITATIONS

While experts have identified many benefits associated with CBT, one potential disadvantage of this approach is the need for specialized and fairly complex training of therapists so that they can use CBT techniques effectively with patients. CBT may have limited usefulness in patients who have higher levels of cognitive impairment or in those who are not prepared to undertake the work that is required for learning new thoughts and behaviors.

Katherine Hauswirth, RN, MSN

FURTHER READING

Ball, Samuel A. "Psychotherapy Models for Substance Abuse." *Psychiatric Times* 20 (2003): 171. Print.

Carroll, Kathleen M. "Cognitive-Behavioral Therapies." *The American Psychiatric Publishing Textbook of Substance Abuse Treatment.* Ed. Marc Galanter and Herbert D. Kleber. 4th ed. 2011. Web. 16 Apr. 2011. http://www.psychiatryonline.com/resourceToc. aspx?resourceID=33.

Larimer, Mary E., Rebekka S. Palmer, and G. Alan Marlatt. "Relapse Prevention: An Overview of Marlatt's Cognitive-Behavioral Model." *Alcohol Research and Health* 23 (1999): 151–60. Print.

Magill, Molly, and Lara A. Ray. "Cognitive-Behavioral Treatment with Adult Alcohol and Illicit Drug

Users: A Meta-Analysis of Randomized Controlled Trials." *Journal of Studies on Alcohol and Drugs* 70 (1999): 516–27. Print.

National Association of Cognitive-Behavioral Therapists. "What Is Cognitive-Behavioral Therapy?" Web. 16 Apr. 2012. http://www.nacbt.org/whatiscbt.htm.

WEBSITES OF INTEREST

Association for Behavioral and Cognitive Therapies
http://www.abct.org

Beck Institute for Cognitive Behavior Therapy
http://www.beckinstitute.org

National Association of Cognitive-Behavioral Therapists
http://www.nacbt.org

See also: Addiction medicine; Alcohol abuse and alcoholism: Treatment; Behavioral addictions: Treatment; Behavioral therapies for addiction; Treatment methods and research

---

College and substance abuse

CATEGORY: Social issues

DEFINITION: Alcohol is the substance most abused by college students. Some studies suggest that up to 80 percent of the student population uses alcohol and that about thirty-three percent uses various other drugs. College students have a higher rate of alcohol and drug abuse and addiction than does the general population, and white students abuse substances in greater numbers than do students of color.

BACKGROUND

Young adults who leave home to live at a college or university are presented with many new experiences and with first-time exposure to major decision-making. One of the biggest challenges and decisions for the traditionally aged college student (typically defined as those age seventeen to twenty-five years) is how to deal with the college subculture that involves alcohol and drugs. Parties, Greek organizations, and bars and dance clubs provide temptations to use alcohol and other substances, such as marijuana or other illicit drugs.

For some students, these new experiences and decision-making opportunities result in poor judgment and eventual abuse of alcohol and drugs. A further complication is that students in the United States reach legal drinking age of twenty-one years while in college.

TYPICAL SUBSTANCES OF ABUSE

While the use and abuse of marijuana and prescription drugs has increased markedly since the mid-1990s, alcohol is, by far, the drug most abused by college students. Furthermore, large numbers of violations of campus policies, and arrests on campus, involve alcohol intoxication.

Students, like the majority of the general population, also often abuse caffeine in the form of coffee and caffeine-fortified drinks. Beginning around 2000, the consumer market for energy drinks increased dramatically. Energy drinks contain extraordinarily high amounts of caffeine (which can cause heart attacks) and were quickly embraced by college students as a way to stay awake. These drinks are now raising medical concerns.

When many people think of substance abuse, they typically think of hard drugs. However, commonly abused substances, particularly by college students, are prescription drugs such as Percocet, Vicodin, OxyContin, Ritalin, Adderall, Ephedra, and anabolic steroids. These legal drugs are used to get high and, depending on the drug, to stay awake for studying, to enhance athletic ability, to lose weight, or to self-medicate for anxiety, depression, and related mental stresses. Drugs not ingested by the person possessing them, but which are substances abused to help initiate sexual assault, are GHB, ketamine, and Rohypnol. These drugs incapacitate the person who, most often unknowingly, ingests them and they are often used in date rapes.

Abuse of hard and prescription drugs by college students does occur, but the main concern among college and other officials is related to alcohol, especially heavy alcohol use known as binge drinking. Colleges typically define *binge drinking* as excessive consumption of alcohol in a relatively short period of time. The definition of *excessive* varies across law enforcement and other agencies and organizations.

College students receive the most attention of any group for their binge drinking. Data suggest that the greatest alcohol consumption by college students occurs when binge drinking and is greatest among students aged eighteen to twenty year olds. Binge drinking is a significant problem because of the numbers of other kinds of violations of social norms that occur in conjunction with binge drinking. These violations include sexual assault, driving while intoxicated and driving under the influence, and violations of college policies. Other consequences may include injuries from falls and vehicle accidents and drowning (either in a body of water or on one's own vomit). These are the more immediate physical consequences of binge drinking. Students who binge drink are also likely to see their academic performance deteriorate. As with any abusive behavior, there are many reasons given for why binge drinking occurs. Students often experiment with different things, including drinking alcohol. Many who are away from home for the first time want to "fit in," and they consider binge drinking to be one way to be socially accepted. Some people binge drink as a way to deal with other social and emotional issues, such as stress, isolation, and loneliness.

A particular group of students engages in binge drinking because it is, or may be, a part of the pledging process for Greek organizations or the initiation (hazing) of athletes. These behaviors still occur, even though they violate the charters and rules of Greek organizations, the codes for behavior for athletes, and the behavioral policies of colleges. Some students have died from these rituals.

COLLEGE OFFICIALS' RESPONSE

Colleges and universities are acutely aware of substance abuse and how it affects both the individual and the college community. Because of their missions to educate, institutions across the United States address substance abuse from the moment students first arrive on campus during orientation until they graduate.

Colleges and universities develop alternatives to the bar and party scenes by educating students about the possibilities of "having fun" without using substances. Colleges and universities also review and revise their policies about substance use and abuse, aiming for prevention of abuse and education rather than punishment (though judicial action is always possible). Specific information about the drug and alcohol policies of a particular college or university can be obtained from that institution.

Mary Frances Stuck, PhD

FURTHER READING

Borsari, Brian, and Kate B. Carey. "Peer Influences on College Drinking: A Review of the Research." *Journal of Substance Abuse* 13.4 (2001): 391–424. Print. Examines three factors related to peer pressure and student drinking.

Harrington, Cleveland H., et al., eds. *Substance Abuse Recovery in College.* New York: Springer, 2010. Addresses the need for and describes recovery programs and processes in college.

Lewis, Beth A., and H. Katherine O'Neil. "Alcohol Expectancies and Social Deficits Relating to Problem Drinking among College Students." *Addictive Behaviors* 25.2 (2000): 295–299. Print. Discusses the relationship of alcohol use to alcohol expectations and social deficits.

McCabe, Sean Esteban, et al. "Non-Medical Use of Prescription Stimulants among US College Students: Prevalence and Correlates from a National Survey." *Addiction* 100.1 (2005): 96–106. Print. Examines nonmedical uses of stimulates related to student and college characteristics.

Perkins, H. Wesley, ed. *The Social Norms Approach to Preventing School and College Age Substance Abuse: A Handbook for Educators, Counselors, and Clinicians.* San Francisco: Jossey-Bass, 2003. Looks at students' misperceptions of social norms and how these misperceptions promote problematic substance behaviors and how these can be changed.

WEBSITES OF INTEREST

College Drinking: Changing the Culture
http://www.collegedrinkingprevention.gov

Higher Education Center for Alcohol, Drug Abuse, and Violence Prevention
http://www.higheredcenter.org

National Institute on Alcohol Abuse and Alcoholism
http://www.niaaa.nih.gov

National Institute on Drug Abuse
http://www.drugabuse.gov

See also: Club drugs; Designer drugs; Prescription drug addiction: In depth; Stimulant abuse; Teens/young adults and alcohol abuse; Teens/young adults and drug abuse

Compulsions

CATEGORY: Psychological issues and behaviors

DEFINITION: Compulsions are strong, irresistible, and often persistent impulses to perform an act that can be irrational or that can conflict with self-will. Compulsions are distinct from habits and addictions.

COMPULSIVE BEHAVIOR

Compulsions are repetitive behaviors or mental acts to prevent or reduce anxiety rather than to provide pleasure or gratification. The most common compulsive behaviors include washing and cleaning, hoarding, checking, requesting or demanding assurance, and ordering. The acts can last a few minutes or an entire day, often disrupting the compulsive person's work, family, or social roles. Some compulsive acts also can cause physical harm. For example, harm can occur when a person repetitively washes his or her hands so that they become raw or when a person repetitively bites his or her fingernails.

COMPULSIONS VERSUS HABITS

Although people normally perform tasks repetitively, these tasks are not necessarily compulsive. Daily routines and practices are not compulsions; instead, they are normal habits. The difference between compulsions and habits can be recognized contextually. Habits bring efficiency to one's life and compulsions tend to disrupt one's life.

Researchers sometimes distinguish between habits and compulsions as normal compulsions and abnormal compulsions; habits are considered normal compulsions. As such, normal and abnormal compulsions are often similarly diagnosed as compulsive behavior and are distinguished only contextually.

That is, if the behavior is detrimental, it is considered an abnormal compulsion.

COMPULSION VERSUS ADDICTION

The use of both *compulsion* and *addiction* in everyday language is the most likely cause of confusion between the terms. Common and analogous use has led to the terms *compulsion* and *addiction* being both misused and misunderstood. A history of the change in the use of the word *addiction* can also be to blame, as *compulsion* was sometimes substituted for *addiction* to add legitimacy to the treatment of addiction.

Since the 1990s, research by scientists and clinicians has looked into differentiating and disentangling these behaviors. The American Psychological Association, for example, substitutes the term *dependency* for *addiction* to reflect the change in the definition of addiction to include behavioral addiction. Nevertheless, the difference between compulsion and addiction can be simplified. Compulsion is the repetitive behavior or mental act that prevents or reduces anxiety; addiction is a repetitive compulsive condition. Compulsion, or repetitive behavior, is a part of addiction, or repetitive compulsion. Although new research is expanding the definition of the two terms, the complexity of these disorders makes it difficult to propose a single model that could account for all their characteristic features.

COMPULSIVE DISORDERS

The basic mechanisms underlying compulsive and addictive disorders overlap in their phenomenology, their genetics and family history, and in their co-morbidity and pathophysiology. Compulsion is most often coupled with obsession to form obsessive-compulsive disorder (OCD).

OCD is characterized by obsessions and compulsions. Obsessions are unwanted persistent thoughts that produce distress and compulsions are repetitive behaviors that prevent or reduce distressing situations. Persons with OCD often use compulsive behaviors to rid themselves of obsessive thoughts; however, the relief is often temporary.

Symptoms of OCD include excessive washing or cleaning, extreme hoarding, repetitive checking, and preoccupation with limited but specific thoughts, such as sex or violence. OCD is the fourth most common mental disorder in the United States; one in fifty adults in the United States has the disorder. Many people with OCD often remain undiagnosed because of their ability to cope with and function with the disorder.

There is considerable overlap in the co-occurrence of compulsion and addiction. Addiction is a recurring and persistent compulsive condition in which a person engages in a specific activity or uses a substance despite its negative or dangerous effects. Moreover, compulsion is the behavioral aspect of addiction, while further characterization of addiction includes dependency and changes in brain chemistry. A person becomes initially addicted to a substance or behavior as it provides pleasure. Through continued use of the substance or performance of the behavior, the person develops a dependency. Soon after, involvement with the substance or procedure is necessary for the person to provide relief, thereby developing a compulsion. Studies have found that 27 percent of people under treatment for OCD also met the criteria for substance abuse disorder.

Multiple studies have linked compulsive behavior to dysregulation of frontostriatal neurocircuitry in the brain and the associated monoamine systems. The pathological neurochemistry underlying these disorders is caused by dysfunction in serotonin-, dopamine-, and glutamate-dependent neurotransmission. Therefore, first-line pharmacologic treatment involves the use of selective serotonin reuptake inhibitors and clomipramine. Cognitive behavioral therapy is another popular approach. It is being extensively investigated for dealing with different aspects of this disorder. However, the clinical picture for persons with compulsive disorder is complex, as it is marked with wide heterogeneity of the presenting symptoms.

Poonam Bhandari, PhD

FURTHER READING

Abramowitz, Jonathan S., Dean McKay, and Steven Taylor, eds. *Obsessive-Compulsive Disorder: Subtypes and Spectrum Conditions*. Boston: Elsevier, 2008. This book describes in detail the etiology and various subtypes of the compulsive behaviors.

Fontenelle, Leonardo F., et al. "Obsessive-Compulsive Disorder, Impulse Control Disorders, and Drug Addiction." *Drugs* 71 (2011): 827–40. Print. Compares and contrasts the basic concepts underlying compulsive and addictive behaviors.

Franklin, Martin E., and Edna B. Foa. "Treatment of Obsessive Compulsive Disorder." *Annual Review of Clinical Psychology* 7 (2011): 229–43. Print. Reviews the details of existing psychosocial treatments and discusses the efficiency of combining cognitive and pharmacological therapies.

Hyman, Steven E., and Robert C. Malenka. "Addiction and the Brain: The Neurobiology of Compulsion and Its Persistence." *Nature Reviews Neuroscience* 2 (2001): 695–703. Print. Describes the role of compulsion and its persistence in leading to addictive behaviors.

Markarian, Yeraz, Michael J. Larson, and Mirela A. Alde. "Multiple Pathways to Functional Impairment in Obsessive-Compulsive Disorder." *Clinical Psychology Review* 30 (2010): 78–88. Print. Describes basic OCD subtypes, underlying neuropsychological functioning, and recommendations for future research.

WEBSITES OF INTEREST

National Alliance on Mental Illness
http://namimi.org/obsessive-compulsive-disorder

National Institute of Mental Health
http://www.nimh.nih.gov/health/topics/obsessive-compulsive-disorder-ocd

WebMD.com
http://www.webmd.com/anxiety-panic/guide

See also: Addiction; Anxiety; Behavioral addictions: Overview; Obsessive-compulsive disorder (OCD)

Computer addiction

CATEGORY: Psychological issues and behaviors
ALSO KNOWN AS: Pathological computer use; video game addiction; video game overuse
DEFINITION: Obsessive use of computer programs, especially video games, has been proposed as a behavioral addiction similar to compulsive gambling. Disregarding Internet use, computer addiction is a concern of industries that lose productivity and

of parents and teachers who see a decrease in the academics and social skills of boys especially, who are more likely to develop a computer addiction.

CAUSES

With personal computers becoming commonplace in the 1990s came an increase in the numbers of children who appeared to be obsessive computer users, primarily focused on video games. Children and teenagers moved from nonelectronic fantasy games to video arcades to home computers, dramatically increasing the numbers of children and teens playing video games.

These games are purchased or are resident programs in desktop computers, laptop computers, and dedicated video gaming units, or consoles. While some video games are available over the Internet, many are sold in packaged software for use with a general purpose computer or a dedicated computer unit; other computers are designed and advertised as gaming computers.

Computer addiction and particularly video game addiction continue to expand as electronic media use increases and as more computers come in smaller and more portable sizes, such as tablets and smartphones. A survey by the Kaiser Family Foundation found media use by American preteens and teenagers has surged to almost 11 hours per day. The results surprised researchers because they thought that 8.5 hours of electronic media use in 2004 represented the maximum time left in a student's average day.

Students have been able to push their electronic life several hours higher by multitasking with electronic devices. Home computer ownership has reached 84 percent. Ownership of laptop computers rose from 12 to 29 percent from 2004 to 2010. Cell phones (or smartphones) are now handheld computers and hold many resident games. In 2004, only 18 percent of students owned a cell phone; that number is now 66 percent. Furthermore, the main use of cell phones for youths is not to make calls. Tasks that tend to take more of their time on the phone include texting (text messaging), watching other media, and video gaming.

Also problematic is video gaming in the workplace. Depending on the availability of computers, work time and productivity lost to video games and other non–work-related computer use can exceed 10 percent.

Customers wait in line for the grand opening of an Apple Store. Apple products have cultivated a following among users that some experts equate to addicton. (Reuters/Landov)

RISK FACTORS

Researcher Douglas A. Gentile published a survey of eight to eighteen year olds in the United States and found that 12 percent of boys were addicted to video games. Only 3 percent of girls were video game addicts. Also, insofar as computers require a level of affluence, computer addiction is a problem mainly for developed and advanced-developing countries.

A Kaiser Family Foundation survey found that while daily use of all electronic media did not vary much by gender (eleven hours, twelve minutes for boys versus ten hours, seventeen minutes for girls), girls lost interest in computer video games and played far less as teenagers, averaging only three minutes per day. Some researchers suggest that computer addiction is a major cause of the worldwide "boy problem," in which boys are dropping out of academics and girls predominating in the higher levels of education. The decline in boys in academics parallels the rise of personal computer technology.

SYMPTOMS

Researcher Margaret A. Shotton was the first to extensively document computer addiction and dependency, although primarily through anecdotal cases and with references to early video arcade games. Ricardo A. Tejeiro Salguero proposed a PVP, or problem video-game-playing, scale in 2002. Because video gaming is a behavioral addiction (in contrast with a chemical addiction), video gaming was more closely associated with gambling. Gentile developed a similar scale of eleven self-reported negative factors. Having a minimum of six symptoms of the eleven on the scale was set as the threshold for addiction.

The correlation between computer addiction as determined by Gentile's scale and poorer grades in school, for example, could have been an indication of comorbidity; that is, a child might spend more time on the computer and get poor grades because of a separate, but common factor.

Proof that pathological video game addiction causes a decline in academics was established by Robert Weis and Brittany C. Cerankosky. After establishing a group of boys' academic baseline achievement, they gave one-half of the boys access to computer video games and saw their academics decline. The control group continued on with solid schoolwork.

An extensive Kaiser Family Foundation survey found an inverse relationship between electronic media use and good grades, with 51 percent of heavy users getting good grades versus 66 percent of light users getting good grades. Heavy users are less likely to get along with their parents, are less happy at school, are more often bored, get into trouble at twice the average rate, and are often sad or unhappy compared with light users.

SCREENING AND DIAGNOSIS

Salguero and Gentile both proposed a multiple-factor scale to designate pathological computer video gaming. Extensive time spent playing computer games is not a sufficient indicator of addiction. However, when combined with risk factors of low social competence and higher impulsivity, there is a greater chance of pathological gaming that can result in anxiety, depression, social phobia, and poor school performance. There may be a correlation of computer addiction and attention deficit hyperactivity disorder that may be related to a child's difficulty relating normally in social settings, but these are a minority of cases.

TREATMENT AND THERAPY

At the public policy level, Western countries appear little concerned with computer addiction beyond lost workplace productivity. The main societal concerns are in Asia, where there is much more focus on the pool of intellectual talent and more concern with children's academic success. Several Asian nations have attempted to place limits on the amount of time that teenagers can spend on computers per day; most indications are that these limits are easily circumvented by tech-savvy students.

Modeled on summer camps for overweight children are China's experimental summer camps for weaning students from computer addiction. Programs beginning in the United States attempt to use counseling to treat, for example, the psychological problems and antisocial feelings that may coexist with computer addiction. Other programs use outdoor wilderness experiences. No evidence exists of the success of these types of programs.

PREVENTION

Because computers and the evolving tablets, e-readers, cell phones, and other media that are primarily small computers are presumed to be technical advances, little likelihood exists of establishing regulatory measures or controls on the availability of computers and video games. In 2011, the US Supreme Court rejected regulation of violent computer video games in the United States. This leaves the control of children's access in the hands of teachers and parents. Surveys show many parents have a low level of concern about or have little desire to regulate their children's computer activities.

John Richard Schrock, PhD

FURTHER READING

Chiu, Shao-I, Jie-Zhi Lee, and Der-Hsiang Huang. "Video Game Addiction in Children and Teenagers in Taiwan." *Cyberpsychology and Behavior* 7 (2004): 571–81. Print. Associates computer video gaming with hostility, animosity, lower social skills, and lower academic achievement.

Gentile, Douglas A. "Pathological Video-Game Use among Youths Ages 8 to 18: A National Study." *Psychological Science* 20 (2009): 594–602. Print. This extensive study used a Harris Poll to determine the extent that 1,178 American youth met "clinical-style criteria" for pathological gaming.

Gentile, Douglas A., et al. "Pathological Video-Game Use among Youths: A Two-Year Longitudinal Study." *Pediatrics* 127 (2011): 319–29. Print. Both risk and protective factors were measured in this long-term study of 3,034 Singapore school children in grades three, four, seven, and eight. The results show that the addiction "can last for years."

Rideout, Victoria J., Ulla G. Foehr, and Donald F. Roberts. "'Generation M2': Media in the Lives of 8- to 18-Year-Olds—A Kaiser Family Foundation Study." Jan. 2010. Web. 16 Apr. 2012. http://www.kff.org/entmedia/upload/8010.pdf. Although this study focuses on Internet issues, it provides data on game consoles, desktop and laptop computers, and other portable gaming devices.

Salguero, Ricardo A. Tejeiro, and Rosa M. Bersabe Moran. "Measuring Problem Video Game Playing in Adolescents." *Addiction* 97 (2002): 1601–6. Print. The first proposal that excessive use of computer video games resembles a dependence syndrome. Proposes a PVP or problem video-game-playing scale.

Shotton, Margaret A. *Computer Addiction? A Study of Computer Dependency.* New York: Taylor, 1989. The first serious study of computer addiction although relying on video arcade observations and anecdotal data as well.

---. "The Costs and Benefits of 'Computer Addiction.'" *Behaviour and Information Technology* 10 (1991): 219–30. Print. Extension of studies as personal computers became more common.

Weis, Robert, and Brittany C. Cerankosky. "Effects of Video-Game Ownership on Young Boys' Academic and Behavioral Functioning: A Randomized, Controlled Study." *Psychological Science* 21 (2010): 463–70. Print. Results of a study of how video gaming affected academic performance in boys.

WEBSITES OF INTEREST

Pew Internet and American Life Project
http://www.pewinternet.org

VideoGameAddiction.Org
http://www.video-game-addiction.org

See also: Behavioral addictions: Overview; Gaming addiction; Internet addiction; Social media addiction

Conduct disorders

CATEGORY: Psychological issues and behaviors

ALSO KNOWN AS: Disruptive behavior disorders; juvenile delinquency

DEFINITION: Conduct disorders are psychiatric disorders based on different types of callous and aggressive behaviors: physical harm to others, substantial damage to property, pervasive dishonesty or stealing, and breaking rules or defying authority. Substantial evidence suggests that conduct disorders have both neurobiological and environmental causes.

BACKGROUND

Conduct disorder (CD) is characterized by pervasive dishonesty, aggression, and callous disregard for others and for rules. These behaviors are more intense and longer-lasting than the occasional rule-breaking behavior associated with young people, for example. Also, CD is two to three times more common in boys than in girls.

The disorder exists in a continuum with two closely related disorders, one of which—oppositional defiant disorder (ODD)—tends to appear in younger children and the other of which—antisocial personality disorder—is not strictly diagnosable until adulthood. It is believed that some children with ODD "grow into" CD in their teenage years; later, some teens with CD demonstrate an antisocial personality when they become adults.

In practical terms, some children with high levels of irritability, developmentally inappropriate tantrum-like behaviors, and defiance of adults may demonstrate (as they age) a continuing lack of empathy, increasing callousness, and difficulty in restraining from cruel impulses. If these tendencies manifest in three or more different types of serious misbehavior that are repeated multiple times for more than one year, clinicians may consider a diagnosis of CD. Even in this case, the behaviors must be substantially worse than occasional acts of petty cruelty or vandalism and the behaviors cannot be caused by underlying mood problems, attention deficit hyperactivity disorder, or post-traumatic stress disorder. Usually, the earlier the problem behaviors appear, the more severe the disorder is likely to be.

CAUSES

Most mental illnesses emerge from the interaction of internal and external causes. Traditionally, some of the internal causes for aggressive behavior are believed to be low self-esteem, aberrant moral judgment, low frustration tolerance, low IQ, and concomitant low school achievement. CD is highly heritable. A person with a sibling or parent with conduct, hyperactivity, or substance abuse problems is more likely to have a CD.

Other studies have pointed to neurological dysfunctions as important in CD. One study of extremely violent men has offered evidence that the neural pathways associated with recognizing and interpreting facial cues are not particularly effective in these men. Although the data are arguable, it is possible that persons with CD may be similarly unable to correctly interpret facial cues and are therefore more likely to believe that neutral persons are hostile.

Other neurologic studies suggest that the brains of antisocial persons experience difficulty with regulating stress and maintaining appropriate levels of certain neurotransmitters, including serotonin and norepinephrine. Low levels of these brain chemicals have been associated with depression. Persons who experience increased levels of serotonin and norepinephrine after engaging in risky behaviors may increasingly seek out those behaviors to avoid low moods. Other studies have examined problems in neural pathways linking those parts of the brain responsible for overall decision making with other parts of the brain associated with rewards and with learning.

Even someone prone to aggression or dishonesty may not demonstrate significant behavioral problems without environmental stress. Among the more commonly accepted environmental contributors to CD are poor parenting, especially ineffective monitoring or inappropriate discipline; family problems, including conflict between parents or other disruptions in family life; economic problems like family poverty and poor and crime-ridden neighborhoods; and school problems, including schools that are plagued with high rates of criminal or deviant behavior among students. Not all who experience these environmental issues demonstrate conduct problems, however.

Typically a diagnosis of CD will be based on extensive problems with aggression, property destruction, dishonesty, and rule-breaking behaviors. These problems are discussed here.

TYPES

Aggression Toward People and Animals. The first group of behaviors associated with CD has to do with repetitive viciousness toward people and animals. These behaviors indicate deep unconcern with the basic rights of others to be safe from physical harm. Hence, persons with CD may enjoy bullying or threatening. Beyond just threats, however, many will start fights and may use whatever weapons are available to wound or kill others. Other vicious behaviors in this group include the perpetration of other serious criminal acts in the course of physically harming or threatening others. Armed robbery, rape, and extortion are some examples.

Destruction of Property. Those with little regard for others' physical well-being frequently demonstrate even less respect for others' property. This second group of behaviors associated with CD involves arson, vandalism, and other forms of property destruction. However, this group does not include vandalism that is better explained as thrill-seeking behavior; instead, it includes vandalism for the purpose of destruction and to deprive others.

Dishonesty and Stealing. When confronted with their behavior, many with CD either minimize the severity of their actions or project the blame onto the victim. This basic dishonesty characterizes the third group of behaviors used to diagnose CD. These behaviors include house breaking, lying, forgery, writing worthless checks, and stealing when victims are not present.

Rule-Breaking Behaviors. As the previous sets of behaviors demonstrate, someone diagnosed with CD may often perceive others as unimportant, so, rules developed in society to protect others will be likewise unimportant. However, this fourth group of diagnostically significant behaviors involves the transgression of rules designed to maintain the safety of the young person with CD him- or herself. These behaviors include eloping from school or from home multiple times, especially overnight and often before age thirteen years.

There are other deviant or dangerous behaviors associated with CD that are not diagnostically definitive but nonetheless important. Persons with CD are more likely to engage in several risky behaviors, including risky sexual behaviors, substance abuse, and other criminal behaviors.

TREATMENT

Persons with CD do not appear to respond well to medications. At its most basic level, no medication can help someone who refuses to take it, and with persons who have problems with honesty, compliance can be difficult to determine. Moreover, although they may help with mood lability or poor impulse control, medications are unlikely to help a person unlearn aberrant behavior patterns.

The more effective forms of treatment for children or adolescents with CD involve the entire family. Parents or other caregivers are taught to set appropriate limits, to encourage and reward good choices, and to use sensible and consistent discipline. Sometimes caregivers are taught the importance of spending more time with their children with CD, involving them in socially appropriate activities to lessen the amount of time they can spend with bad influences. Other therapies emphasize the importance for the person with CD of learning impulse control and stress management skills.

Michael R. Meyers, PhD

FURTHER READING

Diagnostic and Statistical Manual of Mental Disorders. 4ᵗʰ ed. Arlington, VA: American Psychiatric Association, 2000.

Finger, E. C., et al. "Disrupted Reinforcement Signaling in the Orbitofrontal Cortex and Caudate in Youths with Conduct Disorder or Oppositional Defiant Disorder and a High Level of Psychopathic Traits." *American Journal of Psychiatry* 168.2 (2011): 152–62. Print.

Murray, Joseph, and David P. Farrington. "Risk Factors for Conduct Disorder and Delinquency: Key Findings from Longitudinal Studies." *Canadian Journal of Psychology* 55.10 (2010): 633–42. Print.

"Options for Managing Conduct Disorder." *Harvard Mental Health Letter* 27.9 (2011): 1–3. Print.

Scheepers, Floortje E., Jan K. Buitelaar, and Walter Matthys. "Conduct Disorder and the Specifier Callous and Unemotional Traits in the DSM-5." *European Child and Adolescent Psychiatry* 20.2 (2011): 89–93. Print.

Van Goozen, Stephanie, et al. "The Evidence for a Neurobiological Model of Childhood Antisocial Behavior." *Psychological Bulletin* 133.1 (2007): 149–82. Print.

WEBSITES OF INTEREST

American Academy of Child and Adolescent Psychiatry
http://www.aacap.org/galleries/FactsForFamilies/33_conduct_disorder.pdf

Mental Health America
http://www.nmha.org/go/conduct-disorder

National Alliance on Mental Illness
http://www.nami.org

PubMed Health: "Conduct Disorder"
http://www.ncbi.nlm.nih.gov/pubmedhealth/PMH0001917

See also: Children and behavioral addictions; Crime and behavioral addictions; Pyromania

Controlled Substances Act (CSA)

CATEGORY: Social issues

DEFINITION: The Controlled Substances Act was passed by the US Congress as part of the Comprehensive Drug Abuse Prevention and Control Act of 1970. Its purpose is to regulate the production, importation, distribution, use, exportation, and possession of certain drugs and substances.

DATE: Effective October 27, 1970

BACKGROUND

Not until the 1960s did drug abuse become a major federal-government issue in the United States. Before this time, drug abuse was considered mostly an unacceptable behavior. The 1960s, however, saw an escalation in drug-related crime, including the smuggling of drugs into the United States.

In response, in 1970, Congress passed the Comprehensive Drug Abuse Prevention and Control Act. The Controlled Substances Act (CSA) was part F of this law. To enforce this legislation US president Richard M. Nixon created the Drug Enforcement Administration (DEA) in 1973. Before the establishment of the DEA, the United States had several federal agencies involved in drug regulation and control. The DEA was formed to group all drug-control activities under a single federal agency.

The DEA is responsible for achieving the mission of the CSA. Also involved in activities related to the CSA are the Department of Health and Human Services (including its National Institute on Drug Abuse, part of the National Institutes of Health) and the Food and Drug Administration (FDA), both of which help determine what substances are to be covered by the CSA.

The CSA established five schedules to classify controlled substances. Controlled substances are narcotics, hallucinogens, anabolic steroids, stimulants, and tranquilizers. Controlled substances are assigned to a schedule based on three factors: their potential for abuse, whether they have a medical use, and whether the substance can be safely used.

Schedule I drugs have no medical use, have a high potential for abuse, and have no accepted safety levels. Prescriptions cannot be written for schedule I drugs. Some examples of Schedule I drugs are cannabis, heroin, 3,4-methylenedioxymethamphetamine, lysergic acid diethylamide, mescaline, and methaqualone.

Schedule II drugs have a high potential for abuse, have either no medical use or may have a medical use in certain conditions, and have a high potential for addiction. Some examples of schedule II drugs are cocaine, opium, morphine, methamphetamine, methylphenidate, and methadone. Schedule III drugs have less potential for abuse, are used for medical treatment, and have a moderate risk for addiction. Some examples of schedule III drugs are anabolic steroids, ketamine, and dihydrocodeine.

Schedule IV drugs are much less likely to be abused, have a medical use, and are less likely to lead to addiction. Some examples of schedule IV drugs are benzodiazepines, modafinil, zolpidem, and meprobamate. Schedule V drugs are even less likely to be abused, have a medical use, and are unlikely to lead to addiction. Some examples of schedule V drugs are diphenoxylate, pregabalin, and cough suppressants with codeine.

In addition to drug schedules, the CSA has other provisions related to drug use. The CSA requires that all persons involved with drug production, distribution, possession, use, importation, and exportation be registered with the DEA. The CSA includes the specifications for storage of controlled drugs and the security for this storage. It describes the records that must be kept for the use of controlled drugs. The CSA describes how controlled drugs are to be disposed of.

In addition, the CSA discusses penalties for abuse of controlled drugs, procedures for importing and exporting controlled drugs, procedures for producing controlled drugs, and the provision for the taking of the violator's assets.

The CSA has been amended several times since 1970, to include major changes in the law and to reflect amendments of CSA rules, such as to add new drugs or substances or to change the schedule of a drug or substance based on new information. Later changes have included permitting electronic and facsimile prescriptions for schedule II drugs and limiting the amount of pseudoephedrine that may be purchased at one time. This last change requires that the purchaser present a picture identification card at the point of sale.

MISSIONS AND GOALS

The mission of the CSA is to regulate the production, importation, use, possession, and distribution of certain drugs and substances; to enable the United States to meet its obligations under international treaties; to classify drugs according to their addiction potential and danger, and whether they have a medical use; to protect the public safety; to create a closed system of distribution for those authorized to handle controlled substances; and to identify key officials in international and national drug enforcement.

The CSA identifies the World Health Organization (WHO) as the international authority on controlled drug classification and enforcement and includes a provision to automatically add any measures requested by WHO. International treaties play a major role in the development of US drug policy.

Christine M. Carroll, RN, BSN, MBA

FURTHER READING

Controlled Substances Act. Web. 14 Apr. 2012. http://www.deadiversion.usdoj.gov/21cfr/21usc.

National Substance Abuse Index. "Controlled Substances Act (1970)." Web. 14 Apr. 2012. http://nationalsubstanceabuseindex.org/act1970.htm.

US Drug Enforcement Administration. *Pharmacist's Manual: An Informational Outline of the Controlled Substances Act.* Springfield, VA: DEA, 2010.

Van Dusen, Virgil, and Alan R. Spies. "An Overview and Update of the Controlled Substances Act of 1970." 1 Feb. 2007. Web. 14 Apr. 2012. http://www.pharmacytimes.com/publications/issue/2007/2007-02/2007-02-6309.

See also: Controlled substances and precursor chemicals; Drug Enforcement Administration (DEA); Legislation and substance abuse

Controlled substances and precursor chemicals

CATEGORY: Substance abuse
DEFINITION: Controlled substances are drugs that are regulated by the US Controlled Substances Act and by state laws. The laws aim to interdict the trafficking of illegal drugs and to minimize the danger of abuse and addiction to drugs that have valid medical uses. Precursor chemicals are used in the manufacture of controlled substances.

CONTROLLED SUBSTANCES AND THE LAW
The Controlled Substances Act (part of the Comprehensive Drug Abuse Prevention and Control Act of 1970), consists of many laws regulating the manufacture and distribution of substances that are illegal or that can become addictive or abusive. The term *substance* is used in the act rather than the term *drug* because *substance* is a more encompassing term.

Substances listed in the act are classified into five schedules. Schedule I substances have a high potential for abuse and have no accepted medical use. They are therefore illegal drugs and cannot be sold or used; violators of schedule I are prosecuted.

Schedules II through V substances have acceptable medicinal uses and are progressively less likely to be abused or to cause physical or psychological dependence. The rules for prescribing and dispensing of controlled drugs by physicians and pharmacists are most rigorous for schedule I drugs and are progressively less rigorous for schedule II to V substances.

Physicians must be registered with the US Drug Enforcement Agency to prescribe controlled substances, and they must maintain detailed records of all transactions. The number of authorized refills (if any) must be stated and adhered to. The act has been modified several times since its enactment in 1970, and the classification of specific substances is subject to change.

CONTROLLED SUBSTANCES ACT: SCHEDULE CHARACTERISTICS
Schedule I includes a large number of substances classified as opioid drugs and hallucinogens and also a few depressants and stimulants. Opioid drugs have a chemical structure and physiological activity similar to opium that are derived from the poppy plant. Opioid drugs also are known as narcotic drugs or narcotics.

Opioid drugs such as heroin and several morphine and codeine drugs are useful in treating moderate to severe pain, but these drugs are listed in schedule I because of their potential for abuse and dependence.

Hallucinogens include the synthetic compound LSD (lysergic acid diethylamide) and also peyote and mescaline, which are found naturally in certain cacti. Marijuana is a popular drug of abuse, whose classification is controversial. Some people believe that marijuana has valid medicinal uses and should therefore be reclassified or even legalized.

Schedule II drugs include the opium poppy and the purified opium derived from the poppy. Other opioid drugs in schedule II include cocaine, methadone, oxycodone, hydrocodone, hydromorphone, and natural coca leaves. Oxycodone, sold under the trade name OxyContin, is a valuable drug for relieving chronic pain, but the drug has become popular with abusers.

Included in schedule II are the amphetamines, which act as stimulants. Methamphetamine is a synthetic compound made from amphetamine. Short-acting barbiturates, such as pentobarbital, also are in this schedule.

Schedule III substances include anabolic steroids, stimulants, and depressants. Drugs that have a depressant effect on the central nervous system act as sedatives. Intermediate-acting barbiturates are included in this category. Drugs that have a stimulant effect on the central nervous system include amphetamines and methamphetamines. Also included are drug formulations or preparations that have a limited quantity of narcotics.

Schedule IV drugs act as central nervous system depressants and produce sedation, induce sleep, and reduce anxiety. The most common drugs in this group are the barbiturates, including barbital, phenobarbital, and methylphenobarbital. Also included in this schedule are other drugs that have a similar effect, such as chloral betaine, meprobamate, and ethchlorvynol.

Schedule V drugs include formulations containing limited quantities of narcotic drugs in combination with other medically active drugs. The levels of narcotic drugs allowed are less than those in schedule III.

Many prescription drugs are controlled substances, and the diversion of these drugs for nonmedical uses is increasing rapidly. Opioids are by far the most common prescription drugs that are diverted to illicit uses. Some professionals in the medical community believe pain is actually undertreated. This belief is controversial because increased prescriptions for opioid drugs increases the supply for diverted uses. The overall effectiveness of opioids for pain relief remains a topic of debate.

The diversion of prescription drugs can occur by persons who sell or give their drugs to friends or associates. Diversion also can occur by theft or by what is called doctor shopping, visiting several doctors to obtain multiple prescriptions. The White House Office of National Drug Control Policy, established in 1989, addresses problems in illicit drug supply and use and coordinates efforts to control the problem.

PRECURSOR CHEMICALS

Precursor chemicals are chemicals used in the synthesis and manufacture of controlled substances. They become part of the drug's chemical structure. It is difficult to regulate these precursor chemicals because they also have valid commercial uses.

Also of concern to drug enforcement officials are essential chemicals. These chemicals are used in the extraction, purification, and concentration of drugs from natural sources. Essential chemicals do not become part of the molecular structure of a drug. Methamphetamine precursors such as pseudoephedrine, phenylpropanolamine, and ephedrine are most problematic.

The US Chemical Diversion and Trafficking Act (1988), which amended the Controlled Substances Act of 1970, regulates forty chemicals as list 1 and list 2 chemicals in the US Code of Federal Regulations. In addition to administering regulatory controls, the act administers criminal sanctions that control the diversion of precursor chemicals; the act permits, however, access to chemicals necessary for legitimate commerce.

David A. Olle, MS

FURTHER READING

Manchikanti, Laxmaiah. "National Drug Control Policy and Prescription Drug Abuse: Facts and Fallacies." *Pain Physician* 10 (2007): 399–424. Print. Extensive statistics on the increasing problems of prescription drug abuse. Discusses the diversion of prescription drugs for illicit use, and discusses national drug control strategy.

Sevick, James R. "Precursor and Essential Chemicals in Illicit Drug Production: Approaches to Enforcement." Washington, DC: Department of Justice, 1993. Print. An excellent discussion of illicit drug production and the distinction between precursor and essential chemicals. Includes a comprehensive list of chemicals used in the production of illicit drugs.

WEBSITES OF INTEREST

Controlled Substance Schedules. US Drug Enforcement Administration
http://www.deadiversion.usdoj.gov/schedules

"Controlling Precursor Chemicals." *Office of National Drug Control Policy*
http://www.whitehouse.gov/ondcp/precursor-chemicals

See also: Anabolic steroids; Barbiturates; Codeine; Controlled Substances Act (CSA); Gateway drugs; Hydrocodone; Methadone; Methamphetamine

Co-occurring disorders

CATEGORY: Psychological issues and behaviors
ALSO KNOWN AS: Chemical abuse and mental illness; comorbid disorder; co-occurring psychiatric and substance disorders; dual diagnosis
DEFINITION: Co-occurring disorders (CODs) refer to diagnoses of one or more mental disorders with

the use of alcohol and drugs of abuse. A COD diagnosis applies when one or more of each of the two types of disorders can be established independently of the other. Comorbidity of substance abuse disorders and mental illness is common, although individual conditions may vary in terms of severity, chronicity, disability, and degree of impairment in functioning.

OVERVIEW

Persons who have been diagnosed with a substance abuse disorder are twice as likely to also have a serious mental illness, compared with the general population. Moreover, the reverse holds true—people diagnosed with a serious mental illness are twice as likely to also have a substance abuse disorder. When two (or more) separate disorders occur simultaneously or concomitantly in the same person, they are said to be comorbid or co-occurring, although one illness does not directly cause the other.

Despite this, the two disorders do interact, and each can affect the course and outcome of the other. Substance abuse disorders and serious mental illnesses are caused by overlapping factors, such as underlying deficits in the brain and genetic vulnerabilities, and both affect similar neurotransmitters and signaling pathways. Substance abuse can acerbate or trigger psychosis and mood and affective disorders; worsening or untreated mental illness can intensify the drug or alcohol problem.

Experience has shown that mental health issues tend to surface before the onset of substance abuse, which then becomes a conscious or subconscious form of self-medication to alleviate symptoms of mental anguish. People with COD have a poorer prognosis and higher rates of drug relapse, and they are more prone to treatment noncompliance and violent behaviors. Risk factors for having CODs include family history of substance use; multidrug use; antisocial personality disorder; being a young, single, adult male; having a lower level of education; homelessness; incarceration; and limited access to treatment.

EVOLVING EVIDENCE

The association between substance abuse disorder and serious mental illness has been well established, supported by several major studies first conducted during the late 1990s. These studies include the landmark Epidemiologic Catchment Area Study and the National Comorbidity Survey, both sponsored by the National Institute of Mental Health. Also, the Substance Abuse and Mental Health Services Administration (SAMHSA), part of the US Department of Health and Human Services, issues its annual National Survey on Drug Use and Health (NSDUH), which provides data on health and the use of tobacco, alcohol, and illicit drugs in the United States.

According to the NSDUH, 2.5 million adults aged eighteen years or older had a COD in 2008. In general, adults with a past-year serious mental illness had higher rates of past-year illicit drug use (30.3 versus 12.9 percent), higher rates of past-year cigarette use (50.5 versus 28.5 percent), higher rates of heavy alcohol use (11.6 versus 7.3 percent), and higher rates of binge drinking (29.4 versus 4.6 percent), compared with those without a serious mental illness.

Among adults with past-year major depressive episode (MDE), 20.3 percent abused or were dependent on alcohol or illicit drugs, compared with 7.8 percent without MDE. More specifically, adults with MDE had higher rates of past-year illicit drug use (27.2 versus 13.0 percent), past-thirty-day heavy alcohol use (9.6 versus 7.1 percent), and past-thirty-day cigarette use (29.1 versus 15.2 percent), compared with those without MDE. Adults with past-year serious psychological distress (SPD) had higher rates of past-thirty-day illicit drug use (19.6 versus 7.3 percent, and, excluding marijuana, 12.3 versus 2.9 percent), heavy alcohol use (12.1 versus 7.3 percent), binge drinking (30.9 versus 24.6 percent), and cigarette use (47.6 versus 24.5 percent), compared with adults without SPD.

Furthermore, the NSDUH reports that two million youths aged twelve to seventeen years had MDE in 2008, and of that figure, 21.3 percent had illicit drug or alcohol dependence or abuse, indicating that there were 426,000 youths with CODs in 2008. For those who did not have MDE, the rate of dependence or abuse was only 6.4 percent. Youths with MDE also had higher rates of illicit drug use (37.4 versus 17.2 percent), past-thirty-day cigarette use (3.6 versus 1.8 percent), and past-thirty-day heavy alcohol use (3.4 versus 1.8 percent), compared with those without MDE.

TREATMENT APPROACHES

Researchers now have a better understanding of the prevalence of CODs, of the specific issues related to CODs, and of how CODs affect treatment and treatment outcome. Of the 2.5 million adults with COD in 2008, 60.5 percent received treatment at a specialty facility, but only 11.4 percent received treatment at a facility equipped to treat both substance abuse disorders and serious mental illnesses. However, efforts to provide targeted treatment for both disorders concurrently is gaining favor, as mental health professionals realize the need to address the interrelationships among the two disorders and begin to focus more attention on their shared neurobiological aspects.

Integrated treatment involves combining COD treatment with a primary treatment relationship or service setting. The intention is to treat the whole person. SAMSHA states that integrated COD treatment "is an evidence-based approach to care, which recognizes that individuals go through different stages on their way to recovery." These stages include engagement (establishing a working alliance), persuasion (forming a trusting relationship), active treatment (seeing the problem and making positive changes), and relapse prevention (creating a relapse prevention plan and building on positive behaviors). Such practices as integrated screening and assessment techniques, treatment planning strategies, motivational interviewing, cognitive-behavioral therapy, and peer support are part of the treatment program. Integrated stage-wise treatment is proving to be a viable path to recovery and is helping individuals with COD improve the quality of their lives.

Barbara Woldin, BS

FURTHER READING

Galanter, Marc, and Herbert D. Kleber, eds. *Psychotherapy for the Treatment of Substance Abuse.* Arlington, VA: American Psychiatric, 2011. A condensed version of *The American Psychiatric Publishing Textbook of Substance Abuse Treatment* (2008).

Hendrickson, Edward L. *Designing, Implementing, and Managing Co-Occurring Treatment Services for Individuals with Mental Health and Substance Use Disorders.* Binghamton, NY: Haworth, 2006. Details "blueprints for action" on developing co-occurring treatment programs; geared to clinicians working in treatment centers.

Smith, John. *Co-Occurring Substance Abuse and Mental Disorders: A Practitioner's Guide.* Lanham, MD: Aronson, 2007. An overview of evidence-based practices for screening, assessing, and treating co-occurring disorders; interesting read through use of patient vignettes.

WEBSITES OF INTEREST

"Co-Occurring Disorders." *Substance Abuse and Mental Health Services Administration*
http://www.samhsa.gov

"Drug Abuse and Mental Illness (Comorbidity)." *National Institute on Drug Abuse*
http://www.drugabuse.gov/related-topics/comorbidity

See also: Depression; Mental illness; Risk factors for addiction; Substance Abuse and Mental Health Services Administration (SAMHSA)

Cough and cold medications

CATEGORY: Substances

ALSO KNOWN AS: Dextromethorphan; DXM; poor man's PCP; red devils; robo; skittles; triple C; tuss

DEFINITION: Dextromethorphan hydrobromide (DXM HBr) is an active ingredient (cough suppressant) in a variety of over-the-counter (OTC) cough and cold medications sold under such trade names as Robitussin, NyQuil, Dimetapp, and Coricidin. DXM also can be purchased on the Internet in pure powder form. In high doses, DXM is a dissociative hallucinogen that produces effects similar to those of ketamine and phencyclidine, or PCP.

STATUS: OTC medications containing DXM are legal worldwide; some US states require proof of age to purchase

CLASSIFICATION: Noncontrolled substance

SOURCE: Synthetic compound

TRANSMISSION ROUTE: Oral

HISTORY OF USE

Dextromethorphan (DXM) was developed by the US Navy in the early 1950s as a nonaddictive substitute for codeine. It was patented in 1954 and approved by the US Food and Drug Administration for over-the-counter (OTC) sale as an antitussive (cough suppressant) in 1958.

DXM has been widely used since as an active ingredient in cough and cold medications. More than 140 OTC medications containing DXM are sold in the United States. DXM in powder form can be purchased on the Internet in 1 gram multiples.

DXM abuse was first noted in the 1960s with the use of Romilar, an OTC tablet form of DXM. Romilar was taken off the market in the United States in 1973. Abuse of DXM in liquid and capsule forms of cough and cold medications was first observed among teenagers in the 1990s. These preparations are appealing to adolescents because they are inexpensive (compared with other drugs of abuse) and are easy to purchase (or shoplift). In addition, many teenagers think DXM is safe because it can be obtained without a prescription; websites promote its abuse and offer recipes for extracting the substance from cold tablets.

Between 1999 and 2004, the number of reported cases of DXM abuse among adolescents increased tenfold; some experts consider it the most commonly abused dissociative drug in North America. About 10 percent of teenagers in the United States report abusing cough and cold medications. On average, fifty-five hundred adolescents are taken to emergency rooms each year in the United States because of a DXM overdose.

The average age of DXM abusers is fifteen years, although there are also reported cases of middle-aged adults abusing the drug. Most teenagers, however, stop using DXM in their early twenties because harder drugs are readily available to young adults.

EFFECTS AND POTENTIAL RISKS

DXM in therapeutic doses (15–30 milligrams) suppresses coughing by acting on the area in the brain that controls coughing rather than directly on the respiratory tract. It can cause drowsiness or dizziness at the therapeutic level.

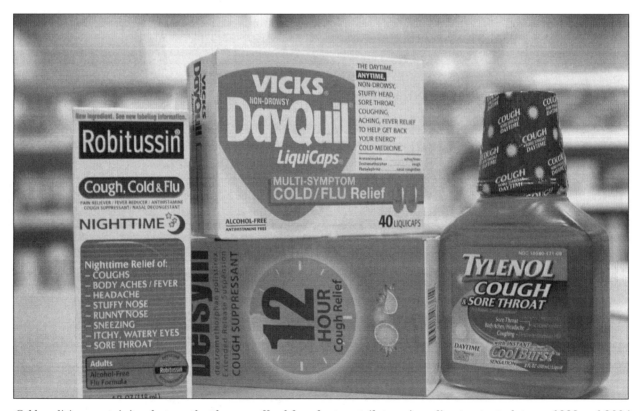

Cold medicines containing dextromethorphan are offered for sale at a retail store. According to reports, between 1999 and 2004 the abuse of over-the-counter cough medicines, many containing dextromethorphan, has risen 50% a year, mostly among youths. (Getty Images)

Because it affects the brain, it can cause hallucinations, blurred vision, feelings of unreality, out-of-body sensations, loss of sense of time, excitement, euphoria, and distortions of perception when taken in high doses (between thirteen and seventy-five times the normal therapeutic dose). DXM also can cause paranoia, high blood pressure, heavy sweating, nausea, fever, vomiting, headache, skin rash or itching, seizures, loss of consciousness, and death.

DXM is unusual among dissociative drugs of abuse in that users experience its effects in a series of distinct stages or plateaus rather than in a gradual fashion. Users at the first plateau typically experience DXM as a stimulant, while those at the second plateau are more likely to feel a dreamlike state and be detached from reality. Abusers at the third plateau may report serious disruptions of cognitive function (such as inability to perform simple arithmetic) and other frightening experiences.

Several specific risks are associated with DXM abuse. First, teenagers who use it in the form of OTC preparations are taking it in combination with antihistamines, pain relievers (usually acetaminophen), and fever reducers. These other ingredients considerably increase the risk of overdose or damage to the liver from the acetaminophen. DXM also is dangerous when taken in combination with ecstasy because of the risk of overheating and dehydration, particularly when taken at raves or in hot weather.

Second, about 5 percent of Caucasians are genetically unable to metabolize the drug normally, which leads to the rapid development of toxic levels of DXM in the bloodstream. Third, because DXM affects an abuser's sense of reality and awareness of his or her surroundings, it can lead to impaired driving, risk-taking, and fatal accidents.

DXM in OTC medications is safe for use by most persons when the products are taken as directed. It should not, however, be taken by persons using monoamine oxidase inhibitors or selective serotonin reuptake inhibitors because it has potentially dangerous interactions with these drugs.

Rebecca J. Frey, PhD

FURTHER READING

Bryner, Jodi K., et al. "Dextromethorphan Abuse in Adolescence." *Archives of Pediatric and Adolescent Medicine* 160.12 (2006): 1217–22. Print. An account of recent trends in abuse of cough and cold medications by teenagers in the United States that includes descriptions of the effects of DXM abuse and overdose symptoms.

Finn, Robert. "Easy Availability Driving Dextromethorphan Abuse: Hallucinations, Dystonia." *Pediatric News* 38.5 (2004): 24. Print. Brief overview of DXM abuse that includes descriptions of the various experienced plateaus.

Miller, S. C. "Dextromethorphan Psychosis, Dependence, and Physical Withdrawal." *Addiction Biology* 10.4 (2005): 325–27. Print. A brief article on the potential for addiction to DXM and its long-term complications.

Shannon, Joyce Brennfleck, ed. *Drug Abuse Sourcebook*. 3rd ed. Detroit: Omnigraphics, 2010. A comprehensive standard reference work for college students about all known drugs of abuse, including OTCs, prescription medications, and illegal substances.

WEBSITES OF INTEREST

KidsHealth.org
http://kidshealth.org/parent/h1n1_center/h1n1_center_treatment/cough_cold_medicine_abuse.html#

The Partnership at Drugfree.org
http://www.dxmstories.com

Web MD: "Teen Drug Abuse of Cough and Cold Medicine"
http://www.webmd.com/parenting/teen-abuse-cough-medicine-9/teens-and-dxm-drug-abuse

See also: Controlled substances and precursor chemicals; Dextromethorphan; Over-the-counter drugs of abuse; Teens/young adults and drug abuse

Crack

CATEGORY: Substances

ALSO KNOWN AS: Rock

DEFINITION: Crack is a solid form of cocaine made by dissolving powdered cocaine in a mixture of baking soda or ammonia with water. The mixture is boiled into a solid form and then broken into chunks. Crack is a powerful stimulant that reaches the brain in about eight seconds and produces an intense high that lasts between five and ten minutes.

STATUS: Illegal in the United States, Canada, and Europe

CLASSIFICATION: Schedule II drug in the United States because of its high abuse potential; has medicinal purposes (as an anesthetic). Crack and cocaine are considered the same drugs. Canada classifies crack as a schedule I drug. Since 1961, the United Nations has identified cocaine as a schedule I drug. In the United Kingdom, crack is a class A drug, and in the Netherlands it is a list 1 drug under that country's opium law.

SOURCE: A chemically altered form of cocaine, which is derived from the leaves of the coca plant, commonly found in South America. Cocaine also can be biosynthesized in a laboratory.

TRANSMISSION ROUTE: Inhalation; intravenous (of the liquid form of crack, also called freebase)

HISTORY OF USE

Crack first appeared in the US cities of Los Angeles, San Diego, and Houston in the early 1980s, reportedly as a means of moving a large amount of cocaine that was available in the United States in the 1970s. The major crack epidemic, as it came to be called, took place between 1984 and 1990, mostly in poor, urban areas in the United States. By 2002, the United Kingdom reported a crack epidemic, and today, crack is used worldwide.

Since about 2000, the use of crack has decreased substantially, though it has not disappeared. Young adults (at levels as high as 65 percent) report having tried crack at least once; however, repeat-usage percentages are significantly lower. Arrest rates for crack possession are also dramatically lower than those of the 1980s and 1990s, with some cities showing crack-arrest percentages in the single digits.

There are several explanations for these lowered rates, including higher prices for cocaine and also changes in how the law handles charges for crack possession. However, the most significant cause for the decrease in the use of crack is the dramatic rise in methamphetamine use. Methamphetamine's low cost, easy availability, and extremely addictive nature make it popular among drug abusers.

EFFECTS OF USE

Crack is a stimulant that artificially increases the levels of dopamine released from the brain. Also, crack prevents dopamine from being "recycled" by the body, leading to an excess of dopamine with repeated use. This excess causes an overamplification of the dopamine-receptor neurons and leads to a disruption of normal neural communications. For example, the brain loses the ability to properly respond to pleasurable stimuli, which causes the drug user to seek more drugs to feel any pleasure. While the initial response of the brain to this massive dopamine buildup is a drug-induced euphoria, an increase in self-confidence, and increased high energy, these effects become harder and harder to attain as the dopamine system becomes damaged, leading to addiction and tolerance.

RISKS OF USE

Crack affects not just the brain but also almost every system in the body. One of the most strongly affected is the pulmonary system. Because crack is inhaled using high temperatures (90 degrees Celsius, or 194 degrees Fahrenheit), users often suffer burned lips, tongue, and airways. Another common side effect of crack use is a cough with black sputum, which is caused by the butane torches used to heat the smoking pipes. Other crack-related respiratory illnesses include pulmonary edema (also known as crack lung), asthma, and adult respiratory distress syndrome.

Sudden death from cardiac arrest is another danger to crack users, especially those who drink alcoholic beverages while using crack. (Any polydrug use increases the risk of sudden cardiac arrest.) Psychiatric trauma also is common in crack users and may include severe paranoia, violent behavior, and hallucinations (including delusional parasitosis, or Ekbom's syndrome, the belief that one is infested with parasites; this can cause a person to violently scratch themselves).

Crack users are especially at risk for infections with the human immunodeficiency and hepatitis viruses. Shared needles are one source; the other source is the exchange of sex for drugs. This often places women at an especially high risk. Another danger is tuberculosis and other saliva-borne diseases, which are passed by sharing a common crack pipe.

The so-called crack-babies epidemic has been weighted by myth and misinformation, leading people to believe that a generation of children became an essentially lost generation. Studies show that the stereotype of the crack baby, born addicted to crack and facing insurmountable developmental issues and an inability to bond, is simply false. The reality is more complicated. Independent of other issues, such as alcohol and tobacco abuse and poor physical environment, many of these babies are living normal lives.

Further research shows that the area of the body most affected in these children is the dopamine system that develops early in the fetal cycle; the system may show long-term effects of crack and cocaine exposure. A child also may have a mild behavioral disorder or a subtler developmental phenotype that resembles attention deficit hyperactivity disorder. Cognitive and attention systems may be affected, and these children may require help from a special-needs program.

S. M. Willis, MS, MA

FURTHER READING

Laposata, Elizabeth A., and George L. Mayo. "A Review of Pulmonary Pathology and Mechanisms Associated with Inhalation of Freebase Cocaine ('Crack')." *American Journal of Forensic Medicine and Pathology* 14 (1993): 1–9. Print. A review of the respiratory conditions that result from inhalation of crack, ranging from burned lips and airways from the crack pipe to pulmonary edema and hemorrhage.

Lejuez, C. W., et al. "Risk Factors in the Relationship between Gender and Crack/Cocaine." *Experimental and Clinical Psychopharmacology* 15 (2007): 165–75. Print. A study that examines the psychological and socioeconomic reasons why women are more at risk from using crack.

Thompson, Barbara L., Pat Levitt, and Gregg D. Stanwood. "Prenatal Exposure to Drugs: Effects on Brain Development and Implications for Policy and Education." *Nature* 10 (2009): 303–12. Print. A comprehensive look at the effects of several different types of prenatal drug use, including how crack use specifically affects the development of the dopamine system, which can have long-term effects on cognitive and attention systems.

WEBSITES OF INTEREST

National Institute on Drug Abuse
http://www.drugabuse.gov

Office of National Drug Control Policy
http://www.whitehouse.gov/ondcp

See also: Cocaine use disorder; Dopamine and addiction; Recreational drugs

---

Crime and behavioral addictions

CATEGORY: Social issues

DEFINITION: Behavioral addictions involve the compulsive repetition of negative behaviors independent of the ingestion of drugs and alcohol. While far less prevalent than substance abuse addictions, behavioral addictions, when they involve criminal acts, can be equally destructive to the addict, the addicts' family, and society in general. Several particular facets of behavioral addiction commonly result in criminal activity; they include gambling addiction, sex addiction, kleptomania, and pyromania. However, not all behavioral addictions are attributable to criminal behavior.

INTRODUCTION

Behavioral addictions are closely related to maladapted impulse-control abilities as defined by the repeated failure or inability to resist harmful behavior or impulsive actions. Behavioral addictions involve a variety of both common behaviors and peculiar activities.

Many behavioral addicts become hooked on activities that other persons engage in only occasionally, such as shopping, sexual activity, eating, or gambling. According to the US Department of Health and Human Services, nearly 16 million Americans demonstrate compulsive sexual behaviors. Additionally, one in twenty Americans is a compulsive shopper, while 4 to 8 million Americans are considered problem gamblers. Behavioral addictions to food, shopping, technological devices, exercise, and appearance are conventionally only harmful to the addicts themselves. Several addictions, however, result in criminal activity.

CRIMINAL BEHAVIOR AND COMPULSIVE GAMBLING

Compulsive gambling is a behavioral addiction that manifests itself as an obsession with placing financial wagers for the possibility, however scant, of a profitable return. Gambling addiction spans the entire gamut of games of chance, from sports betting and card games to billiards, casino gaming, and lotteries. Legal gambling has been one of the fastest growing industries in the United States for several decades, while illegal wagering has maintained a cultural presence so large for so long that law enforcement agencies can only contain it rather than try to prevent it.

Conventionally, compulsive gamblers resort to criminal behavior only after all other avenues of potential income are no longer available. This behavior includes the sale of personal property, the sale of property of friends and family, or petty theft from spouses and family.

Aside from engaging in such illicit acts as petty and grand theft, compulsive gamblers, according to researchers, also engage in a variety of other criminal activities. These activities range from fabricating auto accident claims to health insurance fraud, arson, and making false claims about thefts, fires, and property damage. Data indicate that compulsive gambling also can lead to involvement in drug trafficking, assault, and prostitution. Many parallels can be made between gambling addicts and substance addicts, because each addiction lends itself to the erratic tendencies, poor judgment, and violent behavior that often can result in criminal activity.

CRIMINAL BEHAVIOR AND SEX ADDICTION

Research indicates that as much as 6 percent of all adults in the United States have some form of sex addiction. Sex addiction can range from the constant desire for sexual activity or stimulation to an inability to control sexual urges, behaviors, and thoughts.

Sex addiction enters the realm of criminal behavior when it involves the improper coercion, exploitation, or duress of other persons. It also involves forcing others to act out sexual behaviors in a public forum without discretion or respect for societal norms.

Not all sex addicts partake in criminal activities or are addicted to perverse sexual behaviors, but some sex addicts are involved in criminal behaviors including rape and sexual assault, prostitution, incest, pedophilia, harassment, voyeurism, and exhibitionism. Like many other behavioral and substance addictions, sex addiction may be related to the effect of dopamine on the brain.

KLEPTOMANIA

Kleptomania, or compulsive stealing, is by definition an addiction to a criminal behavior. While petty thieves and shoplifters customarily steal for want of items they cannot afford or steal for profit, kleptomaniacs impulsively steal from all locations and for any reason; they steal for the sake of stealing. According to 2007 statistics from researchers at Stanford University, nearly 1.2 million Americans have this behavioral addiction.

The cause of kleptomania is unknown and widely debated among both medical and sociological professionals. While some experts believe it is related to the release of dopamine during the act of theft, others believe it also may be a behavior symptomatic of other underlying psychological or social development problems.

PYROMANIA

Pyromania is an extremely rare but potentially lethal behavioral addiction involving the compulsive starting of fires. According to a study in the *British Journal of Criminology*, pyromaniacs account for only about 1 to 4 percent of all arsonists in the United States each year. Unlike arsonists, who ignite fires for personal or financial gain or as an act of assault, pyromaniacs achieve a perverse euphoria from creating fire as a destructive force. Pyromaniacs also take pleasure in surveying the damage left behind from fires.

Much like kleptomania, pyromania is believed to be rooted in underlying psychological trauma or impaired social development of some kind. This trauma often includes a childhood history of psychological, physical, or sexual abuse. Experts believe that pyromania may be caused by an aggression rooted in childhood abuse and by poorly developed problem-solving skills and cognitive maladjustment.

STRATEGIES FOR TREATMENT

Although persons with behavioral addictions have several similarities with persons with substance abuse addictions, there remains a great deal of debate on whether behavioral addictions can be classified as addictive behavior. A wide sociological and scientific gap exists between the concept of addiction and impulse control disorders.

Research indicates that the neurological patterns between substance abusers and behavioral addicts have many similarities, but not enough is known about these neurological functions to present a clear delineation between the two. It is perhaps because of these similarities that the treatment strategy for behavioral addictions closely mirrors that of substance abuse recovery.

Treatment for gambling, sex, shopping, and other compulsive behaviors often involves cognitive therapy to attempt to highlight the underlying psychological factors that lead a person to act on such impulses. This connection has been further established by the effective use of substance abuse treatments such as group therapy and by the use of antidepressant medications in persons with impulse control disorders.

Individualized therapy coupled with immersion in support groups also has shown to be beneficial for impulse control addicts. Like their substance abuse counterparts, behavioral addiction support groups strive to deconstruct the common repetitive cycle of isolation and shame inherent in addictive behavioral patterns. These programs also focus on the development of new coping skills with which to combat the anxieties that may lead to compulsive behaviors.

Much of the debate lies in the neurological function in the brain of pleasure-inducing chemicals such as beta-endorphins and serotonin. Scientific research has shown that persons on medications that boost production of such chemicals are more likely to develop addictive behavioral patterns.

A major disruption to the development of early screening, treatment, and prevention of impulse control behaviors is the lack of agreement in determining what behaviors constitute the diagnosis of addiction and where behavioral addictions land on this spectrum. Another source of disruption is determining the relationship between these disorders and criminal behavior.

John Pritchard

FURTHER READING

DiClemente, Carlo. *Addiction and Change: How Addictions Develop and Addicted People Recover.* New York: Guilford, 2003.

Grant, Jon E. *Impulse Control Disorders: A Clinician's Guide to Understanding and Treating Behavioral Addictions.* New York: W. W. Norton, 2008.

Grant, Jon E., and Marc N. Potenza, eds. *The Oxford Handbook of Impulse Control Disorders.* New York: Oxford UP, 2012.

WEBSITES OF INTEREST

Bureau of Justice Statistics
http://bjs.ojp.usdoj.gov/content/dcf/contents.cfm

PubMed Health: "Conduct Disorder"
http://www.ncbi.nlm.nih.gov/pubmedhealth/PMH0001917

See also: Behavioral addictions: Overview; Crime and substance abuse; Socioeconomic status and addiction

Crime and substance abuse

CATEGORY: Social issues

DEFINITION: Alcohol and illicit drugs are involved in approximately 80 percent of all criminal offenses leading to arrest and incarceration in the United States. Common crimes involving substance abuse are domestic violence, driving under the influence, assault and battery, and property offenses such as theft and burglary.

BACKGROUND

The precise relationship between substance abuse and crime is difficult to define. First, the cultivation, manufacturing, possession, and sale of illicit drugs are each crimes in their own right. This fact is aligned with numerous studies that have connected the propensity of persons who abuse illicit drugs to commit crimes. Similarly, laws dictating the appropriate distribution and consumption of alcoholic beverages exist throughout the United States. While these statutes themselves are often violated, there exists a well-established parallel between abusive alcohol use and criminal behavior.

It is widely accepted that the behavior of persons impaired by illicit drug and alcohol abuse are prone to erratic tendencies, poor judgment, impulsivity, and violence that lends itself to criminal activity. Repeated abuse of alcohol and drugs also decreases the self-control and inhibitions that distinguish criminals from law-abiding citizens.

Data acquired from the prison population in the United States illustrates that a considerable number of criminals and prison inmates were under the influence of drugs or alcohol, or both, when committing offenses of all kinds. According to a 2009 survey of ten metropolitan areas in the United States by the Office of National Drug Control Policy, the number of criminals who tested positive for at least one controlled

An alcoholic stealing gin from supermarket. (Peter Dazeley)

CRIME AND ALCOHOL ABUSE

Motor vehicle violations make up the majority of alcohol-related crimes in the United States. The National Partnership on Alcohol Misuse and Crime (NPAMC) reports that more than 1 million Americans are arrested for driving while intoxicated each year, cases that result in 780,000 criminal convictions. NPAMC findings also note that alcohol-related automobile accidents cost taxpayers more than $100 billion in law enforcement expenses annually. A staggering thirteen thousand people die in drunk-driving-related accidents in the United States each year.

While decades of public interest campaigns led by national law enforcement agencies like the National Highway Traffic Safety Administration (NHTSA) and nonprofit organizations such as Mothers Against Drunk Driving (MADD) and the DUI Foundation have kept the dangers of drunk driving in the public eye, alcohol abuse is also ubiquitous in a wide variety of non-vehicle-related crimes. Domestic violence,

underage drinking, and assault are the most frequently occurring non-vehicle-related but alcohol-related crimes in the United States.

While research has uncovered a recurring coexistence between domestic violence and alcohol abuse, not all domestic abusers are alcoholics and not all alcoholics are domestic abusers. A contrary rationale is that while alcohol abuse is regularly a contributing factor in many acts of domestic violence, there also are cases in which alcohol abuse is used as an excuse or an avoidance of accountability by its perpetrators.

There is less scholarly gray area between alcohol use and criminal behavior by underage people. Consumption of alcohol by persons younger than age twenty-one years is itself a commonly perpetrated crime. According to the Centers for Disease Control and Prevention (CDC), underage drinkers consume 11 percent of all the alcohol consumed in the United States each year, despite the illegality of doing so. CDC data also indicate that underage alcohol abuse leads to higher rates of school absence and reckless sexual behavior, and to brain development and memory problems.

Like their adult counterparts, abusive underage drinkers also have a higher propensity to violate laws against drunk driving and to engage in or be victimized by physical assault. The risk of criminal behavior appears to follow underage drinkers into adulthood, according to a 2011 study by the University of Miami that linked abusive underage alcohol consumption with a greater probability of committing property crimes like theft or predatory crimes like assault later in adulthood.

A 2008 report by the Pew Center on the States reported that more than 5 million incarcerated adults were drinking at the time of committing their offense, a group that constitutes 36 percent of the entire US prison population. The research also showed trends indicating that the more violent a crime, the more likely alcohol was involved.

CRIME AND DRUG ABUSE

Drug-related offenses are broken down into three categories by the National Institute on Drug Abuse (NIDA): drug possession and sales, offenses committed to support preexisting drug abuse, and drug-related involvement in criminal activities not related to drugs. In 2011, thirty-one thousand people were arrested in the United States on federal drug charges. The US Drug Enforcement Administration (DEA) arrests more than twenty-six thousand people for possession each year, and has done so every year since 1986.

A majority of illicit drug abusers rely on petty crimes to support their habit. These crimes range from petty theft to burglary to grand theft auto. Data from the US Bureau of Justice Statistics (2002) indicate that one-quarter of convicted property and drug offenders commit their crimes to get money for drugs. NIDA research also ties drug use to several other felony convictions, including money laundering, grand theft, and counterfeiting.

While a majority of drug-related crimes can be attributed to the illegality of drugs themselves, research shows that a majority of criminal acts are carried out by persons acting under the influence of or in the pursuit of many types of illicit drugs. That said, the relationship between drugs and crime remains extremely difficult to determine from a research perspective and remains a topic of debate among criminologists and sociologists.

YOUTH-ORIENTED PREVENTION

Federal, state, and local law enforcement agencies have developed numerous systems and processes aimed at reducing the appeal of drug use in hopes of simultaneously halting the various criminal activities that accompany that use. Aimed largely at school-age children and young adults, the agencies' primary goals have been to prevent persons from entering into the culture of drugs. These programs, which involve coursework and demonstrations of the negative aspects of drug use, have met with varying degrees of success.

The Drug Abuse Resistance Education program (D.A.R.E.) is an example of a failed nationwide effort to curtail drug use and violence. Founded in 1983 by former Los Angeles Police Department chief Daryl Gates, the program was widely utilized in public schools in the United States to explicitly educate young people on the dangers of drug use and activity through lecture-style lessons, drug identification demonstrations, and attempts at building trusting relationships with local police officers through in-school interactions.

By the late 1990s research began to show that the D.A.R.E. program not only was ineffective in decreasing drug use in the majority of communities in which it was utilized but also contributed to a rise in alcohol and drug use among its participants. Evaluation studies demonstrating the program's ineffectiveness were made by several federal agencies, including the US Office of the Surgeon General and US Department of Education (DE). The program's widespread reputation for ineffectiveness led the DE to prohibit schools from utilizing federal funds for the program in 1998.

New strategies fostered by the National Youth Anti-Drug Media Campaign in online campaigns, such as TheAntiDrug.com and AboveTheInfluence.com, detract from the communal, schoolroom-oriented strategies of previous programs like D.A.R.E.. The AntiDrug.com program emphasizes positive parental influence as a crucial dissuasion from the temptations of drug-related activity, while AbovetheInfluence.com seeks to tear down the status of illegal drug use as a popular counterculture.

John Pritchard

FURTHER READING

Andrews, D. A. *The Psychology of Criminal Conduct.* Cincinnati, OH: Anderson, 2010.

Galanter, Mark, ed. *Alcoholism and Violence: Epidemiology, Neurobiology, Psychology, Family Issues.* Recent Developments in Alcoholism 13. New York: Springer, 1997.

Hammersley, Richard. *Drugs and Crime.* London: Polity, 2008.

Hanson, Glen, Peter J. Venturelli, and Annette E. Fleckenstein. *Drugs and Society.* 11th ed. Sudbury, MA: Jones, 2012.

US Department of Justice. "The Systems Approach to Crime and Drug Prevention: A Path to Community Policing." Sep. 1993. Web. 12 Apr. 2012. https://www.ncjrs.gov/pdffiles/systems.pdf.

WEBSITES OF INTEREST

AlcoholFacts.org
http://alcoholfacts.org/D.A.R.E..html

Centers for Disease Control and Prevention
http://www.cdc.gov/alcohol/fact-sheets/
    underage-drinking.htm

National Center for Victims of Crime
http://www.ncvc.org

National Institute on Drug Abuse
http://www.drugabuse.gov

National Partnership on Alcohol Misuse and Crime
http://www.alcoholandcrime.org/npamc/issues/
    alcohol-and-crime

*Substance Abuse, Mental Health, and Criminal Justice
    Studies*
http://www.norc.org/Research/Departments/Pages/
    substance-abuse-mental-health-and-criminal-justice-
    studies.aspx

US Drug Enforcement Administration
http://www.justice.gov/dea/statistics.html#arrests

See also: Crime and behavioral addictions; Prison and substance abuse; Socioeconomic status and addiction

---

Cross-addiction

CATEGORY: Health issues and physiology
ALSO KNOWN AS: Addiction transfer
DEFINITION: Cross-addiction involves the transfer of an addiction from one harmful substance or behavior to another. It also involves the abuse of more than one mind-altering substance at a time.

CAUSES

Scientists now understand that addiction is a physiological problem caused both by nature and by nurture. A person who becomes an addict often inherits a sensitive brain and develops behavioral habits that lead to chemical changes in the brain. These changes, in turn, lead the person to use toxic substances against his or her will.

Research confirms that all drugs of abuse, including alcohol, marijuana, nicotine, amphetamines, barbiturates, opiates, and heroin, work on the same neurological pathways in key areas of the brain—in particular, dopamine receptors and the limbic system, a primitive area focused on meeting basic needs. Dopamine is a "feel-good" chemical that tricks the limbic system into equating drugs with pleasure or relief, and even with survival.

In people who are genetically predisposed to addiction, the release of dopamine is more intense, and it unleashes what is known as the phenomenon of craving. Such persons cannot limit their intake of an addictive drug because of this craving. People who do not come from a family of addicts or alcoholics can, through force of habit, still become addicted to toxic drugs and experience the same phenomenon.

Often when a person attempts to quit a drug of choice, he or she will use another drug to satisfy the craving and essentially keep the reward pathways of the brain in hypersensitive mode. Alternatively, cross addicts who have no desire to quit will mix a cocktail of drugs to get a desired effect.

RISK FACTORS

The dopamine hypothesis suggests that if a person is addicted to one drug, they are at higher risk of becoming addicted to another. For people who are trying to quit a particular drug, cross-addiction can lead to a relapse of the original drug-taking behavior because of the sustained craving and because of impaired decision-making abilities.

SYMPTOMS

The symptoms of addiction feature three characteristics: chemical dependency, drug-taking habits, and denial of dependency and habits. Chemical dependency involves four components: craving, or the compulsion to ingest a mood-altering substance; impaired control of the amount ingested on any given occasion; physical dependence, which produces a period of withdrawal when the drug is discontinued; and tolerance, or the need for more of the drug to feel its effects.

Cross addicts are often in extreme denial. They tend to be more secretive than alcoholics and will hide their behavior from friends and family members. Because most drugs are illegal, cross addicts often suffer from paranoia.

SCREENING AND DIAGNOSIS

Cross-addictions are far more dangerous than alcoholism alone, because mixing drugs and alcohol can lead to death sooner. As with alcoholism, cross-addiction requires a certain amount of self-diagnosis to be treatable.

Dependence can be diagnosed when the person admits to three or more of the following: taking substances in greater amounts than intended; a persistent desire to cut down or stop using fails to change the behavior; frequent intoxication or presence of withdrawal symptoms that interfere with functioning; spending significant amounts of time acquiring drugs or dealing with the consequences of use; giving up activities in order to use drugs; persistent use despite adverse consequences; marked tolerance; withdrawal symptoms; and the use of drugs to treat withdrawal symptoms.

TREATMENT AND THERAPY

Intensive therapy and treatment are required to break an addiction without transferring that addiction. The first step is building self-awareness and an understanding of the nature of addiction. Sobriety must be the first priority, and it should be affirmed and nurtured daily.

If a person transfers an addiction from one substance to another, the brain remains in addictive mode; the neural associations and pathways have no opportunity to become disabled and dormant. Thus, the cycle of cross-addiction can be broken only by stopping the drug-taking and by remaining totally abstinent from all mind-altering drugs.

Acute withdrawal symptoms, such as sweating and nausea, can last a couple of weeks. Postacute withdrawal symptoms can happen for two years. These bouts tend to last three or four days and produce irritability, mood swings, variable energy, low enthusiasm, disturbed sleep, and difficulty concentrating. The first two years are the most difficult; after five years of abstinence, relapse is uncommon.

PREVENTION

Recovery is a lifelong process that requires new coping skills. Relaxation is chief among them; rigorous honesty and avoiding high-risk situations also will help prevent a relapse.

People who have been addicted to one drug must be vigilant, because cross-addiction can occur by happenstance. A recovering alcoholic, for example, may go to the dentist and be prescribed pain medicine,

to which he or she develops a chemical dependency. Without thinking about it, the patient begins to increase the dosage and frequency of the pain medication and may seek unnecessary refills. Not all doctors learn about the physiology of addiction, so to protect oneself, a recovering addict must be wary when taking prescription medications.

Laura B. Smith

FURTHER READING

Christopher, James. *How to Stay Sober: Recovery without Religion.* New York: Prometheus, 1988. Approaching recovery from a secular point of view, this book counsels self-reliance and self-respect instead of reliance on a higher power. Suggests new coping skills and provides a weekly diary for the first year of sobriety.

Johnson, Marlys C., and Phyllis Alberici. *Cross-Addiction: The Hidden Risk of Multiple Addictions.* New York: Rosen, 1999. Discusses the nature of drug addiction, how addiction to one substance can be transferred to another, and how to recover from addiction.

Kipper, David, and Steven Whitney. "Cross-Addiction." *The Addiction Solution: Unraveling the Mysteries of Addiction through Cutting-Edge Brain Science.* Kipper, David, and Steven Whitney. New York: Rodale, 2010. Draws on composite case histories to illustrate how the innovative personal recovery program works by customizing treatment for a diverse group of addicts abusing a variety of substances, from the first day of treatment to successful resolution.

Ries, Richard, and Shannon C. Miller. *Principles of Addiction Medicine.* Philadelphia: Lippincott, 2009. A text for physicians and mental health professionals on all aspects of drug and alcohol addiction from the American Society of Addiction Medicine.

WEBSITES OF INTEREST

Alcoholics Anonymous
http://www.aa.org

American Society of Addiction Medicine
http://www.asam.org

Drug Addiction Center
http://www.drugaddictioncenter.org

Narcotics Anonymous
http://www.na.org

See also: Addiction; Addictive personality; Co-occurring disorders; Relapse

---

Cutting and self-mutilation

CATEGORY: Psychological issues and behaviors
ALSO KNOWN AS: Self-injury
DEFINITION: Cutting and self-mutilation are behaviors in which a person injures his or her own body; these behaviors are not usually suicide attempts. Some examples of self-injury are cutting, burning, hair pulling, and head banging.

RISK FACTORS AND RELATED CONDITIONS

Although self-injury can occur at any age, it usually begins in adolescence. It was originally thought that women were more likely than men to engage in self-injury, but later research indicates that the incidence is equal among women and men. The research also indicates that about 1 percent of the US population engages in various types of self-injury.

Persons who self-injure commonly have a history of abuse, including sexual, physical, or emotional abuse. Self-injury is often associated with other mental health problems, such as eating disorders, substance abuse, obsessive-compulsive disorders, schizophrenia, depression, bipolar disorder, borderline personality disorder, anxiety disorders, post-traumatic stress disorder, dissociative disorders, panic disorder, and phobias.

Persons who engage in self-injury often come from homes where expressing anger and other emotions is (or was) forbidden. They frequently have low self-esteem and exhibit perfectionism. Also, they are likely to be impulsive and to have poor problem-solving skills. However, self-injury does not indicate the severity of mental illness or the ability of the person to function and lead a relatively normal life.

WHY PERSONS SELF-INJURE

There are many reasons for self-injury. One is using the behavior to provide a way to deal with overwhelming feelings, such as anger, extreme sadness, anxiety, depression, stress, sense of failure, self-hatred, or the helplessness of a trauma. Persons who self-injure have difficulty coping with severe emotional pain.

Self-injury can serve as a distraction from emotional pain, a way to express feelings that the person is unable to describe, or a way to feel a sense of control over something that is uncontrollable. Persons who self-injure often describe a feeling of calmness and relief of their intense feelings after they have injured themselves. Other self-injurers describe feeling emotionally numb and empty. For these persons, the self-injury allows them to feel something. Some are communicating their distress and expressing a need for help through self-injury. Others are punishing themselves for some imagined wrong.

Other persons use self-injury to prevent something worse from happening to them. This is unrealistic thinking, in which the person feels that if something bad is happening to him or her now, nothing else bad can happen. Others use self-injury to separate themselves from their feelings, which fade in the face of the physical pain. Most likely self-injury leads to the release of endorphins in the brain. These substances are natural pain relievers and tranquilizers.

It is thought that some persons self-injure to seek attention and to manipulate others. This is unlikely because most self-injurers are ashamed of the injuries that they cause, and they will hide their self-inflicted injuries. It is common for self-injurers to wear shirts with long sleeves and full-length pants in all types of weather to hide their injuries. The exceptions to this are persons who are developmentally disabled and persons with organic brain disease. They are likely to engage in self-injury without also trying to hide the injury or the behavior. In these instances, the behavior is caused by their brain injury.

SYMPTOMS AND TREATMENT

No single therapy exists to treat persons who self-injure, and there is no consensus as to the most effective treatment. Typically, treatment must be developed based on the needs and other mental health conditions of the self-injurer. Possible helpful medications include antidepressants, antipsychotic drugs, and minor tranquilizers.

Often-used psychotherapeutic approaches include cognitive-behavioral therapy, dialectical-behavior therapy, and psychodynamic psychotherapy. The type of psychotherapy also depends on the other psychological illnesses of the client. In severe cases of self-injury, the person may be hospitalized to exert some control over the behavior.

Psychotherapy usually begins with an exploration of why the person self-injures. The therapist will teach alternative behaviors to use when the person feels like self-injuring. These alternatives include physical activities, journaling, and talking with friends or family members. Alternative actions also may be taught, such as snapping an elastic band that is wrapped around the self-injurer's wrist. While this action does cause some pain, it does not cause injury. Biofeedback may be used to help the person identify the feelings that lead to the urge to self-injure.

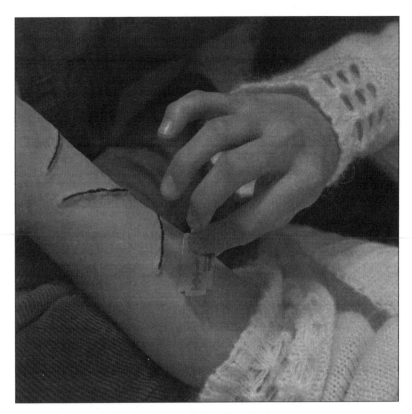

Girl cutting herself. (Raider Peter/DPA/Landov)

It is important that the person understands that treatment, especially self-treatment, takes time, hard work, and motivation. If the self-injurer is an adolescent or child, family therapy may be necessary to identify what triggers the self-injuring behavior. Group therapy also may be used to provide the person with supportive relationships with others who are dealing with similar issues. Self-injurers who are developmentally disabled can be taught how to accomplish goals without using self-harming behaviors.

Christine M. Carroll, RN, BSN, MBA

FURTHER READING

Hollander, Michael. *Helping Teens Who Cut: Understanding and Ending Self-Injury.* New York: Guilford, 2008. Explains self-injury and debunks the many myths surrounding self-mutilation and cutting behavior. Outlines advanced treatment principles.

Smith, Melinda, and Jeanne Segal. "Cutting and Self-Harm." Jan. 2012. Web. 17 Apr. 2012. http://www.helpguide.org/mental/self_injury. htm. This article is aimed at helping the self-injurer understand why he or she self-injures. Includes information on obtaining support and assistance.

Strong, Marilee. *A Bright Red Scream: Self-Mutilation and the Language of Pain.* New York: Virago, 2005. First published in 1999, this work examines self-injury and the psychology of pain through case studies.

Sutton, Jan. *Healing the Hurt Within: Understanding Self-Injury and Self-Harm, and Heal the Emotional Wounds.* 3rd ed. Oxford, England: How to Books, 2007. The author, a psychotherapist, describes the reasons for self-injury with case studies and includes information on helping the self-injurer.

WEBSITES OF INTEREST

KidsHealth.org
http://kidshealth.org/teen/your_mind/mental_
    health/cutting.html

National Center for PTSD
http://www.ptsd.va.gov/professional/pages/
    self-harm-trauma.asp

SAFE Alternatives
http://www.selfinjury.com

See also: Behavioral addictions: Overview; Body modification addiction; Self-destructive behavior and addiction

D

D.A.R.E. (Drug Abuse Resistance Education)

CATEGORY: Diagnosis and prevention

DEFINITION: Drug Abuse Resistance Education is a combined program of law enforcement agencies and school systems around the world educating students about the consequences of drug use, gangs, and violence.

DATE: Established in 1983

BACKGROUND

The Drug Abuse Resistance Education (D.A.R.E.) program was established by the Los Angeles Police Department (LAPD) and the Los Angeles Unified School District in 1983 to address drug addiction and violence among children and adolescents. The program received early support from the Robert Wood Johnson Foundation and many private donors. In its early days, D.A.R.E., under its cofounders, LAPD officers Glenn Levant and Daryl Gates (who later became LAPD chief), focused both on demand reduction (decreasing the desire for drugs by making students aware of the physical, personal, and social consequences of drug use) and, with law enforcement agencies, on supply reduction (decreasing drug availability to potential addicts of all ages).

Early research investigating the effectiveness of D.A.R.E. programs indicates that the effect of these programs has been minimal, and one study (published in 2004) argued that the program does not warrant being funded. The authors of this critical study also indicated, however, that most studies of D.A.R.E. have not used a pretest/post-test format. If D.A.R.E. were to be studied using this more rigorous format, the study authors added, it might be shown to be more effective.

In the early 1980s, before the existence of programs like D.A.R.E., 66 percent of high school students had used illegal drugs; in 2008, illegal drug use among high school students had decreased to about 47 percent. The program was revamped in 2001, and

Celebrity D.A.R.E. ammbassadors have included actor Steven Seagal. (Getty Images)

again in 2008, to make it function more effectively. D.A.R.E. now operates in every state in the United States and in close to fifty other countries. Ongoing reviews of effectiveness are continuing.

MISSION AND GOALS

The mission of D.A.R.E. is to provide students with information and skills for making good and healthy decisions for safer and healthier lives. While the program originally dealt with the topics of drug use and violence, it has been expanded to include gangs, Internet safety, and the prevention of cyberbullying.

D.A.R.E. also attempts to establish positive relationships between police officers and school children.

This allows the officers to visit schools to speak in a friendly, informative manner about the importance of a drug-free life. The D.A.R.E. curriculum consists of seventeen lessons presented to the students by police officers once a week in classrooms. The officers also teach decision-making skills.

All officers have mentors who are senior D.A.R.E. officers. Mentors teach the classroom officers how to effectively present material to children, inform them of helpful interactive activities, and provide further tips on teaching about drugs and violence. All D.A.R.E. officers provide students with skills to help them make informed decisions in and out of the school environment. Doing so helps the students build self-esteem, stand firm against peer pressure, and develop the courage to refuse drugs or to refuse to participate in violent activities.

Robin Kamienny Montvilo, PhD

FURTHER READING

Ennett Susan T., et al. "How Effective Is Drug Abuse Resistance Education? A Meta-Analysis of Project D.A.R.E. Outcome Evaluations." *American Journal of Public Health* 84 (1994): 1394–1401. Print.

Hanson, David J. "Drug Abuse Resistance Education: The Effectiveness of D.A.R.E.." Web. 29 Feb. 2012. http://alcoholfacts.org/D.A.R.E..html.

Kanof, Marjorie E. "Youth Illicit Drug Use Prevention: D.A.R.E. Long-Term Evaluations and Federal Efforts to Identify Effective Programs." Washington D.C.: GAO, January 15, 2003.

Levant, Glenn A. *Keeping Kids Drug Free: D.A.R.E. Official Parent's Guide.* San Diego: Advantage, 1998.

West, Steven L., and K. K. O'Neal. "Project D.A.R.E. Outcome Effectiveness Revisited." *American Journal of Public Health* 94 (2004): 1027–29. Print.

WEBSITES OF INTEREST

American Council for Drug Education
http://www.acde.org

Drug Abuse Resistance Education
http://www.dare.com

Office of Safe and Drug-Free Schools
http://www2.ed.gov/about/offices/list/osdfs

The Partnership at DrugFree.org
http://www.drugfree.org

See also: Education about substance abuse; Just Say No campaign; Law enforcement and drugs; Prevention methods and research; Schools and substance abuse

Date rape drugs

CATEGORY: Substances
ALSO KNOWN AS: Club drugs; ecstasy; flunitrazepam; gamma hydroxybutyrate; ketamine; Rohypnol
DEFINITION: Date rape drugs are typically odorless, colorless, and tasteless substances that are often combined with alcohol and other drinks to commit sexual assaults. The drugs sedate and incapacitate an unsuspecting person, leaving that person unable to resist a sexual assault.

COMMON DATE RAPE DRUGS

Rohypnol (flunitrazepam), gamma hydroxybutyrate (GHB), and ketamine are common date rape drugs. Alcohol and ecstasy are also used to commit sexual assaults. All of these drugs affect judgment and behavior and can put a person at risk for sexual assault or risky sexual activity.

Rohypnol use began to gain popularity in the United States in the early 1990s. It is a benzodiazepine (chemically similar to sedative-hypnotic drugs such as Valium or Xanax) and is illegal in the United States. It is legal in Europe and Mexico, where it is prescribed for sleep problems and used for anesthesia. It is exported to the United States illegally.

Rohypnol is a pill that dissolves in liquid. Some of these pills are small, round, and white. Newer pills are oval and green-gray in color. When placed into a drink, the pills' dye makes clear liquids turn bright blue and dark drinks turn cloudy. However, this color change is often difficult to see in a dark drink, such as cola or dark beer, or in a darkened room, such as a nightclub or bar. Also, pills with no dye are still available. The pills also can be ground into a powder.

GHB (Xyrem) is a central nervous system depressant that was approved by the US Food and Drug Administration (FDA) in 2002 for use in the treatment of narcolepsy (a sleep disorder). This approval came with severe restrictions, including its use only for the treatment of narcolepsy, and with the requirement that it be monitored by the FDA through a patient registry.

GHB also is a metabolite of the inhibitory neurotransmitter gamma-aminobutyric acid. It exists naturally in the brain, but at much lower concentrations than those found when GHB is abused. GHB comes in a few forms: a liquid with no odor or color, a white powder, and a pill. It can make a drink taste slightly salty.

Ketamine is legal in the United States for use as an anesthetic for humans and animals. It is mostly used with animals. Veterinary clinics are sometimes burglarized for their ketamine supplies. Ketamine comes as a liquid and a white powder.

EFFECTS ON THE HUMAN BODY

The sedative-hypnotic effects of date rape drugs are powerful. The drugs can affect a person quickly and without that person's knowledge, which makes them especially appealing to potential perpetrators of assault. The length of time that the effects last varies and depends on how much of the drug is taken and if the drug is mixed with other drugs or alcohol. Alcohol makes the drugs even stronger and can cause serious health problems, even death.

The effects of Rohypnol occur within thirty minutes of ingestion and can last for several hours. A victim may look and act like someone who is drunk. He or she might have trouble standing, might have slurred speech, or might pass out. GHB takes effect in about fifteen minutes and can last three or four hours. A small amount of GHB can have a big effect. Ketamine is fast-acting. A victim might be aware of what is happening but unable to move. Ketamine also causes memory problems. Later, a victim might not remember what occurred while drugged.

It is often difficult for a person to know if he or she has been drugged and assaulted. Most victims do not remember details of the incident. The victim might not be aware of the attack until eight or twelve hours after it occurred, after the drug effects wear off.

Date rape drugs can leave the body quickly. By the time a victim receives help, the drug involved in the attack is likely out of the person's system. However, there are other signs that indicate a person might have been drugged, including the following, in which the person feels drunk and has not had any alcohol or feels like the effects of drinking alcohol are stronger than usual; wakes up feeling hung over and disoriented or having no memory of a period of time;

remembers having a drink, but cannot recall anything after that; finds that his or her clothes are torn or are not fitting properly; or feels like he or she had sex but cannot remember having sex.

Persons who have ingested a date rape drug should get medical care immediately. As with any sexual assault, it is important that the victim not urinate, douche, bathe or shower, brush teeth, wash hands, change clothes, or eat or drink before seeing a medical professional. Doing so may destroy evidence of the assault. The hospital will use a rape kit to collect any evidence. The victim should ask the hospital to take a urine sample that can be used to test for date rape drugs. Rohypnol stays in the body for several hours and can be detected in the urine up to seventy-two hours after ingestion. GHB leaves the body within twelve hours.

Claudia Daileader Ruland, MA

FURTHER READING

Adams, Colleen. *Rohypnol: Roofies—"The Date Rape Drug."* New York: Rosen, 2007.

Albright, J. A., S. A. Stevens, and D. J. Beussman. "Detecting Ketamine in Beverage Residues: Application in Date Rape Detection." *Drug Testing and Analysis* 4.3–4 (2011). Print.

Németh, Z., B. Kun, and Z. Demetrovics. "The Involvement of Gamma-Hydroxybutyrate in Reported Sexual Assaults: A Systematic Review." *Journal of Psychopharmacology* 24.9 (2010): 1281–87. Print.

WEBSITES OF INTEREST

Center for Substance Abuse Research
http://www.cesar.umd.edu/cesar/drugs/rohypnol.asp

National Institute on Drug Abuse
http://www.drugabuse.gov/publications/infofacts/club-drugs-ghb-ketamine-rohypnol

Project GHB
http://www.projectghb.org

WomensHealth.gov
http://www.womenshealth.gov/publications/our-publications/fact-sheet/date-rape-drugs.pdf

See also: Club drugs; GHB; Ketamine; Rohypnol; Sexual assault and drug use

Debtors Anonymous

CATEGORY: Treatment

DEFINITION: Debtors Anonymous is a twelve-step recovery program modeled on Alcoholics Anonymous, which helps people overcome the accumulation of unmanageable, unsecured debt.

ESTABLISHED: April 1976

BACKGROUND

Debtors Anonymous (DA) owes its inception to a group of recovering alcoholics in New York City who, in 1968, organized an informal support group, under the leadership of John H., to explore members' self-destructive behavior with money. After trying various approaches (at one time the group called itself Penny Pinchers and emphasized thrift, and it later called itself Capital Builders, emphasizing savings and income maximization), group members concluded that the central problem was accumulating unmanageable, unsecured debt.

In April of 1976 the group formally inaugurated DA, a program based on the twelve-step recovery model of Alcoholics Anonymous (AA). The early, central aim of DA was to help its members avoid accumulating additional unsecured debt and clearing up past debts through negotiations with creditors and repayment, when feasible.

The organization grew slowly. By 1982, five meetings were being held, all in Manhattan. At this time the founders established a board of trustees and a general service conference. DA now provides about five hundred meetings in twelve countries, but it remains concentrated in urban areas in the United States.

The organization has published the book *A Currency of Hope* (1999), a compendium of thirty-eight stories about recovery from debt through DA participation, and also a number of pamphlets, mainly on the mechanics of working the program. For general information on twelve-step programs, members are referred to AA literature, to which DA publications are considered supplemental.

Most of DA's growth occurred before 1996. A number of explanations have been offered concerning why interest in DA has leveled off or even declined since the mid-1990s. One possibility is that it treats the act of incurring debt as if it were an addiction, a model that remains questionable. Indebtedness often accompanies addictive behaviors, as prudent financial management is overcome by compulsion; the act of borrowing itself is secondary. As long as the bulk of DA membership was drawn from the ranks of alcoholics, who were accustomed to using the twelve-step model to combat a "real" addiction, people would accept the type of program (like DA) that demanded total abstinence and strenuous efforts to clear up old debts, because it had worked for them. An increase in the number of people without twelve-step experience who expected general financial management support and rejected abstinence in favor of moderation, has shifted DA's focus, and that shift introduced terms such as *self-debting*, *financial anorexia*, and *situational debting*. There is a movement within DA to return to a more strict concentration on monetary debt.

MISSION AND GOALS

The aim of DA is twofold. First, it provides recovery tools for people who are struggling with debt, and second, it provides a support structure within which recovering members can share their experiences with newcomers.

A key feature of the program is awareness, both of individual finances and of the climate in which people operate. Members are encouraged to keep a daily journal in which they note every expenditure and keep receipts. Although the organization does not lobby publicly against the often-deceptive practices of the credit industry (one of DA's traditions, borrowed from AA, is avoiding politics), it does play an active role in educating members about how the industry encourages people to incur debt.

A person wishing to receive help from DA should first start attending meetings, or, if none are available, should explore meetings online or by telephone. Upon joining, a debtor will connect with a sponsor, a more experienced member who guides him or her through the twelve steps. The new member will then be asked to join a pressure relief group, comprising three people who have gone a minimum of ninety days without accumulating unsecured debt. The new member will work with other group members to formulate a spending and action plan. Ideally, a spending plan allocates funds to meet needs, retire debt, and save for the future, and it also includes ways to increase income.

People become financially indebted for many reasons, not all under personal control. One pattern of behavior that has addictive characteristics and can lead to spiraling credit card debt is compulsive spending disorder. The *Diagnostic and Statistical Manual of Mental Disorders* of the American Psychiatric Association (APA) includes compulsive spending under the diagnostic category of impulse control disorders not specified, but the APA may recognize the disorder as distinct in revised manuals. DA addresses spending compulsion indirectly, through a strict program of budgeting and prohibition against credit card use for consumer purchases.

Since the collapse of the housing market in the United States and the ensuing global recession beginning in 2007/2008, the availability of consumer credit has contracted considerably, and the realities of debt in the United States have changed. Overconsumption and lack of impulse control play a smaller role now, while declining income, declining home values, medical debt, and student loans have become more prominent. This shift may be another reason why fewer people are using the services of DA.

DA considers legal bankruptcy proceedings to be an outside issue and has no position for or against it. Declaring bankruptcy would force a debtor into the sort of careful budgeting and economizing that DA encourages. It is often the only realistic option for people with large involuntary, primarily medical, debts.

Martha A. Sherwood, PhD

FURTHER READING

Bill W. *Alcoholics Anonymous.* 4th ed. New York: Alcoholics Anonymous, 2002. The first 168 pages of this oft-referenced text contain a blueprint for twelve-step recovery programs, including Debtors Anonymous.

Debtors Anonymous. *A Currency of Hope.* Needham, MA: Author, 1999. A collection of thirty-eight personal stories of recovery from debt, plus an explanation of the Debtors Anonymous program.

Geisst, Charles R. *Collateral Damaged: The Marketing of Consumer Debt to America.* New York: Bloomberg, 2009. Explains how the United States turned from a nation of savers into a nation of consumers addicted to debt.

Manning, Robert D. *Credit Card Nation: The Consequences of America's Addiction to Credit.* New York: Basic, 2003. A mostly historical look at the problem of consumer debt in the United States.

Morenberg, Adam D. "Governing Wayward Consumers: Self-Change and Recovery in Debtors Anonymous." MA thesis. UP of South Florida, 2004. Print. A sociological analysis of Debtors Anonymous.

WEBSITE OF INTEREST

Debtors Anonymous
http://www.debtorsanonymous.org

See also: Group therapy for behavioral addictions; Self-destructive behavior and addiction; Support groups; Twelve-step programs for addicts

Decriminalization of drugs in the United States

CATEGORY: Social issues

DEFINITION: Decriminalization refers to a reduction in or an elimination of the criminal classification or status of any activity considered a criminal offense. Decriminalization of drugs specifically refers to reducing or eliminating legal restrictions placed on the possession, distribution, and use of illicit substances, most notably marijuana.

OVERVIEW

For much of the twentieth century and into the twenty-first century, the United States has been engaged in a pronounced effort to stop the flow of illicit substances into the country, to curb the use of such substances, and to reduce the number of crimes related to their use. This effort has been characterized as the War on Drugs.

Increasingly, however, many activists have called attention to the belief that this "war" has thus far proved ineffective at best and even counterproductive in reducing drug-related crime. In response, a substantial movement in favor of the decriminalization of drugs has developed and turned the question of the appropriate legal status of illicit substances into one of the most hotly debated issues in contemporary politics.

At the center of this debate is marijuana, one of the most widely used drugs. Reports estimate that nearly 100 million Americans have experimented with marijuana at least once in their lifetime. Proponents of decriminalization argue that marijuana is a largely harmless substance that has been unjustly maligned in the arena of public opinion and should thus be legalized.

Opponents of the decriminalization of marijuana argue that marijuana is potentially as harmful as other drugs and that its legalization would only encourage more drug-related crime and other social problems. Further intensifying this debate is medical marijuana, which has benefits for persons with certain ailments and diseases. To fully understand the debate over the decriminalization of marijuana and other drugs, it is critically important to view the issue from both sides of the argument and carefully study the potential benefits and consequences such legislation would likely have.

ARGUMENTS FOR DECRIMINALIZATION

According to an October 2011 Gallup poll, 50 percent of Americans are in favor of legalizing the use of marijuana, a record number. Those in favor of decriminalizing marijuana argue that the legalization of its use would be beneficial in many ways.

Among the chief and often most persuasive of these arguments is the belief that decriminalization would save governments and law enforcement agencies much money. The enforcement of laws related to marijuana costs an estimated $10 billion to $15 billion annually. Proponents of marijuana decriminalization argue that legalizing marijuana would eliminate these costs, thus allowing for the reallocation of these funds for other, more useful purposes, including taxpayer savings.

To some extent, this theory of cost reduction has been proven. Since 1973, twelve US states (Alaska, California, Colorado, Maine, Minnesota, Mississippi, New York, Nebraska, Nevada, North Carolina, Ohio, and Oregon) have either decriminalized marijuana or have otherwise amended state marijuana regulations. In California, where the possession of small amounts of marijuana has been partially decriminalized, reports have shown that the state saves close to $30 million annually—funds that would otherwise be used to prosecute small-time marijuana offenders.

In addition to highlighting the potential financial benefits of the decriminalization of marijuana, proponents also frequently target what they see as misconceptions about the drug's use. First and foremost, to counter the claim that decriminalization would likely result in a dramatic upsurge in the number of marijuana users, proponents respond by arguing that marijuana is already a widely used drug, with about 25.8 million people using the drug at least once per month.

Proponents also point out that those who use marijuana often do so responsibly, and without dependence. For example, whereas most people who use alcohol or tobacco generally consume these addictive substances daily, most marijuana users consume marijuana on a monthly or weekly basis only. This, supporters claim, shows that marijuana is not as addictive as alcohol or tobacco and is not as likely to lead to abuse or dependence.

Another common concern many people have about the decriminalization of marijuana or other drugs is that decriminalizing drugs might lead to an increase in crime. Proponents of decriminalization, however, argue that this concern is based on a misconception, one that is based primarily on the belief that because many people who have committed crimes have also used drugs that drugs must directly cause people to commit criminal acts. Proponents of decriminalization say that drug use is only one of many factors that leads people to crime and should not be considered a sole cause.

In addition, studies have shown that marijuana is the least likely of the major illicit drugs to result in criminal activities of any kind (alcohol, on the other hand, has been implicated in 40 percent of violent crimes in the United States). Persons who are high on marijuana are unlikely to become violent.

Finally, proponents of decriminalizing marijuana also argue that doing so would, to some degree, lighten the workload and general burdens of the criminal justice system. Though the number of marijuana-related crimes is relatively low in comparison with other types of crime, the elimination of these cases would reduce the workload of police and the courts, free up much needed space in correctional facilities, and save the criminal justice system, governments, and taxpayers money.

It also is important to note that the proponents of decriminalization support the legalization of marijuana for medicinal purposes. Research has shown that marijuana does improve the painful symptoms of certain illnesses. Marijuana supporters often strongly believe that, even if marijuana were not decriminalized for recreational use, it should be legalized for those with a legitimate medical need for the substance.

Opposition to Decriminalization

For all those who support the decriminalization of marijuana and other drugs in the United States, there are nearly as many people who oppose decriminalization. Opponents cite a variety of reasons why such legislation would fail and, possibly, lead to even larger social concerns.

Opponents of decriminalization argue that legalizing marijuana would lead to a significant increase in drug use across the United States. They also believe that decriminalization also would lead to an increase in the number of teenagers who experiment with marijuana, a claim that proponents refute (arguing that only a minimal, if any, increase in use would occur among teens).

Finally, opponents argue that marijuana is a gateway drug and that legal use of the substance would eventually lead to an increase in the use of harder drugs. However, proponents refute this claim also, claiming that statistics show the rate of usage of harder drugs is much lower than the rate of use of marijuana, which suggests that most marijuana users never move on to more dangerous substances.

Another argument made regularly by opponents is that decriminalization would cause a dramatic increase in the crime rate. They believe that the majority of those crimes labeled as drug-related are actually crimes committed by persons under the influence of a mind-altering substance, and are not committed as part of the sale of drugs. Opponents believe that legalizing a drug will not stop related crimes.

Opponents also argue that drugs should remain illegal because of the medical issues surrounding drug use. In answer to the claim made by proponents of decriminalization that legalization has economic advantages, opponents argue that any financial savings incurred would be offset by increased expenses related to health costs, traffic and industrial accidents, decreased productivity, domestic violence, and other issues. Finally, in regard to medical marijuana, those who oppose decriminalization, even for persons with legitimate medical conditions, argue that there exist safer alternatives to marijuana, some of which use the same ingredients found in marijuana itself.

Jack A. Lasky

Further Reading

Caulkins, Jonathan P., et al. *Marijuana Legalization: What Everyone Needs to Know.* New York: Oxford UP, 2012. An updated look at the issue of marijuana decriminalization.

Evans, Rod L., and Irwin M. Berent, eds. *Drug Legalization: For and Against.* La Salle, IL: Open Court, 1994. Provides a look at the pros and cons of drug decriminalization from both sides of the issue.

Fisher, Gary L. *Rethinking Our War on Drugs: Candid Talk about Controversial Issues.* Westport, CT: Praeger, 2006. A comprehensive look at the war on drugs and issues surrounding modern drug policies.

Husak, Douglas N. *Legalize This! The Case for Decriminalizing Drugs.* New York: Verso, 2002. An argument for the decriminalization of drugs in the United States.

Websites of Interest

Center for Medicinal Cannabis Research
http://www.cmcr.ucsd.edu

Drug Policy Alliance
http://www.drugpolicy.org

Law Enforcement Against Prohibition
http://www.leap.cc

NORML
http://norml.org

US Drug Enforcement Administration
http://www.justice.gov/dea

See also: Crime and substance abuse; Law enforcement and drugs; Legislation and substance abuse; Medical marijuana

Dependence

CATEGORY: Substance abuse
ALSO KNOWN AS: Addiction
DEFINITION: Chemical dependence is a primary, progressive, and potentially fatal condition resulting from the chronic abuse of a toxic substance. Compulsive and repetitive use of a substance, whether drugs or alcohol, results in a loss of control over the amount ingested on any given occasion, leading to a higher tolerance so that more of the drug is needed for the person to feel its effects. Once chemical dependence has developed, suddenly stopping the substance use will produce withdrawal symptoms such as anxiety and other unpleasant physical symptoms.

CAUSES

Dependence is caused by a combination of factors, including inherited genes, environmental stressors, and, often, an underlying or pre-existing mental health issue, such as depression or anxiety. Social factors, such as peer pressure to experiment, also come into play. Environmental stress, whether at work or home, is also a major contributor to cravings that drive a person to abuse substances.

Personal choice also is a cause. A person chooses a particular drug for its pharmacological effect in reducing stress or uncomfortable feelings. Psychoanalyst Sigmund Freud was the first to raise this self-medication hypothesis after noting the antidepressive properties of cocaine. Since this time, psychoanalysts and biological researchers have agreed that people use addictive substances to relieve undesirable states of mind and, through continued use, often become chemically dependent.

Physiologically, addictive substances flood the brain's reward circuit, primarily with the hormone dopamine. When these reward pathways are continually overstimulated, the brain produces less of its own hormones and dopamine receptors. Without the drug, the person is then unable to enjoy the things that brought pleasure. The person progressively takes greater amounts of the substance to overcome tolerance, which leads to profound chemical changes in neurons and brain circuits that compromise the long-term functioning and health of the brain.

RISK FACTORS

Aside from genetics, risk factors for dependence include surviving a disaster or experiencing psychic trauma. Disaster and trauma survivors are prone to stress-related disorders such as post-traumatic stress disorder and depression. Such persons may self-medicate with alcohol or other drugs to relieve unbearable symptoms.

Social development also may play a role in drug abuse and addiction. Typically, over one's lifetime, certain developmental milestones are met in which a person gains the confidence and skills needed to mature and progress in life. When these milestones are not met, the developmental perspective predicts that such diversions from the norm lead to less-than-satisfactory adjustment, possibly increasing the risk of substance dependence.

SYMPTOMS

The four primary symptoms of drug dependence are the presence of cravings, loss of control over the amount ingested, tolerance to the drug's effects, and withdrawal symptoms when the substance is not available. Behavioral symptoms include hostility when confronted about drug abuse or making excuses; missing work or school with decreasing performance; becoming secretive; and neglecting to eat, groom, or take part in activities.

SCREENING AND DIAGNOSIS

Toxicology screens, known as drug tests, can be used to determine whether substances are present in the body. The sensitivity of these tests depends on the drug itself, when it was taken, and whether the test is done on blood or urine. Blood tests are more successful at detecting toxic substances, but urine tests are used more often, in part because they can be done at home, and are cheaper and less invasive to perform than drawing blood samples.

TREATMENT AND THERAPY

It can be difficult to convince a chemically dependent person that he or she needs treatment. Denial, a common indicator of addiction, is less of a hurdle when the person is approached and treated with empathy and respect.

Once a problem has been acknowledged, treatment involves stopping the substance use either gradually or abruptly (with a period of detoxification) and providing support for the person to remain drug-free. Dependence is characterized by relapse, and many people who want to quit have to try several times. Even after long periods of sobriety, relapses are possible.

The term *detoxification* refers to a controlled environment in which people may be monitored as their bodily systems return to normal. Medications are often used to control withdrawal symptoms, especially with heavy alcohol use or opioid dependence, because suddenly stopping the substance can lead to death in extreme cases. Medications are available for treating dependence to nicotine, alcohol, and opiates, but not to stimulants or marijuana.

Treatment programs exist as in-patient or out-patient services and should be evaluated based on the type of drug abused, the duration of dependence, and whether the goal is to quit entirely or to minimize a habit's deleterious effects. Twelve-step programs such as Alcoholics Anonymous and Narcotics Anonymous provide networks of support for total abstinence through reliance on a higher power; some people, however, do not respond to the spiritual underpinnings of these programs.

Individual and group therapies that employ cognitive-behavioral therapy focus on changing thoughts to alter behaviors, often with the goal of reducing the habit's impact on work and family. Rehabilitation (or rehab) centers exist to separate more seriously dependent patients.

PREVENTION

Education on drug dependence is important for prevention, as are strategies for coping with stress. These strategies can include meditation, yoga, cognitive-behavioral strategies, physical exercise, and progressive-relaxation techniques. For those who are recovering from dependence, relapse prevention involves avoiding places frequented by people abusing drugs and developing a new social network that supports the recovering addict in leading a drug-free lifestyle.

Laura B. Smith

FURTHER READING

Essau, Cecelia A. *Substance Abuse and Dependence in Adolescence: Epidemiology, Risk Factors, and Treatment.* New York: Taylor, 2002. The author, along with an eminent group of international researchers and clinicians, summarizes the most recent empirical findings and knowledge on substance abuse and dependence in adolescence. Includes comprehensive information on prevention and treatment.

Kleber, Herbert, et al. "Treatment of Patients with Substance Use Disorders." *American Journal of Psychiatry* 164 (2007): 5–123. Print. Published as a supplement, this practice guideline was developed by psychiatrists who are in active clinical practice and by contributors involved in research or other academic endeavors.

Liptak, John J., Ester Leutenberg, and Amy Brodsky. *The Substance Abuse and Recovery Workbook.* Duluth, MN: Whole Person, 2008. Contains self-assessment exercises, exploratory activities, reflective journaling exercises, and educational handouts to help readers discover habitual and effective methods of managing substance abuse and to explore new ways of healing.

White, Jason M. *Drug Dependence.* Upper Saddle River, NJ: Prentice Hall, 1990. This thorough, nonjudgmental overview of drug dependence approaches the subject from biological, psychological, and social perspectives. Appropriate for undergraduate-level courses in drug abuse, society and behavior, psychopharmacology, and behavioral pharmacology.

WEBSITES OF INTEREST

Medline Plus: Drug Dependence
http://www.nlm.nih.gov/medlineplus/ency/article/001522.htm

National Institute on Drug Abuse
http://www.drugabuse.gov

Native Alcohol and Drug Abuse Counseling Association of Nova Scotia
http://nadaca.ca

See also: Codependency; Physiological dependence; Psychological dependence; Science of addiction; Substance abuse

Depressants abuse

Category: Substance abuse

ALSO KNOWN AS: Sedative-hypnotic abuse; tranquilizer abuse

DEFINITION: Depressants represent a broad category of substances, with or without clinical use, which reduce the activity of the central nervous system. Included in this category of substances are ethanol, sedative-hypnotics (barbiturates, benzodiazepines), barbiturate-like compounds (chloral hydrate, methaqualone, meprobamate), narcotics (opium, morphine, codeine), marijuana, antihistamines, and some inhalants. Frequently, the term depressants abuse is used in a restricted sense, to designate specifically the nonmedical use of sedative-hypnotic drugs.

CAUSES

Humans have always sought to alleviate the effects of stress and to reduce anxiety, depression, restlessness, and tension. Alcohol and kava kava are two of the oldest depressant agents. The nineteenth century brought synthetic substances such as bromide salts and chloral hydrate. These were followed by barbiturates and benzodiazepines, which were introduced in the twentieth century.

Depressant abuse is on the rise because of the wide availability of drugs by prescription or through the illicit marketplace. Examples of illegal depressants of abuse include the date rape drugs flunitrazepam (Rohypnol) and gamma-hydroxybutyric acid (GHB, a natural depressant).

Overall, short-acting agents are more likely to be used nonmedically than those with long-lasting effects. Because of their wider margin of safety, benzodiazepines have largely replaced barbiturates. They now constitute the most prescribed central nervous system (CNS) depressants—and the most frequently abused, usually to achieve a general feeling of relaxation. However, barbiturates and barbiturate-like drugs still pose clinical problems, as many young people underestimate the risks these drugs carry. Non-benzodiazepine sedatives, such as zolpidem (Ambien), also can generate misuse and dependence.

Most sedative-hypnotic drugs work by enhancing the inhibitory activity of the neurotransmitter gamma-aminobutyric acid, thus reducing CNS activity and promoting relaxation and sleep. They are usually prescribed to treat sleep disorders, anxiety, acute stress reactions, panic attacks, and seizures. In higher doses, some agents become general anesthetics. Chronic use results in tolerance and dependence (both psychological and physical).

RISK FACTORS

Barbiturate abuse occurs most commonly in mature adults with a long history of use, while benzodiazepines are favored by younger persons (those younger than forty years of age). Two main categories of people misuse depressant drugs. The first category comprises people who receive depressant prescriptions for psychiatric disorders or who obtain them illicitly to cope with stressful life situations. These persons have a high risk of becoming dependent, especially if they receive high doses, take the drug for longer than one month, and have a history of substance abuse or a family history of alcoholism. However, if dose escalation is not evident and drugs are not used to achieve a state of intoxication, chronic benzodiazepine users should not be considered abusers.

A second important category comprises people who use sedative drugs in the context of alcohol or multiple-drug abuse. These people may take benzodiazepines to alleviate insomnia and anxiety (sometimes induced by stimulants), to increase the euphoric effects of opioids, and to diminish cocaine (or alcohol) withdrawal symptoms.

SYMPTOMS

People who abuse depressants often engage in drug-seeking behaviors that include frequently requesting, borrowing, stealing, or forging prescriptions; ordering and purchasing medication online; and visiting several doctors to obtain prescriptions. These behaviors often accompany changes in sleep patterns and irritable mood and increased alcohol consumption. Recreational use and self-medication with depressants may lead to accidental overdoses and suicide attempts. Many persons use a "cocktail" of alcohol and depressant medications for enhanced relaxation and euphoria. This practice is dangerous, as it carries a high risk of overdose.

Sedative-hypnotic drug intoxication resembles alcohol, painkillers, and antihistamine intoxication. It presents with impaired judgment, confusion, drowsiness, dizziness, unsteady movements, slurred speech, and visual disturbances. Young adults attempting to get high may show excitement, loss of inhibition, and even aggressive behavior. Acute GHB intoxication leads to sleep and memory loss. These manifestations occur without alcohol odor on the breath, unless the abuser combined the drug with alcohol. In the case of barbiturates, the behavioral effects of intoxication can vary depending on the time of day, the surroundings, and even the user's expectations.

Tolerance to barbiturates is not accompanied by an increase in lethal dose, as it is with opiates. For this reason, an overdose can be fatal. Signs and symptoms of barbiturate overdose vary, and they include lethargy, decreased heart rate, diminished reflexes, respiratory depression, and cardiovascular collapse.

All sedative-hypnotics can induce physical dependence if taken in sufficient dosage over a long time. Withdrawal from depressant medication results in a "rebound" of nervous system activity. In a mild form, this leads to anxiety and insomnia. In cases of more severe dependence, withdrawal manifests with nausea, vomiting, tremors, seizures, delirium, and ultimately, death. Therefore, discontinuation of prescription drugs necessitates close medical supervision.

SCREENING AND DIAGNOSIS

To evaluate a person who might abuse depressant medication, a doctor will obtain a thorough medical history, ask questions about current and previous drug and alcohol use, and perform a physical examination. A psychiatric evaluation may also be required. The diagnosis of depressant drug abuse relies on evidence of dose escalation, on obtaining multiple prescriptions, and on taking the drug for purposes other than those stated in the prescription.

Multiple tests detect the presence of drugs and also potential medical complications. These include drug screening (urine and blood), electrolyte and liver profiles, an electrocardiogram, and X-ray and magnetic resonance imaging.

TREATMENT AND THERAPY

Therapeutic strategies for depressants abuse vary according to the drug used, the severity of the manifestations, and the duration of drug action. Common therapies include detoxification, which involves the use of agents that reverse the effects of the drug (for example, using Flumazenil for benzodiazepine abuse and using Naloxone for narcotics abuse). Other common therapies include the use of medications that mitigate withdrawal symptoms, counseling in inpatient or outpatient settings, support groups, and relaxation training. When a person receiving treatment has combined a CNS depressant with alcohol or other drugs, all aspects of this addiction have to be addressed and treated.

PREVENTION

Sedative-hypnotic medication should be used only as prescribed. Combinations of CNS depressants (such as alcohol/drug or over-the-counter drug/prescription medication) pose high risks and should be avoided.

People who are unsure of a drug's effects, or who suspect dependence, should consult a pharmacist or a doctor. Those people who are contemplating the discontinuation of a CNS depressant or who are experiencing withdrawal symptoms should seek medical care immediately.

A careful assessment is necessary before prescribing depressant medication in persons with a history of drug abuse. These individuals require close monitoring. Also, caregivers and health care providers should verify that there are no alternative sources for obtaining the drug of abuse.

Mihaela Avramut, MD, PhD

FURTHER READING

Hanson, Glen R., Peter J. Venturelli, and Annette E. Fleckenstein. *Drugs and Society.* 9th ed. Sudbury, MA: Jones, 2006. An easy-to-read textbook that includes a comprehensive review of CNS depressants and their effects and patterns of abuse.

Parker, James N., and Philip M. Parker. *The Official Patient's Sourcebook on Prescription CNS Depressants Dependence.* San Diego, CA: Icon, 2002. Useful resource for patients and caregivers, covering all aspects of depressant dependence.

Sadock, Benjamin J., and Virginia A. Sadock. *Kaplan and Sadock's Synopsis of Psychiatry: Behavioral Sciences/Clinical Psychiatry.* 10th ed. Philadelphia: Lippincott, 2007. Popular psychiatry textbook for students and health care practitioners that discusses depressants abuse.

Sue, David, Derald Wing Sue, and Stanley Sue. *Understanding Abnormal Behavior.* Boston: Wadsworth, 2010. Accessible textbook that includes a well-written discussion of depressants misuse.

WEBSITES OF INTEREST

National Institute on Drug Abuse

http://www.drugabuse.gov/publications/research-reports/prescription-drugs/cns-depressants

US Drug Enforcement Administration

http://www.justice.gov/dea/concern/depressants.html

See also: Prescription drug addiction: Overview; Psychosis and substance abuse; Sedative-Hypnotic abuse

Depression

CATEGORY: Psychological issues and behaviors

DEFINITION: Depression, or clinical depression, is a serious mental illness that can lead to self-neglect and self-abuse, including substance abuse, which can lead to addiction.

INTRODUCTION

Severe depression that is acute and of short duration is known as major depression. Seasonal adjustment disorder is a type of acute major depression, and mild chronic depression lasting more than two years is known as dysthymia. Clinical depression is thought to be caused in most cases by a chemical imbalance in the brain. This imbalance can occur among a number of naturally occurring chemicals, including neurotransmitters, vitamins, and amino acids.

Symptoms of depression include loss of interest in normal activities, fatigue, sleeping problems, weight loss or gain, sexual dysfunction, and thoughts of death and suicide.

The National Alliance on Mental Illness estimates that as many as 15 million Americans suffer from depression in a given year. The 2004 *World Health Report* (World Health Organization) reported that major depressive orders affect 6.7 percent of adults in the United States, about 14.8 million people. Depression is the major cause of disability in people age fifteen to forty-four years in the United States and in Canada.

ADDICTION

Addiction is roughly defined as a chronic, relapsing disease that affects both the brain and behavior.

Like depression, addiction has a biochemical component and is considered a mental illness. The accepted scientific model of addiction suggests that addiction is involved with the pleasure centers of the brain. Chemicals in these centers are activated when a person ingests certain substances or engages in certain behaviors.

Many pleasure-inducing substances, such as chocolate, and pleasurable behaviors, such as listening to music, cause no harm. However, some substances and behaviors are destructive and can become addictions. Addiction to nicotine, alcohol, and certain illegal and prescription drugs is well documented. People also can become addicted to activities such as gambling, sex, web surfing, pornography, and shopping. People with destructive addictions generally have little or no control over their addiction and spend a great deal of time obsessing over it.

When a person uses a pleasure-inducing substance excessively and repeatedly, his or her body becomes saturated with metabolites, the chemicals in a substance that the body converts (metabolizes) into nutrients or energy. Some metabolites, especially those found in alcohol and certain drugs, become trapped in fatty tissue in the body. If a person stops using the substance, the metabolites are released back into the bloodstream, causing the brain to react as if the body were withdrawing from the substance. The pleasure centers in the brain accustomed to dealing with large amounts of the metabolites now must cope with only a small amount of the available chemicals. The brain then calls for, even demands, the substance. This is known as a craving, an uncomfortable and sometimes agonizing biological response accompanied by mental distress. The only way to end the craving is to take more of the substance, and the addictive cycle repeats. In medical terms, the user relapses.

DEPRESSION WITH ADDICTION

Some people suffer from both depression and addiction in varying degrees. This condition is known as a dual diagnosis or a co-occurring disorder. These terms apply to a condition in which a person has at least one addictive disorder, such as alcoholism, and one major mental disorder, such as depression. Questions then arise: How common are these co-occurring disorders? What is the relationship between depression and addiction? Does one cause or contribute to the other?

As might be expected, the exact number of diagnosed cases of co-occurring disorders for any given period or population is difficult to determine. More studies need to be done. However, a small number of studies conducted since the 1980s reveals some interesting data.

One study found that, when compared with the general population, people with mood disorders like depression were twice as likely to also have an addictive disorder, and people with an addictive disorder were about twice as likely to have a mood disorder. Another study found that about 53 percent of drug abusers and 37 percent of alcohol abusers suffered from at least one serious mental illness. A series of national household surveys on health and drug use conducted by the US Department of Health and Human Services in the early 2000s revealed co-occurring disorders in about 5.2 million adults, 2.4 percent of

full-time employed adults, and 31 percent of adults using homeless services. In 2004 an estimated 192,690 persons in emergency rooms for drug-related incidents had co-occurring disorders.

Chemical changes and imbalances are characteristic of both depression and addiction. Studies have shown that depression and other mental illnesses can trigger addiction, that addiction can contribute to depression, and that depression and addiction share common risk factors. It is not clear, however, that one disorder actually causes the other, or which disorder came first.

DEPRESSION AS RISK

A common cause of clinical depression is the imbalance or dysregulation of the chemicals serotonin and dopamine. Among their many functions in the human body, these chemicals are involved with mood,

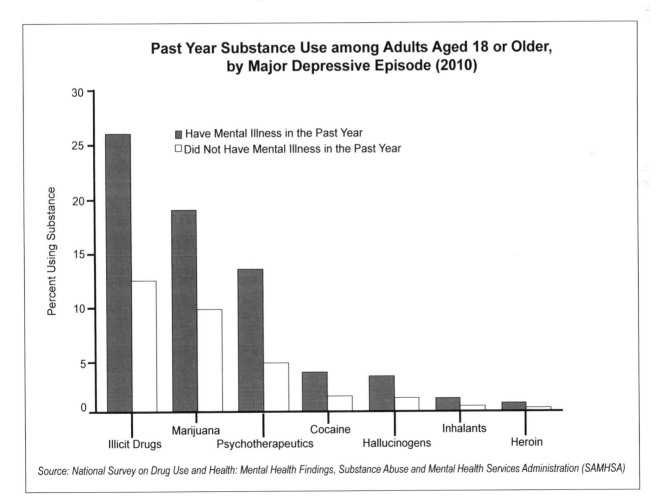

Past Year Substance Use among Adults Aged 18 or Older, by Major Depressive Episode (2010)

■ Have Mental Illness in the Past Year
□ Did Not Have Mental Illness in the Past Year

Source: National Survey on Drug Use and Health: Mental Health Findings, Substance Abuse and Mental Health Services Administration (SAMHSA)

emotions, and the experience of pain and pleasure. They are sometimes called the reward molecules. The lack or dysfunction of either of these chemicals can trigger depression symptoms.

To relieve the symptoms, many people with clinical depression self-medicate, turning to food or drugs or alcohol to boost themselves, as these substances react positively on the pleasure receptors of the brain. This sometimes works for a while. Eventually, however, symptoms return and the addictive cycle continues. Alcohol, in particular, is counterproductive. Because it is a depressant, it can lessen the effect of antidepressant medications (a common treatment for depression).

ADDICTION AS RISK

Addiction can intensify or trigger depression and other mental illness symptoms. Addicts often experience depression and anxiety over their lack of control. A well-documented example is the prevalence of depression among obese people, especially children. Food is a pleasure-inducing substance, and out-of-control overeaters are as much addicts as are alcoholics.

Many alcoholics have depression because of the harmful effects of alcohol on their relationships, careers, and physical and emotional health. As a drug, alcohol is classified as a depressant. It slows brain activity and the function of the central nervous system, which affects a person's movement, perception, and emotions.

Drug users also risk depression. Marijuana, cocaine, and hallucinogens raise dopamine levels and provide short-lived pleasure. Abusers often "crash," however, and sink into a depression when they stop using. Also, abuse of some of these drugs can result in psychosis and other forms of severe mental illness.

COMMON RISKS

Depression and addiction can stem from the same source separately or simultaneously. Research has found shared risk factors between the two disorders. Genetic factors, for example, make it more likely that some people will develop either disorder or that one disorder will develop once the other has surfaced. Brain development problems can lead an adolescent, or even a child, to early drug use, which can lead to depression later in life. Environmental factors such as trauma and stress can trigger both depression and addiction. Certain regions of the brain, such as the area

that handles response to stress, are adversely affected by both depression and addiction.

TREATMENT

Both depression and addiction can be treated separately, although focusing on one does not mean the other will disappear. Many medical and behavioral professionals maintain that dysthymia (chronic depression) and addiction can only be treated, not cured. Nevertheless, research has found that an integrated approach to treatment for both disorders (that is, treatment that occurs at the same time and in the same setting) can be effective. Successful integrated treatment is individualized, coordinated, and long term.

A specialized team of health care professionals and service providers, working with each patient, creates a personalized illness model and treatment program. In addition to the traditional medications and talk therapy, interventions and services might include detoxification, behavioral modification therapy, pain management, family counseling, diet and wellness counseling, job training, and the teaching of relationship and money-management skills. Family involvement and peer support are important components of integrated treatment. Each patient proceeds at his or her own pace, often taking years to recover. Relapses are common, even expected, because of the complex nature of treating two disorders simultaneously.

A number of integrated treatment centers have formed across the United States. Many centers accept insurance from most providers. This relatively new approach to treating co-occurring disorders shows much promise.

Wendell Anderson, BA

FURTHER READING

Dosh, Tyanne, et al. "Comparison of the Associations of Caffeine and Cigarette Use with Depressive and ADHD Symptoms in a Sample of Young Adult Smokers." *Journal of Addiction Medicine* 4 (2010): 52–54. Print. Report on a study of the relationship between caffeine use and psychiatric symptoms in young adult cigarette smokers.

Schwartz, Thomas L., and Timothy Petersen, eds. "Depression and Addiction." *Depression: Treatment Strategies and Management.* 2nd ed. London: Informa, 2009. This chapter reviews evidence of genetic causes of depression and addiction.

Westermeyer, Joseph J., Roger D. Weiss, and Douglas M. Ziedonis, eds. *Integrated Treatment for Mood and Substance Use Disorders.* Baltimore: Johns Hopkins UP, 2003. Clinicians discuss co-occurring disorders and their treatment.

WEBSITES OF INTEREST

National Alliance on Mental Illness
http://www.nami.org

National Institute on Drug Abuse
http://www.drugabuse.gov

See also: Co-occurring disorders; Depressants abuse; Mental illness

Designated drivers

CATEGORY: Social issues
DEFINITION: Designated drivers are sober drivers who are designated to transport people who have consumed alcohol. The concept was spearheaded as a public safety campaign at the national level in the United States.

HISTORY

The National Highway Transportation Safety Administration (NHTSA), the US Department of Transportation (DOT), and the Ad Council were the lead agencies in bringing public attention to the dangers of impaired driving in the United States. The Ad Council has worked with relevant US government agencies in using the power of media to enhance awareness and foster action against drinking and driving.

The Friends Don't Let Friends Drive Drunk campaign, formed by the DOT and the Ad Council, effectively illuminated problems associated with drinking and driving. The public service announcement (PSA) campaign called Innocent Victims focused on the victims of alcohol-related automobile accidents. Moving beyond television, PSAs have been delivered through radio, print, and online.

MISSION AND GOALS

Designated driver programs alert the public about designating a driver to remain sober on all outings involving alcohol consumption, so that those who choose to consume alcohol at such outings will not later drive a vehicle while drunk or will not ride in a vehicle driven by an impaired driver. This safe ride concept, which also involves variously funded, alternative transportation, is an important component of community-based, designated-driver programs.

Support for designated-driver programs comes from civic organizations, foundations, community groups, local residents, and businesses. The scope of this support ranges from community-wide efforts to independent programs. Endorsement can come from law enforcement, public health, education, and service groups. The NHTSA's Safe Communities program involves forming coalitions that promote issues associated with traffic, road, highway, and personal safety.

EFFECTIVENESS

The NHTSA notes that almost 80 percent of drivers report being influenced by the Friends Don't Let Friends Drive Drunk campaign of the DOT. These drivers took steps to prevent others from driving under the influence of alcohol. In addition, 25 percent of drivers report that the campaign helped them to refrain from drinking and driving. The importance of such campaigns is underscored by data provided in a NHTSA report that about sixteen thousand people die in the United States each year in alcohol-related motor vehicle accidents. Furthermore, a three-component program recently announced by the NHTSA offers the public a program of enhanced law enforcement, offender prosecution and adjudication, and relevant medical and mental health services.

Ronna F. Dillon, PhD
Laurel D. Dillon-Sumner, BA

FURTHER READING

DeJong, William, and Jay A. Winsten. "The Use of Designated Drivers by US College Students: A National Study." *Journal of American College Health* 47.4 (1999): 151–56. Print.

Kazbour, Richard R., and Jon S. Bailey. "An Analysis of a Contingency Program on Designated Drivers at a College Bar." *Journal of Applied Behavior Analysis* 43.2 (2010). Print.

Lange, James E., et al. "The Efficacy of Experimental Interventions Designed to Reduce Drinking among Designated Drivers." *Journal of Studies on Alcohol* 67.2 (2006): 261–68. Print.

See also: Drugged driving; Drunk driving; Prevention methods and research

Designer drugs

CATEGORY: Substance abuse
ALSO KNOWN AS: Club drugs; party drugs; recreational drugs
DEFINITION: Designer drugs are illegal synthetic analogs of controlled substances that possess similar pharmacological qualities. Designer drugs encompass a wide range of potent, unpredictable, and potentially deadly stimulants, depressants, hallucinogens, and opiates. Common designer drugs include methamphetamine, ecstasy, China white, lysergic acid diethylamide (LSD), phencyclidine (PCP), ketamine, and gamma hydroxybutyric acid (GHB).

HISTORY OF USE

Designer drugs became popular in the 1970s as a way to bypass existing regulations on controlled substances. After the Controlled Substances Act (1970) restricted the availability of illicit substances, clandestine chemists began modifying and manufacturing synthetic alternatives with similar pharmacological effects. Designer-drug production and trafficking became widespread, producing cheaper and stronger alternatives.

Some designer drugs were originally intended for medical use; others were created strictly for recreational use. The first designer drugs included hallucinogens and synthetic substitutes for heroin and amphetamine.

By the 1980s, many designer drugs became known as club drugs and gained popularity among young abusers at underground dance parties, bars, and nightclubs called raves. These raves became the place to sell and use club drugs, such as ecstasy, to enhance the club experience. The combining of designer drugs emerged as a common practice to enhance euphoric effects. Mixing ketamine, a hallucinogenic tranquillizer, with the stimulant methamphetamine became known as trail mix, while using ecstasy with LSD was called candy flipping.

Designer drugs remained legal until the 1980s, when their psychological and physical hazards became fully recognized. The drugs caused numerous overdose deaths worldwide. By 1986, the widespread manufacture and misuse of designer drugs prompted legislators in the United States to modify the Controlled Substances Act and add the Federal Analog Act to include all chemically similar substances and possible derivatives as controlled substances.

Designer drugs make up a substantial portion of the illegal drug market. Newer classes of designer drugs such as spice, K2, 2C-B, and bath salts are continually being developed, marketed, and sold by illegal chemists. Despite efforts to curb designer drug production, their abuse and popularity continues to be a concern.

COMMON DESIGNER DRUGS

Common designer drugs include hallucinogens and depressants as well as synthetic substitutes for heroin and amphetamine. The most popular amphetamine or speed analogs include methamphetamine and methylenedioxymethamphetamine (MDMA, or ecstasy).

Methamphetamine, known as meth, crystal, ice, speed, and crank, is one of the most addictive designer drugs available. It is commonly used at clubs for its intense rush of euphoria. By the 1960s, methamphetamine abuse reached epidemic proportions.

MDMA has both stimulant and hallucinogenic properties and is related to amphetamine and mescaline. Ecstasy is a party drug designed to produce a rush of euphoria followed by heightened sociability and hallucinations.

A popular synthetic heroin alternative is China white, which encompasses a variety of fentanyl derivatives (painkillers with opiate-like properties similar to but more potent than heroin). China white gained popularity as a recreational drug among heroin users as a cheaper alternative.

Hallucinogenic designer drugs include LSD and PCP. LSD, or acid, is the most widely known of the hallucinogenic drugs. It is an extremely potent semisynthetic psychedelic drug derived from lysergic acid. PCP, or angel dust, derivatives were popular in the 1970s. PCP, originally developed as a surgical anesthetic, is a dangerous and unpredictable hallucinogen; users typically experience horrifying and violent hallucinations.

Several designer drugs, such as ketamine and GHB, exhibit depressant and hallucinogenic qualities. Ketamine is a tranquilizer with powerful hallucinogenic properties that is known to induce out-of-body and dreamlike states. GHB, known as cherry meth and liquid ecstasy, initially was used as a bodybuilding agent to stimulate muscle growth. GHB is a popular recreational drug at nightclubs and is sometimes used as a "date rape" drug.

EFFECTS AND POTENTIAL RISKS

Designer drugs are often lethal substitutes; they are mixed with unknown impurities and are many times more potent than the original substance they mimic. Designer drugs can act as stimulants, depressants, hallucinogens, and painkillers (opiates).

Designer drugs exhibit different effects at varying doses. Stimulants, like methamphetamines, increase brain activity by increasing the neurotransmitter dopamine, producing euphoria, excitement, and increased energy. Depressants, such as GHB, slow the central nervous system through endorphin-like mechanisms, inducing relaxation, contentment, and sedation. Hallucinogens, such as LSD, bind to serotonin receptors in the brain, producing sensory distortions. Opiates, including China white, act through opioid receptors to alter pain responses. Although the effects of each designer drug are different, all can be lethal.

Designer drugs are abused for their intoxicating effects. The short-term effects of designer drugs include increased euphoria, excitement, and energy. Negative short-term effects include nausea, vomiting, anxiety, depression, confusion, irritability, amnesia, dilated pupils, impaired speech, visual disturbances, hallucinations, behavioral changes, disturbed sleep, muscle cramps, panic attacks, shaking, clenched teeth, drooling, chills, increased perspiration, increased heart rate, hypertension, and sudden death.

Long-term designer drug use can lead to anorexia, dehydration, social withdrawal, anhedonia (inability to experience pleasure), violent behavior, suicidal behavior, paranoia, psychosis, stroke, seizures, convulsions, paralysis, coma, lung disease, kidney, heart, and respiratory failure, blood vessel damage, permanent brain damage, and death.

Most designer drugs are highly addictive; physical and psychological tolerance and dependence develops quickly. Users crave larger doses of the drug to achieve the original high. Mixing designer drugs with other substances increases the risk of accidental overdose and death.

Rose Ciulla-Bohling, PhD

FURTHER READING

Clayton, Lawrence. *Designer Drugs.* New York: Rosen, 1998. Provides basic information about the various types of designer drugs, their effects, and causes for abuse and addiction.

Gahlinger, Paul M. *Illegal Drugs: A Complete Guide to Their History, Chemistry, Use, and Abuse.* New York: Plume, 2004. A comprehensive guide to the history, chemical properties, health effects, and medical uses of both legal and illegal drugs.

Goldberg, Raymond. *Drugs across the Spectrum.* 6th ed. Belmont, CA: Wadsworth, 2010. Discusses the history, health effects, treatment, prevention, and legal issues associated with drug addiction and its effects on society.

Foxy

Foxy is a hallucinogenic drug in the tryptamine family, similar to psilocybin (mushrooms). It is used recreationally as a psychedelic.

Foxy most frequently appears in tablet or capsule form. The drug was first synthesized by Alexander Shulgin, and its chemical creation was reported by him in 1980. With the placement of MDMA (ecstasy) under legal control in the United States in 1985, foxy began to appear in the illicit-drug street trade.

Foxy, named in 1999, was first called Eve to contrast with Adam, a name used occasionally for ecstasy. Foxy soon became more widely known as a designer street drug and became popular in dance clubs and raves and other such venues, where the use of club drugs, particularly ecstasy, was well established.

Hanson, Glen R., Peter J. Venturelli, and Annette E. Fleckenstein. *Drugs and Society*. 10th ed. Sudbury, MA: Jones, 2009. Examines the effects of drug use and abuse on individuals and society. Provides detailed information on drug laws, commonly abused drugs, and substance abuse treatment and prevention options.

Olive, M. Foster. *Designer Drugs*. Philadelphia: Chelsea House, 2004. Presents information on the history, health effects, production, distribution, and regulations associated with designer drugs.

WEBSITES OF INTEREST

eMedicineHealth.com
http://www.emedicinehealth.com/club_drugs/article_em.htm

National Institute on Drug Abuse
http://www.drugabuse.gov

See also: Club drugs; Ketamine; LSD; MDMA; Rohypnol; Teens/young adults and drug abuse

Detoxification

CATEGORY: Treatment
DEFINITION: Detoxification, also referred to as detox, is the removal of harmful substances from the body with necessary supportive care, which may include the administration of medication or other therapies, such as hemodialysis.

OVERVIEW

Detoxification (detox) is applied to chronic situations of substance abuse, such as alcoholism and drug addiction. It also applies to acute conditions such as alcohol poisoning caused by binge drinking and drug overdoses. Detox is only the first step in the resolution of a substance abuse problem. It removes the substance from the body and restores homeostasis (a state of normalcy), but it does not remove the person's desire to ingest the substance again. Follow-up care is essential to reduce the likelihood of continued substance abuse.

ALCOHOL DETOXIFICATION

Alcohol detox is necessary in cases of alcohol poisoning caused by the rapid ingestion of a large quantity of alcohol over a short time and in cases of long-term alcohol abuse (alcoholism). Most cases of alcohol poisoning are caused by ingestion of ethanol (C_2H_5OH), which is a component of beer, wine, and hard liquor. Ethanol is produced by the fermentation of sugar.

Some cases of alcohol poisoning are caused by methanol (CH_3OH) or isopropyl alcohol (C_3H_8O). Methanol is primarily used in the production of other chemicals; it is sometimes used as an automotive fuel. Isopropyl alcohol is a component of rubbing alcohol and is widely used as a solvent and cleaning fluid.

The amount of alcohol in the body is usually measured as the blood alcohol content (BAC). The BAC is expressed as the percentage of alcohol per liter of blood. Alcohol consumption is also measured by the number of drinks consumed.

Alcohol Poisoning. Treatment of alcohol poisoning consists of supportive measures as the body metabolizes the alcohol. These measures include insertion of an airway (endotracheal tube) to prevent vomiting and aspiration of stomach contents into the lungs; close monitoring of vital signs (temperature, heart rate, and blood pressure); oxygen; medication to increase blood pressure and heart rate, if necessary; respiratory support, if necessary; maintenance of body temperature (blankets or warming devices); and intravenous fluids to prevent dehydration. Glucose should be added to fluids if the patient is hypoglycemic (has low blood sugar). Thiamine is often added to fluids to reduce the risk of a seizure. A final measure is hemodialysis (blood cleansing), which might be needed in cases of dangerously high BACs (more than 0.4 percent). Hemodialysis is also necessary if methanol or isopropyl alcohol has been ingested.

Alcoholism. Withdrawal symptoms from long-term alcohol abuse may range in severity from mild tremors to seizures, which can be life-threatening. Approximately 5 percent of patients undergoing alcohol withdrawal have delirium tremens (DTs), which are characterized by shaking, confusion, and hallucinations. DTs also cause large increases in heart rate, respiration, pulse, and blood pressure. These symptoms usually appear two to four days after abstinence from alcohol. Withdrawal may require up to one week.

Patients suffering from DTs require inpatient care at a hospital or a treatment center.

Although some patients with less severe symptoms also receive inpatient care, many can be successfully treated as outpatients. Sedatives are administered to control withdrawal symptoms, which range from anxiety to seizures.

DRUG DETOXIFICATION

A patient in need of detox can be either a long-term substance abuser or a person who has had an acute drug-related episode (for example, an overdose). Drugs requiring detox include both illegal substances such as heroin and cocaine and prescription medications used inappropriately. Most cases of drug abuse involve psychoactive (mood-altering) substances. Psychoactive substances are either central nervous system (CNS) stimulants (cocaine and methamphetamine) or CNS depressants (heroin or barbiturates). Many substance abusers ingest more than one drug with different properties, which complicates detox measures. Drugs are sometimes ingested with alcohol, which is a CNS depressant.

Long-term substance abusers are admitted voluntarily to a health care facility, through the prompting of friends or relatives, or by court order. Initially, health care staff take a complete medical history (with particular attention to substances abused). This history is followed by a physical examination and laboratory tests, which check for levels of substances in the bloodstream. A treatment plan is formulated based on the duration of abuse and on the substances involved.

The condition of persons experiencing an acute drug-related episode ranges from euphoric to comatose; furthermore, the status may change rapidly. For example, a relatively alert person may lapse into a coma, have a seizure, or suffer cardiac arrest. For a person with a drug overdose, detox consists of supportive measures similar to those for alcohol poisoning. If a CNS stimulant was ingested, medication may need to be administered to lower the patient's heart rate, blood pressure, and respiration. If a CNS depressant was ingested, medication may need to be administered to raise these parameters.

The first step of detox is to evaluate the patient's physical and mental status and determine the types of substances involved. In some cases, information can be obtained from the person, witnesses, or physical evidence (such as syringes or pill containers). If this information is not available, medical staff conduct laboratory tests to determine the substances (and amount) present in the bloodstream.

If necessary, supportive measures such as oxygen administration, respiratory assistance, and intravenous medication will be initiated. Usually, medication is required to guide the patient through the detox process. Patients will be told of the medications used during treatment. The detox process may take one or two weeks and can be done on an inpatient or outpatient basis, or in combination.

For people with a serious substance abuse problem, inpatient care is often necessary. These programs include detox followed by counseling, group therapy, and medical treatment. A benefit of an inpatient program is that it greatly reduces the risk of a patient gaining access to harmful substances. For anyone who receives inpatient care, regular outpatient follow-up is essential. Many medical centers include treatment for substance abuse. Stand-alone facilities also are present throughout the United States and in other developed nations. Some provide care in a basic, clinical setting while others function in a resort-like setting. One well-known facility is the Betty Ford Center (in Rancho Mirage, California), which was founded by former US First Lady Betty Ford. The one-hundred-bed non-profit residential facility offers inpatient, outpatient, and day treatment for substance abusers. It also provides prevention and education programs for family members (including children) of substance abusers.

RAPID DETOXIFICATION

Rapid detox is a controversial treatment method for addiction to opiates such as heroin. In rapid detox, the patient is placed under a general anesthetic and is administered drugs such as naltrexone, which block the brain's opiate receptors from any circulating opiates. Additional medications are administered to accelerate the physical reactions to the rapid withdrawal while the patient is unconscious. Proponents of the process state that the procedure not only shortens the withdrawal process but also avoids much of the associated pain, which can be severe. Opponents point to studies that some patients undergo serious complications and death, and to other studies that describe the return of withdrawal symptoms after the patient awakens from the anesthetic. Critics also note that the treatment can be expensive.

NICOTINE DETOXIFICATION

Nicotine, which is contained in tobacco leaves, is highly addictive. In addition, cigarette smoking (or chewing) has pleasurable associations and induces stress relief. This component of smoking markedly increases the likelihood of a relapse. Detox occurs on an outpatient basis with the use of aids such as nicotine patches or gum, which are gradually decreased in amount.

Innumerable resources are available to a smoker who desires to quit. These resources include personal physicians, smoking-cessation clinics, and self-help groups. Some people can simply quit smoking on their own and endure the withdrawal symptoms, which include strong cravings for a cigarette, restlessness, and irritability. Withdrawal from nicotine takes one to two weeks after last dose.

Robin L. Wulffson, MD

FURTHER READING

Bean, Philip, and Teresa Nemitz. *Drug Treatment: What Works?* New York: Routledge, 2004. An introduction to the complex issues surrounding substance abuse. Addresses treatment options and outcome measures.

Fisher, Gary, and Thomas Harrison. *Substance Abuse: Information for School Counselors, Social Workers, Therapists, and Counselors.* 4th ed. Boston: Allyn & Bacon, 2008. Incorporating actual clinical examples with solid research, this text provides counselors and social workers with a detailed overview of drug addictions.

Liptak, John, et al. *Substance Abuse and Recovery Workbook.* Whole Person, 2008. Contains self-assessments, exploratory activities, reflective journaling exercises and educational handouts to help participants discover the habitual and ineffective methods of managing substance abuse, and to explore new ways for healing.

Miller, William. *Rethinking Substance Abuse: What the Science Shows, and What We Should Do About It.* New York: Guilford, 2010. Reviews what is known about substance abuse and offers overviews of biological, psychological, and social factors involved in the treatment of substance abuse. Also anticipates future developments and evaluates them for their impact on prevention and treatment.

Seixas, Judith. *Children of Alcoholism: A Survivor's Manual.* New York: Harper & Row, 1986. Focuses on children of alcoholics and the unique problems they face.

WEBSITES OF INTEREST

Al-Anon and Alateen
http://www.al-anon.alateen.org

Alcoholics Anonymous
http://www.aa.org

National Institute on Alcohol Abuse and Alcoholism
http://www.niaaa.nih.gov

National Institute on Drug Abuse
http://www.drugabuse.gov

See also: Addiction medications; Alcohol abuse and alcoholism: Treatment; Alcohol poisoning; Treatment methods and research

---

Dextroamphetamine

CATEGORY: Substances

ALSO KNOWN AS: Dexedrine

DEFINITION: Dextroamphetamine is a stimulant used medically for narcolepsy, attention-deficit hyperactivity disorder, and in the treatment of depression.

STATUS: Legal in the United States and in other countries, including Australia and Great Britain

CLASSIFICATION: Schedule II controlled substance

SOURCE: Dextroamphetamine sulfate is the dextro-isomer of the compound d,1-amphetamine sulfate. Dextroamphetamine is categorized as an amphetamine and is a sympathomimetic amine of the amphetamine group.

TRANSMISSION ROUTE: Oral ingestion of tablets, capsules, or solution. Crushed tablets can be snorted or injected.

HISTORY OF USE

Dextroamphetamine is classified as a stimulant. The drug was approved by the US Food and Drug Administration (FDA) in 1976 and is available in generic and brand formulations. The abuse of this and other stimulant pharmacologic compounds, and the prescription rates for attention deficit hyperactivity disorder (ADHD) medications, has increased since 2000. Prescription amphetamines, including dextroamphetamine, are abused to enhance focus, to lose weight, and to get high.

EFFECTS AND POTENTIAL RISKS

Dextroamphetamine produces both central nervous system (CNS) and peripheral effects. In the CNS, dextroamphetamine has a stimulant effect; peripherally it raises blood pressure and produces weak brochodilatory and respiratory stimulation. Additionally, stimulants in general are known to increase focus and attention, which can help students during their studies. Dextroamphetamine is abused by teenagers and young adults as a diet aid. The drug suppresses feelings of hunger, leading the abuser to eat less and lose weight.

Short-term risks associated with dextroamphetamine are similar to those seen with other stimulants. Persons with preexisting hypertension or cardiovascular conditions are at a higher risk for cardiac complications. Increased aggression, hostility, and mixed or manic episodes in people with preexisting psychiatric conditions have been reported. Long-term use can lead to dependence, and abruptly stopping the medication can cause withdrawal symptoms, including fatigue, depression, and sleep abnormalities.

Allison C. Bennett, PharmD

FURTHER READING

Grabowski, John, et al. "Dextroamphetamine for Cocaine-Dependence Treatment: A Double-Blind Randomized Clinical Trial." *Journal of Clinical Psychopharmacology* 21 (2001): 522–26. Print.

Williams, Robert J., et al. "Methylphenidate and Dextroamphetamine Abuse in Substance-Abusing Adolescents." *American Journal of Addictions* 13 (2004): 381–89. Print.

Wu, Li-Tzy, et al. "Misuse of Methamphetamine and Prescription Stimulants among Youths and Young Adults in the Community." *Drug and Alcohol Dependence* 89 (2007): 195–205. Print.

WEBSITES OF INTEREST

National Institute on Drug Abuse
http://www.drugabuse.gov

National Survey on Drug Use and Health
https://nsduhweb.rti.org

Substance Abuse and Mental Health Services Administration
http://www.samhsa.gov

See also: Depression; Prescription drug addiction: Overview; Stimulant abuse; Stimulants: Short- and long-term effects on the body

Dextromethorphan

CATEGORY: Substances

ALSO KNOWN AS: CCC; DXM; poor man's PCP; robo; skittles; triple C

DEFINITION: Dextromethorphan is a cough suppressant contained in dozens of over-the-counter medications, and it is increasingly being abused for its dissociative opioid effects.

STATUS: Legal in many countries worldwide

CLASSIFICATION: Unclassified

SOURCE: Widely produced as an additive to cough and cold preparations in the form of liquids, tablets, and capsules

TRANSMISSION ROUTE: Oral ingestion

HISTORY OF USE

Familiar since the 1950s to people with coughs and colds, dextromethorphan (DXM) was originally developed as a safer alternative to the codeine cough syrups that were then common. DXM was long considered devoid of any potential for abuse, even though it is an opioid derivative. When taken at higher than recommended doses, however, DXM produces dissociative hallucinogenic effects. As a result, since the 1990s, abuse of over-the-counter (OTC) medications, including DXM, has grown. In 2011, only alcohol, tobacco, and cannabis were abused more frequently than OTC medications.

EFFECTS AND POTENTIAL RISKS

DXM acts in the brain and spinal cord to inhibit receptors for N-methyl-d-aspartate (NMDA). As such, DXM—along with other NMDA antagonists—alters distribution of the neurotransmitter glutamate throughout the brain, in turn altering the user's perception of pain, the user's understanding of the environment, and the user's memory. Subjective effects include euphoria, hallucinations, paranoid delusions, confusion, agitation, altered moods, difficulty concentrating, nightmares, catatonia, ataxia, and anesthesia. The typical clinical presentation of DXM intoxication involves hyperexcitability, lethargy, ataxia, slurred speech, sweating, hypertension, and nystagmus.

Abusers of DXM describe the following dose-dependent plateaus: mild stimulation at a dosage between 100 and 200 milligrams (mg); euphoria and hallucinations begin at a dosage of between 200 and 400 mg; between 300 and 600 mg, the user will experience distorted visual perception and loss of motor coordination; and between 500 and 1,500 mg, the user will experience dissociative sedation. These effects are experienced only when a person has consumed vastly more DXM than recommended for normal therapeutic use.

This consumptive practice is particularly dangerous when DXM is combined with other active ingredients, such as pseudoephedrine, acetaminophen, or guaifenesin. Health risks associated with abusing these latter substances include increased blood pressure (pseudoephedrine), potential liver damage (acetaminophen), and central nervous system toxicity, cardiovascular toxicity, and anticholinergic toxicity (antihistamines).

Michael R. Meyers, PhD

FURTHER READING

Cherkes, Joseph. "Dextromethorphan-Induced Neurological Illness in a Patient with Negative Toxicology Findings." *Neurology* 66 (2006): 1952–53. Print.

Lachover, Leonard. "Deciphering a Psychosis: A Case of Dextromethorphan-Induced Symptoms." *Primary Psychiatry* 14 (2007): 70–72. Print.

Zawertailo, Laurie A., et al. "Effect of Metabolic Blockade on the Psychoactive Effects of Dextromethorphan." *Human Psychopharmacology* 25 (2010): 71–79. Print.

WEBSITES OF INTEREST

PubMed Health
http://www.ncbi.nlm.nih.gov/pubmedhealth/
PMH0000695

US Drug Enforcement Administration
http://www.deadiversion.usdoj.gov/drugs_concern/dextro_m/dextro_m.htm

See also: Cough and cold medications; Over-the-counter drugs of abuse; Teens/young adults and drug abuse

Diagnosis methods

CATEGORY: Diagnosis and prevention

DEFINITION: Before treating addictions, health practitioners must be sure that the addiction actually exists. They must differentiate between alcohol and drug abuse and alcohol and drug addiction. To do this, health practitioners must complete an initial assessment of their patients' conditions and then make their diagnosis. A diagnosis is the identification of an illness or a condition. After a health practitioner diagnoses a patient, he or she must develop a suggested method of treatment for the patient's condition.

ASSESSMENT METHODS

The diagnosis process is typically initiated by the patient or the patient's loved ones. The patient and his or her family may request the help of their family doctor. Depending on the family doctor's knowledge of and experience with diagnosing alcohol and drug addictions, the doctor may decide to perform the addiction assessment him- or herself or may refer the patient to a specialist or therapist.

Physicians perform addiction assessments to determine whether the patient is abusing or is addicted to drugs or alcohol. Though the general public does not typically differentiate between these two conditions, medical professionals adhere to strict guidelines that define abuse and addiction. This is important, as the treatment that the professional recommends is affected by whether he or she believes the patient is abusing drugs or is addicted to them.

To make this determination, the physician performing the addiction assessment instructs the patient to think about his or her behavior during a twelve-month period. The physician then asks the patient a series of questions based on one of many assessment tools. The most commonly used addiction-assessment tools are surveys known as CAGE, T-ACE, AUDIT, and AA20. While these surveys were initially developed to diagnose alcohol addiction, they can be altered and used to uncover a drug addiction.

CAGE. This short four question survey is meant to identify a drinking problem in the lifetime of the patient. The physician will ask the patient each of the following questions, expecting a yes or no response:

C—Have you ever felt you should **cut down** on your drinking?

A—Have people **annoyed** you by criticizing your drinking?

G—Have you ever felt bad or **guilty** about your drinking?

E—**Eye opener**: Have you ever had a drink first thing in the morning to steady your nerves or to get rid of a hangover?

Answering yes to two of these questions indicates that the patient has a serious drinking problem. CAGE is a popular test because it can be administered in any setting and is useful for persons all of genders, ages, races, and socioeconomic backgrounds.

T-ACE. This survey is based on CAGE and also consists of four short questions; however, it is used to uncover a drinking or drug problem in pregnant women. This survey helps physicians identify a drinking problem in the woman's lifetime and during pregnancy. The physician will ask the patient to answer the following questions:

T—**Tolerance**: How many drinks does it take to make you feel high?

A—Have people **annoyed** you by criticizing your drinking?

C—Have you ever felt you ought to **cut down** on your drinking?

E—**Eye opener**: Have you ever had a drink first thing in the morning to steady your nerves or to get rid of a hangover?

The physician scores the patient's responses to these questions. If the patient has a score of two or higher, the physician can assume that the patient may have a drinking problem and will need further assessment. The scores attributed to these questions are as follows: 1 point for a positive answer for A, C, or E; 2 points for answering T with a number higher than 2.

Craving

Craving denotes an intense desire or need for a specific substance of abuse (such as alcohol, cocaine, heroin, and nicotine), following a period of abstinence or cessation of substance use. Craving may be elicited by exposure to cues (triggers) associated with that substance, by stress, or by a low (priming) dose of the self-administered drug. Craving may motivate drug-seeking behaviors and is thought to contribute to relapse even in long-abstinent persons.

Many researchers consider drug craving within a Pavlovian conditioning framework of drug addiction, in which the drug is the unconditioned stimulus. Environmental cues paired with drug consumption are conditioned stimuli that come to evoke conditioned responses, one of which is craving. In a 1992 study by Ronald Ehrman and colleagues, men addicted to cocaine but with no history of heroin use reported craving in response to cocaine-related stimuli but not to heroin-related or nondrug stimuli.

Craving also can be elicited by the initial effects of a drug experience that signal a more intense later drug effect. These conditioned cravings make it difficult for addicts to use drugs in moderation.

AUDIT (Alcohol Use Disorder Identification Test). This survey is favored by medical professionals because it provides more details about the patient's drinking habits than other shorter surveys. It consists of ten questions and presents five answer options for the first eight questions and three answer options for the last two questions. The patient is to select the option that best captures his or her honest answers. Like CAGE, AUDIT can be used to assess patients of all genders, ages, races, and backgrounds. The questions on the AUDIT are the following:

1. How often do you have a drink containing alcohol?
2. How many drinks containing alcohol do you have on a typical day when you are drinking?
3. How often do you have six or more drinks on one occasion?
4. How often during the last year have you found that you were not able to stop drinking once you started?

5. How often during the last year have you failed to do what was normally expected from you because of drinking?

6. How often during the last year have you needed a first drink in the morning to get yourself going after a heavy drinking session?

7. How often during the last year have you had a feeling of guilt or remorse after drinking?

8. How often during the last year have you been unable to remember what happened the night before you had been drinking?

9. Have you or someone else been injured as a result of your drinking?

10. Has a relative or friend, or a doctor or other health worker, been concerned about your drinking or suggested you cut down?

A score of 8 or more on AUDIT tells the physician that the patient may have a drinking problem that needs to be addressed. Scores for the first eight questions can be 0 to 4 points each. Scores for the last two questions are worth 0, 2, or 4 points.

AA20. An assessment survey developed and distributed by Alcoholic Anonymous (AA). As its name indicates, the survey includes twenty questions designed to determine whether a person has a drinking problem. In a clinical setting, the physician asks the patients to answer yes or no to the following questions:

1. Do you lose time from work due to drinking?
2. Is drinking making your home life unhappy?
3. Do you drink because you are shy with other people?
4. Is drinking affecting your reputation?
5. Have you ever felt remorse after drinking?
6. Have you gotten into financial difficulties as a result of drinking?
7. Do you turn to lower companions and an inferior environment when drinking?
8. Does your drinking make you careless of your family's welfare?
9. Has your ambition decreased since drinking?
10. Do you crave a drink at a definite time daily?
11. Do you want a drink the next morning?
12. Does drinking cause you to have difficulty sleeping?
13. Has your efficiency decreased since drinking?
14. Is drinking jeopardizing your job or business?
15. Do you drink to escape from worries or trouble?
16. Do you drink alone?

17. Have you ever had a complete loss of memory as a result of drinking?
18. Has your physician ever treated you for drinking?
19. Do you drink to build up your self-confidence?
20. Have you ever been to a hospital or institution on account of drinking?

According to AA, answering yes to three of these questions indicates a serious drinking problem. The physician should order further assessment to determine if the patient is abusing alcohol or is addicted to alcohol.

ABUSE VERSUS ADDICTION

Medical professionals rely on criteria set by the *Diagnostic and Statistical Manual of Mental Disorders* to determine if a patient is combating alcohol or drug abuse or addiction. To make an accurate diagnosis, physicians urge their patients to answer all questions honestly.

A physician may diagnose a patient as a substance or drug abuser if the patient has been in one or more of the following situations within the past year:

- The patient has failed to meet obligations, such as skipping classes at school, missing shifts at work, or neglecting to spend scheduled time with a friend or family member.
- The patient has engaged in reckless activities, such as driving or starting a fight while under the influence of drugs or alcohol.
- The patient has encountered legal troubles, such as being accused of a serious crime, getting arrested, or neglecting to pay fines.
- The patient has continued to drink or take drugs even though he or she has encountered personal difficulties or problems, such as frequent disagreements with family members or coworkers.

A physician may diagnose a patient with a substance or drug addiction if the patient has experienced two specific psychological factors—withdrawal and an increased tolerance for his or her drink or drug of choice—and one or more of the following behavioral patterns:

- Inability to stop once using starts
- Failure to adhere to self-imposed limits
- Limiting time spent on other activities to consume drugs or alcohol
- Spending a disproportionate amount of time consuming drugs or alcohol
- Continuing to use a drug or drink even though the patient is in poor health

Once the physician has diagnosed the patient with either a substance or drug abuse problem or an addiction, the physician can then speak with the patient about the next course of action: treatment. Addictions may require more aggressive treatments, such as medications and various types of therapy. Abusers will be encouraged to seek help for their problems through group therapy, drug and alcohol counseling, and familial support.

Nicole Frail

FURTHER READING

American Psychiatric Association. *Diagnostic and Statistical Manual of Mental Disorders.* 4th ed. Washington: APA, 1994.

Hoffman, John, and Susan Froemke, eds. *Why Can't They Just Stop?* New York: Rodale, 2007.

National Institute on Alcohol Abuse and Alcoholism. *Assessing Alcohol Problems: A Guide for Clinicians and Researchers.* 2nd ed. Washington, DC: DHHS, 2003.

Orford, Jim. *Excessive Appetites: A Psychological View of Addictions.* New York: 2nd ed. Wiley, 2001.

WEBSITES OF INTEREST

National Council on Alcoholism and Drug Dependence
http://www.ncadd.org

National Institute on Alcohol Abuse and Alcoholism
http://niaaa.nih.gov

Substance Abuse and Mental Health Services Administration
http://www.samhsa.gov

See also: Drug testing; Prevention methods and research; Screening for behavioral addictions

DMT

CATEGORY: Substances

ALSO KNOWN AS: Businessman's special; N,N-dimethyltryptamine

DEFINITION: DMT is a naturally occurring compound with hallucinogenic properties. It is also produced synthetically.

STATUS: Illegal except for use in controlled research; no approved medical indication in the United States

CLASSIFICATION: Schedule I controlled substance in the United States; schedule 3 drug in Canada

SOURCE: Found in a number of plants, especially in the American tropics, and in trace amounts in humans and other animals. Its natural function in the human body has not been determined. Structurally, it is analogous to the neurotransmitter serotonin.

TRANSMISSION ROUTE: Ingested as a tea or mixed with marijuana and smoked; also snorted and, when liquefied, injected

HISTORY OF USE

Europeans who first arrived in the Caribbean and in Central and South America came into contact with indigenous peoples who used DMT derived from plants to induce hallucinations as part of their religious experience. The explorers tried to suppress these practices, which persisted, often in secretive settings.

DMT was first synthesized in a laboratory in 1931 by chemist Richard Manske. It gained popularity as a drug of abuse in the counterculture of the 1960s. According to US government statistics, the abuse of DMT in the United States increased between 2007 and 2010.

EFFECTS AND POTENTIAL RISKS

DMT is the shortest-acting of commonly abused hallucinogens. Its effects are evident within ten minutes, peak at about thirty minutes, and usually end within an hour. Hence the street name businessman's special.

Physical effects of DMT abuse include increased blood pressure and heart rate, agitation, dizziness, nystagmus (involuntary, rapid eye movement), and incoordination. At high doses, seizures and respiratory arrests have occurred. Psychological effects of DMT abuse include intense visual hallucinations,

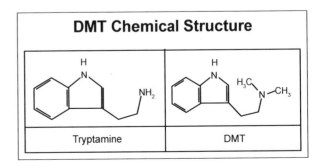

DMT Chemical Structure

Tryptamine | DMT

depersonalization, auditory distortions, and altered sense of time and body image. DMT causes anxiety attacks far more frequently than does the hallucinogen LSD (acid).

Ernest Kohlmetz, MA

FURTHER READING

Abadinsky, Howard. *Drug Use and Abuse: A Comprehensive Introduction*. 7th ed. Belmont, CA: Wadsworth, 2011. Focuses on what drugs are abused, how they are abused, and how abuse is treated or prevented. Hallucinogen abuse, including DMT, is covered in chapter 6.

Julien, Robert M. *A Primer of Drug Actions*. 11th ed. New York: Worth, 2008. A concise, nontechnical guide to the mechanisms of action, side effects, uses, and abuses of psychoactive drugs. Chapter 12 covers hallucinogens, including DMT.

Kuhn, Cynthia, Scott Swartwelder, and Wilkie Wilson. *Buzzed: The Straight Facts About the Most Used and Abused Drugs from Alcohol to Ecstasy*. 3rd ed. New York: W.W. Norton, 2008. Contains an informative, easy-to-read section on hallucinogens, including DMT, and their effects.

Lowinson, Joyce W., et al., eds. *Substance Abuse: A Comprehensive Textbook*. 4th ed. Philadelphia: Lippincott, 2005. A comprehensive textbook. Chapter 18 covers hallucinogens, including DMT.

WEBSITES OF INTEREST

National Institute on Drug Abuse
http://www.drugabuse.gov

US Drug Enforcement Administration
http://www.deadiversion.usdoj.gov/drugs_
  concern/dmt/dmt.htm

See also: Hallucinogen abuse; Hallucinogens: Short- and long-term effects on the body; Psychosis and substance abuse

Domestic violence and addiction

CATEGORY: Social issues
DEFINITION: Domestic violence occurs when a person in an intimate relationship physically, sexually, mentally, emotionally, psychologically, or verbally assaults his or her partner. Family violence occurs when most members of the same household—spouses, children, or the elderly—are abused. Women are more likely than men to be abused. Research has shown that the presence of alcohol or drug addictions in the home increases the likelihood of domestic or family violence.

DOMESTIC VIOLENCE IN THE UNITED STATES

Domestic violence is one of the most underreported and most common crimes in the United States. According to researchers Jennifer P. Schneider and Richard Irons, in the article "When Is Domestic Violence a Hidden Face of Addiction?" (1997), more than one-quarter of women in the United States will be abused in their lifetimes. More than 54 percent of married women in violent households will be sexually assaulted repeatedly. Although an estimated 25 to 35 percent of all women who visit emergency rooms have been abused through acts of domestic or family violence, only 5 percent of these women admit that their partners or spouses are responsible for their injuries.

When a person struggling with an addiction to drugs or alcohol is present in the household, many of these numbers increase. In 2010, *Addiction Treatment* magazine reported that 80 percent or more of all cases of domestic violence are somehow connected to the use of drugs or alcohol. The US Department of Justice (DOJ) has reported that 61 percent of domestic violence offenders are addicted to drugs or alcohol. Schneider and Irons found that 75 percent of women living with addicts have been threatened with violence, while 45 percent have been physically or sexually assaulted by their partners.

Regardless of whether an addiction coexists with violence in a household, women are typically abused thirty-five times or more before they make a formal complaint to police. In addition, 47 percent of men—those with and without a substance abuse problem—who beat their wives do so three times or more each year.

As time passes, violence is likely to escalate in a home where a family member is dealing with an addiction to drugs or alcohol. In extreme cases, this leads to the murder of a spouse. The DOJ estimates that one-half or more of persons accused of killing their spouses admit that they were drunk or high at the time of the murder.

Women are not the only victims of domestic violence; children are victimized too. The National Coalition Against Domestic Violence (NCADV) reported that children living in a home with an addict are more likely to suffer physical, mental, or emotional abuse than those in a household where substance abuse is not present. More than 80 percent of child abuse cases involve an abuser who was under the influence of drugs or alcohol at the time of the abuse.

DOMESTIC VIOLENCE AND ADDICTION

Domestic violence and addiction do not have a causal relationship; throughout the years, experts have established that these problems are closely related, but these same experts have not and cannot prove that domestic or family violence is a direct result of a drug or alcohol addiction. It is true, however, that domestic violence is more likely to occur in homes in which a member of the family has become dependent on a particular substance.

Experts cannot call the relationship between domestic violence and addiction causal because it is unclear what factor is the cause and what is the effect. Questions such as the following remain: Did the abuser commit an act of violence because he or she was drunk? Or did the abuser begin drinking because he or she felt guilty for acting violently?

Even though experts have tried to inform the public that evidence of a causal relationship between addiction and domestic violence does not exist, the general public continues to view this relationship as such. Many people do not consider that violence is present in homes where addictions are not. They take no issue with blaming the violence on alcohol and drug abuse; they view abusers as weak and controlled by their substance or drugs of choice. According to the Center for Substance Abuse Treatment, this view has facilitated a "learned disinhibition." Essentially, society has provided abusers with an excuse for their violence. This view also provides abusers with expectations that they will become violent if they drink or get high.

Although society may continue to view this relationship as causal, experts remain unconvinced. Researchers have discovered, however, that cases of domestic violence and addiction do appear to be connected through behavioral parallels. According to Schneider and Irons, the relationship between an addict and his or her drug of choice is similar to the relationship between an abuser and his or her violent tendencies in the following ways:

- In both substance abuse and domestic violence, the user/abuser experiences a loss of control. The abuser loses control of his or her emotions and anger, while the addict loses control of his or her drinking or drug use.
- Both the addict and the abuser continue their behaviors despite recognizing negative consequences of their actions. The addict and abuser feel remorse or guilt regarding their actions, and abusers are aware that their victims may have experienced emotional, sexual, or physical damage or discomfort because of their behaviors.
- The addict and the abuser develop a preoccupation or obsession with their behaviors. Addicts become obsessed with being drunk or high, while abusers become obsessed with the idea of controlling their victims—especially in circumstances where the abuse is sexual. This preoccupation often erases all guilt or remorse the addict and abuser may feel about their behaviors.
- Both the addict and abuser become tolerant. The addict requires higher doses of his or her substance of choice to reach a mental state in which he or she is content. The abuser becomes increasingly more violent; the abuse may become more frequent, more intense, or more diverse in nature. The victim, too, becomes more tolerant of and desensitized to the abuse.

Because of these, and a number of other similarities between domestic violence and addiction, it is easy for both of these conditions to present themselves in a single household. In many cases, the person with the addiction is also the abuser; however, the addict also can become the victim. Sober members of the household who are unhappy with the addict's behavior are also capable of losing control. This may lead to abuse of the addict.

TREATING COEXISTING CONDITIONS

When treating a person addicted to drugs or alcohol who is also a domestic violence offender, it is important that both the violent tendencies and the addiction receive attention. In these cases, drug and alcohol counselors, physicians, and domestic violence counselors should work together to determine the proper approach to treatment.

Physicians may prescribe medications to help treat the addiction and eliminate any rage or depression. Therapists and other treatment professionals may recommend one-on-one counseling or group therapy. They may even require their patients to be active in multiple groups, such as a domestic violence group and an addiction group, in addition to taking medication and speaking with a therapist.

Professionals, regardless of the course of treatment chosen, should ensure that both the violence and the addiction are being treated. Because medical professionals do not view addiction as the cause of family violence or vice versa, they should be able to separate each factor and assign specific treatments to each. Many experts agree that once the addiction is under control, the persons who are abused can be part of the treatment process. The abused person might attend therapy sessions with the patient and are often expected to support the patient as best as they can.

Providing patients with both domestic violence and substance abuse counseling in a single setting is the ideal way to treat these coexisting conditions; however, the number of patients who receive both of these services in one location is quite low across the United States. The DOJ reported that 80 percent of domestic violence programs do not offer services to help their patients deal with substance abuse, though 92 percent of the program directors surveyed wish the programs did. These numbers are low because of a lack of financial resources and the absence of staff members who know how to counsel both family violence and addictions.

THE FUTURE?

Schneider and Irons found that 63 percent of abusive men admitted to seeing their fathers abuse their mothers when they were children. Many of these men were abused by their fathers too. Both witnesses and victims of family violence are more likely to form a dependency on drugs and alcohol than those who did not grow up in violent homes. This increases the likelihood that they will then abuse their own family members.

Children who no longer wish to see their parents abused—in addition to children who wish to escape a household in which they are abused—often run away from home. The NCADV has determined that runaways have a high risk of becoming addicted to

drugs and alcohol. This substance abuse, combined with memories of abusive childhoods, may place these persons on destructive paths to violent future homes of their own.

Nicole Frail

FURTHER READING

Center for Substance Abuse Treatment. *Substance Abuse Treatment and Domestic Violence.* Rockville, MD: SAMHSA, 1997. Print.

Irons, Richard, and Jennifer P. Schneider. "When Is Domestic Violence a Hidden Face of Addiction?" *Journal of Psychoactive Drugs* 29 (1997): 337–44. Print.

McCollum, Eric E., and Terry S. Trepper. *Family Solutions for Substance Abuse: Clinical and Counseling Approaches.* New York: Haworth, 2001. Print.

Sanders, Mark. *Slipping through the Cracks: Intervention Strategies for Clients with Multiple Addictions and Disorders.* Deerfield Beach, FL: HCI, 2011. Print.

WEBSITES OF INTEREST

Addiction Treatment
http://www.addictiontreatmentmagazine.com

American Psychological Association
http://www.apa.org/topics/violence

National Coalition Against Domestic Violence
http://www.ncadv.org

Substance Abuse and Mental Health Services Administration
http://www.samhsa.gov

See also: Children and behavioral addictions; Families and behavioral addictions; Families and substance abuse; Gender and addiction

Dopamine and addiction

CATEGORY: Health issues and physiology
ALSO KNOWN AS: Dihydroxyphenylethylamine
DEFINITION: Dopamine, a catecholamine neurotransmitter, is the brain's reward and anticipation (craving) molecule. It plays an important role

in the reinforcing effect of drugs and in the powerful cycle of brain dysfunction they cause.

THE DOPAMINE SYSTEM

In the central nervous system, dopaminergic (dopamine-producing) neurons reside only in a few areas, such as the substantia nigra of the midbrain, but establish connections with numerous brain regions. Dopamine (DA) dysfunctions in Parkinson's disease and schizophrenia, for example, suggest that projections from midbrain to certain brain regions (such as the striatum and frontal cortex) are involved in behavioral reactions controlled by rewards. Extensive studies conducted since the mid-twentieth century revealed that DA is involved in the generation of movement, cognition, attention, mood, reward, reward expectation, addiction, and stress.

Pleasant behavioral events (natural reinforcers such as eating, drinking, exercising, and sexual activity) stimulate the brain's reward (limbic) circuitry, causing DA release from dopaminergic neuron terminals. The information is relayed to the frontal lobe of the brain and stored in memory. The stored memory leads to behaviors directed at procuring the reward.

DOPAMINE IN ADDICTION

Dopamine involvement in multiple stages of addiction is a complex phenomenon and the subject of intense research efforts. The need for DA and its pleasurable effect can be satisfied by substances that mimic the action of this molecule on its receptor.

These substances (addictive drugs) induce transitory, exaggerated increases in DA outside the cells in a deep brain area called nucleus accumbens, a key component of the reward system. This occurs through enhanced release or decreased recycling of the neurotransmitter. The DA surges mimic or exceed the physiological responses that follow natural rewards.

Human-brain imaging studies demonstrate that the subjective feeling of euphoria occurring during intoxication associated with DA increases in deep brain nuclei. The drug-induced surge of the neurotransmitter is especially rewarding for persons with abnormally low densities of certain DA receptors (such as D2DR). Low receptor availability is associated with an increased risk for abuse of cocaine, heroin, methamphetamine, alcohol, and methylphenidate.

The euphoria triggers a reinforcing pattern that "instructs" the person to repeat the rewarding behavior of abusing drugs. As the abuse continues, long-lasting and significant adaptive decreases in DA brain function occur. These decreased levels reduce the effect of the neurotransmitter on the reward system and force the addicted person to keep abusing drugs in an attempt to normalize DA function.

When larger amounts of the drug are required to achieve the same DA high, desensitization (tolerance) occurs. Chronic drug use ultimately produces cellular and molecular adaptations in higher-processing areas of the brain, leading to disruptions in learning, mood, inhibitory control, and many other functions.

Mihaela Avramut, MD, PhD

FURTHER READING

Kipper, David, and Steven Whitney. *The Addiction Solution.* New York: Rodale, 2010.

Koob, George F., and Nora D. Volkow. "Neurocircuitry of Addiction." *Neuropsychopharmacology* 35 (2010): 217–38. Print.

Renner, John A. Jr., and E. Nalan Ward. "Drug Addiction." *Massachusetts General Hospital Comprehensive Clinical Psychiatry.* Eds. Theodore A. Stern et al. St. Louis, MO: Mosby, 2008.

WEBSITES OF INTEREST

Addiction Science Research and Education Center
http://www.utexas.edu/research/asrec/dopamine.html

National Institute on Drug Abuse
http://www.nida.nih.gov/infofacts/understand.html

See also: Brain changes with addiction; Drug interactions; Science of addiction; Symptoms of substance abuse

Drug abuse and addiction: In depth

CATEGORY: Substance abuse

DEFINITION: Although drug abuse and drug addiction are related in many ways, these conditions are viewed independently by experts. While it is true that drug abuse may lead to drug addiction, many circumstances can cause a person to only experiment with drugs and alcohol and not become addicted. Some people may have a biological predisposition for substance addiction, but there are a number of initiatives that aim to prevent the development of this disease.

CAUSES

The reasons people abuse drugs and alcohol are innumerable. Some people become hooked on a drug they once used recreationally or decided to try experimentally. Others find comfort in the escape that the effects of drugs and alcohol provide them: They become numb to any physical or emotional pain they feel and are distracted from any thoughts or emotions that may be causing them stress. Still others abuse medications that doctors prescribe for particular ailments or illnesses.

One of the most common reasons people abuse drugs is to escape reality. Research has shown that a high percentage of drug users did not have a stable childhood. Many have memories of being physically, verbally, or sexually abused as children or adolescents. Others recall violent households and quarreling parents. Women in physically or sexually abusive marriages are more likely to seek comfort in drugs and alcohol than are women in healthy relationships.

Men who are domestic violence offenders also are more likely to abuse drugs and alcohol—and act violently toward others while intoxicated—than men who are not violent. It is important to note, however, that drug and alcohol abuse is not a proven cause of domestic violence and that domestic violence is not a proven cause of drug and alcohol abuse. These situations are known as correlated rather than causal.

Gay, lesbian, bisexual, and transgendered men and women are more likely to use drugs—and continue to use them throughout their lifetime—than are heterosexual individuals. This drug use is often in response to the frequent discrimination and abuse that sexual minorities may face because of their sexual orientation or gender expression.

When a person abuses a drug too frequently, he or she can become addicted to that substance. Another cause of drug addiction is genetics. It is true that some people are predisposed to addiction because of family history and genetics. Abuse also may lead to addiction if the person has a mental illness, such as antisocial personality disorder, bipolar disorder, or schizophrenia.

Drugs may ease the symptoms of these conditions or can make living with them more bearable. Thus, people may become addicted to drugs or alcohol as they attempt to self-medicate their disorders.

People also are more likely to abuse drugs if they enjoy the effects the substances have on their brains. Opioids, for example, block the nerve receptors in the brain that help the body to sense pain. Opioids also engage the receptors in the brain that detect pleasure. The drug causes users to enter a euphoric state, in which they experience stress relief and a carefree emotional state. People who enjoy this sensation may come to think they need the drug to be happy. Frequent and repetitive use leads to abuse of the drug. Users may then become addicted to it, which causes their brains to undergo physiological changes in response to the continued drug exposure, causing them to feel as though their bodies truly need the drug to survive.

RISK FACTORS

As discussed, risk factors to drug abuse and addiction, specifically addiction, include a genetic predisposition to addictive behavior. If a person with an addictive personality has a child, chances are high that the child also will form addictions in his or her adult life.

Considering the argument of nature versus nurture, both play a crucial role in the development of an addiction. Genetics are extremely important, but so is the environment in which a child is raised. If a child witnesses uncorrected addictive behavior, he or she is more likely to adopt that behavior at a later point in life. However, not all men and women who become drug abusers and addicts grew up in a household with a drug or alcohol addict. Witnessing a parent with a behavioral addiction, such as to gambling or sex, also may influence a child's later addiction to a substance, and not to a behavior.

Other factors that lead to drug and alcohol abuse and addiction include peer pressure and drug use at a young age. The earlier one starts smoking cigarettes and marijuana or drinking alcohol, the more likely that person will become addicted to those drugs in the future. Also, persons who start abusing drugs during adolescence are more likely to experiment with harder drugs.

The diagnosis of a mental disorder of various types—anything from anxiety to multiple personality disorder—also increases the chances that a person will begin abusing (and possibly become addicted to) drugs or alcohol. Persons who are prescribed medications for mental illnesses or for pain relief may become addicted to their prescriptions. Persons who wish to ignore treatment of their mental conditions may fall into the habit of smoking, injecting, snorting, or drinking substances that offer relief from their present stresses.

Social risk factors for drug and alcohol abuse include being between the ages of eighteen and forty-four years, being of low socioeconomic status, and being single (not married). According to the US Department of Justice, men are more likely than women to abuse or become addicted to drugs and alcohol.

SYMPTOMS

The difference between drug abuse and drug addiction lies within the physical symptoms of each condition. Medical professionals use guidelines defined by the *Diagnostic and Statistical Manual of Mental Disorders* (DSM) to determine whether a person is addicted to a substance or is abusing a substance. According to the DSM, a person cannot be abusing and depending on a substance simultaneously. Once a person crosses into addictive behaviors, they are no longer just abusing

---

Drug Abuse Screening Test

Created in 1982 by Harvey Skinner, the drug abuse screening test (DAST) is a self-report questionnaire that assesses problems associated with the lifetime abuse of over-the-counter, prescription, and illicit drugs. The test does not directly assess the specific type, frequency or quantity of drug use, and it does not assess for problems related exclusively to alcohol use.

DAST is a self-administered questionnaire. Items on the test parallel questions on the Michigan alcoholism screening test. Questions require a yes or no response. Each response is assigned one point when answered in a manner consistent with drug use problems. A scoring system recommended by Skinner suggests that scores greater than five indicate problems with drug use.

DAST may be used either for research or for clinical purposes. Because DAST is a screening instrument only, the confirmation of DAST scores with more thorough diagnostic procedures is often necessary for clinical purposes.

---

the substance.

Because drug abuse leads to drug addiction, one can easily understand that addiction is the more serious condition when it comes to treatment. When persons are physically addicted to a substance, they may feel as though they cannot live without that substance in their system. People can become physically ill, and emotionally and mentally unstable, if their bodies crave a substance and do not receive it. This experience is called withdrawal. People who are abusing drugs do not experience withdrawal, as they are not yet physically dependent on the drug.

Another symptom that differs between drug abuse and drug addiction is related to tolerance levels. A person who is addicted to a substance becomes increasingly tolerant of that substance. To achieve a high from the drug, that person must increase the amount he or she takes. As time passes, the person becomes tolerant of this larger amount and again increases the amount consumed. People who abuse drugs may occasionally consume a larger amount in one sitting than they do normally, but they do so to achieve a more intense high; they do not consume more drugs because they can no longer get high with the amount they regularly use.

Symptoms of drug abuse include:
- failure to meet obligations, such as missing a meeting with a family member or friend, purposely skipping classes at school, or neglecting to arrive on time for a shift at work
- engaging in reckless activities, such as driving under the influence of drugs or alcohol
- developing legal or financial troubles, such as getting arrested, being accused of a serious crime, or failing to secure or keep track of personal funds
- continuing to use drugs even after encountering personal difficulties or issues, such as fighting with family members, friends, or coworkers

When a person becomes addicted to the substance, he or she will experience withdrawal without the drug and an increased tolerance for the drug in addition to some or all the following behavioral symptoms:
- inability to stop using
- failure to follow self-imposed limits
- decreased time spent on other activities that do not include drugs
- spending an excessive amount of time consuming drugs or alcohol

- continuing to consume a substance despite the presence of other illnesses or poor health

These symptoms will be present along with the symptoms belonging to the individual substances the person is using. If someone is addicted to opioids, for example, that person may exhibit slurred speech, itching, paranoia, depression, confusion, low blood pressure, and excessive sleeping.

SCREENING AND DIAGNOSIS

The first step in treating drug abusers and addicts typically involves their loved ones—people who take notice of their behavioral changes, physical appearance, and drug use. These persons may convince the drug user to seek treatment.

The user may call his or her primary physician or family doctor. After an initial screening in which the doctor runs a series of tests and asks the patient questions about his or her drug use, the doctor may refer the patient to a specialist for an accurate diagnosis.

Before treatment can begin, the patient must be diagnosed as an abuser or an addict. This step is crucial, as treatments for drug abuse and drug addiction are different because of the physical withdrawal that accompanies drug addiction. Withdrawal requires its own special form of treatment, including medications and sometimes short stays in rehabilitation facilities.

To determine abuse or addiction, medical professionals adhere to the criteria defined by the DSM. They also use a series of surveys consisting of yes-or-no answers that help them to uncover how significant the substance is to the patient's life. Some of the most popular surveys used are the CAGE, T-ACE, AUDIT, and AA20. Before administering these surveys, medical professionals advise their patients to be honest about any drugs they have abused in the past twelve months. Then, using a point system associated with the given survey, the medical professional can see if the patient has become dependent on drugs or alcohol.

Another important part of the screening and diagnosis process is the discovery of other physical ailments, coexisting drug addictions, or comorbidity. This discovery occurs through both laboratory testing and psychotherapy. Specific medications and methods used in addiction treatment may counteract other drugs the patient is using or interfere with other conditions the patient may have; it is crucial to discover all illnesses, diseases, and dependencies before treatment begins.

Through laboratory screenings, medical professionals may discover that vital organs such as the lungs, liver, or heart have been damaged by repetitive drug abuse. They also may discover conditions such as tuberculosis or human immunodeficiency virus infection, which could have been obtained through the sharing of drugs and drug paraphernalia, such as needles.

Diagnosing comorbidity is a critical step in addictions treatment; treating a patient addicted to cocaine requires a different approach than the one taken to treat a patient addicted to prescription painkillers who is simultaneously struggling to overcome depression, anxiety, or a personality disorder. According to the National Institute on Drug Abuse, 60 percent of substance abusers also have a mental illness. A mental illness may be present before a person starts using drugs, or a person might start using drugs before becoming mentally ill. Both conditions also may be the result of similar risk factors, such as genetic predisposition and environmental triggers (such as high stress or trauma).

People living with mood disorders are more likely to develop a drug habit. In addition, patients with drug disorders are two times as likely to be diagnosed with a mood or anxiety disorder. Men seeking help for drug abuse are often diagnosed with antisocial personality disorders while women are likely to exhibit behavior indicative of depression, anxiety, or posttraumatic stress disorder.

TREATMENT AND THERAPY

Ideally, a person who is abusing or addicted to a substance and who is also dealing with an additional addiction, physical illness, or mental illness should be treated for these issues by the same health professionals at a single facility. This does not often occur in the United States, however. Patients' conditions are viewed as unrelated, and patients are sent to multiple facilities to speak to a variety of medical professionals, from physicians to psychotherapists to drug and alcohol counselors.

If a person is abusing and not yet addicted to drugs or alcohol, he or she will not go through the stages of withdrawal. Most drug abusers are assigned to group therapy sessions, in which they speak about their drug use in front of other persons who understand what they are going through. If they are uncomfortable with—or in are in need of supplementing—group therapy, a drug and alcohol counselor or psychologist may counsel them independently. Therapy helps patients learn to deal with their cravings and to live a drug-free life. It enables them to set goals for the future and to repair strained or broken relationships with friends and family members. Although millions of people abuse drugs and alcohol each year, only 10 percent of abusers seek help for their conditions.

Persons dependent on substances experience withdrawal when they stop using the substance. Oftentimes, this is a painful process, as receptors in the brain "beg" for the drug of choice. Patients are often admitted to a medical facility for observation when they are about to enter withdrawal, as the symptoms can range from headaches to strokes, seizures, and heart attacks, depending on the drug of choice. Depending on the severity of the patient's situation, doctors may prescribe medications that help the patient during the withdrawal process. The most common withdrawal medications are methadone, clonidine, subutex, and suboxone.

After an addict's body is free of all drugs and alcohol, the patient may begin treatment for his or her condition. This treatment may be similar to therapies embraced by drug abusers—either group therapy or individual meetings with drug and alcohol counselors. Doctors also can choose to place some patients on medications to help calm cravings, fight depression, or reduce anxiety. Naltrexone, acamprosate, and disulfiram are common drugs administered to alcohol addicts. Naltrexone also can be distributed to opioid addicts. Even those addicted to nicotine can use bupropion or varenicline in addition to nicotine gum, patches, and nose sprays.

Each year about 40 percent of people who have become dependent on drugs or alcohol seek help for their problems. Research has found that the majority of those seeking help are men, as women are less likely to admit that they have substance abuse problems. They also, in general, have to ensure their children are cared for, which often keeps them from leaving home and joining treatment groups. Most rehabilitation facilities or drug and alcohol centers are not equipped to care for children and do not offer babysitting or daycare services.

To prevent relapse, people recovering from substance abuse and addiction are reminded to pay attention to their bodies and minds and to ask for help when they need it. The relapse process includes three stages: emotional, mental, and physical. If a patient feels anxious, defensive, or angry and misses group meetings or doctors' visits, he or she could be in the first stage of relapse. Combined with poor sleeping and eating habits and mood swings, this first stage may lead a patient to postacute withdrawal. Patients are instructed to reach out to medical professionals, friends, or family members if they feel they are in danger of relapse.

Nicole Frail

FURTHER READING

American Psychiatric Association. *Diagnostic and Statistical Manual of Mental Disorders.* 4th ed. Washington, DC: APA, 1994. The official guide all medical professionals use to diagnose mental illnesses and conditions.

Ghodse, Hamid. *Ghodse's Drugs and Addictive Behaviour: A Guide to Treatment.* New York: Cambridge UP, 2010. Examines in detail various types of drug addictions and behavioral addictions, presents treatment options, and suggests methods of preventing substance misuse.

Gwinnell, Esther, and Christine A. Adamec, eds. *The Encyclopedia of Addictions and Addictive Behaviors.* New York: Infobase, 2005. Provides information about more than three hundred types of addictions; discusses the historical and modern-day treatments of each addiction.

Hoffman, John, and Susan Froemke, eds. *Why Can't They Just Stop?* New York: Rodale, 2007. Written to supplement an HBO television documentary of the same name, this book offers insight into how a chemical dependency affects the lives of all involved; includes personal narratives and success stories.

Ries, Richard K., ed. *Principles of Addiction Medicine.* Philadelphia: Lippincott, 2009. Textbook that provides information on how to diagnose, manage, and treat patients experiencing various types of addictions.

WEBSITES OF INTEREST

AddictionsandRecovery.org
http://www.addictionsandrecovery.org

American Pharmacists Association
http://www.pharmacist.com

Centers for Disease Control and Prevention
http://www.cdc.gov

HelpGuide.org
http://www.helpguide.org

MedicineNet.com
http://www.medicinenet.com

National Institute on Drug Abuse
http://www.drugabuse.gov

National Institutes of Health: MedlinePlus
http://www.nlm.nih.gov/medlineplus

See also: Anxiety medication abuse; Gateway drugs; Hallucinogen abuse; Narcotics abuse; Opioid abuse; Painkiller abuse; Recreational drugs; Substance abuse

Drug abuse and addiction: Overview

CATEGORY: Substance abuse

ALSO KNOWN AS: Drug dependence

DEFINITION: Drug abuse is a disease characterized by continued misuse of drugs even when faced with drug-related occupational, legal, health, or family difficulties. Problems associated with drug abuse must be present for a minimum of twelve months to meet the diagnosis, according to the fourth edition of the American Psychiatric Association's *Diagnostic and Statistical Manual of Mental Disorders* (DSM-IV). Drug dependence refers to long-term, compulsive drug use, with attempts to stop that end in repeated returns to use. Drug dependence also indicates that the user's body has begun to develop a tolerance to the drug and may require the drug in higher doses to achieve the same effects and to avoid withdrawal symptoms. Drug abuse and drug dependence are not terms that should be used to describe people who are taking appropriate dosages of prescribed drugs (pain medication, for example) and who have become physically dependent on them. Diagnosis of both drug abuse and drug dependence requires the presence of specific behavioral symptoms.

CAUSES

The cause of drug abuse and dependence is unknown, although there are a variety of theories. One theory holds that there may be a genetic component that predisposes a person to developing a drug addiction. Another theory is that drug abuse is a learned behavior and that people begin to use drugs by copying the behavior of those around them. Medical professionals have not been able to target a specific cause. Long-term drug use alters the brain's structure and chemistry, which may reinforce the desire to keep using drugs regardless of the consequences.

RISK FACTORS AND SYMPTOMS

A risk factor is something that increases the chances of getting a disease or condition. For drug abuse and addiction, young males are at a greater risk, as are those who have family members with substance abuse problems. Other risk factors include social and peer pressure, early antisocial behavior, stress, and easy access to drugs. Anxiety, depression, and panic disorders are also risk factors associated with drug abuse and addiction.

Denial that a drug problem exists is common. Drug abuse can occur without physical dependence and often progresses to drug dependence. To diagnose drug abuse, the symptoms must have lasted for at least twelve months and may include repeated work, school, or home problems due to drug use; continued use of drugs even though it means risking physical safety; recurring trouble with the law related to drug use, including impaired driving; and continued use of drugs despite drug-related problems in personal relationships.

Symptoms of drug dependence include at least three of the following: craving for the substance; inability to stop or limit drug use; tolerance, or taking greater amounts to feel the same effect; withdrawal symptoms that occur when the drug is stopped; significant amounts of time trying to acquire drugs and recover from their effects; and giving up activities to use drugs or recover from their effects. Drug use continues even when it causes or worsens health and/or psychological problems.

DIAGNOSIS

To help with diagnosis, doctors ask a series of questions regarding drug-related problems, specifically:
- how often the patient uses drugs
- which drugs the patient uses

- what amount and if the patient has increased the amount to receive the same desired effect
- emotional problems that may have occurred while using drugs
- problems with a job, family, or the law

Tests may include blood and urine tests to check for the presence of drugs.

TREATMENT

There is no cure for drug abuse or drug dependence. Treatment consists of three main goals: to help patients stop using drugs, to decrease the toxic effects of the drugs being used and to aid in symptoms of drug withdrawal ("detoxification"), and to prevent relapse. Successful treatment depends on the drug user's recognition of the problem and desire to change. Recovery takes a long time and is not an easy process. Patients may need multiple courses of treatment.

Therapies include medications, counseling, and self-help organizations. Drugs may help to alleviate some of the symptoms of withdrawal. In some cases, medication may be ordered to prevent relapse. People addicted to heroin may be given methadone to help taper them off. Methadone may also be given on a long-term basis to improve the chance of staying in treatment. Methadone is a narcotic that blocks cravings as well as the pleasurable effects of heroin and other opiates. Other drugs that are used in treatment are naltrexone (e. g., ReVia, which blocks the effect of opiates) and buprenorphine (e. g., Subutex, which is similar to methadone).

Therapy raises awareness of the underlying issues and lifestyles that promote drug use. Therapy also works to improve coping and problem-solving skills and works to develop other ways of dealing with stress or pain. Through counseling, a person can learn how to handle situations associated with drug use and replace drug-using activities with other activities that are more meaningful. Family support is encouraged.

There are numerous organizations and support groups dedicated to helping people stop using drugs. Two examples are Narcotics Anonymous and Cocaine Anonymous. These are twelve-step programs. Members of these organizations meet regularly to talk about their drug-related troubles and provide a network of support for each other.

Debra Wood, RN

Drug-Seeking Behavior

Drug-seeking behavior (DSB) is a symptom of drug abuse and addiction. A person with DSB will continuously try to access narcotic pain medication or tranquilizers even though he or she may have no medical need for these drugs. In order to obtain the desired drug from a pharmacy or doctor, a person with DSB may exhibit the following behavior:

- complaints about severe pain
- repeated requests for "lost" prescriptions
- use of forged prescriptions and false identification
- assertiveness, including demands to see a doctor immediately
- evasiveness in answering questions about medical history and references
- giving exaggerated accounts of textbook symptoms
- becoming violent if requests are denied

FURTHER READING

Fisher, Gary, and Nancy Roget. *Encyclopedia of Substance Abuse Prevention, Treatment, and Recovery.* Thousand Oaks, CA: Sage, 2009. An encyclopedia of key concepts and approaches used in the field of substance abuse.

Shapiro, Harry. *Recreational drugs: A Directory.* London: Collins & Brown, 2004. A compendium of all major recreational drugs, including facts about use, effects, risks, and legal status.

Thombs, Dennis. *Introduction to Addictive Behaviors.* 3rd ed. New York: Guilford Press, 2006. Covers theories of addiction, prevention, comorbidity, motivation enhancement, and harm reduction. Also covers psychoanalytic, cognitive, family, and social/cultural issues.

WEBSITES OF INTEREST

Cocaine Anonymous
http://www.ca.org/

Narcotics Anonymous
http://www.na.org

National Institute on Drug Abuse
http://www.nida.nih.gov

See also: Addiction; Narcotics abuse; Routes of administration; Substance abuse

---

Drug Enforcement Administration (DEA)

CATEGORY: Social issues
DEFINITION: The Drug Enforcement Administration (DEA) is an agency of the US government that enforces the controlled substances laws and regulations of the United States.
DATE: Established in July 1973

BACKGROUND

The enforcement of federal drug laws in the United States began in 1915 within the Bureau of Internal Revenue (now the Internal Revenue Service). By the 1960s, two agencies were responsible for drug law enforcement: the Bureau of Drug Abuse Control within the Department of Health, Education, and Welfare and the Federal Bureau of Narcotics within the Treasury Department. In 1968, these agencies were combined as the Bureau of Narcotics and Dangerous Drugs (BNDD) within the Department of Justice, giving the US attorney general full authority and responsibility for enforcing all federal laws on narcotics and dangerous drugs.

The Drug Enforcement Administration (DEA), which superseded the BNDD, was created by US president Richard M. Nixon by executive order in July 1973, to establish a single, unified command to enforce federal drug laws and to consolidate and coordinate the government's drug control activities. Nixon called on the new agency to launch a global "war" on drugs.

In 1982, jurisdiction over drug investigations was coordinated between the DEA and the Federal Bureau of Investigation, greatly expanding the number of agents and technical support focused on this effort. The DEA also works closely with Immigration and Customs Enforcement. In 1984, the DEA was given expanded authority to work with parents, teachers, and other concerned citizens on drug education and prevention strategies.

The DEA is headed by an administrator of drug enforcement, who is appointed by the president and confirmed by the US Senate. The president also appoints the DEA's deputy administrator. All other DEA officials are career government employees. Those directly involved in drug-law enforcement outside the legal branch are special agents, diversion investigators, and intelligence research specialists.

Special agents are the primary criminal investigation and enforcement officers of the DEA. Most are assigned to regional or international offices. They enforce the controlled substances laws and regulations of the United States, identify and immobilize drug traffickers, and seize and dismantle the financial assets of drug traffickers.

Diversion investigators conduct investigations of the illicit sales and abuse of controlled substances. They work within the Office of Diversion Control of the DEA. A relatively new concern and area of investigation for this office is the rise of Internet sites offering controlled substances openly or with little pretense of control. Many of these sites are based in Canada. Diversion investigators are authorized to take administrative, civil, and criminal actions against people and organizations in violation of controlled substances regulations.

Intelligence research specialists work closely with special agents to conduct major drug investigations, both in the United States and abroad. Areas in which intelligence research specialists conduct and manage research projects include drug cultivation and production, methods of transportation, trafficking routes, and the structure and working operations of trafficking organizations.

MISSION AND GOALS

The mission of the DEA is to enforce the controlled substances laws and regulations of the United States and to bring to the appropriate criminal and civil justice system those organizations and principal members of organizations involved in the growing, manufacture, or distribution (including smuggling) of controlled substances within or destined for illicit traffic in the United States. Additionally, the DEA is empowered to recommend and support educational and training programs aimed at reducing the availability of illicit controlled substances on the domestic and international markets.

The DEA has a number of primary responsibilities, starting with the investigation and preparation for prosecution of two types of offenders: major violators of controlled substances laws operating at interstate and international levels and criminals and drug gangs who perpetrate violence in local communities. The DEA manages a national drug intelligence program in cooperation with federal, state, local, and foreign officials that collects, analyzes, and disseminates strategic and operational drug intelligence information. It is mandated to seize and divest assets derived from, traceable to, or intended to be used for illicit drug trafficking. The DEA enforces the provisions of the Controlled Substances Act (1970) as they pertain to the manufacture, distribution, and dispensing of legally produced controlled substances.

The DEA coordinates the work of federal, state, and local law enforcement officials on mutual drug enforcement efforts. It works with foreign governments in developing and carrying out programs designed to reduce the availability of illicit abuse-type drugs in the United States through such methods as crop eradication and substitution, and through training foreign officials. Under the policy guidance of the US secretary of state and US ambassadors, the DEA is responsible for all programs associated with drug counterparts in foreign countries. The DEA acts as a liaison with the United Nations, with Interpol, and with other organizations on matters relating to international drug control programs.

Ernest Kohlmetz, MA

FURTHER READING

Clifford, Tom. *Inside the DEA*. Bloomington, IN: Authorhouse, 2006. The narrative of a former DEA agent who began working with the agency in 1971.

Robbins, David. *Heavy Traffic: 30 Years of Headlines and Major Ops from the Case Files of the DEA*. New York: Chamberlin, 2005. Presents the history of the agency through 2005 and examines possible future challenges.

WEBSITES OF INTEREST

National Institute on Drug Abuse
http://www.drugabuse.gov

US Drug Enforcement Administration
http://www.justice.gov/dea

See also: Controlled Substances Act (CSA); Education about substance abuse; Law enforcement and drugs; Legislation and substance abuse

Drugged driving

CATEGORY: Social issues

ALSO KNOWN AS: Driving under the influence; impaired driving

DEFINITION: Drugged driving is the operation of a vehicle with a measurable quantity of an abusive or nonabusive substance in the body. Impaired driving results from any amount of illicit substance, such as heroin, cocaine, and marijuana, and impairing amounts of legal substances, such as sedatives or prescription painkillers. Driving under the influence of drugs can be particularly pronounced when the substance or substances are combined with alcohol.

STATISTICS

Drugged driving has become a growing problem in the United States and across the globe; twenty-first-century rates in the United States approach those of drunk driving, and the US Centers for Disease Control and Prevention estimates that 18 percent of vehicle accidents annually are related to drugs. Data collected by survey and reporting organizations, such as the Fatality Analysis Reporting System and the Monitoring the Future drug-use survey in teenagers, suggest that drugs are identified seven times more often than alcohol in youth drivers on weekend nights.

Nearly one-third of high school seniors admit to riding with an impaired driver or driving a car while impaired from drug use. Marijuana is the primary drug associated with drugged driving in youth and all other age groups; the second and third most frequently used are cocaine and methamphetamines, respectively.

A growing concern is the contribution of prescription painkillers and sedatives to drugged driving. In the United States, impaired driving rates from benzodiazepines or opiates approach those of drugged driving with cocaine.

RISK GROUPS

People age fifty-five years and older are at particular risk of impaired driving from the sedating effects of prescription drugs through normal use or misuse. Any person who uses a sedating prescription or nonprescription drug may experience impaired driving; people who obtain multiple prescriptions of painkillers, sedatives, or antidepressants are most likely to experience drug misuse and driving impairment.

The most common drugged-driving risk group, however, is youth, especially new drivers. Approximately 25 percent of vehicle-related fatalities that occur each year involve drivers younger than age twenty-five years. Prior offenders of drunk or drugged driving laws comprise another at-risk population.

TESTING

Documenting drugged driving is complicated, in part because impairment thresholds are frequently unknown and evaluation methods are not standardized. For example, studies show that marijuana and stimulants increase the likelihood of poor decision-making and response times while driving. Connecting the use of these drugs with specific vehicle crashes is difficult, however, because of overlapping use, low testing rates, and poor understanding of the behaviors that cause reckless driving. Better and more frequent drug testing can support the connection between drug use and impaired driving.

Testing for drug impairment is more complex than testing for blood alcohol concentrations. Choices about what drugs to test for and what methods to use remain unclear. Because drug levels in the body fluctuate nonlinearly, tested concentrations are not always predictive of effect. In addition, circulating drug metabolites can impair ability at least as much as the original drug but may not affect test results. Finally, drug testing must be conducted rapidly, because the primary drug can dissipate within hours despite lingering impairment.

Testing can be performed on urine, blood, or oral fluids. Blood tests report the most accurate drug concentrations but are invasive, costly, and time consuming. Urine is less indicative of drug effects and is difficult to test reliably in the field. Both blood and urine testing can require offsite laboratory evaluation, which adds to the cost and timeliness of results.

Oral fluid testing, conversely, is easy to administer and provides reasonable accuracy. However, these tests still do not evaluate metabolites, and they do not always have evidence-based cut points that reflect impairment. Oral kits have become preferred for field use because they are rapid-use tests that do not require a laboratory. Although rapid tests provide the best option for identifying drugged drivers quickly and are more accessible for law enforcement, they have lower sensitivity and more false positives than laboratory tests.

A barrier to frequent drugged-driving testing is appropriate drug identification. Law enforcement must identify behaviors representing drug use before ordering tests; the ability to distinguish the types of drugs by symptoms is crucial to minimize what drugs are tested for. Drug-recognition-expert programs are being developed to address this need and to educate law enforcement officers about the symptoms of specific drug use.

PREVENTION

Prevention is implemented through the education of three populations: new drivers, who are often unaware that drugged driving poses risks and consequences similar to those of drunk driving; law enforcement professionals, who need to identify and test persons who are suspected of drugged driving; and health professionals, who can identify risks associated with specific prescriptions or persons on multiple high-risk drugs.

The National Drug Control Strategy has set a prevention goal of 10 percent lower drugged-driving rates by 2015. Supporting this goal requires improved testing technology and application, greater professional education and outreach efforts, and broad public-health awareness campaigns. These efforts can be supplemented by clear legal restrictions, especially zero tolerance policies for illicit drug use while driving. Partnered efforts for public education, especially youth antidrug campaigns, are necessary deterrents, as are fines and arrests for drugged driving.

Over-the-counter and prescription drugs pose a greater challenge for prevention and legislation, as these drugs are legal and common. However, even therapeutic dosages can affect driving in some people. The efforts of health professionals to educate the public about the sedating effects of legal drugs and about the risks of misuse and drugged driving should be at the forefront.

Nicole M. Van Hoey, PharmD

FURTHER READING

Institute for Behavior and Health. "Drugged Driving Research: A White Paper." 31 Mar. 2011. Web. 2 Apr. 2012. http://www.whitehouse.gov/sites/default/files/ondcp/issues-content/drugged-driving/nida_dd_paper.pdf. Summarizes drugged driving statistics and requirements for future testing and prevention. Identifies public policies to implement for increased awareness of drugged driving risks and consequences.

Maxwell, J. C. "Drunk Versus Drugged: How Different Are the Drivers?" *Drug and Alcohol Dependence* 121 (2012): 68–72. Print. Report on drug choices and target populations that distinguish drugged from drunk drivers to direct prevention campaigns.

National Institute on Drug Abuse. "What Is Drugged Driving?" Dec. 2010. Web. 2 Apr. 2012. http://www.drugabuse.gov/publications/infofacts/drugged-driving. An informative web guide to drugged driving.

Office of National Drug Control Policy. "Teen Drugged Driving Toolkit: Parent, Coalition, and Community Group Activity Guide." Web. http://whitehouse.gov/ondcp/drugged-driving. Describes the risks of drugged driving particular to youth drivers. Identifies resources and guides for community organizations to use for educational campaigns and programs.

WEBSITES OF INTEREST

DruggedDriving.org
http://www.druggeddriving.org/ddp.html

US Drug Enforcement Administration
http://www.justice.gov/dea/driving_drugged.html

See also: Designated drivers; Drunk driving; Law enforcement and drugs

Drug interactions

CATEGORY: Health issues and physiology
DEFINITION: Drug interactions occur when two or more medications or drugs are taken simultaneously or near simultaneously, causing interference with the metabolism of one or both agents. Drug interactions can cause the concentrations of one or both agents to either increase or decrease, potentially resulting in unforeseen negative reactions, including fatalities.

INTERACTIONS AND DRUG METABOLISM

Medications and recreational drugs are metabolized in the body into pharmacologically active chemical components; nonpharmacologically active chemical moieties are then excreted from the body. Most medications are either metabolized by the kidney (renal metabolism) or by the liver (hepatic metabolism).

Within the liver and intestines exist multiple enzymes and pathways responsible for breaking down medications. Some of the enzymes that are most commonly involved in drug metabolism are the cytochrome P450 (CYP) enzymes. Of the CYP enzymes, CYP3A4 is most commonly involved in drug metabolism. It has been estimated that this enzyme is at least partly responsible for the metabolism of almost 50 percent of medications. The rate and amount of drug that can be metabolized depends on a number of factors, including the amount of enzyme present and the speed at which these enzymes are working.

When a person ingests multiple medications metabolized through the same pathway, the enzymes may not be able to metabolize all the medications simultaneously, leading to elevated, possibly toxic, levels of the drugs. For example, alprazolam (Xanax) is metabolized through CYP3A4. If a patient taking alprazolam is prescribed clarithromycin (Biaxin) for sinusitis and takes the two medications together, the clarithromycin, a CYP3A4 inhibitor, will effectively slow the breakdown of alprazolam, leading to increased sedation and central nervous system (CNS) depression. If the patient continues to take alprazolam, unaware that drug levels are building up in his or her system, dangerous consequences can occur.

DRUG-FOOD INTERACTIONS

In addition to the medications that may interact with one another, drugs also can have interactions with food. Milk and other calcium- and magnesium-containing products can interact with certain medications, including fluoroquinolone antibiotics such as ciprofloxacin (Cipro) and levofloxacin (Levaquin). Divalent cations such as calcium and magnesium can bind the antibiotic, keeping it from being absorbed by the body.

Another example of drug and food interactions is the heightened CNS depressant effects of alcohol when combined with medications that already produce CNS depressant effects, such as benzodiazepines (alprazolam, or Xanax, and lorazepam, or Ativan) and morphine or morphine derivatives (such as the hydrocodone products Vicodin, Norco, and Loratab and the oxycodone products Percocet and Percodan).

CNS depressant medications and substances, such as alcohol, slow down certain brain processes. This can lead to decreased motor function and coordination, drowsiness, confusion, and respiratory depression. CNS effects are cumulative, which is why the addition of alcohol to the system of a person taking either chronic or recreational (and legal) CNS depressants can be so dangerous. These medications and the resulting sensations can have addictive properties, leading the user to purposely combine the two in an unsafe and potentially fatal manner.

DRUG AND HERBAL SUPPLEMENTS INTERACTIONS

Herbal medications are often assumed to be more natural and, therefore, safer than pharmacologically produced medications. The use of these agents has continued to increase, although the exact number of people using supplements is hard to gauge because these agents are available without a prescription (over the counter).

Some of the most popular supplements have serious interactions with common medications. These supplements include St. John's wort, *Ginkgo biloba*, ginseng, and garlic. St. John's wort, which is used to treat many ailments, most commonly depression, is metabolized through CYP 3A4 and 2E1 and, therefore, can be unsafe when used with some anticoagulants, including warfarin, and with some medications used to treat human immunodeficiency virus (including protease inhibitors and non-nucleoside reverse transcriptase inhibitors). Ginkgo is commonly used for memory enhancement. There have been numerous reports of bleeding in patients taking ginkgo while also taking anticoagulants, and in patients with clotting disorders.

It is important that patients understand that herbal supplements, although generally safe, can dangerously interact with over-the-counter and prescription medications. Patients should alert their doctors, pharmacists, and other providers about what supplements they are taking to help prevent serious interactions.

Allison Armagan, PharmD

FURTHER READING

Izzo, Angelo, and Edzard Ernst. "Interactions between Herbal Medicines and Prescribed Drugs." *Drugs* 61.15 (2001): 2163–75. Print. A systematic review of the seven best-selling herbal products: garlic, ginkgo, ginseng, kava, St. John's wort, echinacea, and saw palmetto. Reports adverse reactions and interactions for each of the herbal products, if any.

Saito, Mitsuo, et al. "Undesirable Effects of Citrus Juice on the Pharmacokinetics of Drugs." *Drug Safety* 28.8 (2005): 677–94. Print. A systematic review of grapefruit and other citrus juices' effect on the metabolism of drugs. Includes a review of the cytochrome P450 3A4, p-glycoprotein, and organic anion transporting polypeptide.

Wallace, Allison W., Jennifer M. Victory, and Guy W. Amsden. "Lack of Bioequivalence When Levofloxacin and Calcium-Fortified Orange Juice Are Coadministered to Healthy Volunteers." *Journal of Clinical Pharmacology* 43 (2003): 539–44. Print. A study of the pharmacokinetics of an antibiotic, levofloxacin, in twelve healthy volunteers given either twelve ounces of calcium-fortified orange juice, non-calcium-fortified orange juice, or water.

WEBSITES OF INTEREST

Drugs.com: Drug Interactions Checker
http://www.drugs.com/drug_interactions.html

National Institute on Drug Abuse
http://www.drugabuse.gov

US Food and Drug Administration
http://www.fda.gov/drugs/resourcesforyou/ucm163354.htm

See also: Brain changes with addiction; Dopamine and addiction; Science of addiction

Drug paraphernalia

CATEGORY: Substance abuse

DEFINITION: Drug paraphernalia encompasses any product, device, or material that enables illicit drug use, concealment, or manufacturing. Most drug paraphernalia are illegal. The most common drug paraphernalia include hypodermic needles and syringes, bongs, pipes, spoons, roach clips, mirrors, razor blades, and scales.

HISTORY OF USE

Drug paraphernalia have a long history of use. By the 1970s in the United States, recreational drug use reached epidemic proportions, giving rise to drug paraphernalia stores known as "head shops." These stores, which often also sold music, sold a variety of specialized drug-related items. These items, which included water pipes called "bongs" and marijuana cigarette holders known as "roach clips," catered to, enhanced, and glamorized drug use. Head shops openly displayed other items that advertised and promoted drug culture, including clothing, jewelry, tattoo designs, posters, and publications.

The commercial distribution of drug paraphernalia and the growing drug problem prompted antiparaphernalia laws. In 1979, the US Drug Enforcement Agency (DEA) enacted the Model Drug Paraphernalia Act to help states prohibit the sale and possession of any article used to prepare and consume illicit drugs. The act defined drug paraphernalia, listed criteria to determine the presence of drug paraphernalia, and prohibited advertisements for drug paraphernalia. By the 1980s, many states required businesses to obtain a license to sell drug paraphernalia, forcing many head shops to close.

To further restrict access to drug paraphernalia, the DEA drafted the Federal Drug Paraphernalia Statute as part of the Controlled Substances Act (1970) to regulate the possession, selling, offering, and transport of illegal drug paraphernalia. Many US states enacted their own regulations prohibiting drug paraphernalia.

Drug paraphernalia are frequently designed with bright and colorful logos to attract teenagers and young adults. Various drug paraphernalia can be acquired on the Internet, through mail-order businesses, and in tobacco and specialty shops. Sometimes, drug paraphernalia are labeled with misleading disclaimers to minimize the dangers associated with illicit drug use. Drug paraphernalia items are continually evolving along with illegal drug activity.

COMMON DRUG PARAPHERNALIA

Drug paraphernalia can be categorized as user or dealer specific. User paraphernalia consists of items that facilitate drug use, such as hypodermic needles and syringes, pipes (metal, wooden, acrylic, glass, stone, plastic, ceramic), pipe screens, bongs, roach clips, spoons, tubes, razor blades, mirrors, rolling papers, and drug kits. Dealer paraphernalia consists of items that facilitate the production, trafficking, and concealment of illicit drugs and include blenders, scales, bowls, baggies, capsules, balloons, vials, and diluents and adulterants for mixing illegal drugs.

Drug paraphernalia also encompasses drug storage or "stash cans" to conceal drugs. These items include bags, envelopes or flaps, purses, pen cases, small vials and containers, cigarette packs, pill bottles, film canisters, water bottles, gum and candy wrappers, pagers, soda cans, lipstick dispensers, and make-up kits. Stash cans may be specially constructed with hidden compartments to conceal drugs.

Drug paraphernalia can be difficult to identify because ordinary household products can be used to disguise illicit drug use. Sunglasses can be used to hide pupil dilation and red eyes. Breath sprays, mints, air fresheners, perfumes, and incense can be used to mask drug-related odors. Clothing may have hidden drug compartments.

DRUG-SPECIFIC PARAPHERNALIA

Different drug paraphernalia can be associated with different methods of drug transmission, such as inhaling, smoking, and injecting. Drug paraphernalia designed to aid in the inhalation and smoking of illicit drugs such as marijuana, crack, and cocaine includes pipes, smoking masks, roach clips, miniature spoons, bongs, hoses, tubes, and lighters. Hypodermic syringes, needles, and lighters are well-known drug paraphernalia for preparing and injecting drugs such as heroin and methamphetamine.

Drug paraphernalia can be associated with specific drugs such as ecstasy, cocaine, and marijuana and with methamphetamine production and inhalant use. Ecstasy paraphernalia includes pacifiers, lollipops, and mouth guards to aid in relieving jaw clenching, teeth

Drug paraphernalia. (Southern Illinois University)

grinding, and dry mouth. Glow sticks, flash lights, vapor rubs, and masks enhance stimulation while candy pieces and jewelry can be used to hide pills.

Cocaine paraphernalia includes pipes, glass tubes, small spoons, and lighters for smoking. Razor blades, cards, and mirrors are typically used to organize cocaine into lines for snorting through straws. Marijuana paraphernalia includes chillums or cone-shaped pipes, rolling papers to form cigarettes, stash cans, roach clips to hold the joint, and deodorizers or incense to disguise the odor.

Drug paraphernalia associated with methamphetamine production includes flasks, funnels, tubing, adaptors, joints, cooking equipment, and thermometers. Drug paraphernalia associated with inhalant use includes rags for sniffing, spray cans, glue, paint, plastic bags, balloons, nozzles, and bottles.

Rose Ciulla-Bohling, PhD

FURTHER READING

Ginther, Catherine. *Drug Abuse Sourcebook.* 2nd ed. Detroit: Omnigraphics, 2004. This book provides basic information about illegal drugs, health and treatment issues, and drug prevention programs.

Hagan, Holly, et al. "Sharing of Drug Preparation Equipment as a Risk Factor for Hepatitis C." *American Journal of Public Health* 91.1 (2001): 42–46. Print. Discusses the link between sharing injection paraphernalia and hepatitis C infection.

Inciardi, James A., ed. *Handbook of Drug Control in the United States.* Westport, CT: Greenwood, 1990. Outlines the history, scheduling, and regulation of illegal drugs in the United States.

Korsmeyer, Pamela, and Henry R. Kranzler, eds. *Encyclopedia of Drugs, Alcohol, and Addictive Behavior.* 3rd ed. Detroit: Macmillan, 2009. A general resource addressing the history and medical and legal issues associated with drug use and addiction.

Scheb, John M., and John M. Scheb II. *Criminal Law and Procedure.* 7th ed. Belmont, CA: Wadsworth, 2010. A practical resource for learning about the criminal justice system and the prohibition of drug paraphernalia.

WEBSITES OF INTEREST
GetSmartAboutDrugs.com
http://www.getsmartaboutdrugs.com/identify/
   paraphernalia.html

National Drug Intelligence Center
http://www.justice.gov/ndic/pubs6/6445/index.
   htm

US Drug Enforcement Administration
http://www.justice.gov/dea/concern/
   paraphernaliafact.html

See also: Gateway drugs; Intravenous drug use and blood-borne diseases; Meth labs; Pipes and hookahs; Routes of administration

Drug testing

CATEGORY: Diagnosis and prevention
ALSO KNOWN AS: Drug screening; toxicology screening
DEFINITION: Drug testing is the screening of human body fluids, primarily blood, urine, and saliva but also hair, to identify the presence of illicit drugs, including marijuana, phencyclidine, methamphetamine, and cocaine. Drug screens also detect the presence of frequently abused prescription drugs, such as amphetamines or opiates. Additional screens for alcohol, hydrocodone, barbiturates, benzodiazepines, and other drugs may be used by federal agencies, and federal contractors use urine screens only, based on the provisions of the Drug-Free Workplace Act of 1988.

DRUG SCREENING BASICS
Many organizations testing for drugs use a drug panel that tests urine for multiple drugs. Drug screens often test for the metabolites of substances, or the chemical results that are found within the body after the drug is processed. A positive urine test is followed by a confirming test for the specific drug. For example, the metabolite for marijuana is tetrahydrocannibinol (THC). If the first test is positive for THC, then a confirming test for delta-9-tetrahydrocannabinol-9-carboxylic acid is performed, confirming (or denying) marijuana use. The opiate screening will test

for opiate metabolites, and a confirming test will test specifically for the opiate drugs codeine or morphine.

Government and private employers are major users of drug testing methods, and many private firms have created their own drug testing programs. The American Management Association estimates nearly two-thirds (62 percent) of employers in the United States use drug testing.

Drug screens are used for six primary reasons. The first reason is to prescreen potential job candidates for drug use. The second reason is to randomly test workers as a deterrent to drug use on the job and to identify safety hazards in persons in high-risk occupations. Third, tests may be performed if there is a reasonable suspicion that a specific person is abusing drugs. Fourth, tests may be ordered subsequent to an employee accident, and fifth, upon the return to work of an employee involved in an earlier accident. Sixth, employers will use a follow-up test to recheck an employee following a positive drug screen. Employers will often use toxicology screens to test an employee before a promotion or to test an employee during that employee's annual physical examination.

One key reason for the implementation of drug testing in the twentieth century was to deter workplace drug use, and screening appears to be working. According to the US Substance Abuse and Mental Health Services Administration (SAMHSA), the number of positive drug tests at worksites around the United States plummeted from 13.6 percent in 1998 to 3.6 percent in 2009.

Any positive test for drugs is often followed by a more sophisticated test, one that uses gas chromatography/mass spectrometry (GS/MS) to test for specific substances. If this test is positive too, it will be given to a physician knowledgeable about drug abuse for further review.

LAW ENFORCEMENT DRUG SCREENING
Law enforcement officials test for drugs among persons involved in automobile and other vehicle accidents to determine if alcohol or drugs may have been a factor in causing the accident. Law enforcement often uses drug screens to test persons who have been arrested to determine if that person was under the influence of drugs at the time the alleged crime was committed. Incarcerated persons are subject to drug screening, as are those who are on probation or parole. A positive drug screen for a person on probation

or parole often means he or she will be sent back to jail or prison, because a positive drug screen is usually a violation of the terms of probation or parole.

Drug courts throughout the United States manage the cases of persons convicted of drug offenses, and drug testing is an integral part of the program. It is estimated that more than one thousand courts have drug courts to manage drug offenders.

Drug testing also may be sought by law enforcement because some drugs are known to escalate the risk of violence. As a result, a person in custody for committing a violent act may be tested for recent drug use, especially for the use of a drug, such as methamphetamine or cocaine, that is linked to violent behavior. According to research by SAMHSA (2002–2004), among adolescents age twelve to seventeen years, all of whom had engaged in violent behavior in the past year, 69.3 percent had abused methamphetamine, 61.8 percent had abused cocaine, and 61.4 percent had abused hallucinogens in the past year. Marijuana was found to be used by nearly one-half (49.7 percent) of the adolescents deemed violent.

OTHER REASONS FOR DRUG TESTING

Competitive athletes are barred from using drugs such as anabolic steroids, which are known to increase muscle mass and endurance but which also have many serious health effects. Also, athletic organizations use drug screening to ensure that high school, college, and professional athletes remain drug free because drugs affect athletic performance and can provide an unfair advantage in competition.

A 2002 ruling by the US Supreme Court (*Pottawatomie County v. Earls*) allows schools to test students who are not athletes, through random drug tests. Schools that adopt such programs believe that random testing can deter students from abusing drugs and also believe that testing allows for the identification of students with drug problems, who would benefit from counseling.

Pain management doctors may test their patients to ensure they are taking only the drugs that are prescribed to them and not taking any additional drugs of abuse. Some people who are prescribed drugs such as opiates, amphetamines, and benzodiazepines divert (mostly sell) their drugs to others. In this case, a negative test for the prescribed drug is problematic, indicating that the person is not taking the prescribed drug. Pain management doctors also want their patients to take only scheduled drugs that are

---

Drug Testing and Poppy Seeds

Eating pastries and other food products with poppy seeds can cause positive test results for heroin. Opiates (such as heroin, morphine, and codeine) can be found in urine samples for as long as two days after eating poppy-seed-containing foods and for up to sixty hours if large quantities of the seeds are consumed.

Hair analysis is a more accurate, but less commonly used method of testing for recent heroin use. In a hair analysis, a false-positive test result would not occur after eating food containing poppy seeds.

One high-profile demonstration of the validity of poppy seed drug-test claims was conducted on the Discovery Channel's television program *MythBusters*. One participant ate a poppy seed cake and tested positive for opiates one-half hour later. The other participant ate three poppy seed bagels and tested positive two hours later. Both participants continued to test positive for sixteen hours.

---

prescribed; doctors are alerted if the test reveals the presence of nonprescribed drugs of abuse. Some pain management doctors require patients to sign a contract that they are willing to be tested randomly for drugs. If the patient refuses to sign the contract, the doctor will not provide treatment.

Persons admitted to emergency rooms with an altered mental state are often tested for drugs to help medical professionals determine whether the behavior is likely caused by drug abuse or by mental illness. One complicating factor is that some mentally ill persons also abuse drugs. It should be noted, however, that few mentally ill persons are violent. However, research has indicated that the abuse of alcohol and drugs escalates the risk for violence among people with mental illness.

Substance abuse treatment facilities may require drug screening to ensure that patients in the facility are not using drugs that they have acquired illicitly, that is, drugs brought to the facility by visitors or others. Child protection workers may request drug screening to verify that former addicts who had abused or neglected their children in the past are no longer using drugs of abuse. Sometimes young children are tested for drugs, particularly if it is known that a parent has abused drugs in the past. Investigators may test the child's hair or urine for traces of drug use. If drugs are found in the body fluids or hair of a child, the child may be removed from his or her home. Additionally, small children sometimes ingest drugs carelessly left out by drug abusers; these children are at risk of cardiovascular or neurological symptoms, even death.

PROS AND CONS OF TESTING METHODS

Although urine is the most common fluid screened, organizations do seek other means for screening for drugs; each screening method has advantages and disadvantages. For example, because hair grows about one-half inch per month, testing of the hair can determine the presence of drugs from several months prior to the test. In contrast, screens of the urine can detect drugs used within hours or days only, with some exceptions. As a result, if recent abuse of drugs is sought, then tests of the urine or blood are preferable; if information on long-term drug abuse detection is sought, then hair testing for drugs may be preferable.

Another factor in determining what test to use is the speed at which the test results are needed. Urine and blood test results usually can be obtained rapidly. In contrast, hair must be sent to a specialized laboratory for analysis. Oral fluid testing, often referred to as saliva testing, can be done on-site, although this test is not as commonly used as urine or blood testing.

The reliability of a given test is another factor. For example, hair testing can be affected by the use of hair bleaches and dyes by the person providing a sample. Up to 60 percent of drugs may be removed through such processes. The drugs least affected by the use of cosmetic substances for the hair include cannabis (marijuana and hashish) and opiates. Urine testing and blood testing are highly reliable, although false positives can occur with urine testing. In addition, often there is no first-hand observation of the collection of urine for testing, as is with testing of the blood, hair, or oral fluids. As a result, some people deliberately attempt to alter urine test results by, for example, submitting the urine of another (likely drug-free) person.

The invasiveness of a given test is sometimes a consideration in choosing the type of test. Saliva testing is considered noninvasive because it requires that the person simply spit multiple times into a special container. Hair testing is noninvasive because it requires cutting only a few strands of hair close to the scalp. Urine testing is not considered invasive but it can be embarrassing if the examiner listens outside the door. Conversely, blood testing is the most invasive form of blood testing because it requires the penetration of the skin with a needle to collect the blood.

DRUG POSITIVES AND FALSE POSITIVES

In most cases, a person who tests positive for a drug most likely used the drug. Positive drug screens may lead to job termination or to not being hired for a job. Some people may test positive for a drug, especially with a urine screen, even if they have not used the drug in question.

It also is true that a person will test positive for a drug that they have been prescribed. A person being treated for attention-deficit hyperactivity disorder, for example, will test positive for amphetamine use. While tests can determine the presence of, in this case, amphetamine, tests cannot determine if the person is using the drug lawfully.

Some medications may cause a false positive on a urine screen. For example, nonsteroidal anti-inflammatory drugs (NSAIDs) may give a false positive for the use of marijuana. NSAIDs may also give a false positive urine result for barbiturates, a type of controlled drug that is included in some drug screens. The use of a Vicks inhaler may give a false positive result in the urine for an amphetamine. The use of sertraline (Zoloft), a commonly used antidepressant, may give a false positive for benzodiazepine. Other antidepressants, such as bupropion, desipramine, and trazadone, may give a false positive result for amphetamine use.

Christine Adamec, BA, MBA

FURTHER READING

American Management Association. "Medical Testing 2004 Survey." Web. 11 Mar. 2011. http://www. amanet.org/training/articles/printversion/2004-Medical-Testing-Survey-17.aspx. Summarizes major research by the American Management Association on organizations using drug testing in the United States.

Heller, Jacob. "Toxicology Screen." *MedlinePlus*. 12 Feb. 2009. Web. 8 Mar. 2011. http://www.nlm. nih.gov/medlineplus/ency/article/003578.htm. A physician offers basic, helpful information on drug screening.

Moller, Monique, Joey Gareri, and Gideon Koren. "A Review of Substance Abuse Monitoring in a Social Services Context: A Primer for Child Protection Workers." *Canadian Journal of Clinical Pharmacology* 17.1 (2010): 177–93. Web. 5 Mar. 2012. http://www.cjcp.ca/pubmed.php?articleId=260. Discusses key factors in drug testing based on the unique perspective of a state child-protection worker.

Nasky, Kevin M., George L. Cowan, and Douglas R. Knittel. "False-Positive Urine Screening for Benzodiazepines: An Association with Sertraline? A Two-Year Retrospective Chart Analysis." *Psychiatry* 6.7 (2009): 36–39. Print. Discusses a two-year study of false-positive urine screenings for benzodiazepines among persons taking sertraline, finding positive evidence for an association.

Reynolds, Lawrence A. "Historical Aspects of Drugs-of-Abuse Testing in the United States." *Drugs of Abuse: Body Fluid Testing.* Eds. Raphael C. Wong and Harley Y. Tse. Totowa, NJ: Humana, 2010. A comprehensive source on drug testing.

US Department of Health and Human Services. "Mandatory Guidelines for Federal Workplace Drug Testing Programs." *Federal Register.* 25 Nov. 2008. Web. 11 Mar. 2011. http://edocket. access.gpo.gov/2008/pdf/E8-26726.pdf. Provides numerous and detailed questions and answers related to the federal drug screening program.

Vincent, E. Chris, Arthur Zebelman, and Cheryl Goodwin. "What Common Substances Can Cause False Positives on Urine Screens for Drugs of Abuse?" *Journal of Family Practice* 55.10 (2006). Web. 5 Mar. 2012. http://www.jfponline.com/Pages. asp?AID=4455. Discusses common substances that can cause a false-positive reading on a urine drug screen.

WEBSITES OF INTEREST

National Institute on Drug Abuse
http://www.drugabuse.gov/drugpages/testingfaqs. html

US Preventive Services Task Force
http://www.uspreventiveservicestaskforce.org/ uspstf08/druguse/drugrs.pdf

See also: Diagnosis methods; Law enforcement and drugs; Legislation and substance abuse; Prevention methods and research; Screening for behavioral addictions

Drunk driving

CATEGORY: Social issues

ALSO KNOWN AS: Alcohol-impaired driving; driving under the influence; driving while intoxicated

DEFINITION: By law, a driver is considered to be impaired by alcohol if his or her blood alcohol content is 0.08 percent (0.08 grams of alcohol per 100 milliliters of blood) or higher. A *driver* is any operator of a motor vehicle, which includes motorcycle, truck, and passenger vehicle.

DRUNK DRIVING LAWS

Every US state has enacted a law making it illegal to drive with a blood alcohol content (BAC) of 0.08 percent or higher. Also, each US state has set the minimum drinking age to twenty-one years and has established a zero-tolerance law that prohibits people less than twenty-one years of age from driving after drinking. The majority of zero-tolerance laws set the drinking limit to a BAC of 0.02 percent. Drivers convicted of alcohol-impaired driving face suspension or revocation of their license.

Drivers who refuse to undergo BAC testing or who fail the test can have their license taken away immediately under a process called administrative license suspension. This process is practiced in forty-one states and the District of Columbia, and the length of time a license is suspended ranges from seven days to one year, depending on the state. Many states will consider restoring driving privileges during a suspension if the person demonstrates a special hardship (such as needing to drive to work).

A mechanism that prevents suspended or probationary drivers from operating a vehicle while impaired by alcohol is the ignition interlock device. This device is attached to the vehicle's ignition and forces the driver, before being able to start the vehicle, to blow into the device for an analysis of the driver's blood alcohol level; a device that registers a BAC of 0.08 or above will lock the vehicle's ignition.

EFFECTS OF ALCOHOL

Alcohol is quickly absorbed into the bloodstream and travels throughout the body and to the brain within thirty to seventy minutes of having an alcoholic drink. A standard alcoholic beverage (such as a twelve-ounce beer, a five-ounce glass of wine, or one shot of liquor) contains about one-half ounce (exactly 0.54 ounces) of alcohol.

All of these types of alcohol will affect BAC in the same way. How quickly a person's BAC rises will depend on how quickly he or she drinks the beverage, on the amount he or she drinks, on the amount of food in the person's stomach, and on his or her weight and gender. Having food in the stomach helps slow the absorption of alcohol through the stomach walls into the bloodstream. Moreover, heavier people have more water in their body, and this water dilutes their BAC. Females typically have less water and more body fat than men, and alcohol is not easily absorbed into fat cells, so more alcohol is absorbed into the bloodstream.

The effects brought on by alcohol start to appear with a BAC of 0.02 percent. These effects include a loss of judgment and a decline in the driver's ability to quickly track moving objects or perform two tasks at a time. Once a person's BAC reaches 0.05, the risk of a fatal crash substantially increases. At this level, the person is less alert and coordinated, has trouble focusing, has trouble steering the vehicle, and is slower to respond to emergency driving situations. At a BAC of 0.08 percent, muscle coordination is poor and the driver will have problems concentrating and controlling the vehicle, will have short-term memory loss, will have problems processing information (for example, signal detection), and will show impaired reasoning and depth perception. With a BAC of 0.10 the driver's reaction time and control deteriorates, thinking slows further, and driving becomes even more difficult. By the time a driver's BAC reaches 0.15 percent, he or she shows a major loss of balance, impaired processing of information, inattention, and little control of the vehicle.

STATISTICS

The National Highway Traffic Safety Administration's National Center for Statistics and Analysis (NCSA) tracks statistics on alcohol-impaired driving and reports these results annually. The NCSA states that any fatal crash in which a driver has a BAC of 0.08 percent or higher is an alcohol-impaired-driving crash, and fatalities resulting from this crash are alcohol-impaired-driving fatalities. They further clarify that *alcohol-impaired* does not mean that the crash or the fatality was solely caused by alcohol impairment.

Another source that monitors and reports statistics annually is the Insurance Institute for Highway Safety (IIHS). This organization uses data from the US Department of Transportation's Fatality Analysis Reporting System to analyze and report statistics.

FATALITIES

Some progress has been made to reduce alcohol-impaired driving and related injuries and deaths since about 1980. Reports from the NCSA and the IIHS show that from 1982 to 1994, the United States had a 32 percent decline in deaths among drivers with a BAC at or above 0.08. This decline has leveled off in fatalities per year and has ranged from 22 to 25 percent since 1994 through 2009. Looking at overall alcohol-impaired traffic fatalities (drivers or non-drivers), the United States had a 7.4 percent decline between 2008 and 2009.

The year 2009 had 10,839 alcohol-impaired traffic fatalities (or one death every forty-eight minutes), accounting for 32 percent of the total

Sobriety Checkpoints

The sobriety checkpoint, or roadblock, is a law enforcement tool used to arrest drunk drivers and to deter driving while intoxicated. Specifically, sobriety checkpoints occur when law enforcement officers set up a roadblock and stop cars to determine if their drivers have been drinking alcohol. According to the US Centers for Disease Control and Prevention, accidents involving drunk drivers were reduced by 20 percent in US states that have sobriety checkpoints.

Sobriety checkpoints raise a number of concerns, however. One is racial profiling and another is the targeting of unlicensed drivers. If a driver is unlicensed, his or her car can be impounded, making money for the state but penalizing drivers stopped at checkpoints who were not drunk. A third issue is the constitutionality of a sobriety checkpoint. Opponents say it violates the constitutional (Fourth Amendment) right against unreasonable searches.

motor vehicle traffic fatalities in the United States. Drunk drivers made up sixty-seven percent of persons killed; 16 percent were passengers in the drunk drivers' vehicles, 10 percent were occupants in other vehicles, and 6 percent were not in a motor vehicle.

Time of day and day of the week also were important indicators of an increased incidence of alcohol-related-deaths. Midnight to 3 a.m. was the deadliest time for intoxicated drivers involved in crashes: 72 percent of these drivers had a BAC at or above 0.08 and 46 percent had a BAC at or above 0.15. The incidence of alcohol-impaired drivers involved in fatal crashes was four times higher at night (37 percent) than at daytime (9 percent) and was two times higher on weekends (31 percent) than on weekdays (16 percent).

The NCSA defined *nighttime* as starting at 6 p.m. and ending at 5:59 a.m. (daytime began at 6 a.m. and ended at 5:59 p.m.) and defined *weekend* as starting Friday at 6 p.m. and as ending Monday at 5:50 a.m. (*Weekday* was defined as Monday from 5 a.m. to Friday at 5:59 p.m.). The IIHS narrowed the timeframe for what defined *nighttime* (9 p.m. to 6 a.m.) and found that 62 percent of drivers with a BAC at or above 0.08 had died and 46 percent of drivers with a BAC at or above 0.15 had died during that time.

Of 1,314 children age fourteen years and younger who were killed in motor vehicle crashes, 181 (or 14 percent) died in crashes involving alcohol-impaired drivers. Fifty-one percent of these 181 children were in the vehicle of the alcohol-impaired driver and 15 percent were struck by the alcohol-impaired driver's vehicle (data not reported on the remaining 34 percent).

DRIVER CHARACTERISTICS

Of the 12,012 drivers involved in a fatal crash with a recorded BAC of 0.01 percent or higher, 84 percent had a BAC of at least 0.08 and 56 percent had a BAC of 0.15 or higher. The most common BAC recorded for drunk drivers involved in fatal crashes was 0.17 percent.

Age was a significant predictor of a person driving drunk and being involved in a fatal crash. Drivers between twenty-one and twenty-four years of age with a BAC of 0.08 or higher topped the list of fatalities at 35 percent, followed by twenty-five

to thirty-four year olds (32 percent), thirty-five to forty-four year olds (26 percent), forty-four to fifty-four year olds (22 percent), sixteen to twenty year olds (19 percent), fifty-five to sixty-four year olds (13 percent), sixty-five to seventy-four year olds (7 percent), and age seventy-five years or older (3 percent). There was a consistently higher percentage of male drivers with a BAC at or above 0.08 percent who were involved in fatal crashes in every age group. More than one-half of men age twenty-one to thirty years (58 percent) and age thirty-one to forty years (53 percent) with a BAC at or above 0.08 and involved in a crash were killed.

For overall deaths of drunk drivers with 0.08 or higher, 40 percent were male and 22 percent were female, 29 percent were motorcyclists, 23 percent were drivers of passenger vehicles, 23 percent were drivers of light trucks, and 2 percent were drivers of large trucks. Drivers involved in a fatal crash with a reported BAC level of 0.08 or higher were eight times more likely than nondrinking drivers to have a previous impaired-driving conviction.

Christine G. Holzmueller, BLA

FURTHER READING

"The ABCs of BAC: A Guide to Understanding Blood Alcohol Concentration and Alcohol Impairment." 17 Feb. 2012. Web. http://www.stopimpaired-driving.org/ABCsBACWeb. Clearly explains the effects of alcohol and how it affects a person's driving abilities at different BAC levels.

Dasgupta, Amitava. *The Science of Drinking: How Alcohol Affects Your Body and Mind*. Lanham, MD: Rowman & Littlefield, 2011. A comprehensive study of the science of alcohol impairment.

"Impaired Driving." 17 Feb. 2012. Web. http://www.nhtsa.gov/Impaired. Features manuals, brochures, and toolkits on impaired driving.

"Traffic Safety Facts 2009 Data: Alcohol-Impaired Driving." 17 Feb. 2012. Web. http://www-nrd.nhtsa.dot.gov/pubs/811385.pdf. Provides detailed descriptive data and summaries on alcohol-impaired driving fatality by role, type of vehicle, gender, age, BAC levels, and US state.

WEBSITES OF INTEREST

Insurance Institute for Highway Safety
http://www.iihs.org

Mothers Against Drunk Driving
http://www.madd.org

National Commission Against Drunk Driving
http://www.ncadd.com

National Highway Traffic Safety Administration
http://www.nhtsa.gov

National Institute on Alcohol Abuse and Alcoholism
http://www.niaaa.nih.gov

See also: Designated drivers; Drugged driving; Mothers Against Drunk Driving (MADD); Students Against Destructive Decisions (SADD)

DSM-IV criteria for behavioral addictions

CATEGORY: Diagnosis and prevention

DEFINITION: Behavioral addictions are behaviors that a person feels compelled to complete even if those behaviors result in long-term negative consequences. Behavioral addictions are not substance related but have a compulsive quality. These behaviors are often focused on gambling, stealing, food intake, Internet or web use, pornography and sex, and self-mutilation.

BEHAVIORAL ADDICTIONS IN THE DSM-IV

The DSM-IV (*Diagnostic and Statistical Manual of Mental Disorders,* fourth edition) is published by the American Psychiatric Association. The DSM-IV provides a classification system for the identification and diagnosis of mental disorders. (The updated version of the fourth edition of the DSM-IV has the additional designation of *TR*, meaning *text revision*). The DSM-IV provides specific criteria for the diagnosis of mental disorders that are used in clinical and forensic settings.

Behavioral addictions do not have a specific category in the DSM-IV. Also, some controversy exists over the use of the term *addiction* in describing these conditions. Behavioral addictions can be found in the DSM-IV within the impulse control disorders classification. Advocates of applying the term *addiction* to

various behaviors have suggested that the category of behavioral addictions be included in the revision of the DSM.

For each mental disorder that can be considered a behavioral addiction, the DSM-IV provides specific information related to diagnosis. The DSM-IV gives specific diagnostic features or symptoms of the disorder, followed by a section describing associated features that are not central for making a diagnosis. Following a general presentation of the mental disorder, the DSM-IV includes information concerning the disorder's prevalence, familial patterns, and prognosis, as well as cultural, age, and gender issues surrounding the disorder.

IMPULSE CONTROL DISORDERS

The diagnostic category in the DSM-IV that includes the largest number of mental disorders that can be considered to be behavioral addictions is the impulse control disorder section. This group of mental disorders shares the major characteristic of having an irresistible impulse as the core symptom.

Persons with this type of mental disorder report the inability to resist an urge to engage in some action that may be harmful to themselves or others. An internal state of mounting tension precedes the action, and the behavior is followed by a sense of pleasure and satisfaction. As the state of tension grows, the person may actively plan a course of action to relieve the tension and experience the pleasurable aftermath of the behavior.

Persons diagnosed with impulse control disorder typically do not voluntarily seek treatment for the condition because they consider these actions to be a part of their self-identity. *Ego-syntonic* is the psychiatric term used to indicate this state of congruence between actions and personal perception found among persons with impulse control disorders.

PATHOLOGICAL GAMBLING

One of the most common impulse control disorders considered to be a behavioral addiction is pathological gambling. This diagnosis is used with persons who engage in persistent and recurrent gambling despite the negative personal, social, financial, or occupational consequences. Persons diagnosed as pathological gamblers have a preoccupation with gambling, feel an excitement from gambling that requires an ever increasing amount of money used in betting, may engage in illegal activities to finance the gambling activities, gamble excessively to try to recoup losses, and will rely on others to cover mounting financial debts.

This behavioral addiction leads to frequent lies to hide the extensive involvement with gambling and creates disruptions or loss of personal and vocational relationships. Persons with this disorder typically show a pattern of numerous failed attempts to stop or reduce their involvement with gambling.

Pathological gamblers share a number of personal characteristics, including having a high level of energy, being overconfident when placing gambling bets, and being a free spender. Pathological gamblers fail to develop sound plans for saving money and fail to follow any realistic budget. For them, money becomes a major pathway to happiness and the solution to all of life's problems.

When gambling debts begin to reach excessive levels, the pathological gambler will engage in antisocial actions to finance the gambling. Usually the antisocial actions are nonviolent and can include fraud, embezzlement, and forgery. It should be noted that the person always states an intention to repay the money gained through illegal means, but the addiction to gambling prohibits the repayments, as any winnings are used to finance additional gaming behaviors.

It has been found that pathological gambling usually begins in adolescence and goes through a pattern of four phases in its development and continuation. First is the winning phase, which is marked with a substantial amount of money being won through gambling. A second phase then emerges as a progressive pattern of loss takes place. During this time, persons whose lives are structured around gambling will progressively make foolish bets. It is during this phase that persons begin to miss occupational or social responsibilities and start to borrow money.

The third phase involves a sense of desperation that is marked with frenzied gambling, increasing debt, and possible illegal activities. The final phase in pathological gambling is reached when the gambler becomes hopeless about his or her situation. Even in this phase, the gambling continues, as it is tied closely to arousal and excitement. Persons with this disorder are addicted to the arousal and excitement provided through gambling.

Treatment for pathological gambling can be difficult because persons with this disorder often do not voluntarily want treatment. Entry into treatment is usually the result of legal or family pressures. The treatment of choice for pathological gambling is group therapy through Gamblers Anonymous (GA), which is based upon the principles of Alcoholics Anonymous and includes therapy that is centered on public confession of problematic behaviors, on peer support and pressure for change, and on the involvement of persons recovering from the disorder. Even with GA treatment, the dropout rate of participants is high, and pathological gambling is often seen as a long-term problem once established.

Pyromania

Another impulse control disorder that fits into the behavioral addiction classification is pyromania. Persons diagnosed with pyromania engage in the recurrent, deliberate, and intentional setting of fires. Persons with this disorder are physically aroused and excited before setting fires and find gratification and pleasure when witnessing the resulting fire. Sexual arousal commonly takes place when watching the fire. The fire starter feels no remorse or guilt and lacks concern for the losses experienced by others.

It is common for the fire starter to make elaborate plans and to carefully schedule the timing of a fire. In general, persons with this disorder also have a general fascination and curiosity about fires and anything associated with fire fighting. They will routinely travel to watch fires, and they frequently set false alarms. Pyromania is considered to be distinct from arson, as arson is a crime, not an addiction, associated with setting a fire for financial gain.

Pyromania usually begins in childhood and varies in severity during adolescence and adulthood. The disorder, however, has a chronic course that is maintained through the pattern of arousal and satisfaction gained from the fire setting. It is common for persons with this disorder to deny their problems and to avoid treatment for the condition. Treatment options for pyromania are limited, and for programs that are available, treatment focuses on techniques to quell the undesirable behaviors.

Trichotillomania

Also included in the DSM-IV category of impulse control disorders is trichotillomania: recurrently pulling out one's hair. The pulling out of one's hair is preceded with a sense of tension that is followed with a sensation of pleasure when the hair is actually pulled from the scalp. Persons with trichotillomania typically develop bald patches, and the disorder is most often diagnosed in girls and women.

Although all areas of the body with hair can be the target for this behavior, the scalp is the most common area involved. Some persons with trichotillomania ingest the hair after it is pulled. This process, known as trichophagy, can produce intestinal blockage. The occurrence of trichotillomania is often associated with depression, and the process of self-stimulation appears to be an essential factor in its development.

Trichotillomania is usually first seen in adolescence but can develop in childhood. Persons with this disorder usually receive a combination of psychopharmacological agents and behavioral treatment. Treatment includes anti-anxiety and antidepressant medications, and the behavioral therapy option focuses on breaking the cycle of tension and its relief through the pulling of hair.

KLEPTOMANIA

The behavioral addiction of kleptomania is also included in the DSM-IV within the impulse control disorder category. Kleptomania is the recurrent failure to resist the impulse to steal things. The thoughts of stealing are usually intrusive and are lessened only through the act of stealing. In most cases, the stolen objects are not needed, and often there is no goal of achieving financial gain from the acquisition. Persons with kleptomania often are financially able to purchase the stolen objects.

Before stealing an object, the person feels increasing tension that is relieved through stealing. The person feels no guilt or remorse for stealing. It is not uncommon for a person to continue stealing despite repeated arrests; however, the person may feel humiliation and anxiety after being caught in the act.

Females more commonly have this disorder. Kleptomania, which appears to be closely tied to the amount of stress in a person's life, usually first develops in late adolescence and becomes chronic with periods of varying degrees of severity. Persons with kleptomania seldom voluntarily seek treatment. When treatment is undertaken, the person usually receives some combination of antidepressant medication and behavior therapy, which is designed to help the person resist impulses.

OTHER IMPULSE CONTROL DISORDERS

Additional behavioral addictions are diagnosed as impulse disorder not otherwise specified (NOS). This is a general diagnosis that includes a variety of disorders related to behavioral addiction. A number of NOS behaviors are considered to have a compulsive quality. This means that persons with this disorder feel compelled to act out in a problematic fashion despite knowing that doing so is not in their best interests. The NOS diagnosis covers compulsive buying, Internet compulsion, cellular phone compulsion, compulsive sexual behavior, and repetitive self-mutilation.

Compulsive buying involves a frequent preoccupation with buying or an irresistible impulse to purchase things. It also can be diagnosed in persons who frequently buy objects they cannot afford or do not need. Credit card abuse is usually associated with this diagnosis.

Internet compulsion is also known as Internet addiction. The person with this disorder spends the majority of his or her waking hours on the web. Internet addiction usually involves specific web content, such as pornography, shopping, or interactive games.

Cellular phone addiction involves the compulsive use of mobile phone devices. Frequently contacting friends, family, business associates, or acquaintances, the person with this addiction usually tries to justify his or her actions with a variety of excuses. Persons with this addiction appear to have high dependency needs and fears of being alone.

Compulsive sexual behavior, or sexual addiction, is another NOS disorder, one that involves repeatedly seeking sexual gratification in a socially unacceptable fashion. The person with sexual addiction is identified through a pattern of out-of-control sexual behavior, adverse consequences for the sexual behavior, persistent pursuit of high-risk sexual behavior, increasing sexual activity, severe mood swings associated with having or not having sexual activity, and excessive time spent in sexual activity.

Treatment for sexual addiction (which can include Internet addiction that is focused on pornographic websites) usually involves self-help groups modeled on the twelve-step approach of Alcoholics Anonymous. The self-help programs specializing in sexual addiction are Sexaholics Anonymous, Sex and Love Addicts Anonymous, and Sex Addicts Anonymous.

FURTHER READING

Grant, Jon E., et al. "Legal Consequences of Kleptomania." *Psychiatry Quarterly* 80 (2009): 251–59. Print. The researchers discovered that kleptomania has significant legal outcomes that include incarceration. Recurrence was common with progressively severe legal consequences for the perpetrators.

Hook, Joshua N., et al. "Measuring Sexual Addiction and Compulsivity: A Critical Review of Instruments." *Journal of Sex and Marital Therapy* 36 (2010): 227–60. Print. A number of objective instruments have been developed to assess sexual addiction. This review provides descriptions and critiques of seventeen instruments.

Kafka, Martin P. "Hypersexual Disorder: A Proposed Diagnosis for DSM-V." *Archives of Sexual Behavior* 39 (2010): 377–400. Print. The author proposes that when the DSM-IV is revised, it should include sexual addiction as a hypersexual disorder. This proposed diagnosis would emphasize the dysregulation of sexual arousal and behavior apparent in this condition.

Lin, Chien-Hsin, et al. "The Effects of Parental Monitoring and Leisure Boredom on Adolescents' Internet Addiction." *Adolescence* 44 (2009): 993–1004. Print. The authors found that increasing amounts of leisure time available to adolescents contributes to Internet addiction. Recommends ways to increase family activities and outdoor recreation to reduce the effects of Internet addiction.

MacKay, Sherri, et al. "Epidemiology of Firesetting in Adolescents: Mental Health and Substance Use Correlates." *Journal of Child Psychology and Psychiatry* 50 (2009): 1282–90. Print. The authors examined adolescents in grades 7 through 12 who engaged in fire setting. These adolescents showed high levels of psychological distress, patterns of binge drinking, and high rates of delinquent behaviors.

Nover, Lia, et al. "Recovery in Pathological Gambling: An Imprecise Concept." *Substance Use and Misuse* 43 (2008): 1844–64. Print. Pathological gambling is considered to be poorly defined in terms of having imprecise diagnostic criteria. The lack of clear criteria makes is difficult to determine treatment effectiveness for pathological gambling.

Weinstock, Jeremiah, et al. "College Students' Gambling Behavior: When Does It Become Harmful?" *Journal of American College Health* 56 (2008): 513–21. Print. The authors examined pathological gambling among college students. Risk factors in the development of this condition included the frequency of gambling on a monthly basis, time spent in gambling activities, percentage of income spent on gambling, existence of a gambling plan, and time spent gambling beyond the initial plan.

WEBSITES OF INTEREST

AddictionInfo.org
http://www.addictioninfo.org

Diagnostic and Statistical Manual of Mental Disorders
http://www.psych.org/MainMenu/Research/DSMIV

Gamblers Anonymous
http://www.gamblersanonymous.org

See also: Behavioral addictions: Overview; Diagnosis methods; Gambling addiction; Impulse control disorders; Kleptomania; Pyromania; Trichotillomania

---

DSM-IV criteria for substance use disorders

CATEGORY: Diagnosis and prevention

DEFINITION: Published in 1994 by the American Psychiatric Association, the fourth edition of the *Diagnostic and Statistical Manual of Mental Disorders* (DSM-IV) outlines the necessary clinical features for the diagnosis of substance use and other disorders.

SUBSTANCE USE DISORDERS

The criteria for substance use disorders can be found in the DSM-IV section on substance-related disorders. The substance use disorders include substance dependence and substance abuse. While the typical course of a substance use disorder is for a person to develop substance dependence following a period of repeated use and abuse, this progression is not a requirement for a dependence diagnosis; it is possible for someone to become dependent on a substance without having first abused that substance.

A person can become physiologically dependent on a prescribed pain medication without ever having used that substance in a manner other than prescribed. Once physiological dependence is established, the person also may become psychologically dependent and may then begin to engage in the adverse behaviors indicative of abuse. In this scenario, the dependence actually preceded what would typically be considered abusive behavior.

The DSM-IV's substance use disorders section is organized such that the general criteria sets for substance dependence and abuse across all substances are presented first, and substance-specific information follows. Despite minor differences between substance classes (for example, cannabis dependence is rarely associated with clinically significant withdrawal symptoms and amphetamine dependence is sometimes associated with reverse tolerance or sensitization), the general criteria for dependence and abuse appear to apply equally well across substance categories.

Substances of dependence and abuse are categorized into ten classes: alcohol, amphetamine, cannabis, cocaine, hallucinogens, inhalants, nicotine, opioids, phencyclidine (PCP), and sedatives, hypnotics, or anxiolytics. Many prescription and over-the-counter medications also can be the source of a substance use disorder.

SUBSTANCE DEPENDENCE

Also known as addiction, substance dependence is typically classified as the continued use of a substance despite the presence of significant substance-related problems. The core features of addiction include physiological dependence (tolerance or withdrawal) and psychological dependence (compulsive drug-taking behavior). Furthermore, while not a specified symptom of dependence, craving (the urge to use a substance) is typical among addicts.

While dependence is possible for all substances, the specific symptoms may vary somewhat from one class of substance to another (for example, withdrawal symptoms are generally not present in hallucinogen dependence). The criteria for dependence include tolerance (the need for increased amounts of the substance to achieve intoxication), withdrawal

(characteristic substance-specific symptoms when use is discontinued or reduced), taking more of the substance and for a longer period of time than was intended, and a desire and unsuccessful attempts to discontinue substance use. The criteria also include devoting an inordinate amount of time to obtaining, using, or recovering from the substance; impaired activities (occupational, social, familial) because of substance use; and continued substance use despite the knowledge of significant physical and psychological substance-related problems (such as, continued alcohol use following medical diagnosis of cirrhosis of the liver).

To meet criteria for a clinical diagnosis of substance dependence, three or more of the above symptoms must be present for a minimum of twelve months. Furthermore, diagnosis can be specified as being with or without physiological dependence (that is, tolerance or withdrawal). Several independent empirical investigations have supported the continued use of this subtyping distinction, noting that persons with physiological dependence tend to have a greater severity of disorder than those without.

SUBSTANCE ABUSE

Substance abuse is characterized by substance use that significantly interferes with the user's life. For example, use that results in significant disruptions in school, work, or family; use in situations that are physically dangerous (driving while intoxicated); and use resulting in legal problems. The primary difference between abuse and dependence is that abuse focuses exclusively on the presence of harmful consequences associated with substance use, and abuse does not include physiological and psychological dependence.

Although substance abuse is more common in persons who have only recently begun regular or heavy use, some people never develop substance dependence despite showing continued negative consequences associated with repeated substance use. While abuse is possible for all substances—with the exception of nicotine—specific symptoms may vary somewhat from one class of substance to another (for example, recurrent legal problems may be more apparent, especially initially, with illicit drug abuse compared with alcohol abuse).

The criteria for substance abuse include recurrent substance use that results in a failure to fulfill major obligations at work, school, or home; recurrent substance use in physically dangerous situations; recurrent legal problems associated with substance use; and continued substance use despite problems in social and interpersonal relationships. To meet criteria for a clinical diagnosis of substance abuse, one or more of the above symptoms must be present for a minimum of twelve months.

In an empirical investigation of the abuse criteria, researchers have reported on the validity of the criteria in identifying persons with substance-related problems and on the predictive ability of the criteria to identify future problems. Most persons (approximately 80 percent) with substance abuse meet criteria for only one symptom, and the most commonly diagnosed abuse symptom is recurrent use in physically dangerous situations. Persons meeting criteria for two or more symptoms, however, typically report a greater number of substance-related problems and may be more likely to develop dependence.

PREVALENCE ESTIMATES

True prevalence statistics for substance use disorders may be difficult to obtain. Many persons who meet diagnostic criteria for substance dependence or abuse remain unknown because they are homeless, suffer from comorbid psychiatric illnesses, do not seek treatment, or underreport their substance use and substance-related problems out of shame and social stigma.

The Substance Abuse and Mental Health Services Administration (SAMHSA) reported on data collected during the 2009 administration of the National Survey on Drug Use and Health (NSDUH). The NSDUH is an annual survey of civilians in the United States age twelve years and older; it includes national estimates of substance use, dependence, and abuse.

Based on its findings, SAMHSA reported an estimated 22.5 million people (8.9 percent of the population) with a substance use disorder in 2009. Of these 22.5 million people, 3.2 million were dependent on or abused both alcohol and illicit drugs, 3.9 million were dependent on or abused illicit drugs only, and 15.4 million were dependent on or abused alcohol only.

In a comparison of these statistics since 2002, the overall rate of substance use disorders has remained virtually unchanged. The most common illicit substance of dependence or abuse was marijuana (4.3 million), followed by pain relievers (1.9 million) and

cocaine (1.1 million). Younger age at first use of alcohol or marijuana (fourteen years and younger versus eighteen years and older) was associated with increased likelihood for the development of dependence or abuse for alcohol and illicit drugs, respectively. The rates of substance dependence or abuse were highest among persons age eighteen to twenty-five years and among men (twice as many men as women), Native Americans, persons with less than a high school education, and persons who were unemployed. Rates of substance dependence or abuse did not vary by geographic region.

LIMITATIONS AND FUTURE CONSIDERATIONS

DSM-IV (and, previously, DSM-III-R) criteria for substance use disorders are based on a scientific literature that favored a bi-axial approach to alcohol and drug use disorders in which the causes of a dependence syndrome were viewed as distinct from the adverse consequences associated with heavy and recurrent use. Despite previous research indicating the empirical validity of this distinction, later research suggests that this categorical approach to the diagnosis of substance-related problems may not be warranted.

Other problems with the current classification system include the existence of diagnostic "orphans" and "imposters." The former category includes persons who meet criteria for only one or two dependence symptoms and none of the abuse symptoms. Within the DSM-IV diagnostic structure, these persons remain undiagnosed. However, research suggests that these persons later demonstrate substance-related problems as significant as those meeting criteria for substance abuse. The latter category includes people who may be too readily diagnosed with abuse under the current one-symptom threshold.

As noted, substance abuse is most often diagnosed when the sole criterion for physically hazardous substance use is met (typically, driving while intoxicated). Some have argued that, while certainly a risky behavior, driving after drinking may not in and of itself warrant psychiatric diagnosis.

As the American Psychiatric Association prepares for the publication of the fifth edition of the DSM, substantive revisions to the substance use disorders are being proposed. The most notable proposal is the elimination of the division between dependence and abuse. The proposed revision would create a single diagnosis of substance use disorder that would subsume the fourth edition's criteria for both substance dependence and abuse. Furthermore, minor changes to the fourth edition's criteria have been proposed. For example, the abuse criterion for recurrent legal problems associated with substance use may be omitted, while a symptom regarding cravings or a desire to use may be added.

Finally, in an attempt to include a more dimensional approach to the diagnosis of substance use disorders, an additional severity specifier has been proposed such that persons meeting criteria for two or three symptoms would be considered moderately affected. Persons meeting criteria for four or more symptoms would be considered severely affected.

Stefanie M. Keen, PhD

FURTHER READING

American Psychiatric Association. *Diagnostic and Statistical Manual of Mental Disorders.* 4th ed. Washington, DC: Author, 1994. This manual provides detailed information necessary for the diagnosis of mental health disorders for children, adolescents, and adults. In addition to the specific symptom criteria for each disorder, the DSM-IV includes prevalence estimates; information regarding course and prognosis; specific culture, gender, and age features; information regarding familial patterns; and important considerations when making differential diagnoses. The manual is typically considered the gold-standard for mental health professionals.

Martin, Christopher S., Tammy Chung, and James W. Langenbucher. "How Should We Revise Diagnostic Criteria for Substance Use Disorders in DSM-V?" *Journal of Abnormal Psychology* 117.3 (2008): 561–75. Print. A literature review of the DSM-IV criteria for substance use disorders. This article specifically focuses on the validity of these criteria and proposes empirically based revisions to the diagnostic structure of substance use disorders for the fifth edition of the DSM.

Saunders, John B. "Substance Dependence and Non-Dependence in the *Diagnostic and Statistical Manual of Mental Disorders* (DSM) and the International Classification of Diseases (ICD): Can an Identical Conceptualization Be Achieved?" *Addiction* 101, suppl. 1 (2006): 48–58. Print. A comparison of the criteria for substance use disorders between the DSM and ICD diagnostic systems. This review of the literature supports the inclusion of both dependence and abuse diagnoses, although it suggests that abuse criteria may be culturally dependent.

Schuckit, Marc A., et al. "Prospective Evaluation of the Four DSM-IV Criteria for Alcohol Abuse in a Large Population." *American Journal of Psychiatry* 162.2 (2005): 350–60. Print. An examination of the performance characteristics for each of the four DSM-IV substance abuse criteria, as they pertain to alcohol abuse. Results showed that each of the four criteria performed well over a five-year period with respect to identifying individuals with alcohol abuse diagnoses.

WEBSITES OF INTEREST

American Psychiatric Association. DSM-5 Development: Substance-Related Disorders
http://www.dsm5.org/ProposedRevisions/Pages/Substance-RelatedDisorders.aspx

National Institute on Alcohol Abuse and Alcoholism
http://www.niaaa.nih.gov

National Institute on Drug Abuse
http://www.drugabuse.gov

Substance Abuse and Mental Health Services Administration
http://www.samhsa.gov

See also: Addiction; Alcohol abuse and alcoholism: Overview; Diagnosis methods; Drug abuse and addiction: Overview; Substance abuse

E

Economic impact of addiction

CATEGORY: Social issues

DEFINITION: The economic impact of addiction is the cost associated with substance abuse and addiction as expressed in US dollars, both in dollars spent (also called direct or resource costs) and in dollars not earned (also called indirect or productivity costs).

ESTIMATES

The first step in estimating the economic impact of addiction is to determine what costs and what addictions will be included in that analysis. The broadest estimate would include all the costs associated with the following:

- medical care (treatment for addiction and treatment for the health consequences of substance abuse, such as cirrhosis of the liver)
- criminal justice (such as enforcement of laws, consequences of property crimes, and costs of incarceration)
- social services (for example, foster care for children of methamphetamine addicts)
- employee absenteeism and lost productivity (both for substance abusers and their families)
- excess substance abuse-related deaths (such as lost earnings for addicts who die prematurely)
- substances or behaviors themselves

Key to this process is to separate out the excess, addiction-related costs from the general, population-level, "background" costs. For example, bankruptcy costs for pathological gamblers should take into account the risk of bankruptcy associated with gambling in excess of the general population-level risk of bankruptcy.

To estimate the economic burden of all addictions, these costs are calculated for each type of substance abuser or addict, including tobacco users, alcohol abusers, drug addicts, and problem or pathological gamblers. Although many people think only of illicit drug users when they discuss the economic costs of addiction, the costs associated with alcohol problems, tobacco use, and other addictive behaviors are also relevant. In this article, the specific population of addicts or users for each cost estimate will be explicitly stated wherever possible. Because research on the economic costs associated with food and sex addiction are lacking, potential costs associated with disordered eating and with addictive sexual behaviors will not be discussed here.

It can be difficult to determine whether costs incurred by a substance user are related to addiction per se. For example, not everyone who has an alcohol-related car accident is necessarily addicted to or dependent on alcohol in a physical sense. However, one definition of substance addiction is the continued use of a substance despite negative consequences. In that respect, some would argue that any cost incurred by a substance user is therefore an addiction-related cost.

There are two additional difficulties associated with calculating the costs of addiction. First, many people have multiple addictions. For example, many gamblers are also likely to have alcohol or drug problems and to be smokers. Therefore, it may be somewhat misleading to simply sum up the costs associated with each addiction and consider that sum to be the total economic impact of addiction; in reality, the total is likely to be less than the sum of its parts. Second, it is difficult to determine causal relationships between addiction and some of the costs associated with addiction. Do criminals gamble or do gamblers become criminals, or is there a separate causal factor that results in both gambling and crime? In short, it is important to remember that attributing costs to specific pathologies is a complex exercise.

Finally, a true estimate of the economic impact of addiction at the societal level would take into account both the costs of addiction and the economic benefits. From a strictly economic point of view, the money legally spent by addicts on alcohol, tobacco, food, and gambling provides jobs, economic development, tax revenue, and funding for social goods. The central issue is whether the increase in one party's income is worth the costs to another party. Because such an analysis for addiction in general does not appear to have been conducted, this question is beyond the scope of this article.

An analysis of the economic burden of addiction can be done using a bottom-up or top-down approach. For a bottom-up approach, estimates for all the possible risks for each of the potential consequences and the costs associated with each consequence are calculated at an individual level to arrive at a cost per addict. Once that cost has been estimated, it is multiplied by the prevalence (percentage of the population with the addiction at a particular time). For the top-down approach, the total amount spent in each category is multiplied by the percentage attributable to people with addictions. For example, if the annual cost of traffic accidents is $164.2 billion, and if an estimated 7 percent of all traffic accidents involve alcohol, then the alcohol-related cost of traffic accidents would be $11.49 billion per year.

ECONOMIC IMPACT ON SOCIETY

According to a report from the US Department of Health and Human Services (DHHS), the total economic impact of alcohol, tobacco, and other drugs in 1999 was approximately $511.4 billion. Alcohol abuse was responsible for $191.6 billion (37.5 percent), tobacco use for $167.8 billion (32.9 percent), and drug abuse for $151.4 billion (29.6 percent). Adding in problem gambling (at an estimated $40 billion per year) would bring the total to more than $551.4 billion per year. Adjusted for inflation and assuming all other trends were the same, the total would be about 33 percent higher in 2011 dollars (approximately $733.4 billion). It is important to note that this total does not account for overlap between addictions.

The National Institutes of Health rank alcohol second, tobacco sixth, and drug disorders seventh among estimated costs of illness for thirty-three diseases and conditions. Even though fewer people die from alcohol-related causes than from tobacco-related causes, alcohol-related costs are higher because alcohol-related deaths tend to occur at younger ages than do smoking-related deaths. The combined total of approximately $511 billion per year for alcohol, tobacco, and other drugs overshadows the annual cost of the most costly illness, cardiovascular disease ($393.5 billion per year; 2004 estimate).

According to the DHHS report, the costs associated with alcohol abuse are broken down as follows: direct costs (4 percent for alcoholism treatment, 10 percent for treatment of the medical consequences of alcohol abuse, and 13 percent for crashes, fires, criminal justice) and indirect costs (67 percent due to lost earnings from premature deaths and disability and 6 percent for lost earnings due to crime). The costs associated with tobacco use include 45 percent for treatment of medical consequences and 55 percent for productivity losses due to illness and premature deaths. No estimates were available for amounts spent on treatment, prevention, fires, or tobacco-related crime aside from approximately $600 million in state spending driven by tobacco settlement funds. As for illicit drugs, the costs in the DHHS report were attributed as follows: direct costs (5 percent for addiction treatment and prevention, 4 percent for treatment of medical consequences, and 21 percent for crashes, fires, and criminal justice) and indirect costs (31 percent due to lost earnings from premature deaths and disability and 39 percent for lost productivity related to criminal acts).

Abuse of alcohol and other drugs is associated with an increased risk for numerous adverse outcomes, including premature deaths, hospitalizations, and incarceration. In 2000, it was estimated that tobacco was the number one actual cause of death (435,000 persons, or 18.5 percent of all deaths), alcohol consumption was third (85,000 deaths, or 3.5 percent), and illicit drug use was ninth (17,000 deaths, or 0.7 percent). According to another source, 38,396 persons died from substance abuse (excluding accidents, homicides, and infant mortality) in 2006, marking a death rate of 12.8 per 100,000. An estimated 25 to 40 percent of patients in general wards are being treated for alcohol-related medical issues at any given time.

In 2002, there were 670,307 emergency room visits for causes directly related to illicit drugs, with an additional 1.2 million emergency room visits in which an illicit drug was implicated in the reason for the visit. In 2008, there were 971,914 emergency department visits involving nonmedical use of pharmaceutical drugs; of these, 68 percent involved pharmaceutical drugs only, 13 percent involved both pharmaceutical and illicit drugs, 13 percent involved both alcohol and pharmaceuticals, and 6 percent involved all three. Among inmates of jails and prisons, 64 to 69 percent admit to being regular drug users, with 26 to

32 percent saying that they were using a drug at the time of their offense. In 2008, 12 percent of all arrests were for drug-related violations, and an estimated 20 percent of state and 53 percent of federal inmates had a drug offense as their most serious offense in 2006.

A 2002 estimate of the economic impact of substance abuse (illicit and pharmaceutical drugs) from the Office of National Drug Control Policy (ONDCP) found the total cost was $180.6 billion: $52 billion in direct costs and $128.6 billion in indirect costs. Adjusted for inflation, this would be approximately $222 billion in 2011 dollars, a higher estimate than the DHHS report estimate for the cost of drug abuse of approximately $201.4 billion in 2011 dollars. The costs were separated into the following categories: direct costs (9 percent for treatment of medical consequences and 20 percent for other direct costs, such as the cost of goods and services lost to crime and social welfare costs) and indirect costs (33 percent due to lost earnings from premature deaths and disability and 38 percent for lost productivity related to criminal acts).

On a per capita basis, the economic impact of drug abuse varies substantially from state to state. The US average, as of 2002, was $628 per person per year. The top four states and their corresponding per capita costs are Louisiana ($815), Illinois ($767), Maryland ($763), and Delaware ($756). The bottom four states are North Dakota ($350), Iowa ($385), South Dakota ($407), and Minnesota ($442).

In 2009, the US government budget for illicit drug control was $15.3 billion and covered the following categories: 23 percent for treatment (in the form of grants to states), 12 percent for prevention (education and outreach), 25 percent for domestic law enforcement, 26 percent for interdiction (mainly border enforcement), and 14 percent for international drug-control efforts.

Economic analyses for substance abuse treatment and prevention programs have been produced by many different local, state, and federal entities, often because of requirements that budgets be justified in terms of return on investment and cost-benefit ratio. Many substance abuse prevention programs exist, but not all have been proven effective. For example, although 80 percent of students in the United States were exposed to school-based substance abuse prevention programs in 2002, only 20 percent were exposed to programs proven effective. According to a report from the DHHS, the average effective school-based program in 2002 cost $220 per student. If implemented nationwide, effective school-based prevention programs could save an estimated $18 per $1 invested.

The economic cost of gambling addiction has been estimated at $40 billion per year. These costs are attributable to job losses, unemployment insurance, welfare benefits, bankruptcy, divorce, physical and mental health, arrests, and incarceration. This figure does not include the actual monies spent on gambling activities (legal gambling revenue in the United States was $68.7 billion in 2002). The total also does not include lost productivity costs, although surveys suggest that more than two-thirds of gamblers have missed work to gamble. Criminal activities by gambling addicts also are not included, and these activities may be substantial. For example, one survey of four hundred Gamblers Anonymous members found that 57 percent admitted to stealing to finance their gambling, with an average theft of $135,000 and a total theft of $30 million among the respondents.

TRENDS

From 1992 to 2002, according to the ONDCP, the costs associated with illicit drug abuse increased from $107.5 to $180.8 billion—an average of 5.3 percent per year. During the same period, the size of the adult population and consumer prices (inflation) increased by 3.5 percent, so the costs associated with drug abuse increased more than would be expected. Components of the costs associated with illicit drug abuse that are readily available from year to year include the amount spent on treatment and on the federal drug-control budget. Both of these components continue to increase every year. From 1986 to 2005, spending on substance abuse treatment grew by about 4.8 percent annually, compared with 6.9 percent annual growth in mental health spending and 7.9 percent annual growth in overall health spending. From 2002 to 2010, the federal drug-control budget increased from $10.8 billion to $15 billion, or about 4.4 percent per year.

Individual users spent an estimated $64 billion to purchase illicit drugs in 2000. This amount is a substantial reduction from $154 billion, the amount spent in 1988. The majority of the decline is related to declines in the amount spent on cocaine, which dropped from $107 billion in 1988 to $35 billion in

2001. This appears to have been caused by decreases in both the price of the cocaine and in the volume purchased. In 1988, a person would have paid about $250 per gram of powder cocaine or $270 per gram of crack cocaine, but by 2001, the price would have been $194 per gram of powder and $226 per gram of crack. In 1988, users in the United States consumed 660 metric tons of cocaine, compared with 259 metric tons in 2000.

The total amount spent on heroin also declined, from $26 billion in 1988 to $10 billion in 2001. Unlike with cocaine, most of the decline appears to have been in the price of the heroin, which fell from around $1,126 per gram in 1988 to $432 per gram in 2001. Heroin consumption remained fairly steady, from 15 metric tons in 1988 to 13 metric tons in 2000.

Amounts spent on marijuana, methamphetamine, and other drugs remained mostly constant from 1988 to 2001, aside from a short-term increase in the mid-1990s for methamphetamine. In contrast with heroin and cocaine, the mostly steady total spent on marijuana and methamphetamine does not reflect the fluctuations seen in the prices paid by individual users. For example, marijuana prices per gram fell from $14 to $9 between 1988 and 2001, and the price of methamphetamine fell from $317 to $213 per gram in the same period. The amount of marijuana consumed in the United States has increased from an estimated 894 metric tons in 1988 to 1,047 tons in 2000. The amount of methamphetamine consumed in 2000 (20 tons) is slightly less than consumed in 1988 (23 tons), but less than the amount consumed at the peak in the mid-1990s (54 tons).

Lisa M. Lines, MPH

Further Reading

Cartwright, William S. "Cost-Benefit Analysis of Drug Treatment Services: Review of the Literature." *Journal of Mental Health Policy and Economics* 3 (2000): 11–26. Print. Provides a review of studies evaluating the costs and benefits of treatment for substance abuse.

Miller, Ted R., and Delia Hendrie. "Substance Abuse Prevention Dollars and Cents: A Cost-Benefit Analysis." Rockville, MD: Center for Substance Abuse Prevention, 2008. Web. 5 Mar. 2012. http://store.samhsa.gov/shin/content//SMA07-4298/SMA07-4298.pdf. Provides estimates of the costs associated with the use of alcohol, tobacco, and illicit drugs.

National Gambling Impact Study Commission. Final Report. 18 Jun. 1999. Web. 5 Mar. 2012. http://govinfo.library.unt.edu/ngisc/reports/fullrpt.html. Comprehensive report on the social and economic effects of gambling on society.

Office of National Drug Control Policy. "The Economic Costs of Drug Abuse in the United States, 1992–2002." Washington, DC: Office of the President, 2004. Web. 5 Mar. 2012. http://www.ncjrs.gov/ondcppubs/publications/pdf/economic_costs.pdf. Provides updated estimates for the economic costs associated with illicit drug abuse.

Websites of Interest

Alcohol Cost Calculator
http://alcoholcostcalculator.org

Drug Abuse Treatment Cost Analysis Program
http://datcap.com

See also: Addiction; Families and behavioral addictions; Families and substance abuse; Poverty and substance abuse; Socioeconomic status and addiction; Work issues and behavioral addictions; Work issues and substance abuse

---

Education about substance abuse

Category: Diagnosis and prevention

Definition: The methods for substance abuse education vary widely. Education can be as informal as a community-based health fair to practitioner-oriented education sessions and workshops at conferences. Colleges and universities offer highly formal and structured education and instruction. Media messages are often used to educate the public on the multiple issues related to substance abuse.

Overview

Throughout recent history, efforts have been developed to educate the public on the dangers of substance abuse. Much of this work has been targeted to youth populations, especially in school settings. Substance abuse prevention educators have assumed that educating people on the dangers and harmful nature of substance abuse alone will actually prevent drug use and addiction. However, many studies have questioned the effectiveness of this approach.

Traditionally, a common technique was to bring to the classroom a recovering addict to talk about drug use and how it negatively affected that person's life. This approach was thought to be effective for preventing substance use. Another approach was for a teacher to show a film on substance abuse, a film that often included a number of scare tactics believed to deter youth from drug experimentation. Generally, the teacher would follow the film with a discussion of the dangers of drugs.

Another common method once believed to prevent substance abuse was for substance abuse educators to attend health fairs and simply hand out brochures to passersby. Health educators believed that if people knew about the negative effects of drug use, they would not use drugs. Much money and resources were spent in the hopes that educational brochures would deter people, primarily young people, from using tobacco, alcohol, or other drugs.

However, studies showed that these educational efforts were mostly ineffective. Substance abuse education is informative, but is not effective as a single, stand-alone approach to preventing substance use. Practitioners, who began to question their approach, also began to explore the nexus between substance abuse education and the prevention of drug abuse. In some cases, popular approaches to prevention education, such as the original Drug and Alcohol Resistance Education (D.A.R.E.) program and other singularly focused educational curricula, were shown to have adverse outcomes. For this reason, the National Institute on Drug Abuse (NIDA) substantially changed the D.A.R.E. curriculum.

Substance abuse education can be effective if the goal is to inform people of the facts of drug use and to train students of health care about the best practices associated with the substance abuse profession. Different disciplines offer their own perspectives on the issue of substance abuse. Some courses, in substance abuse counseling for example, teach student therapists how to work with clients who abuse substances.

CENTER FOR SUBSTANCE ABUSE PREVENTION
The Center for Substance Abuse Prevention (CSAP), part of the US Substance Abuse and Mental Health Services Administration (SAMHSA), created six

strategies that many US states use to channel funding to their respective regions, counties, and community groups that conduct prevention programs. One of these areas is prevention education. This strategy includes two-way or multidirectional communication about substance abuse topics, including prevention programs that cover parenting techniques, social skills, and peer resistance skills.

Prevention education is one of six overall strategies that CSAP attaches to the Substance Abuse Prevention and Treatment block grant. The other five strategies include information dissemination, alternative activities, community-based processes, environmental approaches, and problem identification and referral.

The focus of prevention education is to provide substantive information. Simply passing out a brochure, for example, is considered information dissemination only. Adequate prevention education occurs in settings with interactive communication that leads, for example, to programs such as Life Skills Training (LST), which has been replicated nationally. This program has proven effective across multiple sites.

The LST program is a school-based program that prevents substance abuse and violence by targeting risky behaviors. The curriculum includes multiple sessions, over time, with interactive role-playing scenarios that engage the students in the program. A number of evidence-based educational programs in substance abuse exist on the National Registry of Evidence-based Programs and Practices (NREPP), which is sponsored by SAMHSA.

NATIONAL INSTITUTE ON DRUG ABUSE (NIDA)
NIDA, part of the National Institutes of Health, also provides some definitions and descriptions on substance abuse education and dissemination efforts. NIDA has two critical focuses. The first is the strategic support and conduct of research across a broad range of disciplines. The second is ensuring the rapid and effective dissemination and use of the results of that research to significantly improve prevention, treatment, and policy as it relates to drug abuse and addiction. Specifically, NIDA funds education and dissemination efforts that inform adults and youth about the neuroscience of addiction. Youth-focused curricula include Brain Power and NIDA Goes Back to School, programs with a substance-abuse educational component.

Many of the early programs identified by NREPP were programs that were funded in part by NIDA, which also published the book *Preventing Drug Use among Children and Adolescents* (1997). This work highlights a number of evidence-based, substance-abuse prevention programs, many of which have an educational focus. A number of programs have since been created and are being studied for effectiveness. The contributions and research funding that NIDA provides is crucial. Research results are interpreted and then transferred to the field to influence educational practice.

NIDA's publication also highlights the risk-and-protective-factor approach to prevention. This approach, which has been adopted by most in the field of substance abuse prevention as the framework for programming, argues that there are multiple risk and protective factors in a person's life that can influence each stage of youth development. These factors operate across a number of domains, some of which include substance abuse. The implications for prevention specialists is that these factors must be assessed and understood before implementing a prevention program or a strategy designed to decrease risk factors and to increase protective factors. This is exciting research, and NIDA was one of the first federal agencies to disseminate information on this approach.

GUIDING PRINCIPLES AND BEST PRACTICES

As prevention knowledge continues to grow, new findings are being presented that have a role in guiding decision-making about funding and implementing prevention programs. Early findings on prevention education include the following:

- Providing information and educating people on the harms and risks associated with substance abuse is not an effective strategy when used in isolation from other approaches. Skill development in combination with education is preferred.
- Didactic approaches are not effective at preventing substance abuse. Interactive educational approaches are encouraged.
- When educating youth, peer approaches are preferred but require training and oversight.
- When implementing education programming in schools, lengthy curricula, including booster sessions, are preferred to short-term or one-time-only types of events.

- Social skills programs that include numerous risk-and-protective-factor approaches are preferred.
- Booster sessions are encouraged after the prevention education session has concluded.
- Role-playing components to substance abuse education programs are recommended.
- Educational programs that include parents and students are recommended.

This early work helped to guide the field of substance abuse prevention. Much of the early work of the Center for the Application of Prevention Technology, under CSAP contract, was to coordinate with states, jurisdictions, and tribal entities to transfer evidence-based information on substance abuse prevention programs and best practices to state leadership. It is within this context that education about substance abuse is often discussed. Communication covers what is effective and ineffective in this area.

COLLEGE AND UNIVERSITY EDUCATION

Substance abuse education is growing. Colleges and universities offer many educational courses in substance abuse prevention and treatment, and the content of these courses varies widely. Some focus on substance abuse prevention, others focus on pharmacology, and still others focus on substance abuse treatment. Courses cover the sociology of substance abuse, criminal justice solutions to substance abuse problems, the medical implications for patients with substance abuse disorders, and substance abuse counseling. Courses are being taught traditionally, in the classroom, but also online.

Substance abuse certification and licensure requirements have driven much of this increased activity in substance abuse education. Professional education in substance abuse prevention could not happen without careful pedagogical approaches and scientific findings to guide effective practice in the field.

NATIONAL YOUTH ANTI-DRUG MEDIA CAMPAIGN

The National Youth Anti-Drug Media Campaign is an educational vehicle for substance abuse messages in the United States. Millions of dollars are spent annually to create, distribute, and broadcast messages across the country. The campaign is part of the

Office of National Drug Control Policy (ONDCP) in Washington.

A number of messages are offered as part of a comprehensive media campaign. Although the vast majority of these messages are one-way communication episodes, substance abuse organizations use the material too. Also, the ONDCP and state authorities discuss how media messages can support substance abuse services regionally.

Julie A. Hogan, PhD

FURTHER READING

Brounstein, P., Janet Zweig, and Steve Gardner. *Science-Based Practices in Substance Abuse Prevention: A Guide*. Rockville, MD: Center for Substance Abuse Prevention, 1998. Provides overviews of a number of research-based principles that prevention professionals are encouraged to follow when implementing prevention programs. Includes prevention education recommended strategies.

Fisher, Gary, and Nancy Roget. *Encyclopedia of Substance Abuse Prevention, Treatment, and Recovery*. Thousand Oaks, CA: Sage, 2009. An encyclopedia of key concepts and approaches used in the field of substance abuse.

Hogan, Julie, et al. *Substance Abuse Prevention: The Intersection of Science and Practice*. Boston: Allyn & Bacon, 2003. A textbook that orients students and prevention specialists through the science of substance abuse prevention.

National Institute on Drug Abuse. *Preventing Drug Use among Children and Adolescents: A Research-Based Guide for Parents, Educators, and Community Leaders*. 2nd ed. Bethesda, MD: DHHS, 2003. A handbook that highlights a number of substance abuse prevention programs that have been proven effective.

WEBSITES OF INTEREST

National Institute on Drug Abuse
http://www.drugabuse.gov

National Registry of Evidence-based Programs and Practices
http://nrepp.samhsa.gov

National Youth Anti-Drug Media Campaign
http://www.whitehousedrugpolicy.gov/mediacampaign

US Substance Abuse and Mental Health Services Administration
http://www.samhsa.gov

See also: Center for Substance Abuse Prevention (CSAP); Center for Substance Abuse Treatment (CSAT); Centre for Addiction and Mental Health (Canada); College and substance abuse; D.A.R.E. (Drug Abuse Resistance Education); Just Say No campaign; Media and substance abuse; National Institute on Alcohol Abuse and Alcoholism (NIAAA); National Institute on Drug Abuse (NIDA); Schools and substance abuse

---

Elderly and addictions

CATEGORY: Social issues
ALSO KNOWN AS: Elderly substance abuse
DEFINITION: The elderly populations of developed nations experience high rates of addiction and substance abuse, which often go unnoticed by society at large. These addictions are made more problematic by associated health problems and by generational attitudes that keep the elderly from seeking treatment.

TYPES OF ELDERLY SUBSTANCE ABUSE

In all industrialized countries, the fastest growing age segment comprises persons age sixty-five years and older. Societal aging in the United States, for example, is projected to increase the proportion of the elderly from around 13 percent in 2010 to 20 percent by 2030, as baby boomers (persons born from 1946 through 1964) add about 70 million people to this age group. An estimated 17 percent of the elderly have health problems related to the abuse of alcohol and of legal drugs, including nicotine and over-the-counter (OTC) medications.

Alcohol. Researchers have long recognized the difficulties of accurately estimating rates of alcohol abuse among the elderly, rates that range from less than 2 percent to more than 20 percent. Elderly alcohol abusers often remain unnoticed compared with younger adults because they often drink at home and are less likely to have their problem drinking revealed by intervention at work or by legal problems, such as an arrest for drunk drinking. The elderly also are more self-conscious about their drinking and are reluctant to seek help because they view their addiction as a sign of low moral character.

Evidence that elderly alcoholism is a significant problem is the high rate of hospitalization for alcohol-related conditions among the elderly. Elderly alcoholics are characterized as either chronic or situational addicts. Chronic addicts are those who began abusing alcohol while young or middle aged; they typically have serious emotional or physical health problems as a result. Furthermore, their lives will be shortened if they do not significantly moderate their alcohol consumption. Situational addicts are those who began drinking in old age in response to disconcerting life events, such as the death of loved ones, dissatisfaction with retirement, or health problems.

Prescription and OTC drugs. The abuse of both prescription and OTC medications is a significant health problem for elderly Americans. Approximately 25 percent of all drugs prescribed are prescribed to the elderly. These drugs include highly addictive psychotropics and narcotics, such as benzodiazepines, Valium, and Librium.

Confidential surveys indicate that almost one-half of the elderly take prescription drugs at higher dosages than prescribed, and that many elderly respond to their increasing addiction by inadvertently or deliberately obtaining duplicate prescriptions from more than one doctor. Prescription drug abuse is detected in only about 37 percent of elderly patients, compared with 60 percent of young adults, and serious negative health effects are more common for the elderly.

Many older people believe that the recommended dosages of OTC medications are irrelevant because they do not require prescriptions. The excessive use of some of the most popular OTCs, such as antihistamines, cold medications, and laxatives, can cause confusion, increased probability of stroke and heart problems, potassium and sodium deficiencies, and

A support group for older adults at an addiction treatment and rehab center in Florida is shown. The number of older adults reporting substance abuse problems is on the rise in the early twenty-first century. (AP Photo)

chronic diarrhea. Furthermore, many OTCs contain caffeine, which can lead to the abuse of OTC sleep aids.

The use of prescription and OTC medications combined with alcohol significantly increases the probability of addiction-related health problems for the elderly. Physiological changes that occur with aging, such as reductions in body mass, liver and kidney function, and body water, result in higher concentrations of drugs and alcohol for longer periods of time. Combinations of alcohol and drugs that remain in older persons' systems for up to twice as long as in younger adults can have serious consequences, including emotional and mental problems, injuries from falling, and dangerous overdosing.

Nicotine. The elderly suffer from more serious nicotine-related health problems than any other type of substance abuse. When the first rolled packaged cigarettes were marketed in 1913, few Americans smoked. Elderly cohorts still living came of age during the tobacco industry's aggressive, effective, and deceptive advertising campaigns, which began in the 1920s. Among those endorsing smoking were actors, athletes, and physicians, who repeated the industry's claims that cigarette processing eliminated the health risks and that smoking was part of a sexy, successful, fun-filled, and glamorous lifestyle. Also, tobaccos were being blended to maximize cigarettes' addictiveness. By the 1960s, close to 50 percent of American adults were nicotine addicts.

About 10 million older American smokers now know that smoking is causally related to all of the leading debilitating and fatal medical pathologies. Only 10 percent report success in quitting, and 80 percent say that they wish they had never started smoking. Smokers live twelve years less, on average, than nonsmokers. A study by Columbia University's Center on Addiction and Substance Abuse found that substance-abuse-related hospitalizations (from 1994 through 2014) will cost Medicare $1 trillion. Smoking accounts for 80 percent, or $800 billion dollars, of this amount.

DIAGNOSIS AND TREATMENT CHALLENGES

Among the reasons that elderly substance abuse is diagnosed at much lower rates than for younger abusers is the way in which many doctors respond to the symptoms of older patients. Research has shown that conditions like loss of balance or memory, physical or mental illness, and sexual dysfunction are often attributed to the normal decrements of aging rather than to addiction. Furthermore, many elderly abusers hide their addiction because they consider it stigmatizing. Many were functional abusers for decades and refuse to acknowledge the more pronounced effects on their health because of advancing age. In addition, some doctors and caregivers admit to ignoring the problem because they do not want to deny a source of pleasure to their elderly patients and clients.

Furthermore, many doctors are reluctant to diagnose elderly patients' substance abuse problems because they are not convinced that the common rehabilitation approach, which involves peer groups and self-help programs like Alcoholics Anonymous, works well for the elderly. Older participants in these programs often assert that they think their abuse problem is different from those of younger group members, and they report feeling self-conscious and out of place. While self-help groups made up entirely of elderly participants do have higher success rates, physicians posit that these groups should be used in conjunction with interactive therapy by health care professionals.

Geriatric specialists point out that the treatment of elderly addicts can be complex. For example, emotional illness may cause substance abuse, but treating the underlying problem often involves prescribing addictive drugs, a true dilemma for physicians and other health professionals. Experts also point out the necessity of creating a treatment program that will probably require the interaction of medical and mental-health-care professionals and family members if an elderly abuser is to return to a healthy, abuse-free life.

IMPLICATIONS

In addition to the general concerns regarding the effects that the projected growth of the elderly population will have on the funding of elderly benefit programs such as Social Security and Medicare, there are concerns that future elderly cohorts will contain a much higher proportion of substance abusers. Baby boomers abuse licit and illicit drugs at much higher rates than do earlier generations, which may significantly increase elderly addiction-related policy issues.

Experts assert that the most daunting of these policy challenges involves the need for health care specific to substance abuse by the elderly. Current programs' provisions are inadequate, and expanding such services to meet increased needs will be difficult, especially since cutting program expenditures is the focus of most initiatives.

Substance abuse and emotional illness often co-exist, and Medicare requires a 50 percent copayment for mental health care and substance abuse treatment, compared with a 20 percent copayment in other cases. Therefore, many elderly addicts go untreated, and those who opt for substance abuse treatment often receive no follow-up mental health care. Elderly advocates have long argued that doctors too often dismiss elderly patients' complaints about depression because their reported symptoms do not meet the requirements for a diagnosis of "major, or clinical, depression." However, the elderly experience "minor, or reactive, depression" because of loss or other life changes at rates higher than any other age group. The elderly also commit suicide more than any other age group. One study found that 75 percent of elderly suicides had seen a doctor within one month of their death. Researchers estimate that baby boomers exhibit rates of addiction and emotional illness that are at least three times those of the current elderly population.

The federal agency that analyzes substance abuse by older Americans is the Substance Abuse and Mental Health Services Administration (SAMHSA). This agency evaluates the need for and promotes the availability of substance abuse services for this population. Since its creation in 1992, SAMHSA has published numerous reports that document the growing magnitude of the elderly addiction problem. After reviewing the available studies, consulting with experts, and identifying gaps in relevant data, SAMHSA publications have projected a significant increase in elderly substance abuse and call for policy initiatives that would greatly increase the availability of substance abuse prevention and treatment options for elderly cohorts.

Jack Carter, PhD

FURTHER READING

Barry, Kristen Lawton, David W. Oslin, and Frederic C. Blow. *Alcohol Problems in Older Adults: Prevention and Management.* New York: Springer, 2001. Provides information on how to prevent, recognize, and treat elderly alcohol addiction.

Colleran, Carol, and Debra Jay. *Aging and Addiction: Helping Older Adults Overcome Alcohol or Medication Dependence.* Center City, MN: Hazelden, 2002. Highlights the magnitude of substance abuse problems among the elderly, and provides guidelines for recognizing problems with older family members and for finding the appropriate treatment.

Gurnack, Anne M., Roland Atkinson, and Nancy J. Osgood, eds. *Treating Alcohol and Drug Abuse in the Elderly.* New York: Springer, 2002. Explains approaches to treating the elderly who are addicted to alcohol, prescription drugs, and tobacco, with case studies.

WEBSITES OF INTEREST

RecoveryConnection.org
http://www.recoveryconnection.org/senior-citizens-alcohol-drug-rehab

Substance Abuse and Mental Health Services Administration
http://www.samhsa.gov

See also: Age and addiction; Gender and addiction; Nicotine addiction; Over-the-counter drugs of abuse; Socioeconomic status and addiction

Emergency treatment

CATEGORY: Treatment
ALSO KNOWN AS: Critical care; urgent care
DEFINITION: Emergency treatment of drug and alcohol overdose requires urgent care for the particular drugs and other substances ingested, medical stabilization of patients, and subsequent follow-up care with substance abuse treatment centers.

EMERGENCY TREATMENT OVERVIEW

A person who has overdosed on a drug requires emergency treatment. Oftentimes, this treatment is initiated by friends, family, or coworkers. Emergency rooms (ERs) can be a challenging maze for persons not familiar with them, but some characteristics are common to most ERs.

Triage yields the first ER assessment, determining illness severity. *Triage* is a French word meaning "to pick or cull." Triage nurses record information related to the patient. Any family or friends accompanying the overdosed patient can be particularly helpful at this time by providing information they have about the overdosed patient. Medications, health history, allergies, and any drug paraphernalia found with the overdosed patient can help with diagnosis. The patient's vital signs are taken and recorded in triage, including his or her pulse, temperature, respiratory rate, and blood pressure.

Illness severity is usually broken into the following categories at triage: critical and immediately life threatening, such as a heart attack or a heroin overdose in which the patient is not breathing well; urgent but not immediately life threatening, such as most cases of abdominal pain or many cases of alcoholic intoxication; and less urgent, or the "walking wounded," including those with lacerations, coughs, and sore throats.

The emergency treatment of addictions and substance abuse is at first concerned with treating overdoses. After treatment of an overdosed patient and after medical stabilization, secondary care is initiated. Common substance abuse problems resulting in emergency treatment include alcohol intoxication, cocaine abuse, and heroin abuse. The following information outlines what can be expected if confronted with the care of an overdosed person.

A person overdosed on alcohol will often be obtunded (that is, will have a decreased mental status and will show lethargy and stupor). He or she may be vomiting, may lack muscle coordination, or may be passed out (unconscious). Severely intoxicated persons, who sometimes have a blood alcohol content (BAC) level above 0.35 percent and as high as 0.50 percent, should be transported to an ER as soon as possible. Alcohol levels in that high of a range often mean alcohol poisoning. (Legal limits of alcohol intoxication while driving in the United States is 80 milligrams of ethanol per 100 milliliters of blood, or a BAC of 0.08 percent.) Upon arrival at the ER, the alcohol-poisoned person is first assessed in triage.

An obtunded alcohol-intoxicated patient who is still conscious would most likely be assessed as a category two patient. A person overdosed on heroin, unconscious with the pinpoint pupils characteristic of narcotic overdoses, and with a severely depressed respiratory status, would be advanced to the category one or resuscitation section of the ER. Cocaine intoxication can lead to compromised cardiovascular dynamics. In such cases, pupils are dilated (large), breathing rates speed up, blood pressure elevates, and abnormal heart rates and rhythms occur with cocaine use. A person overdosed on cocaine and with a compromised cardiovascular function would be advanced to category one for emergency care and stabilization.

BASIC STABILIZATION

Overdose precautions taken "in the street" do not (and should not) typically include inserting a needle into the heart (as featured in films and on television). Street methods, which should not be used, sometimes include forced milk ingestion in an unconscious, narcotic-overdosed person, ice packing, or the injection of milk or saltwater (saline) solutions. Serious side effects can ensue, including aspiration pneumonia (milk vomited up from the stomach and into the lungs), hypothermia (dangerously low body temperature), blood infections, and cellulitis (skin infections).

Substance abuse overdose is a serious emergency requiring hospital treatment and evaluation. Someone trained in cardiopulmonary resuscitation (CPR) can check for a pulse in the unconscious person and initiate CPR after calling 911 for assistance; any home or street care should first be guided by accessing the emergency health care system. Recent programs have placed naloxone, a drug that treats narcotic overdoses, in the hands of nonmedical personnel so that they can treat life-threatening overdoses in the street. Training programs for this type of treatment exist in urban areas. A doctor-supervised training program organized through the Chicago Recovery Alliance, for example, has dispensed naloxone to drug users in an effort to provide lifesaving narcotic reversal on the streets.

EMERGENCY CARE

Initial ER treatment of a nonresponsive patient involves intravenous (IV) line insertion, oxygen administration, and heart monitoring. An IV provides direct access to blood vessels for medication injection and allows intravenous fluid replenishment if needed. Many obtunded overdose patients have depressed respirations, and oxygen applied through a mask or nasal cannula helps deliver oxygen to the brain and body. Cardiac or heart monitoring along with oxygen-saturation measuring devices offer valuable information related to blood transport in the body.

Emergency treatment of narcotic overdoses requires naloxone. Naloxone blocks the opiate receptors in the nervous system and reverses comas and breathing problems caused by opiates like heroin. Naloxone is rapidly effective, usually reversing the coma and respiratory depression within one or two minutes. A glucose solution is often administered intravenously to unresponsive patients to treat the possibility that low blood sugar is causing or contributing to the unconscious state.

Naloxone is helpful for narcotic overdoses, but it does not readily block alcohol poisoning. An alcoholic will be treated with IV fluids to replenish fluids and minerals and with the vitamin thiamine and multivitamins, and he or she will be observed for many hours until the excess alcohol is metabolized by the person's liver. Generally, a person's BAC level will drop from 0.20 to 0.10 in about five hours. This rate of metabolism will vary, and alcoholics often metabolize alcohol at a faster rate.

Cocaine overdose often leads to cardiac arrhythmias, requiring cardiac monitoring, analysis of abnormal rates and rhythms, and appropriate interventions to stabilize the heart. These interventions include IV medications or electrical defibrillation and cardioversion.

All of these treatments are subject to ongoing evaluation and reassessment. A category two alcohol-intoxicated patient could progress to a category one patient with no pulse or blood pressure, requiring advanced CPR and intervention. Narcotic overdosed patients may rapidly improve with naloxone treatments but could "crash" from secondary problems caused by the effects of multiple drug ingestions or by underlying heart, lung, kidney, or brain problems.

Emergency treatment is often followed by inpatient hospitalization, depending on the problems and recovery course. Follow-up care with substance abuse treatment centers is necessary to prevent recurrence of these life-threatening overdoses.

Richard P. Capriccioso, MD

FURTHER READING

Capriccioso, Richard P. "Emergency Rooms." *Magill's Medical Guide*. Ed. Brandon P. Brown et al. 6th ed. Pasadena, CA: Salem, 2011. Comprehensive overview of emergency rooms including the background and history of emergency medicine development, diagnostic and treatment techniques used in emergency medicine, and perspectives on the multidisciplinary role of emergency medicine in all fields of medical care. Detailed descriptions of various types of emergency departments.

Marx, John. *Rosen's Emergency Medicine: Concepts and Clinical Practice*. 7th ed. Philadelphia: Mosby, 2010. A textbook covering all areas of emergency treatment and medicine.

Samet, J. A. "Drug Abuse and Dependence." *Goldman's Cecil Medicine*. Eds. Lee Goldman and Andrew I. Schafer. 24th ed. Philadelphia: Saunders, 2012. A textbook presentation related to epidemiology, diagnosis, and treatment of drug abuse.

Terry, Don. "A Shot That Saves the Lives of Addicts Is Now in Their Hands." *New York Times*, 24 Jul. 2010. Web. 6 Mar. 2012. http://www.nytimes.com/2010/07/25/us/25cncnaloxone.html?_r=1. A timely discussion of a program designed to provide heroin abusers with naloxone so that heroin overdoses can be treated in the street, in a well-timed and perhaps life-saving fashion.

WEBSITES OF INTEREST

Medscape: Alcohol and Substance Abuse Evaluation
http://emedicine.medscape.com/article/805084-overview

National Association of Emergency Medical Technicians
http://www.naemt.org

National Institute on Drug Abuse
http://www.drugabuse.gov

See also: Alcohol poisoning; Naloxone; Overdose

Emetic abuse

CATEGORY: Substance abuse

ALSO KNOWN AS: Ipecac abuse

DEFINITION: Emetic abuse is typically diagnosed in persons with psychological disorders such as bulimia nervosa, which affect eating behaviors. Emetics, which are poisonous irritants designed to induce intense vomiting by irritating the stomach, are regularly consumed to control weight through purging the body of consumables and their unwanted calories. Emetic abuse is a dangerous and damaging form of purging, but it is treatable.

CAUSES

Emetic abuse primarily affects adolescent girls and young women between the ages of twelve and twenty-five years who are exploring weight loss methods or who have an eating disorder such as bulimia nervosa. Childhood sexual abuse, food digestion problems, substance abuse, family history, and involvement in activities that value thinness, such as ballet, gymnastics, and modeling, also play a role in emetic abuse.

The best-known over-the-counter emetic is ipecac. Emetics are typically administered orally or by injection. These agents force vomiting by stimulating the gastric nerve endings responsible for muscle contraction and the brain chemoreceptor trigger zone. Emetics are officially prescribed in emergencies, for one-time-use only, to eliminate the absorption of poisonous toxins.

With repeated use, emetics can be lethal. They can accumulate in the body because of their long half-lives and can cause progressive weakening of the muscles. Misuse may lead to severe dehydration, electrolyte imbalances, and serious life-threatening cardiac complications, including heart muscle wastage. Some injuries can improve if the abuse stops.

RISK FACTORS

In addition to desired weight loss, as already discussed, other risk factors for emetic abuse include mental health issues such as depression, anxiety, low self-esteem, and obsessive-compulsive disorder.

SYMPTOMS

The short-term effects associated with emetic abuse and repeated vomiting include dental problems such as cavities, gum disease, bad breath, and staining and discoloration from stomach acids. Other health consequences include swollen glands, throat and esophageal irritation and inflammation, eye problems, muscle weakness, dizziness, fatigue, dry skin, blackouts, chest pain, and irregular heart beat.

Long-term effects associated with emetic abuse include electrolyte, mineral, and vitamin imbalances; alkalosis (loss of chloride); hypokalemia (low blood potassium); hypoglycemia (low blood sugar); dehydration; hypertension; menstrual abnormalities; gastric reflux; stomach ulcers; and esophageal tearing and bleeding (Mallory-Weiss syndrome).

Serious medical complications may result from repeated emetic use. These complications include seizures, stroke, paralysis, pancreatitis, kidney and liver damage, respiratory failure, heart arrhythmias, heart muscle wastage and poisoning (myocardial toxicity), cardiac arrest, and sudden death.

SCREENING AND DIAGNOSIS

Emetic abusers are usually secretive about their abuse and about the reasons for their abuse; health professionals should be familiar with behaviors and conditions associated with eating disorders. Primary care physicians should consult with a mental health professional and behavioral therapist for diagnosis and treatment.

Evaluation includes a medical history and physical examination to establish evidence of purging. Diagnostic screenings may include blood, urine, and electrolyte analysis to confirm emetic abuse and an electrocardiogram and echocardiogram to detect heart muscle damage.

TREATMENT AND THERAPY

Treatment for emetic abuse can be long and difficult and depends on the duration and severity of use. Emetic abuse tends to be chronic, so early intervention is critical for a successful recovery. Optimal care usually requires close patient monitoring and a combination of medical care, nutritional counseling, and psychotherapy. Withdrawal from emetics can be accomplished in an inpatient, outpatient, or residential setting specializing in eating disorders; most abusers can be managed as outpatients.

Antidepressant medications used to treat depression and reduce anxiety may be helpful in treating emetic abuse and in preventing relapse. Fluoxetine (Prozac) appears to reduce binge-purge behaviors and to improve eating perceptions. Other medications may be required to manage the physical complications associated with emetic abuse.

Cognitive-behavioral therapies are essential in eliminating binging-purging behaviors, restoring normal eating patterns, identifying and changing negative self images, and targeting the emotional issues that triggered the abuse. Therapy may be individual, family, or group based.

PREVENTION

The best preventive measure is to avoid using emetics and to better manage underlying illnesses associated with the abuse. Patients should be educated about possible health hazards related to emetic use, such as toxicity and potential for abuse.

Rose Ciulla-Bohling, PhD

FURTHER READING

Bulik, Cynthia M. "Abuse of Drugs Associated with Eating Disorders." *Journal of Substance Abuse* 4.1 (1992): 69–90. Print. Discusses the problem of drug use among women with bulimia nervosa.

Flomenbaum, Neal E., et al. *Goldfrank's Toxicologic Emergencies.* 8th ed. New York: McGraw-Hill, 2006. A comprehensive guide covering how toxins affect the body. Also covers clinical symptoms, emergency treatment guidelines, antidotes, and case studies.

Manoguerra, Anthony S., et al. "Guideline on the Use of Ipecac Syrup in the Out-of-Hospital Management of Ingested Poisons." *Clinical Toxicology* 43.1 (2005): 1–10. Print. Reviews the benefits and risks associated with ipecac use in the home.

Pritts, Sarah D., and Jeffrey Susman. "Diagnosis of Eating Disorders in Primary Care." *American Family Physician* 67.2 (2003): 297–304. Print. Examines the importance of the family physician in identifying, diagnosing, and treating patients with eating disorders.

Silber, Tomas J. "Ipecac Syrup Abuse, Morbidity, and Mortality: Isn't It Time to Repeal Its Over-the-Counter Status?" *Journal of Adolescent Health* 37.3 (2005): 256–60. Print. A literature overview of the clinical characteristics associated with ipecac abuse among young women and ways to eliminate it.

Steffen, Kristine J., et al. "The Eating Disorders Medicine Cabinet Revisited: A Clinician's Guide to Ipecac and Laxatives." *International Journal of Eating Disorders* 40.4 (2007): 360–68. Print. Reviews patterns of abuse and toxicities related to over-the-counter emetic and laxative use in persons with bulimia nervosa.

Yager, Joel, Harry E. Gwirtsman, and Carole K. Edelstein, eds. *Special Problems in Managing Eating Disorders.* Washington, DC: American Psychiatric, 1992. Describes the physical and psychological complications associated with diagnosing and treating eating disorders.

WEBSITES OF INTEREST

Drugs.com
http://www.drugs.com/monograph/ipecac-syrup.html

National Association of Anorexia Nervosa and Associated Disorders
http://www.anad.org/get-information/eating-disorder-signs-and-symptoms

National Institute of Mental Health
http://www.nimh.nih.gov/health/publications/eating-disorders/complete-index.shtml

See also: Behavioral addictions: Overview; Bulimia; Laxative abuse

Emphysema

CATEGORY: Health issues

DEFINITION: Emphysema is a chronic obstructive disease of the lungs. The lungs contain millions of tiny air sacs called alveoli. In emphysema, these sacs lose their elasticity and air becomes trapped within. It becomes difficult to expel oxygen-depleted air from the lungs, which diminishes the normal exchange of air. Emphysema is classified as a chronic obstructive pulmonary disease (COPD).

CAUSES

Emphysema develops due to smoking; inhaling toxins or other irritants; and apha1-antitrypsin deficiency (A1AD), a genetic defect which can cause emphysema at an early age in nonsmokers.

RISK FACTORS

Factors such as smoking, exposure to long-term secondhand or passive smoke, and exposure to pollutants in the environment increase the chances of developing emphysema. Other risk factors include a family history of emphysema, a medical history of frequent childhood lung infections, HIV infection, and connective tissue disorders. Individuals at age fifty years or older also have a greater risk of developing emphysema.

SYMPTOMS

Early symptoms of emphysema include coughing in the morning, coughing up clear sputum (mucus from deep in the lungs), wheezing, and shortness of breath with physical activity. As the disease progresses, symptoms experienced may include increased shortness of breath, rapid breathing, fatigue, and a choking sensation when lying flat. Other symptoms include trouble concentrating, increase in chest size (barrel chest), enlargement of the right chamber of the heart, heart failure, swelling in the legs, weight loss, breathing through pursed lips, a desire to lean forward to improve breathing, and more frequent flare-ups (periods of more severe symptoms).

SCREENING AND DIAGNOSIS

A thorough review of the patient's medical history and a physical examination are performed. The examination may include testing, such as chest X-rays, a test that uses radiation to take pictures of structures inside the chest; CT scan, a type of X-ray that uses a computer to generate 3-D images of the internal organs; arterial blood gas test, a blood test used to assess the amount of oxygen and carbon dioxide in the blood; and lung function tests (spirometry).

TREATMENT AND THERAPY

There is no cure for emphysema. Instead, treatment aims to ease symptoms and improve one's quality of life. Treatments involve smoking cessation, which slows the progression of the disease; environmental management, or limiting the number of irritants in the air to make breathing easier; and medication, which helps to ease the symptoms and reduce complications. Medications include bronchodilators to relax the airways and open breathing passages (may be given as pills or inhaled), corticosteroids to decrease inflammation and swelling in the breathing passages, antibiotics to fight bacterial infections, and expectorants to loosen mucus and make it easier to cough up.

Living with Emphysema: An Interview

Sandy, a fifty-year-old woman, is married with three grown children. She started smoking at age fourteen and continued until she was forty-eight years old. She quit for one full year, but has recently started smoking again. She says that one cigarette was all it took to return to smoking. She is struggling to quit again, and she is retired because of her emphysema. The following is a brief interview with Sandy:

Q. What was your first sign that something was wrong? What symptoms did you experience?

A. My first sign was being short of breath. I had been short of breath for years, but it became much worse over two years ago. I found it increasingly difficult to climb stairs or walk for any distance. I noticed that I could not even walk a whole city block without having to stop and rest. Surprisingly, it was after I had quit smoking for a month that I really noticed an increase in my shortness of breath. It was strange to me that I was more short of breath when my expectation was that I would be breathing easier.

Q. What was the diagnosis experience like?

A. I saw my primary care provider first. I wasn't referred to a specialist right away. My doctor felt that I probably was in the early stages of emphysema and decided to treat me first with medication and inhalers. He didn't feel that my condition was severe enough to require a specialist. I wasn't completely happy with that but felt that he must know what he was talking about. It wasn't until eight or nine months later, when I had a cold and possible lung infection, that I was referred to a specialist and given a pulmonary function test. When the test results came back, my primary care doctor admitted that he had not realized how bad my condition was.

Q. How do you manage your disease?

A. I am currently seeing a pulmonary specialist. This is my second pulmonary specialist; I was not happy with the attitude of the first specialist, so I switched. I am seen every three months and usually have a spirometry done in the office. I am on three different inhalers: Advair, Combivent, and Flovent. I also use Accolate twice a day and I keep prednisone on hand for flare-ups. I have had blood work, chest X-rays, and a dobutamine stress test. Next month, I will have a CAT scan on my lungs to see what kind of condition they are in.

Currently, I am operating at 30 percent lung function, and the doctor has told me that this is as good as it gets. I have been fortunate to not need supplemental oxygen yet. Recently, the doctor has mentioned the word *transplant*. He explained that at age fifty, I am young enough to endure a transplant. By the time I'm sixty, I may have only 15 percent lung function left.

I am also taking an antidepressant. So you can see that this illness has caused some stress and depression.

Oxygen may also be given to supplement the air taken in by the body. Increasing the amount of available oxygen helps to increase energy levels and heart and brain function. In addition, because emphysema makes individuals prone to influenza and pneumonia, doctors recommend an annual flu shot and a pneumococcal vaccine.

Lastly, special exercises can strengthen chest muscles and make breathing easier. Physical activity builds endurance and improves quality of life, while special breathing exercises with and without an incentive spirometer can help to bring more air into the lungs and force trapped air out of the lungs. A small number of patients may benefit from surgery, including a bullectomy (removal of a bulla—a large, distended air space in the lung) or a lung transplant.

PREVENTION

Individuals can reduce the chances of developing emphysema by not smoking, avoiding exposure to secondhand smoke, avoiding exposure to air pollution or irritants, and wearing protective gear if exposed to irritants or toxins at work.

Debra Wood, RN

FURTHER READING

Chhabra, S. K., R. K. Gupta, and T. Singh. "Cutis Laxa and Pulmonary Emphysema." *Indian Journal of Chest Diseases & Allied Sciences* 43.4 (2001): 235–47. Discusses cutis laxa, a disorder of the skin due to a defective elastin synthesis, which can occur in those with pulmonary emphysema.

"COPD Resources." *AARC.org*. American Association for Respiratory Care. 2012. Web. 29 Mar. 2012. Information about chronic obstructive pulmonary disease (COPD), including basic facts, causes, diagnosis, comparison to asthma, treatments, patient information, and education about the lungs.

Petrache, I., et al. "HIV Associated Pulmonary Emphysema: A Review of the Literature and Inquiry into Its Mechanism." *Thorax* 63.5 (2008): 463–69. A review of the clinical studies that support a direct association between HIV infection and emphysema. Also reviews developments in the basic understanding of HIV and emphysema.

WEBSITES OF INTEREST

American College of Chest Physicians
http://www.chestnet.org

American Lung Association
http://www.lungusa.org

See also: Chronic obstructive pulmonary disease (COPD); Respiratory diseases and smoking; Smoking: Short- and long-term effects on the body; Tobacco use disorder

Ephedrine

CATEGORY: Substances

ALSO KNOWN AS: Ma huang

DEFINITION: Ephedrine is an alkaloid drug derived from plants of the genus *Ephedra* (family Ephedraceae); it also is produced synthetically. Ephedrine is similar in chemical structure to amphetamine and methamphetamine drugs.

STATUS: Legal (certain formulations by prescription only in the United States and United Kingdom); illegal for use as a dietary supplement; sold over-the-counter in Canada as a nasal decongestant

CLASSIFICATION: Scheduled Listed Chemical Product (SLCP)

SOURCE: Primary natural source of ephedrine is as an extract from plants of the genus *Ephedra*, specifically *E. sinica* and *E. distachya*; most commercial supplies are grown in China. Because of the expense of extracting ephedrine from natural sources, most pharmaceutical sources of the drug are L-ephedrine, which is produced synthetically.

TRANSMISSION ROUTE: Ephedrine occurs as fine white crystals or powder; the drug is readily soluble in water. In capsule form it is administered orally, and when dissolved in water can be administered in a nasal spray. It also can be given subcutaneously or intravenously.

HISTORY OF USE

Ephedrine has been used as an herbal preparation (ma huang) for thousands of years in Chinese medicine as a treatment for asthma and bronchitis. A Japanese chemist, Nagayoshi Nagai, first isolated ephedrine from the plant *E. distachya* in 1885, and it has been used in Western medicine since that time.

Ephedrine acts to increase the activity of nor-adrenaline on adrenergic receptors in the brain. It indirectly stimulates the sympathetic nervous system and can cross the blood-brain barrier and affect the central nervous system directly by causing the release of noradrenaline and dopamine. Thus, its action is similar to that of the drugs amphetamine and methamphetamine.

Ephedrine has been abused by athletes, particularly by weightlifters and bodybuilders, because it is thought to act as an appetite suppressant and may promote fat utilization. Many athletes need to maintain a certain weight and body fat percentage before competition, leading to ephedrine's use, often in combination with caffeine and aspirin. In 2004, the US Food and Drug Administration banned the use of ephedrine in dietary supplements aimed at weight loss.

EFFECTS AND POTENTIAL RISKS

Ephedrine has many legitimate medical uses, primarily in the treatment of respiratory problems but also to treat hypotension, narcolepsy, certain types of depression, and myasthenia gravis (an autoimmune neuromuscular disorder). However, ephedrine has many potentially serious side effects, and persons with heart disease, angina pectoris, hyperthyroidism, diabetes, and enlarged prostate must be closely supervised by their physicians during use of the substance.

Side effects of ephedrine include nervousness, panic disorder, insomnia, vertigo, difficult breathing, headache, tachycardia (rapid and erratic heartbeat), nausea, anorexia, and painful urination. Ephedrine should not be used during pregnancy except under extremely close medical supervision. Negative drug interactions occur between ephedrine and certain antidepressants, namely serotonin-norepinephrine reuptake inhibitors, and monoamine oxidase inhibitors. Ephedrine should not be used with medications for cough and congestion.

Lenela Glass-Godwin, MS

FURTHER READING

Fontanarosa, Phil B., Drummond Rennie, and Catherine D. DeAngelis. "The Need for Regulation of Dietary Supplements: Lessons from Ephedra." *Journal of the American Medical Association* 289 (2003): 1568–70. Print.

Martin, Elizabeth. *An A to Z of Medicinal Drugs.* New York: Oxford UP, 2010.

Maxwell, Jane Carlisle, and Beth A. Rutkowski. "The Prevalence of Amphetamine and Methamphetamine Abuse in North America: A Review of the Indicators, 1992–2007." *Drug and Alcohol Review* 27.3 (2008): 229–35. Print.

WEBSITES OF INTEREST

MayoClinic.com
http://mayoclinic.com/ephedrine

WebMD.com
http://webmd.com/drugs/ephedrine

See also: Amphetamine abuse; Methamphetamine; Stimulant abuse

Esophageal cancer

CATEGORY: Health issues

DEFINITION: The esophagus is the muscular tube that transports food from the throat to the stomach. Esophageal cancer is the growth of cancer cells in the esophagus.

CAUSES

There are two main types of esophageal cancer: squamous cell cancer, which arises from the cells that line the upper part of the esophagus, and adenocarcinoma, which arises from glandular cells that are present at the junction of the esophagus and stomach. Cancer occurs when abnormal or mutated cells in the body divide out of control. If cells keep dividing, a mass of tissue forms. These are called growths, or tumors. If the tumor is malignant, it is cancer. Cancer can invade nearby tissue and spread to other parts of the body.

RISK FACTORS

Factors that may increase the chance of esophageal cancer include tobacco use, including cigarettes, chewing tobacco, or snuff; excessive alcohol consumption; and a history of gastroesophageal reflux, especially if this has caused Barrett's esophagus (a complication of chronic esophagitis, or inflammation of the esophagus). Other factors include achalasia, or chronic dilation of the esophagus; infection with *Helicobacter pylori*, which causes stomach ulcers; certain rare genetic conditions, such as Plummer Vinson syndrome and tylosis; a damaged esophagus from toxic substances, such as lye; a history of cancer of the head or neck; and the human papilloma virus (HPV) infection.

SYMPTOMS

Symptoms of esophageal cancer include trouble swallowing or painful swallowing; coughing, a hoarse voice; pain in the throat, back, and chest; nausea and vomiting; coughing up blood; and weight loss. The structure and location of the esophagus makes it easy for cancer to spread very early. This can make a cure more difficult. People who have related conditions, especially reflux, are encouraged to discuss regular screening tests with their doctors. This may include an endoscopy, in which a tube with a tiny camera is inserted into the body in order to see inside.

SCREENING AND DIAGNOSIS

After a thorough examination and a discussion of the patient's medical history, doctors perform tests to diagnose esophageal cancer. These tests may include a chest X-ray; an upper gastrointestinal series—a series of X-rays of the esophagus, stomach, and duodenum, or the first part of the small intestine; esophagoscopy, the examination of the esophagus using a lighted scope; biopsy, which is the removal of a small sample of esophageal tissue to test for cancer cells; CT scan, a type of X-ray that uses a computer to generate 3-D pictures of structures inside the body; and a bone scan to see if the cancer has spread to the bones.

TREATMENT AND THERAPY

Treatment for esophageal cancer may incorporate surgery to remove the tumor. The doctor may remove all or part of the esophagus, as well. A plastic tube might be used to replace the missing portion of the esophagus. Radiation therapy and chemotherapy are also options. Radiation therapy, or radiotherapy, is used to kill cancer cells and shrink tumors. Radiation may be external radiotherapy, which is radiation directed at the esophagus from a source outside the body, or internal radiotherapy, which is when radioactive materials are placed into the esophagus in or near the cancer cells.

Chemotherapy is the use of drugs to kill cancer cells. Chemotherapy may be given in many forms, including by pill, by injection, and via a catheter. The drugs enter the bloodstream and travel through the body. They will kill mostly cancer cells, but some healthy cells may also be killed. Chemotherapy alone will not cure this type of cancer. It is only used when the cancer has already spread and cannot be cured. At this point, chemotherapy is used to help shrink the tumor and to ease pain or control nausea.

Chemotherapy and radiation therapy together are better than radiotherapy alone. They may also be as effective as surgery alone. Sometimes, chemotherapy and radiation therapy are followed by a surgery. This has been shown to be a most aggressive form of therapy and may be the best way to cure a patient of their disease.

Other treatment options are laser therapy, which is when high-intensity light is used to kill cancer cells, and photodynamic therapy, which is a combination of drugs and special lights used to try to kill cancer cells. This therapy is a promising treatment approach, but is only appropriate in a very small number of patients. There are limits to how far the infrared light source will travel into the cancer itself. The tumor must be very small (smaller than one-quarter-inch thick). It must not involve any lymph nodes or other structures.

PREVENTION

To prevent esophageal cancer, individuals should avoid or quit smoking or using other tobacco products, drink alcohol only in moderation, and seek medical treatment for gastroesophageal reflux disease.

Rosalyn Carson-DeWitt, MD

FURTHER READING

Abeloff, Martin D., et al. *Clinical Oncology*. 2nd ed. New York: Churchill Livingstone, 2000. A clinically focused reference of the latest oncology research. Includes information about esophageal cancer.

Far, A. E., et al. "Frequency of Human Papillomavirus Infection in Oesophageal Squamous Cell Carcinoma in Iranian Patients." *Scandinavian Journal of Infectious Diseases* 39.1 (2007): 58–62. A study of the role of human papilloma virus (HPV) in the development of oesophageal squamous cell carcinoma (ESCC).

Feldman, Mark, Lawrence S. Friedman, and Lawrence J. Brandt, eds. *Sleisenger & Fordtran's Gastroin-*

testinal and Liver Disease. 9th ed. Philadelphia: W.B. Saunders, 2010. A core, updated reference source on the techniques, technologies, and treatments in the fields of gastroenterology and hepatology.

WEBSITES OF INTEREST
American Association of Otolaryngology, Head and Neck Surgery
http://www.entnet.org/

American Cancer Society
http://www.cancer.org/

See also: Alcohol: Short- and long-term effects on the body; Cancer and substance abuse; Lung cancer; Smoking: Short- and long-term effects on the body; Tobacco use disorder

Ethanol

CATEGORY: Substances
ALSO KNOWN AS: Alcohol; ethyl alcohol; EtOH; grain alcohol; neutral spirit
DEFINITION: Ethanol, a small molecule with the chemical formula CH_3CH_2OH, occurs as a natural result of the microbial fermentation of sugars. Humans control fermentation and distillation to produce ethanol for use in alcoholic beverages and for industrial purposes.
STATUS: Usually legal but highly regulated and taxed in the United States and many other countries
CLASSIFICATION: Controlled by various federal, state, and local laws
SOURCE: Produced for human consumption in alcoholic beverages; produced industrially to use as a solvent, a fuel additive, and for other applications; amateur winemakers and brewers may make small quantities legally in the United States; occurs naturally in foods such as fresh bread and some fruit juices
TRANSMISSION ROUTE: Ingestion, almost entirely of ethanol-containing liquids

HISTORY OF USE

Consumption of ethanol predates written human history. Even animals may behave as if inebriated when consuming overripe fruit containing ethanol

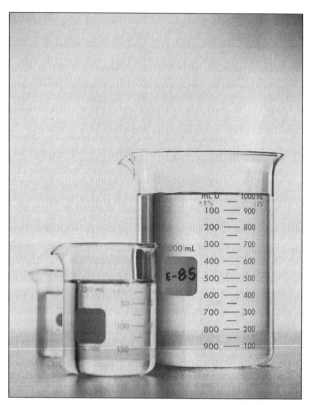

Ethanol, which is found in alcohol, is also used as a fuel. (Paul Eekhoff)

naturally. Characteristic fermented grain and fruit beverages are part of many cultures. A current trend is mixing alcoholic beverages with so-called energy drinks containing caffeine and other pharmacologically active substances.

EFFECTS AND POTENTIAL RISKS

Ethanol metabolizes in a deceptively simple manner in animals, including humans. Ethanol oxidizes in two steps to acetate, which enters normal metabolism without pharmacologic effect. Acetate accounts for the high caloric content of ethanol (7.1 calories per gram). Reduced cofactors generated by oxidizing ethanol explain its fat-sparing ability and how it causes hypoglycemia (high blood sugar) and lactic acidosis when taken in excess.

Oxidative conversions are carried out by two enzymes widely distributed in nature: alcohol dehydrogenase and aldehyde dehydrogenase. The intermediate acetaldehyde is toxic and accounts for some of ethanol's toxic effects, such as hangover symptoms and cirrhosis (irreversible liver damage), and accounts for ethanol sensitivity in some people. Ethanol itself accounts for neurologic effects like inebriation (with loss of inhibition and coordination) and addiction (alcoholism).

After ingestion and absorption from the gut, ethanol in the bloodstream reaches liver, lungs, and other tissues and organs. Ethanol affects the brain directly, in a variety of complex and little-understood interactions. Excess imbibition leads to delayed oxidation in liver, inebriation and other brain effects, and release of acetaldehyde into the blood, which causes headache, nausea, and other delayed symptoms typical of hangovers.

Ethanol's neurologic effects on the brain result from the direct interaction of the ethanol molecule with protein receptors in the membranes of neurons. Several proteins and the genes that encode them have been implicated, including those responsible for neurotransmitters involved in addiction to other substances. Different gene frequencies probably account for ethnogeographic variation of ethanol metabolism and alcoholism among various human groups.

R. L. Bernstein, PhD

FURTHER READING

Berg, Jeremy M., John L. Tymoczko, and Lubert Stryer. *Biochemistry*. 8th ed. New York: Freeman, 2010.

Haseba, T., and Y. Ohno. "A New View of Alcohol Metabolism and Alcoholism: Role of the High-Km Class III Alcohol Dehydrogenase (ADH3)." *International Journal of Environmental Research and Public Health* 10 (2010): 1076–92. Print.

Manzo-Avalos, Salvador, and Alfredo Saavedra-Molina. "Cellular and Mitochondrial Effects of Alcohol Consumption." *International Journal of Environmental Research and Public Health* 12 (2010): 4281–4304. Print.

WEBSITES OF INTEREST

CurrentAlcoholResearch.com
http://www.currentalcoholresearch.com

NutraMed.com
http://www.nutramed.com/alcohol/abchemistry.htm

See also: Alcohol abuse and alcoholism: Overview; Caffeinated alcoholic drinks; Solvents

Exercise addiction

CATEGORY: Psychological issues and behaviors
ALSO KNOWN AS: Compulsive exercise; exercise bulimia; exercise dependence; overtraining
DEFINITION: Exercise addiction is an observable condition characterized by making physical activity central to one's life, often to the detriment of other responsibilities and obligations. Exercise addicts voluntarily and compulsively participate in excessive physical activity, typically of high intensity and duration. Exercise addicts may engage in multiple daily sessions of physical activity, avoid rest days, embrace compulsive thoughts about activity during work or social times, and experience symptoms of withdrawal when exercise patterns are interrupted. Exercise addiction may be a symptom of other emotional disorders or may be a phenomenon in itself.

CAUSES AND RISK FACTORS

Exercise addiction may be caused by emotional disorders, personality characteristics, and social influences. The desire to control one's weight and body image is typically a common rationale for exercise addiction, and the addiction often accompanies eating disorders such as bulimia. The pleasurable sensation associated with endorphin release (for example, the runner's high) can provide the exercise addict with a motivation for pursuing exercise beyond moderation. Oftentimes, regret about lapses in regular activity can give way to inappropriate guilt about missing any opportunity to exercise.

Persons with tendencies toward obsessive-compulsive behavior, persons with body- and self-image concerns, and endurance athletes are most vulnerable to engage in physical activity for its own sake. Participation in extreme exercise beyond that necessary for health benefits, pursuing increasingly greater exercise accomplishments, and comparing progress with others of similar behavior can place one at risk for developing an unhealthy addiction to exercise. Participants in other-than-team sports and those who self-coach are at highest risk.

SIGNS, SYMPTOMS, AND DIAGNOSIS

Exercise addicts may exhibit one or more of the following:

- activity sessions repeatedly lasting over one hour
- feeling remorseful about missing an activity opportunity

- substituting activity for social interaction
- exercising to and through pain
- adherence to a regular and rigid routine
- being overly concerned about exercise goals
- inability to maintain an overall sense of relaxation and acceptance when not active
- amenorrhea (in females), fatigue, and depression

Researchers have estimated that as many as 80 percent of persons diagnosed with bulimia possess tendencies toward exercise addiction (and are therefore considered exercise bulimic). The anxiety felt when not exercising are lifted when one resumes the regimen.

Exercise addiction is not recognized as a primary disorder in the *Diagnostic and Statistical Manual of Mental Disorders* of the American Psychiatric Association, and diagnosis is challenging. The confirmation of exercise addiction ultimately rests with determining the importance and role of activity in a person's life while still exploring other conditions that may be present.

TREATMENT AND THERAPY

Exercise addiction is similar in concept to other addictions in that it shares a link with an underlying condition. Since regular physical activity is a desired behavior of health promotion and maintenance, efforts should be redirected to maintaining an active lifestyle while rebalancing the role that exercise plays in one's life. Because physical exercise is often recommended as a desirable substitute for many compulsive acts, it can become compulsive for those inclined to addictive behavior. Therefore, treating the exercise addict necessitates a multipronged approach, and it is unlikely that self-help or nonprofessional approaches to its cure will be effective.

Initially, a health care provider should determine the person's present state of health, including his or her physical and emotional well-being. Further analyses should focus on the patient's nutritional status and dietary habits, motivation for recovery and redirection of goals, capacity for implementation of coping strategies, and a health-focused activity prescription.

Treatment therapies would include the development of healthy eating habits; strategies for improving and maintaining a healthy self-esteem and body image; gradual incorporation of healthy, alternative recreational pursuits; and the monitoring of progress over time. It is likely that recovery from exercise addiction may take months and even years, and it must address underlying issues or other conditions. Even as the research

into treatment efficacy progresses, individual counseling and monitoring will remain critical to achieving success.

P. Graham Hatcher, PhD

FURTHER READING

Cole, Cheryl. "Addiction, Exercise, and Cyborgs: Technologies of Deviant Bodies." *Sport and Postmodern Times.* Ed. Genevieve Rail. Albany: State U of New York P, 1998. Examines a wide range of cultural and economic influences contributing to the development of exercise addiction.

Friedman, Peach. *Diary of an Exercise Addict.* Guilford, CT: Globe Pequot, 2008. Chronicles one woman's six-year struggle with and recovery from exercise bulimia.

Johnson, Marlys. *Understanding Exercise Addiction.* New York: Rosen, 2000. Written for teenagers, this book includes information on gender-based aspects of exercise addiction and recommendations for treatment.

Kaminker, Laura. *Exercise Addiction: When Fitness Becomes an Obsession.* New York: Rosen, 1998. Written for adolescents, this work describes the conditions associated with preoccupation about weight and body image. Also discusses the role and harm of compulsive exercise.

Powers, Pauline, and Ron Thompson. *The Exercise Balance.* Carlsbad, CA: Gurze, 2008. Provides a framework for identifying and recovering from overtraining.

Skupien, Robert. *Wired to Run.* Kansas City, MO: Andrews, 2006. Written by the founder of Runaholics Anonymous. Explains the specific nature of running addiction, a condition the author claims affects 11 million people in the United States.

WEBSITES OF INTEREST

Active.com
www.active.com/running/Articles/Know_the_signs_of_unhealthy_exercise_addiction

BrainPhysics.com
www.brainphysics.com/exercise-addiction.php

KidsHealth.org
http://kidshealth.org/parent/emotions/behavior/compulsive_exercise.html

See also: Behavioral addictions: Overview; Compulsions; Work addiction

F

Families and behavioral addictions

CATEGORY: Social issues

DEFINITION: Behavioral addictions are those addictions that involve social, observable behaviors but not the abuse of or dependence upon chemical substances. The dynamics and features that characterize chemical addiction also occur in behavioral addiction, but without a person physically ingesting a substance that promotes the addictive response. While a behaviorally addicted person may also have a simultaneous chemical addiction, these are understood as separate addictions even though treatment modalities overlap substantially. The most common behavioral addictions involve food, pornography, video gaming, online social networking, gambling, shopping, serial relationships, kleptomania, and exercise.

SCOPE OF THE ISSUE

While behavioral addictions are well accepted as serious mental and behavioral health problems, this historically was not the case. Mental health and even substance abuse specialists were slow to recognize the addictive properties in these behaviors for several reasons. First, the behaviors, such as shopping, were often routinely engaged in. The activities themselves are usually ordinary, everyday, and common. There is nothing inherently addictive about them.

Second, some behavioral addictions that are not as ordinary (for example, pornography) occur privately, often hidden from public view. Performed in secret, people who are addicted are unseen and unchallenged. Others simply were unaware of the problem. Third, there was a general lack of awareness that such activities could become truly addicting in the same way that alcohol, cocaine, or prescription pain or anti-anxiety medications could become addicting. Among specialists, occasional disagreement still exists about whether behavioral addictions are true addictions.

With increased recognition of the underlying characteristics of behavioral addiction has come more accurate reporting and intervention. Physicians and other health care providers, educational and workplace personnel, friends, and families are now more likely to express concern and acknowledge a serious problem. While varying sources estimate the prevalence of behavioral addictions differently, most addiction specialists conservatively assume that one in ten families has a behaviorally addicted family member. Some specialists believe the prevalence is as high as one family in three.

FAMILIES AND CAUSES

It is established that chemical addictions run in families. That is, having one family member addicted to chemicals increases the likelihood, fourfold, that a first-order relative—a parent or sibling—will develop a chemical addiction at some time in his or her life. Behavioral addictions also run in families, though it is unclear just how much more likely it is that a second family member will develop a behavioral addiction when a first-order relation is addicted to a specific behavior.

The actual connections between one behaviorally addicted family member and a similar addiction in another family member are complex and far from fully delineated. Similarly, how particular family climates promote (or discourage) behavioral addiction is also far from being fully understood. Still, the existence of connections is indisputable.

The first, and most fundamental, connection is family-shared biology and genetics. The response in the brain's pleasure centers tends to be similar in genetically related persons. The enjoyment the video-gaming addict gets will be similar among his or her family members even if the particular source of enjoyment (such as addictive catalog shopping rather than video gaming) is different. The intensity of the reward and its recurrent allure will be similar. However, family genes do not cause addiction.

As many as three-quarters of families with a behaviorally addicted family member do not have a second addicted member. The genetic contribution lies in the degree of likelihood that each family member shares for developing addiction, not that they will develop the addiction. The strength of the tendency to become addicted is largely shared though the outcomes (being addicted to gambling as a primary force in one's life or merely enjoying gambling as a pastime) are not necessarily the same. One is not "doomed" to addiction if a sibling or parent has become addicted.

A second connection lies in what family members are exposed to and learn to imitate. A straightforward example would be how children learn to copy their parents. If a single mother has a relational addiction in which she serially and incessantly dates men regardless of the psychological health of these relationships, her children will gradually learn that their value and sense of safety, security, and meaning is dependent on being in a relationship. Though it could take years for the addictive properties of this behavior to develop in her children, the chances that they eventually will are multiplied.

The woman's children see and experience the emotional anxiety and panic that their mother feels when she lacks an active, current dating relationship. Even if they do not have the language to describe what their mother is doing, they notice their mother's pattern and learn how to ensure they are part of a relationship—any relationship. Even when children come to understand the self-destructive pattern their mother is enduring (and putting her children through), they learn that having a relationship, even a bad one, prevents feelings of insecurity and insignificance that they believe are sure to come if they are not in a relationship. Their addictive pattern of incessant serial dating thus begins.

FAMILIES AND CONTINUATION

Though behavioral addictions are pathological, maladaptive, and harmful to the addicted persons and their families, the addictions persist because the families' way of functioning, how it achieves or fails to achieve what it sets out to do, has accommodated the addictive disease. As much as the family may want the addiction to stop and as much suffering as the addicted member causes, the family responds as a unit (or system, in the jargon of family therapy) in ways

that end up supporting the addictive behaviors. Thus, the behaviors continue.

While this dynamic seems contrary to the well-being of the family and its members, it demonstrates the powerful emotional need within families to hold together for their survival—that no members can be lost. Families achieve this through maintaining a psychic balance, what social psychology describes as homeostasis: the drive within a family to keep itself going, regardless of the existence of harmful and hurtful family patterns (such as abuse, neglect, and addiction).

As the family realizes there is a problematic behavior (for example, one member's addiction to food) it responds initially with efforts to correct the problem. Usually, however, families cannot control a member's overeating or his or her addictive behaviors. As the family experiences repetitive failures, its emotional life becomes threatened, and though members do not consciously and explicitly coordinate their response, they react to the addict in ways that dysfunctionally balances the emotional energy within the family. Members become preoccupied with the addict's food consumption, where he or she is getting the food, where it is hidden, and how much is consumed. This preoccupation involves everyone in the family with the well-intentioned, but unsuccessful, goal of getting the addict to eat normally.

Often, the addiction, known to all, is spoken openly by no one. It becomes this family's "public secret." As a secret, it cannot be effectively addressed. The addict reacts, in turn, to the heightened concern and scrutiny, and because the addiction must be fed, he or she reacts against the family's efforts to help.

These reactions take a variety of predictable forms: angry denial of the problem, in which family members are intimidated and told to mind their own business; avoidance of family encounters and generally being less visible, often in the guise of being too busy to participate in family activities, like meals, and spending large blocks of time at work, school, or in one's room; and helpless proclamations of guilt and shame while vowing to get help or promising to try harder.

This setting involves many negative emotions, including blame, that surface and resurface. Questions are asked by the addict and by family members: Who really cares? Who is really selfish? Who really understands the addict? Who among us will take a stand? The emotional disconnection within the family grows.

FAMILIES AND TREATMENT

Just as families are typically central to the successful treatment of chemical and substance abuse, they are usually central to successful treatment of behavioral addiction. First, open acknowledgement of the problem—that it has reached the stage of addiction—allows the addiction to be treated.

In the early stages of treatment, or recovery, families are often confronted by the behaviorally addicted member's denial that there is a problem, that the problem is as bad as members say, that the addict can control it, or that the behavior is anyone else's business. Addicted video gamers, for example, will likely argue the benefits to their many hours of compulsive playing: It relieves stress for them. They enjoy it. They have friends online who play as much as they do and they enjoy their companionship. They are not bothering anyone else.

In such a case, family members must be supportive but honest in confronting both the addict and themselves, addressing how they have unintentionally enabled the addiction to continue. Family members need to recognize and openly declare what they used to do that allowed the addiction to continue and that they will no longer support the behavior. Members too should seek help, because it is inherently difficult to disengage from a loved one in trouble. Family members should assume a position of full support for helping the addict get help and of zero support for anything the addict does that does not promote recovery.

Paul Moglia, PhD
Eugenia F. Moglia, BA

FURTHER READING

American Academy of Child and Adolescent Psychiatry. "Facts for Families." Washington, DC: AACAP, 2011. An informational guide series for parents and families facing a variety of real-world issues, including behavioral addictions, within families.

Bradshaw, John. *On the Family: A New Way of Creating Solid Self-Esteem.* Deerfield Beach, FL: Health Communications, 1996. One of the best introductions to understanding families as systems with dynamic, reactive energies. Explains in clear, insightful language the family's role in supporting ongoing problematic and addictive behaviors in an individual family member.

Hayes, Steven, and Michael Levin. *Mindfulness and Acceptance for Addictive Behaviors: Applying Contextual CBT to Substance Abuse and Behavioral Addictions.* Oakland, CA: New Harbinger, 2010. Hayes is a pioneer in the application of mindfulness in treatment of substance abuse and addictions in general. A readable work focused on helping the reader apply this approach to many types of behavioral addictions.

Sadock, B. J., and V. A. Sadock, eds. *Kaplan and Sadock's Comprehensive Textbook of Psychiatry.* Philadelphia: Lippincott, 2000. Contains detailed descriptions of various behavioral addictions, written for clinicians but comprehensible to the general reader.

WEBSITES OF INTEREST

Families Anonymous
http://www.familiesanonymous.org

National Institute on Drug Abuse
http://www.drugabuse.gov

Substance Abuse and Mental Health Services Administration
http://www.samhsa.gov

See also: Behavioral addictions: Overview; Children and behavioral addictions; Domestic violence and addiction; Economic impact of addiction; Families and substance abuse; Marriage/partnership and behavioral addictions; Men and behavioral addictions; Women and behavioral addictions

Families and substance abuse

CATEGORY: Substance abuse

DEFINITION: A family with a substance-abusing member often experiences long-lasting, deleterious consequences from that abuse. An individual member's substance abuse or addiction is also the family's substance abuse or addiction. Self-pity, hatred, resentment, guilt, and anger disrupt family life that, while never perfect, should ideally be health-promoting, protective, supportive, and positive. Powerful and dangerous emotions intoxicate and ruin the functional life of the family. Treatment, however, is available for family members and for the addict.

Often the main victims of a family member's drinking problem are the other members of the family itself. (Peter Dazeley)

CAUSES

Initial substance and chemical use is almost always voluntary, as the person decides to consume or not consume a substance; if they do consume, they decide how much. The person is in charge of the choices he or she makes.

Continued choices to use a drug produce chemical and structural changes in the brain that result in involuntary, compulsively driven needs to have the drug. This action compromises the functioning of the areas of the brain involved in the inhibition of drives. The urge is never more than temporarily satisfied, however. The substance, not the person, is in control.

What often starts as an experience of recreation, relaxation, excitement, experimentation, social bonding, or isolated escape from life's challenges becomes a need to satisfy and resupply. Users are now abusers, and abusers often become addicts of the substances they are using.

Substance abuse can involve any chemical, but more often they involve commonly used and legal substances such as tobacco (the nicotine in tobacco is addictive) and coffee or tea (the caffeine in coffee and tea is addictive) or illegal chemicals such as cocaine, heroin, and marijuana. Substances of abuse also include legal medications, such as anti-anxiety and pain medications, which require a physician prescription to obtain, and over-the-counter medications.

Although these substances are chemically quite varied, they all produce the same overt response in the abuser: an unrelenting need to achieve the next altered state of consciousness, be it a high, sleepiness or relaxation, or excitability. Satisfying the need becomes a priority over responsibilities with family, friends, or work. The addict becomes emotionally cut off from family, friends, and coworkers. Addiction and the quest to satiate the next urge control the addict's mental state.

Those struggling with addiction often have legal troubles and frequently use substances in dangerous situations (such as driving under the influence). The ability to resist the impulse to take the drug overtakes users' self-control, and they are left helpless and often beyond the help that their families and friends can typically provide.

RISK FACTORS

While vulnerability to substance addiction can come about for many reasons, the most common involve a prior history of substance abuse in one's family, which is dually suggestive of being exposed to and learning how to use substances (imitative, learned behavior), and a genetic predisposition to responding more strongly to drugs than might be true for the average person. The average person without an addiction is more likely to have been raised in a family free of substance and chemical abuse.

Geneticists are moving closer to identifying several genes and gene clusters that promote a much stronger pleasure response to certain substances than is typical in the average person. Neuroscientists, similarly, are increasing their focus on areas of the brain that become highly excitable in addicted persons exposed to drugs.

One in four families has one or more members who either abuses drugs or is addicted to drugs. This can be explained in part by research that shows that addiction and substance abuse occur more readily in persons with a family history in which a first-order relative is chemically addicted and in which there exists a genetic loading for an unusually pleasurable response to drugs and other substances. This extrapolates to one of every two families having to cope in a major way with a relation or close friend who abuses or is addicted to drugs.

Having a behavioral or mental problem or illness, even common ones like anxiety and depression, also increases the odds that one will develop an addiction. Also more likely to become addicted are persons who were neglected or physically or emotionally abused as children. Research also shows that even the delivery system employed, that is, how the drugs are ingested, puts someone on a faster track to addiction. Snorting and intravenous injection are the most dangerous methods that can lead to drug addiction.

IMPACT ON THE FAMILY

Persons do not intend to become addicts or substance abusers. People most often use substances to change an emotional state, to enhance a state of feeling good, or to combat a state of feeling bad.

Use easily becomes frequent use, frequent use increases the odds that use progresses to abuse; episodes of abuse, in turn, increase—and almost guarantee—the odds that addiction will overcome the person's state of mind and being. They live the life of addictive preoccupation; nothing else matters.

Having a substance-abusing member in a family has long-lasting, deleterious effects that take from the energy, bonds, and nurturance that characterize the traditional family group. The social dynamic in families is that each member reacts to all other members. Mothers react to spouses and their children. Fathers react to spouses and their children. Children react to each parent and their siblings. This mesh of reactions results in a long-term, developmentally progressive, complex social system that has its own lifecycle. A substance-abusing family member has an impact on this cycle, usually in one of three ways. Family members can respond to the substance abuse in a similar fashion.

The most prevalent of these three reactions is the desire to stay engaged with the substance abuser, and to advise, counsel, support, reason with, and show disappointment in the abuser while seeking the promise of abstinence and reform. This response by family members who love and are committed to each other is rarely effective, but nonetheless may last for decades. Engagement often produces depression and hopelessness in the family, which can then produce guilt and shame in the abuser. The pain of the guilt and shame is more than the abuser can withstand, and the negative emotions may drive him or her back to the substance of abuse.

The second most prevalent reaction, confrontation, usually arises some time after the addiction is accepted as a real problem, both for the family member and for the family. Confrontational responses generally have rapid onset with a short half-life. Most people cannot sustain high levels of intense anger and outrage. The addict often recoils in the face of such an emotional onslaught and will nervously try to avoid the drug or not get caught taking the drug. Inevitably, because the addiction or abuse is not being treated, its remission is brief; when it resurfaces, it will again be met by family outrage. The addict will then respond as before: recycling the pattern of abuse.

The third reaction, collaboration, can move family members from being contributors to and enablers of the problem to recognizing that, in the face of the disease, the family has become diseased itself; symptoms are often manifested in a long and varied series of unhelpful, maladaptive, dysfunctional responses that attempt the impossible: Remove the cause of the addiction, try to control the addiction, and find a cure for the addiction.

Engagement initially requires the emotional and psychological detachment from the addict and his or her disease. Genetic loading and family history notwithstanding, family members (often slowly) come to understand that they did not cause the disease, that they cannot (and have never been able to) control the disease, and that they cannot cure the disease.

TREATMENT FOR FAMILIES

Just as families have primary ways of reacting to their drug-abusing members, they also have fairly predictable developmental stages in reacting to these members. In the beginning, as an addict's behavior becomes harder to hide, family members begin to notice that something is wrong.

Family members will feel concerned and worried and will begin genuine attempts to look out for the troubled member's welfare. Families ask, remark, comment, suggest, and obtain promises of reduced or controlled use. Families will protect, make excuses, and try to carry on their normal lives. Slowly, as these efforts only prolong the addiction and delay treatment, families experience extreme emotional dissonance and self-doubt. Families become confused about whether they are tolerating addiction, enabling addiction, or just protecting themselves.

At this stage, families are immersed in the addiction, and treatment becomes necessary, even if the addict refuses. Often family members will employ a strategy of emotional or physical avoidance, a form of denial that parallels that of addicts.

For addicts and their families substance addictions are treatable diseases. As families accept the realities of the addiction, they can begin to make real changes. For most families, the treatment of choice will be a family-centered, twelve-step program such as Al-Anon or Nar-Anon. Individual family members

may get their own treatment by meeting with a mental health specialist skilled at recognizing common dysfunctional family responses. As the family tends to its own health, it gets healthier. With the right kind of help comes healing, and the family can start to return to a normal way of life.

Family life involves intense emotions (good and bad), so it is almost impossible for families to have an engaged response without outside guidance, direction, and support. Help for families coping with addicted members is wide ranging. It comes in the form of twelve-step groups such as Al-Anon and Nar-Anon. Also available are licensed behavioral health care professionals who specialize in substance abuse treatment or specialized treatment centers or programs.

In addition to being an example of those invested in their own recovery, families can be huge catalysts for aiding the addicts' treatment and recovery processes. Ideally, the family should respond to the addiction with support and noninterference.

The role of the family is critical; its reactions will either promote health or enable disease. Though they may never have abused substances themselves, family members should accept that they are coping with more than the substance abuse habits of an individual member. They are facing a family disease, and they should seek help accordingly.

Eugenia F. Moglia, BA
Paul Moglia, PhD

FURTHER READING

American Academy of Child and Adolescent Psychiatry. "Facts for Families." Washington, DC: AACAP, 2011. An informational guide series for parents and families facing a variety of real-world issues, including substance abuse and chemical addictions.

Barnard, Marina. *Drug Addiction and Families*. Philadelphia: Jessica Kingsley, 2007. The author, a senior research fellow at the Centre for Drug Misuse Research at the University of Glasgow, Scotland, has written extensively on the contributory role family environments can play in the development of substance misuse and abuse and how families can respond effectively.

Bradshaw, John. *On the Family: A New Way of Creating Solid Self-Esteem*. Deerfield Beach, FL: Health Communications, 1996. One of the best introductions to understanding families as systems with dynamic, reactive energies. Explains in clear, insightful language the family's role in supporting ongoing problematic and addictive behaviors in an individual family member.

Congers, Beverly. *Addict in the Family: Stories of Loss, Hope, and Recovery.* Deerfield Beach, FL: Health Communications, 2003. Generally regarded as a realistic yet inspirational read, this work includes real-life perspectives from family members coping with a loved one's addiction. Discusses the need for self-care.

Friel, John C., and Linda D. Friel. *Adult Children Secrets of Dysfunctional Families: Secrets of Dysfunctional Families.* Deerfield Beach, FL: Health Communications, 1988. Based in large measure on their extensive clinical experience with families coping with substance abuse, the authors discuss how family dynamics promote conditions that foster substance abuse.

Hayes, Steven, and Michael Levin. *Mindfulness and Acceptance for Addictive Behaviors: Applying Contextual CBT to Substance Abuse and Behavioral Addictions.* Oakland, CA: New Harbinger, 2010. Hayes is a pioneer in the application of mindfulness in treatment of substance abuse and addictions in general. A readable work focused on helping the reader apply this approach to many types of substance addictions.

WEBSITES OF INTEREST

Families Anonymous
http://www.familiesanonymous.org

National Institute on Drug Abuse
http://www.drugabuse.gov

Substance Abuse and Mental Health Services Administration
http://www.samhsa.gov

See also: Domestic violence and addiction; Economic impact of addiction; Families and behavioral addictions; Marriage/partnership and alcoholism; Marriage/partnership and substance abuse; Men and substance abuse; Parenting and alcoholism; Parenting and substance abuse; Substance abuse; Women and substance abuse

Fentanyl

CATEGORY: Substances

ALSO KNOWN AS: Apache; the bomb; China girl; China white; dance fever; friend; goodfella; jackpot; murder 8; perc-a-pop; poison; tango and cash; TNT

DEFINITION: Fentanyl is a highly potent opiate analgesic with biological effects indistinguishable from those of heroin.

STATUS: Legal in approved formulations as an anesthetic and analgesic; other formulations and uses are illegal

CLASSIFICATION: Schedule II controlled substance

SOURCE: Synthetic opiate analgesic with no natural sources. Similar to but more potent than morphine. Illegal formulations are either produced in underground laboratories or smuggled into the United States.

TRANSMISSION ROUTES: Legally administered by intravenous, transdermal (patch), and transmucosal (lozenge) routes; illegal formulations taken intravenously, snorted, or smoked

HISTORY OF USE

Fentanyl was first synthesized in a medical drug research laboratory in Belgium in the late 1950s. The original formulation had an analgesic potency of about eighty times that of morphine. Fentanyl was introduced into medical practice in the 1960s as an intravenous anesthetic. Subsequently, two other fentanyl analogs were developed for medical applications: alfentanil, an ultrashort-acting analgesic (of 5–10 minutes), and sufentanil, an exceptionally potent analgesic (5–10 times more potent than fentanyl) for use in heart surgery. Fentanyls are used now for anesthesia and analgesia. The most widely used formulation is a transdermal patch for relief of chronic pain.

Illicit use of fentanyl first occurred within the medical community in the mid-1970s. Among anesthesiologists, anesthetists, nurses, and other workers in anesthesiology settings, fentanyl and sufentanyl are the two agents most frequently abused. Potential abusers have ready access to these agents in liquid formulations for injection and can divert small quantities with relative ease. Transdermal patches cannot be readily adapted for abuse. The fentanyl lozenge has been

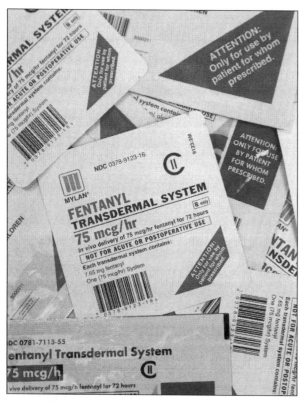

A collection of different brand and dosages of the Fentanyl patch, clearly marked with warnings about non-precribed uses. (AP Photo)

diverted to illegal use. On the street, the lozenge is known as perc-a-pop.

More than one dozen analogs of fentanyl have been produced clandestinely for illegal use outside the medical setting. Since the mid-2000s, fentanyl abuse has emerged as a serious public health problem. Fentanyl-laced heroin or cocaine powders have become the drugs of choice for some addicts.

EFFECTS AND POTENTIAL RISKS

The biological effects of fentanyl are indistinguishable from those of heroin, with the exception that illicit fentanyl analogs may be hundreds of times more potent. Short-term effects of fentanyl abuse include mood changes, euphoria, dysphoria, and hallucinations. Anxiety, confusion, and depression also may occur. High doses or long-term use may impair or interrupt breathing due to respiratory depression. Unconsciousness and even death can occur.

Ernest Kohlmetz, MA

FURTHER READING

Bryson, Ethan O., and Jeffrey H. Silverstein. "Addiction and Substance Abuse in Anesthesiology." *Anesthesiology* 109 (2008): 905–17. Print.

Kuhn, Cynthia, Scott Swartwelder, and Wilkie Wilson. *Buzzed: The Straight Facts about the Most Used and Abused Drugs from Alcohol to Ecstasy.* 3rd ed. New York: W. W. Norton, 2008.

Savelli, Lou. *Street Drugs: Pocketguide.* Flushing, NY: Looseleaf Law, 2008.

WEBSITES OF INTEREST

DrugAbuseHelp.com
http://www.drugabusehelp.com/drugs/fentanyl

US Drug Enforcement Administration
http://www.justice.gov/dea/concern/fentanylp.html

See also: Anesthesia abuse; Narcotics abuse; Opioid abuse

Fetal Alcohol Syndrome

CATEGORY: Health issues

DEFINITION: Fetal alcohol syndrome (FAS) belongs to a group of disorders called fetal alcohol spectrum disorder (FASD). FAS is caused when a woman drinks alcohol during pregnancy. Alcohol can cause birth and developmental defects in the baby. These defects make up FAS.

CAUSES

Alcohol can cross from the mother's blood into the fetus's blood by passing through the placenta. Even a small amount of alcohol can damage the fetus. Doctors do not know how much alcohol it takes to cause defects. The risk increases with moderate to heavy drinking and with binge drinking. Even so, social drinking may pose a danger.

RISK FACTORS

Factors that increase a baby's chance of getting fetal alcohol syndrome include unplanned pregnancy, failure to recognize early pregnancy and continuing to drink, alcoholism, lack of knowledge about the risks of drinking while pregnant, advanced maternal age, and low socioeconomic status.

SYMPTOMS

Birth and developmental defects depend on when the fetus was exposed to alcohol. Babies with fetal alcohol syndrome may have a number of physical symptoms, including low birth weight, delayed growth, small head and eyes, flat cheeks and small jaw, vision and hearing difficulties, heart defects, minor joint defects, and ear infections.

As the infant grows and develops, other symptoms may also appear, including difficulty sleeping and eating, delayed speech, learning disabilities, poor coordination, behavioral problems, and a poor impulse control. Children do not outgrow these effects. Teenagers and adults with FAS often experience social and emotional problems. They may develop secondary conditions, such as mental health problems, the inability to hold a job, alcohol or drug dependence, and anger management issues.

SCREENING AND DIAGNOSIS

A doctor will ask patients about their alcohol intake while pregnant. The child's growth will be assessed and a physical examination will be done. The diagnosis is based on the mother's history of alcohol use and the child's characteristic facial appearance, slow growth, and problems with the nervous system.

Some children with this condition do not have the typical physical features. Their condition is described as fetal alcohol effect (FAE) or alcohol-related neurodevelopment disorder (ARND). An early diagnosis can help a child receive the proper services.

TREATMENT AND THERAPY

There is no specific medical treatment for this condition. Early intervention is helpful, as well as a supportive, nurturing home. The doctor may recommend hearing and vision testing, as well as testing for any other medical problems related to FAS. Professional support helps a family cope with caring for a child with birth defects. Services include respite care and parent training. Parents can learn ways to handle behavior problems and stress management techniques.

PREVENTION

Efforts to prevent fetal alcohol syndrome are important, mainly the avoidance of drinking alcohol if one is pregnant or trying to get pregnant. Women can also take folic acid to prevent other birth defects. Heavy drinking should be avoided when birth control is being used, as damage can occur before a mother knows she is pregnant.

Debra Wood, RN

FURTHER READING

Chaudhuri, J. D. "Alcohol and the Developing Fetus—A Review." *Medical Science Monitor* 6.5 (2000): 1031–41. Describes in detail the various clinical features of fetal alcohol syndrome, based on experimental findings in animals.

"Drinking Alcohol During Pregnancy." *March of Dimes.* March of Dimes Foundation. Nov. 2008. Web. 29 Mar. 2012. Covers the risks of drinking while pregnant, fetal alcohol syndrome (FAS) and fetal alcohol spectrum disorder (FASD), and how to prevent alcohol-related birth defects.

Nayak, Raghavendra B., and Pratima Murthy. "Fetal Alcohol Spectrum Disorder." *Indian Pediatrics* 45.12 (2008): 977–83. Covers the prevalence of FASD, its clinical features, its pathogenesis, and its differential diagnosis.

"Prenatal Exposure to Alcohol." *Alcohol Research & Health* 24.1 (2000):32–41. Reviews how prenatal exposure to alcohol can affect the developing brain of a child in terms of intellect, mental health, and social interactions.

Thackray, Helen M., and Cynthia Tifft. "Fetal Alcohol Syndrome." *Pediatrics in Review* 22 (2001):47–55. Reviews the diagnosis, epidemiology, management, prognosis, and prevention of FAS. Stresses the preventability of maternal alcohol abuse.

WEBSITES OF INTEREST

National Organization on Fetal Alcohol Syndrome
http://www.nofas.org

Pregnancy.org
http://www.pregnancy.org/

See also: Alcohol: Short- and long-term effects on the body; Birth defects and alcohol; Pregnancy and alcohol; Women and substance abuse

Flashbacks

CATEGORY: Health issues and physiology

ALSO KNOWN AS: Déjà vu; hallucinogen persisting perception disorder

DEFINITION: Flashbacks are spontaneous, vivid, sensory (usually visual) or emotional re-experiences, often associated with the past use of psychedelic drugs, such as LSD, or with a past severe trauma.

ACUTE FLASHBACKS

Acute flashbacks are sensory or emotional experiences in which a person relives a past event or experience. Most flashbacks are spontaneous and triggered by a particular sight, sound, or smell. The person undergoing a flashback recalls sounds, smells, images, and feelings often more vivid than they were during the original event or experience. Acute flashbacks are unexpected and short lasting. In most cases, they are benign, pleasant, even comforting. In some cases, however, they are disturbing and can lead to psychotic episodes, severe depression, or schizophrenia.

CHRONIC FLASHBACKS

Hallucinogen persisting perception disorder (HPPD) is a chronic condition in which recurring flashbacks interfere with a person's daily life. In mild cases, flashbacks occur infrequently. In extreme cases, flashbacks occur regularly and begin to distort a person's perception of reality. HPPD is associated with the use of hallucinogenic drugs. Flashbacks can occur any time, from a day to a year after taking a hallucinogen.

HPPD flashbacks cause visual disturbances. The person suffering HPPD may see flashes of intense color; auras around people's heads; dancing geometric shapes; images trailing moving objects; positive afterimages, in which objects remain in the brain after they have left the field of vision; or distortions in which objects appear larger or smaller than they are in actuality.

TRAUMA-RELATED FLASHBACKS

Trauma-related, or nondrug-related, flashbacks were first described medically by doctors treating World War I combat veterans. These types of flashbacks are seen not only in combat veterans but also in other people who have experienced severe trauma, such as witnessing violent death. Flashbacks affect many persons with post-traumatic stress disorder.

DRUG-RELATED FLASHBACKS

Hallucinogens are the drugs most associated with flashbacks. LSD (lysergic acid diethylamide, or acid); psilocybin in certain mushrooms; and PCP (phencyclidine, or angel dust), originally an anesthetic, are the main hallucinogenic, or psychedelic, drugs. By far, LSD is the most commonly used and studied psychedelic.

During LSD flashbacks, users experience an abbreviated version of an earlier drug trip, or experience, without taking the drug. Many users report that the flashbacks are even more intense than the original trips. The flashbacks can be isolated or recurring, brief or drawn-out, pleasant or disturbing, or benign or damaging. Because LSD flashbacks usually appear suddenly, without warning, they can disrupt a person's daily routine and lead to unpredictable behavior.

Chronic LSD users are more prone to flashbacks than occasional users. People with an underlying emotional problem and people highly susceptible to suggestion also are more prone to flashbacks than healthy users. Even emotionally healthy people who have used LSD only once or twice can experience flashbacks more than one year after taking the drug.

CAUSES

Scientists do not fully understand the biochemical processes through which hallucinogens affect the mind and body, and they do not know the causes of LSD flashbacks and HPPD. Research suggests several theories for flashbacks.

First, drugs can remain stored in body fat and in some organs—lungs, kidneys, liver, brain—long after they are taken. When the body burns fat during strenuous activity, the drugs might enter the bloodstream, causing the person to experience some of the drug's effects. Second, LSD might have damaged the brain, causing it to send incorrect signals. Third, LSD may have changed the way the brain functions and processes information, which may account for the accompanying visual disturbances. Another theory holds that flashbacks have nothing to do with psychedelic drugs, but that flashbacks are naturally occurring altered states of consciousness that are not understood and, consequently, mislabeled or misinterpreted by drug users.

TRIGGERS

Although scientists do not know the causes of flashbacks, they are reasonably sure of certain triggers. Common flashback triggers include physical or mental stress; physical or mental fatigue; lack of sleep; marijuana or alcohol binging; the use of certain prescription drugs, including antidepressants; and mild sensory deprivation. People sometimes deliberately induce mild sensory deprivation to alter their consciousness or to deeply relax. To induce mild sensory deprivation, a person might focus intensely on one particular sound, blocking out all other background sound, or might stare at a solid-colored surface without blinking for an extended period.

TREATMENT

No specific treatment exists for flashbacks. Doctors have prescribed certain medications, such as anti-seizure drugs, for people suffering HPPD. However, the effectiveness of these drugs remains debatable because of the unpredictability of flashbacks and because of the uncertainty of their cause. Treatment for trauma-related flashbacks generally follows the protocols for treating mild mental disorders: talk therapy or other forms of psychotherapy.

Wendell Anderson

FURTHER READING

Baggott, Matthew, et al. "Abnormal Visual Experiences in Individuals with Histories of Hallucinogen Use: A Web-Based Questionnaire." *Drug and Alcohol Dependence* 114 (2011): 61–67. Print. Report of a study used to record the symptoms of unusual visual disturbances in hallucinogen users and the relationship to drug use of those disturbances.

"Hallucinogens: LSD, Peyote, Psilocybin, and PCP." 18 Feb. 2012. Web. http://www.drugabuse.gov/infofacts/hallucinogens.html. A brief US government informational report on hallucinogens.

Heaton, Robert. "Subject Expectancy and Environmental Factors as Determinants of Psychedelic Flashback Experiences." *Journal of Nervous and Mental Disease* 161 (1975): 157–65. Print. Report of a study that assessed the roles that expectations, suggestions, and automatic responses play in inducing psychedelic flashbacks while people undergo mild sensory deprivation.

Lerner, Arturo, et al. "Flashback and Hallucinogen Persisting Perception Disorder: Clinical Aspects and Pharmacological Treatment Approach." *Israel Journal of Psychiatry and Related Sciences* 39 (2002): 92–99. Print. A clinical discussion of the differences between acute flashbacks and hallucinogen persisting perception disorder.

Myers, Lin, Shelly Watkins, and Thomas Carter. "Flashbacks in Theory and Practice." *Heffter Review of Psychedelic Research* 1 (1998): 51–57. Print. A short review of some of the effects of mind-altering drugs, concluding that flashbacks, generally, are more benign than they are damaging.

WEBSITES OF INTEREST

National Institute on Drug Abuse
http://www.drugabuse.gov

The Partnership at DrugFree.org
http://www.drugfree.org

See also: Brain changes with addiction; Narcotics: Short- and long-term effects on the body; Science of addiction

Food addiction

CATEGORY: Psychological issues and behaviors
ALSO KNOWN AS: Compulsive overeating
DEFINITION: Food addiction is characterized by the uncontrolled desire for and preoccupation with food. Food addicts are driven by obsessive-compulsive thoughts about food and eating despite knowing the negative effects of excess food intake, including obesity. Dependency on food, as with other dependent substances, occurs when destructive behavior persists despite the negative outcomes associated with repeated use.

CAUSES

Cited causes of food addiction include depression, loneliness, stress, hostility, boredom, childhood sexual or emotional trauma, and low self-esteem. Some scientists believe there is a biological explanation for food addiction that involves dopamine, a neurotransmitter in the brain.

Eating is typically a pleasurable experience, but food addiction is caused by a loss of control over the agent of abuse: food. Persons addicted to food may not recognize their addiction or may feel incapable of breaking the cycle of overeating. They have an undeniable preoccupation with food and are compelled to eat large amounts of food. For food addicts, this cycle eventually becomes the norm.

In an episode of binge eating it is not uncommon to consume in excess of 10,000 calories. These calories lead to obesity if not expended, yet it is not accurate to assume that all obese persons are food addicts. Food addicts continue to engage in compulsive overeating even when aware of its destructive effects. Those who eventually want to break the cycle often feel incapable of doing so, while others feel they can stop but continue to postpone doing so.

Eating habits are established during childhood. The development of poor eating habits, including binge eating, may result from ineffective coping mechanisms. Food serves as a barrier or substitute to dealing with emotionally difficult situations and relationships. Poor eating habits continue into adulthood and become ingrained in behavior.

RISK FACTORS

Binge eating disorder is the most common eating disorder in the United States. This and other forms of food addiction most commonly affect girls and women age fourteen to thirty-five years, perhaps because of society's emphasis on appearance and thinness. Both women and men can be food addicts, but women more often seek treatment. Food addiction affects persons of all body types and body weights.

Although food addiction most often results in obesity, not all obese persons are food addicts. Persons with a family history of overeating and persons who lack adequate coping mechanisms for stress, disappointment, and anger may be more at risk for the disorder. Persons with a genetic predisposition for binge eating are enabled by family members, who often allow the cycle to continue through their own actions and expectations.

SYMPTOMS

Binge eaters differ from bulimics in that they do not attempt to rid themselves of the consumed food after a binge. Binge eaters and food addicts spend overwhelming amounts of time planning and fulfilling food "frenzies," which occur publicly or privately. They may eat a reasonable portion in public

Morbid obesity is one manifestation of food addiction. Food addict Michael Hebranko, one of the heaviest people in the world, weighed nearly 1200 lbs at his heaviest. (NY Daily News via Getty Images)

yet overeat in private. They often eat when they are not hungry or when they are emotionally upset. Feelings of low self-worth and guilt often follow binges, yet these binges are followed by planning for the next episode of eating. Each encounter with food can perpetuate the cycle of destruction.

Though the majority of Americans eat more than what the US Department of Agriculture recommends, food addicts far exceed these same recommendations. Food addicts often feel full but may appear ravished, out of control, or on a high, or they may always claim to be hungry.

The insatiable appetite for food is a manifestation of other underlying problems. Food often becomes a substitute for other aspects of life that addicts do not perceive as fulfilled, including personal goals, finances, and personal and professional relationships. Food has filled these voids and temporarily provides the comfort, completeness, or pleasure that the addict so desperately seeks. Often, the addict makes food the object of obsession in attempts to delay or avoid dealing with uncomfortable situations or emotions.

Foods high in sugar and fat are thought to act as triggers for obsessive, compulsive eating. Therefore, withdrawal from these triggers is real and can cause cramps, tremors, and exaggerated feelings of depression and guilt.

SCREENING AND DIAGNOSIS

Screening tools in the form of questionnaires are available to determine if further evaluation may be necessary to aid in the diagnosis of a food addiction. However, these tools rely on self-reports. Food addicts are typically ashamed or in denial, or they feel they are too out of control to modify their behavior. These facts alter self-assessment tools.

Furthermore, food addiction is not a recognized diagnosis in the American Psychiatric Association's *Diagnostic and Statistical Manual of Mental Disorders*, although there is debate as to whether or not it should be included. Binge eating is a symptom of other well-known eating disorders, such as bulimia, yet the two have distinct differences.

Health care providers are in a unique position to help those who may suffer from food addiction. Obesity is often attributed to other medical problems, such as thyroid disorders. However, appropriate laboratory tests can determine if a causal relationship exists. Among other complications, binge eating may lead to depression, suicidal thoughts and tendencies, obesity, heart disease, hypertension, type 2 diabetes, hypercholesterolemia, and joint problems.

TREATMENT AND THERAPY

Other substances of abuse (such as cocaine and heroin) are harmful to the addict regardless of dose. Treatment and therapy for substance addicts involves the elimination of the abused substance, which not only is detrimental to the body but also is completely unnecessary to sustain life.

Treatment and therapy for food addiction is unique because eating is required for human survival. The abused substance cannot be entirely removed from the person's environment. Also noteworthy is that eating is a social behavior. Eating's social aspects make it more challenging to control, given that humans are immersed in activities involving food and eating. Whether compulsive or not, overeating is

more acceptable when others are also engaging in this behavior.

To sever their dependency on food, addicts must first realize and accept that they have a problem and must willingly receive treatment and support from trained professionals, such as physicians, dieticians, and mental health specialists. Food addicts must reclaim power and learn to control food instead of allowing it to control them.

Obesity that often accompanies binge eating and food addiction should also be addressed. Weight loss and psychological counseling may occur separately or simultaneously, but both are required to optimize the addicts' future.

PREVENTION

Unhealthy foods tend to be more accessible and often are more affordable than sound, nutritious foods. Considering the predominance of hectic lifestyles in developed nations, this limited availability of healthy foods creates the perfect opportunity to make poor food choices. Obesity, the second leading cause of preventable death in the United States, can lead to premature death or disability. It is estimated that the United States spends more than $200 billion on obesity-related health care each year.

Behavioral changes are required to prevent and correct binge eating and obesity. Apart from eating healthy and exercising regularly, several other strategies are suggested. Education is necessary to increase awareness of the problem, and educational efforts should be provided worldwide. Ideally, healthier food choices will be made equally available and healthy eating habits will be taught and reinforced. Also, researchers will continue to explore the underlying reasons behind unnecessary eating or overeating.

Virginia C. Muckler, CRNA, MSN, DNP

FURTHER READING

Costin, Carolyn. *The Eating Disorder Sourcebook.* New York: McGraw-Hill, 2006. Provides information on recognizing eating disorders, on available treatments, and more.

Kessler, David A. *The End of Overeating: Taking Control of the Insatiable American Appetite.* New York: Rodale, 2009. Discusses how Americans have lost control over food and examines how they might regain that control.

Power, Michael L., and Jay Schulkin. *The Evolution of Obesity.* Baltimore: Johns Hopkins UP, 2009. Examines the "trend" of obesity, the reasons behind it, and why individualized methods are required to prevent and reverse it.

Wansink, Brian. *Mindless Eating: Why We Eat More Than We Think.* New York: Bantam, 2010. An exploration of "mindless" eating and how humans can be more cognizant of food intake.

WEBSITES OF INTEREST

HealthyPlace.com
http://www.healthyplace.com/eating disorders

Overeaters Anonymous
http://www.oa.org

See also: Behavioral addictions: Overview; Binge drinking; Overeaters Anonymous; Sugar addiction

G

Gamblers Anonymous

CATEGORY: Treatment

DEFINITION: Gamblers Anonymous is a twelve-step recovery program based on Alcoholics Anonymous. There are no requirements for membership other than the desire to stop gambling. The purpose of Gamblers Anonymous is to support personal changes and daily behaviors that lead to a healthy way of living without gambling.

DATE: Established 1957

BACKGROUND

Gamblers Anonymous (GA) was founded in 1957 in Los Angeles by compulsive gamblers Jim and Sam (no last names are used in any of the anonymous programs). GA is a twelve-step program modeled after Alcoholics Anonymous (AA) and based on spiritual principles.

Following the medical model of addiction as an illness, compulsive gambling is seen as a progressive disease and an overactive behavior symptomatic of an emotional disorder related to low self-esteem and self-destruction. People who gamble compulsively want to be seen as generous (big spenders) and special (lucky), thus adding value to their lives. GA uses a list of twenty basic questions concerning gambling behavior; a person who answers "yes" to seven or more of these questions is considered a compulsive gambler.

Like other twelve-step-program meetings, GA meetings focus on the sharing of what it calls "experience, strength, and hope." Personal stories commonly include episodes of theft, deceit, lost relationships, and self-loathing. Members with some degree of abstinence from gambling describe where they are in working the steps of the program and how they have benefitted from the principles of the program, thus supporting and encouraging newer members.

Although GA is based on spiritual principles, interpretation is individual and independent of any religious dogma. Anonymity is paramount to creating a safe environment for revealing, learning, and growing, and members are reminded not to discuss what they have seen or heard in meetings.

In addition to focusing on emotional problems, GA provides resources to assist members with their financial and legal problems. Members are discouraged from filing for bankruptcy or borrowing money to repay debts. By abstaining from gambling, a person will usually have more earned income available to make restitution, leading to the resolution of financial pressures.

Membership in GA does not require dues payment; however, because GA declines funding from outside sources to remain self-supporting and self-governing, free-will contributions are accepted at meetings. Participants are encouraged to donate toward expenses that include meeting room rental and the cost of refreshments.

MISSION AND GOALS

The official literature of GA states that its members' "primary purpose is to stop gambling and to help other compulsive gamblers do the same." The nonprofit organization does not solicit members; persons must seek out the program. GA does not get involved with financial arrangements; members are responsible for paying off their own debts.

In the United States, one in sixty-two adults has a gambling problem. It has been estimated that six million compulsive gamblers in the United States lose $20 billion annually. However, less than 10 percent seek addiction treatment, and the rates of suicide and attempted suicide among gamblers remain high.

As of 2005, more than one thousand GA meetings were held in twenty-three cities in the United States; GA groups also meet in more than ten other countries. Many chapters are in cities where gambling is legal in some form, including cities in California, Nevada, and New Jersey.

Caesars Entertainment Corporation (formerly Harrah's Entertainment), one of the largest companies in the gaming industry, has been promoting responsible gaming since the late 1990s. While Caesars does not specifically endorse GA, it has been publicizing the signs and symptoms of compulsive gambling, thus helping to reduce the stigma.

An outcome study of GA conducted in 1988 found that less than 8 percent of people who begin attending GA meetings continue to work the program and stay away from gambling for more than one year. One reason may be that the stress of accepting responsibility for financial, legal, and employment problems in spite of abstinence from gambling is overwhelming. Another possible reason is that compulsive gambling also may be compounded by substance abuse: When the concomitant addiction is not addressed, relapse into gambling is easily triggered.

In addition, the recovery rate of GA members is still lower than that of AA members because the medical model of compulsive behavior as a progressive illness is less accepted by society for compulsive gamblers than for alcoholics. The medical community has labeled compulsive (pathological) gambling as an impulse control disorder similar to compulsive eating, kleptomania, and hypersexuality. The increasing incidence of compulsive gambling in persons with Parkinson's disease, for example, has prompted research that has discovered an associated dysfunction in the frontal lobe of the brain. Rat models of impulsivity are being developed to identify potential pharmacological targets and treatments for impulse control disorders.

Bethany Thivierge, MPH

FURTHER READING

A Day at a Time: Gamblers Anonymous. Center City, MN: Hazelden, 1994. Daily affirmations and readings to inspire compulsive gamblers to pursue recovery.

Gamblers Anonymous. *GA Red Book: A New Beginning.* 3rd ed. Los Angeles: Author, 1998. Inspirational stories about persons who have successfully worked GA.

---. *Sharing Recovery through Gamblers Anonymous.* Los Angeles: Author, 1984. Handbook for compulsive gamblers following the twelve-step recovery program.

Sanders, Elizabeth. *Gambling Recovery: Working the Gamblers Anonymous Recovery Program.* Tucson, AZ: Wheatmark, 2010. A guidebook to working the twelve steps of the GA recovery program. Includes exercises at the end of each step.

WEBSITES OF INTEREST

Gamblers Anonymous
http://gamblersanonymous.org

National Council on Problem Gambling
http://www.ncpgambling.org

See also: Behavioral addictions: Treatment; Gambling addiction; Group therapy for behavioral addictions; Support groups; Twelve-step programs for addicts

---

Gambling addiction

CATEGORY: Psychological issues and behaviors
ALSO KNOWN AS: Compulsive gambling; disordered gambling; pathological gambling; problem gambling
DEFINITION: Gambling is an activity that involves a degree of risk and an expenditure of money or goods with the hope of an increased return but with the possibility of a total loss. Some people gamble for pleasure, in a nonaddictive fashion, and suffer no ill effects from gaming activities. Others have a problem with gambling, which is manifested by their increasing desire to gamble, even if doing so creates hardships. These hardships include money and debt problems, difficulties at work, relationship problems, and legal sanctions.

CAUSES

Problem gambling has a familial component because parents with a gambling addiction tend to socialize their children into the gambling world. Many of these young people, in turn, develop disordered gambling behavior. Research with twins suggests that there may be a genetic component underlying gambling addiction, which may be reinforced by cultural norms. Cultural components have also been associated with problem gambling, as have games that can be played without a gambling component, such as mahjongg and bingo.

RISK FACTORS

Greater numbers of men typically experience gambling addiction, although women are also at risk. People with gambling addictions often have other mental health issues (including personality disorders, mood disorders, and anxiety ailments) and other addictive disorders, which increase the challenge in determining what effects were caused by gambling and what were caused by other comorbidities. Problem gamblers often consume alcohol, nonprescription drugs, and tobacco in unhealthy ways, which also contributes to dysfunctional behavior.

Prevalence research in much of the developed world suggests that approximately 1 percent of the world's population may experience gambling problems. The disordered gambling figures for adolescents, in locations where such research has been completed, are much higher, with the implication that gambling-addiction numbers will rise as adolescents age and as increasing means to gamble become available. The growth of Internet gambling is particularly challenging for local authorities to license, control, or measure. Particular concerns with these web-based services are that young players are difficult to identify and, thus, cannot be prevented from accessing these sites, even when local laws do not permit children to gamble.

SYMPTOMS

According to the *Diagnostic and Statistical Manual of Mental Disorders* (DSM-IV), published in 1994 by the American Psychiatric Association (APA), pathological gambling is considered to be an impulse-control disorder. A text revision of this manual, called DSM-IV-TR, appeared in 2000, but this revision did not fundamentally change the definition of pathological gambling. The DSM volumes do not use the term *addiction* in connection with gambling, although other APA publications highlight the similarities to substance addictions.

Pathological gambling is defined operationally by the presence of five of ten criteria. The measures focus on the negative effects of gambling for an individual (such as preoccupation, desire to gamble, and difficulty stopping) and the results for gambler's associates (such as lies, illegal actions, and loss of relationships). It is possible that some of the current criteria may be revised in updated editions of the DSM.

A person may manifest a gambling addiction for a period of time and then gain some control over his or her behavior, only to relapse and begin the cycle yet again. This is a common pattern for other addictive

---

South Oaks Gambling Screen

The most common instrument used to screen for probable pathological-gambling behavior is the South Oaks Gambling Screen (SOGS), developed at South Oaks Hospital in New York. South Oaks Hospital is located on Long Island and is well known for work with psychiatric problems and addictions. SOGS has become one of the most-cited screening instruments in psychological research literature involving the measurement of pathological gambling.

Henry Lesieur, a psychiatrist and certified gambling counselor, and Shelia Blume, medical director at South Oaks Hospital, developed the twenty-item SOGS in the late 1980s to produce a scale that would be consistent and quantifiable. In use, responses to the twenty items are recorded, and agreement with five or more items is interpreted as evidence of the presence of pathological gambling. In the years since its development, SOGS has become the most commonly used scale to measure problem gambling in both clinical and nonclinical settings.

---

disorders, and this cyclical progression is challenging for persons in the gambler's family and social circles, and for the individual gambler.

SCREENING AND DIAGNOSIS

Several dozen screening and diagnostic devices have been used to measure problem gambling. Many of these are based on the DSM criteria for measuring pathological gambling. Two commonly used tools are the South Oaks gambling screen and the modified NORC DSM-IV screen for gambling problems.

Depending on the type of gambling screen used, a diagnosis typically places the person along a continuum of increasingly disordered behavior. At the lowest levels are people who have never gambled, although few people fit into this category at most locations, given the ubiquity of gaming activities in contemporary society. People who do not gamble excessively, or who cause no harm to themselves or others, may be described as recreational or social gamblers. Gamblers who display symptoms are termed *compulsive gamblers, disordered gamblers, excessive gamblers, intemperate gamblers, pathological gamblers,* or *problematic gamblers.* The term *gambling addiction* is not used typically in the social or the health sciences, although the general public uses it. Some treatment centers use this nomenclature as it is readily understood by clients.

TREATMENT AND THERAPY

Treatment traditionally involves talk therapy, although more recent approaches have focused on pharmacological interventions, especially antidepressants. A small number of studies have examined the effects of mood stabilizers and opioid antagonists (specifically naltrexone). Some of these medications had unpleasant side effects for the research volunteers, especially the participants in clinical studies using naltrexone.

Many people with gambling addictions have access to psychological and therapeutic treatments, including psychoanalytic approaches, psychodynamic-based treatments, behavioral therapy, cognitive approaches, addiction-based interventions, and self-help. Much of the research on these types of treatment relies on small sample sizes and no control groups, creating challenges in determining what treatments are most successful.

An additional problem for gamblers is that most treatments are offered at a cost, which can pose difficulties for this group given that, typically, gamblers have little money by the time they need treatment. Free Gamblers Anonymous groups are found in most urban centers, which is helpful for this client group.

In addition to methodological problems with studies that make it difficult to identify the most promising treatment options, there are conceptual issues. Generally, people with gambling addictions have been considered to be a fairly uniform subject group by researchers; however, there are many differences within the group in terms of comorbidity and other factors, which might influence treatment outcomes. Also, there are many problem gamblers who manage to recover without treatment; it would be useful to learn more about this group and what factors account for their improvement.

Treatment efforts also have focused on spouses and other family members of problem gamblers. Because the addict also negatively affects others with his or her addiction, therapists have suggested that family members too could benefit from some intervention.

PREVENTION

It can be argued that the best prevention for gambling addiction is to avoid gambling, since most people do not realize their propensity for unhealthy and problematic gambling until they have a problem. Generally, government dollars have been spent on treatment rather than on prevention, but there are strong public health arguments that support greater efforts in prevention.

Susan J. Wurtzburg, PhD

FURTHER READING

Kaminer, Yifrah, and Oscar G. Bukstein, eds. *Adolescent Substance Abuse: Psychiatric Comorbidity and High-Risk Behaviors*. New York: Routledge, 2008. A broad consideration of substance abuse among adolescents.

Ladouceur, Robert, and Stella Lachance. *Overcoming Pathological Gambling: Therapist Guide*. New York: Oxford UP, 2006. Useful therapeutic information, from a cognitive-behavioral therapy approach, for the therapist, gambler, and affected family members.

Nathan, Peter E., and Jack M. Gorman, eds. *A Guide to Treatments That Work*. 3rd ed. New York: Oxford UP, 2007.

National Research Council. *Pathological Gambling: A Critical Review*. Washington, DC: National Academy, 1999. A clearly written overview of gambling technology, problem gambling, its effects on individuals and communities, and treatment.

Newman, Stephen C., and Angus H. Thompson. "The Association between Pathological Gambling and Attempted Suicide: Findings from a National Survey in Canada." *Canadian Journal of Psychiatry* 52.9 (2007): 605–12. Print. Identifies an association, although causality is unproven, between pathological gambling and attempted suicide.

Petry, Nancy M. *Pathological Gambling: Etiology, Comorbidity, and Treatment*. Washington, DC: American Psychological Association, 2005. Examines pathological gambling from a clinical perspective.

Wong, Irene Lai Kuen. "Internet Gambling: A School-Based Survey among Macau Students." *Social Behavior and Personality* 38.3 (2010): 365–72. Print. Discusses two growing gambling populations, each of which deserves more study: Internet gambling and adolescent participation in gambling.

WEBSITES OF INTEREST

A.D.A.M. Medical Encyclopedia
http://www.ncbi.nlm.nih.gov/pubmedhealth/
PMH0002488

HelpGuide.org
http://www.helpguide.org/mental/gambling_
addiction.htm

National Council on Problem Gambling
http://www.ncpgambling.org

See also: Behavioral addictions: Overview; Compulsions; Gamblers Anonymous; Gaming addiction; Impulse control disorders; Men and behavioral addictions

Gaming addiction

CATEGORY: Psychological issues and behaviors

ALSO KNOWN AS: Pathological video game use; problematic video gaming; video game addiction

DEFINITION: Gaming addiction broadly refers to excessive time playing games, particularly video games. The gaming addict displays a pattern of behavioral addiction (similar to gambling addiction) whereby he or she ignores social, relational, and occupational responsibilities and becomes preoccupied with the game. In general, gaming addiction has a greater connection to video games than to board games, card games, or sports.

CAUSES

Gaming addiction can have several underlying causes. In general, gaming addictions are triggered and cultivated when unmet (or partially met) social and psychological needs are fulfilled by playing games. It is believed that one of the primary functions of playing games is to rehearse real-life situations and circumstances to develop behavioral responses without risk. Reasons for excessive gaming can include stress release, relaxation, anxiety reduction, escapism, autonomy, social interaction, and competence and self-esteem development.

Gaming addiction is considered to be similar to pathological gambling in that it begins as rewarding entertainment. Video gaming, like gambling, activates the brain's reward pathways (and releases dopamine). Another consideration in the cause of video game addiction is the genre of the game. The massively multiplayer online role-playing games (MMORPGs) have a significant mixture of social interaction and open-ended game play that has drawn considerable attention for being addictive. The interactive nature of video games and the increasing potential for realistic depictions of environments that allow for complex social interactions increase the potential that they become salient to the person playing the game.

RISK FACTORS

Research indicates that adolescent and young adult males are predominant users of video games and also show a greater incidence of dependency. Gaming can elicit a cognitive and affective state known as flow, which is characterized by a rewarding, focused sense of control and a loss of sense of time and place. Data demonstrate that pathological gaming can persist over time and is not a "phase." Impulsivity, absence of empathy, low social competence, and inability to regulate emotion are correlated with pathological gaming, although experts differ on the causal relationship of these factors in gaming development. (The factors also may be in response to problematic gaming.)

Addictive or pathological patterns of gaming also appear to predict mental health issues such as depression, anxiety, and social phobias; however, the role of these effects in developing and maintaining gaming problems is unclear. Youth who play games more than thirty hours per week are more likely to develop gaming addiction than are those who game less than twenty hours per week. Games such as MMORPGs, which involve identifying with a gaming character or avatar, are much more likely to become addictive. Open-ended games or those that regularly add content to be mastered, also pose a risk of addiction. Persons with a history of addictions (such as substance abuse and gambling) and persons with extended periods of unstructured time are also considered to be at risk for gaming addiction.

SYMPTOMS

Symptoms for gaming addiction, which range from psychological and social to physiological, include excessive game-binging (gaming for more than six to eight hours at a time with little or no interruption), gaming late into the night, a decreased interest in school or occupational pursuits, anger or frustration when denied access to gaming (for example, when the computer server is not working, when access to a game is denied, or when disengaging), being preoccupied with the next gaming session, downplaying the prevalence or effects of video gaming, a distorted perception of time while gaming, difficulty abstaining from gaming, increased spending on games and gaming platforms and equipment, and feelings of distress when unable to play. Relational symptoms include lying to others about how much time is spent gaming, decreased time spent with family and friends, increased preference given to fellow gamers in their social relationships, and decreased interest in marital and romantic relationships.

Other issues, such as sleeping difficulties or a significant change in sleep habits, dry or red eyes, weight gain, lack of attention to personal hygiene and eating habits, and soreness to the back, neck, hands, or wrists (such as carpal tunnel syndrome), can be symptomatic of pathological gaming. The use of substances such as stimulants (for example, caffeine) to aid in staying awake and alert also may indicate a gaming addiction.

SCREENING AND DIAGNOSIS

Several screening tools have been developed to study gaming addiction, none of which are considered gold standards. These screening tools use measures similar to those used to determine pathological gambling and substance abuse. The gaming addiction scale for adolescents is a Likert scale based on a series of questions that deal with what are suggested to be the core components of gaming addiction. These components include salience, tolerance, mood modification, withdrawal, relapse, conflict, and consequences or problems. Another screening tool is the problematic video game playing scale (PVP). The PVP is a nine-item forced-choice questionnaire that addresses issues related to symptoms of excessive gaming.

The *Diagnostic and Statistical Manual of Mental Disorders* (DSM-IV-TR), published in 2000 by the American Psychiatric Association (APA), does not list video game addiction as an addiction. The APA will reconsider this listing if sufficient data warrants its inclusion in future DSM revisions. In general, proponents of including gaming addiction in the DSM are concerned about the medical, educational, and social well-being of children who spend excessive time gaming.

Given that gaming addiction is not in the DSM, it is not considered a clinical diagnosis. Gaming addiction can be considered comorbid, however, with mood disorders, anxiety disorders, or antisocial disorders. Diagnosis of gaming addiction should consider common addiction criteria, such as tolerance, psychological or physiological withdrawal with gaming abstinence, a progressive increase in time spent gaming, and a cycle of abstinence followed by relapse.

TREATMENT AND THERAPY

The most commonly used treatments are individual psychotherapy and psychoeducation about the effects of gaming consumption. Interpersonal therapy and cognitive-behavioral therapy are commonly employed to treat comorbid psychological issues. In addition, support groups (such as Online Gamers Anonymous) and group therapy can be effective in treating gaming addiction, provided these groups consider matters of access, coping skills, relapse prevention, and recovery.

Online communities for recovery also exist, although computer access and availability and the anonymous nature of this interface, which allows for viewing pornography, can be problematic. To address this, the use of filtering software to monitor use and prevent access to sexually explicit material is commonly regarded as a first-order behavioral or environmental intervention. Pharmacotherapy for gaming addiction or related diagnosis (such as anxiety disorder or mood disorder) should also be considered for severe cases.

PREVENTION

Prevention of gaming addictions is best achieved by avoiding the regular use of video games. Refraining from extended play of video games, especially MMORPGs and those that are open-ended, also is recommended.

William M. Struthers, PhD

FURTHER READING

Block, Jerald J. "Issues for DSM-V: Internet Addiction." *American Journal of Psychiatry* 165.3 (2008): 306–7. Print. Professional commentary on how behavioral addictions such as gaming addiction and Internet addiction should be understood in the development of criteria for the DSM-V.

Clark, Neils, and Scott P. Shavaun. *Game Addiction: The Experience and the Effects.* London: McFarland, 2009. Well-written text that addresses the issues of game addiction, symptomology, and development.

Gentile, Douglas A., et al. "Pathological Videogame Use among Youths: A Two-Year Longitudinal Study." *Pediatrics* 127 (2011): 319–29. Print. A longitudinal study that examined video game use among students in Singapore. Article includes measures that examined social competence, educational outcomes, and mental health issues.

Grüsser, S. M., R. Thalemann, and M. Griffiths. "Excessive Computer Game Playing: Evidence for Addiction and Aggression?" *Cyberpsychology and Behavior* 10 (2007): 290–92. Print. Examines gaming addiction and its connection to aggression and impulsive behavior.

Johnson, Nicola F. *The Multiplicities of Internet Addiction: The Misrecognition of Leisure and Learning.* Burlington, VA: Ashgate, 2009. A comprehensive text that frames gaming within the context of recreation and proficiency.

Skoric, M. M., L. L. Teo, and R. L. Neo. "Children and Video Games: Addiction, Engagement, and Scholastic Achievement." *Cyberpsychology and Behavior* 12.5 (2009): 567–72. Print. Examines the effects of video gaming on educational and scholastic performance.

WEBSITES OF INTEREST
American Psychiatric Association
http://www.psych.org

Online Gamers Anonymous
http://www.olganon.org

See also: Behavioral addictions: Overview; Computer addiction; Gambling addiction; Internet addiction; Social media addiction

Gasoline

CATEGORY: Substances

DEFINITION: Gasoline is a volatile, flammable solvent that is inhaled by abusers of the substance. It is generally a mixture of hydrocarbons derived from petroleum and normally used as fuel in internal-combustion engines. Along with other aromatics, gasoline also contains various benzene compounds.

STATUS: Legal

TRANSMISSION ROUTE: Inhalants are readily absorbed through the lungs and then relatively rapidly metabolized in the liver, whereby different cellular mechanisms lead to pharmacologic and toxicologic effects. Gasoline is inhaled through the mouth and nose and into the trachea, often from a saturated cloth.

HISTORY OF USE

Prevalence of lifetime inhalant use among twelfth-graders has ranged between 10.3 percent in 1976 (when first measured) and 18.0 percent, at the 1990 peak. The 2006 rate of 11.1 percent has been stable since 2002. Abuse of gasoline is one of the most widespread inhalant abuses in the United States.

In the late 1990s it was considered that volatile solvent abuse was among the most difficult and refractory to treat. Inhalant abuse intervention has been characterized by the absence of even a rudimentary treatment model. There is no specific agent that can reverse or alleviate acute solvent intoxication, addiction, or the rare cases that present with withdrawal symptoms. Volatile substance abusers do not fit well within existing treatment regimens.

Reports of the abuse of leaded gasoline have been limited to northern Canada, the southwestern United States, and the Australian outback. To fight rampant gasoline sniffing in the outback, the Australian government introduced Opal, a fuel that has been in use since 2006 and has yielded a 70 percent reduction in the abuse of gasoline across outback communities.

EFFECTS AND POTENTIAL RISKS

Gasoline is a depressant that acts directly on the central nervous system. The vapors from gasoline trigger visual hallucinations, changes in consciousness, euphoria, and nystagmus. The abuser experiences a subconscious state, wherein he or she dreams while aware of his or her surroundings. This euphoric effect has a short duration and compels the user to inhale again. Adverse effects include dizziness, aggressiveness, impaired judgment, weakness, and tremors.

Long-term effects manifest as neurological and cognitive abnormalities in the absence of acute toxic brain diseases, and also include peripheral neuropathies and bone marrow damage. Chronic, heavy abuse of leaded gasoline results in an encephalopathy, cerebellar and corticospinal symptoms and signs, dementia, mental status alterations, and persistent organic psychosis. Chronic abuse also can lead to sudden death.

Stephanie Eckenrode, BA, LLB

FURTHER READING

Doweiko, Harold E. *Concepts of Chemical Dependency.* 8th ed. Belmont, CA: Brooks, 2012.

Fitzhugh, Karla. *Inhalants.* Chicago: Raintree, 2004.

Miller, Norman S., and Mark S. Gold. *Addictive Disorders in Medical Populations.* Hoboken, NJ: Wiley, 2010.

WEBSITES OF INTEREST

Aboriginal Drug and Alcohol Council
http://www.adac.org.au

National Institute on Drug Abuse
http://www.drugabuse.gov

Teens Health
http://kidshealth.org/teen/drug_alcohol/drugs/inhalants.html

See also: Aerosols; Depressants abuse; Household chemicals of abuse; Inhalants abuse; Solvents

Gateway drugs

CATEGORY: Substances

ALSO KNOWN AS: Gateway hypothesis; gateway theory

DEFINITION: Gateway drugs, especially marijuana but also tobacco and alcohol, are drugs thought to lead to the use of other (typically illegal) drugs. The drugs used initially are considered less harmful. The gateway is considered a "tunnel" that leads directly from simple drug use to hard drug use. Another view considers the gateway as a "funnel" that allows (some) people to move more easily to hard drugs. The term *gateway drugs* is thought to have been coined by Robert DuPont, the first director of the National Institute on Drug Abuse.

There is some debate as to whether gateway drugs actually lead to the use of more harmful drugs of abuse.

STATUS: Tobacco and alcohol are legal in the United States; marijuana is illegal except by prescription in some US states. Gateway drugs are governed by certain regulations covering sales, conditions of use, and the minimum age for buying and using.

CLASSIFICATION: Marijuana is a schedule I narcotic; tobacco and alcohol are uncontrolled substances

SOURCE: Tobacco comes from leaves of seventy different species of the *Nicotiana* plant; consumable alcohol is known as ethanol; marijuana comes from the hemp plant *Cannabis sativa*

TRANSMISSION ROUTE: Tobacco is smoked, chewed, snuffed, and dipped; alcohol is ingested; marijuana is smoked and ingested

HISTORY OF USE

Chemicals derived from *Nicotiana* plants were used for medicinal purposes in the sixteenth century. Cigarettes were first made in the 1830s and were popular in the United States by the 1860s. By the 1950s studies showed that tobacco was hazardous to one's health and, in 1965, cigarette advertising in the United States had to include a warning of tobacco's health hazards.

Alcohol, specifically wine, was used as early as 5000 BCE. Alcohol use became rampant and problematic in the United States before 1920, leading to Prohibition. With Prohibition came moonshine, speakeasies, and even more problems, leading to the law's repeal in 1933. Alcohol sales and use were again legal in the United States.

Marijuana, which is often referred to as cannabis or THC (delta 9 tetrahydrocannabinol, its main chemical ingredient), was used for medicinal purposes as early as 3000 BCE and as an intoxicant by 1000 BCE. Marijuana use was illegal in the United States by 1920. It is now legal in certain US states for medicinal purposes and can be obtained by prescription.

One study (2001) found that the progression from alcohol and tobacco use to marijuana and harder drugs was first seen in the United States in people born after World War II, that it peaked in the baby boomers born in the 1960s, and that is has since shown a decline, indicating less of a gateway effect than in the past. Studies do indicate, however, that the younger a person begins smoking or drinking, the more likely he or she will progress to hard drugs.

Smokeless Tobacco

Smokeless tobacco, or snuff, is finely ground or cut tobacco that is sold in three formats: dry, moist, and sachet. Dry snuff is powdered and inhaled through the nose. Moist snuff, also called dipping tobacco, is sold in tins for oral use; sachet snuff is moist snuff packaged in small pouches similar to teabags. Swedish snuff, called snus, is pasteurized rather than fermented and induces less salivation in its users than does moist snuff.

Smokeless tobacco products regained popularity in the 1970s as people learned the dangers of smoking cigarettes and mistakenly thought that smokeless tobacco was a safe alternative to satisfy their nicotine addiction. In the United States in 2009, smokeless tobacco users were 3.5 percent of all adults (7 percent of adult men), 6.1 percent of all high school students (11 percent of males), and 2.6 percent of all middle school students (4.1 percent of males).

EFFECTS AND POTENTIAL RISKS

Smoking causes dry mouth and thirst, after an initial increase in salivation. A sore throat and cough often follows dry mouth. Shortly after beginning the use of tobacco, the body will start to have problems with red-blood-cell production, which is often accompanied by cardiac arrhythmias. Long-term effects of smoking include cardiac problems, stroke, and lung problems, including cancer. According to most research, smoking, over time, affects almost every system in the body.

Alcohol is a sedative and a psychoactive drug, and it affects cells in the cerebral cortex, leading to disinhibition. As such, it tends to impair judgment. Driving under the influence of alcohol (above the legal limit) is illegal, and it is responsible for thousands of motor vehicle accidents and vehicle-related deaths in the United States each year. Long-term alcohol use can lead to liver and pancreatic problems, to cancer of the throat and esophagus, and to brain damage (such as Wernicke-Korsakoff syndrome).

Short-term effects of marijuana use can include disorders of perception, learning, memory, cognition, and coordination, and to symptoms of anxiety. While long-term effects of marijuana are unclear, it is thought that the drug may affect the immune system and the respiratory system, and that it can cause some forms of cancer. Marijuana use also can potentially lead to the use of harder, more dangerous drugs (in accordance with gateway theory).

Robin Kamienny Montvilo, PhD

FURTHER READING

DuPont, Robert L. *Getting Tough on Gateway Drugs: A Guide for the Family.* Washington, DC: American Psychiatric Association, 1984. A classic in the field of gateway drugs. The author discusses the meaning and types of gateway drugs, and examines how parents and communities can prevent the use of gateway drugs by adolescents and young adults.

Golub, Andrew, and Bruce D. Johnson. "Variation in Youthful Risks of Progression from Alcohol and Tobacco to Marijuana and Hard Drugs across Generations." *American Journal of Public Health* 91 (2001): 225–32. Print. Focuses on the likelihood of progression from tobacco or alcohol to marijuana and to harder drugs.

Kandel, Denise B. *Stages and Pathways of Drug Involvement: Examining the Gateway Hypothesis.* New York: Cambridge UP, 2002. This research-based volume looks at different explanations of the gateway hypothesis.

WEBSITES OF INTEREST

DrugWarFacts.org
http://www.drugwarfacts.org/cms/Gateway_Theory

National Institute on Drug Abuse
http://www/drugabuse.gov

See also: Marijuana; Teens/young adults and alcohol abuse; Teens/young adults and drug abuse; Teens/young adults and smoking

Gender and addiction

CATEGORY: Social issues

DEFINITION: Though it is unclear whether men or women are more susceptible to alcohol or drug addiction based on gender-specific biological and environmental factors, data suggest that men and women often become addicted for different reasons. Diagnosis and successful addiction treatment are also gender-sensitive.

BIOLOGICAL DIFFERENCES

Women are generally smaller than men in physical stature and cannot absorb as high a volume of alcohol and drugs as men before becoming intoxicated. Despite this common understanding, women, especially young women, often keep up with their male peers in drinking and consequently sustain a higher level of intoxication.

Scientists learned in a 1999 study that women metabolize alcohol differently than men, leaving them with higher concentrations of alcohol lingering in their blood and a higher susceptibility to cirrhosis of the liver and brain damage. This finding explains how the genders process substances differently, but it does not answer the question of whether gender plays a role in becoming substance dependent.

In a 2010 article in the *American Journal of Public Health*, researchers discussed their study of gender differences in medical conditions and psychiatric and substance-abuse disorders among inhabitants in jails in the United States. The researchers reported that, although gender differences play into the presence of chronic medical and psychiatric conditions, gender differences do not seem to account for the prevalence of substance abuse.

In a 2007 article in *Psychiatric Times*, neuroscience professor Sudie E. Back refuted assertions that rates of substance abuse among men and women were linked to gender differences. She said that for decades there simply has been more data on addiction among men. Male substance abuse is more visible, and through institutions like prisons and the US Department of Veterans Affairs, more data are available. Less research has been done on women but, according to the little that has been done, the prevalence of substance abuse disorders has less to do with gender and more to do with experiences in childhood and adolescence, with mental health, and with stresses in life. To the extent that gender plays a role in understanding substance abuse, the significance is in how addicts are diagnosed and rehabilitated.

Though chemical differences in males and females, such as the presence of testosterone, progesterone, and estrogen, can account for urges to ingest substances and the intensity of their effects, the onset of substance abuse may have much less to do

with gender and more to do with temperament and life experience. When reporting on drivers to ingest substances, females most often attributed an internal emotional stress factor, while men linked an external cue. Also, fewer women than men are likely to enter a substance-abuse treatment program; women seek counseling from a mental health or primary care provider.

ENVIRONMENTAL DIFFERENCES

In a 2006 article in *Canadian Psychology*, researchers presented the results of their review of fifteen studies that analyzed whether any variation in how males and females cope with post-traumatic stress disorder (PTSD) accounts for different rates of substance abuse between the genders. The researchers found that males and females experiencing PTSD were equally at risk for substance-abuse disorders and that, regardless of gender, specialists must be cognizant of the risk for any person with PTSD in engaging in behaviors that can lead to addiction.

According to a 2007 study at the University of Minnesota, women are more inclined to "internalize drinking problems than [are] men." Women tend to hide alcoholism, while men tend to act it out. The study concluded that intervention reaches men more readily than it does women, and suggested that women develop alcoholism later in life than men and spiral into alcohol addiction more rapidly. Data pointed to a stigma related to alcoholism for women that is much less apparent for men. Gretchen Cook reported in a 2003 *Women's E-News* article that,

> Recovery experts often note that while drinking has traditionally almost been a rite of passage for men, it has been considered "unladylike," and that female alcoholics suffered harsher judgments from themselves and society. It's only in the past decade that the institute has added women to their subject pools.

Perhaps entry into alcohol and drug dependence could be reduced simply through raising awareness in how gender-sensitive norms can facilitate behavior leading to addiction. In a 2009 article in the *Journal of Studies on Alcohol and Drugs*, researchers investigated whether social contexts of consuming alcohol influenced college males and females differently in the automatic alcohol associations made in the brain. The researchers found that gender-sensitive social cues trigger a desire to drink. As far as gender differences, researchers found a high general social approval of male heavy drinking and much lower approval for females engaging in heavy drinking. Given the social cognition linked to drinking, the study concluded, this higher social tolerance of males drinking in college creates a higher risk for males developing a lifestyle of heavy drinking.

GENDER-SPECIFIC TREATMENT

In 2007, researchers at the University of North Carolina at Wilmington implemented and then analyzed the results of gender-centric educational initiatives to reduce alcoholism. The project began with awareness-raising events such as small-group meetings to discuss norms associated with gender and to examine how alcohol may be used to enhance or reduce those norms. The project also featured discussions to build cross-gender empathy and understanding of how alcoholism harms individuals of the opposite gender, and it featured studies into gender-based advertising for alcohol products and bars. Both professional- and peer-intervention measures were integrated into the project.

The researchers discovered that, though professional intervention was most effective in reducing gender-based expectations with drinking, peer intervention was much more effective in directly reducing drinking behavior. This suggests that once a person understands the gender-based norms he or she is measuring themselves and others against, that person can process how alcohol consumption plays into those expectations and resist falling into a gender trap of alcoholism.

Melissa Walsh

FURTHER READING

Back, Sudie E. "Substance Abuse in Women: Does Gender Matter?" *Psychiatric Times*, 1 Jan. 2007, 48.

Binswanger, Ingrid A., et al. "Gender Differences in Chronic Medical, Psychiatric, and Substance-Dependence Disorders among Jail Inmates." *American Journal of Public Health* 100.3 (2010): 476–82. Print.

Condor, Bob. "Gender Differences about Alcohol Are Sobering." *Seattle Post-Intelligencer*, 30 Apr. 2007, D1. Print.

Farrington, Elizabeth Leigh. "Using Gender-Based Initiatives to Reduce Campus Drinking." *Women in Higher Education* 16.5 (2007): 22. Print.

Lindgren, Kristen P., et al. "Automatic Alcohol Associations: Gender Differences and the Malleability of Alcohol Associations Following Exposure to a Dating Scenario." *Journal of Studies on Alcohol and Drugs* 70 (2009): 583. Print.

Stewart, Sherry, et al. "Are Gender Differences in Post-Traumatic Stress Disorder Rates Attenuated in Substance Use Disorder Patients?" *Canadian Psychology* 47.2 (2006): 110–24. Print.

WEBSITES OF INTEREST

American Council for Drug Education
http://www.acde.org

Center for Substance Abuse Treatment
http://www.samhsa.gov

See also: Age and addiction; Elderly and addictions; Men and behavioral addictions; Men and smoking; Men and substance abuse; Socioeconomic status and addiction; Suicide and addiction; Women and behavioral addictions; Women and smoking; Women and substance abuse

Genetics and substance abuse

CATEGORY: Health issues and physiology

DEFINITION: Substance abuse is broadly defined as the inappropriate or illegal use of substances, either drugs or alcohol, which may result in legal and safety issues. While historically such abuse has been considered the result of either moral or behavioral failings, evidence has accumulated that suggests some forms of abuse may be caused or exacerbated by genetic factors.

GENETIC EVIDENCE

The response of the human body to specific chemicals has long been known to have a genetic basis. In general, these effects can be considered to fall within two themes: in the presence of receptors on the cell surface that can be activated following the binding of a chemical and in the regulation of a metabolic pathway through the mechanism of chemical activation of specific enzymes. This is particularly true when applied to brain chemistry.

The functions of specific regions within the brain, including those that could include pleasure centers or those that control other forms of reactions to specific drugs, are subject to hereditary control. The expression of cell receptors and the production of enzymes that control pathways in the brain, each regulating the ability to respond to drugs, have an underlying genetic control.

Historically, the treatment of substance abuse, including that involving alcohol and drug addictions (both legal and illegal) has centered primarily on the moral or behavioral aspects of the problem. Treatment once believed that the addicted person has made a choice, first to use the substance and then to continue its use until addiction removes any personal control. While there is certainly a behavioral component to this argument, the initial use of the substance is certainly a voluntary action; increasing evidence suggests a genetic predisposition to the addiction that may follow.

Most historical studies that have attempted to establish a genetic basis for addiction have utilized what were called twin studies. These studies involve a comparison between twins, ideally living separate lives so as to avoid environmental influences in the study, in which the prevalence of substance abuse and addiction may be compared. Numerous epidemiological studies of twins have shown a significantly increased level of risk, even in the absence of environmental influences: If one twin developed an addiction, the other also demonstrated a significantly higher level of risk of doing so.

Adoption studies have reinforced the conclusions reached through twin studies. If a birth parent exhibited problems in the use of alcohol, then the child demonstrated significantly increased risk in exhibiting the same behaviors. However, if the child was adopted and thus did not share genetic features with the adoptive parent, the child exhibited no increased risk. Similar results also were found in cases of drug addiction.

The development of biochemical methods for studying brain chemistry and regulation of pleasure pathways has provided a means to investigate addiction at the molecular level. Studies have shown that some forms of addiction may be exacerbated by the expression of specific genes or pathways in the brain, which are controlled by the drugs in question. Another challenge in attempting to sort out what genes might be involved in addiction is that, often, no single gene is always involved. Rather, the interaction of a variety of genes, and in some cases metabolic pathways in the brain, contributes to addiction.

GENETICS OF ALCOHOL ADDICTION

Though the evidence is largely anecdotal, there is some indication that alcoholism may at some level be subject to genetic factors. It is known that alcoholism frequently repeats through family generations. As noted, studies of twins and comparisons between adoptive or biological children, in which a parent exhibits alcohol problems, support the argument for a genetic component to alcohol addiction. It remains unclear if alcoholism is primarily genetic or whether tendencies to addiction reflect the environment in which the person is raised. Experts agree that alcoholism may result from a combination of factors.

Supporting the argument that genetics may play a role in alcoholism was the discovery of a genetic link between a specific gene that encodes alcohol addiction and a molecule called the cyclic AMP responsive element binding protein (CREB). The CREB gene plays a role in the regulation of brain function during development; in particular, it has an association with the portion of the brain known as the amygdala. The scientific evidence for the role of the CREB gene supports what is known about the function of the amygdala, the region in the central brain that determines a portion of the body's response to emotional disorders and stress.

Persons subject to alcoholism frequently have abnormal reactions to stress, a problem that may be ameliorated by alcohol. Depression and other abnormal responses to stress seem to reflect abnormalities in signaling patterns and gene expression within the amygdala. These abnormalities in turn seem to be caused by improper CREB protein regulation. Alcohol appears to reverse this process. In the presence of increased levels of alcohol, the CREB protein becomes functional, activates the signals within the amygdala, and alleviates the effects of stress. Reduced levels of the CREB protein in the amygdala exacerbates the anxiety levels of the subject, which then increases the subject's desire (and need) for alcohol.

While most of these studies have been carried out in nonhuman animals, many of the identical physiological changes that occur in the brains of test animals, such as rats and mice, have identical counterparts in the human brain and its response to alcohol. Among the questions that should be addressed is whether the need for alcohol forms the basis for its addiction or whether the long-term abuse of alcohol results in the changes found within the brain.

GENETICS AND STIMULANTS

Stimulants such as cocaine, amphetamines (for example, methylene-dioxymethamphetamine, or ecstasy), and even tobacco and caffeine, seem to have in common the ability to utilize common mechanisms within the brain. One mechanism in particular on which addiction studies have focused is the regulation of certain neurotransmitters, chemicals released by neurons in the brain that act to stimulate nerve endings on adjacent nerve cells.

Neurotransmitters such as dopamine, long known for its association with Parkinson's disease, control neural pathways in the portion of the brain known as the striatum, the portion of the forebrain that controls emotions such as pleasure and certain behaviors. Stimulants such as cocaine or amphetamines increase the level of dopamine—cocaine by inhibiting the reuptake of dopamine and amphetamines by increasing their release. Regardless of their mechanism, stimulants cause drug-induced highs.

Studies in mice that have attempted to identify those genes that are particularly sensitive to the presence of stimulants have identified one gene that seems to play a common role: the post-synaptic density-95 (PSD-95) gene. The product of PSD-95 appears to function in regulating the structure of the receptor that serves as the target for dopamine in the pleasure centers of the striatum. Reduced levels of the PSD-95 protein in mice led to an increased response following exposure to cocaine. The sensitivity of mice to cocaine appears to correlate with the level of the PSD-95 protein.

Because most stimulants, including tobacco and alcohol, likewise act in part by increasing the level of dopamine within the striatum, the PSD-95 protein may represent a common feature in the response to the presence of these drugs. Genetic variation in the activity of the PSD-95 gene may be one of the determining factors in both the behavioral response in using stimulants and in the likelihood the user may ultimately become addicted.

Richard Adler, PhD

FURTHER READING

Kendler, Kenneth, and Carol Prescott. *Genes, Environment, and Psychopathology: Understanding the Causes of Psychiatric and Substance Use Disorders.* New York: Guilford, 2007. Relying extensively on twin studies, the authors make the case for genetic influences in many psychiatric disorders, including those of substance abuse. Much of the text deals with epidemiological studies, not molecular mechanisms of addiction.

Kipper, David, and Steven Whitney. *The Addiction Solution: Unraveling the Mysteries of Addiction through Cutting-Edge Brain Science.* New York: Rodale, 2010. The authors address the role of brain chemistry with current applications of neurobiology in an attempt to understand addiction. The authors contend that for treatment of addiction, both the primary cause—brain chemistry—and behavioral changes must be addressed.

Miller, William, and Kathleen Carroll. *Rethinking Substance Abuse.* New York: Guilford, 2006. The authors summarize the contemporary understanding of the role played both by genetics and the environment in development of substance addiction.

Wand, Gary. "The Anxious Amygdala: CREB Signaling and Predisposition to Anxiety and Alcoholism." *Journal of Clinical Investigation* 115 (2005): 2697–99. Print. Report and literature review of the relationship between specific genes and anxiety and alcoholic disorders.

WEBSITES OF INTEREST

Center for Genetic Studies, National Institute on Drug Abuse
http://drugabuse.gov/about/organization/genetics/FAQ_CTN

"Genetic Influences in Drug Abuse." American College of Neuropsychopharmacology
http://www.acnp.org/g4/GN401000174/CH170.html

See also: Adult children of alcoholics; Families and substance abuse; Science of addiction; Substance abuse; Suicide and addiction

GHB

CATEGORY: Substances

ALSO KNOWN AS: Cherry meth; easy lay; fantasy; g; gamma-oh; Georgia home boy; great hormones at bedtime; grievous bodily harm; g-riffick; goop; 4-hydroxybutanoic acid; jib; liquid e; liquid ecstasy; liquid g; liquid x; mils; organic quaalude; salty water; scoop; sleep; sleep-500; sodium oxybate; vita-g; Xyrem

DEFINITION: GHB is a naturally occurring substance that resembles the neurotransmitter and energy metabolism regulator gamma-aminobutyric acid (GABA). GHB generally acts as an intoxicant and as a depressant of the central nervous system. Medically, GHB is used in general anesthesia and to treat narcolepsy, insomnia, clinical depression, and alcoholism. GHB is used illicitly as an intoxicant, euphoriant, "date rape" drug, and body-building supplement.

STATUS: Illegal in the United States, Australia, New Zealand, Canada, and most of Europe

CLASSIFICATION: Schedule I controlled substance; Xylem, the pharmacological preparation of GHB, is a schedule III controlled substance

SOURCE: Naturally occurs in the human central nervous system and in nonhuman animals, wine, beer, and small citrus fruits. Drug suppliers can make GHB easily and cheaply from sodium hydroxide, which is found in drain cleaners and in gamma-hydroxybutyrolactone, a readily available industrial solvent. GHB synthesis kits are available for purchase on the Internet.

TRANSMISSION ROUTE: Ingested as a white powder or a colorless liquid

HISTORY OF USE

Russian chemist Alexander Mikhaylovich Zaytsev first reported the synthesis of GHB (gamma-hydroxybutyric acid) in 1874. French scientist Henri Laborit performed some of the first GHB research in the 1960s. In the late 1980s and 1990s, GHB was sold over-the-counter in the United States as a body-building supplement and sleep aid. Increased incidents of GHB intoxication moved the US Centers for Disease Control and Prevention and the US Food and Drug Administration (FDA) to issue warnings regarding its potential dangers.

In the late 1990s, GHB was used in several highly publicized drug-facilitated cases of sexual assault. Because of this, people labeled GHB a "date rape" drug. Because illicit formulations of GHB are commonly colorless, odorless liquids, surreptitious addition of GHB to drinks in bars and clubs is difficult to detect. Also, several GHB side effects (sedation, euphoria, decreased inhibitions, enhanced sex drive, and mild amnesia) enhance its effectiveness in drug-facilitated sexual assaults. In 2000, the FDA placed Xyrem on the list of schedule III controlled substances and listed nonmedical GHB as a schedule I controlled substance.

Also during the 1990s, GHB became widely used as a club drug. Club or party drugs are used by people who attend nightclubs, raves, and circuit parties. These drugs include methamphetamine, 3,4-methylenedioxymethamphetamine (MDMA, or ecstasy), lysergic acid diethylamide (LSD, or acid), and ketamine (special K). GHB, ecstasy, and ketamine are

GHB is also known as:

Bedtime Scoop	G-Juice	Liquid Ecstasy
Cherry Meth	Gook	Liquid X
Easy Lay	Goop	PM
Energy Drink	Great Hormones	Sat Water
G	Grievous Bodily Harm	Soap
Gamma 10	(GHB)	Somatomax
Georgia Hone Boy	Liquid E	Vita-G

Source: Office on Women's Health in the Department of Health and Human Services

frequently used together, also in combination with alcohol, marijuana, and amphetamines.

The popularity of GHB as a club drug is largely due to the ease of its synthesis and its low cost. GHB is quite popular in dance clubs for persons younger than age twenty-one years, where alcohol is not sold; however, the youth in these clubs can drink water or other nonalcoholic beverages spiked with GHB. Club drugs related to GHB include gamma-butyrolactone (GBL) and 1,4-butanediol, both of which are liquids and found in paint strippers and varnish thinners. These chemicals are known as GHB "prodrugs" because they are converted to GHB by the body after ingestion.

EFFECTS AND POTENTIAL RISKS

In the brain, cells called neurons generate and propagate nerve impulses. GHB exerts its effects by binding to specific receptors on the surfaces of neurons. GHB binds to the $GABA_B$ and GHB receptors. When it binds the $GABA_B$ receptor, GHB causes sedation. Conversely, binding of the GHB receptor increases the release of the neurotransmitter glutamate, which is the principal excitatory neurotransmitter in the brain. Simultaneous activation of both the GHB and $GABA_B$ receptors at low GHB concentrations induces the release of the neurotransmitter dopamine in the ventral tegmental area (VTA). The VTA is one of the key reward regions of the brain, and dopamine release in the VTA produces a feeling of pleasure or satisfaction and is the reason for the addictive nature of GHB.

GHB induces sleep by binding $GABA_B$ receptors in the thalamo-cortical loop, which regulates sleep and arousal. Because GHB binds to the GHB receptor much more tightly than the $GABA_B$ receptor, decreases in the bodily concentration of GHB increase its stimulatory effects relative to its sedative effects. This causes people who have taken GHB to awaken abruptly after a particular time.

The effects of GHB are dose related. At 10 milligrams per kilogram body weight (mg/kg), GHB depresses the central nervous system and causes a general sense of calm and relaxation. GHB doses of 20 to 30 mg/kg induce sleep for two to three hours. A dose of 40 to 50 mg/kg induces even longer periods of sleep, but also causes amnesia, nausea and vomiting, dizziness, weakness, loss of peripheral vision,

confusion, hallucinations, agitation, and low heart rate (bradycardia). Doses above 50 mg/kg cause seizures, unconsciousness, respiratory depression, and coma. GHB effects appear within fifteen minutes of oral ingestion, but the acute symptoms cease after seven hours.

Combining GHB with alcohol increases depression of breathing and can cause death. GHB is rather addictive, and long-term use can cause depression and suicidal tendencies. From 1995 to 2005 in the United Kingdom, the United States, and Canada, there were 226 GHB-related deaths.

Michael A. Buratovich PhD

FURTHER READING

Abadinsky, Howard. *Drug Use and Abuse: A Comprehensive Introduction.* 7th ed. Florence, KY: Wadsworth, 2010. A readable, but erudite, interdisciplinary introduction to drug abuse by a criminal justice academic who spent many years as a parole officer and inspector for the Cook County Sheriff's Office.

Gahlinger, Paul. *Illegal Drugs: A Complete Guide to Their History, Chemistry, Use, and Abuse.* New York: Plume, 2003. An informative compendium on the chemical, medical, and historical aspects of illegal drugs by a physician who is also a certified substance-abuse review officer.

Grim, Ryan. *This Is Your Country on Drugs: The Secret History of Getting High in America.* Hoboken, NJ: Wiley, 2010. A journalist examines illegal drugs, drug supply lines, the culture of drug abuse and drug abusers, the political and economic ramifications of drug abuse, and the problems facing drug enforcement in the United States.

Kuhn, Cynthia, Scott Swartzwelder, and Wilkie Wilson. *Buzzed: The Straight Facts about the Most Used and Abused Drugs from Alcohol to Ecstasy.* 3rd ed. New York: W. W. Norton, 2008. A popular and useful guide to illegal drugs by three professors from Duke University Medical Center.

WEBSITES OF INTEREST

National Institute on Drug Abuse
http://www.drugabuse.gov/infofacts/clubdrugs.html

Project GHB
http://www.projectghb.org

US Drug Enforcement Administration
http://www.justice.gov/dea/concern/ghb.html

See also: Anesthesia abuse; Club drugs; Date rape drugs; Depressants abuse

Government warnings

CATEGORY: Diagnosis and prevention
ALSO KNOWN AS: Health warning labels; US surgeon general warnings; warning labels
DEFINITION: Health warning labels issued by the US government are evidence-based statements of risk associated with the general use of legal substances such as alcohol and tobacco and with the misuse of prescription drugs or other substances of abuse. Warnings are required on products themselves and on related advertisements as a part of public health campaigns. Government warnings are frequently issued through the Office of the Surgeon General as part of the US Department of Health and Human Services.

PURPOSE AND FUNCTIONS

The primary function of a government warning is to increase public knowledge about unsafe use of substances, particularly tobacco and alcohol products that can be purchased without a prescription by adults who have proper identification. These health warnings attempt to minimize dangerous substance activity by discouraging drug misuse and overuse. Warning label goals include the complete cessation of tobacco use and total abstinence from alcohol during any stage of pregnancy.

The first alcohol and tobacco warning labels developed as a result of acts by the US Congress. The Alcoholic Beverage Labeling Act of 1988 was passed in response to birth defects connected with alcohol use during pregnancy. Similarly, tobacco use has been tracked by the Office of the Surgeon General (OSG) since the 1920s. In the 1960s, tobacco use became a public health issue that resulted in government warnings because of early reports about the health damage to nonsmokers from exposure to secondhand smoke.

Government warning labels on alcohol and tobacco are intended to call separate attention to multiple risks. Label text may be decided by the OSG but enforcement is often implemented by affiliate agencies, such as the Alcohol and Tobacco Tax and Trade Bureau (TTB). One goal of the TTB is to protect public safety through oversight of federal laws about alcohol and tobacco product-labeling.

LABEL FORMATS

Product health warnings require text introductions of "Warning" or "Government Warning" in bold type on every package. To ensure visibility, all statements must be placed prominently on high-contrast sections of the package label, separate from other information.

Warning texts expand as evidence builds on the dangers of alcohol and tobacco use. Since 1989, the US government has mandated two warnings on alcoholic products. These warnings are "According to the Surgeon General, women should not drink alcoholic beverages during pregnancy because of the risk of birth defects" and "Consumption of alcoholic beverages impairs your ability to drive a car or operate machinery, and may cause health problems."

In 2001, horizontal boxed text and conspicuous statements with surrounding white space were encouraged on beverage labels to increase attention to the warnings. In 2005, the OSG supplemented alcohol label warnings with an online news advisory to recommend total avoidance of any amount of alcohol during all stages of pregnancy, as evidenced by expanded research on fetal alcohol syndrome disorders.

Like alcohol warnings, tobacco warnings were initiated in Congress and adapted in time. Government warnings about tobacco changed little since the 1960s, until the statements were strengthened by the US Food and Drug Administration in response to the Family Smoking Prevention and Tobacco Control Act of 2009. The new warnings, effective September 2012, comprise nine separate statements, a resource site (1-800-QUIT-NOW), and images of harmful tobacco effects on the body. Each warning contains one statement, one image, and the toll-free quit hotline.

The plain-language warnings, identified through literature review and public commentary, are as follows: cigarettes are addictive, tobacco smoke can harm your children, cigarettes cause fatal lung disease, cigarettes cause cancer, cigarettes cause strokes and heart disease, smoking during pregnancy can harm your baby, smoking can kill you, tobacco smoke causes fatal lung disease in nonsmokers, and quitting smoking now greatly reduces serious risks to your health. These changes, especially the new graphics, are negative reminders to heighten risk awareness, increase quit rates, and empower youth to avoid smoking.

LABEL EFFICACY

Government warnings are updated infrequently, and public awareness of the standard labeling may introduce complacency. Government warnings on alcohol and tobacco are acknowledged by consumers, but effects on behavior are variable. For example, in the Alcoholic Beverage Label Evaluation survey from 1989 to 1995 (which surveyed persons in the Midwest), alcohol risks were noted by participants, but no significant changes in alcohol use resulted. Positive changes, such as lower rates of alcohol use while driving, appeared to level off after approximately three years. Thus, although awareness appears commonplace, the warnings

In this handout from the Food and Drug Administration (FDA), a new FDA warning label for a cigarette packs is seen. (Getty Images)

do not appear to affect any long-term behavioral change.

Strategies for calling greater attention to the health risks include point-of-purchase notices, graphic images to supplement text labels, and even more prominent placement of warnings on the products. For example, cigarette products now require warning label placement on the top half of the front and back of each package or advertisement to pointedly display potential consequences of use. The use of graphics to transmit any health information is known to increase knowledge of risks, increase quit rates, and prevent new smokers.

Even greater distribution of warnings is available through state-regulated point-of-purchase programs, which require establishments that sell alcohol and tobacco to display warning signs at checkouts. For example, businesses that sell liquor must post the government warning about pregnancy and birth defect risks, and tobacco warning signs must be present where the tobacco products are sold.

Nicole M. Van Hoey, PharmD

FURTHER READING

Centers for Disease Control and Prevention. *How Tobacco Smoke Causes Disease: The Biology and Behavioral Basis for Smoking-Attributable Disease.* A Report of the Surgeon General, Executive Summary. Washington, DC: DHHS, 2010. A clinical report of the evidence supporting physical and psychological damage from tobacco, describing disease extent related to tobacco use.

Hammond, David, et al. "Text and Graphic Warnings on Cigarette Packages: Findings from the International Tobacco Control Four Country Survey." *American Journal of Preventive Medicine* 32.3 (2007): 202–9. Print. An international telephone survey that identified the levels of consumer risk awareness about existing tobacco-warning labels compared with changed labels; US labels were associated with the lowest rates of effectiveness.

MacKinnon, David P., and Liva Nohre. "Alcohol and Tobacco Warnings." *Handbook of Warnings.* Ed. M. Wogalter. Mahwah, NJ: Erlbaum, 2006. Discusses effects of warning labels on alcohol and tobacco use in the United States compared with label effects in other countries. Explains the effects of graphic images and the cost-effectiveness of warnings.

WEBSITES OF INTEREST

Alcohol and Tobacco Tax and Trade Bureau
http://www.ttb.gov/tobacco

Center for Science in the Public Interest
http://www.cspinet.org/booze/iss_warn.htm

US Food and Drug Administration
http://www.fda.gov/TobaccoProducts/Labeling/
    CigaretteWarningLabels

See also: Education about substance abuse; Legislation and substance abuse; Prevention methods and research; War on Drugs

Group therapy for behavioral addictions

CATEGORY: Treatment

DEFINITION: As the medical community debates whether behavioral addictions are true addictions, research has proven that support groups (group therapy) that are similar to those for substance abusers can help people to overcome the compulsion for certain unhealthy behaviors. Many of these groups are twelve-step programs. Other behavioral addiction groups focus on cognitive-behavioral therapies, which stress that thoughts precede actions.

OVERCOMING BEHAVIORAL ADDICTIONS

All support groups help a person addicted to a harmful behavior to become aware of the problem, find solace in the company of other people with similar issues, and develop new ways of coping with stress. Behavioral addictions are destructive patterns of behavior that mimic substance abuse. They begin when a person experiences pleasure in association with a behavior and then later engages in that behavior to reduce stress.

Eventually, through frequent and ritualized indulgence, the behavior becomes part of the person's daily routine. A person addicted to behaviors such as gambling, eating, sex, video games, exercise, shopping, or work or affection from another person (codependency) has a strong urge to engage in the behavior to experience relief and euphoria, despite persistent negative consequences.

Whether caused by substances or undesirable behaviors, all addictions have three things in common: physical and mental cravings, a habit, and denial of both craving and habit. Denial is a key factor with behavioral addictions, and it must be overcome if the person is to recover. Group therapy is successful in such cases because sitting in a room and listening to others describe situations and feelings that one has experienced in painful isolation tends to turn denial into identification. People who have recovered from the same affliction can also offer compassion, which is needed to offset feelings of self-loathing in the addict.

Evidence suggests that behavioral addictions involve the same brain mechanisms as substance addictions, although more research is needed to clarify and confirm this. For now, it is clear that behavioral addictions present problems with relationships similar to substance abuse by undermining trust and by putting pressure on family members to compensate for difficulties caused by the addiction.

Unlike treatment for most types of substance abuse, behavioral addiction treatment does not require a detoxification period. A person with a behavioral addiction can stop doing it suddenly without experiencing physical withdrawal symptoms. Psychological withdrawal symptoms are common, however, and include feeling restless or anxious and having a strong desire to engage in the harmful behavior.

PATHOLOGICAL GAMBLING AND GAMBLERS ANONYMOUS

Pathological gambling (PG) is the only behavioral addiction included in the *Diagnostic and Statistical Manual of Mental Disorders* (DSM). PG is classified as an impulse control disorder, in which the "essential feature is the failure to resist an impulse, drive or temptation to perform an act that is harmful to the person or to others." It has been proposed that PG be renamed gambling disorder and moved to a new category, addiction and related disorders.

PG is a serious problem not only for the addict but also for the addict's family and for society at large. The disorder produces financial insecurity, family dysfunction, domestic abuse, legal problems, employment difficulties, psychological distress, and higher rates of suicide. The problem is likely to become more prevalent, as state governments derive significant revenue from and thus promote gambling-related activities, such as lotteries. Also, Internet gambling increases access and anonymity.

Gamblers Anonymous (GA) was founded in Los Angeles in 1957 by two men who focused on fostering a character change within themselves in order to stop gambling. This fellowship of men and women has since grown to thousands of groups in the United States, Australia, Brazil, Israel, Japan, Kenya, Korea, the United Kingdom, and Spain. GA's website offers a questionnaire to help people determine if they need the program.

Family members of compulsive gamblers can attend Gam-Anon, another twelve-step program, founded in 1958. Through Gam-Anon, members come to understand their problem and learn how to give emotional support to the troubled person without enabling him or her in the illness. Children can attend Gam-A-Teen, part of the Gam-Anon program.

OVEREATERS, CODEPENDENTS, AND SEX ADDICTS

The idea for Overeaters Anonymous (OA) came to a woman who attended a GA meeting in 1958 and "heard her story," though she related the speaker's turmoil to her eating compulsion instead of a gambling problem. Not until 1960, though, did she find another person willing to recover from the addiction. OA now offers recovery from compulsive eating through a worldwide fellowship of sixty-five hundred groups in seventy-five countries.

The organization's website includes a fifteen-item questionnaire to help people determine if they have an eating problem. Compulsive eating is a threefold illness, affecting physical condition, mental state, and the spirit. In the mental dimension, a compulsive eater is not "eating down" feelings but is expressing an inner hunger that leads to a loss of spiritual values.

Co-Dependents Anonymous, which celebrated its twenty-fifth anniversary in 2011, is a fellowship of men and women whose common purpose is to develop healthy relationships. Rather than a questionnaire, its website offers a list of patterns and characteristics of codependence, in five categories.

Under the category of denial, for example, codependent behaviors include minimizing one's feelings or expressing negativity in passive-aggressive ways. Low-self-esteem behavior patterns include difficulty making decisions and constantly seeking recognition. Compliance patterns emerge in compromising one's integrity to avoid rejection or anger and being hypervigilant of other people's feelings. Control patterns include freely offering advice and direction to others without being asked and needing to be needed. Avoidance patterns show up in pulling people close and then pushing them away.

Sex and Love Addicts Anonymous, or SLAA, offers help to anyone who has a sex addiction, love addiction, or both, and who wants to recover from that addiction. The fellowship was founded in 1976 by an Alcoholics Anonymous member who was serially unfaithful to his wife. SLAA recognizes that an obsessive-compulsive pattern exists when relationships or sexual activities become destructive to one's career, family, and self-esteem. Advances in computer technology have made it easier for people to access sex-related websites with great anonymity, leading to a problem called Internet-enabled sexual behavior, which affects family relationships, work productivity, and academic success.

INTERNET ADDICTION

Internet addiction is a behavioral problem affecting an estimated 6 percent of people who use the web, according to the American Psychiatric Association. People who lose track of time while using the Internet become more socially isolated, depressed, and challenged by family discord, divorce, academic failure, financial failure, and job loss.

In the United States, one-on-one cognitive-behavioral therapy (CBT) has been shown to reduce the amount of time a person spends online. A study in Shanghai found that group therapy using CBT techniques, which emphasize that thoughts precede actions, was successful in treating teenagers addicted to the Internet.

Laura B. Smith

FURTHER READING

Hecht Orzack, Maressa, et al. "An Ongoing Study of Group Treatment for Men Involved in Problematic Internet-Enabled Sexual Behavior." *Cyberpsychology and Behavior* 9.3 (2006). Print. The first study regarding the effectiveness of group therapy treatment for men with problematic Internet-enabled sexual behavior included five groups of men, 44.5

years old on average. Results showed that group treatment significantly increased members' quality of life and decreased the severity of their depressive symptoms, but did not reduce inappropriate computer use.

Jiménez-Murcia, Susana, et al. "Cognitive-Behavioral Group Treatment for Pathological Gambling: Analysis of Effectiveness and Predictors of Therapy Outcome." *Psychotherapy Research* 17.5 (2007). Print. Examined short- and mid-term effectiveness of group cognitive-behavioral therapy (CBT) for 290 patients suffering from pathological gambling. Outpatient group CBT was found to be effective, with abstinence rates of 76.1 percent by the end of a sixteen-week program and 81.5 percent at six-month follow-up.

Ladouceur, R., et al. "Group Therapy for Pathological Gamblers: A Cognitive Approach." *Behavior Research and Therapy* 41.5 (2003): 587–96. Print. This study evaluated the efficacy of a group cognitive treatment for pathological gambling (PG). Post-treatment results indicated that 88 percent of the treated gamblers no longer met criteria for PG. Discusses recommendations for group interventions, focusing on the cognitive correction of erroneous perceptions toward the notion of randomness.

WEBSITES OF INTEREST

Co-Dependents Anonymous
http://www.coda.org

Gam-Anon
http://www.gam-anon.org

Gamblers Anonymous
http://www.gamblersanonymous.org

Overeaters Anonymous
http://www.oa.org

Sex and Love Addicts Anonymous
http://www.slaafws.org

See also: Behavioral addictions: Treatment; Gamblers Anonymous; Group therapy for substance abuse; Overeaters Anonymous; Support groups; Treatment methods and research

Group therapy for substance abuse

CATEGORY: Treatment

DEFINITION: Group therapy, a critical component of the substance-abuse recovery process, is promoted by the US Substance Abuse and Mental Health Services Administration as a cost-effective treatment for substance abuse. Although group therapy is important to a comprehensive treatment plan, it does not replace core mental health and physician services that focus on substance abuse treatment.

RATIONALE

By the time a person reaches the point of seeking treatment for substance abuse, he or she most likely has become alienated from friends and family because of poor behavior resulting from long-term substance abuse. Therefore, as the recovering abuser steps into a community of persons facing similar concerns, the most important benefit of group therapy is a reduction in the feeling of social isolation.

This sense of community experienced in group therapy rewards participants with peer support and the feeling that they are not alone in the recovery process. Participants benefit by learning how others in recovery are coping with the process, gaining feedback, encouragement, and insight. Group therapy participants also develop or relearn social skills, namely, how to interact with others while sober.

On a practical level, group therapy is cost-effective, as a single psychotherapy professional helps several persons at a time, keeping costs down. By participating in a low-cost group therapy program, substance abusers in recovery may gain a substantial return in treatment for their financial investment.

MODELS

The Substance Abuse and Mental Health Services Administration (SAMHSA), part of the US Department of Health and Human Services, endorses five group-therapy models as effective approaches to substance abuse treatment. These models involve psychoeducational groups, skills development groups, cognitive-behavioral/problem-solving groups, support groups, and interpersonal process groups. The appropriate model for a substance abuser depends on his or her life experience and psychological background.

Psychoeducational groups inform participants about substance abuse and provide them with information about the behaviors, risks, and effects of substance abuse. Psychoeducational groups raise awareness of the science behind the problems of substance abuse, enabling participants to understand why they need medical and psychological help. These groups also help participants understand their own behaviors, the stages of the recovery process, and what resources are available to help them cope during recovery.

Skills development groups help participants develop special skills for recovery. Chiefly, these groups help the abuser learn how to abstain from drug or alcohol use. According to SAMHSA, these development groups should teach social skills and skills that address substance refusal, communications, anger management, parenting, and money management.

Cognitive-behavioral groups are especially important during early recovery, as they help participants identify the psychological factors leading to substance abuse. Participants are guided in exploring their thoughts, beliefs, and feelings as they relate to their substance abuse behavior. Negative thoughts and beliefs, such as feelings of failure and inadequacy, are uncovered and addressed. The goal is for participants to resolve destructive, errant beliefs about their potential and worth so that they can move forward in the recovery process.

Support groups are valuable for treating substance abuse in that they offer a nonjudgmental forum where participants may openly discuss their experiences and struggles with substance abuse. Ground rules for discussion are important for facilitating an environment where recovering substance abusers may freely express feelings and events related to recovery. The psychotherapist leading the support group models active listening, positive feedback, and appropriate, nonjudgmental discussion. Types of group therapy include relapse prevention groups, communal and culturally specific groups, and expressive groups.

Interpersonal process groups apply psychological process-oriented methods to promote substance-abuse recovery. Interpersonal groups focus on individual members, interpersonal interaction among members, and the group dynamic as a whole.

Alcoholics Anonymous. (Larry Mulvehill)

STRUCTURE

Because the appropriate placement of a person into a particular model of group therapy is important, a care provider first evaluates the substance abuser's background, needs, and stage of recovery. Depending on the substance abuser's circumstances and preferences, the care provider matches him or her with a group type and group leader equipped to treat any adjunct issues the person has, such as psychological disorders or traumatic experiences. The caregiver also considers the substance abuser's gender, age, race, ability to cope, stage of recovery, and interpersonal skills.

At the first meeting, the group therapy leader establishes participant expectations and ground rules through a presentation of a "group agreement." Issues addressed in the agreement usually include confidentiality, physical contact, use of substances, contact outside the group, financial obligations, and actions that would lead to expulsion from the group. Though the leader will require that participants accept the agreement, it is unlikely that he or she will discipline or dismiss members for violating the agreement. Rather, if a participant defies the rules of the agreement, the leader will use the situation as a discussion point and a part of the group-therapy process.

There are three phases of group therapy: beginning, middle, and end. The beginning phase includes explanation of the group agreement and ground rules, and an explanation of the rationale and goals for the therapy. The middle phase centers on two things: the leader providing group members with information, including facts about substance abuse or feelings expressed by participants in the group, and on moving participants forward in the process of recovery. The middle phase is the time for participants to connect their experiences and struggles to knowledge about substance abuse and the recovery process. During the end phase, the group leader provides closure by acknowledging what was shared and learned by participants. The leader then summarizes the process and suggests how participants can continue to move forward in the process outside the group therapy environment.

ALTERNATIVE APPROACHES

In 2010, one care provider introduced an online group-therapy community. The interactive twelve-step substance abuse group therapy program, accredited by the Commission on Accreditation of Rehabilitation Facilities, is designed to help abusers who are seeking initial help for the recovery process.

In 2009, the journal *Anthrozoos* published the results of a study of applying animal-assisted therapy (AAT) to group therapy for substance abuse. Researchers concluded that, among clients who had no fear of or abusive tendencies toward dogs, the therapeutic process was significantly improved by adding a therapy dog to sessions. Connection to the recovery process through therapy is critical for clients in overcoming addiction and substance abuse. Toward that end, therapy dogs assist in attaching clients emotionally to the recovery process by reducing their anxiety so that they may disclose feelings and thoughts about their experience of substance abuse.

Researchers, however, urged counselors and psychotherapists to apply AAT not as an isolated or replacement method for group therapy. Rather, AAT should be used as a complementary technique within the group therapy setting and process. A therapy dog becomes valuable as a healing presence in group therapy as he or she performs therapeutic "tricks" during sessions, such as bringing a tissue to a client who is crying and moving to the client who is speaking so that he or she may touch the dog while sharing feelings. "The dog was available when called, was nonjudgmental, and predictable in her responses," the researchers wrote in their study. The dogs provided for an enhanced substance-abuse recovery process, they concluded.

Melissa Walsh

FURTHER READING

Brook, David W., and Henry I. Spitz. *The Group Therapy of Substance Abuse.* New York: Haworth Medical, 2002.

Cleland, Charles, et al. "Moderators of Effects of Motivational Enhancements to Cognitive Behavioral Therapy." *American Journal of Drug and Alcohol Abuse* 31.1 (2005): 35. Print.

Minatrea, Neresa B., Joshua C. Watson, and Martin C. Wesley. "Animal-Assisted Therapy in the Treatment of Substance Dependence." *Anthrozoos* 22.2 (2009): 137. Print.

"SAMHSA Guide Supports Benefits of Group Therapy." *Addiction Professional* 3.3 (2005): 60.

Substance Abuse and Mental Health Services Administration. "Substance Abuse Treatment: Group Therapy, Quick Guide for Clinicians Based on TIP 41." Washington, DC: DHHS, 2005. Print.

WEBSITES OF INTEREST

American Psychological Association
http://www.apa.org/topics/therapy

Substance Abuse and Mental Health Services Administration
http://www.samhsa.gov

See also: Alcohol abuse and alcoholism: Treatment; Alcoholics Anonymous; Cocaine Anonymous; Group therapy for behavioral addictions; Narcotics Anonymous; Support groups; Treatment methods and research

H

Halfway houses

CATEGORY: Treatment

ALSO KNOWN AS: Sober houses; sober-living houses; transitional housing

DEFINITION: Halfway houses are drug- and alcohol-free transitional living environments for people in recovery from drug or alcohol abuse. These houses provide a safe place for addicts and alcoholics to transition back into mainstream society.

BACKGROUND

Recognizing the need for a safe environment for alcoholics in recovery, Alcoholics Anonymous (AA) established the first halfway houses in the 1940s in the United States. These group living facilities were called twelve step houses and provided safety and support for alcoholics who were not ready or able to return to their lives before addiction.

In 1975, Oxford House, established by and for persons in recovery, was established in Silver Spring, Maryland. Sixteen Oxford houses were established between 1975 and 1988. The Oxford House manual for running a group home was first published in 1978.

Several factors led to an expansion in the halfway house movement in the 1990s. One factor was the loss of residential treatment centers because of decreases in government and private insurance funding for these centers. A second factor was the 1988 amendments to the federal Fair Housing Law. These amendments allowed recovering addicts and alcoholics to be considered persons with disabilities, giving those in recovery the right to live together as a "family" of unrelated persons. As part of the 1988 Anti-Drug Abuse Act, all states were required to maintain funds for establishing sober houses based on the Oxford model, and halfway houses are now found throughout the United States.

Halfway houses are not licensed or accredited by the federal government, however, and they are restricted from offering drug and alcohol treatment. Instead, they are permitted to offer a drug- and alcohol-free environment. Also, halfway houses are limited to groups of unrelated adults, disabled through addiction and working toward recovery. To receive government aid, halfway houses can accept only those persons who have completed or who are involved in some type of formal treatment program.

MISSION AND GOALS

Although halfway houses are not licensed to treat alcohol or drug abuse, they do provide support for the recovering addict or alcoholic. Other goals include providing an environment that is safe, structured, and affordable. Most addicts and alcoholics come

Oxford House residents prepare their dinner. (Ross William Hamilton/ *The Oregonian*/Landov)

to a halfway house directly from detoxification and treatment programs. Some continue aftercare and outpatient care at a treatment center while living in the halfway house.

Government-funded halfway houses offer affordable rates, and payment is usually on a month-to-month basis. Although the average stay in a halfway house is three to six months, each house may have different arrangements. Most houses are run by a house manager, who is not required to have a special credential for the position. House manager selection varies greatly, as does the establishment of house rules and regulations.

A person seeking residence at a halfway house often gets a referral from a treatment facility. Houses may cater to men, women, women with children, and to special populations. House rules for residences generally include remaining drug and alcohol free, completing or attending a drug or alcohol treatment program, continuing to make payments for care, and avoiding negative or disruptive behavior. Other house rules may cover check-in times, visitors, attendance at house meetings and twelve-step meetings, and completion of assigned chores and other responsibilities.

Sober living houses are similar to halfway houses but may have less stringent rules. A resident may be admitted without having completed or without involvement in formal treatment. These houses are less likely to be government funded, may be more expensive, and may allow residents to remain indefinitely. Sober living houses provide an alcohol and drug free environment and usually encourage attendance at self-help programs, such as AA.

Numerous studies have documented that the lack of a stable, alcohol- and drug-free environment is a significant barrier to any sustained recovery from addiction. Involvement in twelve-step groups and strong social support remain strong predictors of successful recovery. A variety of studies have shown that halfway houses improve treatment outcomes for both drug and alcohol addiction.

Christopher Iliades, MD

FURTHER READING

Hoffman, John. *Addiction: Why Can't They Just Stop?* New York: Rodale, 2007. Puts a human face on the hidden problem of addiction in the United States and breaks through the myths and misunderstandings that surround the disease and its treatment.

Jason, L. A., et al. "An Examination of Main and Interactive Effects of Substance Abuse Recovery Housing on Multiple Indicators of Adjustment." *Addiction* 102.7 (2007): 1114–21. Print. This study is a twenty-four-month follow-up of residents in early recovery living at Oxford House. The study finds that the house, a self-governed sober living facility, appears to stabilize many persons with substance abuse histories.

Polcin, D., et al. "A Model for Sober Housing During Outpatient Treatment." *Journal of Psychoactive Drugs* 41.2 (2009): 153–61. Print. This study looks at treatment outcomes for forty-six residents in sober housing. Seventy-six percent of the clients who remained in sober housing for five months or more had better outcomes in measurements, such as relapse and employment.

---. "What Did We Learn from Our Study on Sober Living Houses and Where Do We Go from Here?" *Journal of Psychoactive Drugs* 42.4 (2010): 425–33. Print. Reviews a number of studies that confirm the importance of involvement in a supportive environment during early recovery and examines how halfway and sober living houses can improve treatment outcomes.

WEBSITES OF INTEREST

Oxford House
http://www.oxfordhouse.org

SoberShelter.com
http://www.sobershelter.com

"What Are Halfway Houses?" SoberLivingHouses.net
http://soberlivinghouses.net/what-are-halfway-houses

See also: Alcohol abuse and alcoholism: Treatment; Residential treatment; Sober living environments; Treatment methods and research

Hallucinogen abuse

CATEGORY: Substance abuse

ALSO KNOWN AS: Illusionogenic abuse; psychedelic drug abuse

DEFINITION: Hallucinogen abuse is the repeated use of hallucinogens, which are drugs that distort a person's perception of reality after they have caused impairment that undermines the user's ability to fulfill obligations at home, school, and work.

CAUSES

The mechanism by which hallucinogens exert their effects is not fully understood. However, it is recognized that hallucinogens bind with 5-HT serotonin receptors in the brain. Serotonin facilitates transmission of nerve impulses. When a hallucinogen binds with serotonin receptors, it blocks serotonin from these receptor sites, thus altering nerve transmission. Unbound serotonin increases in the brain, contributing to the distortions in vision, hearing, and the perception of time and space, as well as in the alterations in mood and thought processes that occur under the influence of hallucinogens. Abusers regard this as a consciousness-raising experience that can lead to increased creativity and self-awareness.

RISK FACTORS

Hallucinogens are easily and cheaply obtained, making them attractive to adolescents who want to experiment with mind-altering drugs. Older adolescents and young adults use them in the party scene to heighten their experiences. The National Institute on Drug Abuse reports that about 11 percent of high school seniors have tried lysergic acid diethylamide (LSD, or acid) and that about 7 percent have used other hallucinogens. Persons who abuse hallucinogens are also likely to abuse alcohol and marijuana.

SYMPTOMS

Physical symptoms of hallucinogen abuse include increased blood pressure and heart rate; nausea, vomiting, and diarrhea (especially with psilocybin and mescaline); dilated pupils; blurred vision; paraesthesia (burning, tingling, or itching skin); and sweating. With ecstasy (3,4-methylenedioxymethamphetamine, or MDMA), symptoms include muscle cramping, dehydration, and severe elevations in body temperature.

Psychological symptoms of hallucinogen abuse include distortion of sight, sound, and touch; synesthesia, which is confusion of the senses, such as "seeing" sounds; depersonalization, or "out-of-person" experiences; delusions of physical invulnerability (especially with LSD); elation or euphoria; blissful calm or mellowness; reduced inhibitions; poor judgment and increased risk taking; impaired concentration and motivation; anxiety attacks; and paranoia.

Abusers can experience recurring flashbacks of their drug-induced psychological symptoms long after the immediate experience. These flashbacks are referred to as persisting psychosis and perception disorder and posthallucinogenic perceptual disorder. Flashbacks occur in 30 to 50 percent of frequent abusers and far less often in occasional abusers. Use of alcohol or marijuana, or extreme fatigue, can trigger flashbacks. Chronic abuse can affect long-term memory and cause personality changes. Frequent abuse can trigger latent psychiatric disorders, such as depression, anxiety, and psychosis. Frequent abusers can develop psychological dependence on hallucinogens.

SCREENING AND DIAGNOSIS

Most persons who are treated for hallucinogenic abuse are experiencing an acute "bad trip." Key to diagnosis is that their distress will be evident. Routine blood or urine sampling does not detect the use of hallucinogens. Hallucinogen abusers do not develop a tolerance to the drug that would require more frequent and higher dosing. Frequent or high-dose use indicates a psychological rather than a physiological need. Detectable withdrawal symptoms do not occur when an abuser stops using hallucinogens.

TREATMENT AND THERAPY

A bad trip can be a frightening and anxiety-provoking experience, as can flashbacks. The immediate goal of treatment in these situations is to prevent the person from harming the self or others. The abuser needs to be assured that the experience will pass as the drug wears off.

The effects of LSD, the longest-acting hallucinogen, can last up to twelve hours. The abuser should be kept in a quiet, comfortable, and lighted environment and allowed to move around under supervision.

An anti-anxiety drug such as lorazepam or another benzodiazepine may be helpful. An abuser of ecstasy may develop a dangerously high body temperature, which needs to be brought under control.

Persons who have recurrent flashbacks or who were long-term frequent abusers of hallucinogens may require long-term psychotherapy after stopping the abuse. Any underlying psychiatric disorders will have to be addressed. Many people find group support or a twelve-step program to be helpful in the recovery process. Hallucinogen intoxication delirium is a rare syndrome that can occur when a hallucinogen is contaminated with another drug or chemical, such as strychnine.

PREVENTION

Education regarding hallucinogen abuse should begin with children or early adolescents, before they experiment with the drugs. Educators should stress that the effects of hallucinogens cannot be predicted or controlled. Any user, even a first-time user, is at risk of a bad, even life-threatening, trip and of recurrent, disturbing flashbacks.

As all hallucinogen products are prepared in illegal, unregulated laboratories, there is no guarantee of their potency or purity, furthering the user's risk of serious consequences. Parents should be alert to the availability and use of hallucinogens in their communities and should keep children from these sources.

Ernest Kohlmetz, MA

FURTHER READING

Abadinsky, Howard. *Drug Use and Abuse: A Comprehensive Introduction.* 7th ed. Belmont, CA: Wadsworth, 2011. Focuses on what drugs are abused, how they are abused, and how abuse is treated or can be prevented. Hallucinogen abuse is covered in chapter 6.

Julien, Robert M. *A Primer of Drug Actions.* 11th ed. New York: Worth, 2008. A concise, nontechnical guide to the mechanisms of action, side effects, uses, and abuses of psychoactive drugs. Chapter 12 covers hallucinogens.

Kuhn, Cynthia, Scott Swartwelder, and Wilkie Wilson. *Buzzed: The Straight Facts about the Most Used and Abused Drugs from Alcohol to Ecstasy.* 3rd ed. New York: W. W. Norton, 2008. Contains an informative, easy-to-read section on hallucinogens and their effects.

Laing, Richard R., ed. *Hallucinogens: A Forensic Drug Handbook.* San Francisco: Elsevier, 2003. Comprehensive textbook detailing structures, identification techniques, and pharmacologic and pharmacokinetic actions of both common and more unusual hallucinogenic substances of abuse.

Lowinson, Joyce W., et al., eds. *Substance Abuse: A Comprehensive Textbook.* 4th ed. Philadelphia: Lippincott, 2005. A comprehensive textbook. Chapter 18 covers hallucinogens.

National Institute on Drug Abuse. "NIDA InfoFacts: Hallucinogens: LSD, Peyote, Psilocybin, and PCP." 2009. Web. 10 Mar. 2012. http://www.nida.nih.gov/infofacts/hallucinogens.html. An overview of hallucinogens for general readers.

WEBSITES OF INTEREST

AbovetheInfluence.com
http://www.abovetheinfluence.com/facts/drugshallucinogens

National Institute on Drug Abuse
http://www.drugabuse.gov

See also: Flashbacks; Hallucinogens: Short- and long-term effects on the body; LSD; MDMA; Mescaline; Mushrooms/psilocybin; PCP; Psychosis and substance abuse

Hallucinogens: Short- and long-term effects on the body

CATEGORY: Health issues and physiology

ALSO KNOWN AS: Dissociatives; psychoactives; psychomimetics

DEFINITION: Hallucinogens are members of a variable drug class stemming from plant and synthetic sources that induce experiences of fantasy as altered reality and distortions of self and senses.

HALLUCINOGEN SOURCES

Plant sources. LSD, or lysergic acid diethylamide, the prototypical and most potent natural hallucinogen, is extracted from fungal rye. Related hallucinogens are mescaline from peyote cacti, psilocybin and psilocin from mushrooms, and ibogaine from the shrub Tabernanthe. All plant hallucinogens have serotonin-like chemical structures.

Synthetic sources. Of the synthesized hallucinogens, PCP (phencyclidine) and ketamine are key examples. PCP was developed in the 1950s and used through 1965 as an anesthetic, and ketamine was designed as a less potent veterinary anesthetic. Both of these drugs and dextromethorphan induce glutamate-related hallucinations.

Newer designer drugs, including the tryptamines, methylenedioxymethamphetamine (MDMA, or ecstasy), the herbal *Salvia divinorum*, and numerous amphetamine-like drugs, are not specifically members of the hallucinogen drug class. However, they can exert hallucinogenic effects through non-serotonin or non-glutamate pathways.

IMMEDIATE EFFECTS

Hallucinogens distort perceptions of self, emotion, sensations, and moods; they also impair judgment and cause dissociation. Depersonalization, or a disconnection from the physical body and surroundings, and dissociation, or a separation of the mind from the physical self and environment, can lead users to lose control of their body and actions. Each drug experience, or trip, causes unpredictable hallucinations according to the user's environment, the user's emotional state of mind, and the timing, type, and amount of drug used.

LSD, mescaline, psilocybin, and ibogaine affect serotonin (5HT) actions at the 5HT-2 receptors in the cerebral cortex and locus cerebellum to impair control of mood, senses, hunger, and body temperature. The onset of effect is thirty to ninety minutes; LSD and mescaline trips can last up to twelve hours, but psilocybin trips are often only four to six hours. Serotonin blockade results in rapid psychologic fluctuations of fear to euphoria; bizarre but peaceful delusions of enhanced abilities are as likely as time alterations and loss of control that cause panic and terror. Sensory experiences of plant hallucinogens become uniquely confused and overlap. This crossover, called synesthesia, is common and causes an intense and unusual ability to see sounds, to hear or feel colors, and to taste sights.

Unlike these sensory delusions, PCP and ketamine induce primarily dissociative effects by N-methyl-D-aspartic acid antagonism at glutamate brain receptors to cause bizarre distortions of reality. Glutamate blockade results in feelings of power, impaired memory, numbness to pain, detachment from the body and bodily responses, and altered senses. As with plant hallucinogens, out-of-body sensations may be pleasantly empowering or terrifying. Ketamine and PCP both cause an immediate dopamine-related rush of euphoria, followed by anxiety and emotional lability after the dopamine peak. Although PCP is more potent and longer-lasting than ketamine, both drugs are delivered straight to the brain when smoked or snorted, so they take effect within minutes.

PCP-like hallucinogens are known for their quicker onset, shorter duration, and reduced potency compared with plant hallucinogens. For example, dimethyltryptamine (DMT), a designer drug with hallucinatory properties, takes action within two to five minutes, but the effects last only twenty to sixty minutes. Of the PCP-like hallucinogens, dextromethorphan (DXM) alone has specific dose-effect plateaus. Two ounces of 3 milligrams (mg) per milliliter of DXM cough medicine causes mild sensory changes, and complete dissociation occurs at 10 ounces or greater. DXM effects can last for six hours after use and are particularly dangerous because of overdose risk with combination products.

Hallucinogens cause physiologic changes in part through sympathetic nervous system activation. Immediate effects include increased heart rate and blood pressure, sweating and flushing, increased body temperature, nausea and dizziness, pupil dilation, and loss of appetite. Motor changes include tremor, muscle weakness, and ataxia. Mushroom poisoning from psilocybin use can begin within twenty minutes and last for six hours, causing nausea, vomiting, and excessive sleepiness. Increased respiratory rate and shallowness of breathing are particular to PCP and ketamine, and PCP doses greater than 5 mg can induce a dangerous reduction of blood pressure, heart rate, and respiratory rate.

Risk of death from overdose is twofold, through suicidal psychologic impairment of judgment and body dysregulation. At extremely high doses, hallucinogens cause deadly hyperthermia and seizure. Anesthetic nervous system sedation causes coma and dangerously low heart and respiratory rates. Spontaneous muscle contractions lead to muscle breakdown and kidney overload.

DELAYED AND PROLONGED EFFECTS

After the initial trip, adverse psychological and physical effects of drug use last from hours to days. The sense of detachment and the prolonged psychological changes after a trip ends can lead to panic and increased risk of suicide with any drug in the class. Depression, memory loss, visual changes, and long-term psychoses are not uncommon after even a single trip, particularly with LSD or psilocybin. Users with a history of psychiatric disorders more often experience depression and psychoses that can become more pronounced following hallucinogen use.

After use of anesthetic hallucinogens, paranoia and schizophrenic episodes may develop, regardless of the prior state of mind or drug experience. Up to 50 percent of PCP users experience anxiety within forty-eight hours of drug use, and PCP can alter thought, speech, and memory for up to one year after a trip.

Perhaps the most characteristic delayed hallucinogenic response is the psychologic flashback experience. Flashbacks occur primarily after LSD, peyote, or psilocybin use and can occur spontaneously or can be triggered by fatigue, stress, or the use of certain drugs (such as alcohol, barbiturates, and marijuana). These sudden episodes can develop after just a single trip, can occur once or multiple times, and can develop within days or years. A hallucinogenic flashback may repeat the initial trip or may manifest as a visual hallucinatory experience, although any distortion is possible.

Although hallucinogens are considered nonaddictive, serotonin-related tolerance among the plant hallucinogens develops, and dissipates, quickly. Conversely, chronic PCP use leads to addictive cravings and drug-seeking compulsions. Physical dependence on PCP is rare, but PCP may induce reduced heart and respiratory rates as withdrawal.

LONG-TERM IMPAIRMENT

Semipermanent psychological and physical impairments occur as extensions of the drug assault. LSD in particular is associated with psychotic episodes years after drug use has ended; plant hallucinogens induce long-lasting visual changes, disorganized and irrational thought patterns, and fluctuating depression and mania. Conversely, PCP mediates continued depressive symptoms and long-term memory loss.

The flashbacks from natural hallucinogens can recur for up to five years in chronic users and may impact psychological health for much longer. Hallucinogenic persisting perception disorder, or HPPD, is a psychiatric diagnosis of hallucinatory flashbacks that persist for five or more years after a single trip. HPPD flashbacks occur most frequently in persons with a history of LSD use and are typically experienced as repeated false visual sensations and alterations; the effects can be confused with symptoms of neurologic stroke or brain tumor in otherwise healthy persons.

Nicole M. Van Hoey, PharmD

FURTHER READING

Cunningham, Nicola. "Hallucinogenic Plants of Abuse." *Emergency Medicine Australasia* 20 (2008): 167–74. Print. A review of natural hallucinogens that focuses on the drug sources, intoxication effects, and presentation in an emergency medicine setting.

Laing, Richard R., ed. *Hallucinogens: A Forensic Drug Handbook.* San Francisco: Elsevier, 2003. Comprehensive textbook detailing structures, identification techniques, and pharmacologic and pharmacokinetic actions of both common and more unusual hallucinogenic substances of abuse.

Substance Abuse and Mental Health Services Administration. "NSDUH Report: Use of Specific Hallucinogens, 2006." Rockville, MD: Author, 2008. Periodically released government report that discusses hallucinogenic drugs of abuse, in particular the effects of use, drug types used, rates of use, types of users, and results of use. Also includes usage descriptions of new hallucinogenic substances, including herbals and ecstasy.

Wu Li-Tzy, et al. "Recent National Trends in *Salvia divinorum* Use and Substance-Use Disorders among Recent and Former *Salvia divinorum* Users Compared with Nonusers." *Substance Abuse Rehabilitation* 2 (2011): 53–68. Print. Introduces *Salvia divinorum* as a new herbal hallucinogenic substance, identifies the most common users, and discusses adverse health effects.

WEBSITES OF INTEREST

AbovetheInfluence.com
http://www.abovetheinfluence.com/facts/drugshallucinogens

"Hallucinogens: LSD, Peyote, Psilocybin, and PCP."
National Institute on Drug Abuse
http://www.nida.nih.gov/infofacts/hallucinogens.
html

National Substance Abuse Index: Directory of Alcoholism
and Drug Abuse Resources
http://nationalsubstanceabuseindex.org

See also: Brain changes with addiction; Flashbacks; Hallucinogen abuse; LSD; Narcotics: Short- and long-term effects on the body; Psychosis and substance abuse

Harm reduction

CATEGORY: Treatment
DEFINITION: Harm reduction in the context of addiction and substance abuse includes policies and practices that seek to reduce the harm caused by an unhealthy behavior.

BACKGROUND

Harm reduction focuses on behavior that jeopardizes a person's health and public health in general, addressing behaviors such as risky sexual practices and drug abuse. Harm reduction is based in pragmatism, or realism, rather than in the idealism reflected in abstinence-only drug policies.

Harm reduction practices are often controversial in that opponents view them as promoting an unhealthy, immoral, and sometimes illegal behavior. Advocates of harm reduction policies believe that prohibitionist drug policies can increase the risk and danger to users beyond those risks already associated with a drug. Advocates also believe that drug policies based on the prohibition of drugs will not eradicate drug use because people will still break laws and use drugs; drug policies, therefore, should seek to reduce the harm caused by drug use. Harm reduction policies regarding illegal substances are the most contentious in terms of public support.

TYPES OF PROGRAMS

In the United States, harm reduction policies surrounding the use of heroin are among the most controversial, even though many European nations have embraced these policies. Needle exchange programs, in which addicts exchange a used needle for a clean one, are among the most disputed harm reduction programs. Controversy exists even though research consistently shows needle exchange programs minimize the risk of contracting blood-borne diseases such as those caused by the human immunodeficiency and hepatitis viruses.

The US Congress banned federal funding for needle exchange programs in the late 1980s but lifted the ban in 1992 to provide funding for research on exchange programs. Federal money is not, however, used to support exchange programs.

Safe injection rooms, another form of harm reduction for intravenous drug users that exist in some European nations, provide medical personnel and sterile equipment and make referrals to treatment programs. Drug zones have also been implemented in some European cities to contain the spread of drug use into other areas. Additional harm reduction strategies include distributing condoms to students to prevent the spread of sexually transmitted diseases, providing methadone or naloxone to heroin addicts, promoting moderate drinking practices over abstinence for recovering alcoholics, and conducting responsible drinking campaigns on college campuses.

US DRUG POLICY

Overall, drug policy in the United States continues to be shaped around punitive actions that promote zero-tolerance for drug use. The federal government continues to wage a war on drugs that seeks to eradicate drug use. US drug policy has created significant barriers to implementing harm reduction strategies.

Michelle Petrie, PhD

FURTHER READING

Inciardi, James, and Lana D. Harrison, eds. *Harm Reduction: National and International Perspectives.* Thousand Oaks, CA: Sage, 2000.

Marlatt, G. Alan, ed. *Harm Reduction: Pragmatic Strategies for Managing High Risk Behavior.* New York: Guilford, 1998.

Nadelmann, Ethan A. "Common Sense Drug Policy." *Foreign Affairs* 77.1 (1998): 111–26. Print.

See also: Abstinence-based treatment; Alternative therapies for addiction; Treatment methods and research

View of swaths of cannabis near the village of Ketama, northern Morocco. Morocco is the world's largest producer of hashish. (AP Photo)

Hashish

CATEGORY: Substances

ALSO KNOWN AS: Charas; hash; kif

DEFINITION: Hashish is a drug made from the resin, plant oils, or flowers of *Cannabis sativa*, also the source of marijuana.

STATUS: Illegal in the United States and other countries

CLASSIFICATION: Schedule I controlled substance in the United States; schedule II in Canada

SOURCE: Historically, hashish was prepared in the Indo-Iranian regions of Asia, although it now is manufactured in many parts of the world; it is either smuggled into the United States or made in homes or laboratories.

TRANSMISSION ROUTE: Inhaled and ingested

HISTORY OF USE

According to some studies, people have been using cannabis for thousands of years. It now is the most commonly used illicit drug worldwide. Hashish, a potent substance derived from cannabis, has a long history of its own. The word *hashish* is of Arabic origin and refers to preparations made from strong resins, plant oils, and sometimes flowers, which are dried and shaped into various forms; these can then be smoked or, after being dissolved in a liquid, baked into foods.

Hashish originally was used for religious purposes in what is now Pakistan, but its use had spread throughout India and the Middle East by the Middle Ages. Marco Polo and other medieval writers thought that the drug was used to motivate a particularly fierce group of warriors in northern Syria. Somewhat later, hashish was experimented with in Europe, most famously by French writers and doctors in the mid-nineteenth century. Several of these persons believed the hallucinations associated with the drug could be of use in psychotherapy.

EFFECTS AND POTENTIAL RISKS

Like other forms of cannabis, hashish contains dozens of substances called cannabinoids, the general functions of which are not well understood. The most psychoactive substance is delta-9-tetrahydrocannabinol (THC), which binds to specific receptors in the human forebrain and cerebellar cortex. The flowering top and the resins and oils of cannabis are comparably richer in THC than are the other parts of the plant. Once bound to receptors, THC affects motor activity, reward and reinforcement, memory, and the sensation of nausea.

In practical terms, the person consuming small amounts of hashish may experience hallucinations and euphoria. Larger doses may produce increased anxiety and paranoia. With chronic and heavy use, users can experience disorganized or scattered thinking, cognitive deficits, decreased motivation, social withdrawal, and decreased range of affect.

Like other psychoactive substances, THC use can induce dependence. Dependent users tend to experience anxiety, insomnia, and loss of appetite without the drug.

Michael R. Meyers, PhD

FURTHER READING

Benjamin, Walter. *On Hashish*. Ed. Howard Eiland. Cambridge, MA: Harvard UP, 2006.

Breivogel, Chris, and Laura Sim-Selley. "Basic Neuroanatomy and Neuropharmacology of Cannabinoids." *International Review of Psychiatry* 21.2 (2009): 113–21. Print.

Sewell, R. Andrew, Mohini Ranganathan, and Deepak Cyril D'Souza. "Cannabinoids and Psychosis." *International Review of Psychiatry* 21.2 (2009): 152–62. Print.

WEBSITES OF INTEREST

National Institute on Drug Abuse
http://www.drugabuse.gov/drugs-abuse/marijuana

The Partnership at Drugfree.org
http://www.drugfree.org/drug-guide/hashish

See also: Marijuana; Opium; Pipes and hookahs; Psychosis and substance abuse; *Salvia divinorum*

Hazelden Foundation

CATEGORY: Treatment
DEFINITION: The Hazelden Foundation is a nonprofit organization that provides a wide range of programs for alcoholics, drug abusers, and their families. Hazelden has multiple sites in the United States.
DATE: Incorporated on January 10, 1949

BACKGROUND

The Hazelden Foundation was established in an old farm house in Center City, Minnesota, in 1947. It began as a treatment program for men who were alcoholics and was based on the twelve-step program of Alcoholics Anonymous. Initially, Hazelden's founder, Austin Ripley, himself a recovered alcoholic, intended to treat alcoholic Catholic priests, but this plan was quickly dropped.

Hazelden struggled to survive, until several of its key supporters took over the program. The Hazelden Foundation was incorporated in 1949, but it did not begin to grow until 1952, when the Butler family took over. Hazelden soon began to flourish by providing inpatient care for recovering alcoholics, particularly those who needed extended care.

In 1955, Hazelden opened a facility for women called Dia Linn, which was in Dellwood, Minnesota. During the 1960s, Hazelden began providing a comprehensive approach to the treatment of alcoholics, adding psychologists, chaplains, social workers, and family services personnel to its staff. Also during this time, the Hazelden Foundation more than quadrupled the number of beds for its treatment programs. In 1966, Hazelden began treating men and women together and, in 1968, it opened an extended care treatment center for patients who needed a longer period of residential care.

In 1953, Hazelden purchased the rights to *Twenty-Four Hours a Day*, a book of inspirational messages for alcoholics. The publication of this book led the way for Hazelden's own publications business, which started off slowly and did not become successful until the 1970s. Hazelden has published books related to substance abuse, alcoholism, and codependency.

In the 1970s and 1980s, Hazelden expanded further and opened treatment centers in Plymouth, Minnesota; West Palm Beach, Florida; New York City; Chicago; and Newberg, Oregon. The treatment center in Plymouth serves young people (age fourteen to twenty-five years), whose needs may vary from those of adults. In 1984, the foundation opened a retreat center in Center City. In September of 1999 the foundation began a graduate degree program in addiction studies (accredited in 2007). In December of 2003, Hazelden opened a halfway house in St. Paul, Minnesota, and in 2010 it opened a treatment center in Naples, Florida.

The Hazelden treatment programs use the Minnesota model of treatment, which follows the ideas of Alcoholics Anonymous. The Minnesota model is based on the premise that alcoholism is a physical, spiritual, and mental disease, and not a moral failure on the part of the substance abuser. Accordingly, substance abusers are to be treated with dignity and respect. Primarily, the model includes group therapy because it is thought that substance abusers can be helped by discussing their experiences with other addicts. This is a central concept of the model. The goals of treatment include withdrawal from all mood-altering substances, improving the quality of life of the client, helping the client to achieve feelings of self-worth, increasing spiritual awareness in the client, assisting clients in developing relationships with other clients and with therapists, and educating clients in personal choice and responsibility.

The Minnesota model is based on existential philosophy. Existentialism is a philosophy that professes that the individual person determines the meaning of his or her life through the choices he or she makes. The presence of free will is essential to this philosophy. The role of therapists is to provide a comfortable, nurturing, caring, and client-centered environment for therapy.

The Minnesota model is considered the gold standard of treatment for substance abusers, although it does have limitations. One limitation is that its concept of the client having a disease contradicts the assumption of personal responsibility for one's own behavior.

MISSION AND GOALS

The mission of the Hazelden Foundation is to assist persons addicted to alcohol and other drugs in achieving recovery and to assist in maintaining their recovery throughout their lives. The mission includes the goal of helping as many people as possible.

Hazelden intends to achieve this mission through its addiction treatment programs and by publishing books about addiction and codependency, speaking out for persons with addictions, researching addictions and their treatments, providing education for addiction treatment professionals, and sharing research and results with other addiction treatment organizations.

The Hazelden Foundation remains committed to the twelve-step recovery program; to treating clients and their families with dignity and respect; to treating each client as an individual, and not treating their addiction only; and to keeping an open mind to new information and research about addictions. Hazelden continues to maintain a vital presence in the treatment and recovery of addicted persons.

Christine M. Carroll, RN, BSN, MBA

FURTHER READING

McElrath, Damian. *Hazelden: A Spiritual Odyssey.* Center City, MN: Hazelden, 1987. Written by a former administrator at Hazelden, this book provides a history of the Hazelden Foundation and the development of its treatment method for substance abuse, known as the Minnesota model.

National Institute on Drug Abuse. "Minnesota Model: Description of Counseling Approach." Web. 12 Mar. 2012. http://archives.drugabuse.gov/ADAC/ADAC11.html. Provides an outline of the Minnesota model of substance abuse treatment.

Spicer, Jerry. *The Minnesota Model: The Evolution of the Multidisciplinary Approach to Addiction Recovery.* Center City, MN: Hazelden, 1993. A comprehensive overview of the challenges, changes, history, and tenets of the Minnesota model.

Substance Abuse and Mental Health Services Administration. *National Survey of Substance Abuse Treatment Services, 2007: Data on Substance Abuse Treatment Facilities.* 2008. Web. 12 Mar. 2012. http://www.oas.samhsa.gov/nssats2k7/nssats2k7toc.cfm. A US government survey of treatment facilities in the United States.

The Way Home: A Collective Memoir of the Hazelden Experience. Center City, MN: Hazelden, 1997. Four former Hazelden patients describe their recovery from substance abuse.

WEBSITES OF INTEREST

Hazelden Foundation
http://www.hazelden.org

National Association of Addiction Treatment Providers
http://www.naatp.org

See also: Alcohol abuse and alcoholism: Treatment; Alcoholics Anonymous; Minnesota Model; Rehabilitation programs; Treatment methods and research; Twelve-step programs for addicts; Twelve-step programs for family and friends

Health disparities and substance abuse

CATEGORY: Social issues

DEFINITION: Health disparities are those differences in health-related treatment or outcomes that disproportionately affect ethnic and racial minorities, women, the working class and the poor, lesbian and gay persons, and the undereducated.

BACKGROUND

Social service agencies, the government, and researchers define a health disparity differently; however, it typically involves significant differences in treatment or outcomes. The National Institute of Allergy and Infectious Diseases states:

> Health disparities are gaps in the quality of health and health care that mirror differences in socioeconomic status, racial and ethnic background, and education level. These disparities may stem from many factors, including accessibility of health care, increased risk of disease from occupational exposure, and increased risk of disease from underlying genetic, ethnic, or familial factors.

Several studies indicate that health disparity is a problem in the primary care and behavioral healthcare system. Health disparities differentially impact ethnic and racial minorities, women, and other groups who, historically, have not had access to adequate health care.

DIFFERENCES IN HEALTH AND HEALTH CARE

The disparities found for many of these groups differ depending on the indicator or outcome examined; however, there are some underlying trends. Minorities tend to have poorer outcomes when compared with whites; women have poorer outcomes when compared with men; and gay and lesbian individuals have poorer outcomes when compared with heterosexual individuals. These disparities are noted even when other variables, such as socioeconomic status and availability of health care, are controlled for.

Health disparities are especially disconcerting when it comes to substance use. Although racial and ethnic minorities use drugs and alcohol at roughly the same rate as whites, racial and ethnic minorities suffer more ill effects from substance abuse. Health disparities related to substance abuse are noted in several areas, including human immunodeficiency virus (HIV) infection rates, transmission of sexually transmitted diseases (STDs), cardiovascular health as it relates to substance use, hepatitis and tuberculosis infection, and drug-related deaths. Recent statistics include the following:

- African Americans and Latinos are diagnosed with HIV at much higher rates when compared with whites.
- Hispanics/Latinos make up 15 percent of the US population but account for 19 percent of people living with acquired immunodeficiency syndrome (AIDS) and 19 percent of new AIDS diagnoses.
- African Americans make up approximately 13 percent of the US population but account for 44 percent of people living with AIDS; they also represent almost one-half of new AIDS diagnoses.
- African American women incarcerated for drug-related offenses are twice as likely to be HIV-positive when compared with men incarcerated for similar drug-related crimes.
- African Americans (13 percent of the US population) accounted for approximately 70 percent of reported gonorrhea cases and almost one-half of all chlamydia and syphilis cases in 2007.
- African American cocaine users develop more serious cardiovascular problems when compared with whites who also use cocaine.
- In 2007, 83 percent of all tuberculosis cases in the United States occurred in racial and ethnic minorities, particularly among Hispanics, Asians, and African Americans.
- American Indians and Alaska Natives were twice as likely to develop hepatitis C when compared with the white population.
- African Americans account for 22 percent of hepatitis C cases.
- According to the Centers for Disease Control and Prevention, all racial minorities, with the exception of Latinos, had increases in drug-related deaths between 2002 and 2007.

When examining the disparities for lesbian, gay, bisexual, and transgender (LGBT) people, similar results are noted. LGBT persons have higher rates of alcohol and substance abuse when compared with the rates noted among heterosexuals, are less likely to abstain from alcohol and drug use, and are more likely to continue with heavy drinking into later life. All of these behaviors also may contribute to an increased risk for HIV and other STDs.

DIFFERENCES IN TREATMENT

In addition to the disparities noted in health care among minority populations, disparities also are noted in access to and participation in treatment. For example, those of lower socioeconomic status typically access substance abuse treatment at levels significantly lower than persons in higher socioeconomic brackets.

Asian Americans access substance abuse treatment at lower levels than other racial and ethnic groups, even when controlling for prevalence of substance use disorders. Lesbians are less likely to access treatment services for substance use disorders. African American men are less likely to access residential treatment when compared with men of other racial and ethnic groups, and African Americans overall are less likely to complete substance abuse treatment when compared with whites.

Health disparities also affect persons who have both a mental illness and a substance use disorder (co-occurring or comorbid disorders, or COD). Persons with COD have a more difficult time accessing treatment, perhaps because of a lack of adequate training for the professionals who treat substance use and those who treat psychiatric disorders. This is particularly true of persons whose psychiatric illness (such as schizophrenia or bipolar disorder) is more complex and requires medication management.

CONCLUSION

The effect of the disparities noted goes beyond less access to treatment or increased risk of infection with an STD. Disparities significantly impact the individual and community and lead to increased morbidity and mortality.

To address the wide-ranging scope of the problem, the National Institutes of Health, the American Psychological Association, the Office of Minority Health, and other state and federal organizations have made reducing health disparities a priority for the last several years, and this priority continues. Some of the actions taken include developing special task forces, funding for research to examine and address disparities, and

encouraging minority and other scholars to engage in research in this area by offering grants and opportunities for training.

Desirée A. Crèvecoeur-MacPhail, PhD

FURTHER READING

Brown, L. S., et al. "Disparities in Health Services for HIV/AIDS, Hepatitis C virus, and Sexually Transmitted Infections: Role of Substance Abuse Treatment Programs." *Journal of Addiction Medicine* 3.2 (2009): 95–102. Concludes that services do exist that are tailored for special populations, despite barriers.

Burlew, A. K., et al. "Measurement and Data Analysis in Research Addressing Health Disparities in Substance Abuse." *Journal of Substance Abuse Treatment* 36.1 (2009): 25–43. Print. Discusses some of the issues with conducting substance abuse research with ethnic minorities and provides some strategies to increase the validity of such research.

Jacobson, J. O., P. Robinson, and R. N. Bluthenthal. "A Multilevel Decomposition Approach to Estimate the Role of Program Location and Neighborhood Disadvantage in Racial Disparities in Alcohol Treatment Completion." *Social Science and Medicine* 64.2 (2007): 462–76. Print. Attempts to explain the treatment disparities with regards to treatment completion.

Lowman, C., and C. E. Le Fauve. "Health Disparities and the Relationship between Race, Ethnicity, and Substance Abuse Treatment Outcomes." *Alcoholism: Clinical and Experimental Research* 27.8 (2003): 1324–26. Print. Describes some counterintuitive findings concerning disparities research that compared treatment outcomes between whites and African Americans.

WEBSITES OF INTEREST

Institute of Medicine Reports: Disparities
http://www.iom.edu/reports

MedLine Plus: Health Disparities
http://www.nlm.nih.gov/medlineplus/
    healthdisparities.html

National Institute of Allergy and Infectious Diseases
http://www.niaid.nih.gov/topics/minorityhealth/
    pages/disparities.aspx

See also: Gender and addiction; Insurance for addiction treatment; Poverty and substance abuse; Socioeconomic status and addiction

Heart attacks and substance abuse

CATEGORY: Health issues and physiology
ALSO KNOWN AS: Myocardial infarction
DEFINITION: A heart attack is an abrupt interruption of the flow of blood to the heart that results in damage to the heart or death because of a lack of oxygen to the heart muscle. The foods and substances one takes in are major contributors to coronary heart disease. Abuse of four addictive substances in particular—tobacco, alcohol, cocaine, and methamphetamine—increases the risks of a person developing coronary heart disease.

HEART ATTACK

A heart attack occurs when one of the coronary arteries (the vessels that supply blood to the heart) becomes blocked, thus preventing oxygen-rich, or oxygenated, blood from reaching the heart. A lack of oxygenated blood damages heart muscle and kills cells. The severity of a heart attack depends on how much heart muscle dies. For the patient, this could mean a long recovery period, permanent disability, or death. Coronary heart disease, the precursor of heart attack, is the leading cause of death for both women and men in the United States.

Coronary heart disease, also called coronary artery disease, atherosclerosis, or hardening of the arteries, is caused by deposits called plaques that form on the inside walls of coronary arteries. Plaques are a mixture of fat, calcium, cholesterol, and certain white blood cells. Plaques develop gradually over time. All adults have some plaques in their coronary arteries. When plaques are dense enough to restrict the normal healthy flow of oxygenated blood to the heart, coronary heart disease develops. When a section of a plaque deposit suddenly ruptures, blood clots form naturally to seal the crack. When a clot is large enough to block most of or the entire artery, a heart attack follows.

HEART ATTACK AND TOBACCO

Cigarette smoking increases the amount of artery-clogging plaque. An international study in 2007 found that chewing tobacco more than doubles the risk of heart attack, and that smoking and chewing quadruples the risk. The study also found that cigarette smoking triples the risk of heart attack and that the risk increases with every cigarette smoked. Even after quitting, heavy smokers continue to be at risk of heart attack up to twenty years later.

When combined with other risk factors for heart attack, smoking and chewing become even more lethal. Smoking raises blood pressure, increases the likelihood of blood clot formation, lowers the body's ability to benefit from exercise, and decreases high-density lipoprotein (HDL), the good cholesterol. HDL helps to remove bad cholesterol from arteries.

HEART ATTACK AND ALCOHOL

A number of studies have suggested that moderate alcohol consumption, especially of red wine, actually benefits the heart by reducing plaques in the coronary arteries and by increasing HDL cholesterol. How this happens in unclear. Moderate consumption is one drink per day for women and two for men. One drink is generally established as 12 ounces of beer, 5 ounces of wine, or 1.5 ounces of spirits.

However, consuming more than three drinks per day or binge-drinking has a toxic effect on the heart. In addition, heavy drinking over time adds fat to the blood, which increases cholesterol that can settle in the coronary arteries. Heavy drinking also leads to alcoholic cardiomyopathy, a condition in which the heart muscles are weakened and the heart becomes less efficient in pumping oxygenated blood throughout the body and back to the heart. Furthermore, heavy drinking causes high blood pressure, one of the major risks for coronary heart disease.

HEART ATTACK AND COCAINE

Cocaine abuse, whether long-term use or binging, also can lead to a heart attack. One study found that about 66 percent of heart attacks associated with cocaine abuse occurred within three hours of taking the drug, whether by inhaling it or taking it intravenously. A heart attack can occur anywhere from one minute to four days after consuming cocaine.

Cocaine triggers a heart attack in several ways. First, cocaine constricts the coronary arteries, thus reducing the amount of oxygenated blood flowing to the heart. There is no way to measure the amount of cocaine in the system or the duration of use before the constriction becomes so severe that it completely impedes the blood flow. Second, cocaine increases the heart's need for oxygen by speeding up the heart rate and raising blood pressure. Third, cocaine adds to the deposits of plaques in the coronary arteries, and fourth, cocaine produces changes in the blood that make the blood more likely to clot and block arteries.

HEART ATTACK AND METHAMPHETAMINE

Methamphetamine (meth) is dangerous to the heart. Prolonged use or binging leads to rapid heartbeat, irregular heartbeat, inflammation of the heart muscle, inflammation of the lining of the heart, and inflammation of blood vessels within the heart. Meth increases blood pressure and damages blood vessels throughout the body. It also constricts coronary arteries, the major cause of heart attack.

Furthermore, meth's damage to the heart and to the entire cardiovascular system is often irreversible. Even after years of abstaining from the drug, meth users still run a higher risk of suffering a heart attack than does the general population. Furthermore, because meth is so detrimental to every major organ in the body, meth abusers go through a much more difficult and longer recovery period from heart attack than do nonusers.

Wendell Anderson, BA

FURTHER READING

Aslibekyan, Stella, Emily Levitan, and Murray Mittleman. "Prevalent Cocaine Use and Myocardial Infarction." *American Journal of Cardiology* 102.8 (2008): 966–69. Print. Reports on a study of the association between cocaine use and heart attack.

Institute of Medicine. *Secondhand Smoke Exposure and Cardiovascular Effects: Making Sense of the Evidence.* 15 Oct. 2009. Web. 13 Mar. 2012. http://www.nap.edu/catalog.php?record_id=12649. Results of a study showing the link between secondhand smoke and coronary heart disease.

Westover, Arthur, Paul Nakonezny, and Robert Haley. "Acute Myocardial Infarction in Young Adults Who Abuse Amphetamines." *Drug and Alcohol Dependence* 96 (2008): 49–56. Print. Reports on a study of the association between amphetamine abuse and heart attack.

WEBSITES OF INTEREST

American Heart Association
http://www.heart.org

National Institute on Drug Abuse
http://www.drugabuse.gov

Women's Heart Foundation
http://www.womensheart.org

See also: Alcohol: Short- and long-term effects on the body; Cocaine use disorder; Methamphetamine; Smoking: Short- and long-term effects on the body

Heroin

CATEGORY: Substances

ALSO KNOWN AS: Big H; black; black tar heroin; boy; brown sugar; diacetylmorphine; diamorphine; dope; dragon; horse; junk; mud; skag; smack; snow; snowball; tar; white

DEFINITION: Heroin is a highly addictive opioid drug derived from the poppy plant. As an opiate, it functions as a central nervous system depressant similar to morphine, opium, methadone, and hydromorphone (Dilaudid).

STATUS: Illegal in the United States and worldwide

CLASSIFICATION: Schedule I controlled substance

SOURCE: A synthetic derivative of morphine, the most potent constituent of the opium poppy; formed by adding two acetyl groups to the morphine molecule; most of the illicit supply is smuggled into the United States from opium refinement sources in Southeast Asia, Afghanistan, and Mexico or is produced in illegal laboratories

TRANSMISSION ROUTE: Primarily exists in three forms: as a pure white bitter-tasting powder, an impure brown powder, and a black sticky substance called black tar heroin. Most street heroin is mixed or cut with other drugs, additives, and impurities, causing variations in color and potency. Heroin can be smoked, snorted, sniffed, or injected intravenously.

HISTORY OF USE

Diacetylmorphine, later named heroin, was originally synthesized in 1874 in London by the English chemist C. R. Alder Wright. However, it was not until 1898 that Bayer Pharmaceutical Company of Germany commercially introduced heroin as a new pain remedy and nonaddictive substitute for morphine. During the next several decades, heroin was sold legally worldwide and aggressively marketed as a cough medicine and as a safer, more potent form of morphine.

By the early twentieth century, heroin's intense euphoric effects were fully recognized, leading to widespread misuse. Numerous restrictions on the production, use, sale, and distribution of heroin were established to help prevent further abuse. These restrictions included the Harrison Narcotics Act of 1914, the Dangerous Drug Act of 1920, and the Heroin Act of 1924. As a result, heroin consumption briefly declined, but illicit production and trafficking grew. Heroin became one of the most sought after drugs in the world and, by 1970, the US Drug Enforcement

Black tar heroin. (UIG via Getty Images)

Administration classified heroin as a schedule I controlled narcotic. Class I drugs are those with a high abuse potential and no legitimate medical use.

Various methods have been used to gain heroin highs over the years, depending on user preference and drug purity. The most common and economical method of heroin use is injection, or "shooting up." Popular forms of shooting up include "mainlining" (injecting directly into a vein) and "skin-popping" (injecting directly into a muscle or under the skin).

Snorting and smoking heroin became popular as a result of the availability of higher quality heroin, the fear of contracting blood-borne illnesses through needle sharing, and the erroneous belief that inhaling heroin would not lead to addiction. The best-known method of smoking heroin is "chasing the dragon." Originating in the 1950s in Hong Kong, this method involves heating and liquefying the drug on tin foil and inhaling the vapors.

Some users crave an even greater high and engage in "speedballing" or "crisscrossing," which involves simultaneously injecting or snorting alternate lines of heroin and cocaine, respectively. Heroin is considered one of the most dangerous and psychologically and physically addictive drugs available. It remains a serious health issue throughout the world.

EFFECTS AND POTENTIAL RISKS

Heroin is the fastest acting of the opiates; it is three times more potent than morphine. It acts by depressing the central nervous system through an endorphin-like mechanism. Heroin rapidly crosses the blood-brain barrier because of its high lipid solubility. It is quickly metabolized into morphine and binds to the opioid receptors responsible not only for suppressing pain sensation and relieving anxiety but also for critical life processes.

The short-term effects of heroin are attributed to its properties as an opiate. These effects have made heroin one of the most desirable drugs in the world. Heroin produces a warm surge of pleasure and euphoria referred to as a rush. This rush is followed by feelings of peacefulness, well-being, contentment, and physical relaxation. Users go "on the nod," alternating between wakeful and drowsy states while experiencing little sensitivity to pain.

Minor, negative, short-term effects of heroin use include nausea, vomiting, constipation, severe itching, dry mouth, difficulty urinating, heavy extremities, impaired mental functioning, and constricted pupils. Nonpleasurable sensations, such as irritability and depression, can occur as the high dissipates. However, the most serious side effect of heroin use is respiratory depression, which can be fatal.

The most immediate and intense heroin rush is achieved by intravenous injection. However, this transmission route is the most dangerous. The risk of contracting infectious diseases such as human immunodeficiency virus and hepatitis viruses is substantial. Furthermore, illegal street heroin can be contaminated with unknown additives and impurities such as sugar, starch, and poisons, which can cause blood vessel inflammation, blockage, and permanent damage.

Long-term heroin use can lead to adverse physical effects, including collapsed veins, heart and skin infections, liver and kidney disease, and pulmonary complications. Continuous heroin use may affect brain functioning as a result of repeated respiratory suppression and lack of oxygen. However, the most detrimental long-term effect of heroin use is physical and psychological dependence and addiction, which can occur quickly; users crave larger and larger doses of the drug to achieve the original high.

Rose Ciulla-Bohling, PhD

Buprenorphine

Buprenorphine is an opioid analgesic approved for use in the treatment of moderate to severe pain and for treatment of opioid dependence. Buprenorphine has been investigated for treating symptoms associated with opioid and heroin withdrawal. It is available as a sublingual tablet for treating dependence, and it is classified as a schedule III controlled substance.

Buprenorphine therapy is divided into three phases: the induction phase, when treatment is initiated after a patient has abstained from opioid products for twelve to twenty-four hours; the stabilization phase, during which time a patient gradually reduces or discontinues the use of opioid products; and the maintenance phase, in which a patient continues a steady buprenorphine dose for an indefinite time to control cravings and withdrawal symptoms associated with opioid abstinence.

FURTHER READING

Brezina, Corona. *Heroin: The Deadly Addiction*. New York: Rosen, 2009. Discusses the health implications of abusing heroin.

Cobb, Allan B., and Ronald J. Brogan. *Heroin: Junior Drug Awareness*. New York: Chelsea House, 2009. Provides a basic overview of the history of heroin abuse and its addictive nature. Written for younger readers.

Elliot-Wright, Susan. *Heroin*. Chicago: Raintree, 2005. Examines the history, health effects, treatment, and prevention of heroin addiction and its dangerous effect on society.

Libby, Therissa A. *Heroin: The Basics*. Center City, MN: Hazelden, 2007. An introduction to the history, health effects, and addiction risks of heroin use.

Morales, Francis. *The Little Book of Heroin*. Berkeley, CA: Ronin, 2000. Discusses the history and chemistry of heroin and ways to avoid heroin addiction.

WEBSITES OF INTEREST

MedlinePlus: "Heroin"
http://www.nlm.nih.gov/medlineplus/heroin.html

National Institute on Drug Abuse
http://www.drugabuse.gov/infofacts/heroin.html

US Drug Enforcement Administration
http://www.justice.gov/dea/concern/heroin.html#1

See also: Intravenous drug use and blood-borne diseases; Morphine; Narcotics abuse; Recreational drugs

---

History of addiction

CATEGORY: Social issues

DEFINITION: Drugs have been part of human history for centuries, but the nature of addiction and dependence has changed considerably. What might be called drug cults, historically located in traditional cultures and sometimes associated with religious ceremonies, have metamorphosed in some modern societies into alarming mass tendencies. The nature of addictive drugs also has evolved, particularly since the mid- to late twentieth century.

EARLY HISTORY OF DRUG ADDICTION

The history of drug addiction can be traced to prehistoric times. Certain areas of the world, most notably pre-Columbian America, may be said to have developed a culture of drugs as part of religious (or ceremonial) belief systems.

The use of plants with narcotic effects by ruling elites and priests was noted by Spanish conquistadors who came in contact with the Incas of Peru. Drugs such as peyote (derived from a spineless cactus growing in Mexico and parts of Texas) have been used by indigenous populations around the world for their transcendental effects and as meditation.

Probably the most widely known historical example of addiction is the case of so-called opium dens in China. Although popular views may have distorted the image of opium addiction in China, the problem of opium consumption definitely increased during the eighteenth and into the nineteenth century. The Chinese imperial administration, acting in response to a push by India-based British merchants to flood the Chinese market with opium imports, attempted several times to outlaw opium use. Historians also note the use, and the production, of opium in eighteenth century colonial America, in which local militias seem to have used the drug before entering battle. They did so with the knowledge and even encouragement of commanders.

MODERN RISE OF DRUG ADDICTION

Drug addiction in some form was probably present in all societies from ancient times into modern times. A general consensus exists, however, that the socially damaging spread of addiction has become the hallmark of mass modern cultures, particularly in the Western world, beginning in the twentieth century.

Certain addictive drugs have played such a significant role in the modern Western world that each demands its own full history. This is especially the case with marijuana (cannabis and hashish), cocaine (a product of the coca plant), opium (a product of the poppy plant), morphine (derived from opium), and heroin (derived from morphine). Drugs that have spread throughout the world since the mid-twentieth century have shorter but, in terms of their disastrous addictive effects, equally important histories. Among these drugs are methamphetamine and crack cocaine.

In the United States and Canada several addictive drugs became particularly popular in certain periods and among certain population groups. While the dangers of smoking marijuana (or any of the common drugs associated with marijuana) continue to be debated, there is general agreement that, compared with hard drugs, marijuana is not necessarily an addictive drug. This is not the case with other drugs that became popular in recent history.

One side effect of the Prohibition era (1919–1933) in the United States was near glorification of illicit consumption not only of alcohol but also of cocaine and other drugs for partygoers. At a much less glamorous level (in this case both before and after the Prohibition years), both male and female addicts have become prostitutes to obtain money to sustain their habit.

Statistical studies (limited in the first half of the twentieth century) indicate that the number of addicts in the United States and Canada declined between 1940 and 1945, probably because of wartime effects on international supply lines. Drug addiction became an increasing problem, however, in the second half of the century. By the 1950s news of rising drug addiction spread rapidly through the media, particularly when, starting in 1953 in the United States, the Federal Bureau of Narcotics began collecting detailed statistics.

A growing body of statistical reports covering the next five decades of the century would reveal different levels of susceptibility to the dangers of addiction. What was considered alarming in the first years after 1950 was that the use of "soft" drugs (such as marijuana) was becoming almost commonplace; also, the average age of cigarette smokers was decreasing.

Debate about the presumed nonaddictive nature of marijuana and its potential medical benefits continued, and so did debate about the dangers of hard drugs. Addiction was soon an unavoidable subject for government agencies, educational institutions, churches and synagogues, medical treatment centers, and, inevitably, the penal system.

Perhaps foremost on the list of hard drugs associated with addiction before the 1960s is heroin. Initially (around World War I, when chemists discovered a process to derive heroin from morphine to use as a legal painkiller), private users of illegal drugs may have welcomed heroin for its illusory and temporary euphoric effects (later referred to as a heroin rush). Attraction to such sensations had its costs, as heroin users begin to enter alternate periods of wakefulness and drowsiness (a state known as the nod). Mental faculties declined and other bodily functions (such as speech, vision, digestion, and bowel elimination) were affected too. Withdrawal symptoms experienced by an addict (for example, muscle and bone pain, muscle spasms, insomnia, and severe upset stomach) reach their height after about forty-eight hours without new injections.

1960s DRUG CULTURE

Probably more than any other decade, the 1960s stand out as the era both of increasing hard drug addiction and of a rising level of popular experimentation with drugs. Public consumption of marijuana became synonymous with anti-establishment youth rebellion.

The use of dangerous psychedelic drugs, particularly acid, or LSD (lysergic acid diethylamide), was more limited. However, acid was part of a counterculture wave not only among youth but also among the adult population. By the end of the 1960s, however, the term *drug culture* began to be associated not with youth rebellion but with widespread social, economic, and political problems.

Rising levels of addiction in the economically depressed environments of large cities in the United States became increasingly alarming. Also, US military authorities announced a significant number of cases of servicemembers in Vietnam using drugs. For an entire generation of Americans, the decade of the 1960s will be remembered for the presumed attraction of "tripping" and for the growing signs of the psychological, economic, social, and politically destructive effects of addiction.

CRACK COCAINE AND METHAMPHETAMINE

Crack cocaine's appearance on economically depressed inner-city streets in the United States in the mid-1980s marked the beginning of a new and dangerous direction for confirmed addicts and for new drug users. Crack is a highly addictive rock-like substance that is a by-product of a chemical process that converts normal powder-form cocaine. Illicit manufacturers of crack cocaine omit certain steps in the production process and use cheap sodium bicarbonate as a substitute additive. The product can be marketed at lower prices, thus attracting economically disadvantaged drug users.

Methamphetamine (meth) became a significant addictive substance in the 1990s. Synthetic ephedrine

(the basic component of amphetamine) had been produced by chemists in Germany and Japan in the last decades of the nineteenth century. As early as the 1930s the derivative amphetamine became a major prescription drug used to treat a number of illnesses, including epilepsy, schizophrenia, and various forms of depression. Methamphetamine itself became an important new arrival on the drug scene when relatively simple but dangerous chemical methods of producing it became known both to profit-seeking dealers and to a rising number of meth addicts. All such chemical processes are exceedingly dangerous, not only because of risks of fire and explosions but also because of resultant (potentially deadly) contamination of so-called cooking sites and surrounding buildings, some of which must be permanently condemned.

A notorious name associated with this particular sector of the drug culture is Uncle Fester (pseudonym for industrial chemist Steve Preisler, known in his college years for experiments with explosives). In the mid-1980s (following his arrest for purchases of ephedrine and for possession of meth) Preisler wrote the extremely controversial *Secrets of Methamphetamine Manufacture*. His other books have equally alarming titles (*Home Workshop Explosives* and *Silent Death*).

DRUG ADDICTION IN CANADA SINCE 2000

The experiences of Canada with heroin, cocaine, and meth addiction have received less attention than in the United States. Statistics from Canada indicate that, in the case of heroin, a stark contrast exists between recorded drug use nationally (less than 1 percent) compared with drug use in large cities and certain "vulnerable" regions. Northwestern Ontario's figure in 2003 (2.4 percent), for example, was about double the number for the rest of the province. Generally, however, Canadian statistics have shown a gradual decrease in heroin usage in the first years of the twenty-first century.

The picture for meth use in the same period is of more concern. Overall, national statistics indicate that 4.6 percent of the population had tried meth at least once, whereas in certain provinces (Quebec and British Columbia in particular), the figures were not only higher, but instances of addiction were increasing.

Studies of drug addiction in Canada, of meth in particular, note a trend that seems to be emerging in all countries where drug addiction is a serious problem: The relative age of those experimenting with (but not necessarily addicted to) meth is much lower than in previous years. In 2004, for example, more than 10 percent of Canadian youths between the ages of twelve and seventeen years indicated they had tried meth. The situation was even more serious among homeless youth in large cities such as Montreal, where meth use affected more than one-half the persons surveyed.

CRIMINAL INVOLVEMENT IN DRUG ADDICTION

The history of drug addiction includes not only the consideration of specific drugs and their effects but also the effects of addiction on society. Such effects inevitably involve penal violations and legal sanctions to control the effect of drug violations on society as a whole.

At the highest level, large-scale international drug dealings are considered among the most dangerous and harmful arenas of criminal activity, affecting certain areas of the world in particular, namely Latin America, Southeast Asia, and Afghanistan. However, street-level criminality involving drug addicts and drug dealers in many cities of the United States and Europe has at times reached near-epidemic rates.

Because addiction often forces addicts to spend money that goes beyond their means, the temptation to earn money by selling drugs to others is common, even if they are employed. In economically depressed neighborhoods, where more than one-half the potential labor force remains unemployed, this phenomenon can create disastrous consequences, especially when rival gangs (often linked to sponsorship from higher-level drug dealers) defend their "turf" with violence. The victims of this violence have included addicts, dealers, and even bystanders.

Although drug addiction is almost always associated with the use of hard drugs such as crack cocaine and heroin, ample evidence shows that young people who become addicts often had their first experience with drugs by experimenting with chemicals in common over-the-counter substances. Some practices, including the sniffing of certain household chemicals, have occurred for several generations.

New ways to get high with common, legal substances are found regularly. In mid-July 2011, for example, the *New York Times* reported rising evidence that young people were using certain common bath salts containing the dangerous chemicals mephedrone and methylenedioxypyrovalerone as recreational drugs. In this case, harmful effects may be immediate and drastic. Efforts to stop over-the-counter sales of such products have been unevenly successful, varying from state to state.

Byron D. Cannon, PhD

FURTHER READING

"Crack, a Disaster of Historic Dimensions, Still Growing." *New York Times*, 28 May 1989. Print. Brief but thought-provoking coverage of the spread of crack cocaine to different socioeconomic sectors and age groups in the United States.

Diköter, Frank, Lars Laamann, and Zhou Xun. *Narcotic Culture: A History of Drugs in China*. Chicago: U of Chicago P, 2004. A general history of the main aspects of drug addiction in China, with emphasis on its cultural impact in a highly traditional Asian society.

Flynn, John C. *Cocaine*. New York: Birch Lane, 1991. An overview of the history and effects of cocaine written for the general reader.

Hosztafi, S. "The History of Heroin." *Acta Pharmaceutica Hungarica* 2 (1971): 233–42. Print. A concise historical account of heroin usage and its chemical effects on the body.

Kandall, Stephen R. *Substance and Shadow: Women and Addiction in the United States*. Cambridge, MA: Harvard UP, 1996. Although the subject of drug addiction is treated as a general topic, this book focuses on the specific effects of addiction on women.

Weisheit, Ralph, and William L. White. *Methamphetamine: Its History, Pharmacology, and Treatment*. Center City, MN: Hazelden, 2009. Combines fairly technical scientific information on the chemical aspects of methamphetamine with the disastrous social impact and physical dangers of this drug.

WEBSITES OF INTEREST

American Society of Addiction Medicine
http://www.asam.org

History of Cocaine Timeline
http://www.cocaineaddiction.com/cocaine_timeline.html

History of Heroin and Opium Timeline
http://www.heroinaddiction.com/heroin_timeline.html

History of Marijuana and Cannabis Timeline
http://www.addiction2.com/marijuana/history-of-
    marijuana-cannabis-timeline-2.html

History of Methamphetamine and Amphetamine Timeline
http://www.methamphetamineaddiction.com/
    methamphetamine_timeline.html

National Institute on Drug Abuse
http://www.drugabuse.gov

PubMed Health: "Drug Dependence"
http://www.ncbi.nlm.nih.gov/pubmedhealth/
    PMH0002490

See also: Addiction; Just Say No campaign; Trends
and statistics: Alcohol abuse; Trends and statistics: Behavioral addictions; Trends and statistics: Illegal drug
use; Trends and statistics: Prescription drug abuse;
Trends and statistics: Smoking

HIV/AIDS and substance abuse

CATEGORY: Health issues and physiology

DEFINITION: The human immunodeficiency virus
(HIV) is a pathogen. Acquired immune deficiency syndrome (AIDS) is the disease caused by HIV
and is characterized by progressive loss of immune
function and the onset of opportunistic infections
and a variety of cancers. Substance abuse can lead
to high-risk behaviors, including unprotected sex
and sharing drug needles, which increase the
chances of HIV infection.

CAUSES

HIV causes AIDS. The virus enters immune cells, especially CD4 T-helper cells. Dormancy in those cells is
possible, and activation of the virus to the replicative
stage leads to the destruction of those immune cells.
AIDS results when the infected person's T-helper cell
count is reduced to the extent that frequent opportunistic infections occur.

RISK FACTORS

Drug abuse makes addicts vulnerable to infection. The sharing of needles and cocaine straws, for

example, exposes users to each other's body fluids.
Also, intravenous drug abusers inject substances with
immunosuppressive effects.

Immunologic defenses also are compromised by
the simultaneous abuse of alcohol and tobacco and by
personal neglect. The addict also may have impaired
functioning of phagocytosis, reduced superoxide production, and reduced T-cell function, making the immune system ineffective at neutralizing the virus.

Also a risk factor for HIV infection is engaging in
unprotected sex. Anal and vaginal penetration that
causes injury can make a person vulnerable to HIV
infection.

SYMPTOMS

The symptoms of HIV infection can be limited to the
presence of anti-HIV antibodies. After the reduction of
T-helper cell count, otherwise rare cancers, such as Ka-
posi's sarcoma, may result. Numerous bacteria, viruses,
and fungi cause infection when the immune system is
compromised by a reduced count of T-helper cells.

SCREENING AND DIAGNOSIS

Four rapid HIV tests are available. Each has received
marketing approval by the US Food and Drug Administration. These tests are OraQuick Advance Rapid
HIV-1/2 Antibody Test, manufactured by OraSure
Technologies; Reveal G2 Rapid HIV-1 Antibody Test
by MedMira; Uni-Gold Recombigen HIV Test, made
by Trinity BioTech; and Multispot HIV-1/HIV-2 Rapid
Test by Bio-Rad Laboratories. Each of these tests is an
HIV enzyme immunoassay (EIA), and each is considered a screening test. Also, each test mandates additional confirmatory tests if the results are positive.

The basis of these tests is the ability to detect anti-
HIV antibodies in body fluids. Antibodies are products of the immune system that are produced in
response to exposure to a virus and its component
proteins. Antigens, or proteins, from the virus are
embedded in or affixed to a filter. Because antibodies
generated after exposure to HIV bind specifically to
the viral proteins, antibodies in a person's body fluids
will bind to the filter exactly where the protein in the
test kit was placed. To determine if antibodies from
the sample are present on the filter, a second antibody from the test kit is added.

The secondary antibody specifically binds to the
person's antibodies. When an exposed person takes
the test, the secondary antibody binds and creates

a complex. The complex is created only when the person has anti-HIV antibodies in his or her fluids.

Detection of the complex on the filter paper is possible because the secondary antibodies in the test kit come with an enzyme linked to them. This enzyme catalyzes a reaction that results in a color change. The color is detected by visual inspection of the filter paper. Because these kits detect the presence of antibody in the person's fluids and not the virus, a positive result requires additional testing.

The polymerase chain reaction works by detecting the genetic material unique to the HIV virus. This assay works by adding the necessary components for the replication of genetic material to the sample. If HIV genetic material is present, it will be multiplied to generate quantities that can be detected by a color-forming reaction not unlike the EIA tests.

TREATMENT AND THERAPY
Highly active antiretroviral therapy (HAART) is the recommended treatment for HIV. HAART is administered as a combination of three or more anti-HIV medications from a minimum of two different classes. Nucleoside reverse transcriptase inhibitors comprise one class of anti-HIV drug. These drugs inhibit the HIV enzyme reverse transcriptase by means of blockage with a nucleoside. Non-nucleoside reverse transcriptase inhibitors inhibit the same viral enzyme through means other than the addition of nucleosides. Protease inhibitors block another key enzyme from the virus.

Three additional classes of anti-HIV drugs block functions critical to the infection process. They are entry inhibitors, fusion inhibitors, and integrase inhibitors. Because each class of medications blocks the virus in a different way, the combination of several medications increases the chances of preventing viral replication and decreases the chance that the virus will survive long enough to mutate into a resistant form. Some of the drugs are available as a combination pill of two or more different anti-HIV medications from one or more classes.

PREVENTION
Prevention of HIV infection and the development of AIDS in the drug abuser centers on behavior modification. Because HIV is a blood-borne pathogen, one should not share needles. The virus also can be transmitted through sharing cocaine straws among users with damaged nasal mucosa.

Needle Sharing

Intravenous (IV) drug users often share needles (syringes), cookers, and other injection paraphernalia. This practice is associated with the injection of illicit substances, most commonly heroin or other opiates. Users also inject a combination of heroin and cocaine (speedball), cocaine by itself, or any other drug. Needle sharing can lead to blood-borne diseases such as hepatitis and human immunodeficiency virus (HIV) infection.

Needles are shared among users mainly because of a scarcity of clean needles. Needle exchange programs have been implemented in some US states and in some countries outside the United States, but they are controversial. Some persons believe the programs simply enable drug abuse; program advocates disagree, arguing that the availability of clean needles reduces potential harm among users and helps to connect users with treatment programs. Needle exchange programs also distribute needle-cleaning kits among IV-drug users. These kits include materials that help to kill any viruses the needles might contain.

Sexual activity also can expose participants to body fluids and, thus, the virus. The use of condoms is recommended. The close association of drug abuse and prostitution makes prevention difficult. Despite numerous vaccination strategies tested for the prevention of AIDS or reduction of replication of the HIV virus, no effective vaccine has been found to date.

Kimberly A. Napoli, MS

FURTHER READING

Levine, Donald P., and Jack D. Sobel, eds. *Infections in Intravenous Drug Abusers.* New York: Oxford UP, 1999. A comprehensive text for advanced readers and substance abuse specialists.

Ruiz, Pedro, Eric C. Strain, and John G. Langrod. "HIV Infections and AIDS." *The Substance Abuse Handbook.* Philadelphia: Wolters, 2007. Discusses HIV infection and AIDS in the context of substance use and abuse.

Tortora, Gerard J., Berdell R. Funke, and Christine L. Case. *Microbiology: An Introduction.* 9th ed. New York: Pearson, 2007. A microbiology textbook focusing on infectious diseases.

WEBSITES OF INTEREST
Centers for Disease Control and Prevention
http://www.cdc.gov/hiv

Gay and Lesbian Medical Health Association
http://www.glma.org

National Institute on Drug Abuse
http://www.drugabuse.gov

See also: Heroin; Intravenous drug use and blood-borne diseases; Substance abuse

Hoarding

CATEGORY: Psychological issues and behaviors

DEFINITION: Hoarding involves the compulsive acquisition and accumulation of objects, animals, and trash and other debris. The hoarder, who often has a mental illness such as clinical depression, is unable or unwilling to discard anything, resulting in health and safety hazards to all who reside in the dwelling.

ORIGINS AND SYMPTOMS

Not much is known about the cause of hoarding. Research has sought to establish a relationship between the disorder and biological and environmental factors. Some cases of hoarding appear to be responses to grief or loss, while others are considered symptoms of obsessive-compulsive disorder (OCD)—an anxiety disorder in which obsessions and fears promote compulsive or repetitive behaviors the person feels driven to accommodate. Another primary rationale for hoarding is thought to be to avoid waste. The hoarder believes that items should not be discarded because they may be needed later. The idea of an OCD connection with hoarding is quite controversial, as many argue that acquiring items makes hoarders happy.

Common denominators among hoarders, though difficult to identify, do exist. Studies indicate that about one-half of hoarders are clinically depressed. Most have problems with organization. Hoarding shows no real response to early life deprivation, and all thoughts focus upon loss when the hoarder is forced to discard items.

Some hoarders shop compulsively, anticipating a need at some unknown point for the vast number of items brought into the house. Stacks of expired canned food frequently occupy excessive space along with various cooking utensils. Other hoarders save seemingly worthless items and scraps from their past to which they maintain intense emotional attachment. Frequently, items include piles of arts and craft objects—past handiwork of the hoarder, who cannot discard the scraps.

Assorted newspapers, magazines, and articles of clothing line walls in stacks that reach the ceiling, allowing limited access to areas of the house and threatening to collapse upon persons needing access. Hoarded material covers floors, tables, chairs, beds, and eventually all surfaces in the residence. Also, many hoarders collect items that were purchased years earlier and still remain in the original wrapping.

EFFECTS OF HOARDING

Of the more than six million persons in the United States who are thought to be hoarders, many began to exhibit signs of the disorder during adolescence. Some come from homes in which a family member engaged in hoarding. However, most family members of hoarders seem to be embarrassed by the conditions produced by hoarding. Children often leave home as soon as possible and frequently end all communication with the hoarder, who is usually the mother (as most hoarders are women). Spouses seek divorces or become hoarders themselves. A hoarder left alone will often continue to hoard until friends, family, neighbors, or local health authorities intervene.

Animal hoarding involves keeping more pets than can be properly cared for. Animal waste, decayed food and vermin, nonexistent sanitation procedures, and a deteriorating house lead to long-lasting health problems for animals and human residents. The effects on overcrowded, underfed, medically neglected animals legally constitute animal cruelty. Animals that survive such conditions often require extensive rehabilitation; some animals never recover. Humans face high ammonia levels, insect and rodent infestations, parasitic diseases, and food-related illnesses.

Taken in 2010, this photograph shows a home in Chicago, Illinois, where an elderly couple was found buried alive in a hoarded mess. (Alex Garcia/MCT/Landov)

TREATMENT

The main goal of treating people who hoard is to change behaviors, including the compulsion to hoard. Oftentimes, this involves changing the relationship a person has with his or her possessions, which is a long, slow process that can involve discarding one item at a time.

Hoarders sometimes benefit from therapists or professional organizers. Also, therapists could, with the hoarder's help, formulate guidelines for throwing items away. For example, the "two-year rule," frequently a good rule to follow, suggests that if something has not been used in the past two years, chances are it will never be used and should probably be discarded.

Therapists and professional organizers also help hoarders become aware of the buying patterns that encourage hoarding. Hoarders should be urged, for example, to remove magazines and newspapers from the home after a certain period, and mail should be sorted daily (eliminating all junk mail). Filing cabinets should be employed for items such as bills, tax statements, and other important papers. In severe cases of comorbid anxiety, medication can reduce the obsession associated with discarding and with the symptoms of depression. Although hoarding cannot be cured, it can, with behavior modification, medication, and determination, be kept under control.

In cases of animal hoarding, the causes tend to be more serious and, therefore, require more deliberate treatment. Animal hoarders often suffer from dementia, attachment difficulties, and an inability to interpret clearly. Boston veterinarian Gary Patronek considers animal hoarding to be a "pathological human behavior that involves a compulsive need to obtain and control animals, coupled with the failure to recognize their suffering." Extremely difficult to treat successfully, animal hoarding requires extended psychological care long after the animals have been removed from the home. Also, psychologists recommend the involvement of animal welfare, police, health agencies, and the community in continued follow-up measures to work against a recidivist rate that is nearly 100 percent for animal hoarders.

Mary Hurd

FURTHER READING

Arluke, Arnold, and Celeste Killeen. *Inside Animal Hoarding: The Case of Barbara Erickson and Her 552 Dogs.* Lafayette, IN: Purdue UP, 2009. An account of a dog-hoarding case affecting hundreds of starving, ill, and maimed canines.

Bratiotis, Christiana, Cristina Sorrentino Schmalisch, and Gail Steketee. *The Hoarding Handbook: A Guide for Human Service Professionals.* New York: Oxford UP, 2011. Provides tools to assess the hoarding, to coordinate and delegate tasks among helping professionals, and to work directly with reluctant hoarders.

Frost, R. O., G. Patronek, and E. Rosenfield. "Comparison of Object and Animal Hoarding." *Depression and Anxiety* 28.10 (2011): 885–91. Print. Discusses the similarities and differences between object and animal hoarding. Also questions if people who hoard animals meet the same diagnostic criteria proposed for hoarding in general.

Neziroglu, Fugen, Jerome Bubrick, and Jose A. Yaryara-Tobias. *Overcoming Compulsive Hoarding: Why You Save and How You Can Stop.* Oakland, CA: New Harbinger, 2004. Hoarding specialists discuss the causes and patterns of compulsive behavior and provide information on valuable techniques and guidelines for eliminating clutter.

Steketee, Gail, and Randy Frost. *Stuff: Compulsive Hoarding and the Meaning of Things.* New York: Mariner, 2011. An excellent study into the lives of persons who hoard. Seeks causes of hoarding, examines the effects of it on family members, and presents interviews with extreme hoarders who speak of their intimate connection with their hoarded items.

Tompkins, Michael A., and Tamara L. Hartl. *Digging Out: Helping a Loved One Manage Clutter, Hoarding, and Compulsive Acquisitions.* Oakland, CA: New Harbinger, 2009. Psychologists help frustrated family and friends of hoarders who are in denial about their problems. Offers harm reduction strategies to help hoarders, especially the frail and elderly, with health and safety problems, and discusses ways to avoid relationship harm.

WEBSITES OF INTEREST

Clutterers Anonymous
http://www.clutterersanonymous.net

Hoarding of Animals Research Consortium
http://vet.tufts.edu/hoarding

Institute for Challenging Disorganization
http://www.nsgcd.org

International OCD Foundation
http://www.ocfoundation.org/hoarding

See also: Behavioral addictions: Overview; Compulsions; Families and behavioral addictions

Homelessness

CATEGORY: Social issues

DEFINITION: Homelessness is the state of not having a stable, adequate place of residence. Homeless persons include those sleeping outdoors and in buildings not intended as housing and persons temporarily dwelling in shelters or other institutions meant to lodge people without permanent housing. Substance abuse and addiction can both precipitate and develop from homelessness.

PREVALENCE AND PATTERNS OF HOMELESSNESS

Though homelessness is difficult to measure, various governmental and nonprofit agencies estimate that more than 500,000 people are without a place to sleep on any given night in the United States, and between 2.3 and 3.5 million people per year experience homelessness. The majority (more than 70 percent) of people who experience homelessness are located in urban areas, but the phenomenon also exists in suburban and rural areas.

The number of people who face homelessness has risen dramatically since the last decades of the twentieth century, and it continues to increase as the foreclosure crisis in the United States has displaced more and more families. Families with children comprise one of the fastest growing groups among the homeless (more than 20 percent of the total population). Children account for approximately 1.5 million of the yearly homeless population. Women and girls, who comprise about one-third of the single homeless population, make up 65 percent of homeless families. Individuals and families who experience poverty have the highest probability of becoming homeless and demographic groups with high poverty rates are overrepresented among the homeless.

The racial and ethnic makeup of the homeless population reveals a striking disparity, with African Americans being grossly overrepresented. Though African Americans represent only about 12 percent of the total US population, they account for more than 40 percent of homeless persons. Hispanics and Native Americans also are overrepresented, but to a lesser degree, comprising 20 and 4 percent of the homeless, respectively. White and Asian Americans are underrepresented and constitute 38 and 2 percent of the homeless, respectively. Other groups that are overrepresented among the homeless population are military veterans, people with mental illness, and persons with substance abuse problems.

Some people who experience addiction or alcohol and drug misuse, serious mental or physical health conditions, or developmental challenges become chronically homeless, meaning that they are without a stable place to live continuously for one entire year, or are episodically homeless a minimum of four times in the past three years. About 20 percent of the homeless qualify as chronically homeless.

CAUSES OF HOMELESSNESS

Although many factors contribute to homelessness, several factors are particularly prevalent. Poverty is a leading factor. Persons who are unemployed or underemployed, and those who work for less than a living wage, often cannot afford housing. Low wages and insufficient social welfare benefits often cannot match increased costs of living, leaving many in debt and unable to pay their bills. The decreases in the availability of affordable and subsidized housing, along with the increased number of foreclosure-related evictions, have led many families to homelessness.

Health care, domestic violence, incarceration, mental illness, and substance abuse and addiction also are related to homelessness. Lack of affordable health care is one problem that can leave individuals and families with an insurmountable debt that precipitates homelessness. Many women and children are affected by domestic violence, and those who live in poverty may become homeless after leaving an abuser. Domestic violence shelters limit the amount of time a woman and her children can stay, and women without the resources to secure housing confront the prospect of extended homelessness when they leave.

Formerly incarcerated persons often lack the resources and job opportunities needed to acquire housing upon release from jail or prison and face the additional challenge of being ineligible for government-subsidized programs because of their criminal records. Persons who have a severe mental illness are at risk of homelessness, as they often have difficulty living independently and do not have adequate access to programs and supportive housing options. Substance abuse and addiction also can contribute to or extend homelessness, affecting approximately 40 percent of homeless persons. Alcohol is the most commonly used substance among this population.

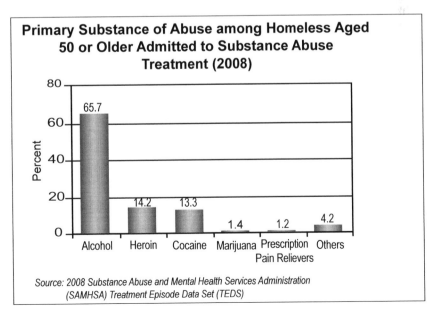

Primary Substance of Abuse among Homeless Aged 50 or Older Admitted to Substance Abuse Treatment (2008)

Source: 2008 Substance Abuse and Mental Health Services Administration (SAMHSA) Treatment Episode Data Set (TEDS)

SUBSTANCE ABUSE AND ADDICTION

Substance abuse and addiction can both precipitate and develop from homelessness. Abuse and addiction can cause problems with family and work relationships, which can lead to homelessness, particularly for those with a limited income. For others, homelessness serves as an introduction to substances of abuse, which are often used to cope with the difficulties of being homeless. Rates of abuse and addiction are substantially higher among the homeless than among the general population, and substance abuse often co-occurs with mental illness. Homelessness can exacerbate addiction or misuse, as the increased pains of homelessness and the immediacy of survival take precedence over treatment.

Treatment options are severely limited for those who cannot finance inpatient programs, and even these involve short stays that often result in a return to the streets or to shelters. A lack of long-term comprehensive care has prompted researchers and advocates to recommend nationwide implementation of integrative housing, treatment, and support programs that address not only issues surrounding substance abuse and addiction but also those additional problems that result from homelessness and mental illness.

Tammi Arford, MA

FURTHER READING

Bourgois, Philippe, and Jeff Schonberg. *Righteous Dopefiend.* Berkeley: U California P, 2010. After more than a decade of research, the authors present a photo-ethnography that chronicles the lives of homeless heroin users in San Francisco.

Hopper, Kim. *Reckoning with Homelessness.* Ithaca, NY: Cornell UP, 2009. Hopper, a scholar-activist, provides a social, historical, and cultural exploration of homelessness in the United States.

Kusmer, Kenneth L. *Down and Out, On the Road: The Homeless in American History.* New York: Oxford UP, 2002. Focusing on structural and cultural issues, this book provides a far-reaching history of homelessness in the United States, ranging from the colonial era to the present.

Levinson, David, ed. *Encyclopedia of Homelessness.* Thousand Oaks, CA: Sage, 2004. A collection of articles on all aspects of homelessness.

Schutt, Russell K., and Stephen M. Goldfinger. *Homelessness, Housing, and Mental Illness.* Cambridge, MA: Harvard UP, 2011. Examines notions of community and isolation and discusses how these issues relate to housing policies for mentally ill and substance-using homeless persons.

WEBSITES OF INTEREST

Homelessness Resource Center
http://www.nrchmi.samhsa.gov

National Alliance to End Homelessness
http://www.endhomelessness.org

National Coalition for the Homeless
http://www.nationalhomeless.org

National Health Care for the Homeless Council
http://www.nhchc.org

See also: Domestic violence and addiction; Mental illness; Poverty and substance abuse; Socioeconomic status and addiction

Household chemicals of abuse

CATEGORY: Substance abuse

DEFINITION: Household chemicals of abuse are commonly found in homes as cleansers, aerosols, beauty products, and adhesives. These substances are inhaled to reach an altered state of consciousness, or high. When used in this manner, household chemicals can produce a number of permanent, negative side effects, including death.

STATUS: Legal to obtain in the United States

CLASSIFICATION: Uncontrolled substances

SOURCES: Household chemicals of abuse include more than one thousand products: hair spray, fabric and room deodorant sprays, nail polish, cough syrup, tub and tile cleanser, correction fluid, felt-tip-marker fluid, compressed-air computer dusters, drain cleaner, video-machine-head cleaner, air freshener, furniture polish, carpet cleaner, canned whipped cream, cooking spray, static cling spray, glass cleaner, all-purpose cleaner, oven cleaner, ant and roach bait, lighter fluid, spray paint, butane, insect spray, paint thinner, gasoline, adhesive, wood stain, motor oil, windshield washer fluid, house paint, antifreeze, Freon, pesticide, weed killer, and pool chemicals.

TRANSMISSION ROUTE: Inhalation

HISTORY OF USE

The main abusers of common household products are teenagers and preteens because these products are mostly inexpensive and readily accessible. Abuse of these chemicals by teens and preteens has steadily increased since the 1980s. More than one million children age twelve to seventeen years use inhalants in a given year, and each year includes about one million new inhalant users of all ages.

A National Household Survey on Drug Abuse found that one in five persons reported having abused common household goods one or more times in their lives. Different products tend to be abused at different ages. Among children age twelve to fifteen years, the most commonly abused inhalants are glue, shoe polish, spray paint, gasoline, and lighter fluid. Among children age sixteen or seventeen years, the most commonly abused product is nitrous oxide, which is found in whipped cream cans. Nitrites are the inhalants most commonly abused by adults.

EFFECTS AND POTENTIAL RISKS

Abused inhalants (except nitrites) act by producing short-term effects similar to barbiturates or anesthetics, which inhibit nervous system functioning. Breathable household chemicals are inhaled by dousing a cloth or bag with the substance and holding it up to the nose and mouth, or by directly spraying the chemicals into the nose or inhaling the vapors to produce a short-term high. This method is known as sniffing, huffing, bagging, or dusting. Because this type of high lasts a few minutes only, users may inhale the chemical again and again to maintain the high.

Abused inhalants are classified into four categories: solvents (fluids that vaporize at room temperature), gases (butane, propane, whipped cream cans, refrigerants), aerosols (spray paint, hair spray), and nitrites (poppers, snappers, room deodorizers). Large quantities of cough syrup containing dextromethorphan also may be directly ingested.

Initial inhalation introduces the substance into the brain and nervous system and produces a stimulating effect, whereas ongoing inhalation may produce a loss of inhibition and control. Because the high of inhalants resembles alcohol intoxication, users may exhibit such symptoms as trouble speaking or walking, dizziness, agitation, increased heart rate, hallucinations, delusions, vomiting, muscle weakness, depression, lightheadedness, confusion, and even loss of consciousness. Nitrites work differently in that they cause vasodilation and muscle relaxation. Dextromethorphan tends to create a feeling of spaciness and, at high doses, hallucinations.

Chronic inhalant abusers tend to exhibit such external signs as loss of appetite, facial rashes and blisters, runny nose, coughing, dilated pupils, extremely bad breath, glassy or glazed eyes, chemical smells, signs of paint or other products on face or fingers, headaches, slurred speech, nosebleeds, and reddened eyes. These signs may indicate intoxication or internal bodily damage caused by use. The chemicals in inhalants cause intoxication by inducing hypoxia (decreased oxygen to the brain), which may lead to brain damage and damage to the heart, liver, lungs, and kidneys. The effects of hypoxia vary according

---

Butane

Butane is a flammable aliphatic hydrocarbon that is a colorless gas at room temperature and at atmospheric pressure. Butane occurs in natural gas and in the atmosphere. It is sold as a bottled fuel for cooking and camping, and it is used as a fuel in cigarette lighters, as a propellant in hair sprays and deodorants, and as a refrigerant in refrigerators and freezers. It was classified as an inhalant drug in 1987.

When used as an inhalant, butane's chemical vapors can produce mind-altering effects. Sniffing, huffing, or spraying of butane allows the gas to enter through the pulmonary system, where it immediately enters the bloodstream. Rapidly absorbed by the body, and being lipid soluble, butane can be trapped in the body's fat cells and continue to be released to the bloodstream in time. If a person sniffs highly concentrated amounts of butane, he or she can die. Sudden sniffing death, as it is called, can result from heart failure within a few minutes.

In 1999, a US law banned the sale of butane lighter-fuel to anyone under the age of eighteen years. By 2000, butane was the most commonly misused volatile substance in the United Kingdom, where it accounted for 52 percent of all solvent-related deaths. Since 2005, butane use has decreased worldwide.

to which regions of the brain are damaged. For example, someone with hippocampal damage may lose the ability to learn new things or to carry on simple conversations.

There are many permanent effects that may be caused by the abuse of inhalants. Some of these include hearing loss, limb spasms, bone marrow damage, brain damage (problem-solving, planning, memory loss, inability to learn new things), loss of sense of smell or hearing, and a breakdown of myelin. Equally serious but potentially reversible effects include heart arrhythmia, liver and kidney damage, blood oxygen depletion, and reduced muscle tone and strength.

Inhalant abuse may be fatal even on the first dose because it may lead to heart failure. This effect is known as sudden sniffing death syndrome and can occur in otherwise healthy persons. This syndrome is mainly associated with aerosols and gases. Inhalants also may cause death by suffocation by displacing oxygen in the lungs. Bagging, or using an inhalant in an enclosed area, increases the chances of suffocation, which is why proper ventilation for the legitimate uses of the products is essential. In addition, death may be caused by the aspiration of vomit.

Eugenia M. Valentine, PhD

FURTHER READING

Foden, Charles R., Jack L. Weddell. *Household Chemicals and Emergency First Aid.* Boca Raton, FL: Lewis, 1993. This manual covers 386 household chemicals, discusses the effects of mixing with other chemicals, and details emergency first aid treatment.

Perron, Brian E., and Matthew O. Howard. "Adolescent Inhalant Use, Abuse, and Dependence." *Addiction* 104 (2009): 1185–92. Print. Provides the demographics and psychological profiles of inhalant users. Personal histories include high levels of trauma, suicidal ideation, distress, antisocial behavior, and other substance-related problems.

Winter, Ruth. *A Consumer's Dictionary of Household, Yard, and Office Chemicals: Complete Information about Harmful and Desirable Chemicals Found in Everyday Home Products, Yard Poisons, and Office Polluters.* Lincoln, NE: iUniverse, 2007. A layperson's guide to the ingredients printed on the labels of certain common products. Listings are cross-indexed by subject and synonym. A directory lists poison con-

trol centers and regional offices of the US Environmental Protection Agency.

WEBSITES OF INTEREST

American Association of Poison Control Centers
http://www.aapcc.org

National Inhalant Prevention Coalition
http://www.inhalants.org

National Institute on Drug Abuse
http://www.drugabuse.gov/drugs-abuse/inhalants

See also: Cough and cold medications; Dextromethorphan; Gasoline; Inhalants abuse; Solvents

Hydrocodone

CATEGORY: Substances

ALSO KNOWN AS: Dihydrocodeinone; Lortab; Vicodin

DEFINITION: Hydrocodone is the most frequently prescribed opiate (narcotic) in the United States. It is an antitussive (cough suppressant) and analgesic (pain relief) agent.

STATUS: Legal

CLASSIFICATION: Formulations containing more than 15 milligrams (mg) per dosage unit are schedule II controlled substances; formulations up to 15 mg per dosage unit in combination with acetaminophen or another noncontrolled substance are schedule III drugs

SOURCE: Semisynthetic with either of two naturally occurring opiates: codeine and thebaine

TRANSMISSION ROUTE: Hydrocodone comes as a tablet, a capsule, a syrup, a solution (clear liquid), an extended-release (long-acting) capsule, and an extended-release (long-acting) suspension (liquid) to take by mouth. Generally abused orally, often in combination with alcohol, but hydrocodone tablets can also be crushed and inhaled.

HISTORY OF USE

Hydrocodone was first synthesized in Germany in 1920 by Carl Mannich and Helene Löwenheim. The first report of euphoria and habituation was published in 1923, and the first report of dependence and addiction was published in 1961. Hydrocodone was approved by the US Food and Drug Administration in 1943 for sale in the United States.

Hydrocodone relieves pain by changing the way the brain and nervous system respond to pain, that is, by binding to the opioid receptor sites in the brain and spinal cord.

Hydrocodone is not usually produced illegally; diverted pharmaceuticals are the primary source for misuse. Misuse comes in the form of fraudulent call-in prescriptions, altered prescriptions, theft, and illicit purchases online. Diversion and abuse have been increasing. In 2008, hydrocodone was the most frequently encountered opioid in drug evidence submitted to state and local forensics laboratories, as reported by the National Forensic Laboratory Information System.

EFFECTS AND POTENTIAL RISKS

Short-term effects are improvement of mood, reduction of pain, euphoria, sedation, light-headedness, and changes in focus and attention. Side effects include nausea, vomiting, constipation, anxiety, dry throat, rash, difficulty urinating, irregular breathing, and chest tightness. When inhaled, burning in nose and sinuses usually occurs. A newborn of a woman who was taking the medication during pregnancy may exhibit breathing problems or withdrawal symptoms.

Symptoms of overdose include cold and clammy skin, circulatory collapse, stupor, coma, depression, respiratory depression, cardiac arrest, and death. Mixing hydrocodone with other substances, including alcohol, can cause severe physical problems or death.

Abuse of hydrocodone is associated with tolerance, dependence, and addiction. There is no ceiling dose for hydrocodone in users tolerant to its effects. Acetaminophen carries the risk of liver toxicity with high, acute doses (of around 4,000 mg per day).

Stephanie Eckenrode, BA, LLB

FURTHER READING

Parker, Phillip M., and James N. Parker. *Hydrocodone: A Medical Dictionary, Bibliography, and Annotated Research Guide to Internet References.* San Diego: Icon Health, 2003.

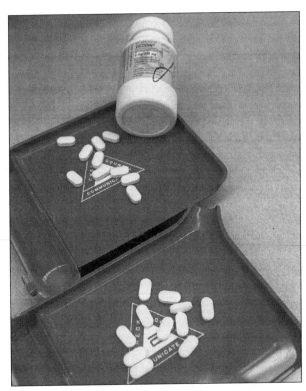

Pain medication Vicodin, top, is shown with its generic equalivent hydrocodone. (Tannen Maury/Landov)

Seppala, Marvin. *Prescription Painkillers: History, Pharmacology, and Treatment.* Center City, MN: Hazelden, 2010.

WEBSITES OF INTEREST

Medline Plus: Hydrocodone
http://www.nlm.nih.gov/medlineplus/druginfo/meds/a601006.html

US Drug Enforcement Administration
http://www.justice.gov/dea/concern/hydrocodone.html

See also: Narcotics abuse; Opioid abuse; Painkiller abuse; Vicodin

I

Impulse control disorders

CATEGORY: Psychological issues and behaviors

DEFINITION: Impulse control disorders (ICDs) comprise a specific group of diagnoses categorized in the fourth edition of the American Psychiatric Association's *Diagnostic and Statistical Manual of Mental Disorders* (DSM). These disorders are pathologic gambling, trichotillomania, pyromania, kleptomania, and intermittent explosive disorder. The DSM category "not otherwise specified" allows the inclusion of rare disorders that share ICD criteria but that do not fit easily into one of the five main diagnoses.

CHARACTERIZATION OF IMPULSE CONTROL DISORDERS

Impulse control disorders (ICDs) are grouped based on the concept of impulsivity. In this context, impulsivity is an urge to engage in a specific behavior that overwhelms normal inhibitions. The behavior is unplanned and is prompted by a stimulus that induces internal tension; the behavior relieves the tension and may bestow a sensation of pleasure. Affected persons are unable to resist the impulse because the usual inhibitions that limit harmful behavior are insufficient or absent.

A key component of an ICD is the disregard for consequences of the behavior, whether by the person with the disorder or by others. For some ICDs, the behavior is by definition a criminal act. The extent of research into individual ICDs varies. Gambling is one ICD that has been extensively studied.

Pathologic Gambling. Gambling is a recreational activity for many people. When it interferes with work, social functioning, and personal relationships, it qualifies as pathologic. Pathologic gambling generally begins in adolescence, with a prevalence estimated at 4 to 7 percent in that age group; the estimate lowers to 1 to 3 percent in adults.

The increasing availability of legalized gambling in North America predicts an increasing frequency of pathologic gambling. Websites offer the convenience of placing bets from virtually anywhere, and casinos are proliferating on cruise ships.

The place of pathologic gambling in the ICD group has been subject to debate. It is often referred to and studied as a behavioral addiction. Researchers find subtypes of pathologic gamblers with low impulsivity, others with traits mirroring substance addictions, and still others with features of obsessive compulsive disorder (OCD). A consistent finding in pathologic gamblers, however, is their choice of immediate monetary rewards over larger, albeit delayed, rewards.

Trichotillomania. Self-targeted, compulsive hair-pulling defines the disordered behavior of trichotillomania. It involves any site on the body, although the scalp, eyebrows, eyelashes, and pubic hair are the most frequent targets. Baldness may result when hair is consistently pulled from the scalp, and if ingested, surgery may be needed to remove hair from the intestinal tract.

Hair pulling is most common in children, with a usual age of onset between eleven and sixteen years. Impulsive hair-pulling can occur at any age, however. It affects more women than men, with the imbalance found in college students and adults younger than age thirty years. Those who seek treatment for trichotillomania also tend to be women.

Pyromania. The media and public often misuse the term *pyromania* to apply to any unlawful fire setting. For a behavior to qualify for a diagnosis of pyromania, several DSM criteria must be met. Early and excessive interest or fascination with fire is one prerequisite. The act of fire setting must be deliberate, repetitive, and without seeming motivation. The fire itself is the reward.

In several studies of arsonists, one-half or more are under the influence of alcohol when they start fires, which precludes the pyromania diagnosis. The disorder as strictly defined, therefore, is extremely rare.

Kleptomania. Kleptomania is the uncontrollable impulse to steal objects that have no personal use. The person with kleptomania disregards the likelihood of incurring legal consequences. Kleptomania should not be confused with shoplifting, in which items are stolen for personal use or monetary gain.

The onset of kleptomania occurs late in adolescence or in early adulthood; more women than men are affected. Impairment in social and occupational functioning is usually significant, and kleptomania appears to have a familial element. First-degree relatives of those affected are more likely than comparison groups to have an alcohol-use problem or other psychiatric disorder.

Intermittent Explosive Disorder. Recently reported and least known of the ICDs, intermittent explosive disorder is thought to be more common than has been recognized; one estimate of prevalence in the adult population is 7 to 11 percent. Features of this disorder are unpredictable, recurrent outbursts of extreme anger, frequently accompanied by unprovoked physical violence. Seemingly normal behavior follows. These episodes commonly result in injuries and property damage. Those affected average forty-three lifetime attacks.

The average onset of intermittent explosive disorder is about fourteen years of age, although most cases may occur in late adolescence to the late twenties. The frequency is higher among men than women.

QUESTIONS ABOUT THE ICD DIAGNOSIS

Impulsivity is a complex trait that is not limited to ICDs; rather, it cuts across a spectrum of psychiatric disorders. Many authors have noted the similarity between ICDs and substance abuse disorders. The occurrence of one or another ICD together with alcohol abuse or drug dependence is common, and much genetic and neurobiologic evidence links ICDs to disorders of substance abuse. According to estimates, ICDs as a group account for as much as 10 percent of psychiatric diagnoses.

For persons who investigate or treat ICDs, the category as listed in the DSM has become confining and questionable. Several heterogeneous behaviors with impulsivity as a hallmark have been proposed for inclusion. These behaviors include compulsive purchasing (items are paid for, as distinguished from kleptomania and shoplifting), compulsive Internet use, compulsive sexual behavior, and compulsive skin-picking and nail-biting.

Compulsions that characterize some ICDs have a strong resemblance to other disorders marked by compulsive behavior, notably OCD. Although compulsive and impulsive disorders have been considered distinctive traits, the behaviors overlap and the theoretical differences are blurring. Behavioral disinhibition marks both impulsive and compulsive disorders.

Shared neurologic and genetic mechanisms are suggested by the occurrence of impulsive and compulsive behaviors in the same person and by their clustering in first-degree family members. Research into the neurobiology of the brain is increasingly finding links among all these disorders.

DRUG-INDUCED ICDs

Dopamine is a neurotransmitter that takes part in regulating behavior linked to pleasure and rewards. When dopaminergic systems fail to work normally, they contribute to ICDs and addiction.

The importance of dopamine to impulse-related disorders is well illustrated by Parkinson's disease, which primarily results from a massive loss of dopaminergic nerve cells in a midbrain structure that is a major player in reward-seeking and addiction. The relevance of Parkinson's disease to ICDs lies in a standard therapy for the disease, which is to replace the lost neurons with dopamine agonists—drugs that mimic the action of dopamine.

Several disorders related to impulsivity and pleasure-seeking have been reported in a significant proportion of persons with Parkinson's disease who have been treated with dopamine agonists. Pathologic gambling, hypersexuality, compulsive shopping, and binge eating are the most frequent behaviors in this subgroup of otherwise low-risk adults. Restless leg syndrome (RLS) is another neurologic disorder that has been treated with dopamine agonists. In one group of one hundred persons undergoing treatment for RLS, 17 percent had one or another ICD.

Overstimulation of the dopaminergic system has been proposed to explain the development of ICDs in these persons; enhanced dopamine release in the brain has been shown with neuroimaging. An addiction to dopamine replacement therapy develops in some persons with Parkinson's disease, who self-administer excessive doses of their prescribed dopamine agonists.

TREATMENT

A variety of pharmacologic agents are being applied to ICDs, but research has been limited and general guidelines are not established. Reports of treatment in the medical and psychiatric literature are often based on a single case or a small patient group.

Studies testing pharmacologic treatments are generally directed to a single disorder, and more than one author has suggested that strategies should focus on targeting underlying mechanisms common to several ICDs. An important consideration that will influence treatment choice is the frequent presence of comorbid psychiatric disorders—mood, substance abuse, and personality disorders—in many persons with an ICD.

In general, treatment has moved away from psychodynamic approaches (talk therapy). Most frequently prescribed are cognitive-behavioral therapy and selective serotonin reuptake inhibitors (SSRIs), which are antidepressants. Treatment with other drug classes is being explored, and mixed success has been reported with opioid antagonists, anticonvulsants, mood stabilizers, atypical antipsychotics, and antidepressants other than SSRIs. Gold-standard, randomized, double-blind, placebo-controlled trials are rare for ICDs, although a few have been reported for pathologic gambling.

Twelve-step, self-help groups and various therapies usually aimed at substance-use disorders have been applied to ICDs, also with varying results. High dropout rates limit the effectiveness of the twelve-step programs.

Judith Weinblatt, MA, MS

FURTHER READING

Cooper-Kahn, Joyce. *Late, Lost, and Unprepared: A Parents' Guide to Helping Children with Executive Functioning.* Bethesda, MD: Woodbine House, 2008. Sets out strategies to help children develop their brain's overall supervisory and behavioral-control system.

Davis, Diane Rae. *Taking Back Your Life: Women and Problem Gambling.* Center City, MN: Hazelden, 2009. Based on accounts of women who were successfully treated for compulsive gambling, this book provides practical avenues to facing and overcoming pathologic gambling.

Grant, Jon E., and Suck Won Kim. *Stop Me Because I Can't Stop Myself: Taking Control of Impulsive Behavior.* New York: McGraw-Hill 2003. Experts cover ICDs

from causes to treatment, ending with where to get help—all in easy-to-understand language.

Linden, David J. *The Compass of Pleasure: How Our Brains Make Fatty Foods, Orgasm, Exercise, Marijuana, Generosity, Vodka, Learning, and Gambling Feel So Good.* New York: Viking, 2011. Explains the evolutionary importance of the brain's pleasure centers and how they influence behavior.

WEBSITES OF INTEREST

International OCD Foundation
http://www.ocfoundation.org

University of Minnesota, Impulse Control Disorders Clinic
http://www.impulsecontroldisorders.org

See also: Behavioral addictions: Overview; Compulsions; Crime and behavioral addictions; Gambling addiction; Kleptomania; Pyromania; Trichotillomania

---

Inhalants abuse

CATEGORY: Substance abuse

ALSO KNOWN AS: Bagging; chroming; dusting; glading; huffing; sniffing; snorting

DEFINITION: Inhalants abuse is the repeated inhalation of fumes, vapors, or gases from common household and commercial products despite evident negative effects.

CAUSES

Inhalation of fumes, vapors, or gases leads to the rapid onset of a high that resembles alcohol intoxication. The chemicals in the inhalants are quickly absorbed from the lungs into the bloodstream and from there to the brain and other organs. The initial high lasts for only a few minutes, so most abusers inhale repeatedly over time to maintain a sustained high. Repeated use builds up tolerance, leading to the need for higher and more frequent dosing.

RISK FACTORS

Inhalant products, such as glues, nail polish removers, hairsprays, felt-tip markers, lighter fluids, and spray paints, are readily available in the home and

Glue

Like other abused inhalants, including cleaning compounds and petroleum products, many adhesives, including glue, contain a potent blend of chemicals, many of which can be intoxicating when inhaled in sufficient quantity. A common way of abusing adhesives is to squeeze an amount into a plastic bag, hold the bag against the nose and mouth, and then inhale the substance, which is made up of various chemicals; inhaling from a bag also limits oxygen intake and increases the effects of the inhalant.

Although their effects pass quickly, several of these chemicals, including toluene and hexane, affect gait and balance, movement, the brain's speech centers, and higher executive functions. In turn, these effects can lead to increased aggression or euphoria.

Many of these effects are augmented by low oxygen levels in the brain, leading to increased loss of balance and coordination and poor decision making. US government studies conducted in the early twenty-first century have shown an increase in inhalant abuse among older adolescents and young adults.

the community. More than one thousand products containing inhalants can be obtained at a low cost and, for the most part, without legal restrictions on purchase or use. US state laws prohibiting the sale of products containing certain inhalants to minors are difficult to enforce. Legal consequences for abusing the few restricted inhalants are minimal.

Most first-time abusers are preteens or young adolescents who begin by experimenting with friends. Among the youngest users, girls are about as likely as boys to try inhalers. In contrast, among young adults, abuse is twice as common among men as among women. The National Institute on Drug Abuse estimates that about 15 percent of all eighth graders have had some experience with abusing inhalants and that 70 percent of abusers were younger than age eighteen years when their inhalants abuse began.

SYMPTOMS

The initial, brief high experienced with inhalants abuse is followed by drowsiness, lightheadedness, and agitation. Short-term adverse effects that can develop include headache, numbness and muscle weakness, nausea, and abdominal pain. Hearing loss and visual disturbances, even hallucinations, may occur.

Long-term use may result in weight loss, disorientation, incoordination, irritability, depression, and irreversible damage to the brain, heart, kidneys, liver, and other organs. Even a first-time user is at risk of death. The abuser can develop a rapid and erratic heartbeat, which can lead to cardiac arrest and death. Abuse also can reduce the body's oxygen level, leading to suffocation.

SCREENING AND DIAGNOSIS

Changes in an abuser's appearance and behavior are the primary indicators of abuse. An abuser may have red or runny eyes and nose, spots or sores around the mouth, paint or other products on the face, lips, nose, or fingers, or unusual breath odor or the odor of chemicals on clothing. The abuser may have slurred speech and appear to be dazed or drunk.

Behavioral changes include increased anxiety, excitability, and irritability. The abuser may become belligerent, even violent, with swings between extreme agitation and lethargy. Speech may be slurred. Disciplinary problems or truancy may develop. Extracurricular activities may be dropped in favor of socializing with friends or staying home. The abuser may develop a new set of friends or become a loner. Conflict with siblings and parents may increase.

No test, such as urinalysis, will detect inhalants abuse. The user has to be confronted and admit to the problem.

TREATMENT AND THERAPY

For most abusers, treatment is community-based and focuses on behavioral changes. One should listen to what an abuser has to say and remain calm and nonjudgmental. This may provide clues to underlying problems, such as peer pressure or problems at home, which can be resolved or redirected. One should focus on the serious health risks of inhalants abuse, not on such behavior being "bad," and should redirect an abuser to constructive, safe, and healthy activities.

A frequent or relapsing abuser will require professional help to identify and address underlying causes for the abuse and any concomitant physical or psychological problems. An initial step is a medical examination to determine if inhalants abuse has caused organ damage. Neurologic, psychological, and cognitive assessments should be part of the initial examination. Family stability, structure, and dynamics may contribute to the abuser's behavior. An effort should be made to obtain constructive participation in treatment by the abuser's family.

Few treatment centers address inhalants abuse. Detoxification may take up to thirty or forty days because inhaled chemicals stored in fatty tissue take a long time to break down and be flushed from the body.

During withdrawal, the abuser may experience headaches, nausea, excessive sweating and chills, tremors, muscle cramps, hallucinations, and even delirium. Relapse is common among heavy abusers, especially if underlying behavioral problems are not addressed.

A warning that a "bitterant" has been added to a can of aerosol dust remover is seen. Companies such as 3M, Imation, and others have been moving to reformulate air dusters to head off what health officials contend has become a widespread abuse problem among adolescents. (AP Photo)

PREVENTION

Children should be informed about the dangers of experimenting with inhalants, preferably before they try them. Inhalants abuse can be the gateway to further substance abuse. Parents, teachers, and other adults involved with children and young adolescents should know and be on guard for warning signs, including behavior changes, and should be prepared to discuss the dangers of inhalants abuse with the young person.

Parents should be aware of what inhalant products are in the home and how they can be used and stored so the risk of abuse is minimized. Similarly, school personnel should assess the use and storage of inhalant products in schools. Programs such as the Alliance for Consumer Education Inhalant Abuse Prevention Program can help parents, teachers, school administrators, and community leaders.

Ernest Kohlmetz, MA

FURTHER READING

Abadinsky, Howard. *Drug Use and Abuse: A Comprehensive Introduction.* 7th ed. Belmont, CA: Wadsworth, 2011. Focuses on what drugs are abused, how they are abused, and how abuse is treated. Inhalants abuse is covered in chapter 6.

Julien, Robert M. *A Primer of Drug Actions.* 11th ed. New York: Worth, 2008. A concise, nontechnical guide to the mechanisms of action, side effects, uses, and abuses of psychoactive drugs. Chapter 4 is on inhalants.

Kuhn, Cynthia, Scott Swartwelder, and Wilkie Wilson. *Buzzed: The Straight Facts about the Most Used and Abused Drugs from Alcohol to Ecstasy.* 3rd ed. New York: W. W. Norton, 2008. Contains an informative, easy-to-read section on the risks involved in inhalants abuse.

Lowinson, Joyce W., et al., eds. *Substance Abuse: A Comprehensive Textbook.* 4th ed. Philadelphia: Lippincott, 2005. A comprehensive textbook on substance abuse. Chapter 20 covers inhalants abuse.

WEBSITES OF INTEREST

Alliance for Consumer Education, Inhalant Abuse Prevention Program
http://www.inhalant.org

National Inhalant Prevention Coalition
http://www.inhalants.com

National Institute on Drug Abuse
http://www.drugabuse.gov

See also: Gasoline; Household chemicals of abuse; Solvents

Insurance for addiction treatment

CATEGORY: Treatment

DEFINITION: Insurance is payment for health care services by a third party payer. Health insurance includes private insurance provided by an employer and Medicare, Medicaid, military health insurance, and individual health insurance. Some health insurance also covers inpatient, outpatient, physician, and counselor care for persons with addictions.

HISTORY

Although experts have known for some time that rehabilitation treatment is important for sustained addiction recovery, not until 2008 did health insurers, on a wider scale, begin to cover addiction treatment. Typically, health insurers contract with health care facilities and providers to obtain a discounted reimbursement rate.

Mental health and addiction treatment facilities and providers have been reluctant to contract with health care insurers because they did not want to accept the reduced reimbursement and because many of their patients did not have health insurance covering mental health and addiction treatment. Less than 70 percent of addiction treatment facilities were contracted with public and private insurers. Health insurers, when they did cover addiction services, only covered detoxification. They provided little or nothing for rehabilitation services for the abuser.

A few US states had mandated that health insurers cover addiction treatment. Other states required that health insurers include options for addiction treatment but did not mandate this form of coverage; still other states did not require coverage at all for addiction services. There were exceptions, however. Self-insured employers opted not to cover addiction services, and employers covered by the Employment Retirement Income Security Act of 1974 (ERISA) were exempt from these state requirements.

ERISA is a federal law that sets minimum standards for pensions and health care insurance in private industry, but it does not require pension plans or health care insurance. Many substance abusers were not employed and had no health insurance. This left addiction treatment facilities and providers without any assurance of payment. As a result, addiction treatment facilities and providers frequently required that persons pay in advance for their treatment.

MENTAL HEALTH AND ADDICTION COVERAGE

In 2008, after years of lobbying by mental health advocates, the Mental Health Parity and Addiction Equity Act (MHPAE) was signed into law in the United States. This federal legislation requires that health insurance policies with coverage for mental health and substance abuse treatment include coverage at the same level as that for physical treatment. This means that co-payments, co-insurance, out-of-pocket expenses, office visit and days-of-service limitations, and in-network and out-of-network benefits, must be comparable to those for care for physical ailments.

In addition, this law requires equal mental health and substance abuse treatment coverage for self-funded health plans and for ERISA employers' health plans; exclusions were no longer permitted. However, MHPAE has a large loophole: Health insurers and employers are not required to offer any mental health and addiction coverage.

Upon enactment of MHPAE, the greatest concern among businesses was that the act would increase the cost of health insurance. Few studies have been performed to determine whether this concern is valid. One study utilizing data from federal employees' health plans has been performed to evaluate this change. Federal employees were granted mental health parity in 2001. The study used claims data from 1999 through 2002. The mental health costs before parity were compared with those after parity. The study found little increase in the utilization and costs of mental health and addiction treatment. However, out-of-pocket costs for members were lowered significantly.

Another flaw in the mental health parity law is the way that health insurers validate and pay for coverage. Often, they have special criteria for claims' reimbursement that interfere with payments. For example, a health insurer might require that the mental health or substance abuse patient receive outpatient care before inpatient care. Only if the outpatient treatment fails can the person be admitted for care. Also, visits to a psychiatrist or a counselor are often limited in number by calendar year.

ISSUES

Even with parity for mental health and addiction treatment, additional reimbursement issues arise. First, a majority of addicted persons have no health insurance. Often they have no job or they have a job that does not provide any health insurance. Second, addicted persons often have relapses. Costs for addiction treatment are controlled through limited admissions for treatment, resulting in limited treatment for relapses.

Third, addiction treatment programs, both outpatient and inpatient, have patient rules. For example, patients cannot take any drugs while they are in the program. They are tested weekly for the presence of drugs in their urine. If they violate this rule, they can be discharged from the addiction treatment program, even if they have health insurance.

Fourth, insurers may require that substance abusers use in-network (contracted) providers. Often, only a few such facilities and providers exist in a given network, and there may be a waiting period for treatment. Programs using cognitive-behavioral therapy are more likely to accept health insurance for payment. If a patient does not respond well to this type of therapy, their health insurance is of little use to them. Fifth, denial is a common symptom of substance abuse. It can be difficult to get the patient to accept their problem and to go for treatment, even if he or she has health insurance.

Christine M. Carroll, RN, BSN, MBA

FURTHER READING

"Acceptance of Private Health Insurance in Substance Abuse Treatment Facilities." 6 Jan. 2011. Web. 21 Feb. 2012. http://www.oas.samhsa.gov/2k11/305/305privateins2k11.htm. Examines data on the extent to which treatment facilities are ready to accept private health insurance for substance abuse treatment services.

"Health Insurance and Substance Use Treatment Need." Substance Abuse and Mental Health Services Administration. 2007. Web. 21 Feb. 2012. http://www.oas.samhsa.gov/2k7/insurance/insurance.htm. Describes health insurance coverage for mental health and addiction services prior to the passing of the mental health parity legislation.

Johnson, Teddi Dineley. "Mental Health Advocates Laud New Federal Parity Law: Equal Coverage for Mental Health Care." *Nation's Health* 38.10 (2008). Print. This article discusses the features of the Federal Mental Health and Substance Abuse parity legislation.

"Understanding the Federal Parity Law." Substance Abuse and Mental Health Services Administration. Web. 21 Feb. 2012. http://www.samhsa.gov/healthreform/docs/ConsumerTipSheetParity508.pdf. A brief overview of the Mental Health Parity and Addiction Equity Act of 2008.

WEBSITES OF INTEREST

Alcohol Policy Information System. National Institute of Alcohol Abuse and Alcoholism
http://alcoholpolicy.niaaa.nih.gov

Substance Abuse and Mental Health Services Administration
http://www.samhsa.gov

See also: Health disparities and substance abuse; Legislation and substance abuse; Mental illness; Socioeconomic status and addiction; Substance Abuse and Mental Health Services Administration (SAMHSA)

Internet addiction

CATEGORY: Psychological issues and behaviors

ALSO KNOWN AS: Compulsive Internet use; excessive Internet use; Internet addiction disorder; Internet-enabled compulsive behavior; pathological Internet use; virtual addiction; web addiction

DEFINITION: Internet addiction (IA) represents a controversial, difficult to define compulsive-impulsive spectrum disorder, characterized by excessive, time-consuming, and uncontrollable use of various Internet applications. This abnormal use results in social, occupational, or financial difficulties. Although not listed in the American Psychiatric Association's *Diagnostic and Statistical Manual* *of Mental Disorders*, the disorder is formally recognized by the American Psychological Association.

CAUSES

Some researchers have suggested that problematic Internet use stems from introversion, inability to communicate directly with others, and social isolation. Other experts have developed models to explain the etiology of this puzzling disorder.

One cognitive-behavioral model states that Internet use provides a way to escape real or perceived problems, mainly for persons who tend to overgeneralize and hold catastrophic and negative views of reality. The anonymous character of the Internet appeals to persons with low self-esteem and with negative thinking. The Internet offers a nonjudgmental environment and induces an artificial feeling of self-worth and belonging.

The compensation theory, promoted by Chinese researchers, maintains that the Internet serves a spiritual compensatory function and represents an avenue for forming social networks in an increasingly demanding and threatening society. Another explanation centers on the neurophysiology of Internet use and the pleasurable, euphoric effect it induces. This effect leads to a host of phenomena, such as reinforcement (in mitigating loneliness or social awkwardness), repeated use, tolerance, and withdrawal, all of which are analogous to other addictions. Finally, some research indicates that situational factors, including the loss of a loved one, unemployment, and relocation, might prompt a person to seek solace on the Internet, thereby precipitating the development of IA.

This photo, taken in 2010, shows a boy sleeping in an Internet café in Weifang, in China's central Shandong province. Internet addiction has become a concern in China. According to a 2010 survey on China's teenagers using the Internet, the number of China's netizens below 19 years old accounted for 33.9 percent of the nation's total Internet users, reaching 115 million in 2009. As of 2010, teenagers under eighteen years old are not allowed to enter the Internet cafes in China. (Sun Shubao/Xinhua/Landov)

RISK FACTORS

Internet access occurs anywhere, anytime. Although fraught with issues of sampling and standardization, a large body of research confirms the existence of problematic Internet use across cultures and age groups. IA, a newer disorder, is more prevalent in young and middle-aged people, especially males and college students. Studies of college students in the United States report IA prevalence rates as high as 26.3 percent. Homemakers also appear to be at risk for the disorder. A nationwide study found that one in eight adults in the United States exhibits signs of problematic Internet use. Up to 9 percent of European children and 18 percent of Asian children have IA.

The status of the Internet in modern culture ensures that all susceptible persons (that is, persons with a genetic predisposition to addiction or those with psychological disturbances) spend time on the Internet and can develop IA. Persons undergoing life-changing events (such as bereavement, divorce, or job loss) are more vulnerable to becoming Internet addicts. In some young persons, studies show, the pressure to succeed can lead to Internet overuse as a means to relieve the stress.

Socially isolated persons and persons with attention deficit hyperactivity disorder (ADHD), depression, and other psychological disorders are at an increased risk for developing IA. Depression, ADHD, social phobia, and hostility predicted the occurrence of IA in follow-up studies. Hostility and ADHD were the most important predictors of IA in male and female adolescents, respectively. Persons with multiple addictions have a high risk of becoming addicted to the Internet and to subsequently relapsing.

SYMPTOMS

IA lacks formal diagnosis criteria. Many researchers still consider excessive Internet use a compulsive, rather than addictive, behavior. In addition, some think of it as a coping mechanism, a symptom of underlying psychological abnormalities, or even a lifestyle change inherent to technological advances. Significant progress has been made, however, in diagnosing IA since it was first described in the mid-1990s.

Overall, the fundamental components of the addictive process, in some ways similar to gambling addiction, are the following: preoccupation with Internet use, greater usage than desired, numerous unsuccessful attempts to reduce usage, withdrawal (with anger and tension when not online), tolerance (including the need for more hours and better equipment), and lying about Internet usage.

Several subtypes of problematic online behavior exist. These subtypes involve excessive gaming, gambling, sexual activities, shopping, and email or text message exchange. Affected persons also may overuse digital devices such as smartphones and tablets. Some of these behaviors likely indicate underlying psychological disorders (such as gambling and compulsive shopping), while others represent Internet-specific behaviors (such as gaming, texting, and browsing). The affected person might turn to the Internet when feeling lonely and might establish online relationships.

Ultimately, the computer or other digital device becomes the person's primary relationship. The affected person undergoes a cycle that rationalizes online behavior and that progresses through regret, abstinence, and relapse. These behaviors can damage relationships with family members and friends, further deepening social isolation. In addition, affected persons may experience difficulty setting and achieving goals, and may display poor attention skills, an inability to delay gratification, and poor school or job performance. One study suggested that young people who are initially free of mental health problems, but who use the Internet pathologically, could develop depression as a consequence. Some people who present with depression, anxiety, or obsessive-compulsive manifestations later show signs of IA upon further examination.

In addition to mental problems, excessive Internet use can lead to physical conditions. Using a computer for extended periods of time leads to weight gain, sleep deprivation, back pain, carpal tunnel syndrome, and vision impairment.

SCREENING AND DIAGNOSIS

Unlike illegal drugs or gambling, for example, the Internet has widespread legitimate uses in fields such as education, research, business, industry, and communications. In this context, IA can be easily masked. Therapists are not likely to detect the disorder unless they look for it. To this end, they obtain a history of symptoms and previous treatment attempts, and information about other potential addictions.

Screening tests used include Young's simple, eight-item questionnaire and multiple clinical interactions. Even so, diagnosing IA can prove difficult because of the lack of rigorous diagnosis criteria. Experts agree, however, that Internet activities become problematic when the person loses his or her ability to control the use and when time spent online impairs daily functions and jeopardizes relationships, employment, education, and personal health. Studies generally indicate significant distress if Internet usage exceeds twenty to twenty-five hours per week.

The first validated instrument to assess the disorder is the IA test (IAT). This questionnaire addresses the duration and frequency of online activities, job productivity, ability to form new offline and online relationships, fear of life offline, attempts to reduce Internet use, and many other behaviors. The person answers each IAT question using a scale of 1 to 5. The higher the final score, the greater the level of addiction. In addition to the severity of the addiction, the therapist identifies the applications (such as gaming, pornography, and chat rooms) that are most problematic for a particular person. The assessment is completed by obtaining a history of earlier treatment attempts, identifying the most detrimental types of usage, analyzing the family environment, and conducting a motivational interview.

TREATMENT AND THERAPY

Hospitals and clinics all over the world have established treatment centers and "detox" facilities for Internet addicts. The programs aim to reconnect Internet-dependent youth and adults to the offline world by temporarily eliminating all avenues for electronic communication or by gradually reducing online time.

Given society's increasingly online nature, many therapists argue that traditional abstinence treatment models may not yield good outcomes, at least for some types of IA. Reorganization of the time periods usually spent online, using timers and reminder cards, and setting goals may help to limit the extent of online activities. Cognitive-behavioral therapy is often recommended as a first therapeutic approach, in addition to couples therapy (especially for networking and "Internet infidelity" addicts), cultivating hobbies, home maintenance skill-building, and socializing opportunities.

More than 85 percent of Internet addicts have an additional psychiatric diagnosis. In these persons, IA remains highly resistant to treatment and, in turn, can render the coexisting psychiatric disorder more difficult to treat. Consequently, any therapeutic attempt should consider the addict's comorbid conditions and address them promptly.

PREVENTION

Despite providing undeniable benefits, the Internet can be detrimental when used inappropriately or obsessively. An expanding body of research aims to clarify the causes, evaluation methods, and treatment outcomes for this phenomenon, which threatens to reach epidemic proportions. Meanwhile, persons at risk of IA, especially youth, can benefit from safeguards that ensure appropriate Internet usage in schools and colleges. Setting limits for usage time is necessary for children and adolescents at home. Guardians and teachers should monitor and limit online time, especially among at-risk children with preexisting psychosocial difficulties.

South Korea has seen about ten cardiopulmonary-related deaths in Internet cafés and one murder related to online gaming. Also, because 210,000 South Korean children age six to nineteen years are affected by and require treatment for IA, that country has identified IA as a prominent public health issue and has started training counselors to address the problem. Competent, aware, technology-savvy professionals now help to identify populations at risk and provide correct diagnoses and therapeutic strategies.

Mihaela Avramut, MD, PhD

FURTHER READING

Aboujaoude, Elias, et al. "Potential Markers for Problematic Internet Use: A Telephone Survey of 2,513 Adults." *CNS Spectrums* 11 (2006): 750–55. Print. Important US study on IA prevalence and addiction markers.

Christakis, Dimitri A. "Internet Addiction: A 21st Century Epidemic?" *BioMed Central Medicine* 8 (2010): 61. Print. Expert article on the prevalence, diagnosis, and prevention of IA.

Young, Kimberly S. *Caught in the Net.* Hoboken, NJ: Wiley. 1998. The first book on IA, authored by a renowned expert in Internet behavior.

Young, Kimberly S., and Cristiano Nabuco de Abreu, eds. *Internet Addiction: A Handbook and Guide to*

Evaluation and Treatment. Hoboken, NJ: Wiley, 2011. Comprehensive guide for professionals and dedicated general readers.

WEBSITES OF INTEREST
Center for Internet Addiction
http://www.netaddiction.com

"Is Internet Addiction Real?" *American Psychological Association*
http://www.apa.org/monitor/apr00/addiction.aspx

See also: Behavioral addictions: Overview; Computer addiction; Gaming addiction; Social media addiction

Intervention

CATEGORY: Treatment
ALSO KNOWN AS: Brief intervention; Johnson model; structured intervention
DEFINITION: In general medicine, intervention can refer to any action intended to produce an effect (such as surgery or administering a medication) or to interrupt or stop the progression of a disease. In the field of addiction and treatment, intervention refers more specifically to an attempt to break the cycle of addiction by persuading the addict to seek professional help. The intervention may be brief and relatively informal or highly structured and led by a professional interventionist.

BRIEF INTERVENTION

There is no universally accepted classification of addiction and substance abuse intervention. However, it is useful to begin with a distinction between brief (sometimes called simple) intervention and formal or structured intervention. This second category can be subdivided into direct and indirect interventions. Although structured interventions were introduced in the 1960s as a method of moving alcoholics into treatment, these intervention models have been increasingly used in treating such behavioral problems as sexual addiction, gambling or shopping addiction, and video gaming addiction.

The term *brief intervention* is sometimes used to include informal attempts by family members or friends to confront the addict or to coax him or her into getting help, but it is more often applied to short, one-on-one counseling sessions between the addict and his or her physician, psychotherapist, social worker, or religious leader in a setting familiar to the addict. Brief interventions in primary care settings are considered to be most appropriate for persons who are not dealing with an immediate legal or social crisis caused by the addiction, are not intoxicated or high at the time of the office visit, and do not have a coexisting major psychiatric disorder. Brief interventions in emergency departments or trauma centers may be helpful, but only with patients who are open to counseling after an alcohol- or drug-related accident or injury.

The National Institute on Alcohol Abuse and Alcoholism (NIAAA) and the National Institute on Drug Abuse (NIDA) have published pamphlets for physicians, psychotherapists, and other helping professionals on conducting brief interventions. Possible settings for such interventions include prenatal care, primary care, emergency care, and college health centers.

The first step in a brief intervention is screening the patient for alcohol or drug use. NIDA has drawn up a "screener" called ASSIST that can be filled out by the patient in the doctor's office on paper or on a computer. After the screener is scored, the doctor then discusses the results with the patient, giving personalized advice according to the patient's likelihood of developing a substance use disorder. NIDA recommends referring high-risk patients to an addiction specialist for further evaluation and treatment, counseling moderate-risk patients to lower their drug or alcohol intake, and advising low-risk patients to continue to be responsible and moderate in their use of alcohol.

After the initial brief intervention, the primary care physician then schedules follow-up visits with ongoing support. Office handouts and other printed educational materials are often given to a patient as part of a brief intervention.

STRUCTURED INTERVENTION

Structured interventions have become increasingly familiar to the general public through such media as reality television shows, popular magazines, social media, and personal memoirs. In a structured intervention, the addicted person is confronted in one of two ways: directly by concerned family members, friends, and possibly employers or religious leaders or indirectly through a professional interventionist's work with the addict's family.

The first type of structured intervention is known as the Johnson model; the second type is variously known as the invitational or family systems model. In actual practice, however, a structured intervention may incorporate features of both the Johnson and the family systems models. The reason for the overlap is that structured interventions are highly individualized; that is, they are tailored to the addict's age, gender, occupation, drug or addictive behavior of choice, living situation, and extended family structure or friendship network.

The goal of a structured intervention is to persuade the addict to enter treatment at once. Plans include transportation to the treatment center and caring for the addict's children, pets, and residence to lower his or her resistance to accepting treatment.

Johnson Model

The Johnson model is named for Vernon Johnson (1920–1999), an Episcopal priest and recovering alcoholic who pioneered the use of structured interventions in alcohol rehabilitation in the 1960s. In the Johnson model, also known as the confrontational or direct model of intervention, those closest to the addict form a team that will confront him or her under the guidance of a trained interventionist. Johnson believed that a confrontational approach is necessary to break through the addict's denial and other psychological defenses.

Members of the team have a pre-intervention meeting in which they learn about the disease model of addiction, decide on treatment options for the addict, and prepare letters or statements in which they describe the effect of the addict's substance abuse (or behavioral addiction) on their lives. They also may prepare a list of the addict's behaviors that they will no longer tolerate, along with specific consequences if the behaviors continue. The statements are written in a straightforward but caring tone that avoids judgmental expressions or accusations.

The actual intervention is usually a surprise to the addict, who may be told that he or she is being taken to lunch or to some other get-together but is instead confronted by the interventionist, family members, and other concerned persons. Following

an introductory explanation by the interventionist, the members of the team take turns reading their prepared statements. At the end, the addict is offered the option of immediate treatment.

Family Systems Model

The family systems model of intervention, also known as the indirect or invitational model, focuses on the addict's family rather than the addict alone. The theory underlying this model is that changes in the family system—the behavior patterns and interactions of family members—will affect the addict also and will reduce the severity of his or her self-destructive behaviors. A common form of this type of structured intervention is to hold an educational workshop for family members, to which the addict is invited; however, the workshop takes place as scheduled even if the addict refuses to attend.

The workshop, which typically lasts for two days, is led by a professional interventionist and includes discussion of intergenerational patterns of addiction and enabling as well as the biological and medical dimensions of addiction. Each family member is helped to understand his or her role within the family system and how his or her behavior may have enabled the addict. The participants may be asked to read some educational materials before the workshop. During the workshop, the various treatment options—including codependency treatment for family members—are explained. If the addict has chosen to attend, treatment is offered to him or her at the end of the workshop.

The general atmosphere of a family systems intervention differs from that of the direct model in that it is nonconfrontational. Interventionists who use this model usually maintain contact and follow-up with the family for as long as one year after the intervention.

PROFESSIONAL INTERVENTIONISTS

While structured interventions can be led by an addict's friend or family member, the chances of success are low because the addict has already had considerable practice in manipulating those close to him or her. Most treatment centers recommend consulting a professional interventionist when brief interventions have failed and when a structured intervention is necessary.

A professional interventionist—who may be a physician, psychotherapist, social worker, nurse, psychologist, or member of the clergy—is a person who has completed training programs and field supervision approved by the Association of Interventionist Specialist Certification Board. After two years of experience in the field, the interventionist may be licensed as a board-certified interventionist, level one. Level-two interventionists have had an additional three years of field experience and have completed an oral or written examination. Lists of certified interventionists can be obtained from treatment centers, community mental health centers, or the Association of Intervention Specialists.

Rebecca J. Frey, PhD

FURTHER READING

Johnson, Vernon. *Intervention: How to Help Someone Who Doesn't Want Help: A Step-by-step Guide for Families and Friends of Chemically Dependent Persons.* Minneapolis: Johnson Institute, 1986. Written by the originator of the direct structured model of intervention, this brief book is a useful introductory guide to the role of interventions in persuading addicts to accept treatment.

Morgan, Oliver J., and Cheryl H. Litzke, eds. *Family Intervention in Substance Abuse.* New York: Haworth, 2008. Intended for family therapists and other mental health professionals, this guide covers several different versions of the family systems model of structured intervention.

Recovery Connection. "Intervention: A Free Resource for Addicts, Friends, and Family." 29 June 2011. Web. 4 Apr. 2012. http://www.recoveryconnection.org/intervention-guide. A booklet that includes guidelines for conducting a successful intervention, worksheets for writing intervention letters, and advice about selecting a treatment center.

Substance Abuse and Mental Health Services Administration. "Brief Interventions and Brief Therapies for Substance Abuse." 2001. Web. 4 Apr. 2012. http://kap.samhsa.gov/products/tools/cl-guides/pdfs/QGC_34.pdf. A guide for professionals who may encounter persons with or at risk for substance use disorders. Describes various types of brief interventions along with their techniques and underlying theories.

WEBSITES OF INTEREST

AddictionIntervention.com
http://www.addiction-intervention.com/category/addiction-intervention

Association of Intervention Specialists
http://www.associationofinterventionspecialists.org

Hazelden Foundation
http://www.hazelden.org

National Institute on Drug Abuse
http://www.drugabuse.gov/publications/resource-guide

See also: Alcohol abuse and alcoholism: Treatment; Drug abuse and addiction: Treatment; Treatment methods and research

Intoxication

CATEGORY: Health issues

ALSO KNOWN AS: Inebriation

DEFINITION: Intoxication is a temporary physical and mental state resulting from having consumed a psychoactive substance. Intoxication is characterized by disruptions to a person's physiological, psychological, and cognitive processes.

CAUSES, SYMPTOMS, AND DIAGNOSIS

Intoxication results from the consumption of substances such as alcohol, caffeine, marijuana and other illicit drugs, some mushrooms and plants, or even over-the-counter and prescription drugs.

Intoxication is diagnosed via identification of the substance in the body system and the observation of characteristic symptoms in the person affected. Specific substances have certain effects on the body and therefore create certain symptoms. Tests of breath and urine samples often are used to detect intoxication. Additionally, simply watching the individual for psychological and behavioral signs of intoxication, or asking the individual to perform certain tasks can help with detection. For instance, police officers suspecting alcohol intoxication may request individuals to try to walk a straight line or to close their eyes and try to stand up straight. Such tests allow the officers to observe the person's balance and body sway. Loss of balance or significant body sway can indicate alcohol intoxication.

Each substance has specific symptoms associated with its intoxication state. Therefore, when testing someone for intoxication, different tests may be needed to determine whether any individual substance has been used.

Alcohol intoxication is marked by symptoms such as slurred speech, coordination problems, unsteady gait, nystagmus (an involuntary condition affecting the eyes in which they do not track the movement of objects smoothly), impairments in memory or attention, and stupor. Stupor is a condition in which the person is in a daze and has numbed senses. With alcohol intoxication, stupor can escalate to a coma. In addition to these symptoms, problematic behaviors may also manifest themselves, such as aggression, impaired judgment, mood problems, or problems interacting socially or at work.

The level of intoxication is directly related to dose, and a substance may produce different symptoms at various doses. For example, whereas small amounts of alcohol have a stimulant effect on behavior, high levels of alcohol cause sedation.

TREATMENT AND THERAPY

Intoxication is short-lived; once a substance has been processed out of the body, the effects dissipate. The intensity of intoxication lessens over several hours after ingestion. Treatment usually consists of a process called detoxification, or detox. This is usually done in inpatient units in hospitals or in treatment centers. Sometimes, however, detoxification may be done in community settings where nonmedical models of intervention are practiced. In all of these settings, symptoms are monitored closely as the person withdraws from the substance, as withdrawal can be dangerous. Withdrawal varies from drug to drug. It also varies depending on how long the person has used the substance and how much has been used. Severe withdrawal from certain substances, such as alcohol, can be fatal without appropriate medical supervision.

PREVENTION

Intoxication for some substances is easier to identify than for others. Increasingly, methods are being developed to identify intoxication with greater ease via objective measures. For instance, technology to assess the iris of the eye to detect marijuana intoxication and the use of patches to detect substance use, such as with drugs that may be excreted in sweat, are two recent developments.

Nancy A. Piotrowski, PhD

FURTHER READING

American Psychiatric Association. *Diagnostic and Statistical Manual of Mental Disorders: DSM-IV-TR.* 4th ed. Arlington, VA.: American Psychiatric, 2000. An updated, comprehensive review of research about mental disorders. Covers the associated characteristics of mental disorders and information on their prevalence, course, and familial patterns.

Julien, Robert M., Claire D. Advokat, and Joseph Comaty. *A Primer of Drug Action: A Comprehensive Guide to the Actions, Uses, and Side Effects of Psychoactive Drugs.* 12th ed. New York: Worth, 2010. A nontechnical guide to drugs, written by a medical professional. Describes the different classes of drugs, their actions in the body, their uses, and their side effects. Basic pharmacologic principles, classifications, and terms are defined and discussed.

Weil, Andrew, and Winifred Rosen. *From Chocolate to Morphine: Everything You Need to Know About Mind-Altering Drugs.* Rev. and updated ed. Boston: Houghton Mifflin, 2004. Identifies and defines psychoactive substances. Also outlines the relationships between different types of drugs, the motivations to use drugs, and associated problems.

WEB SITES OF INTEREST

National Council on Alcoholism and Drug Dependence
http://www.ncadd.org/

National Institute on Drug Abuse
http://www.drugabuse.gov/

See also: Alcohol poisoning; Alcohol: Short- and long-term effects on the body; Blood alcohol content (BAC); Brain changes with addiction; Drug interactions

Intravenous drug use and blood-borne diseases

CATEGORY: Health issues and physiology

DEFINITION: Intravenous drug use is the administration of drugs, usually proscribed substances, by injection directly into the bloodstream. Numerous pathogenic microorganisms are transmitted in this way, which can lead to infectious diseases in the drug abuser.

CAUSES

Blood-borne pathogens such as parasites, viruses, and bacteria can be transmitted by injection drug abuse. Some of these pathogens, and associated diseases, are described here.

Malaria. Plasmodium outbreaks among injection drug addicts have been reported since the early twentieth century, when the first cases were reported in Africa. Needle sharing was suspected, but analysis of blood found in syringes did not show the *Plasmodium falciparum* parasite. Malaria eventually became common in injection drug addicts in New York City, with fatal cases numbering about 135 in the ten-year period preceding US involvement in World War II. Nonfatal cases of *P. vivax* malaria also were reported. The outbreak was limited to intravenous heroin addicts. Cases were typically attributed to sailors who traveled to the tropics. The sharing of needles was the mode of transmission during these outbreaks. The addition of quinine, an antimalarial drug, to cut, or dilute, heroin dramatically reduced cases.

Hepatitis. Sharing of needles by addicts was noted as the cause of hepatitis B virus (HBV) transmission in the mid-nineteenth century. HBV outbreaks associated with injection drug use are still noted today. Research into the prevalence of HBV among injection drug users shows that 50 to 60 percent of all addicts have been exposed to the virus. Combined HBV, hepatitis delta, or hepatitis C virus (HCV) infection causes hepatitis outbreaks among injection drug abusers that are sometimes fatal. HCV is now the most common blood-borne infection in the United States. Each of the hepatides is most common among those exposed to blood, including addicts.

Human immunodeficiency virus (HIV). Intravenous drug users are the second largest risk group for acquired immunodeficiency syndrome (AIDS)

in the United States, comprising one-fourth of all cases. Needle sharing is the greatest risk for exposure and transmission. Forty-three percent of injection drug addicts test positive for the virus. Other human retroviruses, such as human T-cell lymphotropic virus, types I and II, also are transmitted among addicts.

Clostridial disease. Tetanus among addicts is not uncommon in female abusers, though the reason for elevated susceptibility in women is unclear. The *Clostridium tetani* bacterium and spores likely originate in the environment. However, contamination of heroin is possible too. Also, botulism caused by *C. botulinum* infection originating at the injection wound site has been reported among parenteral drug abusers.

Candida. *Candida parapsilosis* is the most common etiologic agent of fungal endocarditis among injection drug addicts. Viable cells have been recovered from both heroin and injection paraphernalia. Because this fungus is a member of the oral flora, addicts may be the reservoirs. *C. albicans* infection of the skin, eyes, bones, and joints has also been noted.

Hepatitis C

Hepatitis C is an infectious disease with a viral etiology that usually leads to chronic infection with persistent liver inflammation (hepatitis). The disease is caused by a ribonucleic acid virus that infects liver cells and has six known genotypes (genetic makeup). Infection is transmitted primarily through exposure to contaminated blood.

Drug users commonly share needles and other drug injection paraphernalia, so a history of current or past use of injectable drugs carries a high risk for hepatitis C. Infection with the human immunodeficiency virus increases vulnerability to the disease, as does alcohol consumption, which accelerates liver damage. Other risk factors include unprotected sexual contact, especially with multiple partners, and nonsterile tattooing techniques.

Most people remain asymptomatic in the early stages of infection, although some may experience mild flu-like symptoms such as fatigue and fever. In time, the infection becomes chronic, and persistent liver inflammation may lead to cirrhosis (scarring of the liver) or liver cancer.

Pseudomonas aeruginosa. Serogroup 0-11 *P. aeruginosa* endocarditis is noted almost exclusively in intravenous drug abusers. Tablets of pentazocine, an analgesic, and tripelennamine, an antihistamine, are crushed, diluted in tap or toilet water without boiling, then injected. The bacterium grows readily in these preparations.

Polymicrobial bacteremia. Seventy percent of blood cultures from injection drug addicts with polymicrobial bacteremia grow *Staphylococcus aureus* along with other bacteria. Therefore, skin contamination and poor hygiene are risk factors. As with *P. aeruginosa* bacteremia, pentazocine and tripelennamine abuse is a risk factor for polymicrobial bacteremia.

Staphylococcus aureus. A common cause of bacterial endocarditis, skin and soft tissue infections, and bacteremia in addicts is *S. aureus.* The source of the bacteria is likely the addict's own skin. Outbreaks of methicillin-resistant *S. aureus* (MRSA) have been reported. Antibiotic abuse, long periods of injection drug abuse, and frequent hospitalizations are associated with MRSA bacteremia.

Mycobacterium tuberculosis. The incidence of active tuberculosis is higher among hospitalized or methadone treatment patients than in the general population. Suppression of the immune system from drug abuse likely leads to an elevated number of infections among those exposed.

RISK FACTORS

The lifestyle of injection drug abusers makes addicts vulnerable to infection. Addicts repeatedly inject substances with immunosuppressive effects that are frequently in contaminated diluents. Immunologic defenses also are compromised by the simultaneous abuse of alcohol and tobacco and by personal neglect.

Several factors may influence the susceptibility in addicts exposed to bacteria, viruses, or parasites. The most important factor in reduced tolerance to infection is the damaged skin of the injection drug abuser. Needle wounds lead to abscesses and result in higher *S. aureus* skin colonization. Destruction of nasal mucosa, depression of cough and gag reflex, and dental carries lead to increased susceptibility. The addict also may have impaired functioning of phagocytosis, reduced superoxide production, and reduced T-cell function.

SYMPTOMS

The symptoms of blood-borne disease vary with the specific diagnosis. General symptoms of infection include fever and inflammation. Also common are body ache, headache, nausea, and vomiting. Hepatides cases can result in jaundice.

SCREENING AND DIAGNOSIS

Diagnosis of infectious diseases among addicts is performed in a manner identical to nonaddicted patients. Fluid or tissue samples must be obtained aseptically and delivered to the microbiology lab. Growth of the specimen is limited to about two hours so that the composition of the flora represents that in the original sample.

A fixed smear is Gram-stained for preliminary identification of Gram-positive or Gram-negative bacteria. Multiple test kits are available for more specific identification of bacterial pathogens. The presence of antibodies directed against a pathogen is used in presumptive diagnosis of hepatitis viruses and HIV. In rare cases, genetic analysis is performed to identify an infectious agent.

A urinalysis and a complete blood count checking white blood cell differential, serum electrolytes, urea, nitrogen, creatinine, glucose, and transaminases should be obtained. A chest X-ray and films of any involved soft tissues and bone should be taken. While bone scans are a valuable diagnostic tool, they are usually not available in emergency rooms, where addicts with infections frequently are treated. A computerized tomography scan of the brain should be ordered if there are neurologic symptoms or signs.

TREATMENT AND THERAPY

The treatment of blood-borne disease in injection drug abusers varies by diagnosis. Chloroquine is frequently used in the treatment of malaria, but quinidine or quinine plus doxycycline, tetracycline, or clindamycin, or atovaquone plus proguanil, are used in the treatment of chloroquine-resistant infections. The hepatitis viruses are treated with antivirals, and HIV is treated with antiretroviral drugs.

Mifepristone and misoprostol are used in the treatment of clostridial disease. Amphotericin B has been the most frequently used antifungal in the treatment of candida infections. Fluconazole is frequently administrated as an alternative to amphotericin B. *P. aeruginosa* is naturally resistant to a host of antibiotics. However, several injectable drugs can be effective. Ceftaroline is a broad-spectrum cephalosporin used in the treatment of MRSA infections. With any infectious disease, treatment of the addiction is essential to the long-term health of the addict.

PREVENTION

It remains difficult to control and prevent infectious diseases among addicts. Most addicts are elusive and seek care in the mainstream health-care system only when very ill or when facing withdrawal. Such socio-economic factors as poverty, illiteracy, and language and cultural barriers are often further impediments to effective care.

With the fear that HIV-infected addicts may be a significant reservoir for the general public, health departments have become innovative. For example, they often employ former addicts to educate current intravenous drug users about blood-borne diseases and risk reduction. If such programs are successful, health experts can anticipate a concomitant reduction in the incidence of other infections associated with needle sharing and patronage of injection-drug "shooting galleries." Hepatitis B and tetanus immunization are effective in the prevention of these diseases.

Kimberly A. Napoli, MS

FURTHER READING

Centers for Disease Control and Prevention. "HIV/AIDS." http://www.cdc.gov/hiv. Comprehensive consumer-based information on HIV and infectious diseases.

Levine, Donald P., and Jack D. Sobel, eds. *Infections in Intravenous Drug Abusers.* New York: Oxford UP, 1999. A comprehensive text written for advanced readers and specialists.

Tortora, Gerard J., Berdell R. Funke, and Christine L. Case. *Microbiology: An Introduction.* 9th ed. New York: Pearson, 2007. A microbiology textbook focusing on infectious diseases.

WEBSITES OF INTEREST

Laboratory Processing of Samples in the Diagnosis of Infection
http://www.bmb.leeds.ac.uk/mbiology/ug/ugteach/icu8/lab/head.html

National Institute on Drug Abuse
http://www.drugabuse.gov

SaferInjecting.net: Harm Reduction Strategies
http://www.saferinjecting.net

See also: Heroin; HIV/AIDS and substance abuse; Substance abuse

J

Jail diversion programs

CATEGORY: Treatment

DEFINITION: Jail diversion programs provide an alternative means of sentencing and rehabilitating certain prisoners, such as nonviolent drug and alcohol offenders and offenders with mental health issues, in order to avoid unnecessary and unproductive jail or prison time.

OVERVIEW

According to the GAINS Center for Behavioral Health and Justice Transformation, an estimated 800,000 people with some form of mental illness are sentenced to serve time in correctional facilities every year in the United States. In 2005, the Bureau of Justice Statistics issued a report stating that more than one-half of all inmates in prisons and jails across the United States had a mental illness.

In large correctional facilities such as the Los Angeles County Jail and the Rikers Island complex in New York City, the population of inmates with mental illness is greater than the number of persons being treated for mental illness in any hospital in the United States. As a result of the modern trend of deinstitutionalization, correctional facilities have become the nation's largest providers of mental health treatment.

In response to this growing problem, many communities have turned to jail diversion programs to better meet the rehabilitation needs of offenders with mental illness and to alleviate some of the strain that housing such inmates places on the criminal justice system. Jail diversion programs are designed to identify and redirect offenders with serious mental health problems and substance abuse problems from jail or prison and toward various community-based treatment and recovery centers. In doing so, these programs allow mentally ill offenders to receive the type of rehabilitative support they need to cope with their illness and to begin to recover instead of being incarcerated, which often only exacerbates their condition.

Along with improved access to quality health care, jail diversion programs are beneficial to offenders with mental illnesses in many other ways. Such programs frequently allow offenders to maintain their employment, which, in turn, provides them with a means of supporting their families and continuing to be productive members of society. In many cases, upon completion of treatment, offenders in jail diversion programs also become eligible to have the charges against them expunged from their records.

Jail diversion programs also are advantageous for the communities in which they operate. In many correctional facilities, the cost of housing a single inmate is often around $100 per day. In communities with active jail diversion programs, which can effectively reduce or eliminate jail time for thousands of offenders, the economic savings for taxpayers is considerable.

TYPES OF JAIL DIVERSION PROGRAMS

Two common types of jail diversion programs are in practice. Each is primarily defined by the point at which diversion occurs during the criminal justice process.

Prebooking diversion takes place before a person is booked into jail and before any charges are filed. The strategies employed within these diversion programs usually focus on the initial contact between an offender and law enforcement officers. As such, prebooking diversion programs require police officers to be specially trained to recognize the indicators of a potential mental illness or substance abuse problem and to make the appropriate judgment as to how an offender should be handled on-scene.

Many of these programs involve collaboration between police and local mental health and substance abuse facilities. This collaboration may come in the form of a team of specifically trained mental health professionals who respond with police to calls that are likely to involve mental illness or substance abuse. In other cases, police officers may simply choose to transport a mentally ill offender directly to a mental health facility instead of to the police station or jail.

The second and more widely utilized type of jail diversion program is postbooking diversion. Postbooking diversion occurs after a person is arrested and formally charged with a crime. Once charged, the offender is screened for mental health and substance abuse problems. If the offender is deemed to be qualified for diversion, those in charge of the diversion program work with prosecutors and court officials to negotiate a reduction in or elimination of jail time for the offender in favor of mental health treatment.

Some criminal justice systems also have separate mental health courts where offenders diagnosed with mental illnesses and charged with nonviolent crimes are tried. In these courts, convicted offenders receive sentences that are specifically designed to allow them to avoid jail or prison time by participating in a voluntary treatment program.

EFFECTIVENESS

Studies have shown that jail diversion programs for offenders with mental illnesses or substance abuse problems have been successful in terms of their ability to rehabilitate offenders and reduce or prevent instances of recidivism following release. One such study, which focused on a jail diversion program operated by the federal prison system and a network of mental health professionals in the city of Baltimore, showed that only 19 percent of offenders who participated in the diversion program went on to violate their probation or parole after completion, as compared with a 56 percent violation rate previously.

Similarly, other studies have shown that offenders who participated in a jail diversion program experienced fewer arrests and fewer days incarcerated or hospitalized after they completed the program than they did in the year prior to their initial arrest. These results show that jail diversion programs do achieve their intended goals of reducing crime among persons with mental illnesses while keeping them out of correctional facilities.

One can, therefore, conclude that jail diversion programs are effective in dealing with mental illness, substance abuse, and crime for all parties involved. Offenders themselves receive the rehabilitation and support they need while avoiding the difficulties associated with serving jail or prison time. Criminal justice systems benefit from the reduction in the number of offenders entering already overcrowded correctional facilities. Communities are, in turn, relieved of some of the economic burdens of paying to support additional inmates. From every perspective, jail diversion programs are effective and worthwhile alternatives to the traditional methods of criminal justice in the United States.

Jack A. Lasky

FURTHER READING

DeLisi, Matt, and Peter John Conis. *American Corrections: Theory, Research, Policy, and Practice.* Sudbury, MA: Jones, 2010. A textbook covering corrections and the justice system in the United States.

Landsberg, Gerald. *Serving Mentally Ill Offenders: Challenges and Opportunities for Mental Health Professionals.* New York: Springer, 2002. A detailed look at how offenders with mental illness are treated in the criminal justice system.

Public Citizens Health Research Group. *Criminalizing the Seriously Mentally Ill: The Abuse of Jails as Mental Hospitals.* Darby, PA: Diane, 1998. A comprehensive study and history of the incarceration of persons with mental illnesses.

WEBSITES OF INTEREST

GAINS Center for Behavioral Health and Justice Transformation
http://gains.prainc.com

National Institute of Corrections
http://www.nic.gov

Substance Abuse, Mental Health, and Criminal Justice Studies
http://www.norc.org/Research/Departments/Pages/substance-abuse-mental-health-and-criminal-justice-studies.aspx

See also: Co-occurring disorders; Crime and behavioral addictions; Crime and substance abuse; Mental illness; Rehabilitation programs; Treatment methods and research

Just Say No campaign

CATEGORY: Diagnosis and prevention

DEFINITION: The Just Say No campaign was a substance-abuse awareness and prevention program for youth promoted by US First Lady Nancy Reagan.

DATE: Established 1982

BACKGROUND

In 1982, Nancy Reagan, then-US First Lady, had been working on the problem of drug abuse through speeches and visits to various national organizations. That same year she was approached by a school girl in Oakland, California, who asked the First Lady what she should say if she were asked to use drugs. Reagan responded with "just say no," which became the name of Reagan's nationwide awareness and prevention program.

Reagan continued her crusade against substance abuse among children. She spoke nationally to parent groups, community groups, schools, and other audiences about drug abuse and its effects on children. In 1986, US president Ronald Reagan signed a proclamation creating the first official Just Say No to Drugs Week. By 1988, more than twelve thousand Just Say No clubs had formed across the nation and around the world.

Early research supported the focus of the Just Say No program. This research, especially the work of Richard Evans on the social inoculation model, supported the claim that these programs "inoculated" students with peer-pressure-resistance skills that included refusing drugs if approached by peers.

In 1989, Reagan established the Nancy Reagan Foundation to continue the campaign against drug abuse. The foundation merged with the BEST Foundation for a Drug-Free Tomorrow in 1994, which developed the Nancy Reagan Afterschool Program, promoting drug prevention and life skills for youth.

MISSION AND GOALS

The Just Say No campaign became a national effort on substance abuse. The mission of the campaign was to teach children to resist drug use by simply teaching them to say "no" to anyone who approached them with the idea of using drugs. The slogan was simple and catchy, and it helped to initiate a national dialogue about the problems of drug abuse in the 1980s.

The program was widely disseminated across the county, but no evidence exists to demonstrate that the program was effective. Also, it is not entirely clear what specific program elements the Just Say No campaign actually contained.

By reviewing numerous sites and old publications, one can see that the Just Say No campaign was linked to a number of early drug prevention efforts. A series of Just Say No media messages was created, and Just Say No clubs were implemented in elementary and secondary schools. A Youth Power program existed, and numerous schools implemented Just Say No afterschool programs. The Just Say No campaign became, in some respects, more of a slogan interwoven with early drug prevention work.

This drug prevention work included the Red Ribbon Campaign of the National Federation of Parents, school-based drug-prevention assemblies, and drug-free weeks that were politically highlighted to bring national attention to the problem of drug use for young people. Although some of these components attempted to teach children positive resistance skills, it is not clear if rigorous evaluations were conducted or if any positive findings exist on the program. Documents link research roots to the development of various programs, but it is not clear what specific components or curricula were created and later evaluated for effectiveness. It appears that the Just Say No campaign evolved into a movement that involved concerned parents and community members.

Dated studies conducted in 1984 concluded the following: One, most substance abuse prevention programs have not contained adequate evaluation components. Two, increased knowledge has virtually no impact on substance abuse or on intentions to smoke, drink, or use drugs. Three, effective education approaches appear to be experiential in their orientation and place too little emphasis on the acquisition of skills necessary to increase personal and social competence, particularly those skills needed to enable students to resist interpersonal pressures to begin using drugs. Four, few studies have demonstrated any success in preventing substance abuse. In the late 1980s and early 1990s drug prevention programs were created based on research ideas but were not commonly evaluated to determine their effectiveness in preventing substance abuse.

A group called Just Say No International, formerly Just Say No Foundation, was formed in Oakland, California, in 1986. This organization was led by Ivy Cohen, who brought attention and focus to the problem of drug abuse internationally. One publication by Far West Laboratory for Educational Research and Development published in 1993 contains an introduction by Cohen unveiling a new Just Say No program entitled Youth Power. Youth Power was developed with the premise that a "whole child" approach to substance abuse prevention was needed. The program is described in this 1993 publication as treating children as individuals with the ability and desire to help provide solutions to drug problems through empowerment models. Again, no evaluation findings were presented in this report.

Information on the Just Say No campaign is difficult to find and locate, and questions remain whether the program actually prevented substance abuse behaviors as measured through rigorous program evaluations. The Substance Abuse and Mental Health Services Administration's National Registry of Evidence-based Programs and Practices does not list the Just Say No campaign as an evidenced-based substance-abuse prevention intervention. The campaign did, however, bring national attention to the problems of drug abuse and American youth in the 1980s and early 1990s.

Julie A. Hogan, PhD

FURTHER READING

Evans, R. I. "A Historical Perspective on Effective Prevention." *Cost-Benefit/Cost-Effectiveness Research on Drug Abuse Prevention: Implications for Programming and Policy.* Eds. W. J. Bukoski and R. I. Evans. National Institute on Drug Abuse Research Monograph Series No. 176. Washington: GPO, 1998. A US-government publication that provides an overview of the history of substance abuse prevention. Also discusses Evans's related work in the 1970s.

Hart, Carl L., and Charles Ksir. *Drugs, Society, and Human Behavior.* 14th ed. New York: McGraw-Hill, 2011. A textbook on drug use in modern society.

National Institute on Drug Abuse. *Preventing Drug Use among Children and Adolescents: A Research-Based Guide for Parents, Educators, and Community Leaders.* 2nd ed. Bethesda, MD: DHHS, 2003. A handbook that highlights a number of substance-abuse prevention programs that have been proven effective.

WEBSITES OF INTEREST

National Registry of Evidence-based Programs and Practices
http:///www.nrepp.samhsa.gov

National Youth Anti-Drug Media Campaign
http://www.whitehousedrugpolicy.gov/mediacampaign

Ronald Reagan Presidential Foundation and Library
http://www.reaganfoundation.org/her-causes.aspx

See also: Education about substance abuse; Government warnings; History of addiction; Prevention methods and research

K

Ketamine

CATEGORY: Substances

ALSO KNOWN AS: K; special K; vitamin K

DEFINITION: Ketamine hydrochloride is a short-acting anesthetic. It has pain-killing and hallucinogenic properties.

STATUS: Legal in the United States for use as an anesthetic in medical settings; nonmedical use is illegal

CLASSIFICATION: Schedule III controlled substance

SOURCE: Synthetic drug with no natural sources; supplies are diverted from legal sources for illegal use

TRANSMISSION ROUTES: Intravenous, intramuscular, ingestion, inhalation

HISTORY OF USE

Ketamine was first synthesized in 1962 in the laboratories of the Parke-Davis pharmaceutical company. It was developed as an alternative to phencyclidine (PCP) for use as an anesthetic. Clinical use in short-term surgery in humans was initiated in 1975. Many patients began reporting hallucinations while under the drug's influence. Its use is now limited in humans, but it has more widespread applications in veterinary medicine. The drug was soon diverted from hospitals, medical offices, and medical supply houses.

Ketamine became a popular drug for recreational use among teenagers and young adults in the club scene. The US Drug Enforcement Administration added ketamine to its list of emerging drugs of abuse in the mid-1990s. It was classified as a schedule III controlled substance in 1999.

EFFECTS AND POTENTIAL RISKS

Primary side effects of ketamine observed in medical settings include increased heart rate and blood pressure, impaired motor function and memory, numbness, nausea, and vomiting. While sedated, patients are unable to move or feel pain. Once the drug wears off, patients have no memory of what occurred while they were sedated.

In unmonitored situations, ketamine produces a dose-related progression of serious adverse effects from a state of dreamy intoxication to hallucinations and delirium. A "trip" on ketamine has been described as being cut-off from reality—"going down into a K hole"—and as an out-of-body or near-death experience. Users may be unable to interact with others around them or even see or hear them. Ketamine has been used as a date rape agent because the victim has no memory of what occurred.

Because abusers feel no pain, they may injure themselves without realizing they are doing so. Chronic use can lead to panic attacks, rage, and

Ketamine is also known as:		
Black Hole	Jet	Psychedelic Heroin
Bump	K	Purple
Cat Valium	K-Hole	Special K
Green	Kit Kat	Super Acid

Source: Office on Women's Health in the Department of Health and Human Services

paranoia. High doses or prolonged dosing can lead to respiratory depression or arrest and even death. Ketamine is often mixed with heroin, cocaine, or ecstasy. Any of these combinations can be lethal.

Ernest Kohlmetz, MA

FURTHER READING

Dillon, Paul, Jan Copeland, and Karl L. R. Jansen. "Patterns of Use and Harms Associated with Non-Medical Ketamine Use." *Alcohol and Drug Dependence* 69 (2003): 23–28. Print.

Kuhn, Cynthia, Scott Swartwelder, and Wilkie Wilson. *Buzzed: The Straight Facts about the Most Used and Abused Drugs from Alcohol to Ecstasy.* 3rd ed. New York: W. W. Norton, 2008.

Savelli, Lou. *Street Drugs: Pocketguide.* Flushing, NY: Looseleaf Law, 2008.

WEBSITES OF INTEREST

DrugAbuseHelp.com
http://www.drugabusehelp.com/drugs/ketamine

Institute on Drug Abuse
http://www.drugabuse.gov

See also: Anesthesia abuse; Club drugs; Date rape drugs; Recreational drugs

Kleptomania

CATEGORY: Psychological issues and behaviors

DEFINITION: Kleptomania is the uncontrollable impulse to steal. Oftentimes it is marked by an inability to stop stealing despite attempts to stop. Kleptomania may be accompanied by other conditions, such as anxiety, mood disorders, eating disorders, and chemical dependency. Other psychological or psychiatric conditions may exacerbate urges to steal and stealing behaviors. Obsessive-compulsive disorder and major depression have been documented to coexist with kleptomania in some cases.

CAUSES AND RISK FACTORS

The causes of kleptomania are not known, although it may have roots in neurobiology, neurochemistry, psychology, and psychiatry. In addition to intrapersonal factors in kleptomania, environmental or situational factors can affect urges to steal. For example, stressful home or work situations may influence urges. More general factors, such as neighborhood violence or environmental overcrowding, also may be involved.

Some researchers have shown that functional-neuroimaging, biochemical, and genetic data implicate multiple neurotransmitter systems in the pathophysiology of impulse control disorders. The existence of multiple systems may elucidate the failure of traditional pharmacotherapy approaches to yield consistently efficacious results. Some researchers propose the development and implementation of targeted therapies to address impulse control disorders. Genetic influences in kleptomania may be present and are being considered, in part, by examinations of stealing behaviors among first-order relatives.

From a psychosocial perspective, stressful childhood experiences, sibling difficulties, and parenting issues may play roles. Failures in impulse control can be addressed through behavioral interventions. Such interventions focus on teaching coping strategies for resisting urges. Cognitive antecedents involve maladaptive thoughts and beliefs. Such interventions involve cognitive-behavioral modification, identifying triggers, avoiding such triggers, and countering maladaptive thoughts and beliefs. Cognitive-behavior therapy is being used in the treatment of kleptomania.

Kleptomania may be a manifestation of underlying conditions such as mood disorders, eating disorders, and anxiety. It is important to note that different factors may be involved for different people. Also, kleptomania may result from more than one factor. Additional causes may underlie the course of kleptomania over time. For example, difficulties with impulse control may underlie kleptomania in its earlier manifestations, while compulsions may develop later in the course of the disorder. Addictive influences may impact people even later in the course of the disorder, with corresponding feelings of anger.

COURSE OF SYMPTOMS

The course of kleptomania reflects sporadic, brief episodes accompanied by long abstinent periods; longer periods of stealing accompanied by periods of abstinence; and chronic stealing with some degree of variability. Prevalence in the general population is believed to be rare, with fewer than 5 percent of individuals who shoplift meeting the criteria for kleptomania. More than 65 percent of affected individuals are female. The age of onset of symptoms and beginning of treatment is younger for women than it is for men.

DIAGNOSIS

According to the DSM-IV-TR, the following five diagnostic criteria must be present for a diagnosis of kleptomania:

- recurrent failure to resist impulses to steal objects that are not needed for personal use or their monetary value
- increasing arousal immediately before committing the act
- pleasure, relief, or gratification at the time the act is committed
- the person is not committed to express anger or vengeance and not committed in response to a delusion or a hallucination
- the act is not better accounted for by a conduct disorder, a manic episode, or by antisocial personality disorder

TREATMENT PROGRAMS

Treatments for kleptomania can be linked to the antecedents of the condition. Treatment methods for kleptomania specifically include the following:

- *Pharmacologic.* While pharmacologic research is ongoing, and drug regimes are administered for some persons, this research has met with complex, sometimes mixed, results. Several classes of drugs are being used.
- *Antidepressants.* Selective serotonin reuptake inhibitors (SSRIs) are the antidepressants most commonly used to treat kleptomania.
- *Mood stabilizers.* Mood stabilizers are intended to reduce rapid or uneven mood changes that may trigger urges.
- *Benzodiazepines.* Such drugs are central nervous system depressants.
- *Antiseizure medications.* Some studies have reported data with respect to possible benefits in addressing kleptomania.
- *Addiction medications.* Opioid antagonists are intended to block the part of the brain that

experiences pleasure during certain addictive behaviors.

- *Covert sensitization.* When an urge to steal arises, patients are instructed to imagine negative consequences until the urge subsides.
- *Aversion therapy.* Patients are taught to hold their breath when they experience the urge to steal until physical discomfort is felt. An association can develop between the urge and the discomfort.
- *Systematic desensitization.* Patients are taught to substitute relaxing feelings for urges to steal.

Ronna F. Dillon, PhD
Laurel D. Dillon-Sumner, BA

FURTHER READING

Grant, Jon E. *Impulse Control Disorders: A Clinician's Guide to Understanding and Treating Behavioral Addictions.* New York: W. W. Norton, 2008. Provides information on impulse control disorders, including extended coverage in treatment.

Halgin, Richard, and Susan Krauss Whitbourne. *Abnormal Psychology: Clinical Perspectives on Psychological Disorders.* 6th ed. Columbus, OH: McGraw-Hill, 2010. Contains material on psychological disorders and how they affect functioning. Includes portrayals and case studies of persons living with the various psychological conditions.

Hollander, Eric, Heather Berlin, and Dan Stein. "Impulse Control Disorders Not Elsewhere Classified." *The American Psychiatric Publishing Textbook of Psychiatry.* Eds. Robert Hales, Stuart Yudofsky, and Glen Gabbard. 5th ed. Arlington, VA: APA, 2008. The range of conditions discussed includes kleptomania, pathological gambling, trichotillomania, and pyromania.

Moore, David. P., and James Jefferson. *Handbook of Medical Psychiatry.* 2nd ed. Philadelphia: Mosby, 2004. Covers psychiatric and neurological conditions and numerous general medical conditions that affect mental functioning.

WEBSITES OF INTEREST

Association for Behavioral and Cognitive Therapies
http://www.abct.org

CNS Spectrums
http://www.cnsspectrums.com/aspx/articledetail.
  aspx?articleid=912

New York University, Langone Medical Center
http://psych.med.nyu.edu/conditions-we-treat/
  conditions/kleptomania

See also: Behavioral addictions: Overview; Compulsions; Crime and behavioral addictions; Gambling addiction; Impulse control disorders; Pyromania; Trichotillomania

L

Laryngeal cancer

CATEGORY: Health issues

ALSO KNOWN AS: Cancer of the larynx, cancer of the vocal chords

DEFINITION: Laryngeal cancer is a disease in which cancer cells grow in the larynx. The larynx is a tube-shaped organ inside the neck that lies between the throat and the windpipe. Its main function is to produce sound for speaking.

CAUSES

Cancer occurs when cells in the body, in this case laryngeal cells, divide without control or order. Normally, cells divide in a regulated manner. If cells keep dividing uncontrollably when new cells are not needed, a mass of tissue forms, called a growth or tumor. The term cancer refers to malignant tumors, which can invade nearby tissues and can spread to other parts of the body. A benign tumor does not invade or spread.

RISK FACTORS

Smoking is by far the most common high-risk behavior associated with laryngeal cancer. Other risk factors include the excessive use of alcohol and occupational exposure to certain air pollutants, such as wood dust, chemicals, and asbestos. Race and age also play a factor: African Americans and people who are age fifty-five years and older have a greater chance of developing laryngeal cancer. Gastroesophageal reflux (stomach acid that backs up into the esophagus and throat where it may come in contact with the larynx) and a weakened immune system are also associated with an increased risk of laryngeal cancer.

SYMPTOMS

The following are symptoms of laryngeal cancer: a persistent cough, hoarseness, or sore throat; an abnormal lump in the throat or neck; difficulty swallowing or pain when swallowing; frequent choking on food; difficulty breathing or noisy breathing; persistent ear pain or an unusual ear fullness, or sensation in and around the skin of the ear; unplanned, significant weight loss; and persistent bad breath.

SCREENING AND DIAGNOSIS

A thorough review of the patient's medical history and a physical examination are performed. Tests may include laryngoscopy, a thin, lighted tube inserted down the throat to examine the larynx; biopsy, the removal of a sample of laryngeal tissue to test for cancer cells; chest X-ray, a test that uses radiation to take a picture of the larynx and nearby structures; CT scan, a type of X-ray that uses a computer to make pictures of the inside of the larynx; or MRI scan, a test that uses magnetic waves to make pictures of the inside of the larynx.

TREATMENT AND THERAPY

Once laryngeal cancer is found, staging tests are performed to find out if the cancer has spread and, if so, to what extent. Treatment depends on the stage of the cancer. For early stage laryngeal cancer, either surgery or radiation alone are the most common and appropriate therapies offered. For more advanced stages of the disease, either radiation with chemotherapy or surgery followed by radiation are the most common treatments given.

Surgery requires the removal of a cancerous tumor and nearby tissue, and possibly nearby lymph nodes. The surgeries for laryngeal cancer are total laryngectomy, which involves the removal of the larynx, including the vocal cords; partial laryngectomy, in which the surgeon removes the cancerous tissue while leaving as much of the vocal cords as possible; tracheotomy, in which a hole is made in the neck below the larynx to assist with breathing; and neck dissection, which involves the removal of the lymph nodes and part of the neck muscles to determine the spread of cancer.

Radiation therapy is the use of radiation to kill cancer cells and shrink tumors. This may mean external radiation therapy, in which the beam is directed at the tumor from a source outside the body. Chemotherapy is the use of drugs to kill cancer cells. This form of treatment may be given in many forms, including pill, injection, or catheter. The drugs enter the bloodstream and travel through the body, killing cancer cells but also some healthy cells. Chemotherapy may be used to reduce the size of a particularly large tumor.

PREVENTION

Since laryngeal cancer is extremely rare in nonsmokers, the best way to prevent this type of cancer is by not smoking. A person can also reduce the risk of laryngeal cancer by avoiding excessive alcohol consumption and by protecting against toxic exposures.

Rick Alan

FURTHER READING

Beers, Mark H., ed. *The Merck Manual of Medical Information.* New York: Gallery Books, 2004. Updated information from medical experts covering numerous medical issues, such as cancer, heart disease, mental illness, pediatric care, eating disorders, and AIDS.

"Laryngeal and Hypopharyngeal Cancer." *American Cancer Society.* American Cancer Society. 2012. Web. 30 Mar. 2012. An overview and detailed guide about laryngeal and hypopharyngeal cancer. Includes information about clinical trials and resources for talking about cancer.

"Laryngeal Cancer Treatment." *National Cancer Institute.* National Institutes of Health. 2012. Web. 30 Mar. 2012. General information about laryngeal cancer as well as its stages, recurrence, treatment options, and resources for more information.

WEBSITES OF INTEREST

American Cancer Society
http://www.cancer.org/

CancerCare
http://www.cancercare.org/

National Cancer Institute
http://www.nci.nih.gov/

See also: Cancer and substance abuse; Esophageal cancer; Lung cancer; Smoking: Short- and long-term effects on the body; Tobacco use disorder

Law enforcement and drugs

CATEGORY: Social issues

DEFINITION: In the United States, the passage of drug laws that define substances as illegal or under the regulatory control of the government necessitated a mechanism for ensuring that these laws are obeyed. Law enforcement agencies at the federal, state, and local levels provide that mechanism. These agencies have been entrusted with the responsibility of enforcing drug laws by interrupting the production, importation, distribution, and sales of drugs in a collective effort known as supply reduction.

HISTORY OF DRUG LAWS

With the passage of the landmark Harrison Narcotics Tax Act in 1914, introduced by US Representative Francis Burton Harrison of New York, the US federal government began its continuous oversight of psychoactive substances. The new law made illegal and began regulating such drugs as narcotics, cocaine, and marijuana and numerous prescription and nonprescription drugs, including amphetamines.

The act taxed physicians only $1.00 annually for the right to legally prescribe opium, morphine, and coca leaves and their various derivatives, mislabeling the latter as a narcotic instead of a stimulant. However, nonphysicians were charged $1,000 for each exchange of any of these drugs, essentially prohibiting exchange under the strict penalty of law for tax evasion. Also, physicians were prohibited from prescribing opiates to treat addicts for maintenance purposes because addiction was not considered a disease, and physicians had to register with the federal government each prescription written and the name of each user.

From its enactment until 1970, the act was the prototypic antidrug law, spawning a succession of legislation drafted to limit the production, distribution, sale, and possession of unlawful substances. Following the legislative model of the 1914 act, the 1937 Marijuana Tax Act was introduced by Robert Doughton of North Carolina and passed over the objections of the American Medical Association. The law prohibited the sale of hemp, cannabis, or marijuana by anyone other than registered and licensed commercial establishments. Each transaction of these products required a transfer tax. The Marijuana Tax Act was repealed by the Comprehensive Drug Prevention and Control Act of 1970, known as the Controlled Substances Act (CSA), which incorporated under one statute many of the extant federal drug laws (for example, the Opium Poppy Control Act of 1942, the Boggs Act of 1951, and the Narcotic Control Act of 1956).

The CSA created a schedule of drugs (I–V) that classified substances, in a hierarchy, according to their widely accepted medical use (ascending order) and potential for abuse and dependence (descending order). According to this hierarchy, drugs in schedule I have no accepted medical use and the highest potential for abuse and dependence, whereas drugs in schedule V have an accepted medical use and the lowest potential for abuse and dependence. Many schedule V drugs (such as codeine) were available as over-the-counter medications (in small amounts in cough syrup). The CSA also transferred the authority for drug regulation from the US Department of Commerce to the Department of Justice, thereby criminalizing all aspects of the drug trade—from production to trafficking, sales, and possession.

FEDERAL ANTI-DRUG AGENCIES

The US Drug Enforcement Administration (DEA) was established in 1973 as the federal government's lead agency for ensuring that domestic drug laws are obeyed and that drug offenders are arrested and punished. With an annual budget of more than $2 billion, the DEA also directs many drug investigations abroad. The forerunner to the DEA was the Federal Bureau of Narcotics (FBN), housed under the Department of Treasury and led by Harry Anslinger. The FBN undertook numerous domestic and international operations in an effort to halt narcotics smuggling.

Reflecting the federal government's abiding and serious interest in eradicating illegal drugs, it created, through the passage of the Anti-Drug Abuse Act of 1986, the White House Office of National Drug Control Policy (ONDCP), which remains under the auspices of the executive branch of the

A crewmember from the Coast Guard Cutter Northland *stands guard next to approximately 3,500 pounds of cocaine confiscated from a 35-foot go-fast vessel in the Caribbean Sea at Base Miami Beach, Florida on March 16, 2012.* (Getty Images)

federal government. The ONDCP sets policy, allocates resources, and engages in public information campaigns to prevent and control drug sales and use throughout the country and to prohibit illegal drugs from entering the United States. The director of the ONDCP, the so-called drug czar, is appointed by the US president to serve as the leading authority on drug enforcement initiatives. The directorship, once a cabinet-level post, has been held by William Bennett (former secretary of education), Barry McCaffrey (a retired US Army general), and John Walters (former assistant to the secretary of education).

Enforcement Activities

The enforcement of drug laws in general occurs at four levels: international, national, state, and local. The international and national levels are under the aegis of the federal government. State and local police departments have specialized units for drug enforcement activities.

In certain instances, resources at each level are combined and coordinated through special task forces that concentrate on a particular drug (such as methamphetamine) or on a particular drug-trafficking enterprise (for example, outlaw motorcycle gangs). To prevent drugs from being smuggled across country or state borders in conveyances (for example, airplanes, boats, cars, trucks, and trains), the government employs agents from the FBI, DEA, Department of Homeland Security (US Customs and Border Patrol), and Transportation Security Administration to perform searches for illegal substances in a multistage interdiction process that involves intelligence gathering, surveillance, pursuit, and capture of smugglers.

To identify smugglers, trained officers implement drug-courier profiling techniques, watching vehicles and persons for telltale signs of drug trafficking. Drugs can be hidden in legitimate cargo or in false compartments in suitcases and in vehicle trunks and door panels. To uncover illegal substances, agents use advanced imaging technologies, trained dogs, pat-downs, body scans, and searches of persons. Drug smugglers have attempted to thwart officials by swallowing drug-filled balloons or by hiding drugs in bodily orifices—a dangerous practice that can result in death if the balloons burst and their contents are absorbed through the stomach or mucosa.

In cooperation with foreign governments, the DEA has engaged in crop eradication efforts that destroy the plants that are later processed into drugs for street sales. Such efforts to destroy crops involve the use of deracination (uprooting) techniques and chemical (for example, paraquat) and incendiary agents. US and foreign governments have subsidized the growers of illegal crops (for example, poppies for opium) to encourage them to cultivate legal crops and to discourage them from participating in the drug trade.

Drug enforcement efforts also focus on interrupting the processing of crops into saleable substances. For example, the milky juice from poppies, which is turned into a brownish gummy matter and then to a powder, becomes heroin for sale and consumption. Other drug factories produce cocaine from coca leaves. More sophisticated factories produce the main ingredient for methamphetamine (pseudoephedrine). The makeshift drug laboratories that produce methamphetamine are usually located in rural areas to hide the noxious odors and toxic, environmentally hazardous chemicals that are by-products of the production process. Drug enforcement agents seize, close, and destroy drug-producing factories of every type.

At the street level, police officers in specialized drug enforcement units gather intelligence from hotlines, local residents, and low-level criminals and informants to uncover drug-selling entities, such as street gangs in urban areas or freelance drug sellers. Officers disrupt operations by raiding houses in which drugs are packaged and stored for sale. Large amounts of drugs and money are seized from these premises as evidence.

In poor communities, drugs are often sold on the street. The public nature of these transactions makes it easier for police to engage in undercover enforcement activities known as buy-and-bust operations. In sting operations, officers pose as drug customers. In reverse-sting operations, officers pose as drug sellers. In both types of activities, an arrest is made after money and drugs are exchanged.

Closed markets are more difficult to police because drug sellers engage in transactions only with known drug customers or those vouched for by trusted friends or criminal associates. Local police can enforce drug laws by implementing other strategies as well, including the use of visible area patrols, crackdowns or sweeps in drug-infested neighborhoods, and partnerships with community-based antidrug programs. Police also can enforce nuisance abatement laws, which close down or seize properties where drugs are stashed or sold, and ordinances that allow them to seal vacant buildings, which are havens for drug sellers and users.

Arthur J. Lurigio, PhD

FURTHER READING

Levinthal, Charles F. *Drugs, Society, and Criminal Justice.* Boston: Prentice Hall, 2012. An extensive primer with many illustrations and reference sources. The content covers drugs and society, legally restricted drugs, legal drugs, and drug policy.

Rowe, Thomas C. *Federal Narcotics Laws and the War on Drugs.* New York: Haworth, 2006. A short history of the war on drugs in the United States. Recommends education and treatment over enforcement and punishment as drug control and prevention strategies.

Zilney, Lisa Anne. *Drugs: Policy, Social Costs, and Justice.* Boston: Prentice Hall, 2011. Examines the major issues surrounding the use and control of illegal substances.

WEBSITES OF INTEREST

US Drug Enforcement Administration
http://www.justice.gov/dea

White House Office of National Drug Control Policy
http://www.ondcp.gov

See also: Crime and substance abuse; Drug Enforcement Administration (DEA); Legislation and substance abuse; War on Drugs

Laxative abuse

CATEGORY: Substance abuse

DEFINITION: Laxative abuse is the repeated and routine use of laxatives to lose weight, shed unwanted calories, feel thin, feel empty, manage bowel movements, or treat constipation. There are different types of laxatives, but stimulant and bulk agents are the most common. Stimulant laxatives and osmotic laxatives physically alter the bowel's ability to function, and with excessive use can cause permanent damage. Bulk agents do not have the same physical effects as stimulant laxatives if taken as directed, but the user may become psychologically dependent on these laxatives.

CAUSES

There are several causative factors associated with the abuse of laxatives. One is the mistaken belief that laxatives will prevent the absorption of calories and help with weight reduction. Another factor is the mistaken belief that daily bowel movements are a necessary part of good health and that laxative use is a harmless remedy to ensure this occurs. A third factor is the repeated use of laxatives to relieve constipation.

RISK FACTORS

There are four groups of people at risk for laxative abuse. The largest group to abuse laxatives includes persons who have an eating disorder, such as anorexia or bulimia nervosa. Adolescents and young adults with low self-esteem and poor body image are particularly prone to disordered eating and laxative abuse. Anorexia nervosa is the severe restriction of food intake to bring about drastic weight loss, which in turn causes dehydration and subsequent constipation. Bulimia nervosa is characterized by a cycle of binge eating followed by behaviors such as vomiting or laxative abuse to compensate or reverse the effects of binge eating.

A second group to abuse laxatives includes athletes who need to stay within a specific weight range; these athletes include wrestlers, boxers, and jockeys. A third group is made up of middle-aged and older people with frequent bouts of constipation. In this group, excessive use often comes with the misperception that daily bowel movements are part of good health. The fourth group includes persons with a factitious disorder, wherein they abuse laxatives to intentionally cause diarrhea.

SYMPTOMS

Several physical warning signs and personality traits indicate laxative abuse. The physical signs include a history of alternating diarrhea and constipation or chronic diarrhea of an unknown origin; physical signs also include gastrointestinal complaints such as cramping or pain, dehydration, and retention of fluids that cause severe bloating and the feeling of being fat.

Certain personality traits are characteristic of those who abuse laxatives. These traits include an obsession with weight and body shape, low self-esteem, impulsiveness, and anxiousness. Exhibiting one of these traits does not mean a person is a laxative abuser, but having a combination of traits may increase the risk of laxative abuse. For example, if a person is obsessed with weight and has low self-esteem, they may binge eat. When this behavior does not make that person feel better, he or she may turn to laxatives to get rid of the calories just consumed.

SCREENING AND DIAGNOSIS

Screening and diagnosis of laxative abuse is tricky and oftentimes difficult because many abusers want to hide the behavior. The best screening tool is a clinician's suspicion. Once a clinician suspects laxative abuse, he or she can order blood tests to check for an electrolyte (potassium, magnesium, sodium, and chloride) imbalance, as chronic diarrhea will remove electrolytes through the stool and will prevent them from being absorbed into the body.

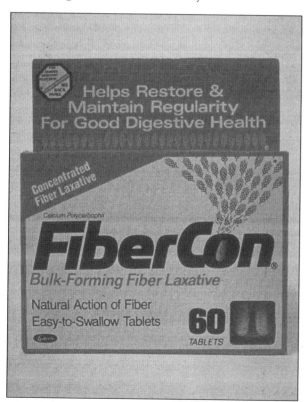

Box of FiberCon fiber laxative. (Time & Life Pictures/ Getty Images)

Persons with an eating disorder typically have low potassium levels in their blood (a condition called hypokalemia). Clinicians can check urine for the presence of a laxative. Another screening method is to perform a personality assessment by having the person complete surveys related to body dissatisfaction, low self-esteem, and level of drive to stay or be thin.

TREATMENT AND THERAPY

To overcome laxative abuse, users will need the medical expertise of a general physician, will need therapy with a psychologist or psychiatrist, and will need consultation with a registered dietician. The most immediate treatment is to stop taking laxatives and to seek a physician's care.

Many people will experience withdrawal symptoms that usually last from one to three weeks; in rare cases symptoms have lasted two days to two or three months. Side effects of withdrawal include constipation, fluid retention, feeling bloated, and temporary weight gain. To treat these side effects one should drink six to ten cups of water per day and decaffeinated beverages to hydrate one's body. (Caffeine is a diuretic and promotes fluid loss, and dehydration causes constipation.) One should eat regular meals and foods that promote normal bowel functioning, such as whole-grain or wheat bran foods with plenty of fluids, vegetables, and fruits.

Routine physical activity also helps regulate the bowel, but a physician should be consulted first because intense exercise can worsen constipation. Physicians may start their patients on fiber and osmotic supplements to help the bowel function properly and to establish normal bowel movements.

PREVENTION

No guaranteed mechanism prevents laxative abuse. However, education can be a powerful tool in helping people understand that laxatives will not prevent the body from absorbing food or losing weight. Moreover, routine laxative use will have a reverse effect on the body, causing dehydration and constipation. Also, social support from friends and family and being aware of the signs and symptoms of abuse are crucial; intervention could prevent long-term laxative abuse and irreversible physical and psychological consequences.

Christine G. Holzmueller, BLA

FURTHER READING

"How to Stop Abusing Laxatives." *EatingDisordersReview.com*. 1999. Web. 22 Feb. 2012. http://www.eatingdisordersreview.com/nl/nl_edr_10_5_14. Presents tips on how to stop abusing laxatives. Outlines common symptoms that will occur once laxatives are discontinued and discusses myths and medical complications about laxative use.

Le Grange, Daniel, and James Lock. *Eating Disorders in Children and Adolescents: A Clinical Handbook*. New York: Guilford, 2011. Chapters examine etiology and neurobiology, epidemiology, diagnosis and classification, medical issues and assessment, treatment, prevention, and parental roles.

Roerig, James L., et al. "Laxative Abuse: Epidemiology, Diagnosis, and Management." *Drugs* 70.12 (2010): 1487–503. Print. A comprehensive medical article about laxative abuse that describes persons at risk of this disorder, examines medical complications from laxative misuse, and discusses treatments for this disorder.

WEBSITES OF INTEREST

Bulimia.com
http://www.bulimia.com

National Eating Disorders Association
http://www.nationaleatingdisorders.org

See also: Bulimia; Emetic abuse

Legislation and substance abuse

CATEGORY: Social issues

DEFINITION: Substance abuse, also known as drug abuse, is characterized by overuse of and dependence on addictive substances, most often narcotic drugs or alcohol. Legislative issues affecting and addressing substance abuse and substance abusers are addressed at the federal, state, and local levels.

SCOPE OF THE ISSUE

More than one-half of persons in prisons in the United States are imprisoned for drug-related crimes. According to the National Substance Abuse Index, the United States is the largest single market in the world for illegal drugs. States generally are left to legislate substance abuse issues.

Federal law, however, may require states to take certain actions, such as tracking specific instances or reporting some types of infractions. Laws also generally distinguish between legal substances, such as alcohol, and illegal substances, including the unlawful use of prescription medication.

Each state chooses what federal laws to enact. Though there are thirty-nine federal laws pertaining to alcohol, for example, states are not bound by them. States also are required to follow the parameters of federal sentencing guidelines.

HISTORY OF SUBSTANCE ABUSE LEGISLATION

The criminalization of drugs in the United States began in 1914 with the Harrison Tax Act. Under this law, a tax of $1,000 was imposed for the nonmedical exchange of certain drugs; the law, however, pertained to tax evasion, not drug use or transfer.

In the early and middle decades of the twentieth century several federal agencies had varying responsibilities and power in drug law enforcement. By the 1960s most of this enforcement was in the hands of the federal Bureau of Narcotics and the Bureau of Drug Abuse Control. Changing attitudes toward drug use during the 1960s and into the 1970s gradually led to increases in crime. Federal law enforcement agencies continued to evolve, as did legislation.

The US Congress passed the Controlled Substances Act, part of the 1970 Comprehensive Drug Abuse Prevention and Control Act, launching national substance control campaigns. The law consolidated legislation that regulates the manufacture and distribution of illicit substances—anabolic steroids, depressants, hallucinogens, narcotics, and stimulants—and some chemicals used to produce controlled substances. As public health threats from other substances became known, the act was amended. In its infancy, the Controlled Substances Act was enforced by the Bureau of Narcotics and Dangerous Drugs under the Department of Justice (DOJ).

In 1973, US president Richard M. Nixon created the Drug Enforcement Administration (DEA) within the DOJ to centralize efforts to combat substance abuse. Interagency rivalry and the necessity of coordinating investigation and prosecution efforts were among the reasons cited for the creation of the DEA. In announcing the DEA, Nixon declared the United States' global war on drugs.

As the war on drugs continued, investigators developed intelligence units and technology to aid agents. Laboratories were built and staffed to support the DEA's efforts. The DEA has continued to monitor substance abuse developments and to respond to emerging trends. In 2011, for example, the DEA took action against three synthetic cathinones, widely called bath salts, following alarming and increasing reports of abuse of the substances.

CLASSIFICATION AND PENALTIES

There are five classifications of controlled substances. Laws mandate the penalties for crimes of trafficking based in part on the classification, or schedule, of the drugs, and in some cases, as with trafficking marijuana, on the amount of drug confiscated. Penalties may include incarceration and fines. Each state sets its own penalties for sale and possession of these substances within the federal guidelines.

Schedule I drugs are classified as substances with high potential for abuse and no accepted medical use in the United States. The law requires that these drugs be tightly controlled, including mandating security for manufacturing and storing them, and establishing quotas and licensing guidelines. Schedule I drugs include heroin, LSD, marijuana, peyote, and ecstasy.

Schedule II substances may have accepted medical use and high potential for abuse; they also are likely to lead to severe physical or psychological dependence. Methadone, oxycodone, amphetamine, methamphetamine, and cocaine are examples of schedule II drugs.

Schedule III drugs include anabolic steroids, codeine with aspirin, and some barbiturates; these substances have less potential for abuse than schedule I and II drugs, have accepted medical uses, and have some potential for dependence.

Schedule IV and V substances have low potential for abuse or dependence and also have accepted medical uses. Valium and Xanax are among the schedule IV drugs. Over-the-counter medicines, such as cough medicines with less than 200 milligrams of codeine per 100 milliliters, are examples of schedule V drugs.

Much of the federal legislation regarding illegal substances pertains to alcohol, marijuana, cocaine, heroin, and methamphetamine. Persons who have been convicted of drug offenses may lose some federal benefits, such as grants and loans, and assistance including food stamps and Social Security benefits. A college or university student receiving federal financial aid, for example, could lose the aid if convicted of a drug offense; the penalty could be temporary for a first offense of possession, but permanent following multiple offenses.

The Controlled Substances Act also includes prohibitions and penalties for selling drugs to minors or near schools and other locations. Federal penalties are often more severe than those for crimes prosecuted at the state level. Local jurisdictions also may pass laws pertaining to drug possession and trafficking.

CURRENT LEGISLATIVE ISSUES

Substance abuse issues continue to arise as chemists develop new synthetic drugs and as others experiment with substances. Such issues often develop in other countries and eventually arrive in the United States. Drug enforcement authorities are continually monitoring and responding to developments.

Designer Drugs

One example of a developing issue is the collection of designer drugs commonly called bath salts, which were first seen in Europe. Hospitals and health care workers reported sharp increases in the number of patients being seen for the effects of bath salts beginning in 2009 and escalating in 2011. These designer drugs were being used for their psychoactive properties.

Under the Comprehensive Crime Control Act of 1984 the US attorney general has the authority to temporarily place substances into schedule I for up to one year. The DEA took action on bath salts in 2011; an order in October temporarily scheduled the bath salt substances into schedule I because the drugs were deemed threats to public safety.

Misuse of Prescription Medicine

Many people who misuse prescription medicine believe that these substances are safe because they are prescribed by doctors. Some people take a larger dose than was recommended because they believe more is better, while others take the medication to induce euphoria. The latter is an example of drug abuse.

Misuse and abuse of prescription medication can cause harm or death. A Centers for Disease Control and Prevention survey found that one in five high school students had taken a prescription medication without a prescription. Among the most common prescription drugs abused are oxycodone, Valium, amphetamine, methamphetamine, and barbiturates.

Penalties for prescription drug abuse vary by state. North Carolina, for instance, mandates prison sentences of seventy to eighty-four months for anyone with more than 4 grams of opium, opium derivatives, or heroin. A person illegally in possession of six Vicodin pills, for example, would be in prison for up to seven years. Penalties increase with the amount of the drug a person has. In contrast, someone caught in North Carolina with more than 10 pounds of marijuana could be sentenced to twenty-five to thirty months in prison.

Prenatal Exposure

According to data from the Substance Abuse and Mental Health Services Administration, a 2007 survey found that 4 percent of pregnant women used illicit drugs and 2.9 percent reported binge drinking. A number of states require health care professionals to screen infants for prenatal drug exposure, and many states go further, requiring that women suspected of prenatal substance abuse be reported to child protective services. Federal laws such as the Child Abuse Prevention and Treatment Act, however, regard such actions as referrals for treatment and investigation of child safety issues, not grounds for criminal prosecution.

Sixteen US states classify substance abuse during pregnancy as child abuse. Some states also require actions including reporting parents to authorities. Responses to substance abuse also vary widely from state to state; some make treatment for pregnant women a priority, others make furnishing drugs to pregnant women crimes. Women who have been charged criminally for prenatal actions often face charges of child endangerment or abuse, fetal murder or manslaughter, or illegal drug delivery to a minor (via umbilical cord), depending on the state.

Federal Alcohol Laws, State Discretion

All fifty states have adopted some federal alcohol laws, such as the law making it illegal to operate motor vehicles with a blood alcohol concentration (BAC) at or above 0.08. Most states have adopted the administrative license revocation law, which suspends licenses of those who fail the BAC test.

Thirty-seven states have adopted the federal law making driving under the influence with a minor child in the vehicle a separate offense or increasing the penalty for doing so. Another federal law mandating jail for a second offense of driving under the influence has been adopted by forty-six states. By 1987, all fifty states had laws making age twenty-one years the legal drinking age; national statistics indicated that per capital consumption of alcohol dropped considerably.

Josephine Campbell

FURTHER READING

Gray, James. *Why Our Drug Laws Have Failed and What We Can Do about It*. Philadelphia: Temple UP, 2011. Former Superior Court judge James Gray addresses drug policy issues including penalties and drug legalization efforts.

Lyon, Joshua. *Pill Head: The Secret Life of a Painkiller Addict*. New York: Hyperion, 2009. A pharmacist and recovering opiate addict describes his downfall and recovery and his positions on various drug treatment and policy issues.

Valverde, Mariana. *Diseases of the Will: Alcohol and the Dilemmas of Freedom*. New York: Cambridge UP, 1998. A history of approaches to alcohol consumption addresses the issue from the perspectives of the individual, society, and the authorities.

WEBSITES OF INTEREST

Centers for Disease Control and Prevention
http://www.cdc.gov

Get Smart About Drugs
http://www.getsmartaboutdrugs.com

National Conference of State Legislatures
http://www.ncsl.org

National Institute on Drug Abuse
http://www.drugabuse.gov

National Substance Abuse Index
http://nationalsubstanceabuseindex.org

Office of National Drug Control Policy
http://www.whitehouse.gov/ondcp

Substance Abuse and Mental Health Services Administration
http://www.samhsa.gov

US Drug Enforcement Administration
http://www.justice.gov/dea

See also: Drunk driving; Opioid abuse; Prescription drug addiction: In depth; Prescription drug addiction: Overview

Leukoplakia

CATEGORY: Health issues

ALSO KNOWN AS: Smoker's keratosis

DEFINITION: Caused by chronic irritation, leukoplakia is a disorder of the mouth's mucous membranes. White patches form on the tongue or inside of the mouth over weeks or months. This can also occur on the vulva in females, but for unknown reasons.

CAUSES

Leukoplakia is caused by chronic irritation. Irritants can come from pipe or cigarette smoking, chewing tobacco or snuff, rough teeth, and rough places on dentures, fillings, or crowns. One type, known as hairy leukoplakia, results from a virus that becomes active in the body when the immune system is weak. This is found primarily in people with the human immunodeficiency virus (HIV) or other types of severe immune deficiency. Infection may play a role in other cases, as well. Most cases of leukoplakia get better once the source of the irritation is removed.

RISK FACTORS

Risk factors that increase the chance of developing leukoplakia are old age (sixty-five years or older); lifestyle, such as tobacco use or long-time alcohol use; and a weakened immune system. More men than women are at risk of developing leukoplakia. In women, the condition more often develops into cancer.

SYMPTOMS

Leukoplakia is usually harmless, but it can lead to cancer. In some cases, leukoplakia resembles oral thrush, an infection also associated with HIV/AIDS and lowered immune function. Symptoms can include a lesion on the tongue or gums, inside of the cheeks, or on the vulva. The lesion can be white, gray, or red in color, and is typically thick and slightly raised, or it may have a hardened surface. Other symptoms include sensitivity to touch, heat, or spicy foods, as well as pain or other signs of infection. With hairy leukoplakia, painless and fuzzy white patches appear on the tongue.

SCREENING AND DIAGNOSIS

In most cases, a dentist can diagnose leukoplakia with a mouth exam. To confirm a diagnosis or to check for cancer, an oral brush biopsy may be needed. This involves removing some cells with a small brush. A pathologist then checks these cells for signs of cancer. Sometimes the dentist uses a scalpel to remove cells after numbing the area.

TREATMENT AND THERAPY

Leukoplakia can be treated by removing the irritant, which may involve quitting smoking or correcting dental problems; removing patches, particularly if signs of cancer are present; and taking medicine. Medicines include valacyclovir and famciclovir or a topical solution, such as podophyllum resin. For hairy leukoplakia, the doctor may prescribe antiviral medicines.

PREVENTION

Smoking cessation, limiting or avoiding alcohol use, good oral hygiene, regular visits to the dentist, and consuming plenty of fruits and vegetables (full of antioxidants) are all effective methods of reducing the chance of developing leukoplakia.

Annie Stuart

FURTHER READING

"Leukoplakia – Overview." *UMMC.* University of Maryland Medical Center. 2011. Web. 30 Mar. 2012. An overview of leukoplakia, as well as its symptoms, treatment, and prevention.

Mayo Clinic Staff. "Leukoplakia." *Mayo Clinic.* Mayo Foundation for Medical Education and Research. A guide to leukoplakia. Covers its definition, symptoms, causes, risk factors, complications, diagnosis, treatments, and prevention.

"Oral Hairy Leukoplakia." *AETC National Resource Center.* AIDS Education & Training Centers National Resource Center. 2012. Web. 30 Mar. 2012. Information about oral hairy leukoplakia. Covers its definition, symptoms, diagnosis, treatment, and patient education.

WEBSITES OF INTEREST
American Dental Association
http://www.ada.org/

National Institute of Dental and Craniofacial Research
http://www.nidcr.nih.gov/

See also: Elderly and addictions; Smoking; Smoking: Short- and long-term effects on the body; Tobacco use disorder

Librium

CATEGORY: Substances

DEFINITION: Librium, trade name for chlordiazepoxide, is a psychoactive drug used to treat anxiety and insomnia. It is also used for agitation, seizures, muscle spasms, alcohol withdrawal, and as a premedication for certain medical and dental procedures. Librium was the first in the class of benzodiazepines, the minor tranquilizers.

STATUS: Available by prescription only

CLASSIFICATION: Schedule IV controlled substance

SOURCE: A chemical structure formed by the fusion of a benzene ring and a diazepine ring; other trade names include Libritabs, Novapam, Risolid, Silibrin, Tropium, and Zetran

TRANSMISSION ROUTE: Ingestion, intravenous, intramuscular, rectal

HISTORY OF USE

Librium works by acting on gamma-aminobutyric acid (GABA), a chemical that occurs naturally in the brain. Brain cells affected by GABA slow down and stop firing, calming the muscles and heart rate and alleviating anxiety and insomnia. When first prescribed, Librium and other benzodiazepines were considered safe and effective. By the 1970s, there were reports of adverse physical and psychological effects. Some persons developed a tolerance to and even a physical dependence on the drug. The US Congress investigated benzodiazepines three times, unusual for a drug legally prescribed. The majority of people taking the drug were middle-class women.

The women's health movement of the 1970s argued that Librium was an agent of social control, a drug that tranquilized women into submission. Addiction specialists considered Librium to be prone to misuse. Emergency rooms often found Librium and other benzodiazepines in persons who overdosed. From a peak of more than 120 million prescriptions per year in the mid-1970s, Librium fell to 60 million prescriptions by 1979. The US Food and Drug Administration now limits Librium to short-term use.

EFFECTS AND POTENTIAL RISKS

Persons taking Librium sometimes experience paradoxical reactions such as seizures, aggression, impulsivity, irritability, or suicidal behavior. Long-term Librium use risks deterioration of physical and mental health. Sudden withdrawal from Librium can cause severe pain in the muscles and joints, insomnia, or suicidal thoughts. A person may experience extrapyramidal symptoms, such as restlessness, involuntary movements, or uncontrollable speech.

Librium may cross the placenta with other substances, putting a fetus at risk for withdrawal, extrapyramidal symptoms, or perinatal complications. Benzodiazepines affect the metabolism of estrogen and may have an association with ovarian cancer.

Benzodiazepines pose the greatest risk to the elderly, causing memory problems, daytime sleepiness, impaired motor coordination, and increased risks of car accidents and falls. Long-term effects may include depression, dementia, and acute anxiety.

Merrill Evans, MA

FURTHER READING

"Drug Abuse and Addiction: Benzodiazepines." *Cleveland Clinic: Current Clinical Medicine.* 2nd ed. Cleveland, OH: Elsevier, 2010.

Harlow, Bernard L., and Daniel W. Cramer. "Self-Reported Use of Antidepressants or Benzodiazepine Tranquilizers and Risk of Epithelial Ovarian Cancer." *Cancer Causes and Control* 6 (1995): 130–34. Print.

Herzberg, David. "The Pill You Love Can Turn on You," *American Quarterly* 58 (2006): 79–103. Print.

Sinclair, Leslie. "Antipsychotic Labels to Cite Risks to Newborns." *Psychiatric News* 46 (2011): 12. Print.

Tallman, John F., et al. "Receptors for the Age of Anxiety: Pharmacology of the Benzodiazepines." *Science*, n.s. 207 (1980): 274–81. Print.

See also: Addiction medications; Anxiety; Anxiety medication abuse; Benzodiazepine abuse; Controlled substances and precursor chemicals

Liver disease and alcohol use

CATEGORY: Health issues and physiology
ALSO KNOWN AS: Alcoholic hepatitis; alcoholic liver disease; cirrhosis; Laennec's cirrhosis; steatohepatitis
DEFINITION: Alcohol (ethanol) is a toxin metabolized in the liver; hence, the organ is the site of major injury from repeated alcohol use. Chronic liver disease and cirrhosis together are ranked as the twelfth leading cause of death in the United States. The course of alcoholic liver disease (ALD) is a continuum of damage in which multiple areas of liver function become impaired, as fatty liver develops into inflammation and necrosis (hepatitis), then fibrosis, and then cirrhosis and liver failure.

THE LIVER

The liver is the largest organ in the body and the only organ able to regenerate itself. Performing more than five hundred vital functions, it is the conduit where blood from the stomach and intestines passes and where toxic substances and waste products are removed from the blood. The liver is responsible for protein, carbohydrate, and lipid metabolism and for detoxification and metabolism of ethanol and its toxic by-products.

The liver consists of two main lobes containing small units called lobules. These hexagonal plate-like structures are made up of hepatocytes (liver cells) and are attached to interconnecting ducts that end in the hepatic duct. Hepatocytes constitute the functional component of the liver, making up 70 to 80 percent of its cytoplasmic mass, and the cells are damaged by prolonged alcohol ingestion. A connective tissue capsule covering the liver acts as scaffolding; its branching extends throughout the liver as septae, enabling vessels and bile ducts to traverse the liver.

DISEASE MANIFESTATION

ALD is a spectrum of evolving liver injuries, progressing from mild steatosis and fatty infiltration to hepatitis and fibrosis, and finally to cirrhosis, which evolves to complications of portal hypertension, hepatic encephalopathy, or hepatocellular carcinoma. Although ALD is often devoid of clinical symptoms and best observed histopathologically, the course of the disease can be insidious.

Steatosis, the abnormal retention of lipid (fat) within a cell, is the earliest manifestation of ALD and is seen in 90 percent of heavy drinkers. The lipid droplets are mostly triglycerides, and as they accumulate in hepatocytes, the liver becomes infiltrated with fatty deposits—hence, the term *fatty liver*. Injury is most evident in the perivenular area (zone three), a diamond-shaped area of the hepatic lobule located around central veins. Fatty liver is a relatively benign condition that reverses itself quickly with abstinence.

Continued drinking causes necroinflammation and the onset of alcoholic hepatitis (AH), an acute form of alcohol-induced liver injury, marked by intralobular inflammation and necrosis. AH is characterized by a group of morphological changes in cell integrity, ranging in severity from detection of distinct necroinflammatory components (steatohepatitis) to evidence of biochemical damage and lesions to fulminant liver failure, triggering sudden and rapid deterioration of liver function.

The pattern of fatty liver development is macrovesicular, such that swelling of the cytoplasm occurs; this process is called ballooning degeneration and it reflects widespread disturbances in lipoprotein transport in and out of hepatocytes. With ballooning, fat accumulation inside hepatocytes is so large it distorts the cell's nucleus and displaces the cytoplasm. In staining it appears as single-shaped white spaces or vacuoles. Ballooning leads to lytic necrosis, causing

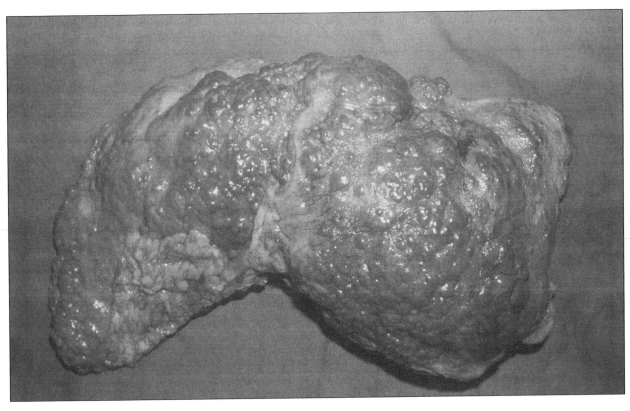

Cirrhosis. (Biophoto Associates)

cell contents to decompose, with subsequent condensation of reticulin fibers (fibrosis). Common lesions in AH are neutrophilic infiltrates, Mallory hyaline inclusions or bodies, megamitochondria, and lipogranulomas that form from ruptured hepatocellular fat.

Clinical diagnosis of AH remains rather nebulous, as there are no positive markers or reliable tests that differentiate simple fatty liver from steatohepatitis or more advanced stages of ALD. The short-term mortality rate for patients with severe AH is high, and the disease is a precursor to cirrhosis, with an associated long-term risk nine times higher in AH than in fatty liver alone.

FIBROSIS

Fibrosis is an exaggerated response to the wound-healing process elicited by liver damage involving the production of excessive type 1 collagen and other extracellular matrix (ECM) proteins and their deposition as scar tissue. Collagen deposition occurs primarily in an area of the liver known as the space of Disse. The fibrosis common to ALD is called sclerosing hyalin necrosis and involves wide pericentral areas of fibrosis extending to portal fields.

With overspreading necrosis, the ECM becomes overwhelmed and loses its ability to express enzymes that degrade lesions. This results in unbalanced synthesis and decomposition of collagen, causing proliferation of connective tissue and, over time, increases to wider bands of collagen that form bridging fibrosis. Lesions then span between septae and cause disturbances in lobular structure, loss of hepatocytes, and deterioration in liver function.

Hepatic stellate cells (HSCs) are known to generate fibrosis. Normally dormant, HSCs become activated in response to liver injury. Activated HSCs are differentiated myofibroblast-like cells with a changed phenotype, characterized by proliferative, fibrogenic, and contractile properties. The process affects a cascade of histologic events in which HSCs elicit inflammatory signaling, cytokine release, and matrix metalloproteinase dysregulation, resulting in increased accumulation of ECM and further fibrosis.

Liver fibrosis is reversible and liver transplantation improves survival. However, most transplant centers do not recommend transplants unless a patient demonstrates a minimum of six months of abstinence from alcohol.

CIRRHOSIS

Cirrhosis is a diffuse pathologic process of architectural disorganization involving the entire liver, whereby normal liver architecture is replaced by abnormal structures called regenerative nodules. These nodules are completely surrounded by fibrous-band bridging between portal tracts. Cirrhosis usually develops over many years and produces a nodular, firm liver. In ALD, cirrhosis is usually micronodular and most prominent in the central vein area. Often called Laennec's cirrhosis, it is characterized by a fine mesh-like pattern of small uniform yellow nodules and narrow, regular fibrous septa.

Decompensated cirrhosis occurs when liver function is overridden by architectural remodeling and is accompanied by complications of portal hypertension or hepatic encephalopathy. Portal hypertension causes phlebosclerosis (hardening of venous walls), resulting from abnormal blood flow patterns of cirrhotic liver, and its effects extend to other organs. Encephalopathy is a clinical state of disordered cerebral function caused by impaired hepatic metabolic function. Decompensated cirrhosis is often further complicated by hepatocellular carcinoma, is irreversible, and has high mortality.

By eliminating alcohol before cirrhosis develops, it is possible for the liver to heal—a sobering fact, considering ALD claimed nearly 14,500 lives in the United States in 2007, according to mortality data from the US Centers for Disease Control and Prevention.

Barbara Woldin, BS

FURTHER READING

"Alcoholic Liver Disease." *Cleveland Clinic: Current Clinical Medicine.* Ed. William Carey. 2nd ed. Philadelphia: Saunders, 2010. Provides comprehensive, easy-to-read coverage of ALD.

Feldman, Mark, Lawrence Friedman, and Lawrence Brandt. *Sleisenger and Fordtran's Gastrointestinal and Liver Disease.* 9th ed. Philadelphia: Saunders, 2010. Discusses pathophysiology, diagnosis, and management of ALD.

Schiff, Eugene, Michael Sorrell, and Willis Maddrey, eds. *Schiff's Diseases of the Liver.* 10th ed. Philadelphia: Lippincott, 2006. Describes clinical and scientific aspects of liver disease, including alcohol-induced injury and transplant section.

WEBSITES OF INTEREST

American Liver Foundation
http://www.liverfoundation.org

MedlinePlus: Liver Diseases
http://www.nlm.nih.gov/medlineplus/liverdiseases.html

National Institute on Alcohol Abuse and Alcoholism
http://pubs.niaaa.nih.gov/publications/aa64/aa64.htm

See also: Alcohol: Short- and long-term effects on the body; Ethanol

Love and relationship addiction

CATEGORY: Psychological issues and behaviors

ALSO KNOWN AS: Codependency; obsessive relationship; pathological relationship; relational dependency; relationship pursuit

DEFINITION: A love or relationship addiction is a behavioral addiction involving an unhealthy preoccupation with a person or an obsession with the idea of romance or love. It can be a one-sided romantic relationship or can involve partners who are codependent, or it can define a nonromantic, pathological relationship, such as that between a child and parent.

CAUSES

A relationship addiction can be caused by many different factors. Common contributors include depression, low self-esteem, loneliness, and a sense of helplessness. Some behavior can be traced to childhood abuse or inadequate bonding experiences with caregivers early in life, which can result in a high level of neediness.

Some people remain in an addicted relationship or fall into a pattern of addicted relationships due to lack of education or social skills, or because of impaired judgment. Pursuers often enjoy exploiting or controlling others, or they seek revenge for being rejected.

Couples who are codependent feed off each other's most vulnerable or negative qualities. In those situations in which a person is obsessed with the idea of romance or love, he or she becomes addicted to the mood-enhancing qualities of "falling in love" and is unable to move forward into a more mature relationship.

RISK FACTORS

People most at risk for relationship addictions are those who have failed to develop a sense of worth and self. Other people at high risk are victims of child abuse or child abandonment or persons who grew up with codependent parents and failed to learn about healthier relationships. Persons with a substance addiction, sexual addiction, or another mental disorder are also at risk, as are those brought up in a fundamentalist religion or a culture that advocates strict passive and dominant gender roles and a sense of martyrdom between spouses.

SYMPTOMS

When a person falls in love, a sense of being "swept away" or losing oneself is common and normal. In a healthy relationship, this state of being is temporary and eventually blossoms into a deeper sense of love and responsibility, qualities of a successful long-term relationship. Also normal is the need to establish multiple relationships before the "right" person comes along.

Those who are addicted to love, however, establish a pattern of leaving partners just when the initial romantic high begins to fall away, never taking a relationship to the next level. Love addicts also can exhibit a pattern of extramarital affairs, tend to spend abnormal amounts of time fantasizing, and may miss work or destroy friendships and family relationships because they are too busy looking for their next attraction.

Signs that one is invested in an unhealthy relationship include situations in which values are being compromised, in which positive rewards are lacking, and in which one's health and safety are at risk. The inability to leave a pathological relationship can cause anxiety, high blood pressure, moodiness, digestive problems, eating disorders, depression, and substance abuse. In some cases, the shame or guilt associated with codependent relationships causes people to withdraw from society. A partner who is manipulative, controlling, and abnormally jealous may stalk the other, invade his or her privacy, and resort to violence or even murder when rejected.

Although it is normal for those who have been rejected in a love relationship to feel sad, worthless, and "lost" for a temporary period of time, the pathological love addict finds the pain so unbearable that he or she has thoughts of suicide and may carry out the act. The dependency upon another can be so overwhelming that it prohibits the person from imagining a life without the partner.

SCREENING AND DIAGNOSIS

There is no official diagnosis of a relationship addiction as determined by the American Psychological Association or any other major professional group. Mental health professionals rely on questionnaires or surveys to measure jealousy, anger, and other emotions, and to uncover related psychological motives.

Examples of surveys that can be administered by professionals or used for self-diagnosis are available from Sex and Love Addicts Anonymous, Co-Dependents Anonymous, and other organizations. As these tests rely upon personal reflection and honest answers, they work best when the client has admitted to a problem. In other situations, family members and current or former partners might be interviewed for additional insight.

When a person has been accused of stalking, the victim may be asked to complete the stalking behavior checklist or similar surveys, which commonly are used in domestic violence cases. Clients will also be screened for mental disorders, including substance abuse, depression, sexual addictions, and borderline personality disorder, which are often present with relationship addicts. A physical examination and medical history also may be conducted.

TREATMENT AND THERAPY

Treatment for a relationship addiction usually involves a twelve-step program similar to the model devised by Alcoholics Anonymous in addition to individual or couples therapy. Twelve-step programs rely on peer support, fellowship, and a belief in a higher power to help the client abstain from the unhealthy behavior or to end an addictive relationship. Individual psychotherapy can help to uncover underlying problems, attitudes, or disorders and to focus on treatment.

An important part of treatment for those who have been involved in an addictive relationship is finding activities that offer a distraction; getting rid of the reminders of a relationship, such as gifts, cards, and music; and participating in a healthy lifestyle. Education is also essential, as clients may need to learn certain coping or interpersonal skills to build healthy relationships. When depression, borderline personality disorder, or another mental disorder is present, treatment also will consist of additional psychotherapy and medication.

PREVENTION

The best way to prevent a relationship addiction is to develop a healthy and happy self-identity. Persons should pursue a career and leisure activities that are fulfilling, should develop a spiritual or humanistic side of life, and should participate in social activities that build healthy relationships. A person who likes and respects him- or herself conveys that and other healthy attitudes to others.

Learning about normal human development and the qualities of healthy relationships, and developing critical thinking skills that can be used to judge relationships, also are important. A person should seek professional help at the first signs of a problem relationship, before a partner becomes abusive or violent, and should be aware that stalking, abuse, and sexual harassment are not only unacceptable, but are also crimes.

Sally Driscoll, MLS

FURTHER READING

Beattie, Melody. *The New Codependency: Help and Guidance for Today's Generation.* New York: Simon & Schuster, 2009. The author, to whom the term *codependency* is attributed, offers self-help advice for leaving unhealthy relationships and dealing with the typical emotional aftermath.

Cupach, William R., and Brian H. Spitzberg. *The Dark Side of Relationship Pursuit: From Attraction to Obsession and Stalking.* Mahwah, NJ: Erlbaum, 2004. This scholarly book discusses obsessive relational intrusion and stalking, including cyber-pursuit, and provides examples of screening tools and an extensive bibliography.

Fisher, Helen. *Why We Love: The Nature and Chemistry of Romantic Love.* New York: Holt, 2004. This pathbreaking book explores the emotional, physical, and biological aspects of healthy romantic love relationships and the sometimes inevitable heartbreaks.

Katz, Dian. "Checking the Health of Your Relationship." *Lesbian News* 29.7 (2004): 51. While intended for lesbian readers, this article is applicable to heterosexual couples too, as it offers generic advice for avoiding and repairing relationship addiction and for developing healthy attitudes.

Moore, John D. *Confusing Love with Obsession: When Being in Love Means Being in Control.* 3rd ed. Center City, MN: Hazelden, 2006. Framed around numerous case studies, this self-help book also includes an index, a recommended reading list, resources for further help, and other useful appendixes.

Peabody, Susan. *Addiction to Love: Overcoming Obsession and Dependency in Relationships.* 3rd ed. New York: Celestial Arts, 2005. This classic self-help book is comprehensive in its coverage of relationship addictions and offers candid advice for prevention and recovery.

Schaeffer, Brenda. *Is It Love or Is It Addiction: The Book that Changed the Way We Think about Romance and Intimacy.* Center City, MN: Hazelden, 2009. A popular psychotherapist compares healthy relationships with addictions and offers an abundance of self-help advice.

Tallis, Frank. *Love Sick: Love as a Mental Illness.* New York: Thunder's Mouth, 2004. A clinical psychologist uses many historical and literary examples to explore jealousy, rejection, obsession, and other emotions and situations related to romantic love, while also discussing their scientific and medical implications.

WEBSITES OF INTEREST

Co-Dependents Anonymous
http://www.coda.org

Sex and Love Addicts Anonymous
http://www.slaafws.org

See also: Behavioral addictions: Treatment; Compulsions; Men and behavioral addictions; Self-destructive behavior and addiction; Sex addiction; Women and behavioral addictions

LSD

CATEGORY: Substances

ALSO KNOWN AS: Acid; lysergic acid diethylamide

DEFINITION: LSD, a synthetic amide of lysergic acid found in ergot, a fungus on grains, is a psychoactive intoxicant, similar to but stronger than psilocybin or mescaline. LSD has powerful mind-altering effects, usually called hallucinogenic or psychedelic.

STATUS: Illegal in the United States and other countries

CLASSIFICATION: Schedule I controlled substance

SOURCE: A synthetic chemical with no natural sources; produced illegally in underground laboratories

TRANSMISSION ROUTE: Crystals are diluted into liquid form and ingested orally; also injected intramuscularly

HISTORY OF USE

LSD was synthesized in 1938 by Albert Hoffman, of Sandoz Laboratories in Basel, Switzerland, as part of a research program seeking new medicines. LSD did not seem to offer such promise, but in 1943 Hoffman accidentally ingested a dose, experienced its psychoactive effects, and described these effects as being surprisingly transformational.

For the next twenty years, Sandoz Laboratories marketed LSD for research purposes. Among early research was that by the US Central Intelligence Agency from the 1950s through the 1970s, in an attempt to discover whether LSD could be used for mind-control purposes. Mostly, however, psychiatry and psychology became involved, initially because LSD seemed to simulate a "model psychosis."

The perceptual distortions induced by LSD, however, are not experienced as hallucinations in the sense of something that is not there; rather, they transform what is given in the perceptual field. This distinction led Canadian psychiatrists Humphry Osmond, Abram Hoffer, and Duncan Blewett to use LSD as a treatment for psychosis. LSD was also studied as an adjunct in psychotherapy, especially by Stanislav Grof in Czechoslovakia. Before its criminalization, more than forty thousand patients were treated with LSD psychotherapy. Notable results occurred in alcoholics, felons, and the terminally ill, persons who normally are resistant to successful therapeutic outcomes.

Albert Hofmann, discoverer of the mind-altering drug LSD and former head of the research department of Swiss chemical company Sandoz in Solothurn, Switzerland. (AP Photo)

In the United States, research was conducted at Harvard University by Timothy Leary, Ralph Metzner, and Richard Alpert (who later became Ram Dass). The trio's 1964 book *The Psychedelic Experience* popularized the view that LSD could be useful in enhancing human potential. Leary, in particular, became a public advocate for LSD with his slogan to "turn on, tune in, drop out."

Soon writers such as Aldous Huxley and Ken Kesey and musicians, most famously the Beatles, also reflected a view of LSD's possibilities. Cary Grant, a major film star, attributed a "new assessment of life" to his experience on LSD. By the 1960s, LSD had become a common drug for American youth, especially in California, where it spread among the burgeoning counterculture. Owsley Stanley, who made and distributed a large amount of LSD in San Francisco in the mid-1960s, is known for fueling the upsurge of interest there. Largely because of this sense that LSD contributed to a rejection of mainstream values, the drug became intensely controversial and the subject of much negative publicity. The manufacture and sale of LSD was made a crime in 1965 and possession was criminalized in 1966.

According to the US Substance Abuse and Mental Health Services Administration, LSD use peaked in the early 1970s, fell slowly to a low in 2003, and has been increasing since. The National Household Survey on Drug Abuse indicated that 20.2 million Americans age twelve years and older used LSD at least once in their lifetime. The most common age of first-time users is eighteen years.

EFFECTS AND POTENTIAL RISKS

The effects of LSD become noticeable within thirty to sixty minutes and last six to eight hours or more. The threshold dose is 25 micrograms (mcg), and 100 to 250 mcg is typical; beyond 400 mcg no further change seems to occur. A feature of LSD is how widely its effects vary. Researchers quickly realized the keys to this variability are the mental set (or state) of the user and the setting in which the drug is used.

The physiological effects of LSD include changes to the pulse rate, muscular tension, blood pressure, constriction of arteries in the periphery, and pupil dilation. These effects tend to be mild and do not last beyond the psychoactive period. Longer term effects have been reported, most spectacularly chromosome breakage, but these claims have not survived rigorous research.

Negative experiential effects of LSD are cognitive and emotional. Judgment is impaired such that the user is not as concerned with safety. Emotionally, a user can become so disoriented as to feel anxiety or panic, a reaction augmented if the setting were conducive to disorientation. A rare longer-term negative effect is the unwelcome vivid memory of an emotionally charged moment from the LSD event, known as a flashback.

The experiential effects of LSD include positive aesthetic, psychological, and spiritual transformations. Aesthetically, the effects center on perceptual changes, especially to the visual field, which is intensely enhanced with greater mobility, colorfulness, transiency, luminosity, energy, swelling, vividness, and synesthesia. Psychologically, the effects of LSD include mood changes, particularly feelings of well-being and euphoria; a new and greater awareness of the world and of self; a deeper understanding of human relationships; a transcendence of time and space; and a sense of ineffability. Spiritually, the effects of LSD include a sense of rebirth; a sense of encounters with divinity; a sense of the world as sacred; and a sense of communion, unity, and nonduality.

These effects tend to be experienced as an inward journey; they are remembered and are felt by the user to be of lasting benefit. The effects are so unmistakable that blinded research studies are impossible. For this reason too, substances other than LSD are rarely sold as LSD.

LSD is not addictive. A tolerance is built up after a few days if used daily, but the tolerance is diminished quickly following cessation of use. Studies of lethal overdose levels in animals indicate it would require an extremely huge amount for humans, and no lethal overdoses have been shown in humans.

Christopher M. Aanstoos, PhD

FURTHER READING

Dobkin de Rios, Marlene, and Oscar Janiger. *LSD, Spirituality, and the Creative Process.* Rochester, VT: Park Street, 2003. A research collection examining the impact of LSD on creativity before LSD was made illegal.

Grof, Stanislav. *LSD: Doorway to the Numinous.* Rochester, VT: Park Street, 2009. A good summary of the clinical research on LSD up to the point it was made illegal. Originally published in 1975.

Hoffman, Albert. *LSD: My Problem Child.* San Francisco: MAPS, 2005. The synthesizer of LSD reflects on its science and mysticism.

WEBSITES OF INTEREST

Multidisciplinary Association for Psychedelic Research
http://www.maps.org

National Institute on Drug Abuse
http://www.drugabuse.gov/infofacts/hallucinogens.html

See also: Flashbacks; Hallucinogen abuse; Hallucinogens: Short- and long-term effects on the body; MDMA/Ecstasy; Mescaline; Mushrooms/psilocybin; PCP; Psychosis and substance abuse

Lung cancer

CATEGORY: Health issues

ALSO KNOWN AS: NSCLC; non-small cell lung cancer; non-small cell bronchogenic carcinoma; small cell lung cancer

DEFINITION: Lung cancer is a disease in which cancer cells grow in the lungs. Cancer occurs when cells in the body divide without control or order. If cells keep dividing uncontrollably, a mass of tissue forms. This is called a growth or tumor. The term cancer refers to malignant tumors. They can invade nearby tissue and spread to other parts of the body.

CAUSES

Cancer is caused by cell division that occurs within the body without control or order. Any damage to the cells in the lungs can lead to the development of lung cancer, including damage caused by first- or secondhand smoke from cigarettes, cigars, or pipes; and exposure to asbestos (a type of mineral), radon (radioactive gas), or other toxins. There are two types of lung cancer: non-small cell lung cancer, which is more common and generally grows and spreads more slowly; and small cell lung cancer, which generally grows more quickly and is more likely to spread to other parts of the body.

RISK FACTORS

There are numerous risk factors that can increase the likelihood of developing lung cancer. They include cigarette, cigar, or pipe smoking; using chewing tobacco; exposure to secondhand smoke; exposure to asbestos or radon; having a lung disease such as tuberculosis; having a family or personal history of lung cancer; exposure to certain air pollutants; exposure to coal dust; radiation therapy (used to treat other cancers); and infection with the human immunodeficiency virus (HIV).

SYMPTOMS

The symptoms of lung cancer are many, and may include a persistent cough, especially one that worsens over time; constant chest pain; coughing up blood; shortness of breath, wheezing, or hoarseness; repeated problems with pneumonia or bronchitis; swelling of the neck and face; loss of appetite or unexpected weight loss; and fatigue. It should be noted that these symptoms might be caused by other conditions.

SCREENING AND DIAGNOSIS

A discussion of symptoms and medical history followed by a medical examination is usually the first step toward a diagnosis. A doctor will also typically inquire about a possible family history of cancer as well as any exposure to environmental and occupational substances. The following tests will help to diagnose lung cancer: chest X-ray, which uses radiation to take a picture of structures inside the body, especially bones; sputum cytology, a test that examines a sample of mucus from the lungs; spiral CT, a special type of X-ray of the internal organs; PET scan, an image created using a tiny amount of radiation that is put into the body; PET/CT scan, a type of imaging test that combines PET and CT scan techniques; bone scintigraphy, a test that detects areas of increased or decreased bone activity; and biopsy, which is the removal of a sample of lung tissue to be tested for cancer cells.

Methods of biopsy include bronchoscopy, in which a thin, lighted tube is inserted into the mouth or nose and through the windpipe to look into the breathing passage and to collect cells or tissue samples; needle aspiration, in which a needle is inserted through the chest into the tumor to remove a sample of tissue; thoracentesis, which involves the use of a needle to remove a sample of the fluid in the lungs to check for cancer cells; and thoracotomy, which is surgery to open the chest and examine the lung tissue.

TREATMENT AND THERAPY

Once lung cancer is found, staging tests are done to find out if the cancer has spread. The goal of treatment is to eliminate the cancer or to control symptoms. Surgery involves removing the tumor and nearby tissue. Lymph nodes may also need to be removed. The type of surgery depends on the location of the tumor. Segmental or wedge resection requires the removal of only a small part of the lung, lobectomy surgery is the removal of an entire lobe of the lung, and pneumonectomy requires the removal of an entire lung.

Radiation therapy and chemotherapy are other possible treatments. Radiation therapy is the use of radiation to kill cancer cells and shrink tumors. This may also be used to relieve symptoms, such as shortness of breath. Radiation may be external, or directed at the tumor from a source outside the body, or internal, using radioactive materials placed into the body in or near the cancer cells. External radiation therapy is more common for treating lung cancer. Chemotherapy is the use of drugs to kill cancer cells. This may be given in many forms, including pill, injection, and via a catheter. Chemotherapy is often used to kill lung cancer cells that have spread to other parts of the body.

There are two newer therapies as well, which are not yet widely used: photodynamic therapy (PDT) and cryosurgery. Photodynamic therapy is a type of laser therapy. A chemical is injected into the bloodstream and is then absorbed by the cells of the body. The chemical rapidly leaves normal cells, but it will remain in cancer cells for a longer time. A laser is aimed at the cancer, activating the chemical. This chemical then kills the cancer cells that have absorbed it. This treatment may also be used to reduce symptoms. Cryosurgery is a treatment that freezes and destroys cancer tissue.

PREVENTION

To help prevent lung cancer, one should cease smoking, avoid places where people are smoking, test for radon gases and asbestos in the home, and avoid workplaces with asbestos. X-rays and CT scans have been studied as methods to screen for lung cancer in smokers; however, as of 2011, no medical organization recommends screening tools for this type of cancer. A recent study has suggested that a type of CT scan may be useful in decreasing mortality rates of lung cancer in smokers.

Laurie LaRusso, MS, ELS

FURTHER READING

Lorigan, P., J. Radford, A. Howell, and N. Thatcher. "Lung Cancer after Treatment for Hodgkin's Lymphoma: A Systematic Review." *Lancet Oncology* 6.10 (2005): 773–79. Reviews various studies that report long-term complications from the treatment of Hodgkin's lymphoma, including a greater risk of lung cancer.

Munden, R. F., S. S. Swisher, C. W. Stevens, and D. J. Stewart. "Imaging of the Patient with Non-Small Cell Lung Cancer." *Radiology* 237.3 (2005): 803–18. Reviews the role of radiologic imaging in patients with NSCLC, which is important for assessing the extent of the disease.

Pantanowitz L., and B. J. Dezube. "Evolving Spectrum and Incidence of Non-AIDS-Defining Malignancies." *Current Opinion in HIV and AIDS* 4.1 (2009): 27–34. Reviews literature about non-AIDS defining cancer (NADC), an increasing cause of morbidity and mortality in HIV patients.

WEBSITES OF INTEREST

American Cancer Society
http://www.cancer.org/

American Lung Association
http://www.lung.org/

Canadian Cancer Society
http://www.cancer.ca

The Canadian Lung Association
http://www.lung.ca

See also: Cancer and substance abuse; Esophageal cancer; Laryngeal cancer; Respiratory diseases and smoking; Smoking; Smoking: Short- and long-term effects on the body